Jim Lyon

D1299374

NETWORK ARCHITECTURE AND
DEVELOPMENT SERIES

Designing Routing and Switching Architectures for Enterprise Networks

Howard C. Berkowitz

MACMILLAN
TECHNICAL
PUBLISHING
U·S·A

Designing Routing and Switching Architectures for Enterprise Networks

By Howard C. Berkowitz

Published by:
Macmillan Technical Publishing
201 West 103rd Street
Indianapolis, Indiana 46290 USA

Copyright © 1999 by Macmillan Technical Publishing

International Standard Book Number: 1-57870-060-4

Library of Congress Catalog Card Number: 98-84221

03 02 01 00 99   7 6 5 4 3 2 1

Interpretation of the printing code: The rightmost double-digit number is the year of the book's printing; the rightmost single-digit number is the number of the book's printing. For example, the printing code 99-1 shows that the first printing of the book occurred in 1999.

Composed in Palatino and MCPdigital by Macmillan Computer Publishing

Printed in the United States of America

Trademark Acknowledgments

All terms mentioned in this book that are known to be trademarks or service marks have been appropriately capitalized. Macmillan Technical Publishing cannot attest to the accuracy of this information. Use of a term in this book should not be regarded as affecting the validity of any trademark or service mark.

Warning and Disclaimer

This book is designed to provide information about wide-area networks. Every effort has been made to make this book as complete and as accurate as possible, but no warranty or fitness is implied.

The information is provided on an as-is basis. The authors and Macmillan Technical Publishing shall have neither liability nor responsibility to any person or entity with respect to any loss or damages arising from the information contained in this book or from the use of the discs or programs that may accompany it.

Feedback Information

At Macmillan Technical Publishing, our goal is to create in-depth technical books of the highest quality and value. Each book is crafted with care and precision, undergoing rigorous development that involves the unique expertise of members from the professional technical community.

Readers' feedback is a natural continuation of this process. If you have any comments regarding how we could improve the quality of this book, or otherwise alter it to better suit your needs, you can contact us at **networktech@mcp.com**. Please make sure to include the book title and ISBN in your message.

We greatly appreciate your assistance.

Publisher
David Dwyer

Executive Editors
Ann Trump Daniel
Linda Engelman

Managing Editors
Patrick Kanouse
Gina Brown

Acquisitions Editor
Amy Lewis

Development Editor
Kitty Wilson Jarrett

Project Editors
Theresa Wehrle
Elise Walter

Copy Editor
Kelli Brooks

Proofreader
Erich Richter

Indexer
Lisa Stumpf

Manufacturing Coordinator
Christine Moos

Book Designer
Gary Adair

Cover Designer
Sandra Schroeder

Compositor
Amy Parker

About the Author

Howard C. Berkowitz is chief technology officer for Gett Communications, where he consults on network architecture with special interests in networking in medicine and in medicine in networking. He is a Certified Cisco Systems Instructor for Internetwork Design, and teaches and has developed advanced routing seminars for enterprises and vendors. He develops analyses and methods used by the entire staff, methods that are also taught to clients. As this book went to press, some of his current design projects included fault-tolerant Internet connectivity for medical content providers, secure virtual private networks for voice and text, and cost-effective means of very large file transfer.

An active participant in the North American Network Operators' Group and Internet Engineering Task Force, he is the author or coauthor of several RFCs in numbering; his current IETF work includes documents on multihoming, virtual private networks, and OSPF network deployment. He continues to give engineering tutorials on these subjects at the North American Network Operators' Group, the USENIX Network Administration conference, and Networld/Interop Europe.

He is the author of *Designing Addressing Architectures for Routing and Switching*, also from Macmillan Technical Publishing. He has written dozens of articles for the industry press and has spoken at numerous trade shows and user groups.

His professional experience includes work as a network management product architect and developer of protocol test systems. He has designed network architecture for large users, including the Library of Congress, Stentor, AT&T, Lucent, Georgetown University Hospital, and US government agencies (including the Labor Department, Environmental Protection Agency, and Agriculture Department).

About the Technical Reviewers

These reviewers contributed their considerable practical, hands-on expertise to the entire development process for *Designing Routing and Switching Architectures for Enterprise Networks*. As the book was being written, these folks reviewed all the material for technical content, organization, and flow. Their feedback was critical to ensuring that *Designing Routing and Switching Architectures for Enterprise Networks* fits our reader's need for the highest quality technical information.

Galina Pildush is a senior network architect at GeoTrain Corporation, a leading Cisco training and consulting partner. After earning her MSc in computer science, she worked for 13 years for major worldwide corporations in the areas of internetwork design, architecture, network optimization, implementation, and project management. She has been an academic teacher at York University, teaching computer science, data communications and computer network courses. Gaining extensive technical experience in internetworking and Cisco products, she reached her CCIE. Currently deploying her passion for teaching, Galina is a senior instructor at GeoTrain, teaching a variety of Cisco courses. Her areas of interest and specialization are ATM, internetwork design and optimization, and voice over IP/Frame. Besides the demanding professional work, Galina, her husband, their two children and their dog, who is a Canadian Champion, all go cycling and on trips around North America and, most of all, they have great times together!

Alexander Marhold is a senior consultant at PRO IN Consulting, a leading provider of high-end telecommunications consulting in Middle Europe. After earning his MSc in engineering, he worked for 10 years in different areas of data processing, CIM, and networking. After achieving his MBA, he worked in different companies as a manager of networking teams. Gaining extensive technical experience in Cisco products and certifications, he reached his CCIE. In addition to his consulting work, he is an academic teacher at a polytechnical university and gives high-end training. His areas of interest and specialization are service provider infrastructure, MPLS, local loop technologies, and network simulation. Besides the demanding professional work, his main areas of interest are his family (with four children), trekking in South America, and Spanish and Latin American culture.

Dedication

To my colleagues in networking, who want to move to greater challenges. My profession is a fellowship; the Internet is a realization to Martin Luther King's dream of a world in which one is judged by the color of their character, not the color of their skin.

To my feline associate, Clifford, who kept up my spirits while writing, and who accepts responsibility from any spelling errors caused by his walking across the keyboard.

Acknowledgments

NANOG has been a continuing inspiration. In particular, I'd like to thank Sue Hares, Susan Harris, and Bill Norton for making me welcome and for encouraging me to present. I've enjoyed sharing the tutorial track with Avi Freedman.

Peer reviewers contributed enormously to the book: Neill Craven, Galina Pildush, and Alexander Marhold.

Stimulating conversations with Priscilla Oppenheimer, Pamela Forsyth, Tom Thomas, Paul Borghese, Leigh Anne Chisholm, and others on the www.groupstudy.com mailing list have helped me refine the ways I present technical concepts and understand the way people learn.

My students in the Cisco Internetwork Design classes helped me formulate the questions to ask in defining requirements and address plans. Ideas also sprang from my participation in revising that course, and I thank Priscilla Oppenheimer, Peter Welcher, and Kip Peterson for thought-provoking discussions.

Mariatu Kamara helped keep my home life and office sane.

Table of Contents

Introduction

I'll dispense with false modesty: I am an excellent cook. As such, it baffles me when I hear people new in the field asking for "cookbook" approaches to switching and routing. True, there are cookbooks that take the cook step by excruciating step through a precisely specified recipe, with absolutely no guidance about substituting ingredients, adjusting for personal tastes, or changing the portion size. But I think of some of my more interesting cookbooks, such as the classic *The Escoffier Cook Book* [Escoffier, 1941]. Recipe 2211 gives a good idea of what a networking professional should look for in a "serious" networking cookbook:

> 2211—Dauphine potato croquettes (*Croquettes de Pommes de Terre a la Dauphine*)
>
> Take the required amount of "Pommes Dauphine" preparation; divide it into 2-oz. portions; mould these to the shape of corks; treat them a l'anglaise; and fry them like ordinary croquettes.

That's it. That's the recipe. You are expected to know how to make *Pommes Dauphine* (or at least where to look it up), what amount is the required amount, how to mould them, what the *l'anglaise* treatment consists of, and how to fry croquettes.

Shall we say that the cookbook doesn't take a "cookbook" approach? Yet the Escoffier cookbook is a valuable reference to me when I want to know how some of the classic French dishes are structured. It is a jumping-off point for me in creating my own recipes.

And so it is in any complex field, be it fine cooking or network design. You must have an adequate background to be able to start with general references and build upon them. All too many people believe in certification models, Novell and Microsoft being well-known examples, that presume if you memorize enough procedures, you can do useful things.

Nonsense, unless your cooking expectations go no further than cooking a Big Mac to McDonald's rigorous rules, or your networking goals will be simple and well-defined.

When I taught introductory Cisco routing classes, I found many students objected to what they called "theory." Theory, to them, turned out to be anything that did not involve hands-on work on a router, typing commands. These students wanted scripts they could follow, filling in the blanks on commands.

The problem they faced is that real-world networks are rarely that simple. Even configuring a router to someone else's design, and certainly troubleshooting it, requires some conceptual understanding of what the box is doing.

To me, there is a level of conceptual understanding that I hesitate to call "theory." In a time long ago, in a data center far away, when I was an IBM mainframe systems programmer, IBM had documents called "principles of operation" that told how a piece of hardware or software worked, at a level that let you plan its use and enhancement. Principles of operation, however, rarely described *why* the product was designed the way it was.

In my experience, there is a spectrum from operational procedures to principles of operation to true theory. Theoretical material in networking includes formal concepts from computer science, mathematics and statistics, and electronic engineering. Theory enters into why protocols are designed the way they are. You cannot look seriously into performance analysis, for example, without having some understanding of statistics and probability, queuing theory as applied to buffering and servers, and so on.

At the same time, this understanding doesn't need to be advanced academic training. In my first year of high school, I nearly failed elementary algebra. My algebra teacher happened to be my guidance counselor, who advised me to stay in the less quantitative sciences, such as biology. He felt I'd never handle the abstraction in my then-intended-field, chemistry. Yet I can function adequately in formal performance analysis, and have at least a passing knowledge of the principles of modern cryptography. It can be done!

At introductions to the North American Network Operators' Group (NANOG), an engineering forum for service providers, a spectrum of meetings usually is presented. The leading edge of theory is presented in such forums as the Association for Computing Machinery Special Interest Group in Communications (ACM SIGCOMM). The next level of protocol design would be seen in the Internet Engineering Task Force (IETF) and the ATM Forum. NANOG is a very technical forum that assumes the protocols developed in the IETF are what they are, and focuses on how to use them in bleeding-edge networks. The next level of meeting is the trade show, such as Networld/InterOp, which focuses on products for beginners to moderately advanced practitioners. Every level in this spectrum, from theory to product details, can be useful in designing networks.

This book is targeted at the principles of operation and "applied theory" of networking. Where configurations are given, they are presented as an example of a technique, and are not intended to be a fill-in-the-blank recipe. My goal is to give you enough understanding of why protocols and products are designed the way they are to be able to select the appropriate methods, but not to overload you with information that really is appropriate only to people actually doing product design.

The technology discussion in Part II begins with the mechanisms that actually forward traffic from interface to interface, both at OSI Layer 2 and Layer 3. Think of Chapter 3 as the rules for driving a car, with another person reading the map and giving directions. The directions you hear are specific and straightforward, such as "take the second right."

Chapters 4 and 5 deal with the map and its navigation. Chapter 4 examines the basic list of directions that are built from several sources, and Chapter 5 tells how dynamic routing protocols help obtain information about potential routes in a changing network. Chapter 6 considers both the interactions of hosts with routing and switching, and routing and switching methods appropriate for interconnecting only a few devices.

After you have selected the technologies on which you can build your architecture, your next task is to prepare the working plans from which the new network is to be built. This is the thrust of Part III, which covers defining what is already there and then drawing the overall plan to include both old and new. Chapter 7 considers how you can combine routing and switching techniques into a workable network. This chapter begins defining the requirements for relays—routers and switches—in terms of their connectivity. Chapter 8 deals with the requirements for making the relays manageable.

It is now time to build. Part IV deals with current deployment practices. With the routing and switching architecture in hand, you can now deal with the detailed subsystem design. Chapter 9 covers techniques used with connection-oriented switches at Layers 1 through 3, discussing both user devices and provider functions to which the user devices may connect. Chapter 9 primarily deals with WAN switching technology.

ATM considerations are also in Chapter 9. ATM can operate both as a LAN or WAN protocol, and many beers have been drunk during engineering arguments about which it is. My feeling is that ATM and related techniques, such as DWDM and SONET, are rather like the sleeping arrangements for an 800-pound gorilla: He sleeps wherever he wants.

Chapter 10 deals with connectionless switches, which are almost exclusively LAN devices. Chapters 11 and 12 move into routing; Chapter 11 establishes basic principles for a "flat" routed network and Chapter 12 moves to consider hierarchical routing, as well as special topological methods, such as tunneling.

Finally, in Part V, the book helps you plan for new technologies that should be available in products in the relatively near term. The chapters of Part V are organized not as WAN and LAN technologies but as the evolving model of edge versus core. Chapter 13 emphasizes devices to which user hosts connect or that are used in the local environment close to the user. Chapter 14 focuses on the internal backbone devices that interconnect relays at the edge.

PART I

Why Route? Why Switch?

CHAPTER 1

What Is the Problem You Are Trying to Solve?

Ready, fire, aim.
—A proverb in many organizations.

A problem is something you have some chance of changing.
Anything else is a fact of life.
—C. R. Smith

If you do not think about the future, you cannot have one.
—John Galsworthy

When you design a network, you must ensure that you understand the user requirements that justify the rest of the network. At the beginning of the design process, you assume that the internal structure of the network will magically meet the user requirements, if those requirements are well known. For example, when we speak of the telephone network as a whole, the usual emphasis is on speaking over the telephone, not on the details, such as the fact that the wire from the telephone goes to an AT&T 5-ESS or Nortel DMS-100 switch. When you begin translating these requirements into the elements of network design, do not leap immediately to selecting specific routers and switches, or even necessarily whether Layer 3 routing or Layer 2 switching is appropriate at a given point. Routers, local-area network (LAN) switches, connection-oriented Layer 2 and Layer 1 switches, and other network interconnection devices are means of controlling the traffic flow on the streets of your network.

These are the fundamental aspects. Other issues that refine the relay structure include several choices:

questions to be asked when defining a relay device

* How does the relay find the destination of a PDU to be forwarded? *routing rules*

* How does the relay ensure that its forwarding rules continue to match reality? *route table updates*

* When the relay tries to forward a PDU out an interface (or medium) that is busy transmitting another PDU, what happens? *queuing rules*

* Will the relay accept new traffic when it is busy processing other traffic? How does it reject excess traffic (if it does)? *congestion rules*

There are operational and economic aspects of specific implementations:

* If the destination in the PDU is logical, not physical, how does the relay select the physical interface on which to forward the PDU? *routing rules*

* How quickly can these decisions be made? *switching times / routing times*

* How important is it for devices in the relaying environment to recognize, without human intervention, their place in the map? *automatic route table updates*

* How much overhead is necessary for the relay to keep track of the map? *internal table sizes*

Relay Types and OSI Reference Model Layers

Formally, relays are defined at the physical, data link, network, transport, and application layers [ISO 10000]. Relays connect two peer entities at the same layer. There are names for the types of relays used at each layer. Some meaningful types of relays do not fit neatly into OSI layers, but their names are still relevant. See Figure 1.2 for the placement of various relays.

Repeaters connect entities at the physical layer. They are primarily concerned with extending cable lengths or otherwise managing wiring. *Multiport repeaters* interconnect more than two Layer 1 entities and are commonly called *hubs*. Do be aware that many vendors use the term hub much more generically, in the sense of an interconnection point at multiple layers.

relay types

Network
address
translator
(NAT)

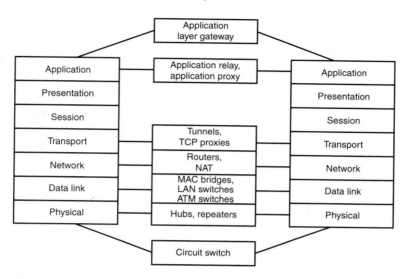

FIGURE 1.2 *Relay types are defined for many OSI layers, as well as above and below the OSI stack.*

MAC bridges connect LAN MAC-entities at Layer 2 of the OSI model. *LAN switches* are bridges on steroids that enhance performance over basic bridges. See Chapter 10, "Connectionless LAN Switching," for a discussion of bridges and LAN switches. Just as hub is a term that vendors have defined in many confusing ways, switch is also a term with many vendor-specific meanings and no single rigorously defined one. In this book, a switch without further qualification is a connectionless Layer 2 relay. Other types of switches include connection-oriented switches used for WAN connectivity. The term *Layer 3 switching* is a hybrid of Layer 2 and Layer 3 concepts.

WAN switches for frame relay, X.25, and arguably ATM also operate at this layer. There is quite a bit of controversy about where ATM layering fits against the OSI model, but it is considered a Layer 2 technology in this book. See Chapter 9 for more information on ATM layering.

Warning

The OSI reference model was developed in the late 1970s and published in 1984. Although the seven layers of OSI are often repeated as a networking mantra—which I consciously do not list in this book—they have been refined over time. The Internal Organization of the Network Layer document, for example, is an OSI document that refines relationships between OSI Layers 2 and 3, sublayering them more meaningfully. Other documents extend OSI to deal with management and routing, which were not really addressed in the basic model.

continues

> *The Institute for Electrical and Electronic Engineers (IEEE) Project 802 committee evolved an architecture for LANs that sublayers Layers 1 and 2. Originally, IEEE 802 work was separate from OSI work; the two were not harmonized until the mid- to late-1980s.*
>
> *ATM and ISDN architectural work also proceeded separately from OSI architecture and has differences in layers and approaches to layering.*
>
> *The point here is that you shouldn't try too hard to force a networking concept, especially one internal to the network, into the basic OSI model. See Chapters 2 and 4 of* Designing Addressing Architectures for Routing and Switching, *also from MTP, for an extensive discussion of these more modern models.*

Routers (or *intermediate systems*, in formal OSI terminology) connect network entities at Layer 3. Other devices that interconnect Layer 3 entities include *network address translators* (NATs).

Basic routers operate on a basic IP assumption that there is a one-to-one mapping between logical subnets and physical media. Still, with conventional routers, it is not uncommon to have more than one logical network map to a single physical medium.

Virtual LANs (VLANs) extend this basic assumption by allowing one or more logical networks to map to a set of linked physical media (see Figure 1.3).

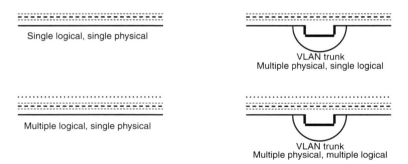

F I G U R E 1 . 3   *Relationships between physical and logical assumptions.*

Transport relays interconnect entities at the transport layer. The most common realization of a transport layer is as tunneling software, which carries a payload in one protocol over a delivery network. Other transport relaying is done in firewalls, as proxy servers.

Application relays interconnect application entities. There are two main types of application relays: pure application relays that pass along application information based on protocol header information and *application layer gateways* (ALGs) that manipulate the contents of application data. Think of the first as a post office and the second as one that opens the mail and forwards a translation in another language.

Proxies

Proxies interrupt the stream at a given layer and manipulate the contents at that layer. There can be proxy functions at different OSI layers. No single definition of a proxy is universally accepted, but I generally consider the basic definition a proxy as a function that terminates an association from a source to a destination, representing itself to the real source as the real destination, and to the real destination as the real source.

Some devices do not truly terminate the protocol stream, but make on-the-fly changes. This behavior is characteristic of network address translators that substitute IP addresses and change appropriate TCP and UDP checksums, but do not terminate TCP connections.

A proxy can be transparent to the user or nontransparent. Nontransparent proxies do identify themselves to at least one real endpoint as other than the true other endpoint.

In Figure 1.4, a proxy at Point A might be in the mailroom, whose staff is not authorized to open mail but can make decisions based on the envelope. For example, they might only forward letters with a known reply address. In networking terms, this would be a transport proxy.

A proxy at Point B, equivalent to an application proxy in networking, represents Madonna's personal assistant. She is authorized to open mail and decide the ultimate handling of a letter:

- Deliver it to Madonna, perhaps putting it into a folder. This would be a transparent proxy.

- Send me a form letter response apparently signed by Madonna. This also would be a transparent proxy.

- Send me a form letter response thanking me for the mail but explaining Madonna cannot answer personal mail. This is not transparent.

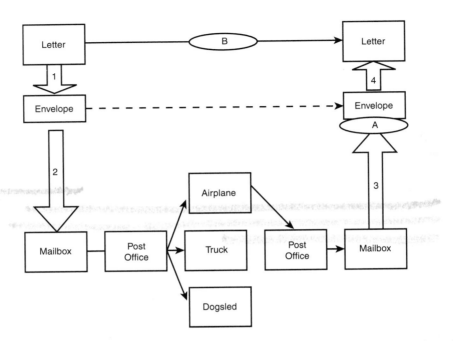

FIGURE 1.4 *Proxies terminate the source-to-destination association at a given layer, but can create a new protocol flow to the ultimate destination.*

Transparency is one aspect of a proxy: the characteristic of whether the end user is or is not aware of the proxy. Figure 1.5 shows a different aspect of proxies: how they operate.

The left side of Figure 1.5 shows a *static proxy*, in which the response to protocol messages is preconfigured.

On the right side of Figure 1.5, the proxy is *dynamic*. In other words, it learns what response to give based on protocol flow that it monitors.

In the static proxy, all definitions are on the local router. In the dynamic proxy case, the first request to locate the mainframe goes through the network to the mainframe, but the local router remembers the mainframe location and responds directly to Host 2's query.

In the static case, whenever a local client requests the address of a server (Point 1), the router responds directly (Point 2) with that address, which the router obtains from a preconfigured or previously dynamically learned table. If the real server is down, the router still responds with its address, and other mechanisms, such as application timeouts, are required to detect the failure.

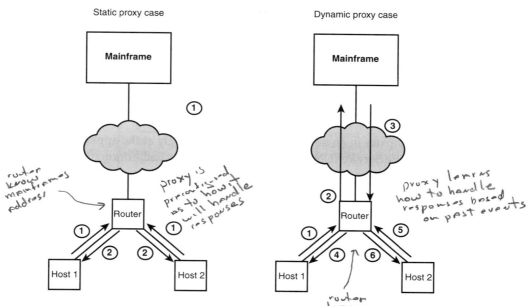

FIGURE 1.5 *Proxies can be either static or dynamic.*

Note

In this text, Points 1, 2, 3, and so on refer to circled numbers in the illustration.

The dynamic case is more complex and timing sensitive. Host 1 issues the first request, which Router 1 forwards to the real destination, the mainframe (Point 2). When the mainframe responds (Point 3), Router 1 forwards it to Host 1 (Point 4) but retains the information in a table inside Router 1.

Subsequently, when Host 2 requests the mainframe's address (Point 5), Router 1 responds from its local cache (Point 6) and suppresses the request to the mainframe. Real implementations are more complex than this, because it is normal practice to age out entries in the proxy cache, periodically sending out a new request to the real destination to confirm the cache contents.

Proxies normally are incompatible with end-to-end encryption. If your security policy permits, it is possible for the proxy to decrypt traffic, apply criteria, and then re-encrypt traffic intended to be forwarded.

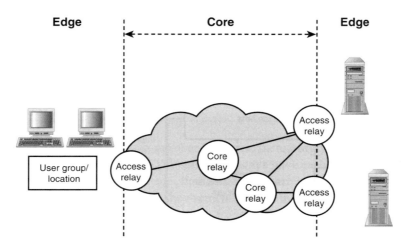

FIGURE 1.7   *End hosts connect to edge devices, whereas core devices connect to edge devices and other core devices.*

The *edge* of a network is the point at which end hosts connect. The backbone interconnects the sites of edge networking.

Another commonly used hierarchical model uses three tiers, *access*, *distribution*, and *core*, shown in Figure 1.8. Access tier functions are at the edge of the network. They need to be close to the end host, because they interact directly with the end host. Typical access layer functions include default routers, broadcast and multicast filters, proxy services, and so on.

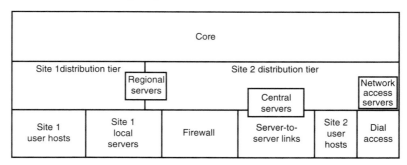

FIGURE 1.8   *Access, distribution, and core devices.*

Access devices connect to end hosts, core devices provide efficient transfer among sites, and distribution devices interface between the two. At Site 1, there are end-user hosts as well as local servers such as printers. The access tier has express communications among the local clients and servers. In most modern installations with appreciable numbers of end-user devices, these express communications are provided by LAN switches. In small installations, the end-user devices can be interconnected with shared-media hubs. See Chapter 10 for details of local interconnection.

In general, you will find switches primarily inside a tier. Routers are more likely to provide the interface between tiers, as are servers with multiple LAN interfaces. These are not strict rules. LAN switches can concentrate into a backbone and thus provide access and distribution, or distribution and core, functions. Routers can be used inside tiers when hierarchy inside the tier makes sense.

Dialup clients are usually placed in the access tier, with their *network access servers* (NASs) in the distribution tier. Look at the central server connections in Figure 1.8 for another example of interfacing between distribution and access tiers. Clients reach the central servers at the distribution tier, but server interfaces used for local server-to-server communications are isolated in the access tier.

Core devices do minimal protocol processing such as filtering or bandwidth management. They are primarily concerned with transfer rather than filtering or traffic management. They can be fast or slow devices depending on network traffic patterns; the key aspect is they are optimized for efficient transfer. A core device can be a low-end router if the core is a low-speed WAN. Other core devices are high-end LAN or ATM switches for campus networks.

Distribution tier devices do protocol translation, bandwidth management, and complex filtering between the core and access tiers. They serve as points of concentration, accepting many access-tier connections and combining their data into high-speed trunks.

To build the appropriate backbone, you need to know the user requirements and map these into a backbone design. You also need to select the technologies and devices you use to connect the edge to the backbone. The next section introduces a methodology for learning those requirements and making those selections.

Formulating a Design Methodology

The design methodology we will use has several major phases. Boundaries between phases might not be clear, and information learned in the later phases is apt to refine information collected and decisions made in earlier phases. One of the fine arts of network design, largely taught by experience, is when to stop a phase and go on to the next.

If your background comes from operating and configuring network devices, be sensitive to the different ways in which design, especially high-level design, is done. It is not a simple cookbook process in which you can plug values into a formula and come up with a final design. To continue a culinary analogy, I am a serious cook. Some of my classic French cookbooks include the directions "take a sufficient quantity of potatoes and cook until done." At my experience level in the kitchen, this is useful information, because it is combined with suggestions on garnishes, sauces, and other matters where I can use independent judgment. As you move to more and more advanced levels of design, you often find that references simply give guidelines that you need to interpret.

Often, even more experience is needed to know when the results of an earlier phase are simply too flawed to build upon. In such a case, you need to go back, refine the information in the earlier phase, and redo the subsequent phases of design. This is apt to ruin an overly optimistic schedule, and you should plan on a certain amount of going back to refine.

I cannot emphasize strongly enough that jumping immediately to the finest technical design, without first understanding the user criteria for success, dooms the project to failure. I use an informal six-phase design approach:

- Step 1. Determine the top management goals, expectations, budget, and fears. In this step, you define the answer to "What is the problem you are trying to solve?" from the perspective of the people who pay the bills and ultimately judge success.

- Step 2. With information technology staff, refine the top management goals. Identify application users and servers and define the topology among them. Collect information about end hosts. Organize the data by end host name, not address, establishing naming conventions as needed. Here, you are answering the question "What is the problem you are trying to solve?" based on the realities of user applications and end host software.

[handwritten margin note: High level design]

- Step 3. Design the addressing structure for all relevant layers and then decide on the routing and switching techniques to use. *Do not yet focus on specific routing and switching products.* This step deals with the question "What internal connectivity problem are you trying to solve?"

[handwritten margin note: Identity from solutions end points]

- Step 4. Select communications software on end hosts and internetworking devices. Consider tradeoffs between doing functions in end hosts versus on internetworking devices. You are asking the question "What problems do you want specific software to solve?"

[handwritten margin note: Select required network hardware]

- Step 5. Select hardware and circuitry, considering tradeoffs between the cost of raw bandwidth and the cost of bandwidth control on internetworking devices. There is likely to be significant back-and-forth analysis between Steps 4 and 5. Step 5 is devoted to the question, "What problems need to be solved by which hardware component?"

[handwritten margin note: deploy network]

- Step 6. Plan deployment. As a sub-step here, you might consider a proof-of-concept demonstration. In many respects, this step poses the question "Have I solved the right problem?"

In this book, we focus on Steps 3 through 6 and on refining Steps 1 and 2.

Designers are often under strong pressure to "get the design done" by executives and middle managers who conceive that design is a matter of selecting boxes and connections among them. Without first knowing the real business requirements, however, there is a much greater chance the project will fail. There are some systematic ways to learn the ultimate requirements, starting with learning the top-level criteria for success and failure.

Step 1: Learning Top-Level Requirements   *[handwritten: High Level Requirements]*

One of the more profound books in political science is Fred Ikle's *Every War Must End* [Ikle, 1991]. This author, who has been a senior official in the U.S. government, draws attention to the point that countries that start wars tend to lose them. The same countries have initial successes. Why, then, is there a conflict?

Countries that start wars have reasons to start ones, but often do not have a well-articulated definition of when they have achieved their objectives and should end the war, even if that requires compromise with their opponents. Many enterprise network designs fail because the executives involved have no clear-cut definition of success, and the objectives begin to vary, then thrash into chaos, during deployment.

If the network designer does not have a clear set of requirements, the customer is not likely to be satisfied with the end product. Some customers, however, want to leap into the internals before the requirements are understood. Sadly, it's not that uncommon for sales representatives of vendor organizations to stress the internal technology, because that internal technology is what they are selling. As a network architect, your most important job is to articulate the real requirements, not glibly to throw networking technology at an undefined problem.

See the sections "Defining Application Requirements" and "Qualitative Factors: The 'Abilities'" later in this chapter to get a more specific idea what you need to learn in Steps 1 and 2. These are not detailed here because Steps 1 and 2 are closely related tasks in which you obtain the same general categories of information, but from different audiences. Step 1 is about getting high-level business requirements, whereas Step 2 refines these into specific requirements for the edge of the network.

You might notice that I consider you, the reader, as having a customer. This role is true even if you are providing design services to someone in your own organization. There is still a process of understanding requirements and negotiating an agreement on what the customer wants and can afford.

Sometimes the Telemarketers Have the Right Idea

To reinforce the idea that most top-level executive decisions about enterprise networks do not focus initially on the routing and switching infrastructure, I offer one of my solutions for dealing with annoying telemarketers.

It seems that I get an almost daily call from long-distance services telemarketers, urging me to change my service to their long-distance service. Their arguments are almost always that heir company can provide service at a lower cost.

I am concerned with the quality and availability of service as well as its cost. So, with some malice in mind, I interrupt their "We will save you 20 percent" with my "Do you have your own national SONET facilities? Do you provide alternative local loop? Where's your POP?"

Usually, there is a pause, followed by "We will save you 20 percent." If the apparent recording begins again, I hang up.

But there is some truth to the sales strategy they use. Cost is a fundamental driver of network design. As annoying as the telemarketer might be, he focuses on the problem most people want to solve—minimizing cost—rather than the mechanics of solving that problem.

Of course, if your only consideration is lowest cost, you also can get a solution of low quality. Cost versus quality is a fundamental tradeoff that you should be discussing with top-level executives.

Detailed Requirements

Step 2: Application Topology and Naming

Step 1 of the methodology identifies a skeleton of key executive concerns. The next step is putting flesh around those bones, typically working with specialists in the applications. Again, it is premature to try to go into the internal implementation of the network, which is the next major step. At this point of analysis, the internals of the network that interconnects these endpoints are magic. The point of this book is realizing that magic. First, of course, you need to identify the endpoints, which are users and servers. User here is a more general term than client. Remember that not all applications are client/server; dumb terminal applications have long been with us. The popular industry term network computer has more in common with some terminal-to-host designs than client/server models.

Second, as you collect this information, introduce a naming structure to organize what you collect. In the IP world, the naming convention for network design is defined by the DNS [Albitz, 1992; Berkowitz, 1998a Chapter 3; RFC 1034].

Third, although the major emphasis should be the applications themselves, you should also collect information on the computer hardware type, operating systems, and networking software type and version being used on those computers. There are times when you have no real statistics on the traffic generated by a given user, but you can establish an upper bound on it when you know the maximum amount of traffic a computer of that type can generate.

Knowing the system and networking software gives you insight into latency and overhead characteristics of the end computers. A computer running SNA or LAT is usually much more sensitive to latency than is one running TCP. A computer running NetBIOS/NetBEUI or NetWare 3.x generates many more broadcasts than a computer running NetBIOS over TCP (NBT) or NetWare 4.x.

You need to establish goals for performance among application hosts. See Chapter 2, "Performance Objectives and Performance Components," for approaches to quantifying these goals, which include response time for interactive application and throughput for bulk data transfer. Availability requirements are another important aspect driven by the needs of applications.

Step 3: Addressing, Routing, and Switching   *Network Design*

Now, it is time to look inside magical clouds and understand their principles, so you can cast your own spells and create a working cloud that interconnects your users and meets their needs.

The backbone provides connectivity among the user endpoints. Its characteristics need to be matched to the user application requirements. Think of flying between two airports. The application requirement is to get between a pair of airports. The backbone is the airplane type and the route it takes.

If you want to fly between Toronto and Tokyo, carrying a large number of people, a Boeing 747 would be an appropriate backbone technology. Taking four commuters between two rural airports is more appropriate for a commuter aircraft.

A staple of spy thrillers, of course, is rushing the hero between two military airports using a supersonic fighter. The 747 is likely to be far more comfortable, but if speed is the most important factor, an F-14 might be a far better choice.

The backbone is optimized for best connectivity among all the users; its structure does not necessarily match specific user requirements. Think of the North American airline system: most airlines concentrate their traffic into flowing among major hubs, rather than directly from small airport to small airport. Connectivity needs of the users are set by the total number of paths through the backbone, the performance and availability needs of those paths, and the available transmission technologies.

In Steps 1 and 2, you deal with a user-oriented worldview. Inside the network, the requirements for efficient and reliable transmission are paramount.

Remember your high-level goal is cost-effectiveness. Avoid pressures from some managers who might be overly concerned with accounting and charge-back, not realizing that a well-designed network shares resources and might not associate individual resources with individual users. They do not realize that attempting to micromanage resource accounting can drive their costs skywards, because so many resources are needed to track usage.

Of course, in much of corporate America, the drive to micromanage is quite independent of any realities of costs and benefits.

In Step 3, you want to be concerned with cost-effective information transfer. Detailed accounting functions should be considered no earlier than Step 4.

Our focus in this book is on Internet Protocol (IP) routing and on a variety of forwarding (often called *switching*) techniques at Layer 2 of the OSI reference model. Evolving methods such as label and cut-through switching are also covered. Do take the use of OSI terminology with discretion, as the OSI definitions have blurred as technology advances. Also, technological advances have blurred the distinction between routers and bridges. *Switch* is a vague term that most commonly is a bridge on steroids, or enhanced connectionless bridge. Designing with connectionless Layer 2 switches is discussed in Chapter 10. Switches also can switch physical media or control virtual circuits, as discussed in Chapter 9.

This chapter helps you start delving into the traffic-flow maps for your network city streets.

End point Needs To Allow Operation on Network

Step 4: Software

After you have decided on the routing structure and where to use switches to optimize performance, you need to select software functions to enable on the routers and switches. Such software decisions do not take place in a vacuum, but involve tradeoffs with software on end hosts and on network management servers. Let's look at some representative decisions.

For routers, a major software decision is the mechanism(s) they will use to find paths. Routers can use preconfigured static information, dynamic routing information exchange, or both. See Chapter 4, "How Do Switches and Routers Find Paths?" for an overall discussion of path determination. Chapter 5, "Dynamic Interior Routing Information Mechanisms," goes into additional detail on alternatives after you decide dynamic routing is appropriate. Chapter 7, "Selecting the Routing/Switching Architecture," discusses the appropriate mix of static and dynamic mechanisms, and the choice of dynamic mechanisms.

How to configure routers

Addressing, as discussed in Step 3, heavily interacts with software selection. If you choose to use unregistered addresses at the edge of the network, but use the global Internet for at least some of your connectivity, you need either to tunnel or translate some of those addresses.

End point address selection

An important part of software selection is handling non-IP protocols at the edge. Do you run them natively through the backbone, coexisting with IP, or do you tunnel the non-IP protocols while wrapped in IP?

Tradeoffs are especially important in dealing with non-IP protocols in your network. For example, Novell NetWare 3.x generates a large volume of broadcast Service Advertisement Protocol (SAP) packets. The entire SAP table is broadcast every 60 seconds. NetWare 4.x, however, sends a much smaller volume of SAPs, only when the SAP information changes.

You can use router software features to reduce SAP volume with filtering and proxying techniques. Converting end hosts to NetWare 4.x dramatically reduces the SAP load. Converting to 4.x, however, requires new software on all hosts, and a substantial amount of system administrator work. This is a good example of a tradeoff between host and network software. If you do not need the additional features of NetWare 4.x, it may be reasonable to implement SAP control on the routers and keep the hosts at 3.x. If you want 4.x for other reasons, you might be able to use much simpler router configurations.

There is a distinct iteration between Steps 4 and 5. You might, for example, decide to use link compression in Step 4. Compression requires appreciable processing power. When you do an initial hardware selection, and discover that a router with substantial CPU or compression coprocessor power is more expensive than additional bandwidth, you might decide to go without compression. The reverse is true; you might, in Step 5, find that uncompressed bandwidth is too expensive and go back to Step 4 to specify compression.

Step 5: Hardware and Media

The most basic part of hardware and media selection is "speeds and feeds." Your preliminary analysis will usually suggest the speeds of the media that need to be connected, and you will have a count of the number of data streams feeding into each internetworking device. Speeds and feeds is a good first pass at selecting particular routing or switching platforms. Remember to include the growth factors you have decided are appropriate.

Major vendors such as 3Com, Nortel/Bay, and Cisco have huge numbers of products. Long ago, I stopped trying to memorize their catalogs; instead, I first decide on the speeds and feeds and then go through the catalog and find devices that match those capabilities.

Just as you will want to trade off doing some software functions on end hosts rather than on routers and switches, you will want to trade off capabilities of the routers and switches versus the transmission medium. One major vendor suggests the appropriate solution to limited bandwidth on LANs is to use LAN switching. If the bandwidth limitation is on Ethernet, however, it might be appropriate to go to Fast Ethernet on selected interfaces and leave most user devices on shared-medium hubs.

As mentioned in Step 4, tradeoffs between compression and raw bandwidth form an important aspect of hardware and medium selection. Another part of selecting the appropriate mix of medium and device capability comes when you have WAN connections from one site to more than one other site. Assume that you need 64 Kbps links to three other cities. You could have three physical interfaces and three local loops to the WAN provider, or you could use Frame Relay with a single T1 local loop over which the three data streams could be multiplexed. By using Frame Relay, you might be able to use a router with one, not three, serial interfaces and also save money on the local loops.

On the other hand, if Frame Relay service is not available in the geographic area where you need the router, it is not a viable alternative. Yet another trade-off involves asking whether you need the 64 Kbps bandwidth continuously or if ISDN on-demand connections might be adequate. If dedicated Frame Relay access is more expensive than the connection time charges for ISDN, ISDN might be a good choice, especially if you only need to connect to one of the other routers at a time.

Step 6: Deployment

Although the First Law of Plumbing says, "If it don't leak, don't fix it," there are times you have to extend plumbing systems. A fairly basic rule of plumbing is to "turn the water off before you cut the pipe."

The parallel in network plumbing is that you don't want to break existing operational services when you add new capabilities. When you are working with a qualitatively new function, such as adding switching to a network that previously has only had routers, you want to familiarize operations staff with the function in a controlled environment. This can be a training class or a test-bed laboratory.

When you begin to introduce the new capability to the operational network, avoid doing massive cutovers, certainly during times that real users are on the network. In hierarchical networks, it is best to start in one area, then add the core, and then add other areas.

There are some good parallels in drug testing and licensing. The Food and Drug Administration has four phases of evaluation:

- Phase 1: Evaluate the absorption and side effects of the drug in healthy volunteers.

- Phase 2: Clinical trials in a small number of patients, evaluating the behavior of the drug in a sick patient.

- Phase 3: Large-scale clinical trials, to establish safety and efficacy.

- Phase 4: Post-marketing surveillance, looking for additional uses and side effects that only show up rarely.

Phase 1 testing for a network capability is the initial learning phase for the designer and operations staff. Phase 2 corresponds to the initial trials with live data.

Phase 3 is just before the full cutover and should reflect workloads close to the expected real environment. In Phase 3 of a network test, the operations staff should be ready to cut back immediately to the legacy environment, should problems occur.

As in drug testing, Phase 4 follows production-level implementation. Certain problems might only show up rarely and be detectable only under full load. As you gain familiarity with the technology, you also can find new applications.

Although drug testing focuses on problems and capabilities, the fourth phase of network deployment should include an additional aspect of monitoring: capacity planning. You want to measure workload and utilization and check these measurements against your assumptions about growth. The goal of capacity measurement and planning is to predict when new resources are needed and to implement them before users are affected.

Defining Application Requirements

In subsequent chapters, we will delve more deeply into technology selection. In this section, however, we detail techniques of application analysis that are relevant to Steps 1 and 2. Both these steps deal with application analysis, but with different audiences and at different levels of detail.

Conceptually, application requirements analysis involves defining which users communicate with which servers, how much traffic will be sent, the expectations of performance for the exchanges between users and servers, and the expectations of availability of the network. With executives, you are concerned with determining the critical services, the budget, and the expectations for security, availability, and performance. You may find quickly that the expectations do not match the budget, and it is critical for you as an architect to manage realistic expectations.

Executives give you the skeleton of requirements, which you flesh out with the information technology staff. Even in a small organization that buys off-the-shelf software, there still should be staff that knows where users are located, an operational necessity. You might need to talk to software vendors to learn capabilities of purchased software.

During the discussions with IT staff, you want to learn about the current system software as well as the applications. There are significant differences in networking capability, for example, among Windows 3.11, Windows 95, and Windows NT.

End users do not see the internals of the network. They should be aware of the communities of interest to which they belong: the sets of services available to them.

Identifying Users and Servers

Begin the analysis with a free-form listing of users and services. It's a good idea to begin this process at the highest possible executive level, encouraging them to brainstorm and recording the results on flip charts.

Although the full application design identifies sets of users and the services they use—communities of interest—remember that your first goal is to find what executives regard as success or failure. Executives often do not conceptualize a systematic relationship between users and services.

It's critical to find out which users and services the executives think of first. By making this discussion free-form and not forcing correlations, you can get very useful information about which users and services first occur to executives, and thus need to be part of a successful solution.

Later, in Step 2, you can refine the skeleton of executive-visible with the information technology staff. During this refinement, you want to pin down the users, servers, and flows among them.

Figure 1.9 shows the communications among clients and servers as *flows*. Flows are one-way, end-to-end relationships between sources and destinations. In Chapter 2, you will see how to associate quantitative traffic and performance requirements with flows.

You collect this information to define *communities of interest*, which are functional and/or geographic sets of users that need to reach common sets of services. Figure 1.10 illustrates communities of interest. Users in a community of interest have common performance and availability requirements. It is perfectly plausible that you might have two communities of interest that use the same set of servers, but one community needs much higher availability than the other.

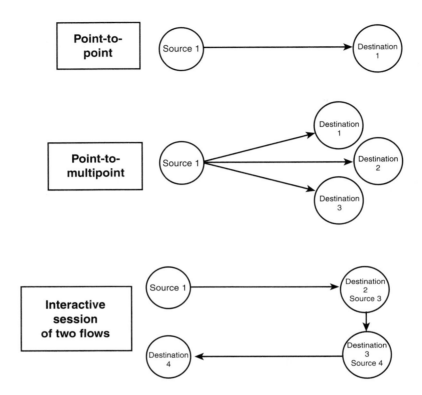

FIGURE 1.9 *Flows are the basic elements of describing application-level requirements.*

one way end-to-end
relationships between
source and destination

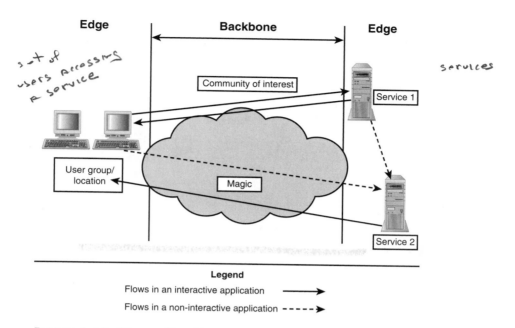

FIGURE 1.10 *Communities of interest are sets of users and servers among which there are flows.*

Administrative Models

One issue in network design is determining the scope of the network design. Networks can't be deployed if no organization is responsible for a given function. Networks turn into chaos when more than one organization is responsible for the same function. The *administrative model* defines responsibilities for different aspects of connectivity, which often involves interconnecting separately managed networks. The administrative model defines the scope of design and operational authority and is at a higher conceptual level than network management.

Like so many architectural concepts in the IP world, these definitions do not come from one central authority. Nevertheless, they reflect my best understanding of the informal consensus of the Internet Engineering Task Force, a perspective of an active participant. Administrative models are summarized in Table 1.1.

Network connection

TABLE 1.1   ADMINISTRATIVE MODELS

Endpoint 1	Core	Endpoint 2	Model
Enterprise 1	Dedicated	Enterprise 1	Intranet[1]
Enterprise 1	Shared provider	Enterprise 1	VPN intranet
Enterprise 1	Dedicated[2]	Enterprise 2	Extranet
Enterprise 1	Shared provider	Enterprise 2	VPN extranet
Enterprise 1	Shared provider	Arbitrary	Internet user
Arbitrary	Shared provider	Enterprise 1	Internet service

[1]*Assumes all IP. If the network mixes protocols, it is a private proprietary network.*

[2]*For purposes of this discussion, a service organization that only services members of the extranet is not considered a shared provider. Shared provider implies a public service provider who provides connectivity under contract.*

The Administrative models include the following:

- Intranets: Single enterprise networks using the IP architecture. Some industry sources consider another property of an intranet: it maximizes the use of Internet tools such as the Web for the human interface, rather than proprietary applications. I do not consider this additional property a requirement.

- Proprietary enterprise networks: Single enterprise networks that include non-IP architecture.

- Extranets: Multiple enterprise networks that communicate using IP architecture over private or contracted facilities, in contrast to the global public Internet.

- Virtual private networks: Single or multiple enterprise networks that establish connectivity over a shared/outsourced infrastructure. Virtual private networks (VPNs) are not directly accessible to the general Internet, although their architecture can include tunnels across the public Internet.

- The global Internet: The set of cooperating Autonomous Systems that use registered IP addresses, DNS-based naming, and BGP routing. There is general public access to the global Internet.

VPN set of user endpoints that communicate over a shared public network

For example, an intranet or a proprietary enterprise network is under the control of a single enterprise. Operational control can be delegated to different parts of the organization, but there is still a central authority.

Extranets involve cooperative relationships among more than one enterprise. There are final authorities within each enterprise that can decide if a given method of connection to other enterprises is acceptable. Depending on the extranet administrative model, there might be a formal organization that manages the inter-enterprise connectivity, such as the VISA or MasterCard networks that interconnect banks. Alternatively, there might be an informal architectural coordination committee.

Do your clients and servers connect only to clients and servers within your own organization? If they are at more than one physical site, how are those sites interconnected? If your users connect to servers outside your organization, how is that connectivity realized? Do you have dedicated lines between your locations?

Are analog dial, Integrated Services Digital Network (ISDN), X.25, or other on-demand physical or data link services used? Do you route to them over Layer 3 services on the global Internet or through a virtual private network (VPN)? A network in which the WAN connections are primarily through dial services often is considered a VPN. Other interpretations of VPN include explicitly engineered networks contracted by service providers or user controlled tunnels through the global Internet. Although an industry-wide definition of VPN does not yet exist, discussions in the IETF VPN Working Group generally are based on it being "a set of user endpoints that communicate over a shared public infrastructure."

If you link computers outside your management's control, but those computers are well-known and are under enforceable common policies, you have an extranet if only authorized employees and partners have access to those machines.

If your end users can access arbitrary hosts in the global Internet, or if arbitrary Internet-connected users can access designated servers you control, you are "on" the global Internet.

Intranets

When you connect clients and servers, the clients and servers are known before they exchange information, and all machines involved are under your top management's administrative control; this is an *intranet*. Figure 1.11 shows the common administrative control inherent in an intranet.

In an intranet, the core is operated by the same organization as the edge networks. A single organization, usually core engineering, is responsible for DNS services for the enterprise. Core engineering and operations also could be outsourced to a third party under the organization's control. Such outsourcing would make it a VPN intranet.

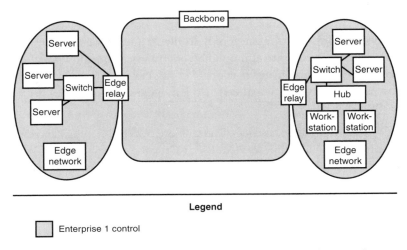

Legend

Enterprise 1 control

FIGURE 1.11 *In an intranet, all components are shown as being under a common administrative control.*

Although this backbone could be tunneled through global internet facilities by either the enterprise or the service provider, the edge networks do not appear on the Internet. Almost any practical WAN involves a service provider, but all requests to that provider come from the organization that owns the LANs. Do note that there is a major difference between tunneled connectivity over arbitrary Internet facilities and tunnels specifically engineered and whose performance is contracted by a service provider.

Extranets

Figure 1.12 shows the more complex administrative responsibilities of an *extranet*, where multiple organizations communicate under a set of bilateral and multilateral agreements on their interfaces. These agreements do not define the internal structure of the participants' networks.

Connectivity between the two organizations could be as simple as a single virtual or dialup circuit. Even with this simple topology, the two organizations
would need to agree on addressing and other parameters. More complex real-
world topologies could link multiple sites of two companies or involve more
than two companies.

In a multiple enterprise organization with significant traffic, or with special
security or other requirements, the various organizations might establish an
organization specifically for managing extranet connectivity. Military organizations in large countries, for example, usually have a joint communications network to which individual bases connect.

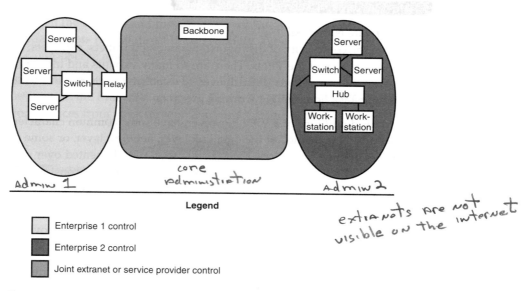

Legend

⬜ Enterprise 1 control

⬛ Enterprise 2 control

▨ Joint extranet or service provider control

FIGURE 1.12

Extranets interconnect multiple enterprises, but are not visible on the global
Internet. In the extranet shown in Figure 1.12, the left and right edge networks
are under different administrative controls. Enterprise 1 runs the left network,
Enterprise 2 runs the right network. Assuming the core is run by a service
organization, both enterprises have to coordinate their network administration
with the core group. In extranets of any appreciable size, a central organization
becomes the only really scalable approach to administration. Otherwise,
each enterprise would have to coordinate with an increasing number of other
enterprises.

The organization owning the visible server name wants it to be highly visible on the general Internet. This server name does not necessarily correspond to a specific machine, but can be distributed across multiple servers, perhaps at different sites. See the later section "Application Distribution Models" for more information.

Having a service Internet-accessible in this manner does not preclude having host-specific login security. Security measures can prevent unauthorized users from using the servers. What makes this different from an intranet or multinet extranet is that the access control is a function of the application or server host, not the network.

In the other common case, shown in Figure 1.14, you, the enterprise network manager, are responsible for providing Internet connectivity to your enterprise's user population, who want to be able to connect to arbitrary Internet machines.

Internet access by the enterprise can be at one or more points of presence.

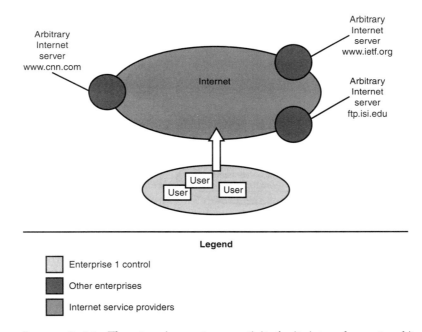

FIGURE 1.14   *The enterprise wants connectivity for its internal users to arbitrary servers on the general Internet.*

Application Distribution Models

Originally, all information processing was centralized in a mainframe. Users connected to the mainframe with dumb terminals that had no local processing capability. Multiple processor applications involved connections among mainframes.

As departmental and personal computers evolved, the industry used the 80/20 rule for networked applications, which suggested that 80 percent of the processing should be done locally and 20 percent done remotely.

More recently, there has been a drive to centralize servers within a campus. The rationale for doing so is to minimize the cost of providing file backups, uninterruptible power, and so on by centralizing operations support resources. Providing physical security for mission-critical servers also drove the trend toward centralized servers. Server centralization has moved the processing ratio closer to 20/80, with 80 percent of the processing done in a server room. Services such as data validation, printing, and cacheing reasonably stay in the workgroup.

The model continues to evolve with increasing workforce distribution and strategic partnerships. In many enterprises, there now can be a mixture of:

- Local processing, including caches

- Campus server processing

- Processing on WAN-connected enterprise servers

- Processing using strategic partner resources in an extranet model

- Processing on Internet-connected hosts

Depending on the specific enterprise, distributions much more complex than 80/20 or 20/80 are common. You might have 20 percent local processing for caches and printing, 50 percent in the campus server farm, 20 percent on WAN-connected internal and partner nodes, and 10 percent on the global Internet.

A highly centralized organization such as a bank might not have any significant Internet or local processing. It might be useful to distinguish between partner and internal WAN-connected resources, and even between regional and central resources within the internal WAN.

It is perfectly reasonable to have a visible server name that does not correspond directly to any single server. There are an assortment of models for distributing workload among multiple servers. Figure 1.15 shows a single virtual
server name that is visible outside the local environment. The actual service,
however, runs on a set of servers within a server farm.

Visibility can mean inside an intranet or an extranet, or on the global Internet.
It is most flexible to refer to the various machines by DNS name, which gives
flexibility in the addresses they resolve to [Berkowitz, 1998a, Chapter 3].

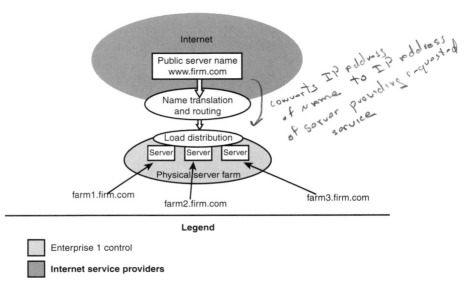

FIGURE 1.15 *The public server name **www.firm.com** maps to multiple machines in a
single server farm. Internal server names in italics need not be visible on the Internet.*

Remember that users looking for service should find services by the name of
the service, not the address of the server. Even when the well-known name
resolves to an address, that address might not be that of an actual server that
does the work. As shown in Figure 1.15, the address to which the name
resolves can be the address of the outside (that is, Internet-visible, registered)
address of some sort of load distribution function. Load distribution functions
can translate external addresses to the internal addresses of actual servers.

The externally visible server name can, in fact, be distributed to different geographic locations, the two server farms shown in Figure 1.16, and then distributed to different servers within these farms. One technique for multiple site spreading is intelligent DNS servers that return a server address based on server load or routing cost. Another technique creates tunnels from server farm to server farm.

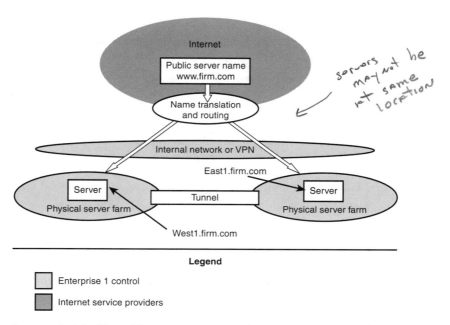

FIGURE 1.16 *The public server name **www.firm.com** can map to machines at multiple locations.*

Public server name maps to multiple machines in a cluster of colocated servers.

When multiple servers are involved in satisfying user requests, the classical disaster recovery model, with a standby mainframe site, does not fit as well. There is no longer the single point of failure that the mainframe recovery site protects against.

Distributed fault tolerance models are excellent when the data and services being provided inherently can be replicated. Many Internet content provider applications fit this model very nicely. The traditional model, however, still can apply best for transaction processing models that involve a master database. Applications in this category include those such as travel reservations or bank operations.

> **Note**
>
> *Allowing general connectivity for users does not mean that your organization cannot impose security policies that prevent access to certain Internet servers. Such prevention can be creative; the security services of one firm with which I worked intercept access requests to sites such as* **www.playboy.com** *and return instead a Web page full of a picture of the firm's CEO, with a snarling audio that says, "Get back to work!"*
>
> *Application caching is another valid technique, hopefully now mostly invisible to your users, that might mean that the server that actually services their request might not be the server they thought they asked for service. Think of a networking group that has all received e-mail of a new technical paper. If their external access mechanism contains a caching facility, the first time the user accesses a Web page containing the paper, it is stored in the cache, and subsequent requests are satisfied by the copy in the cache.*

Network Management Models

Subordinate to administrative models are network management models. Inside enterprises, network management might have centralized or decentralized control. Centralized control is typical of a mainframe data center with a single network control center. An intercontinental network with network control centers in Asia, the Americas, and Europe is a decentralized operation, although there is usually some central point that establishes the network management architecture and deals with enterprise-wide problems.

Too much decentralization leads to an inability to control. For many years, there was a theory that if you put a million monkeys in front of typewriters, one would eventually produce the works of Shakespeare. It is said that this experiment has now been tried and is called the global Internet. The monkey producing Shakespeare theory has been disproved!

Seriously, the global Internet is based on voluntary cooperation among service providers. There is no central authority, which has the implication that no one organization can ensure the quality or availability of the general Internet. Enterprises that rely on the general Internet, as opposed to contractually defined virtual private networks for which specific service providers are responsible, are in great jeopardy if they put mission-critical applications on the Internet.

See the section "Manageability" later in this chapter for more detailed models of the implementation of management. At this point, focus on the administrative assignment of management responsibilities.

Qualitative Factors: The "Abilities"

It would be nice if network designs could be done using a well-defined, quantitative set of technical requirements, and, when these could be met, the design and deployment became a victory. In the real world, successful network design must consider far more than the "size of the pipes."

Think of several less quantitative factors as the abilities of a successful network:

- Scalability: The varied capabilities of adding more users, more sites, and more applications.

- Availability: Often called *reliability*, but I regard the term as more general. I avoid *redundancy* because an English colleague explained that *redundancy* means "no longer needed" in British usage.   *reliability*

- Usability: The ability of users to use network services without difficulty, from the perspectives of both adequate performance and minimum user involvement in connecting to the network. In general, the more secure a network, the less usable it is. A completely secure network is useless, because no traffic can flow over it.

- Compatibility: The ability to support existing equipment and applications.

- Security: The ability to ensure that authorized users have access to resources they need, without compromise of information by unauthorized users, or failure of services for authorized users due to attacks by hostile individuals.

- Manageability: The ability, hopefully invisible to end users, for the operations staff to configure, expand, and troubleshoot the network.

Only after you understand the desires of top management in these areas can you design a winning network. Most of these abilities map into technical requirements, but first look at them in broad terms.

At the edges of the network, users only see the behavior of their applications, not the backbone itself. They have expectations about the performance they want to see. Their expectations can be reasonable only when taken in the context of a defined workload. Their expectations should be met through the life cycle of the network, which is likely to grow significantly during its lifetime.

Scalability is the property of a network that can grow to meet requirements. It is not a trivial task, especially when growth is considered. See the "Scalability" section later in this chapter.

Interactive and non-interactive applications differ, and the interactive ones vary depending on the sort of information they generate. Chapter 2 covers how performance requirements are characterized.

Although service-level agreements define the contract between user and provider, they are not enough. Executive expectations for networks tend to be in qualitative terms, rather than numerical values for response time or other performance parameters.

The most basic ability expectation is *usability*, the property that the network can run the desired applications. The next and lowest quality expectation is *availability*, the assumption that the network will be there to run the applications when needed. *Scalability* is a more subtle quality criterion, because it deals with the life cycle of the network, not just immediate requirements.

Usability is really the most basic criterion as perceived by end users, but scalability is such a basic design requirement that I place it first. Availability is also a fundamental issue, but typically needs to be considered after you know the sizing issues raised by scalability. To understand scalability, you need to understand the size of the existing network and its growth patterns in terms of applications, sites, and users. Only after you have a good idea of the present and future network can you consider all the aspects of availability. Usability is a final test that your design is realistic.

You address compatibility after you learn what end equipment, applications, and existing networking equipment are in place. Although it is essential to have a top-management-defined security policy, the details of security and manageability come as part of network design, after requirements are well defined. Remember that security and manageability intertwine. Classical security mechanisms protect against deliberate attacks on the network, but manageability and availability mechanisms protect against component failures. From the usability standpoint, a network is down whether a deliberate attack or a failure prevents the user from accessing resources. You need to balance your budget for security and management.

Scalability

Many people talk about wanting to be able to grow their networks. In broad terms, scalability is the capability to grow. But there are many dimensions of growth. As a child, I was pleased to watch my mother mark my growth in height with little marks on my closet door. As an adult, I am not pleased to watch my growth when I have to loosen my belt.

I often find that plumbing is a good analogy for networking. Plumbing systems have pipes, the diameter of which determines how much water can flow through them. Plumbing systems have faucets, which determine how much water is allowed to flow out of the pipe into a fixture such as a sink.

Networks have communications media with maximum bandwidths. If you need more bandwidth than a given pipe can provide, you need multiple pipes. Networks have attached hosts that can only accept, or generate, a volume of data from the medium.

Have you ever suddenly shut off a water faucet and heard the pipes vibrate loudly? This is similar to some of the deleterious effects of broadcast on hosts. Just as the plumbing cannot easily handle the bursts of a suddenly closed faucet, but works quietly if it is closed slowly, networks can suffer when they receive traffic in bursts rather than a steady stream. Unfortunately, the nature of both application and much overhead traffic is inherently bursty. Techniques such as buffering smooth bursts into a more even stream that network equipment can handle better.

In contrast, voice and video traffic not only is not bursty, but the silence can be as important as the actual data. Think of the difference between "He is a very nice man" and "He is a very [long pause] nice [long pause] man." A major challenge of voice, video, and data integration is to preserve pauses in the original information streams when the pauses are significant, even though the pauses are opportunities to send information from non-silent sources.

Scaling can simply reflect growth in the number of users. But it also can imply the flexibility to be able to include new types of applications and technologies in the network. Major changes in enterprise organization can affect the administrative, management, and application distribution models. Some upper managers might assume a scalable network can adapt to mergers and acquisition, although there can be even more challenge in divesting parts of an enterprise without major changes to the network.

You might interview the vice president of technical support and first be told, "Oh, we want to be able to grow by 30 percent." On pressing her for further details, you might be told, "We want to move from three to five telephone support centers. The new centers will be in Europe and Australia to give us 24-hour coverage with people who can work on normal shifts. Our current centers each have 30 technicians answering phones, but we want to plan for 50 at each center. The current technician machines use Windows for Workgroups, but we want to migrate to Windows NT, probably 5.0 by the time we are ready."

Not only does this piece of information tell you things about the topology—you need worldwide connectivity—but also scalability needs in the number of sites and the number of users within sites. You also learned a compatibility requirement: The old Windows workstations use nonroutable NetBIOS, but NT 5.0 is IP-based. These are things that are critical in making your technical decisions about media and the routers and switches that interconnect them.

As your interview with the VP progresses, she becomes more comfortable with you and shares more information: "We are also going to add, probably next year, to the force of traveling support specialists. They will need worldwide dial access, which we recognize will probably have to be done through local ISPs. We understand that will require some security for the connections, but we haven't yet determined how much."

You have now learned a scalability requirement in terms of a new application: worldwide secure access. This has implications not just for scalability, but for security and manageability.

How Much Growth?

Part of the art, as opposed to the science, of network design is knowing how much scalability is reasonable in a given environment. Too much scalability can add initial and unneeded complexity and cost. Too little can make upgrading too complex and expensive.

I use an unscientific guideline as a first approximation, refining it as I learn more about the problem and the budget model. For medium-sized enterprise networks, the core architecture should allow for growth by a factor of approximately two orders of magnitude—which is equivalent to a growth of 10 to the power 2, or 100 times. The core implementation should allow for growth of one order of magnitude. This might seem like overkill, but if a network-based application succeeds, explosive growth in a year is quite common.

Remember that this additional growth capability need not involve significant additional cost. In a campus network, the initial expense is installing optical fiber. With rea-

Continues

continued

sonable care, the fiber you run today at 10 Mbps can run at 100 or 1000 Mbps with a change in electronics at the ends.

Small networks should allow for growth of one order of magnitude. Large corporate networks should be architected for two or three orders of magnitude of growth. Internet service providers also should allow for this level of growth.

Architecting for growth doesn't mean that you must install 1000 times the capacity on day one. It means that when you pull cable, you select fiber for which you can use 10-MB Ethernet, Fast Ethernet, and Gigabit Ethernet.

It means you leave rack space in wiring closets to add wiring devices (for example, hubs or switches) for the maximum number of users that can physically fit in the office space fed by the wiring closet. Remember that users might need multiple wiring accesses in individual cubicles, for additional devices such as printers, for migration to new workstations, and as spares.

It means you design an addressing structure that can be changed with growth. It means that you should not need to touch every workstation to renumber the network, but that your workstation addresses come from Dynamic Host Configuration Protocol (DHCP) servers linked to DNS servers.

It means, in general, that your design should be flexible and allow for more powerful equipment to be installed without changing the fundamental architecture.

A network can give perfectly adequate performance at the beginning of its life cycle, but increased load can drive it into collapse. New applications have a great tendency to appear on organizational networks, and the network needs to be sufficiently flexible to cope with reasonable new requirements. Network designers need to educate executives that adding major new applications can require upgrades to the network. Network designers have the responsibility to design a network so that plausible upgrades can be added without total disruption.

Remember that networking devices themselves impose overhead. Without hierarchical design, the workload imposed by routing protocols, server lookup, and so on can increase exponentially and prevent the network from scaling. You might be able to get by with non-hierarchical design with 50 or 500 devices, but at some point of growth, that network is apt to need major restructuring.

Number of Sites

Increasing the number of sites affects your WAN, whether you achieve WAN connectivity over your own facilities, multiplexed provider services such as Frame Relay, virtual private networks, or through the Internet.

Detailed discussions of media are premature when still discussing requirements. Media considerations cannot, however, be ignored if there is an existing
network in place. You need to look at the speeds and topologies of current
links among sites. When you begin to consider growth, you are faced by practical considerations of the growth capability of existing facilities. For example, if
one of your sites has an existing T1 link over which 128 Kbps of Frame Relay
bandwidth is used, the physical medium permits growth to the full 1544 Kbps
available bandwidth. If the existing connectivity uses a full T1, you need to
examine growth requirements for multiple T1s and determine the point when
a higher-speed physical medium such as T3 or ATM is a better choice than
continuing to add T1 links.

User Density at Sites

Knowing where the users are seems a fairly basic requirement. Especially with
the increase in users that telecommute or are mobile, trying to be too detailed
here can be futile. If there are dedicated transmission media that connect
telecommuters to your network, then, indeed, the locations are significant.
Otherwise, it is reasonable to keep track of the locations of their dial-in or other
access points. Even then, you might be less concerned with the location of the
dial-in point than with the service provider that connects them to your network. Remember to distinguish between users that dial in from a fixed location
because they do not generate enough traffic to justify other than dial access,
and the mobile user that is at constantly changing locations. You want to capture the locations of the first kind of user.

As with the WAN connectivity of sites, medium issues enter the discussion of
requirements, although detailed medium design comes later in the design
process. It's essential to know the physical wiring type used for LANs—sub-
Category 5 cable, Category 5, multimode fiber, or single-mode fiber. If the
existing cable plant is Category 3, for example, which does not support Fast
Ethernet over single pairs, you eventually face tradeoffs among installing new
cable, using two pairs for each Fast Ethernet connection, or continuing 10
Mbps operation but make use of workgroup LAN switching.

Locations Are Not Always Known

There are other special cases where you might not know a specific user location. I have worked on military systems where the user was connected by an encrypted dedicated link. When I asked where the other end of the modem link went, I was told "a certain site. Call us if there is a problem." There was a certain implication like "we'd tell you but then we'd have to kill you." I didn't press the matter.

More commonly, you cannot know the locations of some types of users. Telecommuters are at a fixed site, but mobile users are not. It can be useful to split mobile users into two groups: road warriors who dial in from hotels or customer premises and truly mobile users such as FedEx truck drivers.

One aspect of scaling is increasing the number of local users, servers, or both at individual sites. See the section "Application Issues" later in this chapter.

Multicasting and Its Potential for Decreasing and Increasing Traffic

Multicasting has tremendous promise for reducing traffic, but it still is a bleeding-edge topic. Consider a client that sends to a server that has two backup servers, and make the simplifying assumption that the client is unaware of the server resiliency mechanism, simply waiting for a confirmation from the primary server.

Assume that the three servers all must confirm that they have logged the change before the primary server sends back the confirmation. Does the primary send a multicast to the two backup servers and wait for unicast confirmations from each? If so, how do the backup servers let one another know they have made the change? With a confirmed unicast between them?

Or does each server send out an all-server multicast when it writes the record? Does the primary server change the record, send out such a message, and wait for each secondary server to send out a multicast when the secondary server has made the change? By doing it in that manner, a secondary server only needs to send out a single message.

But how does the secondary server know its message has been received? Does it rely on a TCP confirmation over a separate control virtual circuit? If the application protocol runs over UDP, does each server multicast its confirmations as well?

Reliable multicast is not trivial to implement in applications! It has great promise, but it is a new technology.

Remember that multicast can involve one-to-many, many-to-one, or many-to-many relationships. It is usually easiest to model many-to-many relationships as a set of one-to-many or many-to-one trees. Many clients can send to one or more servers, as in fault-tolerant transaction processing.

Users at Large Sites

At large sites, there is apt to be a complex cabling infrastructure. A typical structure, as shown in Figure 1.17, has a hierarchy starting at end user office locations, which connect to horizontal cables, which run to wiring closets. Wiring closets provide a place to interconnect the horizontal feeders to main riser cables. The interconnection usually uses both passive physical patch panels as well as relays.

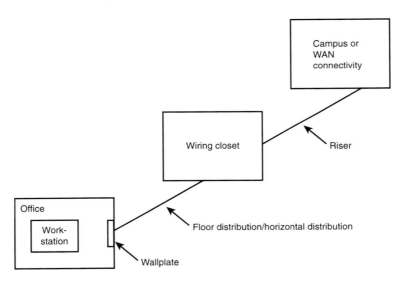

F IGURE 1.17 *Cabling models should be hierarchical.*

See Figure 1.18 for components of a wiring closet. VLANs, discussed later in this chapter, can act as a remotely controllable virtual patch panel and lower your operational cost.

Real patch panels, illustrated in Figure 1.18, are the endpoints in the wiring closets for each cable that runs to a user location. From the patch panel, you connect the cables in use to appropriate relays in the wiring closet. See the section "LAN Media and VLAN Issues" for a further discussion, which includes older media.

In Figure 1.18, patchcords connect the termination of the horizontal distribution cables from the wallplates to appropriate electronic devices, such as hubs, switches, or routers. These relays usually combine multiple office signals into a lesser number of shared equal-speed or higher-speed trunk signals. From the relay output port(s), additional patchcords connect the relay to the riser cable.

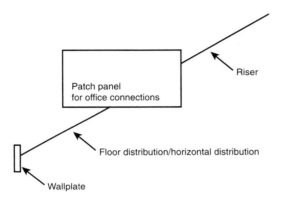

FIGURE 1.18 *Wiring closets have active electronics and passive patch panels.*

Without getting into the details of the cabling, you need to consider how many users can physically be in the area served by each wiring closet. If the enterprise uses modular furniture to create cubicles, you need to consider the potential number of users for each wire closet. This number assumes maximum density of cubicles in the floor area, and potentially multiple connections per cubicle.

One wallplate connection in a cubicle often is not enough. A printer shared by a workgroup frequently goes into an individual's cubicle. When the user's workstation is being transitioned to a newer computer, it's often useful to be able to connect both the old and new devices during the transition. New applications, such as IP telephony, also might need their own wiring.

You will want to consider the horizontal distances between the end-user positions and the wiring closets. Current wiring techniques have a maximum distance of 100 meters, but not all of that distance is available as a pure horizontal straight line between the user location and the wiring closet. Typically, the cable goes horizontally from the wallplate to a bundle of cables taking it to the wall or ceiling; then the horizontal run does not follow a straight line, but goes to the wiring closet through a system of trays that bend around obstacles.

> **Note**
>
> *Remember that 56 Kbps is a theoretical limit. In the United States, you cannot get more than 53 Kbps under ideal circumstances, and 20–40 Kbps might be more typical.*

In workstation-to-main server distributions, interactive, transaction-based applications need access to the main servers, unless cache servers are involved. If the main servers are not co-located, routing or WAN switching is needed to reach them.

Users Who Telecommute

It's important to distinguish between telecommuting and mobile users. Telecommuting users connect to the network from specific sites, often their homes but sometimes telecommuting centers; mobile users connect from arbitrary, unpredictable sites. We talk about mobile users in the next section.

The predictability of telecommuters' connections can be used to improve security. Telecommuters normally use the same phone number, or one of a small set of numbers, analog or ISDN, to dial their access point. At that access point, caller ID or dial-back arrangements can verify the user's location. These are not utterly secure, but generally it is much harder to defeat internal telephone identification than things associated with user computers. If the user computer can be safeguarded and trusted to contain the correct password, using cryptographic authentication extensions of PPP is an excellent idea.

Transmission alternatives that require a fixed installation might be available to the fixed telecommuter, as opposed to the truly mobile user. These alternatives include ISDN, non-mobile cellular radio and cable TV modems, as well as the family of Digital Subscriber Line technologies referred to as xDSL.

> **Warning**
>
> *Don't fall into the trap of assuming that a telecommuter needs only a single IP address that can always be dynamically assigned. Although this is often true, some telecommuting power users have LANs in their homes and need multiple addresses.*
>
> *Techniques variously called port address translation (PAT), network and port address translation (NAPT), or IP masquerade can map multiple local IP addresses to a single global address. These techniques are transparent to most, but not all, applications. [RFC 2391] [Srisuresh, 1998a]*
>
> *Various industry sources have oversimplified address translation techniques. NAT is not transparent to all application protocols; proxies might be needed for transparency.*

Road Warriors

Mobile users can be divided as well, between people who use dial access from arbitrary locations and people and applications that truly communicate while moving. The former can be typified by a sales or customer support person dialing in from a hotel or customer premise during a demonstration, whereas the latter can involve such things as tracking delivery truck position with real-time information from global positioning system (GPS) satellites.

A road warrior is at a fixed location for the entire duration of a communications session. Such a user most commonly accesses your network through public dial facilities with analog modems. For this sort of user, the question is whether he connects to a network access server you operate or whether he calls an Internet service provider and reaches you through the Internet or possibly through a virtual private network.

Hotels, regional corporate offices, and so on are beginning to provide ISDN or LAN access for the road warrior, but such services are in their infancy.

Truly Mobile Users

In contrast with road warriors, the truly mobile user moves physically during a communications session. Unless there are breakthroughs in incredibly elastic extension cords, such users must connect through wireless facilities, such as cellular radio or satellite links.

It can be argued that there is a special case of mobile user, one who uses wireless access within a fixed facility. A good example of this user type is a warehouse worker with a wireless inventory device. Beyond the local environment, however, such a user generally appears to be like one at a large site. It is only their local connectivity that is mobile.

Wireless LANs are becoming more common in fixed locations, because the cost of running cable in old buildings, or for temporary use, can be prohibitive.

Host System Software Issues

You need to be aware of the protocol stacks running on the end hosts, so that you have an idea of how much broadcast traffic they generate. True application programs call upon protocol stacks for actual network transmission and reception.

A single application programming interface, such as NetBIOS, can map to an assortment of lower-layer protocol drivers. The choice of lower-layer driver can have a profound effect on network performance. In Microsoft systems,

NetBIOS can run over the non-routable NetBEUI, over the Novell IPX protocol, or over TCP/IP. NetBEUI is broadcast intensive and does not scale well. Native Novell systems can run NetBIOS over native IPX, over IPX encapsulated in IP, or, in NetWare 5, directly over TCP/IP. Again, the IP drivers are the most scalable.

Application Issues

Interactive and non-interactive applications differ, and the interactive ones vary depending on the sort of information they generate. In Chapter 2, we will detail how performance requirements are characterized.

The more complex the relationship, the more likely it is to generate multicasts or multiple unicast packets. As shown in Figure 1.19, only one host needs the information in an n:1 relationship. In an n:m relationship, m hosts need the information, and in an n:n relationship, (n-1) hosts must receive the information.

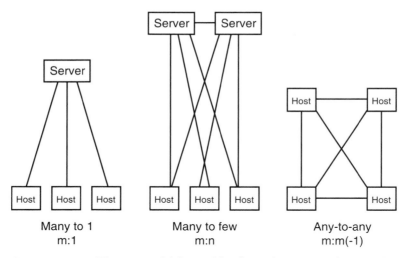

FIGURE 1.19   *There are multiple possible relationships among clients and servers and among peer hosts.*

Your total bandwidth requirement is affected by application topological relationships and the way in which information is sent. A subtle way in which the user workload can increase involves the interactions among the following:

- Basic application record size. Simple text interaction, such as commands sent to a database system, are small. Complex graphics are large.

- The extent to which packets are replicated—copied—so multiple receivers can act on them. An intelligent application should multicast the information, sending one copy that can be heard by all recipients, rather than sending separately to each destination.

Is there one timesharing mainframe, to which all devices are clients or terminals? Is there a small cluster of servers to which all clients send data, and the servers copy it to one another? Is it a collaborative application where all hosts directly exchange data with all other hosts? If multicast mechanisms are not used in the latter two relationships, the data volume increases with the number of hosts.

- Number of users.

It takes more bandwidth to move a large record in the same amount of time that it takes to move a small record. When multiple copies of the same record are needed by multiple servers, as shown in Figure 1.20, the total bandwidth is multiplied.

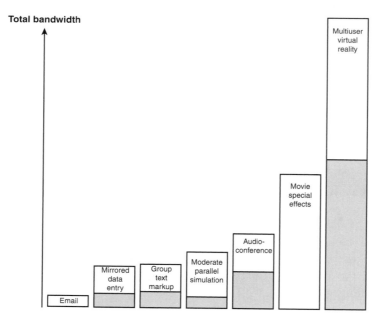

FIGURE 1.20 *For applications that send traffic to multiple destinations, total traffic can be reduced by sending a single multicast (white) rather than multiple unicasts (gray).*

People often incorrectly equate multicast with multimedia. The movie *The Last Starfighter* broke new ground in effectively having all its special effects computer generated, and cinema-quality moving imagery certainly meets most definitions of multimedia. Yet these special effects were generated on point-to-point links from high-quality graphics workstations to a time-sharing super-computer.

When you need to communicate among multiple servers, using multicasting, as shown in Figure 1.20, can reduce the bandwidth requirement. There is an unfortunate tendency in basic networking presentations to suggest that multi-casting automatically imposes undesirable overhead. In actuality, the appropriate use of multicasting reduces overhead. See the section "Broadcast and Multicast Effects" in Chapter 2.

Multicasting and broadcasting both reduce bandwidth in comparison with unicasting the same information to all destinations. Avoid broadcasting in applications, however, because it can impose heavy CPU demands on hosts not interested in the broadcast traffic. Well-designed network interface cards (NICs) and driver software should not impose CPU load for multicast traffic to which a host does not subscribe.

Rules of Thumb for Approximating Data Workload

In the absence of more specific information, there are two fallback techniques you can use to estimate workload. You can consider what the computers on the network can generate as a maximum load. Alternatively, you can look at the general applications being executed and use rules of thumb for the amount of traffic typically generated by that kind of application.

Increased numbers of users can be supported with hubs or switches at the low end. The question is the bandwidth requirements. Purely from the user traffic standpoint, perhaps 100 to 200 66-MHz PCs reasonably can share Ethernets. Taking the processor to 133 MHz with an appropriately sized bus drops to around 10, the number of devices that can share a common 10-Mbps Ethernet medium [Cabletron]. These numbers do *not* consider the application; they are worst-case assumptions based on the capability of the processor to generate data traffic. No application can send more traffic than its computer is capable of transmitting.

Estimating workload by the capabilities of the hosts emphatically does not mean the hosts are adequately sized or will perform well. In the absence of other information on application workloads, however, the host capabilities do establish an upper bound on workload.

From my experience, an approximation based on application type is that a typical office user should get 100–200 Kbps of bandwidth for an office automation application. If there is a requirement for business-quality videoconferencing, the bandwidth requirement grows to roughly 500 Kbps for a single talking head. The 500 Kbps is a rough number for LANs; 384 Kbps is a common videoconferencing speed over WANs. See the later discussion of "Video."

Broadcast effects on a CPU tend to become significant at higher broadcast levels, generally when larger numbers of devices are in the same broadcast domain.

Functions Local to a Workgroup

What information stays local? Printed output is one obvious source of information. Are there printers, read-only files, or other servers intended for local use only? If so, it might be useful to use LAN switches to get efficient access to them. Switches help if LAN congestion is an issue, or if there is a need for speed-shifting on server ports.

For data entry applications, screen formats can reasonably be distributed to local servers. Edit and validation files can be on these servers as well. It can improve performance to cache these files on the workstation.

Surprisingly to some, multimedia data often is best placed on CD-ROMs or local staging disks, with the navigation commands flowing over the WAN. This is surprising because multimedia, in many people's minds, equates to a high bandwidth requirement and thus fast, expensive WAN links.

When defining the problem, explore whether some functions now done remotely can reasonably be moved to the workgroup. Print services are an obvious candidate, but providing application caches can improve performance while reducing bandwidth requirements.

adding latency
" multiple is one
vs single wire y
can help prevent
overloads at a
server or contact
point

Of Course Switches Are Better. Trust me. I Sell Switches.

You should be aware of situations where replacing a hub with a switch can make the local situation worse, not better.

Imagine that you have 100 fast workstations that access a common server. All are interconnected through a 10-Mbps Ethernet.

When the Ethernet driver on each workstation has traffic to send, it detects when the medium is busy and buffers the transmission request. This causes latency, but doesn't necessarily cause packet loss because the workstations have sufficient buffering.

Now, introduce a switch. Why, one might ask, is the manager of this network introducing the switch? In the real world, it might be due to the persistence of the sales representative of a switch vendor, rather than any real understanding of the problem.

Each workstation has dedicated bandwidth to the switch, which means the workstations no longer see traffic from other workstations and the server. The switch delivers traffic even faster to the overloaded server.

If the server can accept a 100-Mbps Fast Ethernet interface and is fast enough to keep up with it, a switch can be useful as a speed-shifting device that creates more bandwidth into the server. Otherwise, the switch can contribute to overloading the server and to the workstations dropping packets that appear to have timed out.

Always remember that an application involves both hosts and networks. Improving the network by adding a switch might not help at all, if the problem is a server that is too slow for its workload. The proper solution here is upgrading the server, but, if that is not immediately possible, you need to realize that a switch can make the problem worse.

You need to investigate further why the switch is a bottleneck. If the processor or disk memory is overloaded, that is a major upgrade for which your customer might not have budgeted.

If it is more a problem of bandwidth into the server, the cost of changing from a 10-Mbps to a 10/100-Mbps NIC is trivial. After the server interface runs at 100 Mbps, a switch does have a value for speed shifting.

You must consider servers and switches as a single system. The bottleneck rarely is at the client end, although there are other good reasons to connect clients directly to switch ports. Switch ports usually provide much better network management capabilities than do hubs.

Switches, routers, and multi-ported application servers can all provide local connectivity. WAN connectivity emphasizes routers, but there are low-end roles for direct host connections to remote access servers, and there are high-end applications for Frame Relay and ATM WAN switches.

Server-to-Server Functionality

Do your application servers talk to one another? This can happen in several ways, not all of which may be obvious. It can be easy to forget about inter-server communications, but these can be major sources of traffic. Perhaps the most common inter-server communications function is backup from application to archival servers.

Another common server-to-server function is resource location. DNS name resolution is a common example, where a local server refers names it does not understand to a more authoritative server. In the case of DNS, the servers are not likely to be at the same physical location.

It is quite common, however, to have application servers in a central server farm, a data center, rather than close to the end user. The industry seems to go through phases where application servers move close to the end user, then back to a data center. Switches can be an excellent way to interconnect co-located servers at one physical location, such as a data center, to optimize inter-server communications. It is quite common to have a specific server or servers used to create backup files and to have a dedicated hub or switch for a backup path.

Other common inter-server functions include resource location and database replication. Both servers and workstations may have to query DNS servers to find information.

Application Replication and Multicasting

Now consider a fault-tolerant application with two real-time backup servers that mirror the primary application server. The application server sends a copy of each transaction it executes to each mirror server. It only does a final update after it receives confirmation that the mirrors have recorded the transactions.

For each user transaction received by the primary server, at least five messages are generated:

- Two copies to mirror servers

- Two confirmations from mirror servers

- One response to client

- Possibly two more confirmations to mirrors that the client response was actually sent

Application replication, at the very least, takes place in a different machine than routing packet replication.

Multicasts Aren't Just for Multimedia

Readers with backgrounds in fault-tolerant transaction processing will recognize that the amount of traffic generated depends on the commitment/recovery mechanisms in use, possible record locks and releases, and so on.

This example assumes that a unicast message was used to send each copy to a separate mirror server. Such copy transmission, however, is an excellent application for sending a single multi-

cast that would be received by both mirrors.

As the technology becomes available, users should consider using mirrored application servers that understand network or data link layer multicasting. This can lead to significant traffic reductions. As you will see in Chapter 5, such multicasting is exactly what the OSPF routing protocol does, quite successfully, to reduce traffic among routers on a shared medium.

Database replication includes both real-time mirroring systems and periodic updates, as found in Lotus Notes. I tend to regard Web caches and replicated databases as subtly different, because the Web caches are essentially anonymous servers, whereas a replicated database should be tightly managed.

Database replication is not the only reason to have application-level replication. Replication can be useful in fault tolerance and in collaborative applications.

C H A P T E R   1   WHAT IS THE PROBLEM YOU ARE TRYING TO SOLVE?

59

Scaling Collaborative Applications

Collaborative applications can indeed involve workstation-to-workstation communications, but this is not a given. A scalable approach is often for workstations to send collaborative application data to a server, as a unicast. The server then sends unicasts to other members of the group and retransmits if necessary.

If you do have collaborative applications, you need to understand their multicast and unicast characteristics. The extreme case is that of a workstation in a collaborative group of n workstations. Assume that these n workstations are part of a larger group of m hosts. To avoid the complexity of Layer 3 broadcasting and multicasting for this workload example, assume all hosts are part of a Layer 2 broadcast domain.

The collaborative application is completely unicast. This means it collaborates with n other workstations, sends each of its $(n-1)$ peers a single unicast packet for an operation it initiates, and receives a single unicast acknowledgement packet from each. Therefore, the total traffic from a single operation is $2\times(n-1)$ packets. If the $(n-1)$ other workstations all respond at an application level, another $(n-1)\times(2\times(n-1))$ packets are generated.

Alternatively, the workstation might send out a single broadcast packet. It would still expect $(n-1)$ responses as acknowledgements. The m hosts all have to process a CPU interrupt when they receive the broadcast.

Using multicasts would improve the situation, assuming that the $(m-n)$ hosts that are not part of the collaboration are smart enough to realize they do not have to process multicast packets sent to a group to which they do not belong. In such a case, one packet goes out and gets $(n-1)$ acknowledgements. Only $(n-1)$ hosts need to process interrupts.

Voice Considerations in Workload

Integration of voice and data tends to involve specialized equipment. Voice over IP is an emerging technology with significant promise. Voice over ATM and Frame Relay are even more mature.

Voice actually does not produce a large amount of traffic, but it is quite sensitive to delay. As a consequence, many network designers give a large amount of bandwidth to voice in the local area, as a simple way to avoid delays caused by congestion.

Direct workstation-to-workstation communications still can occur. Don't neglect this possibility, especially in small offices. This is very common with Apple, NetWare Lite, and early Windows workgroups.

The need for direct communications between workstations can be overstated, but it is there. Other than in a small office, this sort of traffic can appear primarily as an exception case. Workstation-to-workstation file transfers can be useful when upgrading to a new machine. Pings and other network management tools can be useful when troubleshooting the local environment.

Availability

Availability means that the network will continue to provide services in the environment expected for it. The expectation here is one of how hostile the environment might be. Military tactical networks have to cope with the significant probability that individual relays can suddenly become rapidly expanding fireballs. Most community libraries need not worry about such threats.

Expectations of Telephone Networks and the Internet

When you are about to make a telephone call, do you stop to wonder if you will get a dial tone? In developed countries, the telephone system has achieved a level of availability that makes it transparent to its users, who believe it will always be there when needed. In contrast, if you are about to dial in to an ISP, do you wonder if you will be able to get connectivity?

Telephone service is a given in developed countries, but Internet access has not reached the same level of trust. Mission-critical applications should not depend on general Internet connectivity. You can contract with ISPs to provide WAN service, but these services should be quite separate from their general Internet offerings.

Robustness means that your services not only remain available but they remain available at an adequate performance level. Robustness ties to scalability in that a robust system operates effectively when load increases. Robustness ties to reliability in that you are protected against component failures. Robustness ties to security measures that protect your network from deliberate attacks.

Robustness also ties to manageability. Components will fail, and you must be able to diagnose and circumvent problems and then correct the underlying failure. It's a lot easier to be proactive if your network tolerates single failures without intervention.

Fault tolerance guards against failures of clients, servers, and the interconnections among them. Protecting against client and server failures usually requires providing redundant computers.

Threats

You must consider what sort of threats you are trying to protect against. Yes, a Tom Clancy scenario with a 747 crashing into the data center would seriously affect operations, but can you obtain and afford the anti-aircraft defenses to stop it? It might be cheaper to establish a backup data center in a distant city, which also protects you against hurricanes, earthquakes, and freeway gridlock in a way that guns cannot.

The tradeoffs involved are shown in Figure 1.21, in which a noncritical application might have adequate connectivity with a single router and single line. Availability increases with a single router, a single dedicated line (the dotted line), and a dial or ISDN backup. This protects against failures of the dedicated line. If the dedicated line is significantly faster than the dial link, the backup mode is a degraded one.

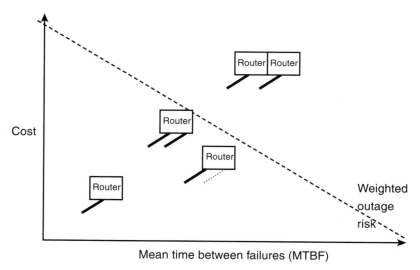

FIGURE 1.21 *Tradeoffs between cost of protection and weighted risk.*

Fully redundant backup lines can protect against communications failures, without loss of performance, as long as the backup link is used only for backup. Typically, there are pressures from financial managers to load share and use the expensive backup line. Such managers don't realize the performance impact if transparent performance is expected.

The amount of backup to provide is complex and subjective. I often find the best way to get top executives to budget for backup is not to concentrate on the overall availability—the mean time between failures (MTBF)—but to ask them to estimate the cost of downtime—mean time to repair (MTTR). After you know the cost of downtime, you can decide if a given mechanism for protecting against failures is cost justified. Downtime at an airline reservation center can cost thousands or millions of dollars an hour, so the cost of backup facilities is much more justifiable than at the public Internet access area of a city library.

Load Sharing

Load sharing is a valid technique, but all its implications need to be considered. Is it the organization's policy, for example, that normal performance is to be expected only when both of two Internet connections are active? If so, top management must understand that performance will drop by at least 50 percent if one connection fails. The performance penalty can be even worse due to heavy congestion of the remaining link.

As a network architect, you need to decide on the role of load sharing, both as a means of delivering bandwidth and as a means of improving availability. Some upper managers find it easier to understand a hot standby, otherwise unused backup facility than the complexity of load sharing. Other upper managers hate the idea of an unused facility and demand load sharing.

If the intention is that both connections can carry the full load, it still might be wise to send some traffic over the backup link, simply to test that it is available.

Load sharing can make troubleshooting more difficult. In connecting to two different Internet service providers, it is quite common that a query to a remote site might go out one link, but the response comes back on the other. This is called *asymmetrical routing*.

If you go to the trouble of having backup lines, try to ensure that they go through your building, and to the streets to your carrier, through separate physical paths.

Relays tend to be much more reliable than lines, but they do fail. A more robust configuration is redundant both in lines and routers. Relays do fail, and hosts need to be able to find alternate routers if they do.

Formal backups definitely have a role. But they are not the only way of achieving fault tolerance. Mirroring and disaster recovery sites are other techniques.

Application Backup

One of the more common excuses in the industry, almost ranking with "The project is 90% complete" is "The network is slow because backup is running." If backup traffic interferes with applications, providing more bandwidth is a viable solution. If the reason applications are slow is that the backup software is locking files or records while they are copied, more bandwidth might not help.

Simple solutions sometimes, but not always, help. Moving backups to the middle of the night is an obvious solution, but one that doesn't fit all environments. For example, what if the application performs real-time weather monitoring, which runs around the clock? What if the data center has no assigned personnel after business hours, and there is no budget for overtime? Unattended backups are not always feasible, because there might need to be a human present to change the physical backup media.

Formal backups definitely have a role. But they are not the only way of achieving fault tolerance. The level of traffic among these redundant computers varies. If the policy is to copy a backup file onto a spare computer and then start running from that computer, the traffic load imposed is that of the original backup, and the exception case of loading the backup onto the spare machine. Backup and restoration are not real-time fault tolerance mechanisms, but can be perfectly reasonable tradeoffs between the cost of protection and the cost of downtime.

When multiple servers are involved in satisfying user requests, the classical disaster recovery model, with a standby mainframe site, does not fit as well. There is no longer the single point of failure that the mainframe recovery site protects against. Distinguish between server farms at a single location, which might provide backup servers but still can have site-wide failures, from multiple server farm sites with traffic distributed among them.

When downtime is more critical, mechanisms such as mirroring can give a much higher level of protection. In addition to the cost of the additional machines needed for mirroring, real-time replication of records to multiple machines can significantly increase network traffic.

Mirroring

Some fault tolerance schemes involve *mirroring*, where every completed transaction is immediately logged to another disk that mirrors the server. There indeed might be a synchronization protocol in use that does not let the client see completion until writing to the mirrored device is confirmed.

High-reliability applications can use multiple mirrors for a given transaction. In such a case, if the original server sends a separate message to each of N mirrors, the total traffic replicates by a factor of N. This is an excellent application for a multicast protocol, because a single packet can be heard by the N mirrors.

This becomes more complex with further examination. It's relatively straightforward to use multicasting to send the record to the mirror machines. If the transfer to mirrors is not a reliable, acknowledged one, this can be perfectly adequate. If there is a need for synchronization, however, the individual mirrors might have to send specific acknowledgements back to the originator, and the originator might need to confirm receipt.

Disaster Recovery Sites

In enterprises that have large server sites, there needs to be protection against failure of the major site, or all connectivity to it. User clients need to go to an alternate site.

Tolerance to major server failure is not strictly a network problem. The network, however, is intimately involved in reconnecting users to the new site.

In a disaster recovery site without mirroring, users, or possibly the user application, are aware of a failure and understand they need to reconnect to the backup site.

There are two basic strategies for rehoming: having the user machines do a DNS name request and obtaining the address of a new server or reactivating the same IP address at the other site. Name-based methods are much more flexible.

In a name-based recovery scenario with user participation, after users detect a failure, they reconnect to the backup site. Assume that your primary site is main.enterprise.com. In the event of failure, the users reconnect to backup.enterprise.com. DNS returns a new address to which your network routes.

In a somewhat less complex name-based recovery scenario, the users reconnect again to main.enterprise.com, but an intelligent DNS system returns a different address, that of the backup site. When this is your backup scenario, be sure that the DNS responses have a short time-to-live value so their machines do not try to go to an old address that they have cached.

time—to— Live

Address-based recovery schemes have the same address for the primary or backup sites, but are designed such that the address is never active in more than one place. When the primary site becomes unreachable, routes to the address active at the primary site age out of the routing tables, and the routers learn paths to the new location. In such a scenario, it is critical that routers at the failed site do not report the site is reachable, even for diagnostics. Maintaining this sort of configuration is far more difficult than one in which there are unique addresses for each site, learned through DNS.

Usability

the network supports the applications that need to be executed

From the user standpoint, *usability* means runs the desired applications. The underlying network implementation is not of concern to end users.

Increasing usability often requires moving responsibilities to new network components, or to network administrators. For example, one of the easiest ways to implement a secure Web browsing capability requires an end user to log in to a firewall and then log in to the remote server from a firewall prompt. Double logons can be avoided by putting proxy client software into the user host, but that can require a change to software on that host. Although most commercial Web browsers contain security clients, the first implementations did not.

When the network runs these applications, it must be responsive. When the applications are interactive, their response time is sufficient for the users to be productive. When the applications are non-interactive, as in the case of file transfer, they are usable if the non-interactive function is carried out in an acceptable period of time. See Chapter 2 for some guidelines on what constitutes acceptability.

Compatibility

Among the most common compatibility issues is the capability to carry non-IP protocols through the backbone. You need to trade off the varying approaches of upgrading end hosts, tunneling legacy protocols through a backbone, and allowing legacy protocols to coexist with IP on a private backbone.

Compatibility issues also arise with networking equipment. It's worth noting that there can be a fair degree of compatibility among different vendors' data exchange protocols, but you might need different management applications to be configured. These issues are discussed further in the section "Compatibility with Existing Network Interconnection Devices."

Another issue is compatibility of management tools. Let's examine that as part of the overall issues of manageability.

Security

In the earlier discussion of "Threats" in the "Availability" section, I discussed the need for balance. Spending too much effort on protecting against one threat to availability cannot give sufficient protection against another. Setting up anti-aircraft defenses against a wayward 747 crashing into your data center is not as cost-effective as providing a geographically dispersed backup data center. Geographic dispersion would protect against a wider range of threats, such as hurricanes and earthquakes.

Many texts treat security and manageability as different problems. I prefer to look at them as the same basic issue: ensuring that your users can get the services they need. Classical security mechanisms protect against deliberate attacks, but network management and fault tolerance mechanism protect against errors and component failures. Making too strong an artificial distinction between deliberate and accidental threats can confuse the situation. If the 747 crashes into the data center, does it really make a difference if a terrorist flew it into a target, or if it fell from the sky because it ran out of fuel?

There is no single security threat, and no single security protective measure. Network security alone cannot protect against all threats; you also need host-based and procedural measures. Security systems provide the following:

- *Identification* of users, *authentication* that they are who they purport to be, and *credentialing* to establish what operations they can perform.

- *Integrity* services that ensure data are not altered. There are two kinds of integrity, *unitary* integrity and *sequential* integrity. Unitary integrity is concerned that individual records are not changed, whereas *sequential* integrity ensures records are not added to or deleted from a stream of records.

- *Confidentiality* services that protect data from unauthorized disclosure.

- *Non-repudiation* services that prove messages were actually sent or received. The first is similar to a receipt for mail sent at the post office and guards against claims such as "the check is in the mail." The other kind of non-repudiation service is similar to a certified mail receipt: a proof of delivery.

- Protection against *denial of service* attacks intended to disable your network or hosts on it. Protections here intertwine tightly with fault tolerance and manageability.

Let me repeat and rephrase that last point. Manageability is closely associated with security. A basic management problem is identifying the specific device that is having problems. A user might need to access the network from several different computers, none of which is under her complete control. At a large site, you might want to implement an authentication scheme that requires such a user to type a password, use a personal one-time password generator based on cryptographic methods, or use other techniques such as biometric identification devices that verify fingerprints, retinal patterns, or hand geometry.

The authentication service could log the physical port from which the user accesses the network. When you know the physical port, you can ask a switch what MAC address is active on it.

Manageability

One of the "abilities" executives rarely see is the ability to do network management. This really is unfortunate, because network management is a major cost factor over the life cycle of your network.

Workforce distribution affects the cost of operating and managing the network. You need to consider your people management of network management! Some industry surveys have suggested the two most expensive parts of the life cycle cost of enterprise networks are WAN bandwidth and operational personnel costs. It is quite common to see total costs of 75 to 85 percent for WAN bandwidth. Because host software often is a major source of bandwidth overhead, WAN costs can be a major motivation for moving from Microsoft NetBEUI to NetBIOS over TCP, or from NetWare 3.x to NetWare 4.x or 5.x. NetWare 4.x removes the major load factor of service advertisements, and NetWare 5.x is IP native as well.

SNMP Management in Perspective

Simple Network Management Protocol (SNMP) management is wonderful in distributed networks, and I recommend it. But as I write this, I can reach over and touch an 8-port Ethernet hub that cost me about $60. It interconnects several computers on two tables in my home office. I am considering at least doubling the range of my network: running some Ethernet cable up to my bedroom and guest room, for times when my visitors or myself would just as soon use my laptop. Even with this massive growth, somehow I don't feel driven to implement SNMP management.

In a network of this size, one proven method to verify connectivity is not to use SNMP, or even simple IP diagnostics such as *ping*—it is to tug on a cable and see if it feels loose. Be realistic.

Specialized interpretation methods might be required for home networks. If you tug on a cable and it tugs back, a four-legged member of your staff might be involved. When I troubleshoot, I don't only check for mouse problems, but also those caused by a cat.

A basic issue in the industry is that people with the skills to diagnose and treat almost any problem do not want to sit and answer phones, or do repetitive configurations.

Smaller remote sites might not have technical staff capable of troubleshooting. Many models should be looked at here, including outsourcing remote troubleshooting to local ISP personnel, implementing remote management tools, or first-level training for remote staff.

Remember the dynamic proxy services discussed earlier? They are a good example of trading off bandwidth against the direct and indirect costs of system administration. Adding caches adds more system administration workload. If a cache product costs $25,000, but it requires $50,000 a year to administer it, your first-year cost is $75,000. Is this more or less than the cost of the bandwidth saved?

It might seem that expending administrator time so bandwidth can be absolutely minimized makes sense, if the actual hands-on administrator time is the only consideration. If the administrator leaves in frustration over the boring work, there can be very substantial costs of temporary coverage, and of hiring and training a replacement.

The "abilities" mentioned up to now are visible to the users and their management. There is a more detailed level of "ability" that is more the province of the network architect. These additional abilities go into the design of the network infrastructure.

Sometimes Simple Solutions Succeed

Remember that no matter how sophisticated remote site management tools are, they are not very useful if no remote site personnel can understand their output and central site personnel cannot access that output because connectivity with the remote site has been lost.

One organization I worked with kept its priorities straight. It had small remote offices with three or four PCs, a dedicated printer for each PC, a shared Ethernet hub, and a single small router linked by Frame Relay to a central site.

When I asked about backup to the Frame Relay connection, they said, "Why? If the router goes down but the Frame Relay is actually up, we waste money on the backup. What we do is give each of the PCs a modem and let them dial directly into the RAS server at the central site. We have good corporate long distance rates, and the workstations don't have much traffic to send and don't connect for long. For us, it's more cost-effective to forgo complex backup and simply let the individual users have dial backup until a support technician can get to the site."

This was creative and practical thinking. Sometimes the low-technology solution is the right one.

Addressing, Switching, and Routing Design

Many books talk of building one's network as if it is a new architectural creation rising from untouched soil. In the real world, the requirement is far more likely to be remodeling one's existing network to meet new demands.

Changes to existing networks tend to be evolutionary rather than revolutionary. There are exceptions, especially when the dominant existing technology does not appear to have future growth. A good example of this appears in large Token Ring shops that commit to a major conversion to Ethernet, with its growth to Fast and Gigabit Ethernet. Still, there are times when you want to create and test a new backbone, or a new campus network, and then transfer existing services to it.

You might notice that we have not yet considered the implementation of the backbone. Many cost, scaling, and technology issues enter into selecting the actual backbone details. The backbone needs to provide the underlying structure that allows the service level to be satisfied, under the defined workload and after reasonable growth.

Begin with the user requirements and then examine the distribution of functions specified by the administrative model. Each separately managed piece contributes to end-to-end performance. Delays in each piece, for example, must sum to be less than or equal to the one-way, end-to-end delay needed to realize the end-to-end delay objective.

Before you select the internetworking devices, you need to take inventory of what you have and develop an addressing plan for the new network.

Relating Application and Network Topologies

Application topology describes the network as seen by its users, remembering that users do not see an integrated enterprise communications utility. Figure 1.22 shows a model that is quite useful for understanding application topology. It is a model and should not be a straitjacket. Chapter 3, "Application Topology: Naming Endpoints," of *Designing Addressing Architectures for Routing and Switching* [Berkowitz, 1998a], deals with this topic. Ideally, users are not aware of network communications at all. Rather than the details of connectivity, they see a certain set of services they can use, and the network simply becomes the underlying magical miracle.

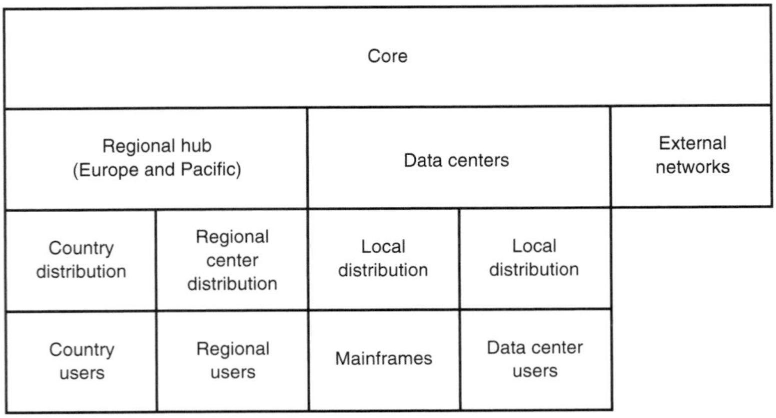

Core			
Regional hub (Europe and Pacific)		Data centers	External networks
Country distribution	Regional center distribution	Local distribution	Local distribution
Country users	Regional users	Mainframes	Data center users

FIGURE 1.22 *A high-level view of an application topology.*

In Figure 1.22, the network core interconnects key user and server endpoints of communities of service. The distribution tiers concentrate groups of users and servers for optimal connection to the core and can contain distributed servers.

I start the process of application analysis with this model and then evolve it to an architectural drawing, as shown in Figure 1.22. The next step in the process of application analysis, shown in Figure 1.23, identifies the general internetworking technologies used at each level of the hierarchy.

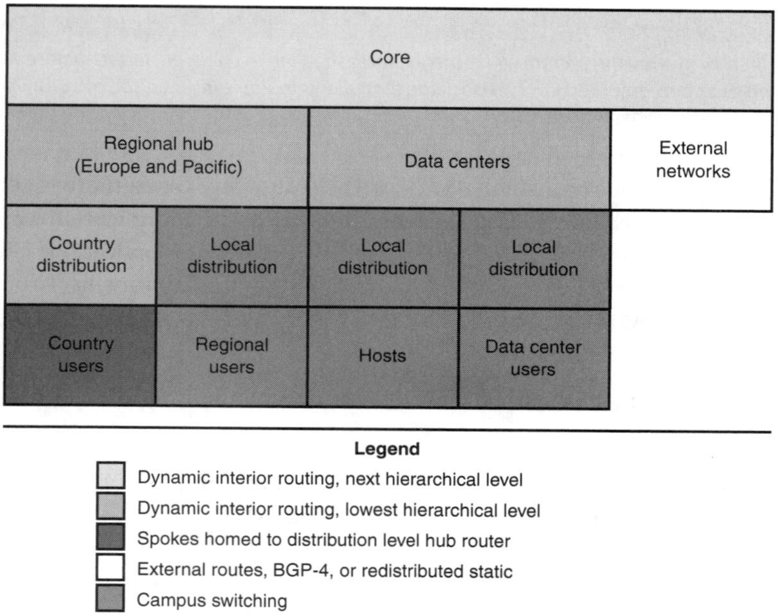

Core			
Regional hub (Europe and Pacific)		Data centers	External networks
Country distribution	Local distribution	Local distribution	Local distribution
Country users	Regional users	Hosts	Data center users

Legend

- Dynamic interior routing, next hierarchical level
- Dynamic interior routing, lowest hierarchical level
- Spokes homed to distribution level hub router
- External routes, BGP-4, or redistributed static
- Campus switching

FIGURE 1.23 *Basic application structure revised to show internetworking technologies.*

The specific technologies used in Figure 1.23 aren't really relevant at this time. Hub and spoke routing with static routes is one routing technique, as is dynamic routing. The method of drawing the architectural relationships is the important point here; you could substitute any number of technologies and have the architectural documentation method here described perfectly well.

Earlier in this chapter, the edge/core and core/distribution/access models were described. You'll note that Figure 1.23 shows a four-level hierarchy. Don't feel as if you are constrained to have a certain number of hierarchical levels in a network. The key point is that the design should reflect a hierarchy, and you should decide the number of levels appropriate for each design.

A given hierarchical level has a significant amount of information that stays inside the boundaries of the level. Typically, you have a large number of elements at the lowest level and concentrate the number of elements as you move upward.

Tip

Often, I literally overlay this picture with other pictures showing the network infrastructure. Most often, I do this on a computer graphics package that allows multiple layers, although drawing it on overhead transparencies works.

A backbone need not be a single WAN or LAN. In many cases, there is actually a hierarchy of backbones. A large concentration of users might have a campus backbone using 100 Mbps FDDI or Ethernet, or possibly faster ATM or Gigabit Ethernet, and yet another relaying device might link this campus backbone to the enterprise WAN backbone. The WAN backbone might consist of a core network plus regional backbones.

With today's products, it can be hard to categorize something as a pure switch or a pure router. It's easier to look for functions:

- Layer 3 (discussed in Chapters 11, "Routing in a Single Area" and 12, "Special and Hierarchical Routing Topologies")

    - Path determination

    - Packet forwarding

- Layer 2

    - Connection-oriented (discussed in Chapter 9)

    - Path determination

    - Frame forwarding

    - Connectionless (discussed in Chapter 10)

- Hybrid techniques (discussed in Chapters 13, "New Methods at the Enterprise Edge," and 14,"New Methods in the Enterprise Core")

    - Label distribution

    - Packet forwarding

Compatibility with Existing Network Interconnection Devices

may use other protocols than IP

The demands of existing equipment, providing operational services, cannot be ignored during such a remodeling. Such demands usually include both IP and non-IP traffic that needs connectivity.

Think of the role of switches as giving high performance in selected areas, whereas routers and gateways convert among different vendors and different media types.

Switch Interoperability

In 1999, switches, realistically, are single-vendor if VLANs are involved and often are single-vendor if the topology is complex or remote management is desired. Non-VLAN LAN switches usually interoperate quite well as long as they all are configured with the IEEE 802.1d spanning tree algorithm. Interoperation does not imply they can be remotely managed; there are often proprietary extensions for management.

A multivendor VLAN standard, IEEE 802.1q, is technically stable and, as vendors implement to the same standard, should allow much more vendor interoperability. It is reasonable to assume that 802.1q VLAN implementations will interoperate, although you will still need different management applications for vendor-specific configuration and troubleshooting. ATM-based LAN Emulation and some proprietary VLAN protocols offer more functions than does 802.1q, so 802.1q can be used more as an inter-vendor link than the primary internal protocol. VLAN design issues are discussed at length in Chapter 10.

ATM switches also interoperate reasonably well in basic connectivity, but might not be able to have a common management system. PVCs generally interoperate, but problems are apt to occur when trying to make SVCs of different vendors interoperate. The problem is less a fundamental incompatibility and more that different vendors support different versions of the ATM Forum standards.

VLANs are most likely to be vendor specific, as the inter-VLAN protocols today are most often proprietary. Deployment of the emerging IEEE 802.1q protocol should result in much better interoperability.

You need to think carefully about the cost impacts of maintaining multiple vendor environments. This goes beyond a need to have potentially different backbone devices, and even beyond a need to have different network management systems. You need to consider the cost of training and retaining people qualified to use these systems.

Does Your Equipment Have Any Class?

IP addressing was long based on the assumption that address allocations were made in units of Class A, B, or C address space. This *classful* approach means that the unit of allocation by central authorities was, in the modern notation, /8, /16, or /24. The number in the new notation specifies how many bits, starting at the left, are used to make routing decisions. Subnetting extends the centrally assigned field.

Slashing Through Subnet Masks

I find that many people have trouble with IP addressing because they are entirely too focused on the decimal representation of IP addresses and subnet masks, rather than the actual binary strings upon which routers and Layer 3 host interfaces make decisions.

An IP address, as seen by a router, has two parts: a *prefix* upon which routing decisions are made and a *host* part with which an endpoint host is located on the last subnet on the route.

Traditionally, subnet masks have been used to determine the length of the prefix. The natural mask of the unsubnetted Class B address 172.16.1.1, for example, is 16 bits long and is written 255.255.0.0. When it is extended with "four bits for subnetting," the mask becomes 255.255.240.0.

The more modern approach is to write the prefix length as a suffix to the address, with the prefix length separated by a slash: 172.16.1.1/20. Unsubnetted Class A addresses have an /8 prefix, Class B have a /16, and Class C have a /24. Subnetting any address adds prefix bits, so "four bits of subnetting on a Class B" is a /20.

The newer, *classless* approach does away with class as a means of allocation. Blocks of address space are assigned based on the amount needed rather than an arbitrary administrative division.

Many IP devices do not fully understand the classless methods. Older routers and especially network access servers might assume that if you have any part of a traditional classful assignment, you own the entire block [RFC 1879].

IP hosts directly interact with routers, although the most common application of this does not involve—or should not involve—full routing table exchanges. Some hosts expect announcements in the Routing Information Protocol (RIP) to learn the location of routers. This introduces several requirements:

- Edge routers must be able to generate RIP.

- The routing system must protect itself against accepting RIP updates inappropriately generated by workstations.

- Operational staff must be on guard to detect security violations from workstations that have created back-door routing to the Internet.

- ISPs should be discouraged strongly from accepting customer RIP announcements and injecting them into the global routing system.

When RIP is used for router discovery, it is usually adequate for routers to generate the default route.

Older hosts might not understand classless addressing. Figure 1.24 shows before and after configurations.

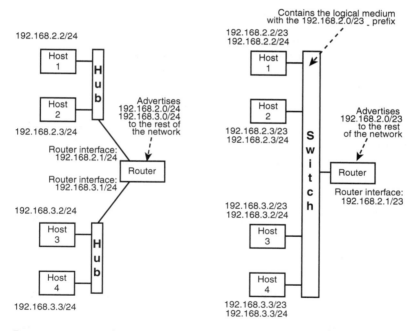

FIGURE 1.24 *Before and after—transition of shared medium hub to flattened LAN-switched environment.*

The left configuration had distinct performance problems before LAN switching was introduced, but it worked slowly. After the "new and improved" switch was installed, performance did not improve as much as expected. More detailed analysis showed that the host-to-host performance was not the same among hosts that seemed to be connected in an identical manner. In the before configuration on the left, two groups of hosts were connected to shared hubs. Each group had a separate Class C address, or, in modern terms, a /24 prefix.

Each shared hub connected to an interface on the router. The router advertised the two separate prefixes, 192.168.2.0/24 and 192.168.2.0/24. The two hubs and the router form a simple hierarchy.

The right side has been flattened, a term beloved by many marketeers. In principle, the router only is used to send traffic leaving the combined switched subnet. This subnet has been assigned the correct CIDR block 192.168.2.0/23, which contains equivalents to the two Class C blocks 192.168.2.0/24 and 192.168.2.0/24.

Hosts in either of the previously separate subnets should be able to communicate with one another through the switch. *Should*, however, often is a red flag when found in an assumption about how a network should work.

If the end hosts on this medium only understand classful addressing, they will insist on sending to one another via the router, because they see each other on different /24 subnets. An assortment of system software does not understand classless addressing. These include older UNIX system and MacTCP (but not Open Transport).

There are various tricks that can work around this restriction, but at this point, focus on the general case. The general case of IP architecture is that devices on the same subnet have Layer 2 connectivity, while routing is necessary to get to different subnets. Classless addressing does not break the IP architecture, because only one subnet is present on the medium.

If the end hosts could not be configured with a /23 prefix, or refused to use it because the IP addresses were in the traditional /24 Class C space, they would try to send to the default router to reach hosts actually in the same broadcast domain.

In an extreme case, if there were no external communications requirement and the network administrator replaced the router with a switch, the hosts simply could not talk to one another. Their communications software would strictly follow the *local versus remote* rule and only would use Address Resolution Protocol (ARP) for a device believed to be on the same subnet. Classful hosts in this situation do not understand that two hosts actually share a common medium. There are workarounds such as forcing the host always to ARP, but the issue here is that classful-only hosts can operate less than optimally in a flattened network.

Non-IP Issues

Many applications have been implemented using proprietary architectures such as NetBIOS/NetBEUI, SNA, AppleTalk, and Novell IPX. SNA was developed for large networks with centralized control. Desktop protocols were originally designed for small networks running over LANs where bandwidth was essentially free and broadcasting was not a performance problem.

Although the vendors involved are migrating their new development to IP-based implementations, there is the reality of an installed base that might not be upgraded immediately. As a network designer, you have to deal with the reality of carrying *legacy protocols* over an IP or modern switched backbone. Legacy protocols tend not to be scalable; but a reasonable strategy is to use them at the edges where necessary, but carry them over a backbone using more scalable techniques.

Microsoft, IBM, Apple, and Novell all have mechanisms for carrying their existing protocols over IP networks. New versions of their software, such as Windows NT 5.0 and NetWare (4 and) 5, run the proprietary upper layer protocols over IP, rather than proprietary transports such as NetBEUI or Internetwork Packet Exchange (IPX).

Multiple requirements become involved with non-IP hosts, especially on the LANs where workgroup machines reside. You'll run into three major categories:

- Workgroup protocols in a local environment

- Client/server LAN

- Mainframe

Several methods are available to deal with non-IP protocols. Protocol translation or tunneling can be a valuable means of keeping the backbone simple, using only IP or appropriate switching methods.

As Samuel Johnson said, "The important thing about a dog walking on his hind legs is not how well he does it, but that he does it at all." Tunnels do add overhead, but can be the only practical way to handle non-IP traffic in an IP backbone. In the long term, the general industry trend is to move toward universal IP.

It might also be reasonable, as shown in Figure 1.25, to terminate the non-IP protocol in an application layer gateway and let the application layer gateway carry the application information in an appropriate IP application protocol.

Electronic mail is a good example of where only application records need to leave the user networks, so there might not be a need for Layer 3 routing connectivity among the user networks. Email is transferred at Layer 7, which is exactly what an application layer gateway does.

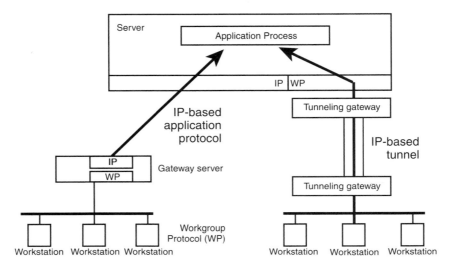

FIGURE 1.25   *Termination versus tunneling.*

Within a local environment, either with old IP addressing or non-IP hosts, there is no need to translate or terminate the old protocol environment. You need to do this only when leaving the local environment.

WAN Media Issues

When the servers to be accessed are across a WAN, it is worth looking at bandwidth conservation measures both at the application and the relaying level. Image compression, for example, really needs to be built in to the applications, either the client or a local server. The more that is known about the data characteristics, the more efficient a compression algorithm can be used.

The workload for different sites tends to put them into different tiers of WAN and metropolitan area network (MAN) connectivity mechanisms (see Table 1.2). The highest bandwidth levels justify asynchronous transfer mode (ATM) or synchronous optical network (SONET) connectivity in the WAN. Interconnection devices for these include ATM switches, SONET add-and-drop-multiplexers (ADMs), and high-performance routers. Speeds at this level

range from DS-3 at the low end, to 100 Mbps, to ATM at 155, 622, and 2048
Mbps. Pure SONET goes higher, with OC-192 links commercially available, and
dense wavelength division multiplexing (DWDM) is a new technology that
pushes bandwidths well above SONET capabilities.

TABLE 1.2   SPEED BANDS FOR WAN AND MAN TECHNOLOGIES

Speed up To	Typical Technology
53 Kbps	V.90 modems
128 Kbps	ISDN, fractional T1
1.5 Mbps	DS-1, xDSL
10 Mbps	xDSL, CATV modems
25 Mbps	ATM
44.7 Mbps	DS-3
100 Mbps	FDDI, ATM
155 Mbps	ATM, SONET
622 Mbps	ATM, SONET
2 Gbps	ATM, SONET
10 Gbps	SONET
100 Gbps	DWDM

At the intermediate tier, up to 1–2 Mbps, where most applications fall, you can
generally meet bandwidth requirements with dedicated lines, Frame Relay, or
similar services. This has usually been the T1 speed band.

Although you might have sub-T1 bandwidths at all your remote sites, carefully
examine the aggregate bandwidth you receive from edge sites at your regional
and central sites. It's quite easy to exceed the capacity of a T1 access pipe by
adding together—aggregating—the bandwidth of many small sites, as in
Figure 1.26. Depending on your provider's traffic management policy, you may
or may not be allowed to burst above the sum of the individual virtual circuit
bandwidths terminating at your central site. Alternatively, you might be able to
burst up to the physical line speed.

There's a saying in aviation, "Peanuts are light, but that doesn't mean you can
carry a billion of them." It might seem that having small sites with a 32-Kbps
access speed should not tax a T1 access line at the central site. If 48 or more
small sites are active, however, the aggregate formed by adding those 32-Kbps
streams equals or exceeds the capacity of the T1.

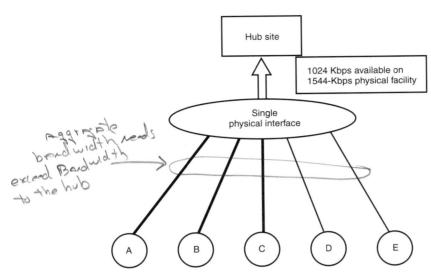

F I G U R E 1 . 2 6 *Bandwidth requirements of many small sites can create a large aggregate at a central site.*

These aggregate assumptions are worst-case. In the real world, especially when different time zones are involved, not all stations transmit at the same time. Detailed measurements can give network designers confidence that a lower total bandwidth to a central site cannot be overloaded by real traffic patterns. This example deals with the extreme case.

Do not simply throw more and more T1 accesses at the problem. Pricing varies very much with the carrier selected, but T3 access makes increasingly good sense. Major providers do offer Frame Relay over DS3, or fractional DS3 services that offer a greater than DS1 but less than DS3 access speed. Again, there are major variations in price in different geographic areas, be they national or local. These DS3 examples are characteristic of U.S. long-haul providers.

LAN Media and VLAN Issues

Bandwidth is much less a factor on LANs and Virtual LANs, although bandwidth still needs to be considered. The physical cabling plant has a major effect.

Cabling

Physical distance from the user desktop to local and distant servers dictates some of the local topology. Older wiring systems using coaxial cable can have cable lengths up to 500 meters, a distance that can be extended with repeaters (see Figure 1.27).

C H A P T E R   1   WHAT IS THE PROBLEM YOU ARE TRYING TO SOLVE?

83

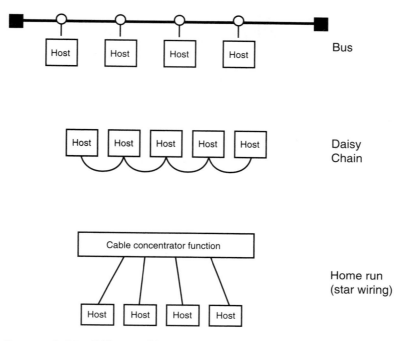

FIGURE 1.27 *Different cabling technologies illustrate various potential large site physical topologies.*

Most current wiring technologies are home-run or star-wired and have a range of 100 meters. This form of wiring runs twisted pair from the user location to the wiring closet, where the pairs are terminated on a patch panel and cross-connected to relays in the wiring closet.

Don't forget that the cable needs to run up from the desktop to a cable tray and then might not take a direct path to the wire closet; you should try to keep your wiring closet-to-desktop range to 80 to 90 meters, rather than try to stretch to a full 100 meters and then find that you are short on length.

If you have large concentrations of equipment, it might not be desirable to home-run each wire to a distant wire closet, putting massive numbers of cable into your cable trays or ducts. Home-run cabling involves independent twisted pair or coaxial cable runs to a cable concentration function in a wire closet. This function can be implemented on a Layer 1 hub, a Layer 2 switch, or possibly a Layer 3 router.

Home-run wiring is by far the most common technique for new installations, but daisy-chain and bus can be found in older Ethernets. At large sites, you should plan on superceding coaxial cable with twisted-pair home-run wiring, which has a lower lifetime cost. Unless you have run out of space in cabling ducts, it is usually most cost-effective simply to abandon the coaxial cable in place, connecting all devices with twisted pair or optical fiber. Removing existing coaxial cable from walls is rarely justifiable.

In the bus topology, each device connects to an external media attachment unit (MAU) that connects to the main coaxial cable using a T-connector or vampire tap. With T-connector wiring, each physical piece of cable ends with a bayonet connector. The bayonet connector mates with a matching connector on a T-shaped splicing connector that joins two cables; it also provides a "pigtail" that connects to a host. Alternatively, the cable ends can be joined directly.

The disadvantage of T-connection is that the medium must be disconnected while changes are made. Vampire taps are an alternative that were primarily used with thicknet, or 10base5 coaxial cables. Their medium-dependent connection consists of two parts of a sleeve that wrap around the cable. As they are tightened by turning a nut, a vampire "fang" penetrates the insulation of the coaxial cable and makes contact with the inner conductor.

Properly installed, a vampire tap can be added to a cable without disrupting communication. It is somewhat harder to install correctly than the T-connector method. I sometimes suspect it fell out of fashion because it seemed so bizarre an approach, but it really does work.

Bus topologies are generally obsolete for building wiring, but you certainly will find obsolete technologies in existing buildings. A friend who was involved in updating wiring at the Pentagon swears she connected a test set to one unlabeled cable and received the message "Many Indians. Send help. (signed) Custer."

In daisy chain cabling, the MAUs are internal and the coaxial cable runs from station to station.

Note

Unfortunately, there are two distinct meanings to the acronym MAU in the context of LANs. In IEEE standards, the MAU is a device that physically connects to the medium. In the case of 802.3, the MAU can be physically separated from the main computer. The MAU, also frequently called a transceiver, has a connection to the computer over an attachment unit interface (AUI) cable. A second interface, called medium-dependent interface in 802.3 and physical medium dependent (PMD) in most later standards, actually connects to the shared medium.

The other usage of MAU comes from IBM's Token Ring specifications, where it stands for multista-tion attachment unit. In the Token Ring case, the MAU is the shared medium, not a connection to it. Multiple MAUs can be interconnected.

The first law of plumbing still applies: If it doesn't leak, don't fix it. If existing equipment is working well on coaxial cable, it doesn't make sense to rip out that cable. It does make sense not to install more.

Switching Versus Routing

A common requirement is shared print services, or access to a read-only file (for example, screen formats) that clearly is for local use only. Switches can help here if the limitation is network bandwidth, or if the inexpensive speed-changing capabilities of switches let a faster server port be implemented. A switch is an inexpensive way to interconnect 10-Mbps devices (typically clients) with 100-Mbps devices (typically servers).

Just as the fashion industry dictates the rise and fall of hemlines, there seem to be fashion cycles in networking. A cycle that varies frequently is where to place application servers: near the user or in a central server farm. Today's trend places campus servers in a server farm, if for no other reason than physical security. Switch-based virtual LANs are an excellent way to provide high bandwidth between users and servers elsewhere on a campus.

Note

When the users are not on the same campus, it can be useful to switch between users and an application cache host that is at their site. The application cache is probably connected to the data center with WAN routers.

Switches need much less configuration than routers and easily allow connectivity for both routable and nonroutable protocols. Figure 1.28 shows how switches can help the local context. Switch and hub relationships are detailed in Chapter 10.

A switch can provide faster, cheaper connectivity to local servers than can a router. In Figure 1.28, the solid line is one subnet and the dashed line another subnet. As long as the frames are unicast, traffic between Clients 1 and 2 and Servers 1 and 2 need only move within their local switch and occupy no bandwidth on the inter-switch trunks. Traffic to Server 5 still only occupies bandwidth from the workgroup switch to the distribution switch. Routing is only needed to get the traffic to servers on different subnets.

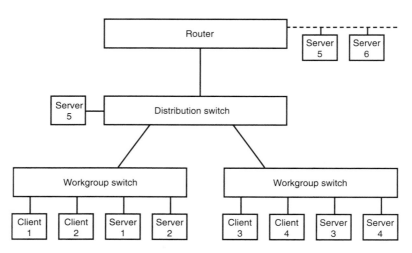

FIGURE 1.28   *Switches provide express local communications.*

When analyzing the connectivity for such devices, first determine that a medium-level bandwidth limitation actually exists and that servers are able to accept the traffic of a dedicated port.

File sharing becomes more complex if you set up a hierarchy of servers or server caches, but it can still be reasonable to use local servers, periodically updated by a "golden copy" master server. It even might make sense to have a local cache server mirroring the master server, with updates in real time using a synchronization protocol. When multiple local users need access to the same data, especially if the data does not change frequently, local caching servers can be extremely cost-effective.

Local Access

As shown in Figure 1.29, local servers sometimes can replace the function of routers in controlling broadcast and multicast traffic, minimizing requirements for routers. Switch ports belonging to VLAN 1 are marked 1 and those belonging to VLAN 2 are marked 2. Although both VLANs 1 and 2 connect users, ports marked 3 are on a third server and support VLAN. On each user VLAN, clients and local printers can broadcast to one another and to the gateway, but not beyond it.

The application layer gateway connects to each VLAN. There is no Layer 3 routing among them. Any traffic among the three VLANs is in the form of an application message created by the gateway.

For example, assume VLAN 1 clients use cc:Mail, VLAN 2 clients use Microsoft Mail, and the backbone mail application is SMTP. For a VLAN 1 client to send a message to a VLAN 2 client, the gateway converts the cc:Mail to Microsoft Mail before delivery. The actual conversion might very well be two-stage: cc:Mail to SMTP and SMTP to Microsoft.

The application layer gateway isolates the user VLAN broadcast domains as well as a router would. In practice, there often is little need for devices on one user workgroup VLAN to send packets directly to devices on another user workgroup. It is more common for the user machine to send to a server, the server to do some processing, and the server to send an application message to another client.

Figure 1.29 shows a simple case where the ALG has a physical NIC for each VLAN. In this case, as opposed to the one shown in Figure 1.30, the ALG is not aware of VLANs.

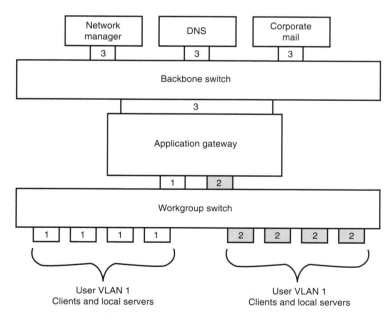

FIGURE 1.29 *VLANs can be interconnected by application layer gateways as well as by routers.*

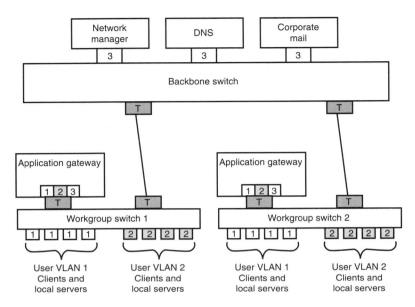

FIGURE 1.30 *Each VLAN-aware application layer gateway server connects two work-group VLANs in a building with a campus-wide backbone VLAN.*

Although it is less common to send application traffic between user work-groups, there is a more common network management requirement to send diagnostic packets to clients and local servers. In Figure 1.29, how does the net-work manager send a **ping** to a device on a client workgroup?

One approach that avoids the expense of adding a routing function is to pro-vide the network manager with the ability to log in to the application layer gateway and issue a **ping** from there. Not all application layer gateways sup-port a diagnostic login function. If such a function is not available, your alter-natives include installing a routing function or making the network management station a member of all VLANs.

Switches can be cascaded into a hierarchy that gives fast bandwidth among workgroups, and to a site-wide server. Building on Figure 1.29, a representative hierarchy without internal routers is shown in Figure 1.30.

The key to this hierarchy being able to scale is its separation of broadcast domains by VLANs combined with the application-level interconnection by multi-ported servers.

The problem in scaling a simple switched hierarchy is that all hosts hear all broadcasts, and there are limits to the number of MAC addresses that can efficiently be handled.

In Figure 1.30, the application gateways are physically connected to VLAN trunks through the ports marked with a T. Smaller boxes inside the ALG, marked 1, 2, and 3, are virtual network interfaces. The physical VLAN-aware network interface cards can decode traffic in the trunk format and switch it to the appropriate virtual interface seen by the server software.

Without proprietary extensions, switches cannot load-share over multiple paths. You might very well, for example, need more bandwidth to the backbone than a single application server port provides. Even with the inverse multiplexing extensions discussed in Chapter 9, load-sharing is usable only in quite restrictive ways.

The more complex the topology, the more routers seem to be needed. Neither routers nor switches alone serve all problems. Application layer gateways, especially when used with VLANs, can be a creative alternative to routers in campus networks.

By using ALGs, you can avoid the cost of Layer 3 routers to reach servers you would, in any case, need to reach anyway. Bandwidth is cheaper in switched networks than routed networks, so your total cost of ownership can be less if you can minimize routers.

Routers, however, have significantly more traffic control and diagnostic capability than switches. Purpose-built routers are often more efficient and more reliable than more general-purpose server software.

A key question in the mix between routers and ALGs is how you use Layer 3 diagnostics on subnets that are only connected to ALGs. Such diagnostics include **ping, traceroute**, and SNMP.

Proxies and Firewalls

Proxy services can be extremely useful in switched networks, allowing frequently used data to be kept local while still retaining the benefits of centralized servers. A large part of the overhead of Novell is the broadcasts emitted by servers and propagated throughout the network. A large part of the overhead generated by NetBIOS is the name searches issued repetitively by clients. Proxy services can greatly reduce this traffic. Assume a client needs to send out a search request to locate a database server. As the network designer, you know many such clients will need to locate the same server. If the session-level protocol were NetBIOS, even tunneled through IP, large numbers of requests would be sent out. The responses to all these requests would be identical.

In a static proxy service, you predefine the response that some set of clients will receive and intercept all of the client requests on a local gateway. This gateway could be implemented in a host or router. The gateway responds to requests as if it were the true end server and does not allow the requests to propagate across the backbone.

Although this approach gives the best traffic reduction, it does need substantial configuration. A variant is a dynamic proxy mechanism, which is more self-configuring but causes more backbone traffic to flow.

Security is another issue. Is the application requirement such that encryption needs to be end-to-end, from workstation-to-end-server, or is router-to-router, or local-to-main server, adequate? Figure 1.31 contrasts these alternatives.

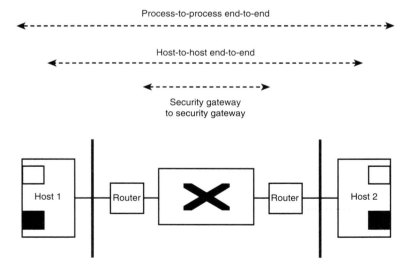

F IGURE 1.31   *Scopes of security trust.*

Each encryption method has pros and cons. End-to-end schemes are best when the application machines are run by a different organization than that which runs the network infrastructure, and the application organization does not trust the network organization. The application group can control the distribution of its cryptographic keys and prescribe physical protection for the end stations. Many government-endorsed encryption systems store the key on a PCMCIA or similar memory card, which can be locked in a safe when not in use.

There are several downsides to end-to-end encryption, the largest being the sheer administrative mechanics of distributing cryptographic keys to all the end stations. In virtually any plausible network, there are much larger numbers of end stations than networking devices.

Policy-Based Routing

Not all relay route selection decisions can be made on purely technical grounds. Different paths can offer different security and performance, for example, whereas bilateral and multilateral agreements can provide a political override. A general term for route selection based on criteria beyond simple metrics is *policy-based routing*. A rule of thumb is that, if a routing decision is made by a test for equality (for example, is traffic of a certain security level?) rather than by comparing numbers (for example, which is the lowest-path cost), policy-based routing is in use. Another way to think of policy-based routing is that it involves decision making that considers factors other than destination and the cost to reach the destination. Policy-based routing, or its close relative flow-based routing, is increasingly important when trying to deliver different qualities of service across the Internet.

Although it is not normally called policy-based routing, one common example is to route traffic depending on the higher-level protocol type. For example, you can examine the TCP port number to determine the application that generated the PDU. Traffic to or from the SMTP mail server port can go on a long-delay path, whereas traffic involving the **telnet** interactive port can go to the lowest-delay path.

[handwritten note: looking at application to determine routing]

A more general way of looking at this example is that you are making forwarding decisions based on flows. For routing purposes, a flow is identified by:

- Source address
- IP protocol type for packet
- Source TCP or UDP port
- Destination address
- Destination port
- IP precedence bits (optional)

[handwritten note: flow identifications — things that might be used to make policy based routing decisions]

Another policy, shown in Figure 1.32, involves bypassing a shared network for certain types of traffic. Bank credit card authorization is a process that involves communications between a merchant's bank (that is, serving the point-of-sale terminal) and the card issuer's bank. There are utility networks (for example, VISA) that interconnect such banks. These utilities charge the banks for each transaction.

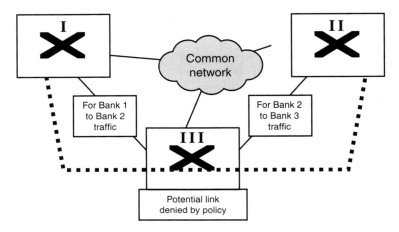

FIGURE 1.32 *Policy routing considers information other than the destination address in selecting paths.*

These considerations include source address and source requirements such as security or quality of service.

In this example, certain large banks recognized that they exchanged large amounts of credit authorization data with other large banks and concluded that the total cost of directly connecting to these other banks would be less than paying the per-transaction cost of the utility network. In this case, Bank II might have a policy that routed:

- Credit authorizations to Bank I via direct line

- All other credit authorizations to common network

- All other traffic (for example, funds transfer) to Bank X via other financial network

Assume that Bank II knows that Bank I is fully connected to the common credit authorization network. From a pure topological standpoint, if the link between Bank II and the common network failed, all other traffic could be sent over the link to Bank I and then to Bank I's link to the common network.

Bank I, however, is a competitor of Bank II. It is perfectly willing to exchange bilateral credit authorization traffic because such exchanges avoid the common network and thus lowers cost. It is quite unwilling, however, to relay other authorizations, because that would free its competitor from the cost of a redundant link to the common network. Bank I pays for its link; why should it be generous to Bank Y?

Considering Cost Factors

A television commercial for automotive repair claims "You can pay me now, or you can pay me later." That is a truism for networks as well. There are definite tradeoffs between spending less at the start of a system's life and paying more over the lifetime of that system.

Acquisition costs include the initial hardware and software, installation effort, and staff training.

Should your routers and switches be fixed-configuration or modular? Fixed-configuration boxes tend to be smaller and cheaper than boxes into which different modules can be plugged, but they must be replaced as units if their capacities are exceeded.

Network management tools range in cost. I feel strongly that configuration management tools are the most important to install at first, because they form the base of any sane change policy. Diagnostic equipment or capabilities can follow.

Design consulting services are another area where a higher initial cost can have major benefits over the project life.

> **"Nurse, the patient has no pulse!"**
>
> **"Doctor, you don't have the stetho-scope in your ears."**
>
> A few years ago, I had to have cardiac bypass surgery. It was reassuring that I was able to have what most studies show is the best predictor of success: a surgeon, team, and hospital that do several bypasses per week. A part-time heart surgeon is one of the more dangerous things in medicine.
>
> In like manner, some design tradeoffs, or the detailed addressing plan, can best be done by someone who does them very frequently. It's been ironic, in my experience working for consulting firms, that top management tended not to want to use the in-house experts who were "rented out" at high dollar figures. Instead, they used cheap outside contractors, who were still working on a design six months later; the true experts might have done that design in a day.

WAN bandwidth is a major part of the system life cycle. In the United States, it is still often cheaper than the processing needed to reduce bandwidth. Optical transmission methods are rapidly increasing the bandwidth that can go on a WAN fiber, so bandwidth cost will probably tend to drop in developed countries. Although you should consider bandwidth in terms of its recurring costs over the life cycle, it can be cheaper to get more bandwidth rather than go to extremes in hardware and software to reduce bandwidth requirements. International circuits are substantially more expensive, although, paradoxically, it can often be cheaper to connect two locations in a country by going through the United States. A colleague found it cheaper to connect Toronto and Vancouver by going south and putting the transcontinental link in the United States. Canada has excellent communications facilities, but pricing tends to be higher than in the United States.

Compression, filtering, and proxy services can reduce bandwidth requirements, typically at the cost of additional CPU, memory, and configuration complexity in routers.

When planning initial installations, consider the cost of the facility between the user location and the carrier end office. It is often wise, even if the initial bandwidth requirement is 64 Kbps or less, to plan for a T1 or E1 local loop and only use part of its bandwidth capability. At higher speeds, where multiple T1 or E1 circuits might be needed, there is a crossover point at which it is reasonable to run a T3 or E3 local loop. At even higher speeds, both performance and reliability can justify a SONET connection to the customer site.

ISDN or modem demand circuits can be quite cost-effective, especially if the application is non-interactive, such as electronic mail or periodic database update.

Looking Forward

In this chapter, you looked at the sorts of hosts and host requirements that live on the edge of the enterprise network. Although some performance requirements were identified, they were not quantified. Chapter 2, "Performance Objectives and Performance Components," introduces methodology for quantifying end-to-end requirements and translating them into the internal design requirements that define your internal structure.

CHAPTER 2

Performance Objectives and Performance Components

186,300 miles per second. It's not just a good idea. It's the law.
—Seen on a button

Why is it important to you to get the wrong answer quickly?
—A frustrated capacity planner to an executive

In the White House, the future rapidly becomes the past,
and delay itself is a decision.
—Theodore Sorenson

In Chapter 1, we decided what needed to be interconnected. In this chapter, we want to pin down the performance requirements of the user devices at the network edge and map them into requirements for the connectivity devices inside the network.

The process of defining an internetwork that meets the user performance requirements is iterative:

- First, you need to quantify the user performance needs, as well as the workload the user presents. You gathered information about these requirements in Steps 1 and 2 of the methodology in Chapter 1. These steps define the endpoints to be connected.

- Second, you need to trace the path that the end-to-end user flow will take through the internetwork. Defining this path involves the addressing, routing, and switching design of Step 3 of the design methodology.

Application Response Time

Response time for interactive applications can be determined as the sum of measurements for a set of one-way transfers. In other words, you sum the performance of a flow from the client to the server, the processing delay in the server, and a flow from the server to the client. These multiple flows define the entire end-to-end, bidirectional path, but in a manner that lets you isolate the components of response time.

A one-way transfer is adequate for describing most non-interactive applications. Interactive applications become difficult when human perceptual factors become involved. These human factors are discussed later in the chapter, in the section "What Values Are Appropriate?"

Not all applications are interactive, and only interactive applications have response time. Performance specification for non-interactive applications is much simpler than for interactive ones. Non-interactive applications tend to be described adequately by throughput and availability measures.

Figure 2.3 shows the minimum components of response time, assuming a single application server:

- Local processing in the client before the first communications are sent
- Queuing for transmission at the server's communications interface
- Network transfer from the client to the server
- Processing in the server
- Network transfer from the server to the client
- Queuing in the client or gateway used by the client

Some response time peremeters for eflow

The first two components are the parts of interest to pure network performance analysts; they are responsible for the true network delay. The reason to identify the other parts is to understand the role they play in overall response time. It might be more cost-effective to reduce host delay with a faster server or software changes than to upgrade an entire network. You cannot meet performance requirements based only on the network; you must ensure that the hosts and the network capabilities are harmonized with one another.

The other delay components can be affected by network performance, such as queuing in a network connection device while the medium is congested. But the focus is on the network paths.

So, if we focus on the network parts, we really have two unidirectional data relationships, one in each direction, for interactive applications. Unidirectional flow really is of interest in characterizing communications requirements. Non-interactive applications are inherently unidirectional, other than for error and flow control in the reverse path.

In error control, the receiver sends acknowledgements to the transmitter. Although acknowledgements are small in volume when compared with file transfers, delaying acknowledgements can have a huge impact on performance. Delays are especially significant in older Layer 2 and Layer 4 protocols that send a single data unit and then wait for the response. Such older protocols include IBM Binary Synchronous Communications (BSC) and Novell NetWare prior to NetWare 3.1.2. Even more modern protocols, such as TCP, SNA FID4 (used between communications processors), and NetWare 3.1.2 and 4.x suffer if the acknowledgements are delayed significantly. See RFC 2001 for a discussion of the interactions between TCP acknowledgement strategies and performance.

The long delay of satellite channels often has a severe performance impact on file transfer. One workaround, discussed in Chapter 11, is to use simplex physical interfaces, one for each direction of transmission. The high-bandwidth, long-delay satellite path is assigned to one interface, and the return path is physically routed over a low-bandwidth, short-delay terrestrial circuit that is assigned to a different physical interface. Error control, however, sees the pair of interfaces as a single interface. This technique is useful when the bulk transfers go only in one direction.

Categorizing Flows

One of the instances in which flows are explicitly requested in modern networks is when machines submit requests in RSVP (Resource Reservation Protocol). See Chapter 13 for a discussion of RSVP. RSVP is an example of the ANSI X3.102 access phase, which is discussed later in the chapter in the section "The X3.102 Model." Other ways to manage flows in the cloud include ATM traffic management, IP differentiated services, and the QoS-aware routing protocols in the research process.

Flows give the network some idea of the workload they will impose. The basic factors used in specifying performance, which, when integrated over time, establish throughput, are

- A sustainable average rate

- A peak rate

- An approximate burst size

factors effecting flow and performance in a network

These parameters were first used in ATM networks and then generalized to any network with quality of service requirements. Current practice is optionally to supplement these parameters with an indication of sensitivity to delay, both absolute delay and delay variability. Additional parameters specify acceptable loss rates.

Supplemental parts of flow specifications include sensitivity to delay variability, also called *jitter*, and sensitivity to data loss.

One useful categorization builds from the RFC 2430 PASTE architecture of the types of flow inside an enterprise, and breaks them into the following categories:

- Network control: Routing updates, SNMP, and so on.

- Priority: Application traffic with special sensitivity to jitter (for example, voice and video), delay and loss (for example, IBM), or delay (for example, LAT). There is an implication that there is an economic penalty to putting flows into the priority category—otherwise everyone would use it.

- Best effort: Data traffic that can be retransmitted, or one-way voice or video transmission such as commercial radio or television.

A flow request using a protocol such as RSVP is an access request. It is subtly different from a connection request. Connection-oriented protocols commit resources, whereas flow-oriented protocols take a more multiplexed or statistical view.

Flows can be set up implicitly or explicitly. Implicit flow setup occurs when a router's software recognizes that significant traffic originates from one source and flows to one or more destinations. Explicit flow setup involves pseudo–virtual-circuit setup with such protocols as RSVP.

What Values Are Appropriate?

Delay sensitivity can be very subjective. Craig Partridge observed that a user perception of distance affects user satisfaction with delay [Partridge, 1992]. Just before I wrote this, I was on the phone from suburban Washington, D.C., to a colleague in Australia. I noticed a slight delay before his responses, but accepted that as understandable given the distance. I would be far less tolerant of the same delay if I were calling across the street. There is a difference between what delay is annoying as opposed to what delay makes it impossible to do work.

two types of delay
fixed
variable (jitter)

There are also different kinds of delay. Variability of delay during a session is far more annoying than a fixed absolute delay. The former is especially disturbing when doing voice or video.

Remember that user-perceived performance depends on the sum of the hop-by-hop unidirectional paths in the network plus any host processing delays.

Subsecond Response Time: A Fad That Didn't Help Productivity

Experience with text-based transaction processing has shown that in certain application contexts, making response time too fast can actually decrease productivity. In the 1970s, one of the catchphrases of the ideal mainframe system was *subsecond response time*.

An insurance company, in cooperation with a university, decided to test the assumption that subsecond response time necessarily was good. The researchers set up a data entry application using a formatted screen on IBM 3270 family terminals, with the ability to adjust the response time seen by the data entry operators. The results were surprising.

Operators were most productive when the response time was approximately three seconds. If response time was less than that, the operators unconsciously began typing at a higher speed and pressing the Enter key before looking at what they had typed, assuming that the computer would validate their input. As a consequence, their typing accuracy dropped and sometimes it would take several repetitions before the data was entered correctly. The operators' productivity, in terms of transactions per hour, dropped because their accuracy dropped.

When the response time slowed to approximately three seconds, the delay was just noticeable and annoying enough that the operators paused and looked at the screen before pressing Enter. At that point, they often saw typographical errors and corrected them locally, before sending the screen.

When the response time grew significantly longer, the operators started having idle time waiting for the mainframe to respond, and their productivity dropped off.

Data entry experiments might not be as applicable today, when intelligent workstations can quickly do local validation. Local validation does need to be programmed and might not be available in all cases. The response time experiments remain thought-provoking and should stay at the back of your mind when you are negotiating response time requirements.

Measuring Workload

Performance requirements should be defined in terms of a particular workload. The tradition in telephony is to define the busy hour as the workload target. ANSI (American National Standards Institute) X3.141 gives a tutorial on the statistical considerations in measuring a network.

When to Measure?

Many people assume that the peak load on a network occurs at the start of the business day, as users initialize their workstations. Observing most offices, however, reveals that the start of individual users' actual work is staggered over a time period significant when looking at network traffic. People start working at different times because they do or do not get a cup of coffee, greet coworkers, or greet coworkers with coffee in hand. I feel strongly, without any evidence whatsoever, that workload in the United States peaks more slowly on Tuesdays that follow telecasts of Monday Night Football.

A more realistic traffic peak usually occurs about 60 to 90 minutes after the official work starting time. By then, people have gotten initial distractions out of the way, returned phone calls, and are concentrating on their routine work. There is often a similar peak around 60 to 90 minutes after the usual return time from lunch.

Flexible working hours, and organizations that operate in multiple time zones and allow flexible working hours, tend to have more blurred peaks. Nevertheless, there still tend to be recognizable peaks. It's not uncommon in North American telephony to see a special peak when the Eastern time zone people can first reach people on Pacific time. In financial applications, there are peaks near the start and end of trading, but also often an after-hours peak for network testing.

People, however, cannot generate traffic as quickly as can unconstrained computers. In many networks, the peak load might take place in the wee hours of the night, when major backups, data distribution, or database updates are in progress.

The term *busy hour* can be a little misleading because most user workloads have two peaks during normal business operations: one in the morning and one in the afternoon. Statistically, this is called a *bimodal distribution*. There often is a third peak, outside normal business hours, caused by backups or other system administration.

There is really no substitute for actual measurements of workload. Realistically, those measurements might not exist, either because the application is new and there is no experience with it or because the application is not instrumented to do the necessary measurements.

One guideline used by some telephone engineers, when fine-grained measurements are not available, is to assume that the busy hour(s) contain 20% of the total daily traffic. Again, this is a rough estimating rule used when nothing better is available.

Guesses, of course, are not as good as actual measurements. Even real measurements can be flawed, because they are taken at times that do not represent the real workload. Ask users what the actual work patterns are. If your client is a public school system, measurements taken during vacation periods do not have much to do with the real workload.

Some manufacturing operations shut down for a week or two annually. These weeks *might* have high loads, however, because they are used for maintenance.

When enterprises do significant financial reporting, you want to be sure that some of your measurements cover a date that ends a month *and* a quarter. Ideally, you want to measure at the end of a fiscal year. If your schedule does not permit waiting this long, you should specifically plan for operational measurements to be done when these events first occur and plan for any tuning needed at those times.

Not Just a Broadcast Storm, but a Hurricane

Truly extreme workloads can come from unusual conditions, especially errors the system was not designed to handle. A major manufacturer's headquarters network went into massive meltdown from traffic overloads and required major manual intervention to correct.

The load had nothing to do with the business. There had been an electrical power failure, and, of course, no activity took place in the dark.

Power was restored simultaneously to all workgroups. The usual staggered start times of the workday did not apply here; all workstations reinitialized at once. The Ethernet-attached devices began broadcasting Address Resolution Protocol (ARP) messages, while the Token Ring devices sent out explorer frames. Diskless workstations sent out Reverse ARP (RARP) and Bootstrap Protocol (BOOTP) requests.

The network had not been engineered to handle simultaneous broadcasts from all devices and soon became congested. Due to congestion, many responses to workstation initialization messages were dropped. When workstation timers expired and had received no response, the workstations retransmitted the requests.

Retransmitting traffic during periods of heavy congestion, as a fault tolerance technique, ranks with pouring gasoline as a means of fighting fire. This is further discussed in the section "Broadcast Storms" later in the chapter.

IETF's Benchmarking Methodology working group (BMWG) has developed a set of specifications for performance measurement. The first of these, RFC 1242, observes the following:

> Vendors often engage in "specsmanship" in an attempt to give their products a better position in the marketplace. This usually involves much "smoke & mirrors" used to confuse the user. This memo and follow-up memos attempt to define a specific set of terminology and tests that vendors can use to measure and report the performance characteristics of network devices. This will provide the user comparable data from different vendors with which to evaluate these devices.

Note

Wherever possible, this book uses standard methodology, primarily from BMWG but also from other standards sources such as national and international standards. Whenever you specify performance requirements, try to use standard terminology.

At the very least, a one-way flow, in any but a trivial path between two end hosts, consists of some set of relays and outgoing links. Figure 2.4 shows a sequence of relays and links in the form of a hierarchy. Hierarchies are far more practical to analyze in real-world networks than are arbitrary series of point-to-point links and network interconnection devices. In most cases, you can characterize the performance of the various hierarchical tiers and add them to find cumulative delay.

As shown in Figure 2.4, the end-to-end path, which involves hosts as well as the network, can be broken into host and network components. The network component can be described with flow specifications. In the real world, enterprise hierarchies are apt to have levels of hierarchy that correspond to levels of the enterprise's organization. From the perspective of the hierarchical design model, most levels of Figure 2.4 are in the distribution tier.

Next, you need to determine whether dynamic routing is sufficient to find the path needed to meet the service requirement, or whether explicit traffic engineering is needed. Most routing follows a closest exit model, which does not consider load or performance requirements.

Research-level efforts are underway to develop routing protocols that do consider quality of service. See Chapter 14 for a discussion of these advanced protocols. Chapters 13 and 14 go into the issues of the interaction of IP networks with lower-layer transmission systems, such as ATM, which do provide quality of service.

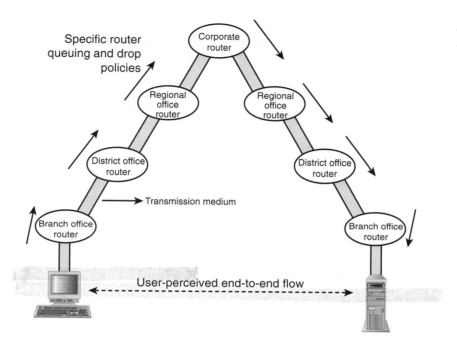

FIGURE 2.4 *Flows are end-to-end. Routers and switches along the end-to-end path can assign different priorities to classes of service to deal with flows they recognize.*

Traffic Engineering and Queuing Policies

Traffic engineering is the process of explicitly assigning traffic to paths other than those that would be selected by ordinary dynamic routing [RFC 2430]. It is usually a manual process, but traffic-aware dynamic routing is emerging as a bleeding-edge technology.

Inside routers and switches along a path, whether that path is dynamically or manually configured, queuing policies describe the handling of flows in routers or switches. The gray medium blocks in Figure 2.4 describe transmission between routers or switches.

When traffic of a given category arrives at a device that can offer differentiated services, queuing policies come into effect primarily when the output port is congested. There can also be policies that affect how much traffic is allowed to enter the device at the input port.

Policies of this sort have long been used in telephone traffic engineering [Kleinrock; Spohn, 1997; Tanner, 1996], and the telephone techniques can be adapted to data networks as long as basically similar assumptions hold. To use the more common telephony methods, you want to use tables or software that predict the probability that a call cannot be serviced because there are no resources to service it. Generally, the most useful statistical characteristic commonly used in telephony is the *Erlang B* distribution that assumes that a call is either serviced or dropped; there is no waiting for access. If the call is dropped, a new access attempt must be made.

Without going into queuing theory, there is a result called *Jackson's Theorem* that shows a way to determine end-to-end capacity by summing the capacity of the relays along the path.

If an output port is busy, traffic destined for it either is dropped or queued (that is, buffered). When the port becomes available, a scheduler selects the queue from which it sends the next packet. There can be multiple queues of different output priorities. Separate algorithms fill queues and empty them.

In Figure 2.4, the paths inside routers are governed by queuing policies; the links between routers are described with media specifications such as bandwidth and delay.

Basic delays are the sum of the link and relay delays in the end-to-end path. When flow-based routing is used, the end-to-end performance of flows depends on the sums of the effect of the queuing and discard policies in each router or switch along the path.

Up to now, we have been concerned with point-to-point flows, admittedly involving chains of flows between the ultimate source and destination. Other flow topologies, and other effects of topology, need to be considered. Dynamic routing mechanisms use simplifying assumptions to pick a path to a destination, and, if there are specific quality of service requirements, manual *traffic engineering* might be necessary to install paths that override dynamic routing to provide the required performance.

More Complex Flow Topologies

Flows are always unidirectional, but can be point-to-multipoint as well as point-to-point. Multiple flows in multiple directions can be combined to build complex topologies, as shown in Figure 2.5, which is an example of a distributed database.

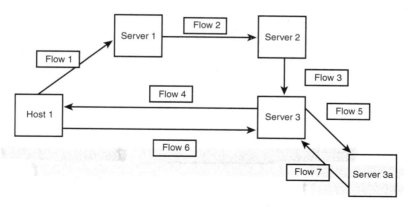

FIGURE 2.5   *An individual application transaction often is composed of multiple flows.*

In Figure 2.5, no routers or switches are shown, simply the endpoints of the flows. Host 1 does not receive a response directly from its local server, Server 1. Instead, a series of flows are involved in the eventual response that Host 1 receives from Server 3. Server 1 receives the request (Flow 1) and searches for an appropriate server by sending a query to Server 2 (Flow 2). Server 2 responds with a referral to Server 3 (Flow 3), and Server 3 responds to Host 1 (Flow 4) and sends a backup message to Server 3a (Flow 5). Host 1 confirms the update, and Server 3 commits the change by both updating its own database and sending a commit message to Server 3a (Flow 6). The process is completed with a confirmation from Server 3a (Flow 7).

This example assumes that host delay is negligible. If it is not, you might want to model the interaction with flows inside the hosts. For example, there could be a Flow 1a in Server 1, which would account for the delay between Flow 1's end and Flow 2's start.

Refining User-Oriented Performance

At the edge of the network, at the user device, there are two basic kinds of application-significant performance: response time for interactive applications and throughput for non-interactive applications.

This section focuses on the quantitative requirements for end-to-end performance. The section "Host Issues" considers some special conditions that can affect host capabilities to participate in the specified end-to-end communications.

The X3.102 Model

Technology-independent, user-oriented communications performance parameters are described in ANSI X3.102, which has been the basis of national and international standards for digital communications performance. Unfortunately, that work has been most associated with telecommunications and the IETF has done a certain amount of reinventing the wheel.

There are three phases of communications:

- Access. The connection setup, or other preparation such as flow requests, necessary before user information can flow from a given source to a given destination. Activities that the destination might have to do before it can receive access requests are not part of this phase. If the destination is not ready for any reason, that is simply considered an overhead factor in measuring performance.

   Different protocols have different access models—X.25, for example, has a two-way handshake in which access implicitly ends with the first user information transfer. ATM and TCP, however, have three-way handshakes that explicitly signal the end of the access phase, when the connection is set up.

- User information transfer. The actual communications of interest. The one-way traffic measurement by X3.102 models is effectively a measurement of throughput.

- Disengagement. The process of disconnecting the measured interface and making it ready for a new connection.

Within each of these phases are the following:

- Successful performance, measured in times
- Misperformance, measured as a probability
- Nonperformance, measured as a probability

Before user information transfer can take place, there must be successful completion of the access phase. If the communications system is connection oriented, this setup time needs to be applied to the overall transfer time to get the real transfer rate.

different protocols have different access methods

The topology of the ANSI model is shown in Figure 2.6. There is a data source, a data destination, and a channel between them. We want to measure the user-oriented performance across that channel.

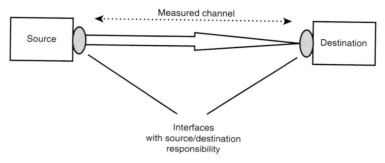

Measured channel

Source

Destination

Interfaces
with source/destination
responsibility

FIGURE 2.6 *A simplified version of the X3.102 measurement topology.*

Measurements taken from this measurement system go into a matrix of user-oriented performance parameters, which is shown in Figure 2.7. User information transfer can be specified as bits or blocks. (User fractions, which are dimensionless ratios that show portions of time not allocated to the measured network, are not shown in Figure 2.7.)

[handwritten: Communication phase]

[handwritten: performance metrics ⇐]

	Speed	**Accuracy**	**Reliability**
Access	Access time	Incorrect access probability	• Access denial probability • Access outage probability
User information transfer	Transfer time	• Error probability • Misdelivery probability • Extra probability	Loss probability
		Transfer denial probability	
Disengagement	Disengagement time	Disengagement denial probability	

FIGURE 2.7 *The X3.102 communications matrix.*

Transfer denial probability is an interesting measurement, which deals not only with the case of communications channel failure, but the case when transfer rates are too low to be useful. It considers both availability and transfer rate.

Establishing Communications

Communications over any unidirectional link involve the ANSI X3.102 three-phase communications process:

1. Access time

2. User information transfer

3. Disengagement

Don't assume that you have no access time because Internet Protocol (IP), Internetwork Packet Exchange (IPX), and other network-layer protocols are connectionless. From the user perspective, name resolution, TCP session establishment, and so on all contribute to delay. There is a certain tendency, in our industry, to consider performance factors such as connection establishment time when dealing with Layer 1 or Layer 2 mechanisms, yet ignore the very real delays that occur as part of higher-level protocol processing.

The Other ATM, and Point of Sale Terminals, Get New Connectivity

Quick query/response applications, such as credit authorization, actually embed user information transfer in the access and disengagement request messages. This technique was introduced many years ago with the X.25 Fast Select facility. Although X.25 networks are becoming less common, although definitely *not* disappearing on a worldwide basis, the Fast Select feature is enjoying a resurgence with automatic teller machine (the *other* ATM) networks.

Fast select is a relatively little-known X.25 feature intended for transaction processing. This feature skips the establishment of a virtual circuit for data transfer. The call request packet contains the query in its user data field. The destination sends a call clearing (that is, refusal) packet, with the response in its user data field.

The impetus to Fast Select in this application is that X.25 packets can be sent over the 16 Kbps D channel of ISDN Basic Rate Interfaces. Low-volume ISDN, which can be provisioned without B channels, is much cheaper than the polled analog multidrop circuits historically used for this application.

Finger-Pointing and Interface Responsibility

An innovation in X3.102 is the idea of *interface responsibility*. If the source host is ready to transmit data through the network interface, it gives responsibility to the outgoing interface to accept the data. Measurement of communications takes place while the channel between the source and destination hosts is responsible for the interface. If the source stops being ready to transmit, or the destination stops being ready to receive, the interface responsibility changes.

Figure 2.8 reminds you of the principle that, unless there is a clear agreement on network performance measurement and the contribution of hosts to user-visible performance, the network provider blames the user for poor performance, and *vice versa*.

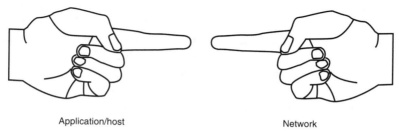

Application/host   Network

FIGURE 2.8 *Interface responsibility is intended to prevent this.*

Assume you want to measure the transfer time between two computers as a measure of network throughput. Picture a stream of packets delivered to an interface by the network. Whenever the interface is ready to receive packets, that is a valid measurement of network performance. When the interface is not ready to receive, and packets either must be buffered or dropped in the network, the delays and losses involved need to be charged against the host, not the network.

The receiving computer exhausts its buffers with each burst transmitted to it and flow-controls the traffic flow for three times the transmission burst time. The observed transfer time is thus four times the true number. By stating the observed transfer time with a receiving user fraction of 0.75, the true value can be extracted from the measured value. In other words, of the total measured value x, the actual network part of it is 0.25 x. Remember that X3.102 is trying to measure the network performance, but practical measurements include host effects such as flow control, pausing a print session to add paper, and so on.

User fractions are dimensionless ratios that show how much of a total "network" measurement is really chargeable to the host. If, for example, the receiving interface were ready to receive traffic only 50% of the time, only 50% of the transfer delay on the channel would truly be charged against the channel.

There are limitations in this technique: What if the channel can only transmit at a peak of 75% in the example above, but the unreadiness of the receiving interface masks this limit? Nevertheless, interface responsibility is a useful idea.

Special Medium Considerations

Most performance models were set up to deal with point-to-point or LAN media. Point-to-point topologies are the most common, but certainly not the only, ones to be considered in performance requirements analysis. In general, performance analysis deals with more complex topologies by treating them as sets of point-to-point media. A point-to-multipoint topology, for example, can be modeled as a set of point-to-point links, all with a common origin and different destinations. We begin by considering connection-oriented and connectionless communications on dedicated point-to-point media and then move to examining on-demand point-to-point connectivity over dialup or virtual circuit media, and multicast connectivity with a variety of media.

Demand

Media that require real or virtual call setup at Layers 1, 2, or 3 are essentially unicast, but have different performance characteristics because the access time is significantly longer than for a dedicated medium. When I had a heart problem, it took longer to stumble to the phone and get the 911 operator than it did to gasp out, "Chest pain. Need ambulance."

Demand services have interesting requirements at the extreme ends of the performance spectrum: analog or ISDN low-bandwidth links and extremely high bandwidth virtual circuit services such as Asynchronous Transfer Mode (ATM). Let's look at each of these in turn. Both have a need for minimizing the duration of connections, although it is a different need in each.

Telephony with modems is the model that most frequently strikes people first considering demand services. Getting a dial tone, dialing, ringing the other end, and completing the connection can take seconds, or even minutes in some international calls.

International calling draws attention to a reality of dealing with low-bandwidth connectivity from public providers. Because calls are charged by connection time, minimizing your costs requires that you minimize connection time. You minimize connection time both by reducing the total volume of traffic to send and ensuring that unnecessary calls are not made.

Be sure that network management and routing protocols do not trigger unnecessary and expensive calls when there is no user data to send. You do *not* want to use routing protocols with periodic updates; these are likely to hold the link up indefinitely. If you have to use a periodic update protocol such as Routing Information Protocol (RIP) or Interior Gateway Routing Protocol (IGRP), you must ensure that the periodic updates do not propagate over the dialup link, either bringing it up or keeping it up. Alternatives for preventing propagation include using static routes, specifying the interface as passive with respect to generating routing updates, and so on.

You should be cautious in using any routing protocol over a dial link, because even update-only protocols use keepalive mechanisms called *hello protocols*. Exceptions are Open Shortest Path First (OSPF) or RIP (version 1 or 2) with demand support, which are aware of the costs of calls and consciously minimize them. EIGRP does not have explicit dial support.

ISDN advocates speak of how access time with ISDN drops to a very few seconds, or below a second, and they are quite correct. ISDN setup speeds are sufficiently fast that the incoming packets sent by the user, which triggered the call, can plausibly be stored in router RAM buffers until the demand circuit is ready to carry them out of the router.

And so it is with technologies such as ATM, with even faster setup times. ATM advocates forget that several things still apply, even with their advanced technology:

- Although setup time is very short, it is not zero.

- Real ATM interfaces can handle a finite number of virtual circuits. A virtual circuit needs, for example, real buffers, and only a finite number of those can be on an interface card.

As we will see in Chapter 13, *cut-through methods* open demand circuits only when there is enough traffic to amortize the access and disengagement time over the life of the flow. If the need is to transmit a single packet query and a single packet response, it is more efficient to send this over existing links, even though the traffic to be transmitted might need to compete with other traffic on those links.

In general, when you want to send a package, you wrap it, label it, and give it to the appropriate carrier. If you are not simply sending a package, but moving the entire contents of your house, it is worthwhile to set up a bulk transfer with a truck, going through the complexity of finding and renting one. For bulk data transfers with critical performance requirements, cut-through methods set up special paths whose setup overhead is justified by their efficiency in transferring large volumes.

When analyzing the user requirement, examine characteristics of the data to see whether router-based measures can help. There are tradeoffs between implementing some of these measures in routers, in local servers, or in workstations. Typical measures include proxy services, filtering overhead packets, and compression.

Multicast Applications

Multicast applications are becoming more and more common. Please do not fall into the widespread misconception that multimedia applications are necessarily multicast, and in turn require high bandwidth. There are high- and low-bandwidth multicast applications; there are high- and low-bandwidth multimedia applications; there are multicast applications carrying only simple text data; there are Hollywood-caliber multimedia applications over point-to-point lines. Modern routing protocols such as OSPF and EIGRP use multicasting.

One operational multicast application is the MBONE, an ad hoc network built of multicast tunnels running over general IP networks. Multicast Backbone (MBONE) is used to videocast the IETF and other professional meetings.

MBONE operation also causes controversy. Because it is sending video, it can create significant bandwidth demands. But because it is implemented in tunnels, it is "stealthy" and not directly visible to Internet service providers (ISPs). Several major ISPs have made MBONE unwelcome on their networks because it creates too much traffic.

There are other cases where tunneling has violated ISP or other external policies, or simply caused unexpected traffic surges. Many new Internet services rely on tunneling, such as mobile IP. Because our focus is on the enterprise network, we do not go into more depth on the subject; simply be aware that Internet-based access to the enterprise might not be ready for mechanisms that put significant traffic through tunnels.

A useful characterization of multicast application topologies starts from the work of Wang [Wang, 1997] and can be extended with the consideration of reliable versus unreliable multicasting. Wang divides the applications into these classes:

- Multipoint-to-multpoint interactive applications
- Point-to-multipoint data distribution applications

Multipoint-to-multipoint applications include computer-to-computer applications including synchronized multiple processor transaction processing and distributed simulation, and human-interactive applications such as collaborative document markup, videoconferencing, and interactive games. Games, of course, range from the purely recreational to the utterly serious military training simulations.

Point-to-multipoint data distribution applications may or may not involve human interaction. They tend not to be interactive, but point-to-multipoint applications such as distance learning or pay-per-view video definitely involve humans and have quality of service requirements characteristic of interactive, non-data applications. Other computer-to-computer point-to-multipoint applications include mail and news delivery, distribution of software updates, stock quotation broadcasts, and so on.

The distinction between point-to-multipoint and multipoint-to-multipoint can sometimes be blurry. The key thing to look for is whether the application flow can be broken into a set of independent point-to-multipoint trees. For example, a fault-tolerant application where each server can originate traffic and send copies to the other servers is not a multipoint-to-multipoint system, but a set of point-to-multipoint trees each rooted in an originating server.

An additional distinction categorizes multicast applications as either reliable or unreliable/best effort. Especially when dealing with non-data applications, reliability is more than simply whether packets are delivered accurately. In many non-data applications such as voice, it is more important not to delay packets than it is to drop occasional packets. The opposite tends to hold true in data applications, where permanent loss is more important than occasional delay. Table 2.1 divides applications using these criteria.

TABLE 2.1   MULTICAST TOPOLOGY VERSUS RELIABILITY

Reliability	Direction	
	Point-to-Multipoint	**Multipoint-to-Multipoint**
Reliable	OSPF routing updates	Distributed simulation
Unreliable	Pay-per-view video	Videoconferencing

An application can use an unreliable transport but still have stringent quality of service requirements. Pay-per-view video and videoconferencing can drop an occasional packet and suffer only a momentary picture problem, but neither can have drops beyond an acceptable limit, nor can they have high or variable delay.

Mobility

Yet another aspect to topology is true mobility, where the end user moves his geographic location. The basic mobility model is that the user logs in at an arbitrary location and creates a tunnel to a home site.

When a mobile node connects to an arbitrary point of attachment, its packets are routed by the access provider to the *home network*, the prefix associated with the source address of the mobile node. The access provider point of attachment becomes known as the *care-of address*. The home network establishes a tunnel to the care-of address and then routes packets received at the home network, destined to the mobile node permanent address, through the tunnel to the most recent care-of address.

Again, capacity and performance planners must consider the effect of tunneling. Remember that some overhead bytes must be used to encapsulate traffic in any tunnel, and the act of encapsulation demands additional CPU cycles in the network interconnection device.

Host Issues

Networks would never become congested if it weren't for those pesky hosts actually sending data over them. Many performance problems are due to host, not network, capacity limitations. It is also useful to have some idea when the hosts simply can't generate enough traffic to cause certain problems. Your customers might be focused on improving the capabilities of their network, rather than trying to understand where application-level performance is being limited. Often, they forget that the design of applications, the processing power of hosts, or the speed of host interfaces is more the problem than network bandwidth.

If you are in the role of a network consultant without authority over the end hosts, do make sure your customer has reasonable expectations of what you can and cannot accomplish with network improvements. It might be worth mentioning to them that simply speeding the network can decrease performance and availability, by delivering traffic faster to overloaded hosts.

Software that runs on hosts can be as much the problem as the host machines themselves. Applications that broadcast packets rather than multicasting or unicasting them simply are not scalable.

End-to-End Protocol Considerations

Ironically, although a connection-oriented transport protocol such as Transmission Control Protocol (TCP) can be a far-better-behaved Internet citizen than User Datagram Protocol (UDP)-based applications that have no mechanisms for proactive or reactive congestion control, TCP is showing its age as it is used at higher and higher speeds. The key paper on TCP performance, RFC 1323, suggests that there might be a theoretical limit at approximately 600 Mbps, but problems have been experienced at 50 Mbps. See RFC 2001 for a discussion of the traffic management mechanisms in TCP.

Happily, there are available software enhancements to TCP that take applications that failed over DS3 ATM and make the applications happy at OC-3, with room for speed growth.

Sliding window transport protocols such as TCP are designed to optimize throughput. In the absence of transmission errors, its throughput is dependent on the *bandwidth×delay* product [RFC 1323]. This value is a good estimate of the buffer space required at the transmitter and receiver, to keep the channel full.

Satellite links show these limitations. At DS1, for example, a DS1-speed satellite channel has a *bandwidth×delay* product of 10^6 bits or more; this corresponds to 100 outstanding TCP segments of 1200 bytes each.

For many TCP implementations, buffer memory has been a performance limitation at high speed or long delay. In most real-world situations, however, speeds have been low enough, or delay short enough, that this is not a practical problem. As 50 Mbps and faster links become more common in wide area networks, common implementations might not be able to achieve more than 50 Mbps throughput per connection.

Even with sufficient memory, TCP still might not be able to exceed 50 Mbps unless the driver knows how to use TCP extension fields to extend the window and sequence number spaces. Although it took three weeks to fill the sequence number space with a 56 Kbps link, this space fills in about 17 seconds at 1 Gbps.

According to RFC 1323, basic TCP implementations have three problems over paths that have a large combined *bandwidth×delay* product:

- Recovery from lost packets

- Window size limit

- Round-trip time measurement

The first problem is caused by the *go-back-N* retransmission used by basic TCP. In this model, if you receive bytes 1 through 1000, and byte 995 is in error, bytes 1 through 995 are retransmitted even though you only need byte 995. Instead, your throughput is degraded by the workload needed to transmit an unneeded 994 bytes. To fix this problem, *selective acknowledgement* only retransmits the specific bytes needed [RFC 2018]. Selective acknowledgement is implemented with a TCP options field.

The second problem comes from the limits of the 16-bit window and 32-bit sequence number field in basic TCP. This was a generous size in the early ARPAnet, when fast lines ran at 56 Kbps, when it could take 3 weeks to fill them. At Gigabit speeds, they can fill in 17 seconds. When the sequence field fills, basic transmission has to stop or there is a danger of having two distinct packets with the same sequence number. When the window size fills, only 64 K can be sent before waiting for acknowledgement. To fix this problem, the *window scaling option* creates an option field that offers to use a larger window buffer, up to 32 bits long [RFC 1323].

The third problem affects various internal timers that TCP uses to optimize its window size without a need for manual configuration. Yet another TCP option, the *timestamping option*, helps with this problem [RFC 1323]. Using the timestamping option makes measurements of round-trip delay for acknowledgements more accurate. Inaccuracies creep into current implementations because typical retransmission timing mechanisms sample arbitrary packets in windows and measure the delay from that sample. Unfortunately, those implementations have no way to tell if they are sampling a packet that has been retransmitted. Adding the delay of retransmission to the real delay skews TCP's perception. The timestamping option actually simplifies TCP implementation. A sender puts a timestamp on an outgoing packet, the receiver copies this timestamp and sends it back in an acknowledgement, and the sender subtracts the received timestamp from its current timer value to get the real round trip delay.

TCP, and its capability to adjust its window size and retransmit packets dropped from congestion, is critical in managing Internet reliability. Special caution should be taken when using Internet voice and other applications that run over UDP and have what can be called a greedy attitude for bandwidth. In contrast, the table manners of TCP are, if not totally immaculate, quite neat.

Some congestion control mechanisms such as random early detect, discussed in Chapter 12 depend on the presence of TCP. They do not affect UDP flows, and there is a consensus that UDP flows should be discouraged in the general Internet.

Traffic Generation Capability

Cabletron published a white paper with some useful guidelines, focusing on the amount of traffic that can be generated by typical Intel platforms running Microsoft Windows and UNIX workstations. To understand the traffic generation potential of a host, consider the following:

- Internal bus (that is, 16 or 32 bit)

- Clock speed (that is, 33 MHz or 133 MHz)

- Processor type

- Network adapter capability

depending on the capabilities of a machine there may be a limit on the amount of traffic generated

This paper makes the important point that a given processor has a physical limit of the amount of traffic it can generate. In the absence of better measurements, which you should try to obtain if at all possible, you can look at your customer's machines and get an upper limit of the traffic they physically can generate.

A low-end workstation with a 16-bit ISA bus and a 66 MHz clock cannot generate more than 2 Mbps–6 Mbps of data even if it is doing nothing but generating Ethernet frames. As Table 2.1 shows, it is unlikely this number of workstations can generate enough broadcasts to cause a significant broadcast radiation problem.

Workstations

Workstations can be connected to a medium that is *oversubscribed*—inadequate to carry the traffic of all workstations if they transmit simultaneously. Because workstation output is largely a function of human activity, oversubscription can be perfectly reasonable. The potential total bandwidth of end user devices (not servers) connected to a LAN switch or shared medium is often two to three times the bandwidth of the medium.

oversubscribed networks are ok if not all end points transmit simultaneously

Alternatively, you can ensure that a medium is not overloaded by looking at the true capacity of workstations to generate traffic. Twenty-four Ethernet-attached workstations theoretically produce 24 Mbps of data. We have said, however, that these clients cannot actually produce that much data. Assuming 5 Mbps, 24 workstations still can theoretically produce 120 Mbps of data. Many older computers of the 486 class, however, cannot produce more than 50 Kbps of data. The real peak workload of 24 of these older computers is 2.4 Mbps.

In practice, it is reasonably safe to oversubscribe a client shared medium, or the equivalent in a switch, because user workstations do not all transmit at once. If all your workstations are this speed, 12 to 24 workstations can share a common medium without congesting it. Simply installing a switch can overload a server even more, because a shared medium hub forces devices to wait for one another.

When workstations move to 100 MHz–200 MHz Pentiums, these devices actually can generate 10 Mbps of actual data, assuming appropriate memory and network interface cards (NICs). Congestion becomes more of a potential problem here, and connecting processors of these speeds to switch ports makes increasing sense. On a shared 10 Mbps medium, 10 to 12 such devices can generate enough data to congest a 10 Mbps Ethernet. Although you could go to shared 100 Mbps media, there are probably enough other reasons to switch—see Chapter 10—that such processors should connect to switched ports rather than a shared medium.

High-End Workstations and Servers

The highest workstation output typically comes from UNIX clients. Servers running UNIX, NT, or other high-end operating systems on high-speed processors can generate even more traffic. In general, there should be little question these devices should be plugged directly into switch ports, and frequently at 100 Mbps. Any one of these devices can fill a 10 Mbps port.

If you can connect clients and servers to the same physical switch, you generally should get the full port speed. Remember to set server ports to full duplex. For increased bandwidth, you might need to consider multiple 100 Mbps ports on servers, or Gigabit Ethernet, or ATM.

Have reasonable expectations of the performance improvements possible with faster media. Although you reduce the latency of transfers into the server, you still face the capability of the server to process more transactions. Early experience with Gigabit Ethernet suggests that Windows NT servers with available NICs can actually process no more than 250 Mbps of data.

See the section "Sizing Uplink Bandwidth" in Chapter 10 for a discussion of the bandwidth required between servers on different switches.

Broadcast and Multicast Effects

Most discussions of broadcasts speak of them flooding the medium, occupying bandwidth. This definitely happens, but often a more subtle problem results from broadcasts and multicasts: The processing load placed on end hosts where each single broadcast packet interrupts the CPU and has to be looked up, which can cause significant problems far earlier than pure broadcast traffic can eat up the available bandwidth. Most discussions of broadcasts focus on Layer 2 broadcasts. It is perfectly possible, however, to have broadcasts in IP, IPX, or other Layer 3 protocols. The scope of local IP broadcasts using the address 255.255.255.255 but not multicasts are limited to the local medium. NetBIOS emulation over IPX, however, floods IPX type 20 packets through all media.

The ways in which non-unicast can affect your performance include the following:

- Volume received at a port

- Volume occupied on shared trunks

- Workload on switches and routers that replicate packets

- Interrupt load on hosts

Traffic Replication at Ports and Trunks

In bridging, broadcast and multicast packets normally flood onto all media, or the broadcast domain emulated by a switch. In Figure 2.9, Workstation 1 is trying to get a reply from Server 1. Workstations 2 and 4, however, are broadcasting.

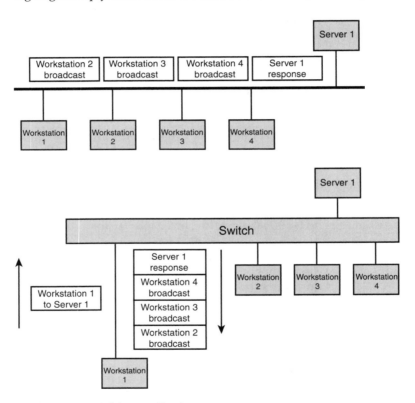

FIGURE 2.9 *Multicast replication.*

In the upper part of the figure, all devices are connected to a shared medium. Depending on the rate at which Workstation 2 through Workstation 4 broadcast, Workstation 1 might wait to gain access to the shared medium, and Server 1 might wait to get access to the medium to send its response. In poorly scalable applications that send many broadcasts, such as NetBIOS, hosts frequently send bursts of seven broadcasts. Even in a small network such as this, there could be 21 or more broadcasts present before Workstation 1 or Server 1 can transmit. Even a minimum-length Ethernet frame, counting preamble and inter-frame gap, takes approximately 72 microseconds to send, so a NetBIOS burst from Workstation 2 through Workstation 4 could cause about 1500 microseconds of waiting time. Full-length Ethernet frames take 1250 microseconds to transmit. If an application sent frames continuously to do a file transfer of a full 64 K NetBIOS window, it would delay all other transmissions by 56 milliseconds.

Adding a switch, as shown in the lower part of Figure 2.9, helps the situation in avoiding waits for the medium, assuming that the port is configured as full-duplex so W1 can send immediately to Server 1. Server 1, however, still hears all broadcasts, which causes Workstation 1 to wait for the server response.

In like manner, Workstation 1 might have to wait for Workstation 2 through Workstation 4 broadcasts before it can receive Server 1's response. You should see that broadcasts have a multiplicative effect on all hosts in a broadcast domain. The single broadcast packet sent out replicates to all receivers.

If the broadcast or multicast truly is needed only on its own segment, vendor-specific filtering can be configured.

Similar behavior can be seen in a system of undersized bridges; the bridges are undersized in the sense that their interface address tables are too small. Such undersizing does not let the bridges keep a full list of local source addresses, so they flood frames destined to nonlocal addresses, even though, if filtering worked properly, these frames would never leave the local medium. Table 2.2 contains a discussion of typical sizing limits.

TABLE 2.2   LIMITING FACTORS FOR BROADCAST DOMAIN SIZE

IP Prefix Length	Usable Host Addresses	Limiting Size Factors
/30	2	Optimal size for point-to-point.
/29	6	—
/28	14	12 hosts is an upper limit on 200 MHz PCs on a shared 10 Mbps Ethernet.
/27	30	20 hosts is a comfortable upper limit for ISA bus, 66 MHz PCs on a shared 10 Mbps Ethernet.
/26	62	—
/25	126	Beginning of broadcast radiation concern given heavy broadcast/multicast.

continues

TABLE 2.2   CONTINUED

IP Prefix Length	Usable Host Addresses	Limiting Size Factors
N/A	200	NetBEUI broadcasts and multicasts can present a significant processing load. Novell 3.x can also create problems with this number of hosts, but the real-world limit tends to be the networkwide number of servers generating Service Advertisement Protocol (SAP) packets.
		Problems can also begin to show when there are substantial numbers of Apple, DECnet, or OSI hosts that issue multicasts, and IP hosts do not ignore these multicasts.
/24	254	Limit of classful awareness if address in Class C range.
/23	510	Usual limit for IP devices that use some broadcasts or multicasts for application data transfer (for example, for NFS).
N/A		Typical broadcast/multicast limit for Novell 4.x devices that only send changed SAPs.
/22	1022	Recommended upper limit for IP. VLAN port size on Bay 28xxx switches.
/21	2046	IETF estimate of upper size of multiserver NHRP system.
/20	4094	—
/19	8190	Typical minimum globally routable prefix.
/18	16382	Pushing extreme range of bridge size. Catalyst 5000 boxwide table size.

Broadcast Storms

A broadcast or multicast storm occurs when multiple stations begin to issue multicasts at a high rate. This is usually due to a host mechanism sending out a critical query, and retransmitting it if no response is received. Unfortunately, the response might have been lost due to network congestion. Establishing source routes in Token Ring networks, where an explorer frame is sent from source to destination, is one example. Another can be periodic ARP cache refreshing in UNIX machines connected to an Ethernet.

It does not take esoteric knowledge of theoretical computer science and mathematical statistics to recognize that systems tend not to recover well, when faced with an overload condition, if you add more of the units that caused the overload.

The best way to avoid broadcast storms is to have protocols that avoid them. Historically, many problems occurred when devices initialized simultaneously and then issued queries at approximately the same 30-second interval. If the devices slightly varied their intervals, by inserting deliberate randomness into their interval timers, breaking synchronization reduced the likelihood of storms. Although such randomization is rarely user-settable, some implementations do randomize, whereas others do not. Another approach is to have the hosts exponentially increase the time between requests when they receive no response to queries. See Chapter 4 for a discussion of inadvertent synchronization in routing protocols.

Several vendors also provide protection against broadcast or multicast storms; they can be configured much more simply. These vendors set a threshold value of broadcast or multicast frames per unit time and block any frames sent in excess of that value. Such features should send an SNMP trap or other notifications when they do this. Be sure not to set the threshold too low, because some broadcasts and multicasts are normal. If you filter too many broadcasts, they are retransmitted. Typical acceptable limits allow perhaps 500 broadcasts per second, which is plausible within a short time interval. If the interface can monitor over longer time periods—one to five minutes—a lower threshold of 100 broadcasts might be more appropriate.

Broadcast and Multicast Load on Hosts

A fairly ugly, but useful, term coined by Cisco for the problem of CPU loading on hosts is *broadcast radiation*. A better name might be *multicast interrupt load*. Remember that a host has to process every broadcast and at least examine every multicast to see if it belongs to that multicast group. Examining multicasts can be distributed onto a suitably intelligent NIC, so that the CPU is not interrupted. Assuming intelligent NICs, multicasting is strongly preferable to broadcasting.

Quantifying Broadcast Radiation

In background materials for its Internetwork Design course, Cisco gave some measurements, admittedly for older systems, that illustrate the problem of broadcast radiation. A broadcast generator was connected to a Sun SparcStation 2 running SunOS 4.1.3 without the multicast kernel. 100 broadcasts per second took up 3% of the CPU, 1000 broadcasts per second took up 23%, and 3800 broadcasts per second, which can be seen in a broadcast storm, crashed the CPU.

Although these measurements were done on a processor much slower than more modern workstations, remember that, although more powerful processors can handle more broadcasts without significant degradation, more powerful processors running badly designed applications can generate more broadcasts.

In current practice, the problem of broadcast load is most likely to be seen on devices that are not general-purpose workstations, but older special-purpose devices with old embedded processors, such as some IBM terminal controllers.

Some vendors have suggested that, with the faster processors available today, broadcast radiation is less of a problem. With faster processors, it probably is in fact less critical for modern workstations, although it still can degrade performance. Whether broadcast radiation is or is not a problem remains controversial, because it is the nature of routing and VLAN technology to restrict the propagation of broadcasts. If a company's product line does not include some capability of limiting broadcasts, it's not surprising that it might tend to minimize the need for that capability. Of course, a given vendor might be completely right that a given capability really is not useful or has been superceded by another technology.

Another thing to consider is the speed of the interface to modern workstations. Although it is true that continuous broadcasts on a 10 Mbps medium might not have a serious effect on a high-speed Pentium II, such high-speed hosts often are connected to a 100 Mbps medium. On such a faster medium, a painful number of broadcasts can arrive.

The potential of being harmed by a broadcast storm is one reason not to default to 100 Mbps connectivity for workstations. Of course, after a device is connected at 100 Mbps, it can also generate broadcasts at high speed.

Not all NIC, interface driver software, or operating system developers deal properly with multicasts and broadcasts. Apple Macintoshes actually do not generate many broadcasts, but they do generate substantial numbers of multicasts. If an IP host on the same medium could not tell the difference between an IP multicast and an AppleTalk multicast, it would have to handle an interrupt for both types of packets. It should have ignored the AppleTalk multicast packets; the device driver was not capable of doing so.

Availability

A device can fail to be available if it, or its connectivity, has failed. Users also see it as not available if it is too slow to handle practical processing.

Requirements tend to be driven by one or more of several major goals for server availability and performance. Availability goals are realized with resiliency mechanisms, to avoid user-perceived failures from single failures in servers, routing systems, or media. Performance goals are realized by mechanisms that distribute the workload among multiple machines such that the load is equalized.

Organization managers need to assign some economic cost to outages. Typically, an incident cost and an incremental cost are based on the length or scope of the connectivity loss. Ideally, this cost is then weighted by the probability of outage. A weighted exposure cost results when the outage cost is multiplied by the probability of the outage. Resiliency measures modify the probability, but increase the cost of operation.

Whether a given failure is worth protecting against depends on the industry. Money trading operations can gain or lose millions of dollars per hour. Life support, manned spaceflight, and military command and control networks incur terrible penalties in the event of failure. A home computer user who wants the latest sports news has the alternative of turning on the television.

Operational costs obviously include the costs of redundant mechanisms (that is, the additional multihomed paths), but also the incremental costs of personnel to administer the more complex mechanisms—their training and salaries. It isn't an either-or question, to provide redundancy or not. A perfectly viable alternative might be to provide two paths and share the load between them. If either path fails, users notice a drop in performance, but not a total failure.

What Is Failure?

A mental image of failure can bring to mind Conan the Barbarian muttering "What is good? To see your enemies scatter before you, to see their huts burn, to hear the lamentation of their women...that is good." Users scattering as a router burns and the operational staff laments clearly is an indication that something failed.

Yet real-world failures are more subtle and do not necessarily require a complete component failure for a devastating problem to exist. Think of a critical interactive application that has become so slow that the user's keystrokes are lost or garbled. The problem might be due to network congestion, an overburdened host, or a high network error rate requiring constant retransmission.

So you should think in terms of service failure as well as component failure. Wang points out that this becomes more complex as service topologies become more complex, discussing separate reliability models for unicast and multicast [Wang, 1997].

How do you characterize reliability in a point-to-multipoint multicast model, when only one receiver fails to receive data? Is the source concerned with ensuring reliable multicast delivery, or is the application more like broadcast television?

There have been several approaches to characterizing the requirements. X3.102 includes a parameter *transfer denial probability*, which measures the probability that a given information transfer will have unacceptable latency. Infinite latency due to a failure is included in this parameter. Wang introduced the idea of a *reliability interval* (RI), which "reflects the connection between reliability and latency, and also defines the policy for dealing with loss recovery." The idea of RI is that it creates a range of reliability requirements, rather than simply calling a requirement reliable or unreliable. For example, if the reliability interval for an audio application is 500 ms, there can be packet retransmission as long as the packets are delivered in no more than 500 ms.

Simpler metrics can be very useful with unicast applications. Complete stoppages of traffic, of course, are failures. But if interactive response time falls below human tolerance, there is an effective service failure. In X3.102 terms, this is a transfer denial event, where the network is either completely down or too slow to be useful.

Defining the Scope of Downtime

Quantifying availability requirements can involve a good deal of contractual clarification, as well as real-world operational reality.

Assume that a router is under normal business-day, 9 a.m. to 5 p.m., maintenance coverage. It fails at 4 p.m. The service technician arrives at 10 a.m. the following morning and repairs it by 11 a.m. How long was it down:

- 19 hours, the wall clock time between the failure event and the repair event?

- 3 hours, the sum of the time from the failure notification to the end of coverage for a given day, and the time from start of the coverage on the next day to the time the device was repaired?

There is no universally accepted answer to this question. The interpretation taken depends on the contract and on business practices.

Reliability and Restful Sleep

Even when there is agreement on how to measure downtime, there is still a great deal of argument about what values of outage time should be set.

In 1981, as a contractor for the U.S. Environmental Protection Agency, I wrote the first formal U.S. government procurement specification for a network whose performance requirements were technology-independent, and specified with X3.102 parameters and supplementary values.

I'm rather pleased with the practical orientation that was given to downtime. We differentiated between failures that did and did not involve the local loop, which very much reflects operational realities. But what were the bases for the actual values, which have been cited in the performance literature as if they have a cosmic significance?

I rather like the use of scientific measurements named for important people in a field: ohms, Hertz, Roentgens, and so on. A little-known fundamental unit for availability can be called the Fulford, in honor of Don Fulford, who was, at the time, the manager of the EPA's data center and indeed one of the best operational managers I've known.

My team agonized over the values to put into contractual requirements for availability. Don stepped in and made it easy.

"My boss," he said, "regards the network as a basic part of the computer service, like printer paper. If the data center ran out of paper and he found out about it, he'd call me at home, regardless of the hour, and complain. I am willing to be awakened N times per year [four, as I recall]. Figure out what the availability would be that will keep me from being awakened more often than that."

So the Fulford became the fundamental reference unit for availability: that level of downtime that causes senior managers to receive a call at any hour of the night. The EPA's network availability was defined as not more than four Fulfords per year, converted into numbers for outage time and time between outages.

Edge Connectivity

Experience shows that small remote edge sites suffer connectivity failures most often because their WAN link fails, not because their relay fails. (This was the reason, when I worked on the EPA network specification, that we differentiated between failures that did and did not involve local loops.) Individual workstation software is not infrequently a problem. The argument is sometimes made that if the automotive industry had progressed as fast as the personal computer industry, we would have $200 cars that get 200 miles per gallon. Unfortunately, we might also have cars that crash twice per day.

A decision needs to be made if having more reliable WAN connectivity is cost-effective. One alternative is to provide individual user workstations with a modem or ISDN access and allow them to dial directly to a remote access server at a major site. If security can be assured, access through an Internet service provider is yet another alternative.

There are both operational and economic reasons to use direct demand access. Operationally, if a failure affects a small site, the users there might not be able to diagnose and correct the failure. Until regular network management staff can work on the problem, the remote users can continue their routine work over the demand link. The demand link directly from the workstation bypasses the LAN, relay, and WAN link.

From an economic standpoint, the cost of maintaining additional backup links can be more than the effective cost of outages caused by link failure. This is especially true at a small site with very few workstations. Outage costs need to be calculated for each enterprise, with its specific business model.

Degraded operation in the case of link failure can be a reasonable compromise, as long as performance is sufficient to allow the users to get some work done. A site might normally have a 256 Kbps service over fractional T1 or Frame Relay. If the regular service is disrupted, 64 (56) Kbps ISDN or 56 (with a maximum achievable 53) Kbps modem connectivity, might be better than no connectivity. Low speed connectivity might not be better than no connectivity if the backup speed is too slow for the application.

When thinking of reliable connectivity to servers, there are several different goals. Some of them involve Internet access, which is really beyond the scope of this book and is discussed only briefly, in the following sections.

High Availability of Your Servers to the General Internet

The first goal when thinking of reliable connectivity to servers involves well-defined applications that run on specific servers visible to the Internet at large. We call this *endpoint multihoming*, emphasizing the need for resilience of connectivity to well-defined endpoints. Solutions here often involve DNS mechanisms, application caches, and so on, rather than routing or switching.

The server name made visible on the Internet might actually map to any of several physical servers in your enterprise.

There are both availability and performance goals to consider here. You must bear in mind, however, that specifying goals only makes sense for things you can control. It is reasonable to set goals for your internal connectivity to server farms, and for your directly connected ISPs. Because you do not control how your external users access the general Internet, and might not have influence over the power of their hosts, it is not reasonable to set user performance expectations that are affected by these factors.

Availability goals arise when there are multiple routing paths that can reach the server, protecting it from single routing failures. Other availability goals involve replicated servers, so that the client reaches a server regardless of single server failures.

Performance goals can include distributing client requests over multiple servers, so that one or more servers do not become overloaded and provide poor service. Load distribution mechanisms can consider actual real-time workload on the server, routing metric from the client to the server, known server capacity, and so on. You can find more information in *Designing Addressing Architectures for Routing and Switching*, also from Macmillan Technical Publishing.

High Availability of Connectivity from Your Users to Arbitrary Internet Servers

The second goal when thinking of reliable connectivity to servers is high availability of general Internet connectivity for enterprise users in your enterprise to arbitrary outside servers. Solutions here tend to involve routing mechanisms.

This is also a case where setting end-to-end performance goals can be difficult because you do not control either the destination servers or parts of the Internet path to reach them. You can set goals for your ISP connectivity.

The ISP might contract to provide end-to-end QoS, but this realistically requires that the VPN provide all services, or contract with other providers. At present, the global Internet does not support QoS.

High Availability Connections Among Selected Partners

Figure 2.10 shows yet another goal related to reliable connectivity to servers; either dedicated facilities, outsourced private networks, or virtual private networks mapped onto the Internet provide connectivity among a set of business partners. I use the term *extranet* to describe such private agreements, which are not visible on the Internet. These partners agree to common interconnection, security, and performance rules, but manage their own network resources.

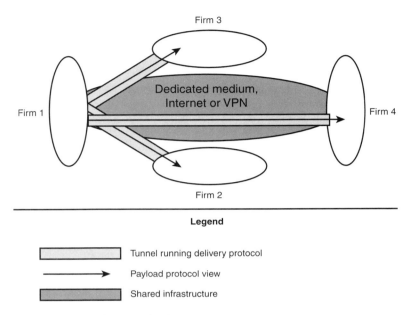

Legend

Tunnel running delivery protocol

Payload protocol view

Shared infrastructure

FIGURE 2.10   *An example of an extranet.*

Extranets depend on tunnels. A *tunnel* is a software construct that carries *payload* information in a payload protocol over a *delivery* communications system with a delivery protocol. There is often a small *glue, shim,* or *encapsulation* protocol header between the end of the delivery packet header and the start of the payload protocol. This small header contains information needed to operate the tunnel. The tunnel usually appears to the end system as a point-to-point line directly to the destination. Alternatively, the tunnel can exist between firewalls or other interconnection devices, and the end systems see one another on a common LAN.

When you characterize the availability of communications in an extranet, you need to consider the needs and reliability of each partner network, plus the characteristics of the network that interconnects them. You need to do those two steps in order, starting with end user requirements:

- Security
- Availability
- Throughput
- Latency

The difference between an extranet and a virtual private network is blurred. Indeed, the industry has not yet come to a generally accepted definition of a VPN. Here, I distinguish an extranet as something primarily constructed by the enterprises using it. They are responsible for its performance, both in implementing tunneling functions and selecting underlying transmission systems that, in combination with tunneling and application software, meet the end-user requirements.

With virtual private networks, however, the service provider is responsible for engineering the network as seen by end hosts and ensuring that requirements are met. I emphasize that these definitions are emerging. It is not a given that consensus exists.

Internet and Virtual Private Network Connectivity Among Enterprise Sites

Another application for Internet connectivity is to use it to provide connectivity among your sites. This is shown in the *virtual private network* (VPN). VPNs have been called *intranets*, but the term *intranet* tends to be more application oriented, emphasizing the use of an IP-enabled application within an enterprise. In this context, an intranet emphasizes Web browsers as the main user interface rather than office automation packages.

Service provider IP tunnels can interconnect the members of a given VPN. If these are carefully engineered, it can be cost-effective. If you expect reliable and predictable performance by tunneling through an arbitrary ISP, you invite disaster.

Although a VPN might seem a very inexpensive way of getting wide area connectivity, it tends to be a bad idea when you simply tunnel through general Internet facilities. Performance can't be controlled. Security is an issue unless you use end-to-end encryption. Tunneling through the Internet can be acceptable, however, for low-volume applications where real-time quality of service is not a requirement. Such applications include a good deal of Internet commerce.

Chapter 11 examines some of the performance affects of the tunnels that a VPN might require.

There are simply too many uncontrolled factors to rely on. It can be quite reasonable to contract with service providers for a VPN that is specifically engineered to interconnect your sites.

The Backbone

Failures in the main connectivity network—the backbone—affect far more users than an individual site connectivity failure. At this point of design, you need to consider what reliability level is needed from the backbone. Design techniques to achieve such reliability are discussed in Chapter 12.

> **Note**
>
> *Increasing redundancy, either of links or routers, does not necessarily increase availability. A node can fail in several ways: sane, dead, or crazy [Berkowitz, 1975]. Sane failures involve situations where the failing component gracefully shuts down, sending alarms and perhaps initiating a backup. Dead failures occur when a component fails abruptly with no warning. Crazy failures take place when the device fails, but continues to operate in some incorrect fashion.*
>
> *Perlman uses the term Byzantine failure to describe crazy failures [Perlman, 1992]. Whichever term is used, will increasing the number of relays or links improve reliability if incorrect information propagates among them?*

Use redundancy where it will help, not for its own sake. Excessive redundancy, as discussed in Chapter 4, can actually increase convergence time. Fault tolerance needs to be considered at the routing and the physical levels. Aspects of redundancy in relation to specific technologies are discussed in Chapters 3 through 14.

Outages at Twelve O'Clock High!

An anecdote from the early days of military operations research puts this into perspective. In 1942–1943, American bombers attacking Germany suffered an excessive loss rate. There was a tactical imperative to make them more survivable, and applying armor was an obvious solution.

Unfortunately, if a B-17 bomber was armored everywhere, it would be too heavy to get off the ground. So, a team of statisticians was told to determine the best places to apply a limited weight budget of armor.

The statisticians drew life-size pictures of bombers on butcher paper, and they waited at each bomber base for the damaged bombers to arrive from missions. They then rushed to the aircraft, noted where the holes were, and plotted them on their paper.

Eventually, the team felt it had enough data and went to the bomber general. It carefully explained that the armor should be applied to specific spots, because these were the places they could demonstrate were hit most often.

The general turned to an aide and said, "armor them everywhere else." He looked at the shocked statisticians, and said "you forgot one thing. These hole locations are on the planes that made it back."

And so it is with network redundancy. One especially blatant problem is that the organization, chuckling with glee on how they get around the telecommunications carriers, carefully selects two different national WAN providers "so there is no common point of failure."

Unfortunately, it is common practice for carriers to lease capacity from one another. Two independent orders for a circuit between Washington and San Francisco might be provisioned in the same fiber cable in which both carriers lease space. In many countries, there might not be diverse facilities between two points, and it can be fruitless to spend money on alternate circuits. When contracting for diverse services, get the carrier to guarantee diversity. See the section "Grooming" in Chapter 9.

If this level of redundancy in the long-distance circuits is appropriate, it is wise to order redundant circuits from a single provider and contractually obligate that carrier to provision them in physically diverse facilities. It is even wiser to put in contractual language that allows you to check periodically how the circuits are physically provisioned, because carriers periodically groom their circuits for better efficiency. Grooming is further discussed in Chapter 9. In the real world, carrier technicians might not notice a diversity requirement for circuits and groom them into the same physical facility.

Realistically, long-distance, high-capacity channels fail far less often than local and in-building connections. It can be a silly expense to lease redundant long-distance channels yet have only a single physical path between your building and the carrier end office.

Service-Level Agreements

Service-level agreements (SLAs) historically have been associated with IBM networking, but have been receiving considerable attention in the industry as a general method. Properly crafted SLAs are excellent tools for requirements definition in the design process. They integrate various factors discussed previously in this chapter with the expectations of upper management that performance goals need to be validated.

Delay sensitivity and other human factors are generally collected into *flow specifications*. Service-level agreements are more global than flow specification. Service-level agreements often involve host application performance as well as the network performance characterized by flow specifications.

The basic SLA defines user performance expectations for a particular application or applications. In relation to Step 1 of the design methodology, it formalizes expectation into a performance contract. For interactive, transaction-based applications, the usual practice is to specify performance goals as a threshold, such as "95% of type X transactions will complete in three seconds or less."

There are statistical advantages to using the threshold technique, rather than stating "average" response time. Using averages tends to assume an underlying normal distribution, which does not fit many applications. Even the term *average* is ambiguous, because it can apply to means, medians, or modes.

Performance goals in a good SLA are associated with workload estimates, both for the specific application and with some consideration of the overall environment. A more complete SLA might read "95% of type X transactions will complete in three seconds or less, assuming 200 active users measured at 10 a.m." This sort of measurement requires instrumented applications or operating systems, or intelligent passive performance monitors. Measurement capabilities of this power have long been available for mainframes, but, aside from sales hype, are not readily available, in a multi-vendor way, for network operating systems.

SLAs consider availability as well as raw performance. Stating goals as threshold values actually does cover many short outages, because a transaction that times out clearly does not complete within the defined threshold. SLAs usually are explicit about expectations of significant periods of downtime, stating them in terms of mean time between (total) failures and mean time to repair.

Looking Ahead

You now know your end-to-end requirements in both qualitative and quantitative terms. Effectively, you have a delay budget that you can spend in various internetworking devices in the path.

The next several chapters provide background for allocating that budget. Chapter 3 deals with the internal forwarding processing of typical switches and routers, each switch and router on the path spending some of your delay budget. Of course, increasing performance of devices tends to increase spending, so you might exhaust your financial budget before exhausting your performance budget if the goals, or finances, are unrealistic.

Chapters 4 and 5 deal with aspects of how the switches and routers make decisions about how to forward. Chapter 6 considers the relationships of hosts to routers and general issues of relaying in small networks. Chapters 7 and 8 deal with the overall relationships and limitations of switches, routers, and servers in networks of various sizes.

After working through Chapter 7, you should be able to decide on the basic architecture of your enterprise network. Part IV deals with specific implementation techniques.

PART II

Selecting Technologies

CHAPTER 3

How Do Switches and
Routers Forward?

He flung himself from the room, flung himself upon his horse,
and rode madly off in all directions.
—Stephen Leacock

Electronic mail is a technology that permits the post office
to lose the mail at the speed of light.
—Howard C. Berkowitz

Dispatch is the soul of business, and nothing contributes
more to Dispatch than Method.
—Lord Chesterfield

Modern relays have two key data structures: the Routing Information Base (RIB) and the Forwarding Information Base (FIB). In low-end devices, these can be the same data structure, but the conceptual distinction still is valid. The RIB is optimized for updating by the routing information mechanisms discussed in the next two chapters, whereas the FIB is optimized for high-speed lookup and is the focus of this chapter.

When you design networks, you need to decide on the relaying functions that are appropriate in various parts of the network and then select specific components to carry out those functions. This chapter examines the ways in which various relays actually forward information, so you can understand the performance characteristics of relays and the advantages and limitations of various types. The emphasis of this chapter is on the relays as standalone boxes. Part III discusses the overall relationships of relaying techniques in your network and then goes into additional component selection issues such as network management. Part IV looks at more specific deployment issues.

In this chapter, an assumption is made that the FIB has been populated by magic. This magic is discussed in Chapter 4. Here, however, the concern is for what a switch or router has been obtained—forwarding information.

Path Determination Versus Forwarding

First, you need to begin by understanding that there is no single thing called *routing*. At the very least, routing consists of two parts:

- *Path determination*, in which the map of the network is, in effect, examined for best paths. The best paths through this map are stored in the RIB.

- *Forwarding*, in which data units are moved from one router or switch port to another, at microsecond or nanosecond speed. Because forwarding applies to every data unit sent through the relay, improving forwarding performance is the key to improving the throughput of relays. It is often useful to distinguish between *packet forwarding* of Layer 3 data units and *frame forwarding* or *cell forwarding* of Layer 2 data units.

This chapter, which emphasizes forwarding, precedes the detailed discussion of path determination. While path determination must happen before anything can be forwarded, it's worth emphasizing the point that forwarding performance affects every packet and frame.

Not all forwarding operations are the same in the same box. The idea of *forwarding paths* is critical in understanding real products, especially those intended for high performance. Such products tend to have one or more distinct hardware-assisted paths through which most packets should flow. Most packets do not need complex handling, such as bandwidth management or filtering. If a packet needs conditional handling, not just forwarding to the destination address, it often must go into a different forwarding path. A conditional handling path can use more processor resources to decide how to handle the packet, but is usually significantly slower than the hardware-assisted path.

Relatively slow WAN links, where bandwidth is a critical constraint, might very well run acceptably through a slower forwarding path, if that path is more intelligent and can provide advanced bandwidth management. As link speed increases to LAN and ATM bandwidths, however, the forwarding path selected can have a major effect on throughput. Cisco routers, in particular, have a substantial number of forwarding paths, and setting a software option that forces your traffic into a slow path can have a huge effect on performance.

One problem router developers face is knowing which packets truly need intelligent handling and which can be dispatched to a fast, stupid, hardware-assisted path. See the section "Deployment Issues and Router Alerts" in Chapter 13 for a discussion of a new IP option that helps routers select the appropriate forwarding path.

As a designer, you must be aware of the effect on the forwarding path when you enable a new feature on a relay. As you will see, adding filters can cause a significant drop in performance, but not nearly as much as traffic prioritization and bandwidth management. Multicast processing also can have major performance impacts.

Figure 3.1 shows the basic model of a relay—in either a router or a bridge—as a box containing the following:

- Some number of input interfaces. Interfaces, as seen by the forwarding logic, can actually be composed of multiple physical interfaces over which information is inverse multiplexed. Alternatively, a physical interface can have several logical streams multiplexed onto it.

- Some number of output interfaces.

- Hardware or software logic to handle protocol behavior at the input and output interfaces.

- Hardware or software logic to determine the destination port(s) for traffic arriving on incoming interfaces.

These are the fundamental aspects of a relay. Other issues that refine the relay structure include several choices:

- How does the relay find the destination of a protocol data unit (PDU) to be forwarded? Routers are concerned with Layer 3 PDUs, whereas bridges and switches are concerned with Layer 2 PDUs.

- How does the relay ensure that its forwarding rules continue to match reality?

- When the relay tries to forward a PDU out an interface (or medium) that is busy transmitting another PDU, what happens?

- Will the relay accept new traffic when it is busy processing other traffic? How does it reject excess traffic (if it does)?

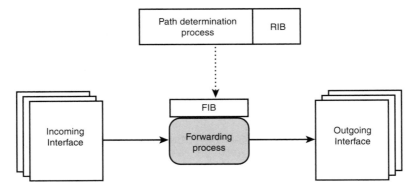

FIGURE 3.1 *In the simplest terms, a relay is a device that takes an input data unit and forwards it to one or more output ports, fragmenting if necessary, and then encapsulating the forwarded information into the frame and data link protocols needed by the output ports.*

There are operational and economic aspects of specific implementations:

- If the destination in the PDU is logical, not physical, how does the relay select the physical interface on which to forward the PDU?

- How quickly can these decisions be made?

- How important is it for devices in the relaying environment to recognize, without human intervention, their place in the map?

- How much overhead is necessary for the relay to keep track of the map?

Most relaying is done under the control of a common administration, or at least exhibiting common routing policies to the world in general. At Layer 3, this is called *interior routing*. *Exterior routing*, using the Border Gateway Protocol (BGP), has additional requirements to allow routing information to flow among independently managed networks.

With WAN technologies such as Frame Relay, Layer 2 forwarding often goes beyond the limits of a single campus or enterprise. There are exterior connectivity mechanisms for Layer 2 WANs, called Network-to-Network Interfaces or Inter-Carrier Interfaces. Layer 2 forwarding for LANs, however, is almost always limited to a single campus of a single enterprise, simply by the limited physical range of LAN technologies.

An important differentiation in WAN Layer 2 forwarding is the idea of user versus provider responsibility. LAN forwarding at Layer 2 is almost always restricted in scope to a single enterprise.

Figure 3.2 shows various administrative and technical arrangements common in WANs. Data terminal equipment (DTE) is a user device that connects to data circuit terminating equipment (DCE) that marks the boundary between provider and user responsibility. The term *DTE-DCE interface* has been used for many years, and User Network Interface (UNI) often describes the same relationship in newer technologies. UNI seems to carry more of a software connotation appropriate for intelligent networks, whereas DTE-DCE interface tends to refer to simpler hardware interconnection; but some protocols, such as X.25, also make DTE and DCE distinctions in their data link and packet level protocol. A packet-level DCE, for example, can issue a diagnostic code of "network congestion," but such a code would be inappropriate for a DTE. Conversely, a DTE can issue a "host cleared call" diagnostic that a DCE would not issue.

As a designer, if you gained your experience with LANs, you must reorient your thinking to realize that some components of the WAN transmission system will be hidden from you. You only can see the behavior at the DTE-DCE interface, perhaps supplemented with management reports or out-of-band monitoring functions provided by the carrier (see Table 3.1).

TABLE 3.1   WAN TERMINOLOGY

DXE	Data switching equipment
IWU	Internetworking unit
NNI	Network-to-network interface
DTE	Data terminal equipment
DCE	Data circuit-terminating equipment
UNI	User-to-network interface

DTE –Data Terminal Equipment
DXE –Data Switching Equipment

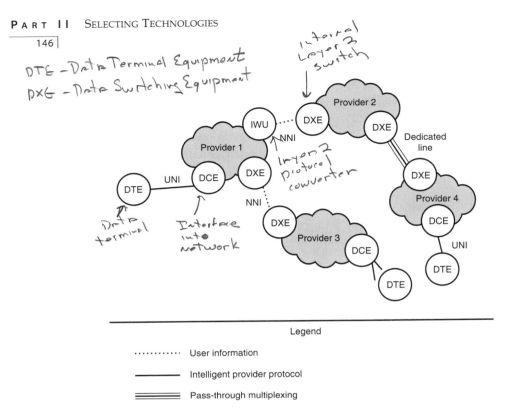

Internal
Layer 2
Switch

Layer 2
protocol
converter

Data
terminal

Interface
into
network

Legend

....   User information

————   Intelligent provider protocol

══════   Pass-through multiplexing

FIGURE 3.2   *User and provider interfaces.*

In Figure 3.2, dotted lines show dedicated or multiplexed channels carrying user protocols. Single lines show inter-carrier protocols. Triple lines show user protocols tunneled through a carrier.

Note

The term Layer 2 is used informally when referring to carrier networks. Many carrier protocols are built against the ISDN, ATM, or other reference models that do not strictly map to OSI reference model layers.

Data switching equipment (DXE) is Layer 2 switches that are usually internal to the carrier, although user networks may contain them okay. IWUs are Layer 2 protocol converters.

Carriers interconnect at the NNI, either with homogeneous protocols on inter-connected DXE or with a DXE at one end and an IWU at the other. As shown between Providers 2 and 4, a user protocol can be tunneled through a provider that does not support that particular protocol. In this example, Provider 4 simply provides a bit pipe for a protocol that Provider 2 supports, but Provider 4 does not. See the section "Demand Backup for PVCs" in Chapter 10 for an example of how tunneling through a carrier can interfere with fault notification—and a way to work around this problem.

Input Interface Processing

There is little difference at the input interface of routers and bridges or switches, as shown in Figure 3.3. Their behavior begins to diverge as the data unit moves higher into the protocol stack, but input logic is similar.

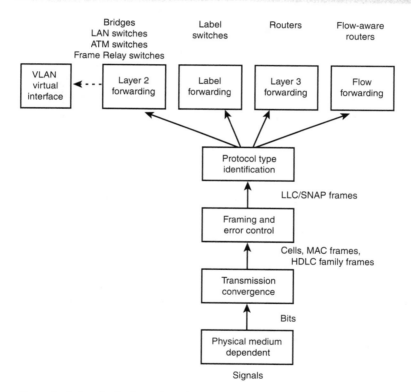

FIGURE 3.3   *At the input interface.*

Various protocol-specific errors can be detected at each of the levels of conversion, from the medium dependent up the protocol stack. Depending on the protocol and the interface implementation, statistics can be kept on some of these errors, and the interface might attempt to correct some or go into a failure condition.

Physical Medium Dependent and Independent Processing

The electrical or optical signals on the transmission medium need to be converted to the internal electronic signals of the forwarding device. Although older technologies such as EIA RS-232C simply specify the "physical layer," newer technologies including LANs split the OSI physical layer into multiple sublayers. In fact, the OSI definitions of Layers 1 and 2 do not always match the structure of newer transmission systems.

The lowest physical sublayer often is called *physical medium dependent* (PMD). Fast Ethernet, for example, operates over two kinds of twisted pair as well as optical fiber. Each is a different PMD. There is a slightly higher medium-independent physical layer, sometimes called the transmission convergence sublayer, that specifies such things as bit timing, low-level diagnostics, and so on. The Synchronous Optical Network (SONET) specification, over which ATM usually runs, has both a PMD and a transmission convergence level. If this is an ATM interface, cells are reassembled into frames before being passed to the frame-level function.

physical layer

Note

As many people go deeper into networking, the OSI reference model conventions they learned in their first data communications courses can be a conceptual straitjacket. The idea of layering remains a good and valid one.

The problem is that the seven traditional layers simply do not fit current practice, especially at the lower layers. There are important sublayering models of the network, data link, and physical layers.

Even the OSI architects themselves recognize this sublayering. There is an all-too-little-known document called the "Internal Organization of the Network Layer" that establishes sublayering and addressing conventions that reflect the realities of intelligent transmission media. This document is discussed further in Chapter 4 of Designing Addressing Architectures for Routing and Switching *[Berkowitz, 1998a].*

At the physical layer, bits may or may not be part of bytes, cells, and frames. Some bits are used purely for the internal operation of the physical layer. Other bits are used for delimiting the start and end of multiplexed channels, of cells, and of frames.

To add even more confusion—and flexibility—there can be multiple physical layers in a single interface. *Dense wavelength division multiplexing* (DWDM) is an emerging, extremely high-speed transmission technology, over which SONET or Gigabit Ethernet can be multiplexed (see Chapter 9).

As a designer, when you evaluate the performance of commercial products, be sure you understand where each layer is processed. Layer, in this context, is arbitrary—levels of abstraction such as transmission convergence and physical medium dependent, rather than OSI layer. A product might have the architectural capability to do some function in hardware or a specialized processor, a given version of its software might not implement this capability. For example, the initial release of one major vendor's campus ATM switch does processing-intensive ATM segmentation and reassembly (SAR) in its general processor, rather than the special-purpose chip on its interface boards. SAR segments variable-length frames into fixed-length cells and reassembles the frames at the destination.

Transmission Convergence

Transmission convergence is also called the medium-independent interface. Typically, it is the place where bits are timed and manipulated in a form independent of the actual electronic or optical signals. It deals with all bits on the interface, not just those that will be used for higher-layer data.

Framing and Error Control

Not all physical layer bits contain data. Some can be used for synchronization and control. Token Ring and FDDI, for example, use a 4B/5B scheme, which means 4 out of every 5 bits are used for data and the 5th is for physical layer control. The 25 Mbps physical layer standard for ATM uses exactly the same chipset as for Token Ring, but uses 5 out of 5 bits for data.

The interface next extracts the data bits from the physical bit stream and follows the rules of the medium access control protocol on LANs, or other protocols such as LAP-F on Frame Relay, to build byte streams and then frames.

ATM has the intermediate level of framing cells at the ATM layer, with SAR being done at the ATM Adaptation Layer (AAL) above it.

It is possible to have bit encoding errors that prevent bits being mapped into a data stream. Such errors can simply be logged or, if persistent, will put the interface into a down condition.

After frames are generated at Layer 2, most data link protocols have some kind of error control. In most modern cases, this means error detection: checking a hardware-calculated error checking field and discarding frames with a bad check field. Some protocols intended for media with a high error rate, such as LAP-B or SDLC, can either directly request retransmission or not acknowledge bad frames, indirectly causing retransmission.

Protocol Type Identification

The next major level is the level at which forwarding decisions are made on frames of data. Different forwarding modes can be used for different protocol types. For example, IP normally would be routed based on Layer 3 information, but NetBIOS would be bridged based on Layer 2 information.

Most data link protocols have some sort of protocol identifier field that can be used to select the appropriate forwarding mode on a specific interface. The Logical Link Control/Subnetwork Access Protocol (LLC/SNAP) defined in IEEE 802.2 is the basis for most identification techniques, not simply the LAN protocols. Other identification methods include the type field in Ethernet or Cisco High-Level Data Link Control (HDLC) frames. There are at least four ways in which decisions can be made, as shown in Figure 3.4.

layer 2

tag
switching

layer 3

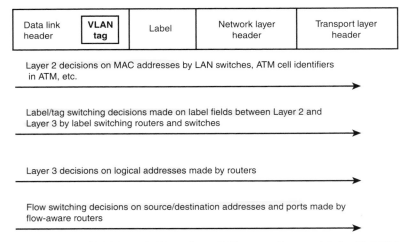

FIGURE 3.4 *Decisions can be made on fields generally associated with OSI Layers 2 through 4. Most commonly, the decision is made on a destination address, but it might involve source-destination address pairs or other fields in the frame.*

In basic LANs, forwarding decisions are based on the destination address field of every frame. The relays forward traffic either directly to a LAN that contains the destination address or to a medium that connects to another relay. Media that interconnect relays and have no end user hosts on them are called *trunks* (see Figure 3.5).

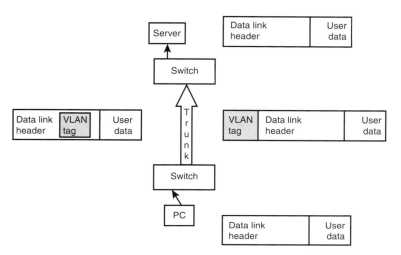

FIGURE 3.5 *Media that interconnect Layer 2 relays are trunks. If virtual LANs (VLANs) are used, frames going over the trunks either have a tag field inserted into, or prepended to, the original frame.*

The data link layer information most commonly used for forwarding decision making is the destination address, such as the destination MAC address in LAN frames, or the data link connection identifier in Frame Relay frames.

Especially when multiplexing over multiple media, decisions can be made on source-destination pairs rather than on destination alone. See Chapters 9 and 10 for further discussion of multiplexing.

When forwarding onto trunks, VLANs make decisions at a higher level of abstraction. They look at a VLAN *tag* field that identifies the VLAN to which the traffic belongs and forward the traffic to a trunk onto which that VLAN is mapped. A given physical interface can have multiple VLANs multiplexed onto them, which it demultiplexes into several virtual interfaces, one for each VLAN. Only when a routing function is present can frames from one VLAN be sent to a different VLAN. Frames from edge networks must be identified in some manner when they traverse *trunks* shared by traffic from multiple edge networks.

This identification is done in VLAN protocols with some sort of protocol-specific header information. In ATM LAN Emulation, the identification is implicit and is associated with the virtual circuit over which trunk traffic is carried.

LAN switches can carry VLAN trunk protocols to other switches, without decoding the individual edge VLANs contained within them. Be careful that any interface through which you send VLAN traffic does support the trunking protocol even if there is no demultiplexing on that switch. The danger of not doing so is that the switch might discard a maximum-length Ethernet frame that now exceeds the 802.3 length specification because it also now is prefixed with a VLAN header (see "Small Giants Roam the Trunks" in Chapter 10).

A VLAN-aware interface appears as a set of virtual interfaces to the input bridging and routing functions described in the following sections. After frames are assembled and error-checked, they are passed to a virtual interface where the bridging or routing logic is applied.

Input Actions Specific to Layers at Which Forwarding Decisions Are Made

Some input actions, such as protocol type identification, must apply to any frame. Other input actions may or may not apply, depending on the layer at which the forwarding decision is made. *Layer*, in this context, is not strictly an OSI layer, but simply a level in some layered architecture. Some of these layer-specific actions are listed in the sections that follow.

Input Actions in Cell Switching

ATM switches look at the virtual path identifier and virtual circuit identifier fields in input frames and look these up in per-interface tables to determine the next hop. Precedence bits are also examined to see if special handling is needed if the output port is congested.

Input Actions in Layer 2 Bridging and Switching

Transparent bridges learn MAC addresses that they see in the source address field of incoming frames. These addresses, and the interfaces on which they appeared, are stored in an address table. Depending on the implementation, the address tables can be per-interface or chassiswide. In transparent bridges, the destination Media Access Control (MAC) address is looked up in the local interface table. If the destination is local to the interface, no further forwarding action is taken. Statistics are updated.

Before a frame is forwarded, it is checked against any configured input filters. These can permit or deny forwarding based on a MAC address, protocol type, Ethernet vendor code, or Logical Link Control (LLC) information. As you will see in Chapter 10, these filtering criteria also can be the basis for assigning frames to VLANs.

If the destination MAC address is not unicast, it is passed on, unless vendor-specific multicast throttling is in effect. Throttling discards the frame if more multicast frames than a given count level are received in a specified time period.

Input Actions in Label Forwarding

Label forwarding, the thrust of the IETF MPLS working group, uses a link-local field inserted between the Layer 2 and Layer 3 headers to make forwarding decisions. MPLS is discussed at greater length in Chapters 13 and 14 but the idea of extracting the label is mentioned here for completeness.

Input Actions in Layer 3 Forwarding

The protocol type is examined to determine whether routing is supported for that protocol family and discarded if it is not. Frame headers and trailers are discarded after the frame has passed error checking.

Pattern-matching rules can be applied to input data, and, if the pattern is matched, an action can be taken. Pattern-matching followed by conditional acceptance of the packet is commonly called filtering or access control. Typical matching parameters include Layer 3 source and/or destination addresses, either explicitly or after a wildcard mask is applied. Other parameters include IP protocol type, type of service/IP precedence bits, and TCP and UDP port values. The latter are actually Layer 4 information, but commonly specified in a Layer 3 context.

The most common action is either discarding or further forwarding data. Other actions might be to manipulate fields in a packet header, such as setting IP precedence bits for differentiated service, or the security option field if the Internet Protocol Security Option is in use.

Remember that you usually have the ability to apply pattern matching and actions on output as well. You can do this sort of filtering on input, output, or both. If an action applies to all packets, it is usually most efficient to do the filtering on input. If it is applied only to some, such as only packets destined for a WAN interface in a router with several LAN interfaces, filtering at the output interface can be more efficient, because that filtering is only necessary on a fraction of packets.

Input traffic shaping functions have been more associated with WAN switches, but now are appearing on routers. Such functions keep track of the amount of data being received on a given physical or virtual interface, comparing the received data rate with average and peak values in a flow specification. Information above those limits is queued or discarded.

Input Actions in Flow Forwarding

In flow-aware forwarding, which can be described either as Layer 4 or Layer 7 aware switching, the input device must go through Layer 2 and 3 processing and then extract and analyze the Layer 3, 4, and sometimes Layer 7 headers. At a minimum, the source and destination Layer 3 addresses need to be considered.

The particular relay might need to do no more than look at the source-destination pair and hash the two together to create an identifier to be used in load sharing. See the section "Load Sharing" later in this chapter and "Source-Destination Hash" in Chapter 11.

If Layer 4 information is being considered, the appropriate Layer 4 fields, such as TCP or UDP source and destination port addresses, need to be extracted. Port information can simply be an input into a source-destination hash mechanism that considers Layer 4 as well as Layer 3 information. The hash can use the full source and destination information as an input or can apply wildcards to source and/or destination to reduce the resulting number of possibilities.

Layer 3 Forwarding

Units of data enter a relay and, in the basic model, their destination address field is extracted and looked up in a pre-populated FIB. Low-end routers can combine the RIB and FIB into one data structure, but the conceptual distinction is valid. Both the RIB and FIB contain destinations and output interfaces to be used in sending to those destinations.

Detailed FIB designs often are proprietary and can be hardware assisted. Various data structures appropriate for FIB use are discussed in the computer science literature, such as Patricia tries [Smith n.d.], radix trees [Sklower, 1999], and so on. These data structures are optimized for speed of lookup, as opposed to RIB designs that are optimized for updating. RIB data structures tend to be linked lists.

Note

Trie is a reasonably obscure computer science term, derived from the middle letters of retrieval. *It is pronounced "tree."*

Patricia tries are well understood and general, but not optimal for every lookup environment. A traditional tree uses large amounts of memory. Variant algorithms use less memory, but large tries still involve many lookups when the number of addresses is large. Host route hashes are very fast for small caches [Torrent, 1999]. Several vendors, including Cisco and Torrent, have lookup algorithms that either are patented or in the patent process. These proprietary algorithms are intended to scale to Gigabit speeds.

Path determination populates the routing information base (RIB) of routers. Depending on the implementation, the RIB and the FIB can be the same data structure. Alternatively, the RIB can be optimized for updating by path determination processes, whereas the FIB is optimized for fast lookup. In specific router examples later in this chapter, you see different ways in which the FIB is implemented.

Generically, a FIB is a data structure organized for high-speed lookup. In most routers, the RIB is what is displayed with a display of the "routing table," whereas certain types of RIBs are displayed with cache displays. I find that the formalism of referring to the RIB and FIB separately helps keep the different functions straight. The term *cache* is also used, with the usual implication that there are fewer entries in a cache than in the RIB. Several high-performance products have a FIB with the same number of entries as the RIB, synchronized with the RIB. It's actually simpler to build a FIB with the same number of entries as the RIB than it is to build a cache with a subset of the RIB.

Note

In traditional routers, the entries in a FIB map to destination prefixes, which can be subnets or aggregates of subnets. An evolving concept, discussed in Chapter 13, is the idea of forwarding equivalence classes (FECs), which can greatly reduce the size and lookup overhead of a FIB. A FEC is a way in which traffic can leave a router. If, for example, a router took 60,000 routes or so as a full BGP feed from two ISPs, it would have only two FECs because a given route would be reached by one ISP or the other ISP.

The idea of a forwarding cache is that a fraction of the routes are most frequently used, and it is productive to store this subset in expensive, high-speed memory. If there are a large number of routes, more than can fit in the cache memory, there is a challenge of keeping the most recently used or most often used routes in the cache. There is a challenge of whether to selectively replace individual cache entries or replace the entire cache when any entry changes. Cache data structures that are optimal for fast lookup are often quite difficult to update incrementally.

Another subtle problem of cache models is they are traffic driven, not topology driven. Given there is not enough room in the cache to hold every route, the only practical method is to keep the most recently used routes in the cache. If, however, there is a sudden change in traffic patterns, perhaps because a major router failed and the network is reconverging around it, the entire cache contents might suddenly become irrelevant and would demand CPU-intensive resources to recalculate the cache.

A *cache miss* condition takes place when a given destination is not found in the cache. The cache miss condition forces a slower lookup in the RIB. If the cache update algorithm invalidates the entire cache when the cache needs to change, all lookups need to go to the RIB while the cache is being updated.

Conceptually, the FIB is organized by destination address. This destination address is a Layer 2 address in a switch or bridge, or a Layer 3 address in a router.

FIBs in real products, however, can use special purpose lookup hardware. The actual data structure usually represents some sort of hash table rather than a simple list, because a FIB is organized for fast lookup rather than fast updating with new destination information.

FIB Lookup

Without exception, routable Layer 3 addresses are hierarchical. They have at least two parts, the more significant part of which is used to make decisions such as which outgoing interface to use to forward the packet on to the *next hop* closer to the destination. The low-order part is evaluated only when the next hop is on to the final destination medium, where the low-order part is used to locate the final host.

In IP routing, the leftmost part of the address is more significant. Traditionally, this was called the *network part*, but use of a pure network part is long obsolete. The part of the IP address used to make routing decisions is called the *prefix*. This prefix is of variable length, from 0 to 32 bits.

When a route is looked up in the FIB, there might be several possible matches, depending on prefix length. See Chapter 4 for a discussion of how routes are installed in this table.

After the table is built, the rule is that the most specific match is always taken. *Most specific* means the maximum number of prefix bits in a table entry that exactly match the prefix extracted from the packet. This is not vendor specific, but defined in RFC 1812.

The most specific possible route is to a specific host. All 32 bits are significant. In classless interdomain routing (CIDR) notation, this is a /32 route.

Of course, a zero-length prefix in a packet makes little sense. By convention, the zero length route is the *default route*, which matches any address but is the least preferable route. The next hop associated with the default route is the address to which you forward when you have no better alternative.

The speed at which an address can be looked up is one of the major determinants of the internal speed of a router. Internal speed, however, is not the most important performance factor in many router applications.

Route lookup algorithms are challenged by the overall size of the routing table. Efficient data structures, algorithms, and often hardware-assisted lookup are critical for Internet backbone routers that must deal with tables of 60,000 routes or more. Internet backbone routers are even more challenged when they must deal with the reality that there is not a higher probability that some routes are used more frequently than others.

The probability of needing specific routes more frequently than all routes is important. It is a valid assumption in most enterprise networks, which might have 1,000 user prefixes but 10 server farms. The most frequently used routes can be cached in software or hardware tables of relatively small capacity, but designed for very fast lookup.

Caching Can Be at Higher Layers, Too!

Don't look at the address cache issue in isolation to switching or routing. Application level proxies and caches can have a significant effect.

There is a hard core of frequently hit sites for which caching helps—the figure of 20 GB cache is thrown out fairly often by experts on the **squid** public domain Web cache. Beyond that, caching does give diminishing returns.

If you think about it, you might get better cache performance on an intranet, where you constrain the range of Web pages that you search for.

Check your premises when evaluating cache schemes. Simply because you have many prefixes doesn't mean every prefix routinely communicates with every other prefix. Typical enterprise networks direct most traffic from users to mainframes or server farms.

Workgroup protocols are more likely than IP to use any-to-any models. Any-to-any models do not scale well. Even in workgroup protocols, it might be that the heaviest traffic is to local servers, and switches might be more effective than routers for accessing local servers. Although LAN switches cannot deal with as complex a topology as routers, LAN switches are less expensive than routers for providing bandwidth within a simple topology such as a workgroup.

Caches can be a highly effective method for small to medium environments, or for routers that connect users to backbones in large environments. In the latter case, the edge router needs to know the relatively small number of routes to the servers. Edge routers that connect the servers, however, are much more likely to need fast access to a large number of routes.

In practice, you control the cache size by selecting a specific router. Low-end routers have a software cache, with a size set by the implementation. The cache size has so many interactions with internals of the implementation that it is rarely practical, or even possible, for the router operator to change it. Higher-end routers have hardware FIBs, either a fixed size or a choice of sizes.

Lookup time might not be a major concern if the transmission media are slow. Transmission medium delay is usually more significant than internal router or switch delay. It is far more likely to see the true performance bottleneck being the speed of the interface to a server, or the processing capability of the server itself, than it is to see a problem due completely to network bandwidth.

Be aware that increasing bandwidth to a server, without full analysis of bottlenecks, can make matters worse by overloading the server with a heavier transaction load. Increasing bandwidth to workstations, without analyzing traffic patterns or workstation capacity, can also create problems. A workstation, for example, might be able to cope with the rate of broadcasts on a 10 Mbps LAN connection, but not on a 100 Mbps connection.

Assume that you have a user site edge router that has two LAN interfaces and a T1-speed Frame Relay interface to eight server sites. At 10 microseconds per lookup, it takes a maximum of 90 microseconds to look up a route using sequential search. Yet it takes approximately 1200 microseconds to clock a full frame onto the Ethernet, and almost 8000 microseconds to send the frame over the T1 assuming no queuing behind frames for other permanent virtual circuits (PVCs).

A maximum-length Ethernet or 802.3 frame has a 14-byte header, composed of destination address, source address, and a 2-byte field used either for type or length information. There is also an 8-byte physical layer preamble, and a 4-byte frame check sequence. The data field can be a maximum of 1500 bytes.

Combining the overhead and data fields, a maximum length frame is 1526 bytes long. Converting bytes to bits, you have to send 12208 bits to send a full frame. At 10 Mbps, this is 1221 microseconds, which for most purposes can be rounded to 1200 microseconds. If full precision is needed, you also want to include the 9.6 microsecond delay required between successive frames, so the true value is closer to 1230 microseconds.

A typical WAN protocol such as PPP, has a starting and terminating frame byte, 1-byte address and control fields, a 2-byte type field, and a 2-byte error checking field for a total of 8 overhead bytes. With a 1500-byte data field, this means you need to transmit 1508 bytes or 12064 bits at a 1.544 Mbps data rate, or 7810 microseconds.

Additional time might be needed to copy the frame internally in the router, or the router might be able to do a pointer swap between input and output interfaces. Clocking the frame into the server, and server processing time, can also be significant.

The important thing is not to overemphasize routing lookup time when it is not the limiting factor. An enterprise network on Frame Relay, with a limited number of server routes, is a quite different situation than a major Internet router with ATM OC-3 and OC-12 links and a 55,000 route table. A router for a small enterprise network, or a router at the edge of a large enterprise network, can work acceptably with a combined RIB/FIB in a reasonable amount of ordinary memory. A large provider router needs large amounts of high-speed memory for its FIB, which will almost certainly be physically separate from the RIB.

Protocol conversion, proxy services, filtering, and other CPU-intensive functions can add to the delay in routers. But most of the delay is apt to be waiting for transmission media.

Note

Traditional routing makes decisions on Layer 3 destination addresses in the headers of incoming packets. Modern routers can consider additional factors such as flow identifiers, precedence fields, and security identifiers.

IP packets contain a Type of Service field in their header. This actually has two parts, four precedence bits and four type of service (TOS) bits.

Little use has ever been made of the TOS bits. The latest OSPF specification dropped support for TOS routing, partially because only Cisco implemented it. At least two implementations must exist before a feature is acceptable as a full standard.

The precedence bits were originally intended for military applications, but have been adopted as a simple way of carrying quality of service information.

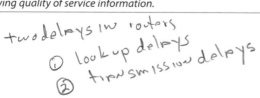

Special Cases in Forwarding

Various exception cases can emerge when the destination is being looked up in the FIB. Several are discussed in the following sections.

Load Sharing

If the output load is to be shared over multiple equal-cost paths, the router must retain the state of the last interface used to send packets to a given destination, so it can select the next in a group of parallel interfaces.

Figure 3.6 shows a generic environment in which you would load balance. A router or switch has two interfaces, 1 and 2, both of which can reach the two destinations, A and B. There is an internal stream of six packets, coming from various Source Addresses, C through E.

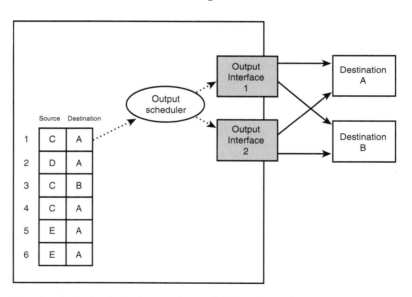

FIGURE 3.6 *Load sharing requires multiple paths to the same destination.*

Figures 3.7 through 3.9 show various forms of load sharing for a stream of packets. They are summarized in Table 3.2.

TABLE 3.2 SUMMARY OF LOAD SHARING MECHANISMS

Method	CPU involvement	Optimality
Per-packet	High	Good for bandwidth and convergence to next link. Bad for keeping packets in sequence.
Per-destination	Low	Good when there is a large number of destinations. Might have unbalanced loads with small number of destinations. Packets stay in sequence. Does not improve convergence.
Source-Destination hash	Moderate	Excellent for spreading load over multiple next-hop links. Packets stay in sequence. Does not improve convergence.
Optimized multipath (see Chapter 14)	High	Allows optimization of load over multiple hops. Coordinates well with label switching.

Round-robin load balancing, the preconditions for which are shown in Figure 3.6, optimizes the use of bandwidth and recovery time after link or interface failures, as shown in Figure 3.7. It also needs more CPU resources, and some load balancing methods increase the probability that packets will be out of order at the destination, requiring additional host resources.

Why does this mechanism tend to cause packets to be out of order? It is bad enough on pairs of links with identical bandwidth and delay, and gets even worse with more than two links or if the links have different bandwidth or delay.

With identical links, you begin sending Packet 1 on the first link, and as soon as you finish sending the packet to the interface, you schedule the second packet for the second link. Next, you schedule the third packet for the first link. If you are lucky and the delays are identical, the receiver receives the first packet, and the second packet is received while the third packet is still being transmitted. If the second link happens to have longer delay, because, for example, the WAN carrier routes them through different media, the third packet could very well arrive before the second.

So far, the assumption has been that the two links are only being used to carry the traffic between one source-destination pair. What if more pairs are involved? You might send the first packet on the first link and schedule the second packet on the second link, but find the second link is busy transmitting a packet from a different source-destination pair. In that case, it is almost certain that the third packet will arrive before the second.

With significantly different delays, such as having two 56 Kbps links, one satellite and one terrestrial, out-of-order delivery becomes much more probable [Berkowitz groupstudy, 26 Jan 1999] (see Table 3.3).

TABLE 3.3 TIMINGS WHEN LOAD BALANCING ACROSS LINKS WITH DIFFERENT DELAY

Time	Sender	Receiver
0	Packet 1 over satellite Packet 2 over terrestrial	
200	Packet 3 over satellite Packet 4 over terrestrial	Packet 2 received (200 bit transmission)
400	Packet 5 over satellite	Packet 1 received (200 bit transmission + 200 satellite delay) Packet 4 received (200 queuing + 200 transmission)
600	Packet 6 over satellite	Packet 3 received (200 bit transmission + 200 queuing + 200 satellite delay)

It's not quite as bad when both links run over terrestrial paths with equal delay (see Table 3.4).

TABLE 3.4 TIMINGS WHEN LOAD BALANCING ACROSS LINKS WITH EQUAL DELAY

Time	Sender	Receiver
0	Packet 1 over terrestrial Packet 2 over terrestrial	
200	Packet 3 over terrestrial	Packet 1 received (200-bit transmission)
	Packet 4 over terrestrial	Packet 2 received (200-bit transmission)
400	Packet 5 over terrestrial	Packet 3 received (200 trans + 200 queue) Packet 4 received (200 queuing + 200-bit transmission)
600	Packet 6 over satellite	Packet 5 received (200 trans + 400 queue

This can get statistically complex with multiple sources sharing the two links. Both configurations give out-of-sequence packets at the destination, but they are more scrambled with different delays.

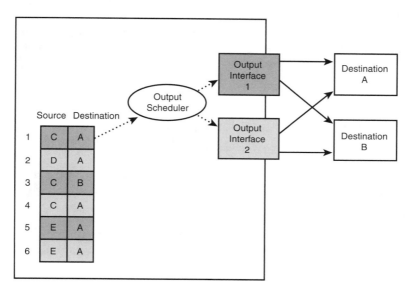

FIGURE 3.7   *Round-robin load balancing equalizes by number of media.*

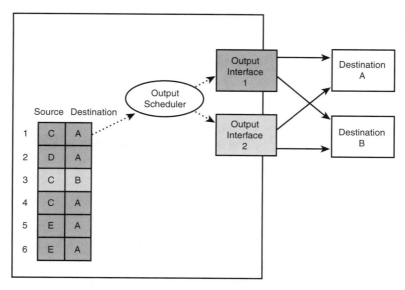

FIGURE 3.8   *In load balancing based on destination address, there are no guarantees that a disproportionate number of destinations might not randomize to one path.*

Statistical load balancing, which is much faster and tends to equalize load if there is a large number of destinations, is called *per-destination load balancing* by Cisco (see Figure 3.9).

The chief problem with destination-only statistical load balancing occurs when there are a small number of destinations. In the worst case, there might be a single destination, but only one medium would be used, with the others being idle.

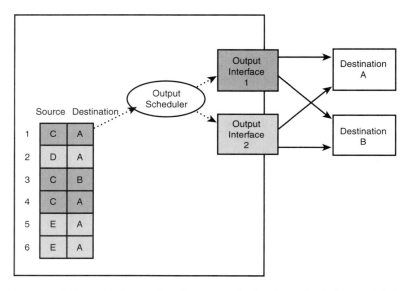

FIGURE 3.9 *Load sharing based on source-destination pairs is far more likely to balance smoothly. Without further information, however, it can send information to a congested link downstream.*

Source-destination pairing removes many of the limitations of destination-only statistical load balancing. Even if there is only one destination, as long as there is more than one source—even multiple processes on the same workstation—the load should spread among the various media.

A given flow tends to go over a single medium, which also reduces the probability of out-of-sequence data units.

Nothing, however, is perfect. The size of a source-destination table is greater than a destination-only table, unless there is only a single source and destination. The size of such a table can grow to be unmanageable or too expensive in resources.

Some sort of wildcarding or aggregation might be necessary to keep the load balancing assignment table manageable. For example, an Internet service provider might define the criterion to be any source address to TCP port 80, the well-known port for HTTP Web traffic, and another load-balancing criterion to be any source to TCP port 25, the SMTP mail port. The more control exerted in this manner, the closer you get to traffic engineering rather than automatic load balancing.

Destination Unreachable

The most obvious special case is that the destination is not found in the FIB, and there is no default route. In this case, the router creates an Internet Control Message Protocol (ICMP) Destination Unreachable message and returns this to the originating host. The source address of this ICMP packet is that of the router interface that received it, and the destination address is that of the origi-nator of the packet that could not be forwarded.

Destination Administratively Prohibited

If a packet fails a filtering test, the RFC 1812 prescribed default action is to return an ICMP Communication Administratively Prohibited message. This can be questioned both from a security and a performance standpoint, but it is the expected behavior. Figure 3.10 shows how filtering can be used to suppress this message returning to the source. The dashed line shows the path taken when the security policy requires suppressing the ICMP response.

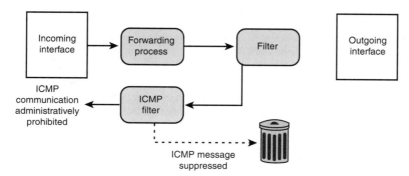

FIGURE 3.10 *Handling the Destination Administratively Prohibited error.*

From the security view, returning the Handling Destination Administratively Prohibited error message reveals to a potential attacker that there is something that the router administrator has gone to the effort of protecting. This can make things interesting to the attacker, while returning a destination unreachable, or simply timing out, does not reveal the protected resource. The destination under probing appears to be a black hole; the cracker does not know if it is down or if it is intelligently rejecting his probes.

Time to Live Exceeded

Time to Live (TTL) Exceeded always reminds me of a router designed by the Godfather. In reality, there are two much more mundane reasons why the TTL message is sent back to a packet's originator.

The most common reason for the Time to Live Exceeded exception to occur is when an outgoing IP header is being constructed, and the TTL field is decremented and hits zero. This is assumed to mean the packet is in an infinite loop and should be discarded. An ICMP message is returned to the originator.

---

traceroute and ping Can Give Different Results

It's worth noting that the common and valuable **traceroute** procedure exploits TTL. **traceroute**'s logic is different from that of **ping** and gives different information, varying with the specific **traceroute** implementation in use.

This diagnostic tool creates User Datagram Protocol (UDP) datagrams and encapsulates them in IP packets. There is no specific UDP port number associated with UDP, but it usually is a high number in the 33,000 range. Some implementations, such as Cisco's, increment the port number on successive transmissions.

On the first **traceroute** pass, the TTL is set to 1, and the packet properly causes an ICMP TTL Exceeded message to be returned from routers one hop away. Different implementations of **traceroute** send the test message in different ways.

On the second pass, the TTL is set to 2, and routers two hops away generate the ICMP response. On successive hops, the TTL continues to be incremented, until either the destination is reached or a hop count limit reached.

Filters and firewalls can affect **traceroute** and **ping** differently. **traceroute** can fail because a strict policy does not permit unexpected traffic to high-numbered UDP ports. **ping** can fail because either inbound or outbound (with respect to the originating device) ICMP is blocked. **traceroute** can fail because the returning ICMP TTL Exceeded is blocked. You should be aware that there are times when you can **ping** but not **traceroute** to a working destination, or **traceroute** but not **ping**. Also be aware that some implementations, particularly Microsoft, have incorrectly used ICMP as the test message, not UDP.

Most people think of TTL expiration as an error condition that probably indicates a packet is in an infinite loop. There are, however, perfectly good reasons to create packets with a TTL of 1.

If you are doing IP multicasting, or any other function where you want to keep the packets limited to the local medium, TTL=1 is a perfectly good technique for doing so. OSPF, for example, multicasts routing information to routers on a common medium and sets TTL to 1.

Redirection

Available path information can cause a host to direct outgoing traffic to some specific router, but the router might "know better" and want the host to send subsequent traffic to some other router. Redirection functions, as seen in Figure 3.11, allow network relays to send traffic to a different router.

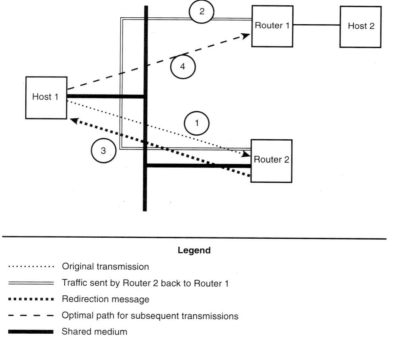

Legend

· · · · · · · · · · ·   Original transmission

═══════════   Traffic sent by Router 2 back to Router 1

■ ■ ■ ■ ■ ■ ■ ■   Redirection message

– – – –   Optimal path for subsequent transmissions

▬▬▬▬▬▬▬   Shared medium

FIGURE 3.11   *Redirection most commonly takes place when a router notices that it is sending a packet back out the same interface on which it was received.*

That next host is accessible to the sending host, because it is on the same medium as defined by the network/subnet number. Because that second router is a better path to the destination than the original receiving router, the first router sends a redirect to the host informing it of the second path.

Note that redirection makes no sense on a point-to-point medium. It is most commonly used on broadcast media, but potentially can be used on nonbroadcast multiaccess media.

Output Processing Actions

Various actions are taken after the destination has been found in the FIB and an output interface selected. The router extracts the data field of the IP packet and any header fields with end-to-end significance and uses these to create one or more new packets. The router reuses most fields of the incoming packet, such as source and destination addresses, in creating the new packets.

More than one packet might need to be created due to IP fragmentation or because the destination is multicast or broadcast.

Some things always occur when forwarding IP packets. The time to live (TTL) field must be decremented, and, if it hits zero, the packet must be discarded and an ICMP error message generated. A new checksum must always be calculated. After a packet is created, it needs to be encapsulated in the appropriate frame type. The frame needs to be converted to bits and sent out. Framing and bit conversion is the reverse of the process described for input processing.

Fragmentation

Fragmentation is the general process of breaking a large data unit into smaller ones appropriate for a particular transmission system. In the ATM context, fragmentation is called segmentation (see Table 3.5).

TABLE 3.5 FRAGMENTATION FEATURES IN PROTOCOLS

Protocol	Optional	Reasons to Fragment
IP	Yes	Interoperability between media with different MTUs.
ATM	No	Fundamental units of transfer, cells, are small.
X.25	Yes	Optimizes retransmission over slow, high-error rate paths.
Frame Relay	Yes	Minimize latency for voice over Frame Relay.

IP fragmentation is a means of making otherwise incompatible media work together. Specifically, it deals with the case where the incoming packet is larger than the maximum transmission unit (MTU) associated with the outgoing medium. The fragmentation message splits the packet into several smaller packets, of a length less than or equal to the outgoing MTU.

Although IP fragmentation certainly works, it tends to be computationally expensive to implement and can generate more traffic than results if hosts do not create packets that need to be fragmented. If a receiving host only receives one fragment out of a sequence, the entire sequence needs to be retransmitted.

Note

There is a general principle here that applies at multiple protocol layers and is especially dramatic with ATM. When you fragment a larger data unit into many smaller ones, send those smaller units into the core, and one of the smaller ones is dropped due to congestion, the entire sequence usually has to be retransmitted.

Newer ATM switches recognize that a cell dropped out of a sequence causes the entire sequence to be retransmitted, so they can discard all cells in the sequence after dropping the first cell.

Stop and look at the illogic here. By definition, you have a problem with congestion because a data unit was dropped. Is it rational, when you know congestion is present, to inject more data into the core?

To avoid such irrationality, it is usually far better to defer or drop traffic at the edge of a network than it is to do so in the core.

Hosts should use MTU path discovery to determine the largest MTU they can send to a given destination, without encountering fragmentation. This value is used to limit the size of packets generated by the host [RFC 1191].

The motivation for using large MTUs, which are likely to be fragmented, is primarily efficiency on the local medium. In principle, using the largest possible frame size on a medium minimizes the overhead of additional frame headers and trailers needed for smaller data fields. For example, Fiber Distributed Data Interface (FDDI) Token Ring often supports frame sizes of 4000 bytes or more, whereas Ethernet is limited to 1500 bytes.

It's worth asking the question, "How valuable is this improvement in overhead?" In practice, it might not be very valuable. The overall cost of requiring IP fragmentation can be greater than the efficiencies achieved on a LAN. Although changing the MTU on many hosts is labor intensive, you should enable MTU path discovery on hosts that support that feature. MTU path discovery automatically sets an appropriate MTU. Another alternative for setting the MTU without excessive manual involvement is to code it as a Dynamic Host Configuration Protocol (DHCP) parameter, assuming your hosts understand that parameter when set in a DHCP response.

Assume that you are on a FDDI medium, where you have selected a 4500 byte maximum frame size, of which 4436 bytes are available for user data.

This user data contains the 8 bytes of LLC/SNAP information, 20-byte IP header, and 20 bytes of TCP. The FDDI frame has 20 bytes of framing overhead not included in the user fields.

The best possible case for transmission efficiency involves a single transmitter sending sequential frames. The maximum possible efficiency of a 4500 byte frame on FDDI is 98.5%.

If the host is limited to 1500 byte frames, it needs to create three frames to carry the same information as the large FDDI frame. Each frame is one packet, so it needs the same LLC, IP, and TCP header information as the large frame. Assuming LLC with SNAP, and IP and TCP with no options, there are 48 bytes of header overhead.

Creating two new packets (for a total of three) adds 96 bytes of user overhead, plus 40 bytes of framing overhead. This is a small fraction of the total volume being sent, but can avoid significant performance problems from fragmentation.

ATM SAR splits variable-length information at the AAL layer into cells for transmission through the cell switching system. When AAL frames are split into cells, information can be added to the cells before segmentation, which can add overhead. ATM headers add 5 bytes of header information to each cell. AAL type 1 adds 1 byte per frame and AAL 3/4 adds 4 bytes, whereas AAL type 5 does not add overhead. AAL 5 relies on a bit in the cell header to signal end of frame.

X.25's packet layer has its own segmentation facility. Although the X.25 default packet size of 128 bytes might horrify people used to efficient sizes for modern networks, packets as small as 128 or 64 bytes actually are more efficient on low-quality links.

Several years ago, I worked on installing Internet access in a developing country, where the fastest line available was 64 Kbps. More importantly, the error rate on these lines was one in 10^5 bits, in contrast with the 1 in 10^{12} or 10^{15} common in modern optical networks.

Link-layer retransmission is more efficient than end-to-end retransmission on slow, high-error rate links. We began by using the LAP-B data link protocols on our router-to-router links. LAP-B, as opposed to PPP or proprietary HDLC protocols, does link-level retransmission.

Even though we enabled link-level retransmission, throughput remained unacceptable until we inserted the X.25 packet layer between IP and LAP-B. By inserting the X.25 packet layer protocol, and enabling its segmentation mechanism, we were able to shorten packet size from the IP minimum MTU of 576 bytes to 128 bytes.

When many packets must be retransmitted, less bandwidth is consumed when an occasional short packet is retransmitted than if every retransmission involves a large number of bytes.

Frame Relay fragmentation is done for a different reason than those of IP or X.25. The reason for Frame Relay fragmentation is very close to the original motivation for ATM cells being small: minimizing latency for digital voice. If cells are small, a given cell does not have to wait for a long frame to be transmitted ahead of it. According to the Frame Relay Forum fragmentation specification [FRF.11], "Frame fragmentation is necessary to control delay and delay variation when real-time traffic such as voice is carried across the same interfaces as data."

Replication for Multicasting and Broadcasting

What if the destination address is a multicast group? This doesn't necessarily mean the local router has to copy it, because the multicast tree involved might have only one output branch.

If the multicast group does include multiple interfaces, the router's forwarding workload goes up significantly. The first problem is that the router must copy packets, which can produce heavy CPU loads.

The second problem has similarities to dealing with IP fragmentation. If the multicast group includes multiple output interfaces, what should the router do when it discovers that some of the output interfaces are busy? There must be buffering available for each output interface.

Medium Issues

Some special cases of forwarding need to be considered. IP routing has long used the local versus remote assumption: If you need to go to a destination outside your own subnet (that is, prefix), go to a router, as shown in Figure 3.12. This router is usually known and configured as the default gateway.

T ABLE 3.6 S UMMARY OF O UTPUT P RIORITIZATION S TRATEGIES

Discipline	Queues	Queuing	Deletion	Service
Class-based	Program-mable.	Programmed. Dropped if queue full.	None.	High to low, servicing each queue up to programmed number of bytes and/or packets.
Weighted fair	2 for interactive vs. non-interactive, 8 when diffserv is implemented.	IP precedence (diffserv) if implemented. Lower-volume flows to higher-priority queue.	None.	High priority as long as there is traffic, low priority for 1 packet before high is checked.
(Weighted) Random Early Detect	Usually 8 or more (diffserv plus RSVP flows plus UDP).	Drop packets in drop-eligible queues trending toward congestion.	Random packets in congested queues.	Some packets dropped with the effect of reducing the amount of data transferred by sources that tend to create congestion.
Guaranteed Maximum Bandwidth	Typically the diffserv number, but may be more.		Packets in excess of burst rate.	Normal traffic up to predefined limit, but traffic above this limit is dropped.

I am not surprised, however, that major vendors have different terminology for the same general case. Cisco IOS speaks of a set of queues of different preference into which packets are placed, and Bay RS describes a single queue with rules specifying how packets are dequeued for transmission. Functionally, these are equivalent.

There are several major strategies for output prioritization, beyond simple FIFO (see the summary in Table 3.6).

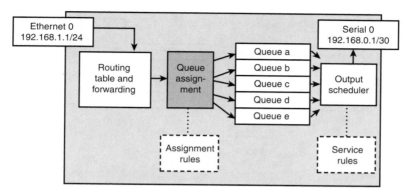

FIGURE 3.14 *All prioritization schemes have basic rules of classifying traffic and assigning them to queues. If the output interface is not busy, most routers send directly to it.*

The first selective prioritization has the drastic policy that certain traffic must go through, even if other traffic is never delivered. The next common strategy guarantees a minimum bandwidth to each type of data; it is a timesharing model. The next model tries to minimize latency for interactive traffic while giving a fair amount of bandwidth to each non-interactive stream. Yet another model avoids overrunning remote sites by limiting the maximum bandwidth that can be used by any flow.

Drastic, Preemptive, or Priority Queuing

Terms for this strategy include drastic, preemptive, strict (Bay's term), and priority queuing (Cisco's term). The basic model is shown in Figure 3.15. When the output interface in Figure 3.15 is busy, traffic is assigned by configured rules to one of a fixed set of queues in priority order. The highest priority queue is serviced until it is empty; other queues are serviced only if all higher priority queues are empty.

No traffic is sent from the second highest priority queue until the highest is empty. Queues are checked after every packet is sent. In pseudocode, the algorithm the scheduler uses after sending each packet is:

```
if HIGH is not empty
  then send next HIGH packet
  else if MEDIUM is not empty
    then send next MEDIUM packet
    else if NORMAL is not empty
      then send next NORMAL packet
      else send next LOW packet
```

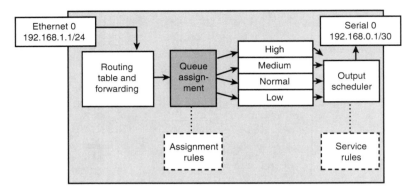

FIGURE 3.15   *Drastic queuing.*

If there is sufficient traffic to keep the highest priority queue from getting empty, no lower priority traffic is sent. This is intentional; the aim of this sort of queuing is to be sure the higher priority traffic is sent, without concern for the requirements of lower priority. This makes a great deal of sense in some situations where the high-priority traffic is time-critical, or critical to network management. Remember that packets that keep the network running, such as routing updates, need a higher priority than any application. If the network goes down, application priorities are useless.

Class-Based, Time-Sharing, or Custom Queuing

The next most common prioritization strategy, shown in Figure 3.16, is variously called class-based queuing, time-sharing, bandwidth (the Bay term), or custom queuing (Cisco's term). When the output interface in Figure 3.16 is busy, traffic is assigned by configured rules to one of a variable set of queues. Each queue has an allocated portion of the total link bandwidth. Where drastic queuing operates on an essentially binary basis—either there is something in a queue or there is not—class-based queuing guarantees a minimum bandwidth to each queue, based on byte counts, or a combination of byte and packet counts.

In pseudocode, the logic of class-based queuing involves n queues, each with a byte count allocation constant **allocation[i]** and a number of bytes sent in the current cycle **sent[i]** is

```
if HIGH is not empty
  then send next HIGH packet
  else if MEDIUM is not empty
    then send next MEDIUM packet
    else if NORMAL is not empty
      then send next NORMAL packet
      else send next LOW packet
```

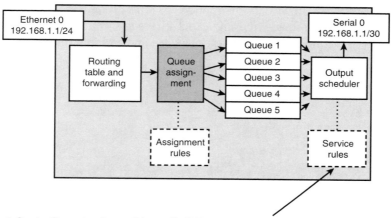

1. Service Queue 1 as long as it has traffic AND the number of bytes sent does not exceed the quota for the cycle.
2. Check next queue. If it is non-empty, send up to the quota number of bytes.
3. Move to the next queue. Service if non-empty. Go back to rule 1 if this is the last queue.

FIGURE 3.16   *Class-based queuing provides a guaranteed minimum bandwidth.*

Packets are, again, queued when the output interface is busy. The output interface, after sending a packet, starts by checking the highest priority queue. If there is traffic in that queue, the output interface services the queue until the number of bytes sent equals or exceeds the allocation of bandwidth to that queue, or the queue is emptied.

After sending the packet that exhausts the allocation for a given queue, the output scheduler checks the next highest priority queue. If there is traffic waiting in that queue, it is serviced again until the allocation is used up or the queue is empty. The scheduler moves through the queue in round-robin order, skipping empty queues and servicing each one until it is empty or its bandwidth allocation for that cycle through the queues is exhausted. After the lowest priority queue is serviced, the scheduler returns to the first queue and repeats the process.

Weighted Fair Queuing

I must confess that when I first saw a description of weighted fair queuing (WFQ), it seemed rather implausible. Its implausibility was that it is so simple. With experience, I have learned it works quite well, as long as its assumptions fit your traffic-handling policy. These assumptions work well for classical IP protocols such as **telnet** and **ftp**, but not as well for native or tunneled IBM protocols. They can be of marginal value when Web applications are transferring large files.

WFQ automatically identifies flows and keeps track of the traffic in each flow. It assumes that interactive applications have low volumes, and that non-interactive, bulk transfer applications have high volumes.

The basic model of WFQ, shown in Figure 3.17, is to start with flow identification on incoming packets.

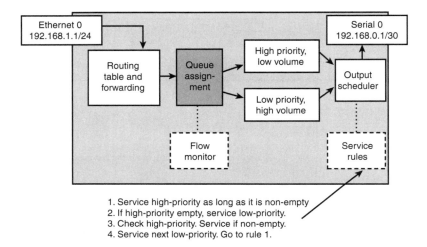

1. Service high-priority as long as it is non-empty
2. If high-priority empty, service low-priority.
3. Check high-priority. Service if non-empty.
4. Service next low-priority. Go to rule 1.

FIGURE 3.17 *WFQ does not need configuration but does categorize traffic into flows, using internal algorithms.*

After packets are assigned to a flow, the flow monitor keeps track of the volume associated with individual flows. Based on their volume, the flows are assigned to high or low volume queues. Low volume flows are prioritized over high volume flows, on the assumption that low volume flows are interactive and high volume flows are bulk transfers that attempt to maximize their window size. This assumption works quite well for most IP-based protocols other than the X Window System and tunneled SNA.

Rate Limiting

You need to specify rules for categorizing traffic into classes of service, and how much bandwidth to give to each class. As shown in Figure 3.18, each class of service is only allowed to send a steady average rate, with an opportunity to send bursts when there is capacity to do so. Traffic that is beyond the average rate, but within the burst rate, is marked with a discard eligibility flag appropriate to the protocol in use.

Different data link protocols, such as ATM and Frame Relay, have header bits that indicate which data units should be discarded first in the event of congestion inside the network. The basic rate limiting algorithm is:

```
If currentVolume ≤ averageRate
then transmit
else
   if currentVolume ≤ burstRate
      then mark discardEligible and transmit
      else drop
```

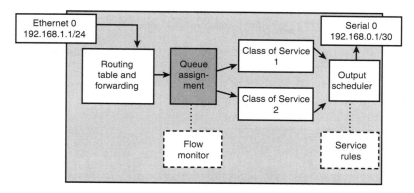

FIGURE 3.18 *When configuring this service, you need to specify both the rules for recognizing classes of service and how much bandwidth to give to each class.*

There are multiple applications for this sort of selective forwarding. You might have customers with access to a high-speed medium such as a 100 Mbps Ethernet, but these customers can be billed based on access bandwidth. Guaranteed maximum bandwidth can restrict them from using more bandwidth than they have paid for.

Another application is to protect "downstream" sites with low-bandwidth access links from being overrun by "upstream" links that otherwise might send large bursts. A data center might, for example, have a DS1 access line with Frame Relay virtual circuits. Although a given virtual circuit might have a committed information rate (CIR) of only 64 Kbps, the data center might be able to dump bursts into the Frame Relay provider network at the DS1 speed of the access link. Guaranteed maximum bandwidth can restrict, in the router or switch before the access link, that traffic does not go out faster than the receiver can accept.

Random Early Detect

Random early detect (RED) always reminds me of a dramatic movie focused on survivors in an overcrowded lifeboat. In the movie, the only way that anyone will live is that someone will die, and the boat officer must make tough decisions.

RED is a bit more cheerful than the movie, because the packets that must die for the many are resurrected by TCP retransmission. Because the largest traffic source on the global Internet is the Hypertext Transfer Protocol (HTTP) used for Web browsing, and HTTP runs over TCP, RED offers significant potential for managing global Internet congestion.

As shown in Figure 3.19, RED requires a means of identifying traffic and a criterion for selecting the priority of flows on which traffic will be dropped. In other words, there are three parts to the mechanism: packet classification, estimation of average queue size, and packet dropping.

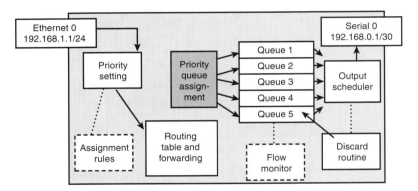

Figure 3.19 *Traffic can be identified as destined for a certain queue either with the Resource Reservation Protocol (RSVP) or by settings of the TOS bits in the IP header.*

Packets are classified using pattern matching, with the action of setting the IP precedence bits in the Type of Service field. Alternatively, packets can be marked through RSVP.

Queue length estimation involves tracking the queue length over time, as an exponentially weighted moving average. In basic, non-weighted RED, this time-averaged queue length is used to select the queue from which traffic is dropped when the congestion threshold is approached.

At the input interface, mark incoming traffic as to type of service, if not already marked or specified by RSVP.

The drop process randomly selects packets for dropping, within two constraints, **minth** and **maxth**. **maxth** is also called the *trigger*. Queues whose average length is less than or equal to **minth** never have packets dropped. In a queue for which the average queue length is greater than **maxth**, all packets are dropped. In the event of congestion, packets in a queue whose length is between **minth** and **maxth** are dropped with a probability proportional to the queue length. See Chapter 14 for a more detailed discussion of applications of RED.

In practice, traffic is identified with settings of the precedence bits in the IP header. These are most commonly set by access routers and acted on by core routers.

What Can Go Wrong?

Hosts and media, of course, unfortunately manage to fail on their own, without assistance from relays. Routers add complexity and additional failure potential, as well as additional flexibility and the potential to recover from errors that simpler devices could not.

Given the realities of routing implementations, it sometimes is difficult to place a given pathological behavior strictly into the path determination or forwarding categories. If an FIB, ostensibly mirroring the RIB, gets out of synchronization with the RIB because the RIB has not yet sent new information to the FIB, is that a path determination or a forwarding problem?

The following list of problems is roughly ordered beginning with problems more associated with path determination to problems more associated with forwarding:

- Route flapping, or routes that are rapidly advertised and withdrawn.

- Routing loops, both transient and persistent.

- Erroneous routing, where packets take a path that is wrong.

- Unworkable routes, which become so long that the time to live is exceeded and packets are discarded, even though the path actually would reach the destination.

- Rapidly changing routing, also called *fluttering*. This is distinct from route flapping and can result in sudden changes in performance. In some cases, this can be a beneficial effect, when it is associated with well-conceived load balancing over equal-cost paths.

- Temporary outages of routers or media.

- Temporary outages of individual routes or interfaces, as might be associated with a FIB frequently being invalidated.

Many of these categories are based on Vern Paxson's work [Paxson, 1997]. Even the first can be unclear—a path determination process might be able to keep up with routing updates, but if forwarding is done by the same processor as path determination, there can be insufficient remaining CPU cycles for adequate forwarding performance. There are no simple answers to these problems. Your job as a designer is to recognize the potential for them to occur and be sure that your network includes the management tools to detect them. Packets can be slowed or dropped in the router due to the indirect effect of a problem in path determination.

Layer 2 Forwarding

Bridges and switches use Layer 2 addresses to make forwarding decisions. Remember that a LAN switch is essentially a bridge on steroids; they work identically at the data link layer. In basic bridging, the forwarding decision-making process is rather simple: send frames out a specific interface if the destination is known to be out that interface. If the destination is unknown, copy the frame and send it out all interfaces. There are more refinements in this model, intended to reduce traffic, discussed in Chapter 10.

MAC bridges logically, but not physically, connect networks at Layer 2. MAC bridges are protocol entities sensitive to the LAN's MAC and link control protocols, but not to protocols above them.

In general, bridges are much less flexible than Layer 3 relays. Following are the major reasons to use a bridge:

- A need to relay protocols, typically proprietary, which do not have network layer headers and thus cannot cooperate with Layer 3 relays. Examples of such protocols include native NetBIOS and local-area transport (LAT).

- Simple point-to-point topologies where there is a need to reduce bandwidth contention, compensate for interconnecting media delay, and fix other performance-related problems not involving complex topologies.

There are two broad families of bridges, which can be combined in a single box:

- Transparent spanning tree bridges, which cooperate to define the bridge-level routing topology, or simply pass data without reference to topology.

- Source-route bridges, for which the topological knowledge remains in the end systems.

Source-route bridges and transparent spanning tree bridges can be made to interoperate, but often have incompatibilities.

A router's model is to store the addresses of destinations, whereas the basic model of a bridge is to store source addresses on a port-by-port basis, to recognize which transmissions are destined to local addresses.

If the destination is known to be local to the medium connected to the interface, the bridge does not forward it through an external port. Different bridge implementations vary in how far inside the bridge a frame goes before it is recognized to be local. As long as the bridge has the processing capacity to handle a local frame that enters the forwarding fabric, there are no negative impacts on the local medium or the overall forwarding performance of the bridge.

The interface selected for forwarding depends on the type of traffic (unicast or multicast) and whether the destination address is known. If the destination is a unicast address and that address is in the address table, traffic only goes out the interface associated with that destination. Traffic to all unknown destinations is flooded out all unblocked interfaces. Unless proprietary extensions to multicast flooding are in use, multicasts are also flooded out all unblocked interfaces.

The Evolution to Transparent Bridges

The earliest bridge type is today called a *simple bridge*. The learning bridge is a refinement of the simple bridge. Two approaches have been standardized for bridge topology management: *transparent bridges* and *source-route bridges*. The former was developed by the IEEE 802.1 group, and the latter was for some time a competitive approach from 802.5. Political harmony was reached by the acceptance by 802.1 of source routing as an optional enhancement to transparent bridges.

What Does *Standard* Mean?

Many formal standards bodies, as opposed to the IETF with its motto "rough consensus and running code," respond to mutually exclusive positions by adopting both and letting the implementers work out the details. To some extent, this happened with the early IEEE 802 bridging specifications.

These are paper documents with substantial variation in vendor implementations, with no formal multivendor compatibility testing.

Newer IEEE 802 standards such as Gigabit Ethernet, 802.1Q VLANs, and 802.1P prioritization are going through multivendor testing.

Most bridges are transparent. When bridging was implemented in software, advocates of source-route bridging argued that it can be faster because source-route bridges need not be burdened with topology management overhead, but this is no longer a practical concern. Source-route bridges are most commonly used in environments where a need exists for compatibility with IBM proprietary LAN protocols. Assume that bridges are transparent unless you find a specific need for IBM protocol support.

How does the transparent bridge decide where to send frames? Each interface records the source address field of every frame that it hears in promiscuous mode. If the interface hears a frame, it can assume that the source address of that frame is physically present on the medium to which the interface is connected.

As the bridge learns which addresses are local to which interface, it begins to match destination addresses against the local source address list, a process illustrated in Figure 3.20. If a destination address matches an address in the local source list, the bridge assumes that both source and destination are local and does not attempt to forward the frame. This blocking of local frames can significantly lower the amount of traffic unnecessarily forwarded to other interfaces.

By capturing the source address field of frames received on an interface, the bridge learns which are associated with each interface. Conceptually, this information is used to populate a local table and a bridge-wide cache. Transparent bridges do not forward packets for local destinations or frames that match administrative filters calling for them to be ignored.

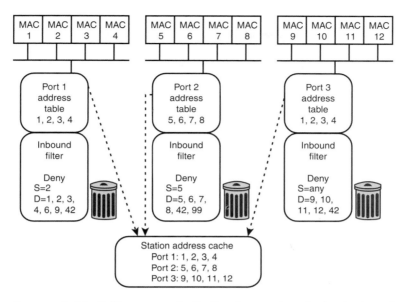

FIGURE 3.20 *Bridges automatically filter frames whose destination is on the same interface on which they were received, as soon as the bridge learns that the source address is on the same medium as the source. Additional filters, applied either to incoming or outgoing filters, can be manually defined.*

Various vendor-specific extensions try to control broadcast and multicast traffic. Switches can learn which specific ports belong to which multicast group and only send multicast frames to those ports that they desire to hear. Other mechanisms can allow only a certain rate of broadcasts or multicasts through a port, assuming any frames above that level are due to a broadcast storm.

A note of caution is in order about one misleading way to describe bridge performance, occasionally seen in sales literature. The metrics packets per second or frames per second are frequently used to describe bridges. If you add up the number of PDUs per second seen at each port of a bridge, the resulting number overstates the throughput. The more meaningful measurement is the total throughput between bridges, inside the bridge and beyond the filter.

Filters themselves can be a performance limitation. Some bridges have relatively small amounts of physical memory available for filter caches, and thus can only filter a certain number of addresses. If, for example, a bridge with a 64-slot memory learns 64 addresses to be forwarded, what does it do when it discovers a 65th?

A transparent bridge learns about the topology and picks the best route. It uses several criteria for forwarding, as shown in Figure 3.21:

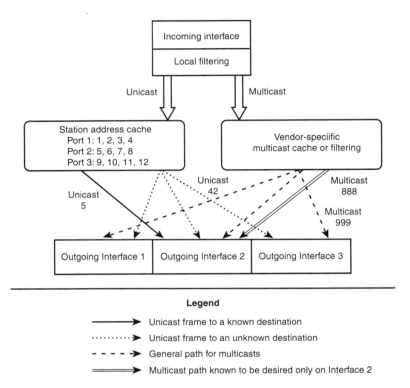

FIGURE 3.21 *The forwarding process in transparent bridges sends frames with known destinations to the port where their address has been cached and forwards frames with unknown unicast addresses out non-blocked ports.*

- Forwarding a unicast frame whose destination address is known to the bridge and is not on the same interface on which the frame was received.

- Forwarding a unicast frame whose destination address is not known to the bridge. The frame is flooded out all unblocked interfaces other than the one on which it arrived.

- Forwarding a multicast frame without vendor-specific multicast control. The frame is flooded out all unblocked interfaces other than the one on which it arrived.

- Forwarding a multicast frame with vendor-specific multicast control, which limits the propagation to the two interfaces where devices have asked to listen to the multicast group.

Unicast frames with known destinations are sent out a single appropriate port. Unicast frames with unknown destinations and all non-unicast frames are flooded out all the non-blocking ports other than the one on which they were received. Flooding can be modified by explicit filtering.

Remote Bridges

The term *remote bridge*, also called *encapsulating bridge*, describes a device that interconnects LAN segments via a medium of a different technology (see Figure 3.22). For example, two 802.3 segments in different buildings might be joined by a high-speed serial line. Each segment would have a bridge with one 802.3 and one serial DTE interface.

IEEE has issued the 802.1g specification for remote bridging, but this specification has many implementer choices and has not so far proven to be a strong standard to ensure multivendor interoperability. In general, either assume that you want the same vendor implementation at both ends of the transit link between two remote bridges or get guarantees from the vendors involved that they have proven interoperability.

> **Note**
>
> *In Token Ring, IBM refers to each of the two boxes that connect to the LAN as a half bridge. I have always found this to be a good metaphor for the general process of encapsulated bridging: two halves of a bridge function joined by a transit medium.*

The IETF has developed a Point-to-Point Protocol (PPP) Bridging Control Protocol that does offer the basis of a multivendor protocol for remote bridging [RFC 1638]. It is a subset of the IEEE 802.1g approach.

In the IEEE model, sets of two or more remote bridges and their interconnecting media are termed *remote bridge groups*. The subset of bridges within that group which actually can exchange frames, a subset selected by the operation of a spanning tree protocol, is called a *remote bridge cluster.*

The PPP bridging control protocol is less general than the IEEE approach. Its model is a pair of remote bridges—connected by a single medium.

Figure 3.22 shows how two Ethernet-connected hosts can communicate across an arbitrary transit network. The transit network between the two bridges shown in Figure 3.22 can actually be a full routed IP network invisible to the bridging functions.

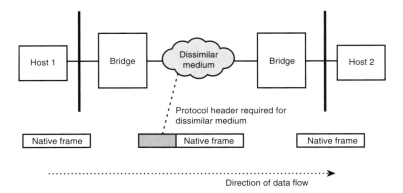

FIGURE 3.22   *An example of an encapsulating bridge where edge Ethernet traffic flows over an arbitrary transit medium.*

Encapsulating bridges are intended for transit only; they are not protocol converters. In Figure 3.23, Hosts 1 and 2 are Ethernet connected, but Host 3 is FDDI connected. Hosts 1 and 2 cannot communicate with Host 3, because Host 3 is not a bridge and does not understand the encapsulated frame. Although the actual behavior of Host 3 varies with the implementation, it might simply assume that the Ethernet header in the encapsulated frame is simply FDDI data.

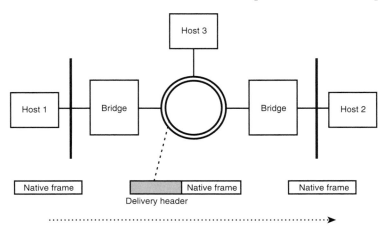

FIGURE 3.23   *The transit medium in remote bridging is just that, transit. Hosts on it are not reachable by hosts on the edge media.*

Translational bridging differs from encapsulating bridging in that it is asymmetrical. A translational bridge converts a frame from one Layer 2 format to another; the original frame is discarded rather than tunneled.

Source-Route Bridges

In source routing, end systems are responsible for determining the path to be taken among bridges and transmitting that path along with data. Source-route bridges are mainly used with IEEE 802.5. The IEEE 802.1 committee has attempted to develop a harmonized approach to transparent and source bridging; transparent bridging is mandatory, and source-route bridging is an additional option.

Standards bodies, of course, do not enforce mandatory requirements. Source-route bridge vendors are most concerned at being compatible with IBM's implementations, which do not always precisely follow the standard.

An important thing to realize about the 802.5 source routing bridge model is that it regards bridges as two-port devices that interconnect pairs of rings.

In Figure 3.24, Ring 1 owns Bridges 1 and 2. The path from Ring 1 to Ring 2 is

```
Ring 1→Bridge 1→Ring 2
```

And the path from Ring 1 to Ring 4 is

```
Ring 1→Bridge 2→Ring 3
Ring 3→Bridge 4→Ring 4
```

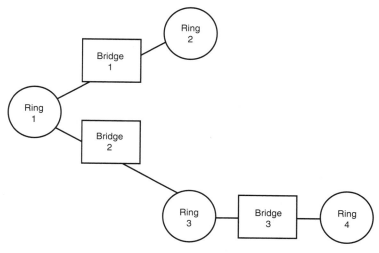

FIGURE 3.24 *A source-route bridging system.*

Source-route bridges have a number range of 1 to 15, but they need to be uniquely identified as a sequence of a ring number, a bridge number, and a ring number. IEEE 802.1/802.5 source routing information is detailed in routing descriptors, which have a field for the bridge number leaving the current ring and the number of the next-hop ring.

The Routing Information field contains the Routing Control field and a set of Routing Descriptors (RDs). The actual source route is contained in the set of RDs. Each RD contains a ring number and a bridge number.

In practical networks, a problem emerges in modeling a multiple-port bridge. Multiple-port bridges are extremely useful devices as central hubs or as major bridging points. There is no good way to define a multiple-bridge with the bridge identification convention of ring-bridge-ring. The problem is shown in Figure 3.25.

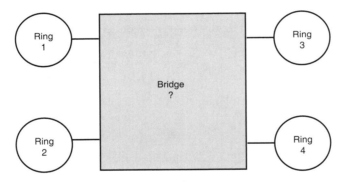

FIGURE 3.25 *Each ring in this multiport bridge problem has an ambiguity about the bridge number necessary to reach the other rings.*

Some recent bridging products do have the intelligence to avoid the ambiguity that a virtual ring solves. Nevertheless, many older devices need a virtual ring to keep things unambiguous. Do put source-route bridging into context. It can be important in pure IBM shops, but fundamentally it is an obsolescent technology. Continuing to enhance source-route bridging, rather than evolving to Ethernet switching and routing, is rather like beautifully streamlining a horse-drawn wagon.

The multiport bridge cannot be represented as a single bridge. How could a two-port device attached to Ring 2, for example, allow selective forwarding to Bridges 1, 3, and 4? A more modern bridge might look at the ordered triplets of <source ring, bridge, destination ring> to disambiguate the bridge, but older bridges might not do so. Virtual rings are a conservative approach.

The answer, shown in Figure 3.26, lies in creating a virtual ring inside the real multiport bridge box.

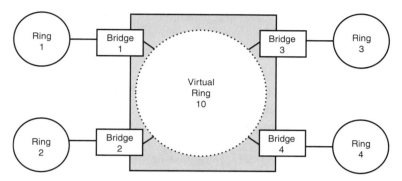

FIGURE 3.26 *The virtual ring in this multiport bridge solution removes the ambiguity, at the cost of adding a hop.*

We can now define the path from Ring 1 to Ring 3 as

```
Ring 1→Bridge 1→Ring 10
Ring 10→Bridge 3→Ring 3
```

The virtual ring can actually be implemented among several physical devices interconnected by physical links not visible to the system of bridges.

Mixed-Media Bridges

There are some known problems and limitations of bridges, typically seen when they are compared to more intelligent routers. For example, a bridge between 802.5 and 802.3 must face several incompatibilities between the two protocols. One of these incompatibilities is bit ordering within the octets of frames, which is different in the two protocols. This tends to be rather confusing. You do not reverse the order of bits from the beginning of the frame to the end of the frame, but you reverse the bits in each octet.

I do not propose to go into every mechanism that has been invented to deal with mixed-media bridging, because mixed media bridging is a fundamentally flawed and obsolete approach. Ethernet and Fast Ethernet products are far cheaper than Token Ring, and designers really need to look at the cost of ownership of a mixture of Ethernet and Token Ring. It's easier to justify Token Ring switches if you have an all-Token Ring environment.

When there is a mixture of Token Ring and Ethernet, my strong advice is to route rather than attempt to bridge between them. If, of course, you are using nonroutable protocols such as NetBIOS/NetBEUI or SNA with LLC-2, this might not be an option. Microsoft and IBM both support IP-based stacks, so consider the total system: it might be wisest to move to IP stacks and get rid of nonroutable protocols. You certainly can route between Token Ring and Ethernet.

If you must do mixed-media bridging, an obvious and relatively simple problem is the different maximum MAC PDU sizes of different protocols. Token Ring can have up to 16 K frames, whereas Ethernet only supports 1500. There is no Layer 2 mechanism that can split a large Token Ring frame into compatible Ethernet frames. Some vendors claim their products can fragment large Token Ring frames, but, if you examine their implementation, you usually find such fragmentation is only supported for IP packets. The fragmentation is really being done at Layer 3. In other words, a bridge that fragments is really a limited-function router.

As illustrated in Figure 3.27, Token Ring and Ethernet have different encoding conventions for MAC addresses. Bit ordering has subtle effects. The IP ARP protocol might not work over bridges between 802.5 and 802.3 LANs, because the bridge cannot know that a MAC address is contained within the LLC data field (that is, in the ARP protocol) and needs to have its bits reordered. Particularly, intelligent bridges and hosts can look at the originating LAN type and do appropriate translations, but I do not recommend depending on all bridges to be this smart.

Other issues include whether bridges should forward frames with bad frame check sequences. Not doing so improves performance on the subnetwork, which does not receive frames in error, but the absence of those frames can interfere with higher-level error recovery mechanisms in the destination subnetwork.

All 802.3 frames are of equal priority, as opposed to 802.4, 802.5, and FDDI, which have priority information in their frames. Priority schemes among these three token-based protocols, however, are all different. The new 802.2P specification does introduce a priority mechanism that can be used to carry frames of any edge protocol.

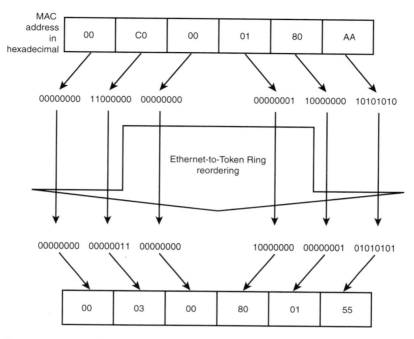

FIGURE 3.27 *Token Ring and Ethernet formats differ not in the order of bytes, but in the order of bits within bytes.*

Forwarding with VLANs

VLANs and emulated LANs (ELANs) really are no more than multiplexing systems that map multiple bridging domains onto a common trunk medium. Interfaces on routers and switches are designated either as trunk or edge.

ELAN technology, also called *LAN emulation* (LANE), allows ATM-unaware devices to transmit over ATM transmission systems. Other transmission systems, intended for building or campus awareness, allow Ethernet or Token Ring LAN devices to communicate over 100 Mbps and faster LANs such as FDDI and Fast Ethernet and Gigabit Ethernet.

VLAN schemes need to build translation tables that map edge LAN MAC addresses to units in the multiplexed trunk system. In the most common (Cisco's) implementation, physical ports on a switch are configured as belonging to specific VLANs. As frames arrive, their real MAC addresses are stored in a table associated with that VLAN.

On a Bay router, one 1024-entry table is associated with each port, so each VLAN can contain a maximum of 1024 MAC addresses. Cisco's approach is to have a larger shared table. Although Cisco does, in principle, allow larger VLANs, VLANs with over 1024 devices can run into other scaling problems.

You can think of the various VLAN/ELAN methods as extensions of encapsulated bridging, with the refinement that several different bridging systems can operate over the same trunks. In other words, the encapsulation is more complex and identifies which edge LAN is sending a particular frame over the trunk.

VLAN trunks are LAN media to which switches connect. Each switch interface has a MAC address appropriate for that medium, and this MAC address conceptually appears as the source address in VLAN headers, when the VLAN trunking protocol encapsulates edge frames as does ISL. The trunk frames can be sent as multicasts or as unicasts to a trunk port on a specific destination VLAN bridge.

ELAN trunking also can be either point-to-point or point-to-multipoint, but is built from virtual circuits rather than the LAN trunks of VLANs.

See Chapter 9 for a discussion of setting up connectivity inside the LANE infrastructure and Chapter 10 for details of how LANE sets up its internal data flows. Chapter 10 also deals with VLANs.

With either VLANs or LANE, existing Ethernet and Token Ring devices do not know about the VLAN structure. The emulated or virtual LAN appears to them as a standard LAN.

Hybrid Forwarding

Numerous techniques are evolving that are not strictly routing or bridging. These are at the leading edge of technology, and some still are in the research phase. Details of these techniques are in Chapters 13 and 14.

Some of these methods physically separate the path determination and forwarding functions. In such cases, information is downloaded to a device that might be called a *switch*, but is given information that lets it look up destinations. The device might recognize the destination from a Layer 2 address, from a *shim* field preceding the Layer 3 header, or from a pattern-matching rule that lets the forwarding engine recognize a flow. Shim fields often define tunnels, in which a packet has two Layer 3 headers, one for the transmission system and one for a user network mapped onto it; the shim field goes between the two headers and describes the tunneling involved.

There are many refinements to this model. Classical routers make decisions on Layer 3 information in the incoming packet, whereas classical bridges and switches make decisions on Layer 2 information in the incoming frame. Hybrid schemes might try to forward based on Layer 2 information as the default and use Layer 3 information only as the exception case.

Alternatively, newer hybrid schemes can use a label or tag that identifies a particular Layer 3 or flow output, but is faster to look up than Layer 3 address or flow identifiers. These techniques, including MPLS and multiprotocol over ATM (MPOA), are discussed in Chapters 13 and 14.

Platform Components

Different vendors have basic design styles, although all major vendors have a range of platform designs to cover the price to performance range. Styles differ if the product is a classic router or a classic bridge/switch. These styles provide a background for evolving hybrid Layer 2/3 devices.

> *Note*
>
> *Specific product examples in this book are neither endorsements of specific vendors, nor do they necessarily reflect the latest product features. Vendor examples are just that: examples chosen to show different design and implementation techniques.*

Interface Processors and Buffering

Electrical or optical signal conversion at the physical layer, and at least part of data link processing, commonly is done in dedicated hardware chips. Integrated circuits that deal with the physical layer are apt to be off-the-shelf. As processing moves higher in the OSI model, chips are more likely to become custom integrated circuits, or some sort of programmable hardware device. Programmable hardware devices range from programmable logic arrays to bit-sliced microsequencers to full RISC, and rarely CISC, processors.

There is no question that performance increases when the interfaces can do significant independent processing. Doing this offloads the CPU, keeping it from becoming a bottleneck, and allows parallel processing on multiple interfaces and in the CPU.

Although it might seem attractive to encourage parallelism, you must ask whether it is cost-effective for specific locations. Edge routers connected by sub-megabit lines are not usually limited by internal processing, but by the WAN line speed. Any reasonable CPU can keep up. The more intelligent the interface processors, the more powerful, and more expensive, the box becomes.

A more common situation is the one shown in Figure 3.29, where the aggregate to a given output port exceeds the port capacity. No matter how fast the fabric is, if it delivers two or more output data units to the same output port, the output port can transmit only one at a time. The output port must either buffer traffic to send or discard it.

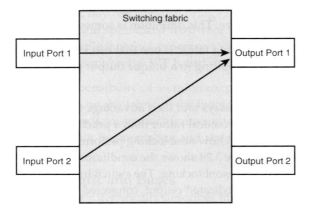

FIGURE 3.29 *In this example of a switch blocking output port, the switch really is not the problem.*

Alternatively, the output port or switch fabric can signal the input port that it is busy, and the input port should buffer the data unit, not letting it enter the fabric. This can be a useful technique, but it can also lead to the problem shown in Figure 3.30.

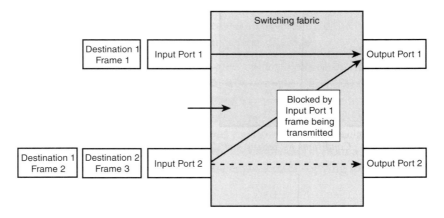

FIGURE 3.30 *An example of head-of-line blocking, where Frame 3 cannot be sent to Output Port 2 until Frame 2 is sent to Output Port 1.*

In this scenario, data units destined to Output Port 1 have arrived on Input Ports 1 and 2. Another data unit destined to Output Port 2 also has arrived on Input Port 1, immediately after the data unit destined to Output Port 1.

In this case, the fabric can transmit only a single data unit at a time to a given output port. Assume that the fabric selected Port 1 and is busy transmitting to a given output port. Input Port 2 has to wait to transmit until the fabric informs Port 2 that it is ready to transmit to Output Port 2.

Head-of-line blocking means that the data unit behind the Port 1 destined data unit on Port 2 has to wait to be transmitted. In principle, while Input Port 2 waits to get a path to Output Port 1, the data unit destined to Output Port 2 could be transmitted in parallel. The reality is that the fabric cannot see the input traffic in the buffer if the input buffer is a FIFO structure. Shared memory buffering in more modern switches tends to avoid head-of-line blocking, because all ports have access to the memory.

You encounter head-of-line blocking in daily life, when you are driving in the right lane and come to a traffic light where you want to turn right. Your car, however, is the second in line, and the car in front of you wants to go straight. If that car were not at the head of the right lane, you could turn right on red. You are, however, blocked at the head of the line.

Given an understanding that blocking can occur even in a nonblocking design, an any-to-any crossbar architecture might not improve performance at lower speeds.

Shared Buses

High-performance routers below the gigapacket range have tended to use shared bus architectures. The important thing to realize about shared buses is that they can only be used for one transfer at a time. A bus might be half- or full-duplex, but even if it is full-duplex, it can transfer only one packet at a time in each direction. Forwarding engines cannot transfer in parallel across the bus.

Cisco's 7x00 series routers are shared buses. The 7000 has a single 533 Mhz half-duplex bus. 7200 series routers effectively have a 600 Mbps bus, whereas 7500 series routers have either one (model 7505) or two (models 7507 and 7513) 1.066 GHz buses.

On its BCN and BLN routers, Bay uses four 256 Mbps buses treated as a single 1 Gbps path. The Cisco 7200 series bridges together three modified PCI buses operating at an effective 200 MHz speed, with an aggregate of 600 MHz.

Bay's ASN series has a 160 Mbps processor interconnect similar to the faster bus in the high-end BCN and BLN.

Cabletron's MMAC Plus has a set of interface modules interconnected with a 2.5 Gbps Internal Network Bus (INB) backplane. This vendor carefully and appropriately states that it is nonblocking when configured with FDDI or Ethernet.

Forwarding Engines

The concept of a fabric tends to be associated with high-performance boxes. As performance requirements drop, there can be a single forwarding processor separate from the main management processor. For yet lower performance requirements, it can be very cost-effective to use a single CPU for both path determination and packet forwarding, although it generally makes sense to use hardware-level Layer 1 and 2 processing.

Management Processors

Higher-performance routers tend to have a separate management processor concerned with path determination and network management functions such as the operator interface and accounting.

On small routers, it is silly to dedicate a special forwarding processor when the CPU has sufficient capacity to handle routing as well as management. A logical extension of this approach is to use general-purpose hosts as routers. This certainly can be comparable to low- to moderate-end routers. UNIX boxes running GateD code, available at **www.merit.edu**, are common in the Internet. Microsoft has introduced its Steelhead/RRAS router code that runs OSPF on Windows boxes. RRAS is a licensed derivative of Bay's code.

Purpose-built routers might not be directly comparable to general-purpose computers doing routing, because the routers can have performance benefits such as a low-overhead specialized operating system, interface cards that do some independent processing, and so on. They also might not incur the cost of disk interfaces and other features necessary in a general-purpose computer.

Platform Design Examples

In the preceding sections, we have looked at forwarding functions of routers and switches. Now, let's look at how specific vendors have implemented some of these functions. In a book, it is neither possible to list every vendor platform, with all their variations, nor desirable. This section considers some general implementation issues and illustrates them with product examples from late 1998. For the most recent information about any vendor's products, contact their sales personnel or look at their Web pages.

You might notice that this discussion does not go deeply into extremely high-performance routers such as the Ascend GRF, Cisco 12000, Juniper MP40, and so on. To put some practical limits on this discussion, I have focused on products intended principally for enterprise rather than ISP or carrier markets. The principles discussed here for high-performance devices, however, do apply to these products.

High-performance enterprise products do blur the line between routers and switches. They actually tend to be a combination of a path determination engine and multiple forwarding processors. FIBs for these processors can contain Layer 2 or Layer 3 information, and for that matter, Layer 4 or label information.

Platforms and Tiers

Major vendors have enormous numbers of products and variations. In teaching Cisco design classes, I long ago gave up on memorizing the product catalog. It's no better with other vendors—it can be enough of a challenge to keep track of which vendors are now one company: Nortel Networks includes products from the former Bay, Nortel, Synoptics and Wellfleet, as well as smaller firms. Digital Equipment Corporation networking products are now split among Cabletron and Compaq. Although most coverage of the Digital split explained that the Digital networking division was sold to Cabletron, some networking technologies, such as a very intense IP version 6 project, were part of Digital's UNIX group and went to Compaq.

The Digital split into Cabletron and Compaq is more like a death followed by probate, distributing things to the heirs. Other splits have been more like bitter divorces. For a long time, Cisco provided router components for hub products to Cabletron, but declined to continue the agreement due to disagreements between the firms.

Some breakups of alliances seem more like broken engagements, or simply dates that didn't work out because of different musical tastes. Before the Bay Networks merger of Synoptics and Wellfleet, there were serious discussions of a joint effort between Cisco and Synoptics, with Cisco Router and Synoptics hub technologies. The joint products were variously called the Rub or the Rubsystem, names which in my opinion were enough to doom the relationship. I recognize both Cisco and Synoptics were California companies with California cultures, but Rubsystem sounded more like something for massage than networking.

Let's say you are responsible for a group of financial traders in a large office building. These traders have the capability of gaining or losing millions of dollars per hour, so their support is absolutely mission-critical.

The office building has two risers. There is a separate server room in each riser. Each workstation connects to two separate floor switches, each of which connects to a single riser. Each server room has a large core switch.

Some switches have total redundancy of all common components. Other switches have some redundant components, such as power supplies, but might have a single management processor.

You might think of having a single switch for the building, assuming it will be highly reliable because it is totally internally redundant. But a disaster such as a fire in one server room can destroy the switch, and no number of redundant components will help. Your availability would be greater if you had two switches, each with lesser internal redundancy, but giving you the ability to have physically separate redundant facilities.

Incidentally, fire can be a more subtle threat than it first seems. Even if you had the ultimate in fire protection systems in your server room, not everyone in the building has such systems, and others rely instead on sprinklers. If there is a fire elsewhere in the building, firefighters are likely to use huge amounts of water to put it out. In my career, I have never had a computer room fire, but I have had three major operational problems caused by fire suppression systems elsewhere in the building.

Look carefully at your needs for component-level redundancy. Redundant power supplies in a switch or router are far less important than ensuring adequate power. Faced with a choice between a second power supply and an uninterruptible power supply (UPS), I will take the UPS every time.

When you install devices that have multiple internal power supplies, do not plug them into the same power strip! Also, be sure the power strips are plugged into different circuit breakers, and preferably that one or all strips are plugged into UPS-protected circuits.

Cisco Platform Examples

When a packet enters a Cisco router interface, its protocol type is determined and it is sent either to bridging or routing for that protocol type.

Based on the hardware type and software configuration, the data unit is sent to a forwarding information base. This forwarding information base can be on the interface processor card, in a special-purpose central switching engine, or on the CPU. CPU-based FIBs can be separate from the RIB, or the RIB and FIB can be the same.

In its higher-end boxes beginning with the AGS and then the 7000 series, Cisco implemented a fast forwarding engine separate from the management and interface processors. This was called the bus controller on the AGS and either the switch processor or silicon switch processor on the 7000. It uses a forwarding application-specific integrated circuit (ASICs) and has a hardware-enabled cache.

In the 7500 series, a single board called the route switch processor (RSP) contains both management and forwarding processors. A variant of the RSP is the route switch module (RSM) and is an option for Catalyst 5000 series switches. Performance is comparable, but the RSM/Catalyst 5000 tends to be more cost-effective when large numbers of LAN interfaces are needed, whereas the RSP/7500 is preferable for WAN-weighted environments.

Another option for routing in the switch boxes such as the Catalyst 5000 is the NetFlow Feature Card (NFFC). This is a *daughter card* or *applique* on the main 5000 processor and enables the 5x00 switch to forward based on Layer 3 addresses at less cost per unit of forwarding power than that of the RSM alone. The NFFC needs to work in concert with a router, which can be as small as a 4500. NFFCs can work with RSMs, providing approximately five times the throughput of an RSM alone.

You should remember that NetFlow means different things on a Cisco switch and router. On a switch, it is a way to add Layer 3 to the forwarding decision. On a router, it is a way to offload forwarding decisions from the main processor to a distributed forwarding processor, or to make Layer 4 decisions.

On-board forwarding modes are fairly new. It's usually informative to begin with three historical switching modes: silicon/autonomous/optimum, fast, and process. This discussion is not specific to a precise Cisco platform, but the first three modes are generally what is done on the Cisco 70xx series. This discussion focuses on routed rather than bridged traffic. Bridged traffic is handled in almost the same manner, except that the units forwarded are frames rather than packets.

Classical Routers

Cisco's pure routers have gone through several generations. I first worked on the xGS series, in which the IGS and CGS were roughly equivalent to today's 2500 series, the MGS roughly equivalent to the 4000 series, and the AGS to the 7000.

The AGS and the 7000 introduced distributed forwarding, although the forwarding was simply offloaded from the main processor into a single forwarding engine.

A Cisco 7000 router, a model that has reached its end of life but is an excellent example to show Cisco's basic switching modes, is shown in Figure 3.31. It has a 533 MHz half-duplex bus. This is nonblocking for a full complement of half-duplex FDDI interfaces, but the five interface slot 7000 cannot be fully populated with OC-3 or full-duplex LAN cards without the danger of exceeding the bandwidth budget.

The 7000 series originally had a Route Processor in one slot and a switch processor or silicon switch processor in another. The route processor does path determination and network management and process and fast switching. The switch processor, or the faster silicon switch processor, do autonomous or silicon switching. An upgrade provides an RSP7000 that combines the RP and SP/SSP functions in a single board, with a faster RISC processor than the original 68040 on the RP. VIPs can extend distributed and express forwarding to the 7000.

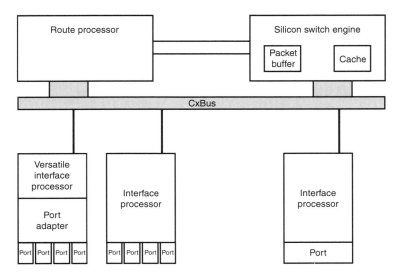

FIGURE 3.31 *A Cisco 7000 is a shared bus machine with a single distributed switching engine and an express path between the route and switching engines.*

Cisco's 7500 series routers, shown in Figure 3.32, have either one or two 1.066 GHz buses, which gives enough additional bandwidth that the router can be fully populated with 100 or 155 Mbps full-duplex interfaces. If all slots used 622 Mbps OC-12, however, there would again be danger of overrunning the bus.

The Route Switch Processor board does path determination in its RP chip, which is also where process and fast switching are done. As shown in Figure 3.32, the RP is shaded because its use as a forwarding engine should be avoided; you should forward on the SP or VIP. A second RSP can be kept in hot standby to back up the active RSP. 7500 series routers always must have at least one RSP, but may or may not have VIPs.

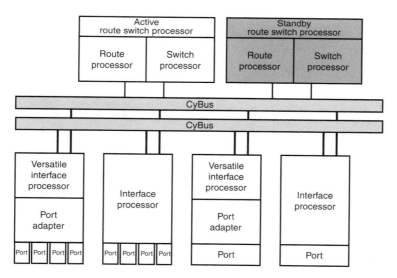

FIGURE 3.32   *A Cisco 7500 has one or two shared buses, one or two RSPs, and zero or more VIPs.*

There is considerable design commonality between high-end routers such as the 7200, 7500, and 12000, and high-end switches such as the 5000, 5500, and 8500. A 5000 can accept an RSM, NFFC, or both. Again, be sensitive to the issue that the marketplace tends to call certain devices switches when they actually have full routing functionality.

In addition to basic Layer 2 switching, an NFFC, or an RSM, a 5500 chassis can accept either a card set equivalent to the Cisco/Lightstream 1010 workgroup/small campus true ATM switch or 8500 series switching modules.

Bus Switching

Figure 3.33 shows what is variously called *autonomous switching, silicon switching,* or *optimum switching* depending on the specific platform and forwarding processor. This switching mode assumes that the interface boards and the forwarding processor are interconnected by a shared half-duplex bus.

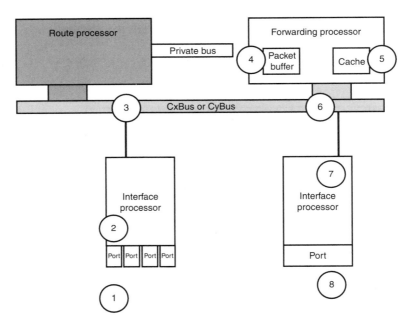

FIGURE 3.33   *In this example of silicon, autonomous bus forwarding, traffic does not flow through the CPU.*

Note

Cisco documentation is inconsistent on the terminology used for the forwarding processor. You might see the same 7000 function described as the silicon switch engine or the silicon switch processor. An earlier forwarding processor for the 7000 was called the switch processor, but the forwarding processor on the combined RSP board is also called the switch processor.

In all the switching modes, the packet is extracted from the frame by hardware on the interface processor (Point 1). The resulting packet is temporarily stored in a hardware buffer on the interface card (Point 2).

At Point 3, the packet is sent onto the bus. In the autonomous switching mode, the interface processor then forwards the packet via the Cisco bus to a switching processor. On the AGS series, this switching engine was called the bus controller and was called the switch processor in early models of the 70xx series. A higher-performance switching engine was called *the silicon switch processor (SSP)*. For practical purposes, these three switching engines have the same function but different speeds.

Just to add confusion, different Cisco documents have referred to the same component as the Silicon Switch Processor and the Silicon Switch Engine. This sort of confusion is not limited to the 7000 series—the modular interface boards for the 4000 series routers, at different times and in different documents, have been called *network interface modules* and *network processor modules*.

More Than Just Confusing Acronyms

Shakespeare's comment "What's in a name?" seems to be a basic part of Cisco's product designation strategy. Many components have had more than one name through their life cycle, often because engineering starts calling it one thing, and sales and marketing change the name to something else.

Even the numbers can be confusing. The first Cisco product called a 4000 was a three-slot modular router with a 68040 processor. Newer models added to the 4000 series routers included the 4500 and 4700, which use the same basic chassis but have faster RISC processors and more memory. The original 4000 has been discontinued.

There is, however, now a new 4000 series, which are Layer 2 switches optimized for Gigabit Ethernet. The first of this series is the 4003. Before the 2500 series was established as a low-end router, there was a 3000 router. The 3000 designation, however, now refers to stackable LAN switches.

5000 series devices were originally high-end LAN switches. The 5500 is indeed a larger LAN switch than the 5000, but 5200, 5300, and 5800 series devices are network access servers. The simple rule in all this: Don't make assumptions about what sort of Cisco device you are dealing with simply based on the first digit.

After the packet arrives at the switching engine, it is stored in a high-speed packet buffer (Point 4). It is looked up in a high-speed cache of destinations (Point 5). Depending on the particular switching engine, this cache can contain 500 to 1000 destinations, hopefully the most frequently used routes. Assuming the destination is found in the cache, the SSP rewrites the packet onto the bus (Point 6) and sends it to a hardware buffer in the outgoing interface processor (Point 7). The interface processor frames the packet and transmits it (Point 8).

If the destination is not found in the cache, it is sent to the route processor over the private bus. The private bus is also used by the route processor to populate the cache.

Notice that the packet traverses the bus twice, effectively cutting the bus speed in half. Newer distributed switching mechanisms can transmit directly to the destination, allowing the bus to be used at full speed.

The idea of small route caches has been unfairly attacked in some competitive sales presentations. True, a small cache thrashes in general Internet applications, where, with proper CIDR aggregation, there is no significant difference in the probability that a given destination will be used.

But in most enterprise networks, especially when addresses are aggregated, there will not be more than this number of routes. A 1000 route cache is certainly cheaper than the memory needed for a full Internet routing table of 50,000 routes or more.

Assuming that the destination is found in the cache, the switch engine then forwards the packet to the outgoing interface processor. Hardware on the outgoing processor does the frame level encapsulation.

If the destination is not found in the switch engine's cache, the packet is sent to the shared I/O memory associated with the route processor. If the fast switching cache, discussed in the next section, does not contain the destination, the destination is then looked up in the RIB using the process switching path.

Optimum switching is often described as similar to fast switching, which is discussed in the next section, but is really closer to bus switching. It is specific to the RSP card on the 7500 series. The reason optimum switching is likened to fast switching is that it is sent to the RSP board rather than to a separate switching board. In reality, however, the RSP contains multiple processors, and optimum switching does not occur in the same processor that fast switching does. Instead, optimum switching uses hardware-assisted route lookup in a processor on the RSP. An RSP can be configured either for fast or optimum switching. The two mechanisms really work alike, but use different processor chips and memory caches on the RSP board.

Optimum switching exploits the specific RISC microprocessor on the RSP. It does route lookup in a content-addressable memory function in the RSP hardware.

Fast Switching

Cisco's default switching mode is generally called *fast switching* and is shown in Figure 3.34. Treat this figure as an example rather than a definitive picture for all routers; it is an example using the basic structure of a 7500. All routers support fast switching. As in bus switching, data link processing is done on the interface processor, but the packet is sent to shared I/O memory (Point 4).

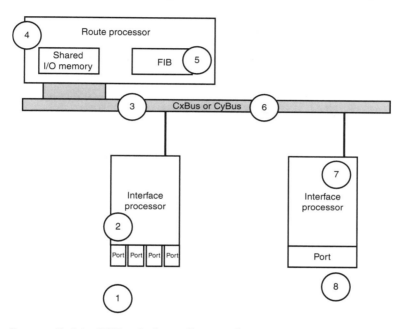

FIGURE 3.34 *CPU cache forwarding uses fast cache in the main processor or on the route processor in an RSP card.*

When in the shared I/O memory, the destination is looked up in a fast switching cache (Point 5). This cache is organized much as is the cache on the switching engine, with the assumption that there will be no more than one output packet for every input packet. The main CPU does the lookup. A new header is created, and the body of the packet is copied from shared I/O memory to the output interface processor (Point 6). The packet does not "move" in the shared I/O memory. The output interface processor does data link processing (Point 7) and physical layer transmission (Point 8).

CPU Hold Queue Forwarding, or Process Switching

The slowest, but most flexible, switching mode is *process switching*, illustrated in Figure 3.35. Process switching does not have the restriction of a single output packet for each input packet of the other basic methods: More than one packet can be output for a single input packet. The flexibility of this method comes, in large part, from the use of separate input and output packet buffering.

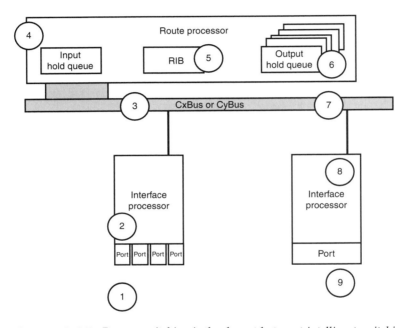

FIGURE 3.35 *Process switching is the slowest but most intelligent switching mode, typically 1/8 to 1/12 the speed of fast switching.*

Each real or virtual interface is allocated a fixed set of input and output buffers called *hold queues*. These buffers are of the smallest size that can contain the specific packet length. When you are estimating memory requirements for a Cisco router, however, assume that the buffers are of the smallest length that can contain the interface MTU.

Depending on the software version, Cisco has five or six pools of internal buffers of various sizes. The number of buffers allocated to input and output hold queues can be set on a per-interface basis; the defaults are 75 for input and 40 for output. Although all Cisco buffers are assigned dynamically, there are relatively more buffers assigned in process switching.

Through Point 3, the processing is identical to that in fast and bus switching. After a packet arrives, it is placed in the appropriate interface's input queue (Point 4). On most platforms, the hold queues are in the main RAM.

Periodically, the input queues are scanned. When a packet in an input hold queue is examined, its destination field is looked up in the main RIB (Point 5), not the FIB. The RIB has more information than the caches, but a longer lookup time.

Assuming that the destination is found, one or more output packets are created. The new output packets are copied to the output interface hold queues of the appropriate outgoing interfaces (Point 7). Although there is additional overhead in copying packets, packets are not copied in fast switching, but only pointers to them are moved. In process switching, there is a place to store multiple packets. As packets are scheduled for transmission, they are sent back over the bus to interface processors in Points 8 through 9.

Conditions that create more than one packet include the following:

- *Multicast or broadcast*. Packets destined for multiple output interfaces.

- *Fragmentation required*. Multiple packets generated for a single output interface.

- *Fragmentation and multicast*. Multiple packets for multiple interfaces.

Another special case where the additional information kept only in the RIB is needed is per-packet load balancing, where packets for a destination are scheduled, in a round-robin manner, for a set of output interfaces. The RIB has the capability to hold state information about the last interface used to send to a destination and the set of interfaces available for that destination.

NetFlow

Cisco's NetFlow is often described in a confusing way. The core technology of NetFlow is the capability to set up fast recognition rules for flows. These rules are then loaded into fast processors. The fast processors can use the recognition rules to do network management or to do forwarding.

Various network management functions, such as IP traffic accounting, need to match variable-length fields in packets. For example, if accounting to the TCP or UDP port level is needed, the router has to locate the port fields. This means that, to move beyond any options fields present in the IP header, it has to understand, and it has to understand enough TCP and UDP to locate the ports. This sort of scanning needs the full involvement of the CPU.

Prior to NetFlow, enabling IP accounting forced the interfaces involved into the process switching path. Cisco engineers realized this was necessary to recognize the first packet of a flow, but this had terrible performance implications for subsequent packets.

NetFlow recognizes the first packets of a flow, but then creates a fixed-length matching pattern that can be downloaded to a switching engine. The switching engine is intelligent enough to recognize port numbers in fixed positions. After this pattern is downloaded, further switching of the packet can be distributed into a much faster VIP switching engine on a 7500 series router, or the NFFC on Catalyst switches.

NetFlow originally moved only the statistics collection function to the switching engine. There are several terms that involve NetFlow. Be aware that NetFlow Data Export (NDE) is not a switching mode, but the mechanism used to export statistics collected on a distributed NetFlow processor. These statistics go to the router's main processor. The switching engine uses its usual cache as its forwarding table.

NetFlow, whether only for network management or also for distributed switching, has two phases. Figures 3.36 and 3.37 show how these are implemented on a 7500 router, whereas Figures 3.38 and 3.39 show an alternate implementation on a 5000 series switch.

In the first phase, illustrated in Figure 3.36, the packet goes through the process switching path. At Point 5b, however, another step is added: creating a recognition rule that is downloaded to the VIP. Recognition rules (that is, filters or access lists) can also be used in the route processor portion of the RSP, although that does not give as good a performance as distributing the function onto VIPs.

Although there are faster forwarding modes on high-end Cisco routers, such as express forwarding, NetFlow switching is generally the fastest mode that can be used if you need to use access lists, detailed IP accounting, or encryption. Supplementary coprocessors are being introduced for the extremely processor-intensive encryption and compression functions.

Warning

All performance numbers given here are purely for the purpose of comparison. Given the time lags of book publishing, these numbers certainly do not reflect the most recent product hardware and software. They are given to give you an idea of the relative performance impact of certain features and architectures.

Real-world performance tests also vary with the conditions of testing as well as the actual product. If the performance metric is packets per second, you tend to have higher performance with short packets. If the performance metric is bytes of throughput, performance tends to be better with long packets.

Informal performance discussions on technical mailing lists often borrow the term from the automotive industry: your mileage may vary (YMMV). YMMV appears after many performance estimates!

The 7200 series routers have the fastest main processor available of any Cisco router, currently the NPE-300, but do not have separate VIPs. NetFlow switching, however, is supported on the 7200. Table 3.7 shows the differences in access list processing with the various switching modes on a 7200 [Morissey, 1999].

TABLE 3.7 REPRESENTATIVE 7200 PERFORMANCE FROM MORISSEY'S GRAPHS (KILOPACKETS PER SECOND, APPROXIMATED FROM BAR GRAPH)

	Optimum	NetFlow 2-packet flow	NetFlow 10-packet flow	NetFlow 30-packet flow
No access list	250	225	225	225
1-line access list	174	175	175	175
25-line access list	110	160	175	190
200-line access list	25	75	125	150

As you can see from this table, there is an initial setup cost for NetFlow. The more packets in the flow, the more this setup cost is amortized among all packets, increasing the overall throughput. If you do not need to monitor flows or use access lists, optimum switching is faster.

In looking at performance numbers, remember that distributed switching modes, such as that done on the VIP, offload processing cycles from the processor that does path determination. With the distributed switching methods, you can generally have higher average processor utilization on the route processor, because the route processor becomes almost completely concerned with routing updates rather than forwarding. You will see bursts of activity when interface processors are initialized or reset, because the route processor needs to rebuild the FIB on the interface processor.

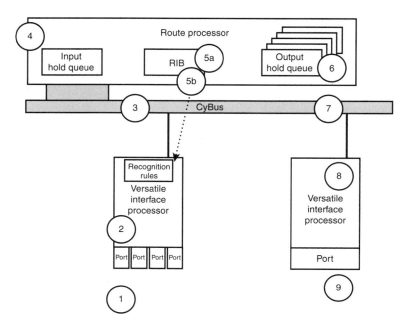

FIGURE **3.36**   *On a router, the first packet of a flow that will be NetFlow switched goes through a modified process switching path.*

The first phase of NetFlow involves recognizing a flow and creating a recognition rule, and downloading the rule and action to a VIP. Steps 1 through 4 are the same as in conventional process switching, Step 5a is the conventional process switching destination lookup in the RIB, and the subsequent steps are in process switching. At Step 5b, however, a recognition rule is generated and downloaded to the forwarding processor. The original implementation of NetFlow distributed flow recognition information to VIP interface cards, not to optimize forwarding but to improve network management.

NetFlow switching can use a cache of MAC addresses, Layer 3 addresses, or source-destination pairs—unique identifiers for flows—rather than the usual cache of destination addresses used by silicon, fast, and optimum switching. Figure 3.37 shows how recognition rules on the VIP are used to handle packets after the first in a flow.

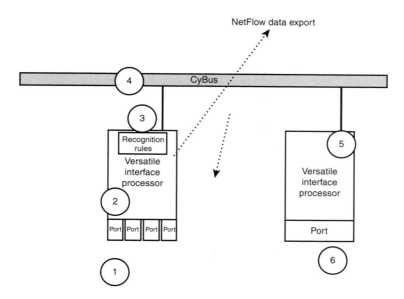

FIGURE 3.37 *The second phase of NetFlow uses the pattern recognition rules down-loaded to distributed processors for forwarding and network management.*

In the second phase of NetFlow switching, the forwarding decision is made at Step 3. The NetFlow rules can be implemented either in the main processor or on a distributed processor, but in either case, the packet is sent directly to the output processor. The most significant performance gains come when the NetFlow processing runs on a distributed processor.

Periodically, a VIP running NetFlow sends statistics to the route processor using the NetFlow Data Export feature.

On 7500 and 7000 series routers, distributed switching, either NetFlow or the Cisco Express Forwarding (CEF) (CEF works on the 7500 series routers only) discussed later in this chapter, offers a major improvement in bus performance. When the incoming interface processor can determine which outgoing processor should receive the packet, the incoming processor sends directly to the outgoing processor. As opposed to silicon switching, the packet is not sent to a switching engine, which then forwards it to the final destination. In silicon switching, the packet traverses the bus twice, but in distributed switching, it traverses the bus only once.

In addition to the doubling of bus performance, if the destination interface port is on the same interface processor as the incoming port, the interface processor can send it out directly without ever putting it on the bus.

In the NFFC application of NetFlow multilayer switching (MLS), the first packet to a destination goes to an external router or a route switch module in the same chassis, as shown in Figure 3.38. An RSM is assumed in this example. This full-capability router is called an MLS route processor (MLS-RP), as opposed to the NFFC, which architecturally is a MLS Switching Engine (MLS-SE).

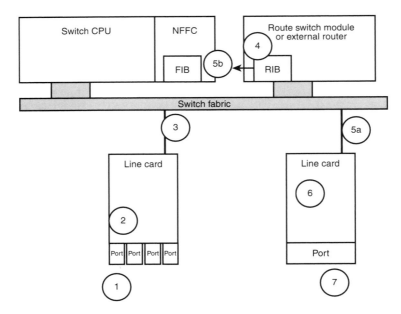

FIGURE 3.38 *The first NetFlow pass uses the RSM for routing.*

An internal management protocol called Multilayer Switching Protocol (MLSP) runs among the MLS-RP and MLS-SE elements. An MLS-RP multicasts its MAC addresses and associated VLAN numbers to all MLS-SE elements.

Originating end hosts send packets to a router MAC address, which is on either a Route Switch Module or external router that supports the MLS-RP server function. The originating host found this router MAC address when it issued an ARP to its default gateway or other router of which it is aware. The first time a given packet is sent to the router, it goes directly to that MAC address (Point 4).

The MLS-RP rewrites the packet and sends it to the destination (Point 5a). When the MLS-RP rewrites the packet and sends it out the backplane of the Layer 3 switch, it puts the MLS-RP MAC address in the source address field of the new frame.

NetFlow switching, however, remembers the MLS-RP address and recognizes a packet is coming from the router. When the NFFC MLS-SE sees such a packet, it builds a cache entry (Point 5b) for the destination MAC address associated with the Layer 3 address. Subsequent packets to the same IP address bypass the MLS-RP and are rewritten to the true destination MAC address, as illustrated in Figure 3.39.

In Figure 3.39, the path taken by packets is shorter and faster. The route lookup is done in the NFFC cache (4), not on the general purpose router. In Step 5, the NFFC sends the packet to the appropriate output interface, where it is buffered (6) and then framed for output (7).

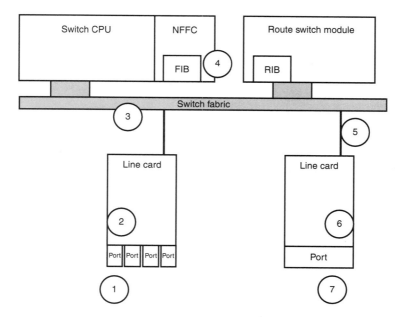

FIGURE 3.39 *Frames or packets beyond the first do not go to the RSM, but are handled by the NFFC.*

CEF

CEF, shown in Figure 3.40, distributes a full FIB copy, not a cache version as in silicon switching, onto each participating VIP. Its algorithm allows the FIB and associated code to be stored in a relatively small amount of memory, suitable for implementation in ASICs. Express forwarding removes the SSP or RSP as a single bottleneck.

Steps 1 through 2 are similar to the other forwarding methods. The difference comes at Point 3, where the destination is looked up in a high-speed memory on the interface processor. An individual VIP can forward between its own ports without involving the bus at all (Point 4a)

If the output port is on another VIP (Point 4b), the receiving VIP can forward over a bus directly to a packet buffer in the output interface processor (Point 5), where the packet is framed and transmitted (Point 6). In such cases, the packet traverses the bus only once, whereas, in silicon switching, the packet traverses the bus from the incoming interface processor to the switch engine and again from the switch engine to the destination interface processor.

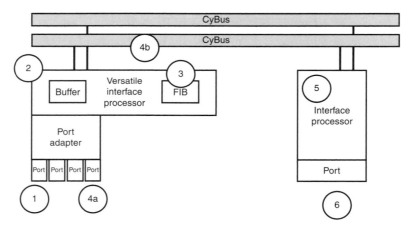

FIGURE 3.40 *CEF emphasizes that the RIB and FIB are in one-to-one correspondence. The distributed FIBs are not caches.*

A VIP has enough RAM that it can contain a full FIB and does not need to use caches. One of the motivations for CEF was to avoid the overhead of cache invalidation and updating. As mentioned earlier, caches work well when there is a relatively small subset of especially active destinations. This is not necessarily a valid assumption for large enterprises (especially at data center routers) or for ISPs.

CEF avoids the dilemma of the complexity of selective cache update versus the performance impact of periodically invalidating the entire cache and reloading it. In CEF, there are two tables, the FIB proper and the adjacency table. Outgoing addresses are looked up in the FIB. The adjacency table contains a table of the Layer 2 address and encapsulating information for each directly connected destination; there is a pointer from each FIB entry to the corresponding adjacency table entry (see Table 3.8).

TABLE 3.8 CISCO FORWARDING MODES

	Rough speed comparison	Intelligence	CPU load	Hardware assisted; hardware dependent?
Process	1	Highest	Substantial	No
Fast	10	Moderate	Light	No
Bus (autonomous, optimum, silicon)	100	Low	None	Yes
NetFlow	100 (faster than bus if there are access lists)	High in setup that creates guidance for dumb	Substantial for 1st packet but 0 for successive	Technically no, although distributing to VIPs needed for best performance
Distributed Flow	200 (faster than bus if there are access lists)	High in setup that creates guidance for dumb forwarding	Substantial for 1st packet but 0 for successive	Yes
CEF	400 (if no access lists)	Low	Moderate for 1st packet to destination, 0 for successive	Yes
Tag/Label	1000	High in setup that creates guidance for less intelligent (but not dumb forwarding	Substantial for setup, 0 for successive for distributed label switching, low for CPU based	No

Multiprotocol Label Switching

In label switching, shown in Figure 3.41, the FIB is populated from a non-local source; messages received from the Tag Distribution Protocol. Because we are dealing with labels rather than conventional routes, the table in which the tags are looked up (Point 3) is called the Tag Forwarding Information Base (TFIB). Tag switching is Cisco's approach to MPLS, discussed in Chapters 13 and 14. I include tag switching here only for completeness in referring to Cisco's platform design.

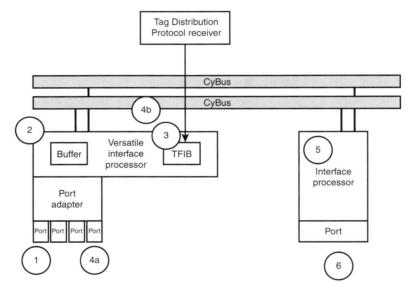

FIGURE 3.41 *An example of tag switching.*

As shown in Figure 3.41, the FIB can be populated from external devices using the Label Distribution Protocol. As a consequence, a single path determination engine could service multiple switch boxes. Effectively, a virtual router is built from a set of forwarding boxes and a path determination processor, which could be in any of the boxes or even stand alone.

High-Performance "Switches"

Cisco's core "switches" include the 5000, 5500, 6000, 6500, and 8500. I put switches in quotes because it can be hard to draw a distinction between high-performance routers like the 7200, 7500, and 12000 and the high-performance switches with Layer 3 awareness. 4000 and 2900 (except the 2926G which does do Layer 3 forwarding) series switches, in contrast, are optimized for Layer 2 only.

In general, the switches are optimized for IP LAN connectivity, whereas the routers support more protocol families and have much more capability for WAN interfacing. The 8500 really is a router, but does not have some of the complex filtering and bandwidth management features of the 7500 and 12000. 7500 and 12000 routers are optimized for the WAN environment, whereas the 8500 is optimized for the campus.

There is upward compatibility among the 5x00 and 8500 series. At Layer 3, the switches support NetFlow and Cisco Express Forwarding.

Collisions do not simply occur on Ethernets, but also in product naming. You need to follow the rules to manage Ethernet collisions, and you simply have to pay attention to vendor rules with product names.

Fore Platform Examples

In its PowerHub products, Fore uses a distributed switching architecture, which is quite appropriate at high speeds. These controllers have a shared memory model, in which a network controller stores a packet in RAM, to which the forwarding processor has access. An interface controller can buffer up to 512 packets for transmission or reception. If the forwarding engine can keep the output memory queue full, the controller can send frames continuously.

Fore's white papers on its architecture draw attention to the reason most commercial routers use a specialized real-time operating system rather than a general-purpose one such as UNIX or NT. Many are custom written for the hardware platform in use. Cisco's IOS was developed by Cisco, although certain related products such as the PIX, obtained through acquisitions, are based on a commercial real-time operating system.

Fore makes the point that it simplifies and speeds its software execution by a relatively straightforward set of rules:

- After a process begins execution, let it run to completion.

- Use a small number of processes and limit the amount of code executed in each so that it does not take a disruptive amount of time to go to completion.

- Use specialized processors to handle line I/O.

The first principle obviates the need for packet-level data locking, which Fore cites can take up to 3 milliseconds for changing the locking context. Some other systems can require multiple locks and releases for the same packet.

The third principle also involves putting simple FIFO memories on interface processors, while using the main shared memory for interprocess communications. Specialized processors that both have local memory and connect to the shared memory carry out other functions such as the actual forwarding.

Fore PowerHub devices have seven separate processes:

- Packet reception, in which medium-specific controllers scan the medium, capture packets, and store them in buffers.

- Receive polling, in which I/O processors poll the receive buffer queues. These processes do error checks and statistical collection on input packet and mark these packets as ready for the next step of processing, forward polling.

- Forward polling takes place in the main processor (MCPU). It examines packet headers, looks them up in the FIB, and forwards them as appropriate to other processes. Fore performs bridging, routing, and filtering in this process. This is the most computationally intensive task and is the limit on PowerHub throughput.

- Management functions such as routing updates and SNMP request handling are done on the MCPU.

- Transmit polling is another IOP function, which scans the shared memory to find packets that have been marked for forwarding. Pointers to these packets, rather than the packets themselves, are moved onto the queue for the outgoing medium processor. If there are no packets waiting for a given outgoing interface processor, a command is sent to it to tell it to transmit anything it has queued.

- Packet transmission. After the actual packet is queued, it is framed and transmitted.

- Transmit clean-up. Buffers and pointers no longer needed are cleared.

Nortel Networks Platform Examples

Nortel Networks is a recent merger of Nortel and Bay Networks. Bay routers evolved from Wellfleet, which long had the slogan, "Switch if you can, route if you must." Where Cisco classifies arriving frames by being either bridged or routed, Bay historically tries to bridge first and then route.

You'll find this section shorter than the Cisco equivalent, simply because Wellfleet/Bay do not have as many different forwarding modes as Cisco.

Wellfleet routers, however, always have had an excellent reputation for forwarding performance, but historically have not had as many traffic management features—filtering, queuing, and so on—as Cisco. Wellfleet emphasized simple and fast and obtained excellent performance.

Classical Routers

Most Bay routers come from the former Wellfleet organization, although Nortel's Passport devices have substantial routing capability.

Core Tier Routers: The Backbone Node Series

Bay's high-end pure routers, the Backbone Node (BN) series, are based on a symmetric multiprocessor architecture illustrated in Figure 3.42. In contrast with Cisco's architecture, where there is a single management processor that does specialized routing but higher-performance routing is distributed to ASICs on switching engines or interface cards, Bay associates a fast routing engine (FRE) or ATM routing engine (ARE) processor module, based on a 680x0 processor, with each interface card. Different models of the FRE have varying processor speeds and memory size.

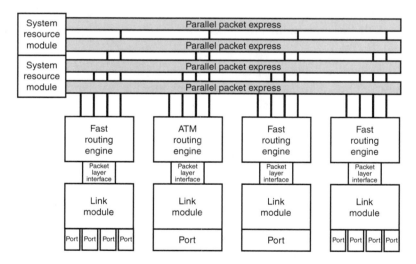

FIGURE 3.42 *Bay/Nortel/Wellfleet BN routers can be configured with different numbers of parallel packet exchange (PPX) paths and routing engines. There is not a separate management processor as on Cisco routers.*

Path determination functions run on the processor modules. The less CPU-intensive routing protocols run on all modules, whereas the more intensive ones, such as OSPF or BGP, are active on a single processor called the *soloist*. Another processor is defined as the *hot standby soloist*. It remains synchronized with the soloist and is able to take over quickly.

ATM engines have a different hardware architecture including two Motorola PowerPC RISC processors and two LSI Logic ATMizer cell processors. These cards also have an additional memory management mechanism for cell and packet buffering.

Interface cards, called *link modules*, have one to eight ports. For a given interface type, such as synchronous or Ethernet, they vary in memory size, processor speed, and whether or not they have a hardware coprocessor for compression. There is a separate 32-bit internal path between each processor module and its associated link module.

There is a separate 32-bit path from each processor module to the inter-module switching fabric, the parallel packet express described later in this section.

In single processor switching, if the output destination is on the same link module as the input port, the FRE processor can send the output frame directly out the output port

Single processor switching, obviously, takes place only when the link module has multiple ports. There are 4- and 8-port link modules for synchronous interfaces, with multiple memory size, processor speed options, and use of a compression coprocessors. There are single and 2-port cards that support fractional T1/E1 or primary rate ISDN.

In addition, there are single and 2-port Fast Ethernet, 2- and 4-port Ethernet and Token Ring cards, and an interesting 2-serial/2-Ethernet card.

Only if the destination is not on the same link module does the main Parallel Packet Express fabric become involved. This fabric is a 1 Gbps parallel packet express fabric composed of four 256 Kbps paths. Transfers from module to module can take different paths in the fabric, because there is no central forwarding module through which all traffic must flow.

A *system resource module* (SRM) arbitrates access to two PPX data paths, randomizing load across them. The basic BLN and BCN routers have a single SRM-L, which also provides a maintenance console interface. An optional second SRM, called the SRM-L, is needed to use all four PPX paths.

Distribution Tier Routers: The Access Node Family

Bay's Access Node of distribution-tier routers also uses the FRE, but in what is at first a single-processor architecture without a switching bus. These products, shown conceptually in Figure 3.43, include System 5000 router modules, the Access Stack Node (ASN), Advanced Remote Node (ARN), and BayStack Access Node (AN) and Access Node Hub (ANH).

This discussion focuses on the ASN, which is stackable into a multiprocessor architecture using Stack Packet Exchange Hot-Swap (SPEX-HS), allowing creation of a configuration with multiple processors. The basic SPEX-HS operates at 256 Kbps, the same as a single PPX path on the Backbone Node family. A second cable can be used to increase the bus bandwidth to 512 Kbps. To put this in perspective, Bay rates an individual ASN as capable of up to 50,000 packets per second, but a stack of four ASN chassis can forward up to 200,000 packets per second.

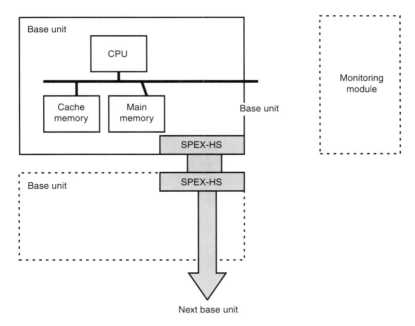

FIGURE 3.43 *A single ASN router has a single routing engine that services multiple interfaces. ASNs can be stacked, however, for greater performance using multiple processors.*

The CPU connects to main memory and an optional 256 KB fast packet cache. The cache can improve route lookup, again with the inherent limitations of cache technology. Compression coprocessors also are available.

Access Tier Routers

For the access tier, Bay has an assortment of smaller routers. They are not stackable, which is perfectly reasonable—devices at this tier are optimized for low cost and tend not to need high performance.

Routers in this family include the Nautica 4000 and 200, the CLAM, and the Marlin. CLAM, incidentally, stands for Corporate LAN Access Module. I confess that, aside from any technical considerations, I often appreciate what Bay chooses to call things!

These routers are based on combinations of MIPS 33000 RISC processors with MC683xx I/O processor chips. Compression coprocessors are available on some models.

Routing Switches

Accelar switches are positioned as routing switches, essentially a marketing term for a highly distributed relay capable of Layer 2 and 3 switching, as well as label and flow forwarding. Marketing-speak, however, does not obscure that Accelar has demonstrated extremely high performance. Figure 3.44 shows the Accelar architecture.

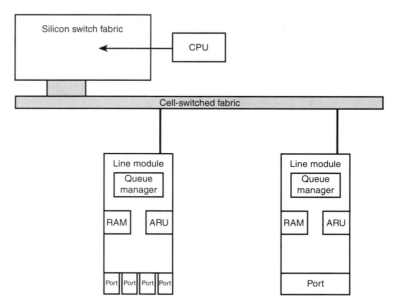

FIGURE 3.44 *As opposed to the frame-switched fabric of Cisco LAN switches, the Accelar uses an ATM cell fabric.*

A 15 Gbps half-duplex, 7 Gpbs full-duplex Silicon Switch Fabric (SSF) processor contains management functions and packet forwarding. It runs routing protocols and stores RIB information in main memory. FIB information is distributed to address resolution unit (ARU) ASICs on the I/O modules. There can be redundant SSFs for high availability. You can see that the term *routing switch* is a marketing rather than technical term. The Accelar can route perfectly well, but the term *router* is avoided because of a strategy of saying "switches are faster than routers."

Actual route lookup is done on the ARUs. The ARUs have up to 24,000 entries, which can be either Layer 2 or Layer 3. If the forwarding engine on the ARU recognizes the destination is on another port of the same module, it sends it directly to that port. Otherwise, it sends the packet to the shared memory fabric.

Before sending the packet to the output destination, the ARU calculates a new checksum and TTL value for packets and inserts a new destination MAC or other Layer 2 address on all frames.

The ARU prepends the packet/frame with an internal header containing the interface identifiers and priority information needed for quality of service. If the packet is multicast or broadcast, the internal label points not at a single output port, but at a list of ports in the multicast group. There are separate lists, distributed to the switch, of membership in a multicast group. Using the two lists, the forwarding engine can send the packet to all involved output ports.

Forwarding through the fabric does not need SSF intervention on a per-packet basis. The actual transfer through the fabric is as cells, not packets, and the queue manager function of the ARU chips perform segmentation and reassembly into packets.

At the output interface, the packet waits in a high or low priority queue, depending on the setting of the priority bit.

Using the MultiLink Trunking (MLT) feature, multiple physical ports can be inverse multiplexed into a single logical stream. An extension, redundant MLT, supports ports on different physical Accelar or BayStack 450 chassis. Although a redundant MLT does not increase the bandwidth, it obviously minimizes single-point-of-failure conditions.

Looking Ahead

In this chapter, we assumed that the RIB was populated by some obscure magic and accepted as a matter of faith that it was. The next two chapters remove the curtains behind which the RIB magician hides. Chapter 4 deals with the general process of installing routes in the RIB, whereas Chapter 5 deals with how the subset of routes determined by dynamic routing protocols are determined.

Chapter 9 focuses on connection-oriented switching, and Chapter 10 deals with connectionless LAN switching. Routing is the focus of Chapters 10 and 11; Chapter 11 deals with Layer 3 forwarding in a relatively flat network, and Chapter 12 examines more formal hierarchical routing methods.

CHAPTER 4

How Do Switches and Routers Find Paths?

Now who will stand on either hand/And guard the bridge with me?
—Macaulay

I like the way you always manage to state the obvious
with a sense of real discovery.
—Gore Vidal

Everybody gets so much information all day long that
they lose their common sense.
—Gertrude Stein

There is a regrettable tendency in the networking industry to apply the same term for several dissimilar ideas. *Route* is certainly an example of this tendency. I use the less common term *path* as a reminder to think about the specific meaning of the term. I define *path* as a sequence of next-hop addresses that lead to a destination. Path is a generalization of *source route* as defined in RFC 791: "a series of Internet addresses." There can be special cases even here, such as unnumbered interfaces and tunnels, but these are beyond the scope of the immediate definition. The IP source route option puts the entire desired path into a packet. For an assortment of reasons, primarily security, source routing is rarely used in IP. Nevertheless, think of a path as the output of a successful **traceroute** to the desired destination.

In the context of an individual router, however, path information is not stored as such. The router stores the destination address and the next hop address (that is, the next address in the path) to the destination.

Route information is stored in one or more Forwarding Information Bases (FIBs) per relay chassis. FIB usage varies with the kind of relay. In low-end devices, the routing information base (RIB) and FIB can actually be the same table in memory, but the conceptual distinction is worthwhile and is the norm in high-end devices. The RIB is optimized for updating by path determination processes, whereas the FIB is optimized for fast route lookup during forwarding. Significant parts of the FIB can be implemented in hardware.

In routers, the FIB usually reflects information at least partially shared among mutiple routers. Based on information that might not be only local to the router, the FIB is defined for the entire chassis. A router FIB is organized to identify the next hop to be taken to get closer to certain specific definitions. A router can have supplemental, exception-case rules for blocking flow to specified destinations, but the basic model of a router FIB is positive: how to forward.

Although bridges still have a chassis-wide FIB, that table is significantly qualified by port-specific information. Where a router's FIB is positive, a bridge FIB in many ways is negative, emphasizing what not to forward. Bridges still cooperate, like routers, in sharing information, but there is as much local decision making as global. The global process emphasizes what paths to block more than what paths to take. Bridge operation is not black and white here; the bridge FIB does contain information on the location of specific MAC addresses. If a bridge with more than one non-blocked output port knows which port leads to the MAC address, it sends (positively) the frame to that port and does not flood it to all output ports as it would if the MAC address were not in the FIB.

A Perspective on Metrics and Costs

Both routers and bridges use a concept of metric, or cost, in their view of the world. Simply speaking, the metric is a number that allows you to speak of multiple paths to the same destination as more or less preferable. See Chapter 5 for a more detailed discussion of metric assignment to dynamically calculated paths.

As a designer, you select the metrics so that traffic takes the most preferred path defined by the minimum path metric. The preferences selected by dynamic routing algorithms may or may not be optimal when there are specific quality of service requirements; see the discussions of traffic engineering in Chapter 14.

Routers, depending on the path determination method they use, can actually evaluate the metric of the entire route. Bridges use metrics to establish their position in the spanning tree topology, looking at the metric to adjacent bridges. Bridges take a more local forwarding view than do routers. *Metric* is a term used in several ways. Figure 4.1 shows the *individual per-interface metrics,* which are summed into a *route metric.*

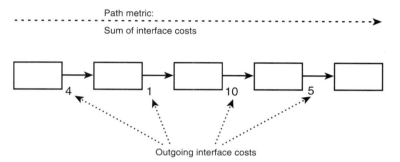

FIGURE 4.1 *Metrics, also called costs, apply both to interfaces and to entire paths.*

Routing mechanisms can compute a metric as a value that applies to an end-to-end path. With this usage, metrics break ties between routes to the same destination and routes calculated by the same path determination method.

Another usage of metric is a cost associated with outgoing interfaces. The two usages are not mutually exclusive. In many routing mechanisms, the end-to-end metric is the sum of interface metrics.

Don't confuse metrics with implementation-specific preference factors used to choose among sources of routing information. Preferences are detailed later in this chapter; see "Installing Routes in the RIB: Administrative Preference Factors." Metrics break ties between different routes to the same destination, which originated with the same source of routing information. Preferences are applied before metrics are considered. Remember what you are doing here. You are using metrics to select the best next hop from the interconnection device where you are, to the ultimate destination address. The next hop really is an outgoing interface, although it is customarily identified by its address, not the interface address, in Layer 3 routing.

The addresses being selected can be Layer 2 or Layer 3. The emerging technique of label switching (see the section "Cut-Through and Label Switching Mechanisms" in Chapter 13) labels represent FEC for specific addresses.

FIBs in Layer 1 and connection-oriented Layer 2 switches are quite different from their connectionless Layer 2 and 3 counterparts. Connectionless Layer 2 switches, used for technologies such as Frame Relay and ATM, are discussed in Chapter 9. See Chapter 10 for a discussion of the LAN switches used at Layer 2. Where Layer 3 routing tries to select the best path to a destination, and possibly load-shares among multiple paths, connection-oriented Layer 1 and Layer 2 switches use a *reachability* rather than a *route* model. There are special cases where the Layer 3 model also is one of reachability, such as Border Gateway Protocol (BGP) path determination.

These lower-layer switches are more concerned with the question of whether a path exists to a destination, and use the first one that will reach the destination. Although there can be some interchange of path information among switch boxes, as with the ATM Private Network-to-Network Interface (PNNI) routing protocol discussed in Chapter 9, the FIBs in connection-oriented switches are port-specific rather than chassis-specific.

This chapter deals with how paths are learned and installed in the forwarding information path. We begin by defining what a path is and next discuss what can go wrong with it.

Chapter 3 describes forwarding using information in the FIB, which is derived from information in the RIB. How does the RIB become populated?

Principles of Layer 3 Paths

A router's RIB service process receives information about potential routes from a variety of sources. What are some of these sources? They certainly are not limited to inter-router dynamic routing protocols. Potential routes can come from the router hardware status, preconfigured information, dynamic routing, or hybrids of switching and routing.

Rout*ing* protocols can provide information for forwarding the packets of the rout*ed* protocol. Dynamic routing information can come from a variety of sources, including the following:

- Routing Information Protocol (RIP).
- Interior Gateway Routing Protocol (IGRP).
- Enhanced Interior Gateway Routing Protocol (EIGRP).
- Open Shortest Path First (OSPF).

- Intermediate System to Intermediate System Intra-Domain Routing Exchange Protocol, to use the formal name and spelling of the protocol more mercifully called IS-IS. We are concerned with the Integrated IS-IS variant that carries IP as well as OSI routes.

- Border Gateway Protocol (BGP).

A router goes through a series of decisions that lets it select the best paths from the larger set of possible ones and installs them in the RIB. Rules are global for the box in picking routes, some of which are prescribed in standard references and some of which are vendor specific.

Before a router actually can forward, it must do the following:

1. Obtain information about potential routes, usually through static configuration or dynamic information exchange that populates the RIB.

2. If dynamic information exchange is used, participate in exchanges with other routers.

3. Install the best of these routes in the RIB, and, if there is a separate FIB, populate the FIB.

4. Look up the destination address of incoming packets in the FIB.

At this level of discussion, assume that there is a process that services the RIB of your router. The process receives information of all sorts, not just dynamic updates from routing protocols, but also from listening to the soft heartbeats of hardware interfaces on your router, or reading manually configured static routes.

This RIB process optionally applies filtering rules to the information it learns. Rules can specify that certain potential routes should be discarded. The rules can even prescribe ways to modify parts of the arriving routing information.

After potential routes pass through any filters, the process installs them in the RIB if they are previously unknown, are in some way "better" than routes currently in the table, or somehow add value to routes already there. Figure 4.2 is the first step in this process.

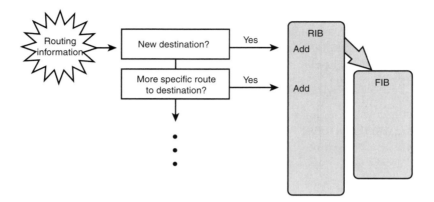

FIGURE 4.2 *The presence of the destination, and the specificity of the reference to the destination, are the first criteria used by the RIB installation process. This is a partial view of the installation process.*

When comparing two routes, the more specific route has a longer prefix (that is, more bits in the subnet mask). For example, 10.0.0.0/16 is more specific than 10.0.0.0/8. The traditional mask would be 255.255.0.0 for the first and 255.0.0.0 for the second.

More formally, potential sources of routes include the following:

- Hardware status and configuration of local interfaces, with local address configuration.

- Software-defined static and quasi-static routes. A quasi-static route is a static route with a preference factor that lets it be more or less preferable to another route.

- Dynamic routing processes.

The basic means of selecting routes is based on specifications in RFC 1812, with vendor extensions. To make the example concrete, Cisco's method is used, but the selection process of most vendors differs only in the details.

When speaking of route selection, there is a subtle difference between selecting routes to be installed in the RIB and looking up the route (in a RIB or derivative FIB) to make the forwarding decision for a specific packet.

There are many sources of routing information, but only those that get installed into the RIB are actually used for forwarding. Various decision factors have been used to select the best route to a destination, and RFC 1812 is the definitive reference on the core set. This RFC does allow for vendor-specific extensions.

The Classic Route Lookup Algorithm

What is documented in RFC 1812 as the classic algorithm is really an algorithm for route lookup rather than route installation. The classic algorithm that RFC 1812 derives from earlier documents does not cover all current practices. Criteria in the classic algorithm are the following:

- *Basic match.* The prefix part of the destination address in the packet is extracted. Any routes that do not include that prefix are rejected. For example, if the destination address is 10.1.0.1/16, a route to 10.2.0.0/16 is rejected, but routes to 10.0.0.0/8 and to the default route, 0.0.0.0/0, are accepted.

- *Longest match.* If there are multiple routes that meet the basic match condition, the route(s) with the longest number of matching bits is selected. In this example, if 10.1.0.0/16 is known, 10.0.0.0/8 is rejected.

- *Weak Type of Service (TOS).* Mechanisms, of historical interest only, used the TOS bits in the IP header, but no routing protocol in current use implements TOS. The use of the IP precedence bits of the TOS field in differentiated service is a different technique concerned with packet prioritization rather than routing.

- *Best metric.* Routes can have some numerical attribute associated with them. The significance of this attribute, called a metric, varies with the routing protocol that generated it. If the router has several potential routes with a metric generated by the same source, that with the best metric is selected. *Best* is defined for each routing protocol, but is usually the arithmetically lowest value.

Which Metric Is Best?

A tax expert friend offered me guidance on how to pick a tax accountant: "You interview all the candidates using the same question: How much is two plus two? Those that blurt 'Three' or 'Five' are immediately eliminated. Politely thank the ones who confidently answer 'Four' and take their names. The one you want is the one who calmly asks, 'How much do you need it to be?'"

So it is with metrics. No one metric is appropriate for all situations. Delay is critical for interactive applications, where efficiency in bandwidth might be more appropriate for file transfer.

Depending on the implementation, static routes may or may not have metrics. Bay's implementation combines static metrics and administrative preference, whereas Cisco's only has administrative preferences among static routes. See the section "Installing Routes in the RIB: Administrative Preference Factors" later in the chapter for a discussion of administrative preferences.

- *Vendor policy.* These are implementation specific.

The most common limitation of the classic algorithm is that it does not deal with categories of routes generated by specific routing protocols. OSPF and IS-IS have classes of routes such as intra-area, inter-area, and external. Any intra-area route, for example, is preferable to any inter-area route. See a discussion of these classes in Chapter 11.

Default Routes

Although we have not yet gone through the full route selection algorithm, we have established enough context so you can see how default routes are installed. Default routes, the least specific possible routes, have many operationally desirable qualities. They minimize configuration and routing overhead on edge routers. Properly used in a hierarchical topology, default routes reduce overall routing overhead.

In other words, the least specific route possible, but one that matches all destinations not matched by a more specific route, is the *default route*.

Sorting Through Default Terminology

A *default route*, by convention, is a route to 0.0.0.0/0. You can have multiple default routes, with different next-hop addresses, in the same router. Only some of the potential default routes can be selected by the RIB installation algorithm if the default routes have different administrative preferences or metrics. If there are multiple equal-preference, equal-cost default routes, most implementations will load-share among them.

The IGRP routing protocol does not understand the 0.0.0.0/0 convention, but internally marks certain destinations as *candidate default networks*. Default networks are functionally equivalent to default routes, as the destination to which to send traffic for which no better destination is known. EIGRP understands both the 0.0.0.0/0 and default network conventions.

On a Cisco router, the only ones that run IGRP and EIGRP, the *gateway of last resort* (GOLR) is the destination to which unknown traffic should be sent. If the most administratively preferred default information comes from IGRP or EIGRP, the GOLR is an IGRP or EIGRP default network. Otherwise, the GOLR is a 0.0.0.0/0 route from BGP, OSPF, IS-IS, or RIP.

Under the architectural assumption of IP, the local versus remote decision, a host (nonrouting device) sends traffic for its own subnet via Layer 2 connectivity, but sends traffic destined outside its subnet to a router. This router is almost always manually configured, or obtained from a Dynamic Host Configuration Protocol (DHCP) server, as a *default gateway*. See Chapter 6 for ways in which a host learns the address of its default router.

Switches, network access servers, and other relays that do not do Layer 3 routing need a default gateway like any other host. These relays need a default gateway not for handling user traffic, but for their own management. Without a default gateway, the relay has no way to reach an SNMP, DNS, or TFTP server not on its own subnet.

Sooner or later, any growing network needs to become hierarchical if it is to scale. This is not only for performance reasons, but for ease of troubleshooting.

We've seen this trend in moving from bridging to routing. In bridging, there is no hierarchy of addressing, although the spanning tree algorithm forces a hierarchical topology. MAC addresses, as opposed to Layer 3 addresses, have no internal structure that imply topology. Layer 3 addresses have at least two levels of hierarchy: prefix and host.

Fully meshing a network does not increase its reliability. If anything, it can decrease reliability.

Real-world relay performance is often limited by the size of the routing table. This is not a problem in small workgroup networks, but can be a major obstacle in scaling to large internetworks. One of the most common ways to keep the routing table to a reasonable size is to use hierarchical addressing structures and the tree organizations they make possible. Hierarchical structure also eases administration by permitting the delegation of address management.

Concern with the size of the routing table is more a matter of the CPU load to recompute it than of looking up individual entries for forwarding. Especially with BGP, and to a lesser practical sense with sanely sized OSPF, the computational load to do a new table calculation goes non-linearly with table size. Also, the greater the number of routes, the greater the probability one of them is going to *flap* (oscillate), requiring frequent recomputation. Smaller routing tables also are easier to troubleshoot.

Without a hierarchy, it is necessary to search tables containing every address in the domain. In a hierarchy, however, the search can break into a relatively small number of sub-searches.

Default routing is a way to keep the routing tables small, often with a side benefit of significant administrative convenience. This technique can, in fact, be used more often for administrative than performance reasons. There are several names for different applications of this technique, including default router, area router, backbone router, and gateway of last resort. They all assume that some router knows more about possible destinations than other routers, so any packet whose destination is not in the local routing table should be forwarded to the default router. They are techniques for building a hierarchical routing model.

Even if the edge router had complete information about all non-local destinations, that router would make no decisions differently—so why burden it with information that simply adds overhead?

The edge router in Figure 4.3 can have one or more static default routes, or it can learn the default from listening to a default route advertised by the backbone router. Both methods work. If you use static default declaration, you should minimize your configuration workload as discussed in the section "Automatically Generating Static Routes" later in this chapter. If you use a dynamic routing protocol to advertise default, you should be sure that the backbone router only advertises the default route on links to edge routers. The distribution router, as shown in Figure 4.3, can participate in full routing with other backbone routers, but should filter out non-default routes from being advertised to edge routers.

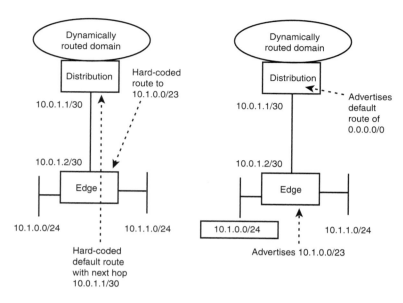

FIGURE 4.3 *In default routing, the edge router knows all directly connected prefixes, but sends traffic for all other destinations to the cloud.*

Default, or hierarchical, routing is convenient administratively because only the higher level core routers need to be updated to know about new networks. This is often a very practical view of the world, as might be seen in a large classroom building on a college campus. In such a building, there might be routers on each floor that link the LANs on each floor. There might be only one router with connectivity outside the building, which would make it the logical default router.

More complex default routing schemes, as shown in Figure 4.4, can associate a metric with multiple instances of a default route. The router can select the best default route, or possibly load-share among multiple default routes. You need to make design decisions whether it is preferable to pick a best route or load share. If the bandwidths or reliability of the links are different, load sharing is rarely desirable.

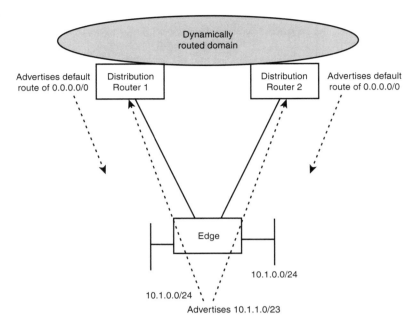

FIGURE 4.4 *Default routes can have metrics, so preferences can be learned from default route advertisements. This can be useful for backup or load sharing.*

Default router schemes reduce routing traffic flow as well, because routers that use a default to get to a set of definitions do not need to receive updates on how to reach each of those destinations. See Chapter 11 for further details.

Installing Routes in the RIB: Administrative Preference Factors

As shown in Figure 4.5, assuming that a candidate route has successfully passed through acceptance filters, the route installation process next checks to see if the destination of this route is not already in the RIB. If this is a new destination, the route is installed. By the time the route installation process sees this information, it refers to a next-hop route rather than the complete path. Complete paths can be considered by the path determination processes, but not by the RIB installation process.

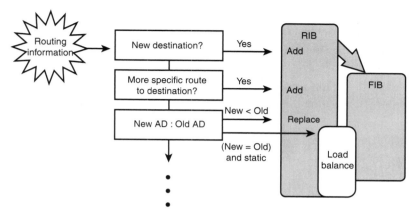

FIGURE 4.5 *Building from Figure 4.2, the next thing considered after specificity of route is the administrative preference among sources of routing information.*

Note

These preference factors do consider protocol-specific factors that we have not yet discussed. At this point, be aware that OSPF has four types of routes, listed in order of preference: intra-area, inter-area, external type 1, and external type 2. See Chapter 12 for details of how these preferences are assigned.

BGP also has a wide range of preference factors, most of which are outside the scope of this text. A fairly basic one, however, is the origin: external versus internal versus unknown, with respect to the current AS.

Bay has preference factors for selecting potential routes, shown in Table 4.1. *Administrative distance* is Cisco's term for preference factor, as shown in Table 4.2.

TABLE 4.1 BAY DEFAULT PREFERENCES (HIGHER VALUE INDICATES MORE PREFERRED) FOR ROUTE DETERMINATION.

Source of Routing Information	Administrative Distance Value
RIP[1], BGP[1], OSPF external[1]	1
Directly connected, static routes[2], OSPF intra-area, OSPF inter-area	16

[1]Can be set to 1–16.
[2]It's important to note that Bay routers cannot have a static route that is more preferred than dynamic routing.

TABLE 4.2 CISCO DEFAULT ADMINISTRATIVE DISTANCE VALUES (LOWER VALUE INDICATES MORE PREFERRED) FOR ROUTE DETERMINATION.

Source of Routing Information	Administrative Distance Value
Directly connected	0
Static routes in the form *interface-name*	0
Static routes in the form *next-hop-ip*	1[1]
EIGRP summary	5
External BGP	20
Floating static (preferred to interior dynamic)	21–89
EIGRP	90
IGRP	100
OSPF	110
IS-IS	115
RIP	120
EGP	140
External EIGRP	170
Internal BGP	200
Floating static (less preferred than dynamic)	201–254
Untrusted	255

[1]*Can be manually configured to any value 1–255.*

Bay RS actually installs routes in its RIB based on the *route weight*. Based on route weight, Bay picks routes in the order from most preferred to least preferred (see Table 4.3).

TABLE 4.3 BAY PREFERENCES.

Source	Preference
Route with highest preference value	1
Direct route with the lowest cost	2
Lowest-metric OSPF intra-area route	3
Lowest-metric OSPF inter-area route	4
Lowest-metric OSPF Type 1 external route	5
The BGP route with the highest LOCAL PREFERENCE value OR the OSPF Type 2 external with origin of BGP and the lowest RIP metric	6
The lowest-metric RIP route OR the OSPF Type 2 external with origin of INTERNAL and the lowest RIP metric	7
The static route with the least metric	8
The OSPF Type 2 external received from a Bay/Wellfleet router of RS 8.0 or earlier	9

GateD's preferences are shown in Table 4.4.

TABLE 4.4 GATED PREFERENCES

Source	Preference
Direct connected	0
OSPF route	10
IS-IS level 1 routes	15
IS-IS level 2 routes	18
Internally generated default	20
Redirects	30
Routes learned via route socket	40
Static routes from config	60
ANS SPF (SLSP) routes	70
HELLO routes	90
RIP routes	100
Point-to-point interface	110
Routes to interfaces that are down	120
Aggregate/generate routes	130
OSPF AS external routes	150
BGP routes	170
EGP	200

Note

Many people are surprised when they change a preference to make a certain route preferable, but it doesn't seem to be installed. This usually occurs because there is a more specific route from a less-preferred source. Such behavior is absolute in keeping with the rules of RFC 1812.

Usually, the default preferences are perfectly adequate for dynamic routing protocols. Note that all the dynamic routing protocols shown in Table 4.1 have different administrative distance defaults. This ensures that metrics are compared only between routes generated by the same dynamic routing protocol. The relative weights given to different sources are not standardized and vary among implementations.

RIP's default administrative distance of 120 on Cisco lets it be replaced by any other interior routing protocol. There is no administrative distance difference between RIPv1 and RIPv2, but prefix lengths advertised by RIPv2 might be longer than, for example, an IGRP route and would replace it.

Preferences in Changing Routing Protocols

One situation in which you might want to set a non-default administrative distance is when converting from IGRP to either OSPF or IS-IS. Although IGRP is an obsolescent and classful dynamic routing protocol, its default administrative distance makes it more attractive than either of these more modern protocols. On most implementations, you can override the preference defaults, either for all information from a given source or for specific routes. On Cisco, this is done with the **distance** subcommand of the **router** major command.

Ideally, when changing routing protocols in a production network, you begin by installing the new protocol on all routers. This assumes that your routers have the resources to run both protocols simultaneously. Set the preference for the new protocol so that it is less desirable than the current one in terms of installing routes in the RIB. With the new protocol running in the routers, check its internal tables, such as the OSPF database, to see that it is correctly finding routes.

In the second step, without removing the old routing protocol, change the preferences so the new one is more preferred than the old. After allowing time for reconvergence, check the active RIBs of all routers and look for routes that are still being learned from the old protocol. If you find any, do detailed troubleshooting until you find out why they are being generated. The most likely cause is a missing command for the new protocol, although another possibility is that the new protocol is importing a route learned from the old protocol.

After you can verify that the new protocol handles all your routes, remove all commands associated with the old protocol. In a hierarchical design, you can do this in stages. In a two-level hierarchy, start in one lower-level hierarchial area, then add the core, then add one lower-level area, and then convert the rest of the lower-level areas.

Load Sharing

Routes must have the same administrative distance even to be considered for load sharing. If the routes were created by dynamic routing protocols, they must also have the same metric.

A common misconception is that the dynamic routing protocols themselves do or do not support load balancing. They can only propose equal-cost paths as eligible for load balancing. The router implementation must permit installation of equal-cost routes in the RIB. IGRP and EIGRP can define unequal-cost routes as eligible for load balancing. All deployed load-sharing mechanisms make decisions about load sharing in relation to neighboring routers, not end-to-end best paths. See Chapter 11 for further discussions of load sharing. Label switching, discussed in Chapter 14, offers the potential of setting up end-to-end optimized paths, which in many respects are virtual circuits. Routing-based load sharing, even with techniques under development, still work on a statistical basis rather than absolutely picking the best end-to-end path.

Some routing mechanisms, such as OSPF external routes or BGP routes, are really not intended to be load balanced. These protocol mechanisms are more concerned with picking a best route and identifying reachability. There is no true load sharing over OSPF external or BGP routes, although there can be approximations in certain specific situations (see Chapter 12).

Metrics in Route Selection

Real routing protocols use different means of computing the metric. Some, like RIP, count the hops (number of routers traversed) between two destinations. Others have no standardized way of computing a metric, making its computation a local implementation choice. Factors used in computing metrics include the following:

- Link bandwidth. Used by IGRP, EIGRP, and often OSPF.

- Link delay. Can be used by IGRP and EIGRP, or as part of a manually computed interface cost for OSPF.

- Administrative preferences, such as monetary cost. Can be manually computed as an OSPF interface cost. Bandwidth for IGRP or EIGRP sometimes is artificially raised or lowered to provide a preference.

- Link error rate. Optionally used by EIGRP and IGRP.

- Link utilization. Optionally used by EIGRP and IGRP. Not recommended.

Routes and metrics vary over time. Relay implementations recognize that such information does not change continuously, but that any such information is likely to become obsolete eventually. Relays exploit the first characteristic by creating caches of relaying information they learn, so they do not continually query sources of information.

Not all these quantitative factors have proved useful in real networks. In particular, link utilization should not be used in the metric. This might seem counterintuitive, but some reflection reveals the problem. You are sending to Destination 1 over Path 1. Path 2 is created and also has connectivity to Destination 1. Assume that both paths have equal bandwidth. If a load-based metric is involved, Path 2 becomes more attractive than the more heavily loaded Path 1. Traffic then migrates to Path 2, making Path 1 less loaded and now more attractive again. This leads to the best path choice alternating between two routes, not balancing between them. See the section "Static Load Sharing" in Chapter 11 for a more detailed discussion.

Metrics are generally comparable only within the same dynamic routing protocol. RIP uses hop count, whereas IGRP and EIGRP use the same complex formula that, in practice, generally is bandwidth based. The complex E/IGRP metric is discussed further in Chapter 5. OSPF is an arbitrary interface cost that, in practice, like IGRP and EIGRP, is bandwidth based. In Cisco's logic, shown in Figure 4.6, metrics are considered after the specificity of the route and its administrative distance.

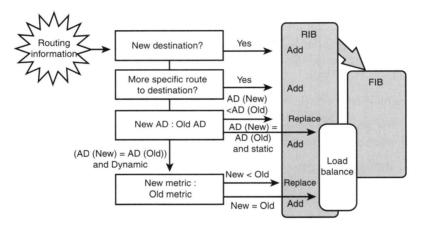

FIGURE 4.6 *Metrics either break ties among routes of equal preference or establish that they are eligible for load balancing.*

RIP overloads the hop count to use it for path cost and loop detection. IGRP tracks the hop count separately from the metric and still uses hop count, but only for loop detection.

Quasi-Static Routes

To have a network with alternate paths, you don't necessarily need to run a dynamic routing protocol. As long as the path selection algorithms support preferences among static routes, you can define static routes that will be used in order of preference.

Quasi-static routes are typified by floating static routes, where there is a set of static routes with different preferences or the same preference when load balancing is desired. *Quasi-static* is a term from the OSI Routing Framework architecture document [ISO 9575], further refined in RFC 1136, and is preferable to *floating static* (a Cisco term) because *floating static* implies routes that are less preferred than dynamic routing. There is no generally accepted term for static routes that are more preferable than dynamic routes; I sometimes call them *anchored static routes.*

Quasi-static routes still need to be configured manually, but when they are used, much of the inflexibility associated with static routing disappears. Chapter 11 gives examples of how quasi-static routes can be used for highly controlled load sharing, dial backup, and other applications for increasing reliability.

Consider an edge router that always defaults toward the backbone. This router can have more than one LAN interface, but it is a stub router: No traffic is sent to it that is not destined for a directly connected medium.

If you want a dial backup to a dedicated WAN connection to the router, you can establish a less-preferred static route to the 0.0.0.0/0 prefix.

The backbone routers need to know how to get to the edge networks. In a simple topology, such as that in Figure 4.3, the distribution router can be configured with explicit routes to the edge prefixes. Quasi-static routes also are useful for dial backup of dedicated facilities when routing updates fail on the dedicated link. Configurations like this might be criticized as maintenance-intensive, but with reasonable administrative procedures, this need not be the case.

Automating the Generation of Static Routes

Remember that you need to administer the subnets assigned to the edge routers. Typically, an installation defines the list of subnets and marks them in a database as they are assigned.

Some general principles of address administration include the following
[Berkowitz, 1998a]:

- Try very hard to avoid entering an address more than once. Sometimes it
  is not possible—a menu-based component might not allow scripting.

- Automate the updating of your router configurations using configurations created from your user address assignment database and loaded
  into routers with **tftp** or **telnet/expect**.

- Generate human-readable reports at the same time, so you have records
  for troubleshooting and for justifying address space allocations.

It can be a fairly simple procedure to write a program that generates static
route configuration statements from the database record. Assume that you are
setting up addressing and routing for the topology in Figure 4.7. When you set
up a new site, your administrative procedure should assign WAN and LAN
subnets. The code-generating program should be able to input the assigned IP
prefixes to an integer, add to that integer, and output the result in the form of a
dotted-decimal IP address. Of course, the IP address structure that underlies
any automatic addressing system must be designed carefully.

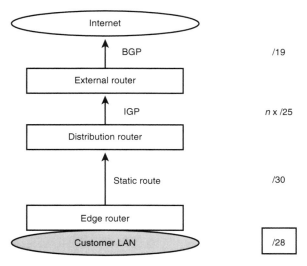

FIGURE 4.7 *An edge-to-concentrator site topology is the basis for writing scripts to generate router configurations.*

This example uses Cisco command language for the router commands and assumes Frame Relay connectivity. **rmtDLCI** is the number of the Frame Relay Data Link Connection Identifier at the remote site, and **distDLCI** is the DLCI at the distribution router. The procedure easily can be extended to generate DNS and other commands, as discussed in my presentation at the November 1998 NANOG conference, "Good ISPs Have No Class." [Berkowitz, 1998a]. For the edge router, generate the following:

```
int e0
ip addr (lanPrefix + 14) 255.255.255.240
int S0.rmtDLCI
ip addr (wanPrefix + 2) 255.255.255.252
ip route 0.0.0.0 0.0.0.0 (wanPrefix+1)
```

For the distribution router, generate the following:

```
ip route (lanPrefix)/0 (wanPrefix + 2)
int S0.distDLCI
ip addr (wanPrefix + 1) 255.255.255.252
! blackhole as appropriate
```

What you are doing here is allocating, for each new user, a /28 for his LAN and a /30 for his access WAN. The /28 and /30 subnets come from blocks of /28 and /30 subnets assigned to distribution routers. These blocks fit inside a /25, which is the block advertised by the distribution router.

Layer 2 Paths

Whereas Layer 3 path determination specifies where to go to the next destination, Layer 2 path determination often specifies where not to go to reach a destination. Spanning trees act more to block looping paths from forming than to identify paths to a destination.

Frames are forwarded over interfaces that are not blocked by the spanning tree algorithm. Individual bridges have station caches that let them forward to MAC addresses known to be reachable from a specific interface. Frames with a non-unicast and unknown unicast destination address must always be flooded out all interfaces except the one on which they were received.

See Chapter 9 for a discussion of basic mechanisms used to set up virtual circuits that underlie connection-oriented Layer 2 services.

Spanning Trees

Several goals were defined for IEEE 802.1D transparent bridge topologies, which are based on a spanning tree algorithm. The strategy results in a bridge with a minimum number of active links; it is assumed that each node and path has adequate capacity to handle all traffic directed to it by the topological algorithm. Adding links between two nodes, either for increased capacity or greater reliability, is not a feature of the basic algorithm. See the section "Resilient Uplinks" later in this chapter for extension to the algorithm that can provide parallel links between two bridges. If you do need parallel links, you might need to use some of these nonstandard extensions that might not work among different vendors. IEEE is working on some multivendor approaches for multi-link. Alternatively, you can route between parts of your network where parallel, partially, or fully meshed links are needed because Layer 3 routing is not subject to the restrictions of the spanning tree topology. The emerging technologies of switching using Layer 3 information downloaded from routers to fast switches tend to combine the cost/performance advantages of switches with the topological flexibility of routers.

Real bridge implementations usually provide a mechanism of giving preference to certain nodes and certain links in forming the tree. It might be desirable, for example, to put the root of the spanning tree at the central server location, so most traffic moves in the direction of servers. It also can be desirable to avoid certain links that are provisioned over packet networks and thus have a per-packet cost. Such links are necessary for backup, but otherwise are too expensive.

One bridge is selected as the root, using the rule of the bridge with the highest priority and, as the second priority, the arbitrary rule of selecting the bridge with the lowest unique address (with the priority field prepended). After this bridge is selected, all other bridges determine their least-cost path and root port leading to that path (defined as lowest metric) from themselves to the root. On each LAN segment, one bridge, if there is more than one, is made the designated bridge; it is the bridge with the least-cost path from the LAN to the root bridge, of all the bridges on that LAN segment. With that, all bridge ports being neither a Designated Port nor a Root port are blocked. After the basic bridge topology is set up, it can be optimized. This process is called *pruning*.

The bridges negotiate among each other and decide on a root. End systems do not participate in this negotiation. The bridge topology is then constructed so that forwarding is done in the direction of the root or through the root, and only one path in the direction of the root is active in any one bridge. Although the tree is drawn toward the root and through it, the paths created are bidirectional.

The IEEE 802.1D standard establishes a method with which a root always is selected automatically. Some implementations only accept the default selections, but many commercial implementations have mechanisms to override the automatic algorithm and force selection of a certain bridge as root, or emphasize the use of certain paths.

There are two parts to the 802.1D model: an initial tree topology definition and continued maintenance of the routing tables. This algorithm's tree grows from a single node, the root bridge. In Figure 4.8, the ports of bridges are shown as numbered circles and the various media connected to the ports as solid or dotted lines. This figure shows a representative spanning tree rooted in Bridge 3, in which one of the Port 5 interfaces between Bridge 1 and Bridge 5 is blocked.

Note

The spanning tree algorithm also does not support parallel links between two bridges, as between Ports A and B. Inverse multiplexing methods, introduced in the "Resilient Uplinks" section later in this chapter, allow the functional equivalent of parallel links to work without confusing the spanning tree algorithm.

Understand what blocking means. It means that only one bridge, in this case Bridge 1, can forward traffic onto the links between Port 5 of Bridge 1 and Port 5 of Bridge 5. To avoid loop formation, Bridge 5 cannot send either to Bridge 1 or Host 1 on the link between the two Port 5s. If a host on Port 2 of Bridge 5 wants to send to Host 1, the traffic has to follow the spanning tree up through the root and down the lefthand branches of the spanning tree.

Blocking does not mean that Host 1 is unreachable, it simply means that the path between the bottom Port 5s cannot be used by bridges to forward to other bridges. Blocking enforces a topology in which there is only one path to one destination.

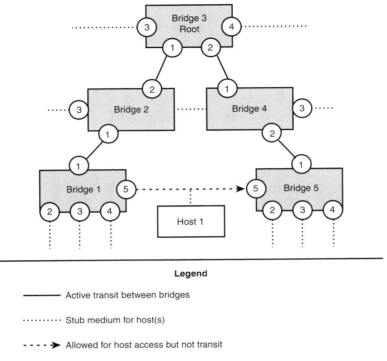

Legend

———— Active transit between bridges

·········· Stub medium for host(s)

- - - - ➤ Allowed for host access but not transit

FIGURE 4.8 *The spanning tree restricts the topology to one active path between any two bridges. Other potential paths are known, but remain in standby.*

Transparent bridges conforming to the IEEE 802.1D standard use a minimal spanning tree. Although this standard does provide mechanisms for bridges to dynamically discover the topology and start working in a plug-and-play manner, the wise designer selects a physical topology and possibly adjusts parameters, so that traffic flows over the most effective path from clients to servers.

You want to have the tree built so that traffic moves through the least number of bridges, and over the fastest links, to reach its destination. This means that you want to affect the factors that will cause the active branches of the tree to be constructed in a manner that matches the hierarchical application topology.

At any given moment, the *active topology* of a bridged LAN is the set of bridges, paths, and ports interconnected by ports in the forwarding state.

Bridge management PDUs distribute information on the existence and reachability of bridges and are being extended in various IEEE 802 working groups to provide activation, deactivation, statistical, and other management functions.

Spanning tree algorithms are discussed in the sections "The 802.1D Protocol" and "Other Spanning Tree Algorithms," but several supporting mechanisms are needed to make spanning tree a reality. These mechanisms deal primarily with the distribution of topological information.

The 802.1D Protocol

IEEE 802.1D bridges multicast status information that defines the spanning tree. Frames containing this information variously are called *hello* or *bridge PDU (BPDU)* frames. This discussion is not intended to give sufficient information to implement code for the protocol, but to help the network designer understand how 802.1D works in practice.

Each bridge has a unique identifier. You can affect the probability of a bridge becoming root by setting a priority field that is part of the bridge identifier. The actual bridge identifiers used in a comparison are actually 8 bytes long: 2 bytes of priority followed by the unique identifier. In theory, you only affect the probability of a bridge becoming root. In practice, if you assign the best (that is, numerically lowest) priority to the bridge you want to become root, and no other bridge has that low a priority, the bridge you configured with the lowest priority becomes root as long as it is operational.

Figure 4.9 illustrates how you can use priority values to impose a certain topology. Assume that Bridge 1 is the most powerful. Bridge 2 is a backup with less forwarding power, but still centrally located. You could set Bridge 1's priority to 1, Bridge 2's to 2, and set all the other bridge priorities to 100.

When a bridge receives a BPDU, it first checks if the information is too old to be considered useful. BPDUs contain the originating bridge ID. These messages have an **age** field, and bridges have a holding time parameter. If the sum of **age** plus the holding time exceeds a limit parameter, **MaxAge**, the hello message is discarded. Because the messages are sent continuously by a normally operating bridge, the table of bridges does not age out in normal operation. Holding time is set to a short value when the bridge perceives the topology is changing, and to a longer value when the topology appears stable.

MaxAge, **HelloTime**, and **ForwardDelay** should have the same value for all bridges in the same spanning tree.

Hellos for typical bridge networks are approximately 50 bytes in length. After initial network setup is done and the topology first stabilizes, only designated bridges transmit a new hello, with a typical **HelloTime** of two seconds.

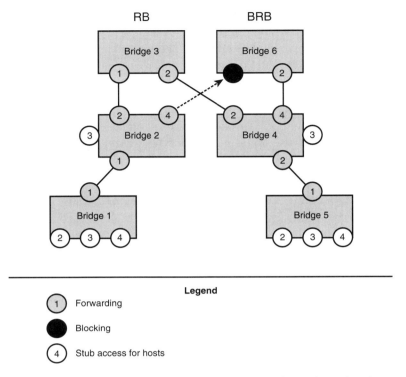

Legend

(1) Forwarding

● Blocking

(4) Stub access for hosts

FIGURE 4.9 *Priorities allow you to cause certain bridges to be preferred as root.*

It seems that reducing timer values would speed convergence, but, in the presence of congested or slow links, tuning timers to their minimum can result in important BPDUs being dropped. If a bridge does not hear BPDUs, it might conclude that a link or bridge is down and transition to a non-forwarding state while it recomputes its view of the spanning tree.

If the information in a valid BPDU offers a lower cost to reach a destination than the receiving bridge has been using, the receiving bridge accepts the new information and sends BPDUs to its downstream bridges, propagating the information.

Figure 4.10 shows the basic finite state machine for 802.1D bridging. The **Blocking** state is entered when the bridge is initialized, or from the **Disabled** state through a bridge management function. Various operations of the spanning tree protocol can cause this state to be entered from **Listening**, **Learning**, or **Forwarding** states. The **Blocking** state is left when the algorithm acts to transition the port into the **Listening** state.

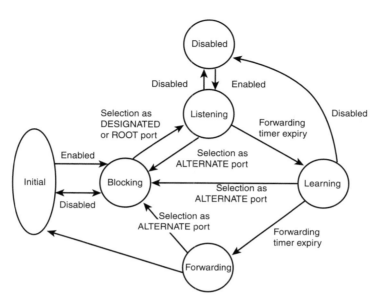

FIGURE 4.10   *802.1D has a relatively simple protocol state machine.*

Note

Although the 802.1D state machines are simple compared to some in routing protocols, they still have many paths, especially for error handling. In these figures, my intention is to show the function of the state machine, and I have omitted some error handling paths in the interest of graphical clarity and showing the main functions.

In the event you are implementing or troubleshooting bridge code, consult the 802.1D standard to find all possible state machine transitions.

After leaving the **Initial/Disabled** or **Blocking** states, bridges enter the **Listening** state with the assumption they are the root bridge. The receiving bridge concatenates its priority to its bridge ID and compares that to the priority and bridge ID. The numerically lower concatenated string wins; if the receiving bridge's string is higher than the advertising bridge's, the receiving bridge assumes the advertising bridge is root.

After the bridge has decided which bridge is the root, it now needs to decide which of its ports are the best paths in the direction of the root. If there is more than one path to the root, in a given direction, the higher-cost paths are put into the **blocking** state.

At this stage, port identifiers are considered. A port that has already been designated for a given medium is not blocked; the bridge hearing such information blocks its own port to that medium. If the costs are the same, the port identifiers are used as a tie-breaker.

After a port is in the **forwarding** state, it can transmit frames received from other ports of the same bridge. In common practice, the received frames are transmitted in first-in, first-out (FIFO) order, but the protocol does contain a user priority field that can be used to implement classes of service. The standard specifies that frames with the same source/destination address and priority should be handled in FIFO order, although separate FIFO queues can be kept for unicast and non-unicast frames. This user priority field is the basis of the 802.1P standard discussed in Chapter 13, a technique for quality of service at Layer 2.

Other Spanning Tree Algorithms

Perlman has written that she disagrees with the final IEEE version of the algorithm she originated [Perlman, 1992]. The IEEE algorithm has two intermediate states before a port goes into the forwarding state. She designed the algorithm with a single intermediate state called *preforwarding*. The IEEE argument is that having a second *learning* state allows the bridge to build up a cache of station addresses, so that the bridge does not flood frames destined to unknown addresses when it enters the forwarding state.

Perlman suggests that the separation into two intermediate states adds unneeded complexity. Having the two intermediate states does increase the delay before a port starts forwarding, and vendors are implementing variants on the original STP algorithm as discussed in the section "Accelerating Access for Host Ports on Switches."

Other issues also affect multivendor interoperability. Most bridges use the 802.1D algorithm. In the past, a substantial number of bridges used an alternate algorithm developed by DEC. Although some implementers claim the DEC algorithm is faster, in the interest of interoperability, it makes sense to use the IEEE algorithm.

Almost all bridges that can speak the DEC algorithm also can be configured to speak 802.1D. Exceptions include the Vitalink TransLAN and the DECbridge 100. If you do have such devices in your network, first consider replacing them to simplify your network. The TransLAN, however, was an interesting implementation optimized for bridging across satellite and other long-delay paths and might have some niche applications.

Many bridges can be configured to run either the IEEE or DEC algorithm. If you have a small group of devices that require the DEC algorithm, you might want to keep that as an island and use a router for connectivity to other spanning trees that use the IEEE algorithm.

There is an IBM proprietary spanning tree algorithm, different from 802.1D, used to control the propagation of source route explorers. See "Finding the Path with Source Route Explorers" later in this chapter.

Accelerating Access for Host Ports on Switches

Bridges (that is, LAN switches) assume, by default, that any device connected to a bridge port is another bridge. By the spanning tree algorithm, the port initially enters the blocking state, then listening, then learning, and finally forwarding. Going through these states takes time.

If the implementation permits, you can designate ports that do not connect to another bridge as not participating in the spanning tree algorithm, or taking a shortcut through the algorithm. In Figure 4.8, the ports that have dotted lines connected to them are eligible for reducing spanning tree initialization time.

When you disable or shortcut the spanning tree, the port goes directly from the initial state to forwarding, avoiding spanning tree processing delays. Figure 4.11 shows the revised state machine for a host port that bypasses the intermediate listening and learning states.

When this extension is not used, it often takes approximately 30 seconds before a host can start forwarding on a switch port. If you do use the extension, you must be very careful that your users do not connect workgroup switches without first informing you. Your administrative practices should emphasize that the network operations center should approve new installations.

This extension also is incompatible with fault tolerance schemes in which a host is connected with two NICs to two different access switches that belong to the spanning tree. In this case, the host relies on the spanning tree to tell it which interface to use and which interface will be blocked. You can avoid this restriction by having a different virtual LAN (VLAN) connected to each interface, but the application needs the intelligence to know which interface to use, or if it should send the traffic out both interfaces to mirrored hosts.

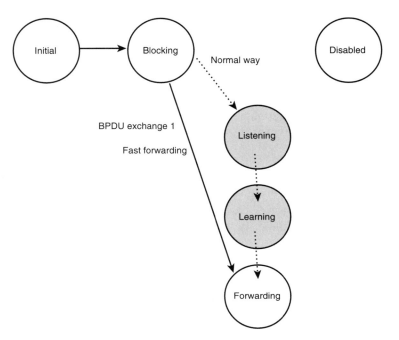

FIGURE 4.11 *In the accelerated access model for hosts, the 802.1D state machine is modified to skip the intermediate states. Again, not all error paths are shown for graphic clarity.*

Resilient Uplinks

Most vendors have a procedure by which the multiple parallel link restriction is not quite violated, but is worked around with inverse multiplexing. Multiple physical links are combined into a single logical path between two adjacent bridges, as shown in the Parallel Link part of Figure 4.12. The spanning tree algorithm sees the multiplexed path as a single link.

This technique, detailed in Chapter 10, provides additional bandwidth. It also is resilient with respect to medium failures, or failures of a port on a bridge. If you do need additional bandwidth, it is probably the best choice. The bridge has to do more work to multiplex, and this can require more expensive bridges or port cards.

If you are primarily interested in fault tolerance rather than additional bandwidth, the technique shown in the right side of Figure 4.12 is another alternative. It can be combined with the parallel link technique on the left side of the figure and comes into play only if all links to the distribution switch, or the distribution switch itself, fail.

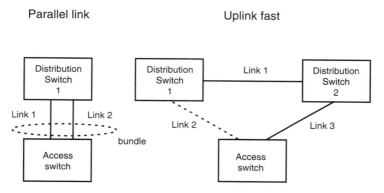

FIGURE 4.12 *Inverse multiplexing and designating uplinks are methods that give different types of resiliency.*

The technique on the right side is resilient in terms of a complete switch failure as well as a failure of a single medium. Several vendors have similar approaches; Cisco calls it *fast uplink switchover*. Consult specific vendor and switch documentation for the range and characteristics of techniques available on specific products. Vendors often support certain techniques on particular parts of their product lines rather than across the board.

In Cisco's fast uplink, one of several spanning tree variants used to improve performance, an *uplink group* of ports is one in which only one port is forwarding at a time. This group consists of the two ports on the access switch.

In Figure 4.12, before a failure, distribution switch 1 is the primary switch and is the root of the spanning tree. After a failure of distribution switch 1 or the link to it, the access switch, which typically is in a wiring closet, knows which is the alternate path to the alternate root. If the primary root link fails, the switches can immediately change uplinks to those that connect them to the alternate route. The changeover works when the primary ports go to the blocked state and the secondary ports go directly to the forwarding state without passing through listening and learning states.

Finding the Path with Source Route Explorers

Source route bridging is really an obsolescent technique, but it is used widely in IBM networks. It requires considerably more configuration than 802.1D transparent bridging, without even beginning to consider the requirements of mainframe-based Token Ring. Mainframe applications often need to know the specific MAC address of the remote host, so you must locally administer host

MAC addresses rather than rely on burned-in addresses. If you do rely on the unique burned-in address, and the network interface card has been changed, the mainframe and front-end processors have no way to know the new burned-in MAC address.

The basic principle is that hosts that want to reach other hosts send an initial *explorer frame* to the destination. Bridges along the way record the path taken to the destination and include this information in the explorer. The receiving host reverses the route and sends a response back to the originator. If some part of the route is busy, the response can come back on an alternative path, which allows a degree of automatic load sharing that spanning trees do not.

The first step in the source route bridging explorer process consists of the originating host sending a **TEST** frame with scope limited to the local medium. If the destination responds to this frame, both source and destination are on the same medium, and source route bridging is not needed.

If there is no response from a local host, a second frame is sent out onto routes. SNA sends an all-rings unicast looking for a specific MAC address, while NetBIOS sends a multicast search for server name. As the explorer goes through bridges, the path it takes is recorded.

The destination host echoes back the response, reversing the path in the arriving explorer. Whichever explorer response arrives first, by definition, has come back on the fastest path, which the originating host now uses as a source route to the destination.

Virtual and Emulated LANs

The most important thing to realize about finding routes for VLANs and emulated LANs (ELANs) is there is no special path determination process. VLANs and ELANs are encapsulation mechanisms that encapsulate a payload protocol such as 802.3 or 802.5 and associate them with a VLAN. The delivery protocol used to carry the VLAN frames (or cells, in the case of ELANs) is a normal one such as Fast Ethernet or Gigabit Ethernet, or ATM in the case of LANE.

In practice, VLANs extend the spanning tree model of user LANs by multiplexing multiple spanning trees onto a system of shared trunks. It can be argued that a LAN switch that contains several broadcast domains is a micro-VLAN, but micro-VLANs can be implemented without the use of VLAN protocols. The easiest way to think of a VLAN is that it is a tunneling mechanism, as shown in Figure 4.13. Frames from edge LANs 1, 2, and 3 enter the

VLAN system on Switch 1. Switch 2 is a transit switch that connects Switch 1 and Switch 3, and also has an edge port for edge LAN 1. Switch 3 has edge ports for edge LANs 2 and 3.

ELANs, or LAN emulation (LANE), is a VLAN technology using ATM trunking. The term *VLAN* is used here to cover both connectionless LAN-based VLANs and ATM ELANs. Do note that LANEv2 has significantly greater capabilities than LANEv1. When coupled with Multiprotocol over ATM (MPOA) mechanisms, LANEv2 is a hybrid Layer 2/Layer 3 technology capable of controlled QoS.

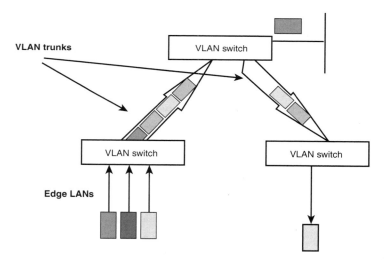

FIGURE 4.13 *Ethernet or Token Ring frames are encapsulated in the high-speed medium format.*

The exact high-speed medium formats available depends on the vendor implementation. Although 802.1Q is in principle independent of the medium being carried, many initial implementations support it only for Ethernet-family frames, not Token Ring or FDDI. Cisco's proprietary ISL does support Token Ring. For FDDI, Cisco uses a variant of 802.1Q.

FDDI with 802.1Q, Fast Ethernet for ISL, or ATM cells for LANE—these encapsulated frames are then bridged through a spanning tree for the high-speed protocol.

Tunneling has the following several components:

- The original *payload* information. In some tunneling mechanisms, such as Data Link Switching, local information such as the Layer 2 header on the originating LAN, can be discarded.

  Another way to look at the payload is that all tunneling mechanisms contain upper-layer payload information, but they do not always preserve the edge protocol header.

- The *tunneling* information. This is information needed to let the receiver know that the incoming PDU contains tunneled information. If the tunneling protocol potentially can multiplex information from different protocols or data streams, there must be information in the tunneling protocol that lets the receiver send the payload to the appropriate destination.

- The *delivery* protocol. This is used to carry the tunneled information over the shared infrastructure. In complex networks, multiple delivery protocols might be used along a path. This is most commonly Fast Ethernet, but also can be FDDI, Gigabit Ethernet, or ATM. ATM, incidentally, can just provide a fast pipe; LANE is not required.

Details of assigning devices to VLANs and ELANs are in Chapter 10.

The spanning tree model still works within VLANs that use LAN protocols such as Fast or Gigabit Ethernet, or FDDI, raw ATM virtual circuits, or ATM LANE as their trunking technique. The trunking LAN protocol follows its own spanning tree, whereas various edge spanning trees are carried through it. Proprietary variants differ as to whether there is a single spanning tree for all VLANs or one for each VLAN.

There are two kinds of VLAN trunking. One method is more clearly a tunneling method. Native frames are prepended with a VLAN header, which contains MAC addresses associated with switch ports. Cisco ISL uses this method, which has advantages and disadvantages. One of the first advantages is that it is transparent to the edge medium MAC format, because the edge format is encapsulated inside the new header. Another advantage is that a separate spanning tree can be established among the MAC addresses of the switch trunk ports, so there can be a single optimization of the topology for trunking. A disadvantage is that the frames tend to be longer and more likely to run into frame length problems.

The other kind, used by 802.1Q, inserts a VLAN tag into the existing header, so that the source and destination MAC addresses are unchanged.

According to the 802.1Q specification [IEEE 802.1Q]:

> The spanning tree formed in a Virtual LAN environment need not be identical to the topology of the VLAN(s). All VLANs are aligned along the spanning tree from which they are formed; a given VLAN is defined by a subset of the topology of the spanning tree upon which it operates.
>
> Second, the topology of the VLAN is dynamic. The structure of the VLAN may change due to new devices requesting or releasing the services available via the VLAN. The dynamic nature of VLANs has the advantages of flexibility and bandwidth conservation, at the cost of network management complexity.
>
> Note: There is a choice to be made as to how many spanning trees operate in a VLAN environment, and how the VLANs in that environment map to those spanning trees. In all cases, a given VLAN maps to a single spanning tree; the mapping choice to be made with multiple spanning trees is whether there is one spanning tree per VLAN, or whether many VLANs map to each spanning tree. Although multiple spanning trees offer some advantages over a single spanning tree in VLAN environments, this Standard avoids the added complexity of defining a mapping function of VLANs to spanning trees by defining a VLAN environment which operates over a single spanning tree. It is the intent of this standard not to preclude future extensions to use multiple spanning trees.

802.1Q and ISL are not significantly different from 802.1D spanning tree path selection. They run on broadcast multiaccess media and operate much as do slower spanning tree protocols. One or more VLANs can map onto the 802.1D spanning tree established among the trunk interfaces of 802.1Q switches. Traffic from all VLANs flows over the trunks. It is the role of configuration information in the edge switches that delivers traffic to specific edge ports.

Trunk interfaces are identified by MAC addresses. The VLAN frame header has information that identifies the particular VLAN that the passenger frame belongs to.

LANEv1 provides essentially the same functionality as VLAN techniques, but exclusively runs over ATM trunks. The basic idea of LANE is setting up virtual circuits among the LAN emulation clients (LECs) and passing unicast frames through these virtual calls. There can be multiple ATM switch hops in a given virtual call path, but the switches are unaware that the cells going through them are associated with LANE. The inter-switch topology is handled as any ATM call setup, either as permanent virtual circuits (PVC) in early implementations or, in modern implementations, as switched virtual circuits (SVC) set up using Q.2931.

Internally, LANE uses a client/server architecture to determine how paths should be set up for unicast frames. It uses other server functions to handle broadcast and multicast traffic.

> ### Note
>
> *For those readers seeking Cisco certifications, there's a bit of Cisco-specific terminology that you need to know. Cisco speaks of demand nodes and resource nodes describing things connected to switches. Demand nodes primarily initiate transmissions. Think of application clients, devices sending SNMP **TRAP** messages and workgroup switches and routers. Resource nodes respond to queries and include things such as application servers, server switches and routers, and network management servers.*
>
> *The servers involved in LANE do not fit precisely into this model because the LANE servers are visible only to LANE devices, not application devices. To be finicky about it, LANE-aware application servers and workstations do see LANE infrastructure servers.*

Establishing connectivity among LANE components is detailed in Chapter 9 and the actual data flow among them in Chapter 10.

ATM and Frame Relay Switches

ATM and Frame Relay switches have FIBs defined for each physical port. The port-specific tables map a field in an incoming data unit—cells in the case of an ATM switch and frames in the case of a Frame Relay switch—to an outgoing port.

In the case of ATM, the incoming and outgoing data units are both cells. The user side of a Frame Relay switch does receive frames, but, depending on the network implementation, the data fields of the frames can be remapped into cells, IP packets, and so on.

ATM switches have per-port FIBs, as shown in Figure 4.14. The tables in Figure 4.14 list VPI/VCI pairs expected on the port and do their destination lookup in these tables. When a destination match is found, the switch rewrites the cell to the designated output port, changing the output VPI/VCI as specified in the input port table.

These tables exist for PVCs, or only after the setup of SVCs. SVCs are established between endpoint addresses. The endpoint addresses use the E.164 international ISDN address format for public ATM networks, or one of several formats under the OSI Network Service Access Point (NSAP) structure for private ATM networks.

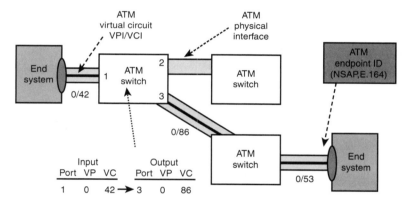

FIGURE 4.14 *ATM switches have port-specific FIBs, which can be populated with manual configuration or an ATM routing protocol such as IISP or PNNI.*

Frame switches are concerned only with true Frame Relay addressing at the edges of the network. Depending on the implementation, they can map Frame Relay DLCIs to ATM virtual circuits, IP addresses associated with tunnels, or even internal DLCIs. The Frame Relay Service in the figure has its own addressing system, to which the Frame Relay switches map.

Looking Ahead

In this chapter, we have looked at how the forwarding tables for routing and switching are populated. Chapter 5 goes into greater detail on the way that routes are dynamically calculated by dynamic routing protocols, to be offered to the route installation process described in this chapter.

Part IV, Chapters 9 through 12, deals with implementing routing and switching in actual network designs.

CHAPTER 5

Dynamic Interior Routing Information Mechanisms

To have his path made clear for him is the aspiration of every human being in
our beclouded and tempestuous existence.
—Joseph Conrad

Many shall run to and fro, and knowledge shall be increased.
—Daniel 12:4

A traveler without knowledge is a bird without wings.
—Sa'Di.

In Chapter 4, we looked at the process of building the routing information base (RIB). Inputs to this process include information from dynamic routing protocols. We treated these protocols as black boxes in Chapter 4, and now we look inside those black boxes. The thrust of this chapter is to review the internals of routing protocols to the extent relevant to network design, not the implementation of the protocol in a router.

Routers are useful because they can forward traffic to nonadjacent, but reachable, destinations. Figure 5.1 illustrates the difference between adjacent and reachable. Adjacent routers are more commonly called *neighbors*. Neighbors share a common transmission medium.

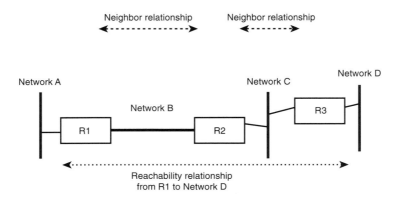

F I G U R E 5 . 1   *Routers 1 and 2, and 2 and 3, are neighbors. Network D and Router 3 are reachable from Router 1.*

A router goes through a series of decisions that lets it winnow the best paths from the possibly larger set of possible ones and installs them in the RIB.

Dynamic Routing Principles

After physical connections to local media, dynamic routing is the most common source of routing information. Dynamic routing is not always the best source. Always remember that static routes can give a fine-grained level of control not available with dynamic routing.

You might want to use a route other than the one that dynamic routing would find because you want traffic to follow a specific path you know will not be congested. You might want to specify paths more specific than dynamic routing to split load across specific media. You will see reasons in virtually every succeeding chapter.

Striking the proper balance between static and dynamic routing reflects the art, as well as the science, of network design. You will evolve your own balance. A frequent argument against static routes is the amount of administration they need, but this can be automated to a significant extent [Berkowitz, 1998b].

Political Philosophy and Routing

The static versus dynamic argument sometimes reminds me of an old political tale, in which one person who believes in government intervention and another person opposed to any regulation, see the same traffic jam.

The first says, "Look, a traffic jam. We need a traffic cop up there." The second says, "Look, a traffic jam. There must be a traffic cop up there." If the first person is a routing architect, she feels that static routes are necessary to direct traffic, whereas routing systems built by the second feature a free market among routers. In the real world, neither architect is always right; a well-designed routing system contains both static and dynamic routing information.

Depending on the protocol architecture, information about nodes can be about specific hosts or routers, or about ranges of addresses.

The path determination part of routing involves several logical steps:

1. *Address discovery*. Routers must discover their own addresses and, if appropriate, their router identifiers. In parallel with neighbor discovery, the routing process generates its initial set of routes, based on its directly connected interfaces. These routes are sent to the RIB acceptance and installation process.

2. *Neighbor discovery*. They must discover neighboring routers, determine if they should exchange routing information, and, if so, do the initial exchanges.

3. *Specialization*. As neighboring routers are discovered, some protocols establish preferences among them for exchanging routing information or forwarding traffic. See the section "Peering and Workload" for more information on OSPF's usage of specialization.

4. *Forwarding*. Each node capable of forwarding PDUs must decide how to forward (that is, route) individual PDUs. It must also recognize when a given PDU is meant for the relaying node itself.

5. *Routing information exchange*. Nodes continue to advertise routes they can reach, listen to information about new routes that other nodes can reach, and possibly announce that certain routes or nodes are no longer reachable.

6. *Dead detection*. This is done with hellos or, in older protocols, the periodic routing updates themselves.

The Router's Own Identity

People secure in their own identities deal better with other people, and this is no less true of routers. When a router sends information to another router, the sending router needs to identify the source of the information. In early protocols, the source IP address of the interface sending the packet was sufficient.

In the more modern protocols, there needs to be a *router identifier* that is associated with no physical interface, but that uniquely identifies the router. Real hardware interfaces can always go down, but software-defined interfaces internal to the router are much more stable. Other routers can generalize about information received from a certain router, even though that router might have parallel paths, or even multiple paths with different costs, to them.

Determining the router's identity is usually the first step of initialization. The router then builds internal data structures and starts loading its tables with information about directly connected media.

Each routing proctocol—if more than one is used—generates a preliminary set of routes and submits them to the RIB installation process. Figure 5.2 shows the important distinction between the routing protocol and the RIB. Chapter 4 deals with the issues of choosing the potential routes to install in the RIB.

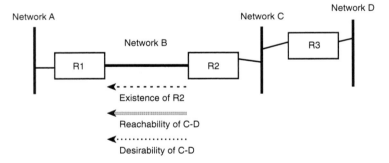

FIGURE 5.2 *Routers exchange information about the routes to which they offer routing services.*

After the local routes are installed, or in parallel to their installation, the router attempts to find neighbors and exchange information with them.

Information to Be Exchanged

As shown in Figure 5.2, when you use a dynamic routing protocol, it always conveys the first two kinds of information in the following list and might carry the third:

Note

I use the term convey rather than carry because there either might be an explicit hello subprotocol that announces the existence of routers, or a router that implies the existence of routers because it hears routing updates from them.

- The existence of neighboring routers.

- The existence of reachable destinations.

- The desirability of paths to reachable destinations.

Figure 5.2 shows the basic kind of information exchange that supports these three types. This figure assumes that a single routing protocol handles all routes. Router R2 sends R1 information about the existence of R2, the routes reachable by R2, and the costs of reaching those routes. There is a mirror-image exchange from R1 to R2.

Depending on the routing protocol, R2 might only tell R1 about the direct route it is using to Network D, or R2 might also tell R1 about the potential route via R3.

Even for a single protocol family such as IP, there might be more than one routing protocol running on a router. One common reason to have multiple routing protocols is transition from an older to a more modern protocol. In some protocol families, there also might be one protocol optimized for LANs with a different one optimized for WANs. The original LAN-optimized protocol for AppleTalk, for example, is the *Routing Table Maintenance Protocol (RTMP)*. *Apple Update-Based Routing Protocol (AURP)* was developed by Apple to complement RTMP by providing better bandwidth utilization on WANs.

Figure 5.3 shows one routing protocol in use. Chapter 4 discusses how to choose among information from different routing protocols.

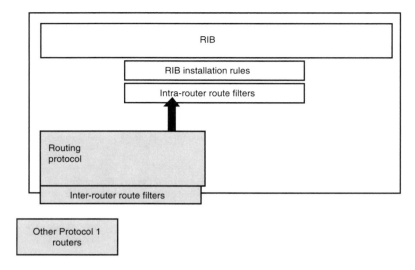

FIGURE 5.3 *The conceptual information exchange between neighboring routers includes existence of each router, the destinations to which that router offers to forward, and the costs of those routes.*

Minimal spanning tree algorithms are adequate for the relatively simple topologies needed for Layer 2 relays, but have limitations when working with more complex topologies of the network layer. Spanning trees can have only one active path between two bridges, although there are vendor extensions that allow multiply physical links to be treated as one path. Routing protocols allow much more complex topologies, the capability to continue forwarding while the RIB is reconverging, and much better load balancing.

The limitation on active paths does not use all the available bandwidth, which routers can do. In all-LAN environments, bandwidth is not as critical a resource as when WANs are involved, so the bandwidth efficiency is acceptable in switched/bridged workgroups and backbones.

Path Calculation and Routing Information Flooding

Two algorithms, using fairly different approaches, are widely used for the latter type of topology calculation: the *distance vector* and the *link-state* algorithms. Perlman characterizes them, respectively, as based on "local propagation of global information," and on "global propagation of local information" [Perlman, 1992]. You do not select whether a given protocol uses one or the other; the choice was made by the protocol designer. Routing Information

Protocol (RIP), Interior Gateway Routing Protocol (IGRP), and Enhanced Interior Gateway Routing Protocol (EIGRP) use distance vector, although EIGRP uses a significant variant called the diffusing update algorithm (DUAL). Open Shortest Path First (OSPF) and Intermediate System-to-Intermediate System (IS-IS) use link state, although OSPF uses distance vector in its core. BGP uses a different algorithm, *path vector*, which is beyond the scope of this discussion.

How does this propagation occur? Before discussing the algorithms involved, it's worth introducing the basic concept of an *area* in hierarchical routing. Area structures become appropriate in any network of appreciable size and are discussed in detail in Chapter 12.

How big does a network have to be before it reaches appreciable size? There is no hard and fast answer, but a reasonable rule is that a network with more than 50 to 100 routers, or more than 500 routes, needs hierarchical structure to function well.

So what is an area? At the very least, it is a collection of routers and routes. The boundary of an area really defines it from a functional standpoint. At a boundary, some routes are suppressed from propagating into other areas. Figure 5.4 illustrates that an area boundary is usually defined by routers that summarize, or aggregate, more-specific routes inside the area into less-specific *supernets* that are advertised into a backbone area. In general, if you inject a supernet into the backbone, you suppress more-specific components of that summary from being injected into the backbone. See "Advertising Holes" in Chapter 12 for an example of when you might want to advertise both a more-specific and a less-specific route.

In a distance-vector algorithm, each network entity generates a map of its paths to all connected nodes in the network, but only sends this map to its adjacent neighbors. Link-state algorithms are a mirror image of distance vector: They create cost maps only of the paths to their adjacent neighbors, but flood the entire routing domain (or area) with these maps.

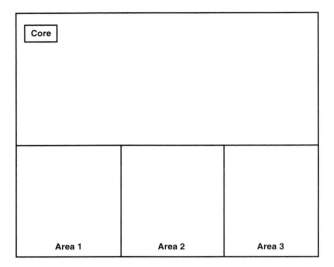

FIGURE 5.4 *Areas are points in a hierarchy at which addresses are summarized, and the resulting supernets are advertised into a backbone.*

Note

The concept of flooding through a routing domain or area is somewhat subtle. It certainly confused me when I first encountered it—how can a router physically flood information to routers that are not directly connected neighbors?

The answer is that a router logically, not physically, floods. In flooding, a router sends information to its neighbors. These neighbors copy the information, without changing it, and send it to their neighbors. In contrast, distance-vector routers always change the information before propagating it.

In contrast, distance-vector protocols create cost tables that contain the router's perception of the cost to all destinations, but pass them only to their neighbors.

Which algorithm is better? This is an example of a high-low architectural decision. There is no clear-cut answer, although most new routing protocols use link-state algorithms. The underlying logic might not be pure, as inter-area routing in OSPF actually uses distance vector [Moy, 1998]. Distance vector is an older idea than link state, but has evolved over time. Proponents of the advanced distance-vector algorithm have challenging arguments that their protocols are superior to link state in some cases. Advanced distance-vector protocols are less common than obsolescent or obsolete distance vector, so there is less operational experience with these approaches. The only commercially available advanced distance-vector protocol is Cisco's proprietary EIGRP, and the single vendor source for this makes the comparison even more difficult.

First-generation distance-vector protocols such as RIP, and second-generation distance-vector protocols such as IGRP, have no idea which router generated a route, and when that route was generated. As a consequence, a router running such a protocol can use old data to build its routing table and generate routes that have loops.

EIGRP has measures to prevent loop formation. Link-state algorithms do not generate routes containing loops, but are more resource intensive and can take longer to establish maps of the routing domain. Link-state routing protocol updates do contain the originator and age of the originator, and the third-generation distance-vector protocol, EIGRP, uses a new mechanism to prevent loops.

Traditional distance-vector algorithms are simpler and less resource intensive than link-state algorithms developed at roughly the same time, but can generate routes with infinite loops.

Assuming that dynamic routing is needed for a large network—and this is not a given—the practical choice for the primary unicast routing protocol is likely to be OSPF or EIGRP.

The OSI IS-IS routing protocol, which has been enhanced as Integrated IS-IS to include IP routes, can be appropriate for some specialized applications, or where it is already the primary dynamic routing protocol. IS-IS is primarily used in large Internet service providers, or in telecommunications operational networks where standards prescribe its use. For example, Synchronous Optical Network (SONET) management requires IS-IS. IS-IS might be gaining new interest, however; see the discussion of its enhancements in Chapter 14.

RIPv1 and IGRP are obsolete for modern applications in large networks. They might be present from older networks and need to coexist with the more modern protocols. Although RIP and IGRP can work in small networks, or in larger networks with extensive tuning, in general they converge much more slowly than modern protocols. They also cannot handle modern classless addressing. RIPv2 can handle classless routes, but does not have a real idea of summarization and does not offer any significant scaling advantages over RIPv1.

> **Note**
>
> *RIP was the first widely used dynamic routing protocol. Its original implementation, however, was not for IP, but for Xerox protocols. Derivatives of RIP are used in several protocol suites, including IP, Novell, and Xerox.*
>
> *Novell RIP is the same as IP or Xerox RIP. Besides the obvious differences that it carries Novell IPX addresses rather than IP addresses, it does not use hop count as its principal metric, only as a tie-breaker.*

There might be special cases for RIP as a host-to-router protocol. RIP version 2 can be adequate for small networks. Applications for RIP are discussed further in Chapter 6. RIP is discussed there, rather than in this chapter, because it is obsolete as a modern routing protocol and does not belong in a discussion of such protocols. RIP does have legitimate niche applications.

Modern routing protocols, such as EIGRP, OSPF, and IS-IS, all have sufficient local information so that they can recompute alternate routes without waiting for periodic updates.

When using modern routing protocols in all but the smallest networks, you want to design hierarchical routing networks. What is small? There is no hard and fast rule, but a small network certainly has no more than 500 routes or 50—100 routers.

In hierarchical routing, discussed at length in Chapter 12, you establish a system in which more-specific routes, those with longer prefixes, are summarized—aggregated—as they propagate to higher levels in a hierarchy. In OSPF and IS-IS, a boundary at which summarization takes place is called an *area*. Both of these protocols have a concept of two levels of areas, with a backbone and some number of non-backbone areas.

OSPF has a persistent topological database, a synchronized copy of which is in each router in an area. If these database copies are not consistent, the link-state algorithm will not work properly, so you must not filter topological announcements inside an area. From the local copy of this database, OSPF creates a transient routing table, and the best routes in it are sent to the RIB to be considered for installation there.

Although the idea of a full-fledged topological database is associated with link-state protocols, EIGRP does have internal topology tables beyond the main routing table. Each EIGRP router maintains a synchronized copy of viable routes in its directly connected neighbors.

Not needing to wait for a routing update to find a new path has important implications for speeding convergence time. Convergence is generally described as the time for a router to find a new set of paths. In detail, there are several meanings of convergence.

Convergence

Defining it very loosely, *convergence* in a router exists when the router has a valid path to all reachable destinations. Unfortunately, the term *convergence* often is used to describe distinct phenomena. These phenomena can be related, but you need to know the distance. Figure 5.5 shows a set of routers where convergence has more than one meaning. Factors involved in convergence include the following:

- Time needed to load an initial set of routes. If R5 were to come up after all the other routers were stable and fully converged, how long would it take for R5 to build a complete RIB?

- Failure detection time after which reconvergence can begin. When the link between R1 and R2 fails (Point 1), how long does it take R1 to detect the failure and begin the search for a new route?

- Time for an announcement of a new route to propagate from the most distant router to the local router. A special case for EIGRP is the time it takes for the local router to request information that is in the most distant router. If Network E (Point 2) fails, how long does it take for R3 and R4 to learn that Network E is no longer reachable? In hierarchical systems, R3 and R4 might never explicitly know that Network E is down, and this is completely appropriate. In Figure 5.5, R2 could be defined as a core router, hiding the left side details from the right. Network E, is shown as a dashed line because it violates the hierarchical model, directly connecting Areas 1 and 2.

- Rules that prevent route announcements for being accepted for a period of time.

- Delays before recomputing routing tables.

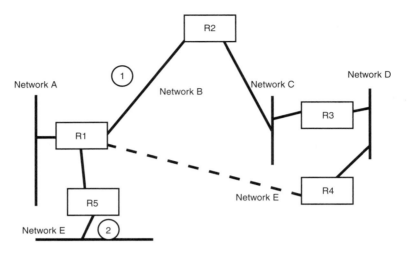

FIGURE 5.5 *You can state convergence time in several meaningful ways for this routing domain: of all routers, of routers in an area, or of a single router.*

The first case of convergence is *initial convergence*: the length of time it takes a router, after initialization, to find all reachable paths. It can be meaningful to differentiate initial convergence both for single routers and for a set of routers initialized at once.

A second basic case is the time it takes a single router to detect a failure and find a new route that takes it around that failure. Assume that the link between R1 and R2 fails. There is a potential route from R1 and R4.

Single router convergence after failure is the length of time that R1 needs to reroute its traffic to R4.

A special case is the time it takes R5 to learn that a directly connected router has an alternate path to the destination. EIGRP is especially fast in this case.

A more general case of convergence is the time it takes all routers to learn the correct routes to all destinations in a single area, or in the full domain. In large networks with unstable media, this *full domain convergence* condition might never be reached. If this condition is frequently not reachable, that forms a good argument to split the domain into smaller hierarchical areas. In a hierarchical routing system, it is meaningful to speak of convergence in individual subordinate or backbone areas. *Area* is used here in a general sense, not limited to formal areas in OSPF or IS-IS but also referring to areas of address aggregation in OSPF. The function of an area can be created in any protocol that supports arbitrary prefix lengths and has a summarization mechanism. EIGRP does not have a formal area mechanism, but it is quite practical to have the effects of areas in EIGRP.

Backbone convergence means that each subordinate area is reachable, although it is possible that some destinations in the area are unreachable. The details of unreachability, however, can be kept local to the area.

Figure 5.6 shows an example where both Areas 1 and 2 have both reachable and unreachable destinations. Areas 1, 2, and 3 are all reachable via the core. Areas 1 and 3 only advertise summaries of their routes into the core area. Area 1 hides the details of its internal reachability from the backbone, whereas Area 2 advertises its detailed routes into the backbone. The core area does not know, due to summarization and the resulting information hiding, that network 10.1.0.0/24 is down.

Perhaps counterintuitively to many beginners, having the 10.1.0.0/24 hidden from the core is usually excellent practice. The core attempts to send to that network by sending it to Area 1, but the actual network is a black hole. Depending on the specific protocols and configuration inside Area 1, either an ICMP destination unreachable is returned or there is no response at all.

Overall stability of the routing domain is the reason it is desirable to suppress details of the internals of Area 1. The core does not need to recompute its routing table whenever an intra-area route goes down.

There still can be legitimate reasons to advertise more-specific, non-summarized routes as done in Area 2. Area 2 has two border routers that give it connectivity to the core. If both routers ABR2a and ABR2b could reach 10.2.0.0/24 and 10.2.2.0/24, but ABR2a has a better intra-area path to the first network and ABR2b has a better path to 10.2.0.0/24, the core could use non-summarized routes to pick the optimal router to reach the Area 2 destination.

In general, stability is more important than obtaining the optimal route. If links are low-bandwidth or congested, as you might see with transoceanic links, the additional routing overhead for the core to pick optimal routes can be justified.

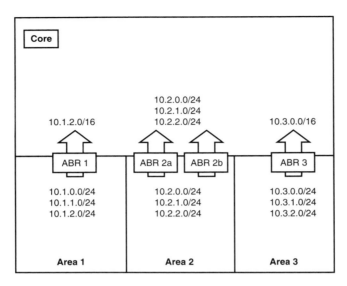

F IGURE 5.6 *Backbone convergence means that area 0.0.0.0 knows how to reach all desti-*
nations in its own area, and the edges of other areas.

When the backbone converges, it does not necessarily mean that all of the
nonzero areas have converged. The job of area 0.0.0.0 is to deliver traffic to the
area border router of a nonzero area that is advertising the destination. That
advertisement can be an explicit or summary route. If the nonzero area cannot
reach the specific destination, that is a problem of convergence in the nonzero
area, not area 0.0.0.0.

See Chapter 12 for a detailed discussion of designing with hierarchical areas. In
general, however, your network is more stable and more scalable if you hide
detailed routes inside areas and avoid frequent propagation of changes into the
backbone.

The Problem of Overloading Protocol Mechanisms

In object-oriented programming, there is an idea called *overloading*, in which
some mechanism that started with a single function has additional functions
assigned to it.

In first-generation routing protocols such as RIP, the mechanism of tracking
hop count served two purposes:

- Loop detection through count-to-infinity
- Route metric

The second-generation of distance vector, IGRP, deleted the second function of hop count. Link-state protocols developed at roughly the same time as IGRP do not use hop count, and EIGRP, a third-generation distance-vector protocol, also does not use hop count.

Hop Count and Loop Detection

Because all nodes in a distance-vector environment do not receive the same information at the same time, timing problems can occur. Unless care is taken, infinite loops could form when a path goes down but other nodes do not realize it. Simplistically, distance vector depends on routers notifying other routers that a path is no longer available. Unfortunately, if the path is not available because the router failed, there is no explicit notification. The connecting router implicitly learns about the remote router's demise, when the connecting router realizes it has not heard several consecutive updates from the failed router.

Routing systems generally follow a model called *hot potato,* or sometimes *closest exit*. The model follows the children's game of hot potato—catch a potato and toss it to the closest person—the object of the game is to get rid of the potato. In Figure 5.7, R2 sends its potato, or packet, to any router that seems capable of taking it. R1 has said it can send to Network C, and R2 does not know how R1 will do that.

Count-to-Infinity

The most basic mechanism that eventually stops the routing loop is called *count-to-infinity*. If, as is the case in RIP, the metric is the hop count, the hop count steadily increments as the routing loop continues. Eventually, the count reaches what is, in the context of a routing protocol, an infinite value. In RIP, this is 16. At 16 hops, a loop is assumed, and the route is marked unreachable.

RIP could have a hop count larger than 15, but if it did, it would take longer to detect loops. The value 16 means the destination is unreachable. Another way to say this is that there is an infinite cost to the destination, hence the term *count-to-infinity*. Count-to-infinity is the most basic loop detection mechanism, although real routing protocols, even RIP, have additional mechanisms such as split horizon and holddown timers. Count-to-infinity detects loops that have formed and removes them from the routing table, whereas newer mechanisms actively try to prevent loops. The mechanisms implemented in first and second generation distance-vector protocols, however, trade off convergence time against loop prevention, or limit the medium topologies that can be used. Fully satisfactory loop control only comes with link-state or third-generation distance-vector protocols. A timing problem, however, can cause loops to form. Remember that R2 also knows how to get to R3 and advertises routes to it. These are expensive routes for R1 that are not normally used.

Look at Figure 5.7 and think about the routing tables created after every medium is operational and the routers are fully converged. R1 knows how to reach the left medium, A, and knows the right medium, C, is reachable through R2.

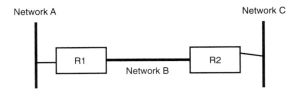

FIGURE 5.7   *A simple interconnected router example where count-to-infinity is the only means of loop detection.*

Now, consider what happens when the right router, R2, detects a failure on Medium C. R2 knows B is down and marks it unreachable.

But assume that just after R2 has marked B unreachable, an update arrives on Link B, and this update contains R1's total routing table. R1's table says it knows how to send to Network C. In a simple case, R2 does not note that R1's way of getting to Network C is to go to R2.

When R1 is told by R2 that Network C is unreachable, R1 marks C unreachable. But suppose that as it does so, R2 updates its table based on the previous update from R1, and now decides C is reachable, not through its directly connected interface, but through R1. Again assuming the most basic model of distance-vector routing, R2 sends an update to R1 saying C is reachable, and R1 assumes it can now reach C. Table 5.1 shows the progression of updates and R2's cost to Network C. It uses the RIP convention of a 15-hop maximum.

TABLE 5.1 R2'S RIB DURING A COUNT-TO-INFINITY.

Iteration	R1's Cost to Reach C Advertised to R2	R2's Computed Cost
1	1	2
2	2	3
3	3	4
4	4	5
5	5	6
6	6	7
7	7	8
8	8	9
9	9	10
10	10	11
11	11	12
12	12	13
13	13	14
14	14	15
15	15	infinite

Because all nodes in a distance-vector environment do not receive the same information at the same time, timing problems can occur. Unless care is taken, infinite loops can form when a path goes down but other nodes do not realize it. Simplistically, distance vector depends on routers notifying other routers that a path is no longer available. Unfortunately, if the path is not available because the router failed, there is no explicit notification. The connecting router implicitly learns about the remote router's demise when the connecting router realizes it has not heard several consecutive updates from the failed router.

Split Horizon

Hop count is being overloaded in the Figure 5.7 example, as both the routing metric and the loop detection mechanism. An early mechanism to prevent loops, other than count-to-infinity, is called *split horizon*. There are two types of split horizon. Simple split horizon prevents one router from re-advertising information about a route to the router from which it first learned it. *Poisoned reverse* sends an update back to the originator, but with an infinite metric to indicate the sending router believes the route to be down.

To see how split horizon works, look at Figure 5.8. The split horizon rule means that a router keeps track of the interface on which it first learned about a route. In Figure 5.5, R1 first learned about the existence of Network C over R1's interface to Network B.

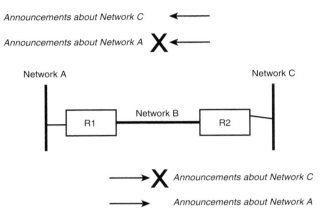

FIGURE 5.8 *Split horizon prevents a router from sending an offer to forward a destination over the same interface over which it first learned about the destination.*

As opposed to some managers I have worked for, R1 applies some common sense, assuming that the entity that first learned about something is apt to know the most about it. It assumes that R2 is closer to Network C, and R1 should not tell R2 about the existence of Network C. R2 is closer to Network C and knows more about it than does R1.

Split horizon has two beneficial effects. It reduces traffic by not sending routing updates to routers that already know about routes, and it prevents some count-to-infinity loops. Split horizon is generally a good thing for periodic-update distance-vector protocols. It is not needed with update-only protocols, be they distance vector or link state. EIGRP has mechanisms that obviate the problems split horizon is needed to correct.

Split horizon creates problems on some media types, as discussed in the section "Media Issues."

Split horizon with poisoned reverse helps prevent problems, but it does increase the size of routing updates because they must contain unreachable as well as reachable paths. The RIP RFC [RFC 1058] cites a horrible example:

Consider the case of a campus backbone connecting a number of different buildings. In each building, there is a gateway connecting the backbone to a local network. Consider what routing updates those gateways should broadcast on the backbone network. All that the rest of the network really needs to know about each gateway is what local networks it is connected to. Using simple split horizon, only those routes would appear in update messages sent by the gateway to the backbone network. If split horizon with poisoned reverse is used, the gateway must mention all routes that it learns from the backbone, with [infinite metrics]. If the system is large, this can result in a large update message, almost all of whose entries indicate unreachable networks.

Both forms of split horizon work. Simple split horizon generates less traffic, but can take longer to identify failures. One potential advantage of poisoned reverse is that it can be used by a router that is shutting down to tell its peers that it is doing so.

The original routing protocols were distance vector. They have continued to evolve. First-generation distance-vector protocols, such as RIP, use periodic update (and might use triggered updates), loop detection through count-to-infinity, hop count metrics, and loop prevention through split horizon and holddown. Perhaps the most important distinction between the two generations is the way in which they use hop count. First-generation protocols use hop count for a wide range of functions, including metrics and loop detection. Second-generation protocols have more intelligent metrics and additional loop detection mechanisms. Second-generation distance-vector protocols, such as IGRP, use a combination of periodic and triggered updates, loop detection by detecting increasing metric, complex metrics, and loop prevention through split horizon and holddown. Holddown can be turned off in most cases because the loop detection mechanism allows only transient loops. Second-generation distance vector does not have a hello mechanism.

Many courses and books are incorrect in the way they describe hello subprotocols, if they say that only link-state protocols have hello mechanisms. Hello subprotocols are an alternative to using periodic updates as a keepalive mechanism and have nothing to do with link-state or distance vector. Historically, hello subprotocols first appeared in link-state protocols, but that is a coincidence.

Holddown

Think of a small child who covers her ears to avoid hearing something that she finds confusing, screaming "I can't hear you!" Holddown is the routing equivalent. *Holddown timers* are another way of reducing loops at the expense of taking longer to recover from failures. After a router hears that a given route is down, it covers its ears for the holddown interval, to allow any confusing and out-of-date updates claiming the route is still up to flush out of the routing system. It allows time for unreliable routing updates to carry the bad news to all routers. RIP and IGRP use holddown in this traditional sense of the term.

OSPF optionally can use a mechanism called holddown, but is quite different from what RIP and IGRP do. In OSPF, the holddown time is the period to wait, after receiving a new update, to recompute the routing table. The intention is to reduce CPU loading by processing several routing updates in one computational batch. In link-state protocols, the time needed to recompute the entire routing table is not strongly linked to the number of new routes received. The new information goes into a database, and the entire database is consulted when recomputing routes.

EIGRP is a special case of distance vector, discussed at more length in the section "Third-Generation Distance Vector/DUAL: EIGRP." Briefly, it has a hello subprotocol, which allows triggered updates only and obviates the loop preventing need for holddown and split horizon.

Metrics in Modern Routing Protocols

Its metric is calculated from the same set of components, although the actual calculated values differ in IGRP and EIGRP. This calculation considers more variables than does the metric calculation in other routing protocols, but operational experience has shown the additional ones not to be terribly useful.

In practice, IGRP and EIGRP primarily base their metrics on bandwidth, as does OSPF in most implementations. In paths with a large number of hops, however, delay becomes a factor. I tend to associate bandwidth with delay, because the default delays are based on a standard bandwidth for the interface type. In other words, the default delay for an interface type does not consider long-delay media such as satellite links or heavily loaded IP over cable TV (CATV).

You can explicitly set a delay and will always want to do so on long-delay media. It is also good practice to estimate delay for slow links. Cisco assumes a default bandwidth of 1.544 Mbps on serial links. You can and should override this with the actual bandwidth. Setting the bandwidth, however, does not change the delay assumption; you need to set that explicitly. The delay of a 56 Kbps line is significantly more than that of a 1.544 Mbps line, and this should be set if your E/IGRP paths have more than two or three hops.

The E/IGRP algorithm does accumulate the delay associated with each hop, and on sufficiently long paths, delay becomes more significant than bandwidth. *Sufficiently* long is not determined by a simple formula; it depends on the actual link bandwidths, delay assumptions, and number of hops.

Periodic Versus Triggered Updates: Dead Routers

Look back at Figure 5.1. After R1 discovers the existence of Network C, does R1 really need to hear, every 30 seconds or so, that Network C is still up? Periodic announcements like that are a source of overhead. Whether they are needed, however, comes back to the classic network design answer, "It depends."

In this case, it depends on whether the routing protocol has another way to find out if R2 is down. Without a dead router detection mechanism, R1 has no way to tell if R2 was down (and Network C thus not reachable) or if Network C was still up because R2 did not tell R1 that Network C was unreachable.

Many references say distance-vector protocols do periodic updates, whereas link-state protocols do updates when something changes. The reality is that first- and second-generation distance-vector protocols happen to do periodic updates, but there is nothing inherent to distance vector that requires periodic updating. They can do triggered updates as well; IGRP does this and better RIP implementations do so.

The key to the matter of periodic updating is how routers handle a more general function, dead router detection. As long as one router knows that a given router is up, "No news is good news." If that router does not send a message that a given prefix is unreachable, the prefix can be assumed to be reachable.

How does a router know that another router is working? In the case of RIP and IGRP, the assumption is that a router sends out periodic updates. If it does not send out these updates, it can be assumed to be down.

More recent routing protocols such as OSPF, IS-IS, and EIGRP separate the dead router detection function from the topological update function. They use a low-overhead keepalive function called the *hello subprotocol*.

OSPF and EIGRP use their hello subprotocol for several purposes. Hello sub-protocol mechanisms are used to detect other routers and establish neighbor and adjacency relationships. After these relationships are established, the hello subprotocol is used for dead router detection.

Neighbor and Adjacency Relationships

Older routing protocols are relatively unselective in the routers they work with. Newer protocols try to be selective to optimize the use of bandwidth. In general, these newer protocols send updates only when they represent a significant change. They send the updates only to the routers affected by the changes. For example, OSPF routers on a multiaccess medium send changes only to designated routers (DRs), and the designated routers only send the most recent significant updates to non-designated routers. EIGRP routers do not propagate updates that do not change the routing table of the router that received the update.

Peering and Workload

Other optimizations can reduce the often significant amount of routing over-head information on links. EIGRP talks to all neighbors, but its diffusing update mechanism limits propagation of information that is not useful.

DR mechanisms in OSPF and IS-IS are a good example of traffic reduction optimization in broadcast networks, as illustrated in Figure 5.9. One of the router interfaces, in this case, is elected DR.

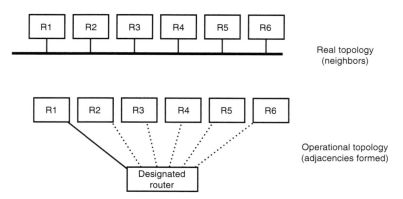

FIGURE 5.9 *On a broadcast multiaccess medium, one router interface is elected as the traffic cop, or designated router, for that medium.*

Conceptually, changes are sent only to that interface, where the designated router determines whether they are significant, and, if they are, sends them to other interfaces on the same medium. The designated router concept means that for N routers connected to a medium, there only needs to be (N-1) adjacencies rather than N×(N-1), if no designated routers were used. The DR listens for changes detected by the routers on its local medium and announces validated changes on their behalf.

There is also a *backup designated router (BDR)*, discussed later in this chapter in the section "Designated Routers." Chapter 11 expands on the designated router mechanism to explain when you should and should not influence which router becomes designated on a medium.

What Is It You Are Designating?

Designated router is inherently a confusing term. The OSPF term is closer to meaning *designated interface* for a specific medium. An OSPF router can be a designated router on some of its interfaces, a backup designated router on others, and a non-designated router on yet others.

After an OSPF router becomes designated, it stays the designated router as long as it is operating. Other routers activating on the same medium do not preempt its designated router status.

That means that trying to specify the DR for a segment is rather pointless, because whether or not the intended router is DR depends on the order in which the routers boot up. As long as a router's priority allows it to become DR, if a router is the first to initialize on a medium, it becomes the DR for that medium.

Media Issues

Although routing, in principle, is a logical process independent of the underlying transmission medium type, real-world routing is definitely affected by the medium. From the standpoint of distributing routing information, there are four basic medium types:

- Broadcast

- Nonbroadcast multiple access (NBMA), such as a packet switching service

- Point-to-point

- Demand, such as dialups

Most routing algorithms assume that a point-to-point or broadcast medium interconnects the relays. The effect of sending routing updates onto such a medium is primarily to reduce the bandwidth available for user traffic. Although the increase in bandwidth might not have a major impact on fast LANs, it can be noticeable on slower NBMA media such as Frame Relay. In addition, although a single multicast is heard by all routers on a hub-and-spokes NBMA medium, the same update needs to be copied by the hub routers to all the non-originating spokes. Such copying can make major processing demands on the hub router, potentially demanding a more expensive router with a more powerful processor.

The design issue here is to be cautious with using dynamic routing on NBMA networks. The main argument against dynamic routing on NBMA, using static routes instead, is that the spokes do not make use of full routing information. Even if a spoke with a full RIB was available, its next hop still is the hub router. More detailed routing information does not change the behavior of the hub router.

Sending detailed routing information to a spoke router, in fact, can be undesirable. Sending substantial information across a WAN consumes bandwidth. In addition, hub-and-spokes NBMA is often used to interconnect a data center site with many small sites. There is a good deal of cost sensitivity in spoke routers, because any small increase in CPU or memory resources, which requires more router hardware, is multiplied by the cost of that additional hardware at a large number of sites.

NBMA connectivity, however, often involves using a service that imposes an actual financial cost based on the amount of data transmitted. This cost can be a true packet or byte count as in X.25 or a charge for bandwidth as in Frame Relay. Transmitting routine routing updates, especially when they reflect no actual change in the topology, can become prohibitively expensive. See the section "RIP Workload and Convergence" in Chapter 6 for an example of the workload produced by RIP.

Active address discovery mechanisms usually depend on the existence of an underlying broadcast medium, as do mechanisms by which dynamic routers find their neighbors and establish adjacencies. Explicit configuration, or special software techniques, are needed to work around these limitations of NBMA and are discussed in Chapter 12.

Stub Media

Yet another scheme for reducing routing traffic recognizes that some routers serve stub networks, parts of a routing environment that do not contain routers that provide transit to other parts, as shown in Figure 5.10. One or more stub routers provide access to the stub area. The key that makes this a stub medium is that R1 and R2 do not exchange information over the shared medium. Their hierarchical superiors are aware of the stub routers, either from dynamic advertisements from the stubs or by static declarations.

Typically, you want to use stub routers for increasing reliability through reliability. You might also use them for load sharing if some of your hosts use one stub while other hosts use another stub as their default router. If you load share in this manner, you need to be protected against the failure of one stub router. See the section "Basic Router Location" in Chapter 6 for a variety of ways in which hosts can find routers, either initially or after a router failure.

Some routing architects call media connected to higher hierarchical levels via stub routers *leaf networks* to avoid confusion with OSPF stub areas, which means something different. Stub network probably is more frequently used.

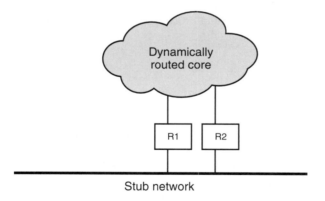

Stub network

FIGURE 5.10 *A stub network is a medium that has only one router on it, or possibly multiple routers if traffic cannot flow through the medium from router to router.*

It makes no sense for a stub router to propagate routing updates onto the stub medium, because there is no router in that area that can use the information. Many routing protocol implementations enable a router to learn that one of its interfaces serves a stub network. Routing updates are blocked from that interface. Within the stub medium, only the default route and local routing information is necessary, unless different stub routers are preferable to go to different destinations.

There is an exception where hosts on the medium listen for routing updates to find the default router. This technique, discussed in Chapter 6, really does not break the stub technique because the hosts listen for routing information but do not generate it.

Sharing Information Among Routing Sources

A route can be created in one routing process, and not only sent to the RIB, but alternatively sent to a different routing process. The receiving routing process can take the advertisement from the sending process and, with appropriate controls, re-advertise it as if the second process originated it. The general process of receiving routing information is *acceptance*. Acceptance most often refers to receiving information from the same routing process, but can refer to receiving information from a different process. The term *acceptance policy* describes the rules used to accept routing information.

When you exchange information between routing processes on the same router, you must ensure there is no feedback between them. Feedback occurs when Process 1 sends a route to Process 2, which (correctly) inserts the route into its own tables (Point 2), but then sends the translated route back to Process 1, as if it were a new route (Point 3). Process 1 now incorrectly assumes the existence of a route to the destination via Process 2, when in fact process 2 would send it back to Process 1.

Note

There is a subtle difference between what information is propagated and what information enters the RIB of a specific router. This difference is most pronounced with link-state routing protocols and with BGP.

A set of link-state routers—an area discussed in Chapter 10—must share the same database of topological information. When you filter routes with link-state protocols, you are suppressing them from entering the RIB, but not suppressing them from being propagated to other routers.

RFC 1812 gives the very good advice "Routing is one of the few places where the Robustness Principle (be liberal in what you accept) does not apply. Routers should be relatively suspicious in accepting routing data from other routing systems." Their level of suspicion should be greatest when they are working with routing information that is originated in one routing mechanism but manipulated by another; RFC 1812 goes on to say, "Routers must be at least a little paranoid about accepting routing data from anyone, and must be especially careful when they distribute routing information provided to them by another party."

When people speaking different languages, or even the same language in different cultures, and try to communicate, errors often occur. Routers that speak IP but with different dynamic routing protocols often have the same problem. *Redistribution* is Cisco's term, widely used in the industry, for the general acceptance of routing information from sources other than the current source. Its command syntax is rather obscure, and we will look at that in detail in Chapter 12.

More general terms are *importing* and *exporting*. One routing process learns from another when it imports routes from the other. Yet another term is to *inject* foreign routes into a routing process. A routing process establishes a relationship to another process and exports when it sends routing. See Figure 5.11 for an example of relationships among the RIB and two different routing processes.

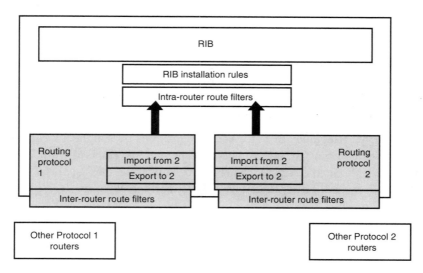

FIGURE 5.11 *Routing processes exchange routing information with peer routing processes, using the same protocol, in other routers. The processes can also exchange with dissimilar protocols in the same router and send some or all routes to the RIB.*

If a routing process imports from a process that does not export anything, no actual transfer takes place. In interior routing, this rarely happens, because the export and import rules usually are set up by the same person. In exterior routing with BGP, which deals with routing between different organizations, mismatches between importing and exporting policies are common errors.

Second, importing is logically just before installation in the RIB. It operates on true routes, not raw topology updates, so does not violate the rules of link-state protocols that all routers must synchronize their databases.

Third, routing protocols include various loop-prevention methods that they use internally. After different routing protocols share information, these automatic safeguards no longer apply. The design of the routing system involving redistribution should minimize the full mutual exchange of routing information and make it hierarchical whenever possible to simplify loop prevention. See Chapter 12 for details on the use of hierarchical redistribution.

Importing and exporting are mechanisms that can cause different routing behavior than might be seen with a single routing mechanism. Other mechanisms come into play when the routing system is hierarchical. Hierarchical design, and exceptions to it, are detailed in Chapter 12.

Dynamic Routing Using Distance Vector

Many people, in their childhood, played "telephone," in which each participant whispers a message to his neighbor, and each neighbor repeats the message to another person. In the game of telephone, the message often changes significantly through errors in *copying*.

Like the game telephone, distance-vector algorithms pass along a message, one in this case describing the cost to varying destinations. Hopefully unlike the game of telephone, the successive neighbors change the message but for the better. Each neighbor adds its additional cost to the costs of reachability in the message it receives.

Distance vector is also known as of the class of the old ARPAnet and the Bellman-Ford algorithm. It involves each node calculating the cost to adjacent or neighbor nodes and, after this computation is done at each distributed node, transmitting the resulting tables of costs (that is, the distance vectors) to all other nodes. Each node, on receiving distance vectors from other nodes, updates its tables to reflect m new destinations or lower-metric routes to previously known destinations.

Early distance-vector implementations did not do reality checks on routing updates. There's an old tale of a man who went into a liquor store and asked for a bottle of Remy Martin VSOP cognac. The merchant quoted him a price of $25, a rather good price!

Our customer, however, said, "The store down the street is offering it for $15." The merchant asked, "So why didn't you buy it?"

"Ah," the customer said, "they were out of stock."

Our hero responded, "My price, then, also is $15 when it's out of stock."

And so it is with some of the earlier distance-vector implementations. Receiving routers considered low price—low metric value—above all else and did not check whether the advertising router would actually provide connectivity to the destination.

In first- and second-generation distance-vector implementations, intermediate systems transmit routing tables (that is, the router's perspective of the network) at fixed times. IP RIP, for example, broadcasts every 30 seconds.

Oh, There Won't Be Any Peak Load Problem...

It has long been assumed that although distance-vector routers send updates at the same interval, that interval timer is relative to the start time on each router. Because the routers are initialized at different times, it was assumed the periodic updates would spread out over time, and there would be no bursts where every router simultaneously sent updates.

These assumptions have proven not to be true. Research by Sally Floyd and Van Jacobson [Floyd, 1994] has shown that periodic update routing mechanisms tend to weak synchronization. Weak synchronization is on the order of a few seconds, not microseconds as with a true time synchronization mechanism.

The gist of the problem is that routers usually reset their update timers when they receive an update from another router, so they can include the new information in the update they send out. Resetting the timer when updates are received turns out to be a working weak synchronization mechanism.

Improved implementations of distance-vector routing protocols, as well as other potentially periodic mechanisms such as ARP cache aging, now jitter, or randomize, the interval before periodic updates. A few seconds of randomization breaks weak synchronization. So, don't be surprised if some of your RIP routers send updates every 31, 33, 30, and 34 seconds on successive updates.

Some distance-vector–based protocols, such as Cisco IGRP, also transmit on an exception basis. This is known as *triggered updates* and is permitted but not required by the RIP standard.

Initially, the router knows about adjacent entities. On receiving a routing table, the router learns about derived entities. Assume that you have a row of four routers connected in a chain, shown in Figure 5.12. The middle routers learn about the stub routers after receiving the first set of updates. From this set, the stub routers learn about the middle router two hops distant.

All routers know about all other routers only after the third iteration of routing updates. This is a very simple example that does not deal with multiple paths or the possibility of a previously advertised route failing. RIP and IGRP do not have a reliable transmission mechanism for their routing updates, so sending repeated updates is also a means of protecting against updates being dropped due to line errors.

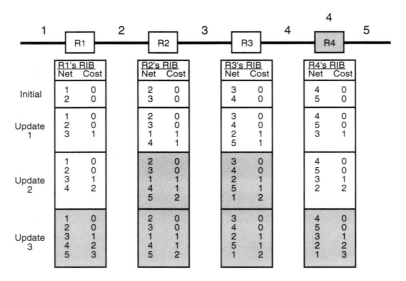

FIGURE 5.12 *Assuming periodic updates, R2 and R3 need two updates to converge (gray area), whereas R1 and R4 need three updates. You can see how this type of routing becomes slower and slower with more routers.*

In Figure 5.12, the middle routers know about all destinations after the second update. R2 and R3 are shaded to show they have reached *convergence*. R1 and R4 do not converge until the third update.

This is an ideal for convergence time. Adding loop avoidance features such as holddown can slow convergence of previously known routes even further.

Loop Detection and Prevention

Because all nodes in a distance-vector environment do not receive the same information at the same time, timing problems can occur. Unless care is taken, infinite loops can form when a path goes down but other nodes do not realize it. Simplistically, distance vector depends on routers notifying other routers that a path is no longer available. Unfortunately, if the path is not available because the router failed, there is no explicit notification. The connecting router implicitly learns about the remote router's demise when the connecting router realizes it has not heard several consecutive updates from the failed router.

These problems have had fixes of increasing efficiency in each generation of routing protocol development.

First-Generation Distance Vector: RIP Versions 1 and 2

RIP is widely implemented both in hardware routers and in software, such as the UNIX **routed** program. It is a simple distance-vector protocol that uses the count of intermediate systems between two endpoints as its routing metric. RIP is limited to networks of moderate size, as it allows no more than 15 router hops in the path between any two entities. All routers in a RIP network have the same view of the network; there is no hierarchy of routers.

RIP generates substantial amounts of routing traffic. As an alternative, OSPF generates much less traffic, but needs more intelligence to make routing decisions.

RIP, a representative distance-vector protocol, uses the following procedure:

- RIP routers keep routing tables with an entry for every possible routing destination in the system. These entries contain the address of next hop router, the router from which the route information came, and the hop count to the destination using that router's address.

- As shown in Figure 5.12, routers periodically send their routing tables to all adjacent routers. When a new update arrives, the receiving router adds 1 to each metric, reflecting the cost of forwarding to the receiving router.

- If the resulting cost to any destination is less than the cost to that destination in the receiving router's current routing table, a cheaper cost to that destination has been discovered. This new and better route replaces the old.

- There are several special cases of updating, some beyond the scope of this discussion. Assume that R2 has been told by R1 that R1 has a route to some destination, and R2 has stored this routing information in its own routing table.

- A distance-vector principle not widely implemented in RIP, but that can be in any RIP and is in IGRP, applies another reality test to updates. If a new update arrives from R1 that contains a cost to the destination that is greater than the cost (via R1) to the destination, R2 substitutes the new cost even if it is higher than the old. The underlying rationale for this is that R1 is in a better position to know the true cost than is R2. Holddown does not apply to updates of lower cost.

Version 1 of RIP (RIPv1) is widely implemented. The new RIPv2 adds variable length subnet mask support, optional authentication, operation over demand media, and the capability to multicast as well as broadcast updates. It still suffers from all the limitations of periodic update and is still a first-generation distance-vector protocol because it uses hop count both as its metric and as a loop prevention mechanism. I regard continued enhancements to RIP as rather like continuing to put processor upgrades into a PC—at some point, the fundamental design can't support better performance, and it is better to move to an entirely new machine.

Figure 5.13 shows the metrics that are computed for a RIP system with links of different speeds. RIP was originally developed for Ethernets of a single speed, so hop count was far more useful than it is in this case.

The routes to Networks 6 through 9 go through a slow link because going through that slow link minimizes hop count. For Network 6, the situation is especially ugly, because the routing system assumes that it has two equal-cost paths to the same destination. Many routers would automatically attempt to load balance over these two links, which are actually of quite different speed. Simple load balancing across lines of different speed can easily lead to performance problems, through such things as a high rate of out-of-sequence packets.

Figure 5.14 shows another ugly problem that can take place with dynamic routing protocols that do not keep information on potential routes, and which implement a holddown timer.

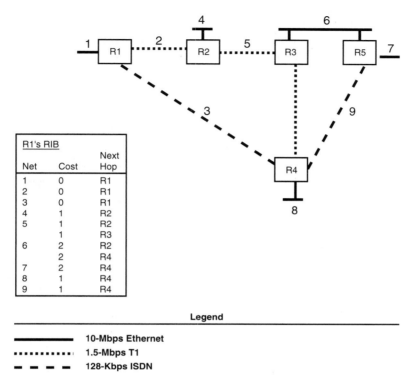

R1's RIB		
Net	Cost	Next Hop
1	0	R1
2	0	R1
3	0	R1
4	1	R2
5	1	R2
	1	R3
6	2	R2
	2	R4
7	2	R4
8	1	R4
9	1	R4

Legend

———————— 10-Mbps Ethernet

•••••••••••• 1.5-Mbps T1

— — — — 128-Kbps ISDN

FIGURE 5.13   *In this example of RIP routing, several routes being used by R1 are less than ideal, because bandwidth is not considered.*

In the symmetrical configuration in Figure 5.14, assume that all paths are equal cost and thus are load balanced. When the path from R1 to R3 fails, which is a path to R4 via R3, R1 is already using another path to R4, the top path via R2. R1 might spend a few seconds to learn the R1-R3 path is down and indeed might send a few packets to the interface now down. In general, however, R1 converges on using the right path within a time defined by the sum of the failure detection time and any delays programmed into interfaces. Interfaces might have programmed delays to avoid shutting down the interface in response to a very transient medium failure.

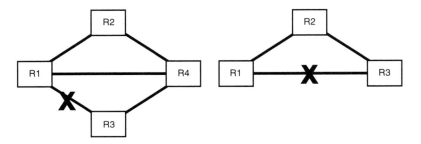

FIGURE 5.14 *There is a radical difference in convergence time between the symmetrical configuration of an even number of routers on the left, and the asymmetrical configuration of an odd number of routers on the right.*

The asymmetrical configuration in Figure 5.14 deals with a very different situation, in which there are no equal-cost paths and thus load balancing is impossible. When the R1-R3 link goes down, R1 is unaware that there is an alternate but more costly path through R2. After the failure detection time, it appears that R1 would learn about a new route to R3 after R1 receives a routing update from R2.

In basic RIP, however, when the failure is detected, a holddown timer is started. The holddown timer has a value of three times the update interval. Although the holddown timer is active, a router does not accept routes to a destination previously known to have failed.

In RIP, assuming instantaneous hardware failure detection, it takes at least 90 seconds (the holddown timer) for R1 to be able to receive the next update from R2, which arrives somewhere between 0 and 30 seconds after the holddown timer expires. Therefore, it takes at least 90 to 120 seconds for R1 to converge. Some RIP implementations use longer values for the holddown timers.

Failure detection times depend highly on the medium. FDDI and Token Ring networks send **beacon** signals when they lose the token, so there is a failure indication in less than one second. On serial interface where the carrier detect or clock signals are significant, or where there must be a certain average one pulse density in the digital stream, failures again can be detected in under one second.

Especially on WAN circuits, there can be transient dropouts of a second or more, but from which the medium recovers. As a result, the failure timer on a WAN link can be set to 5 seconds or more.

If you rely on a Layer 2 keepalive to detect whether a link has gone down, as on a serial link with LAP-B or Cisco HDLC, it usually declares a failure after missing three keepalives. The usual keepalive timer value is 10 seconds, so it takes about 30 seconds to detect a failure.

On Ethernet-family media, where there is no Layer 2 keepalive, you usually have no choice other than to depend on Layer 3 routing protocols as a means of knowing a link is up or down.

So, in RIP, convergence in the asymmetrical case can take as long as 90 seconds of failure detection, 90 seconds of holddown, and 30 seconds of waiting for an update. IGRP's updates are less frequent, so it takes even longer unless IGRP holddown is disabled. Disabling IGRP holddown often is a good idea, because IGRP, as opposed to RIP, has other loop detection mechanisms.

Second-Generation Distance Vector: IGRP

IGRP began the unloading of hop count from the metric calculation. Rather than use hop count, IGRP introduced a complex metric, primarily based on bandwidth but that usually considers delay. IGRP does count hops, but only for the purpose of loop detection. Taking the same network as was used in the RIP horrible example in Figure 5.13, the same topology, when IGRP is used, produces the much better routes of Figure 5.15.

IGRP also unloaded some of the use of topological updating. Although it does use periodic updates to find new usable routes, it sends triggered updates as soon as it detects a failure.

Officially, IGRP is a patented and proprietary protocol. In practice, specifications for it are widely available [Hedrick, 1991]. Cisco appears to have no difficulty with these reverse-engineered specifications being available, although it has insisted on its proprietary rights if anyone tries to implement IGRP on hosts.

IGRP improves on RIP failure handling. Triggered updates and split horizon, in principle, prevent loop formation. But unusually long update propagation times, connectivity failures, and so on can prevent these mechanisms from preventing loops.

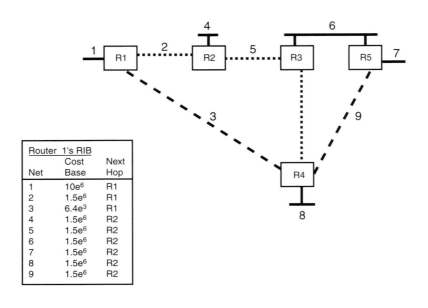

Router 1's RIB		
Net	Cost Base	Next Hop
1	$10e^6$	R1
2	$1.5e^6$	R1
3	$6.4e^3$	R1
4	$1.5e^6$	R2
5	$1.5e^6$	R2
6	$1.5e^6$	R2
7	$1.5e^6$	R2
8	$1.5e^6$	R2
9	$1.5e^6$	R2

Legend

────────	**10-Mbps Ethernet**
··············	**1.5-Mbps T1**
─ ─ ─ ─	**128-Kbps ISDN**

FIGURE 5.15 *IGRP does a much better job than RIP of path determination when links have different bandwidth.*

IGRP was a fine protocol when introduced and offered significant advantages over RIP. IGRP knows the difference between links of different speed and generates less routing update overhead than RIP. Cisco optimized IGRP for stable networks and traded off lowered overhead against slower conversion by transmitting updates less frequently than does RIP. Although IGRP convergence time can be improved with tuning, when its default settings are used, it can take many minutes for it to converge.

Both EIGRP and OSPF offer significant advantages over IGRP, and it makes no sense to implement IGRP in new networks. IGRP runs directly over IP. There is a 12-byte fixed header and 14 bytes per route up to a maximum of 46 updates per packet. By default, the entire routing table, other than routes suppressed by split horizon, is transmitted every 90 seconds.

For details of IGRP packets and debugging, see *CCIE Professional Development: Routing TCP/IP, Volume I* [Doyle, 1998].

IGRP Updates, Timers, and Loop Control

Triggered updates are sent immediately, when an IGRP router detects a topology change such as failure of a route. If this update propagates rapidly, each router that receives an update indicating a route is down marks the route as "possibly down," and blackholes traffic to it. Those receiving routers, in turn, are required to propagate the failure notification.

If holddown is enabled, the blackholed route cannot be replaced by a new route until the holddown timer expires (default holddown timer value 280 seconds) or a route with a lower metric arrives. If the route remains blackholed, it is removed from the RIB after the purge timer expires (default purge timer value 630 seconds).

By default, IGRP does use a holddown timer. One of the second-generation features of IGRP allows it to disable the holddown mechanisms in most cases. IGRP tracks hop count, not as a metric but as a means of hop detection.

It is assumed that if the hop count on a given route begins to increase steadily, or the metric increases by more than 10%, it is a warning that a loop exists. IGRP removes the route when it sees this behavior. Hedrick comments [Hedrick, 1991]: "In general, distance-vector algorithms adopt new routes easily. The problem is completely purging old ones from the system. Thus a rule that is overly aggressive about removing suspicious routes should be safe."

There is at least one case where turning off holddown can be a bad idea. On very low-speed lines, probably 9.6 Kbps or less, disabling holddown causes an increase in the number of poisoned updates sent out. Poison routes have an infinite cost. In networks with a large number of routes that are down, this additional routing traffic can overwhelm a slow link.

The IGRP/EIGRP Metric

IGRP and EIGRP use a complex metric algorithm, with minor scaling differences between the two protocols. In practice, the metric both protocols use is primarily based on bandwidth.

Figure 5.15 shows a practical set of IGRP routes. The actual metric value is a complex and non-obvious value and, in practical cases, reduces to being based on the bandwidth and, to a lesser extent, delay. Figure 5.15, therefore, uses the bandwidth for simplicity rather than the actual IGRP metric.

Bluntly, the IGRP metric was designed to consider factors that are generally beyond the scope of what, today, we reasonably think unicast routing protocols can do well. Some of its ideas were quite reasonable, such as assuming that the interval between routing updates could be increased, in stable networks, to reduce overhead.

In general, IGRP's metric has components that seem like good ideas when first examined, but do not work well when deployed. Delay, utilization, and error rates need dynamic feedback that is not within the view of a single router. For an example of the state of the art in examining these factors, see the section "Dynamic Load Sharing" in Chapter 14.

It certainly can be useful to base a metric on bandwidth in IGRP and EIGRP. In principle, you might want to prefer a low-delay terrestrial path over a long-delay satellite path. In practice, people who have satellite links tend to explicitly traffic-engineer for them with static routes. The delay of which IGRP is aware is manually configured and does not include transient and variable delay due to congestion or bursts of errors. Variable delay, however, tends to be more important than fixed delay in quality of service.

So, to a large extent, this discussion of IGRP/EIGRP metric is historical. Bandwidth is a reasonable basis for a metric, delay can be on occasion, but the other parameters have not proven useful for dynamic routing.

The Cisco **metric weights** command controls which of the metric components are used in calculating the metric on a specific router. Cisco's own *Command Reference* does not define all the values in this command, but simply recommends, "Due to the complexity of this task, we recommend that you only perform it with guidance from an experienced system designer." These weights can be different on different routers; IGRP and EIGRP messages carry the metric components, not the composite metric. This command is written as

```
metric weight tos K1 K2 K3 K4 K5
```

where it can be defined as the following:

- *K1* is the weight for bandwidth, with default value 1.

- *K2* is the weight for utilization, with default value 0.

- *K3* is the weight for delay, with default value 1.

- *K4* and *K5* are used in reliability calculations, with default values of 0.

- **tos** is a type of service value for the TOS bits in the IP header, which are not used in any known network. I refer here to the true TOS bits of the TOS field; the precedence bits are very definitely used in differentiated service (see Chapter 13).

To compute the bandwidth component of the metric, find the lowest bandwidth on any link in the path and divide 10^7 by the lowest bandwidth. Call this value **BW**.

Remember Cisco bandwidths are expressed in kilobits. If you do not set an explicit interface bandwidth, the IOS defaults to an interface-specific default. Unfortunately, this means T1 bandwidth on any serial line that does not have a **bandwidth** statement. Get into the habit of coding bandwidth statements on all serial interfaces and subinterfaces. On Frame Relay subinterfaces, code the Committed Information Rate (CIR) as the bandwidth.

To compute the delay component of the metric, sum all the interface delays in the path and divide by 10. Unless you explicitly configure **interface delay** in units of tens of microseconds, the router assumes a fixed delay value that is a constant for each interface type. To set the delay most accurately for each interface, sum the forwarding delay, the medium propagation delay for 1 bit, and the transmission time for 1500 bits.

In the following metric formula, the weights **K** are coefficients for each of the components. A coefficient of 0 causes the component to be zeroed and drop out of the formula, whereas a coefficient of 1 includes in the calculation:

Metric = (K1 × BW)
+ (K2 *× BW)/(256-load)
+ K3×delay

Using the default weights, the metric reduces to:

Metric = BW + delay

Nonzero values of K5 cause an additional calculation to reflect reliability:

Metric = Metric × [K5/(reliability + K4)]

Third-Generation Distance Vector/DUAL: EIGRP

EIGRP is another evolutionary step in distance vector. Internally, EIGRP is a completely different protocol than IGRP. The only similarities are in the configuration commands and the metric computation. IGRP is upwardly compatible with EIGRP in the sense that EIGRP can accept routing updates sent to it by IGRP, not that the internal algorithms are at all similar. See "IGRP to EIGRP Migration" in Chapter 12.

EIGRP's algorithm is called the *diffusing update algorithm (DUAL). It* was developed by J. J. Garcia-Luna at Stanford Research Institute. Garcia-Luna was not involved in Cisco's implementation of EIGRP. Several of the Cisco product architects have made strong arguments that properly designed distance-vector algorithms have distinct technical superiority over link state. Link-state partisans point to the evolution of their protocol family.

EIGRP completely unloaded hop count and removed it from any role. It uses the same metric as IGRP, but has separate hello subprotocol and reliable update mechanisms that do away with most distance-vector looping problems.

In RIP and IGRP, loops are formed by old information. A significant reason that old information is propagated is the use of periodic updates. When the information distribution mechanism becomes change-only, there is no periodic updating with stale information. To have change-only mechanisms, you need a hello subprotocol so you can detect dead routers. Until you can reliably detect dead routers, you cannot distinguish between not receiving an update because there has been no change and not receiving an update because the router that would have sent it is down or unreachable.

Tip

Like its first OSPF implementation, the first EIGRP release from Cisco had significant problems. To run reliable EIGRP, you must use the rewritten version, which is available in IOS release 10.3(11) and later 10.3 versions, in IOS 11.0(8) and later 11.0, in 11.1(3) and later 11.1, and any 11.2 or later release.

Both OSPF and EIGRP use the term *adjacency*, but in somewhat different ways. An OSPF adjacency is an agreement between two routers that they want to exchange routing information. OSPF does not form adjacencies with all neighbors on the same medium.

EIGRP, on the other hand, does form adjacencies with all of its neighbors, as long as there are no errors. EIGRP considers an adjacency a virtual path over which routing information is exchanged. At initialization, the new router receives all routes and their metrics, known to its neighbors. The receiving router computes a metric of the sum of the route metric sent by the neighbor and the cost of the receiving router's link to the neighbor.

The new router can receive several updates that point to the same destination. It computes the feasible distance (FD) to that destination, which is the lowest computed cost to that destination. For example, a router might receive two updates about the same route, one from R1 with a metric of 100, and the other from R2 of 50. The receiving router's link to R1 might add a cost of 50, but the slow link to R2 might have a cost of 200. The feasible distance is 100, the cost to reach the destination via R1.

When the receiving router evaluates the routes, it applies the feasibility condition (FC) test. FC is true if a neighbor's advertised distance (that is, route metric) to a destination is lower than the current router's feasible distance to the same destination.

When FC is true for a neighbor's advertised route, the neighbor becomes a *feasible successor* for that destination. EIGRP's approach to loop prevention depends on feasible successors and the feasibility condition. A looping path, one that goes back through the current router, always would have a metric greater than the FD. The router rejects such a path, making EIGRP loop-free.

EIGRP Implementation

EIGRP runs directly over IP. There are five packet types, all with a common header shown in Figure 5.16 [Doyle, 1998]. Packets are variable in length, with a fixed header followed by a variable number of variable-length type-length-value (TLV) data elements. Packets are transmitted as unicasts, or as multicasts that do not propagate beyond the local medium. They may or may not be acknowledged, depending on the protocol type. MD5 cryptographic authentication was added in IOS Release 11.3.

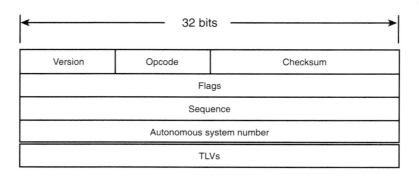

FIGURE 5.16   *The EIGRP Packet Header.*

Following are the five currently used EIGRP packet types:

- Update
- Query
- Reply
- Hello
- IPX SAP

The metric is carried in a TLV structure, which is representative of any information carried in a TLV. Figure 5.17 shows the TLV for the EIGRP metric components. How is this level of detail relevant to design? It's worth knowing that EIGRP updates are fairly small, smaller than link-state updates in OSPF and IS-IS, and that they contain metric components rather than the computed metric.

EIGRP's IPX and AppleTalk TLV's are beyond the scope of this text.

The metrics are calculated with the same algorithm used by IGRP, but scaled by a factor of 256 to allow finer granularity. In other words, the factors that go into computing the metric are the same in IGRP and EIGRP, but the result of the computation is multiplied by 256 in EIGRP.

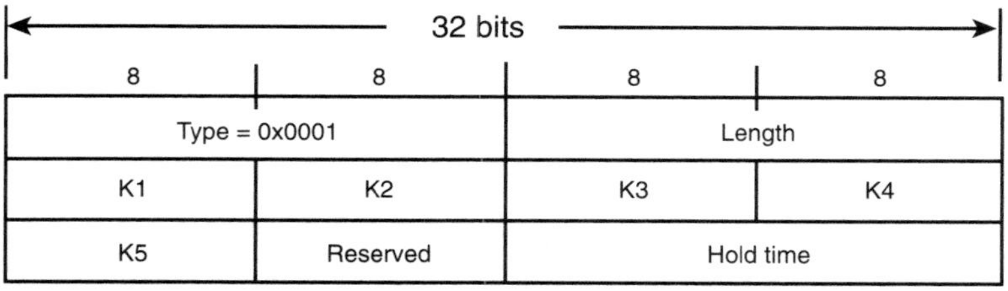

FIGURE 5.17 *EIGRP metric components, not the metric itself, are carried in a TLV structure.*

DUAL has certain requirements for lower-level protocols:

- If a router loses connectivity with a neighbor or gains a new neighbor, the router must detect this within a finite time.

- Protocol messages sent must be received, in a finite time, correctly with respect to bit correctness and packet order.

- When routers send out messages about changes in link cost, link or router failures, or new routers, these change messages are processed one at a time by the receiver, in first-in, first-served sequence.

These requirements are carried out, in Cisco's implementation, by the first two functions listed in the following [Farinacci, 1993]:

- *Neighbor discovery/recovery*. This is done by multicasting hello packets.

- *Reliable Transport Protocol*. EIGRP is selective in requiring all packets to be transferred reliably. The protocol verifies checksums and sequence numbers.

- *DUAL finite state machine*. This is the actual route computation engine.

- *Protocol-dependent modules*. Architecture-specific information for IP, AppleTalk, and Novell IPX. This currently is kept separately, and only if the particular architecture is configured.

A key difference of EIGRP from the routing protocols that preceded it is that EIGRP uses a formal hello subprotocol. This lets it discover neighbors and exchange routes with them secure in the knowledge the peer router is alive.

EIGRP's *topology table* is the list of all routes to all destinations and the identity of routers that have advertised those routes. The EIGRP routing table contains the best routes from the perspective of EIGRP. The EIGRP routing table, in turn, is distinct from the RIB, which contains the routes the router actually uses to forward packets.

For each reachable destination, the topology table contains the following [Doyle, 1998a]:

- Feasible distance of the destination.

- All feasible successors.

- Each feasible successor's advertised distance to the destination.

- The metric to the successor, relative to the current router.

- Information that identifies the interface that connects the current router to the feasible successor.

Next, EIGRP's hello subprotocol discovers the directly connected routers. Figure 5.19 shows, functionally, how copies of the routing tables of the neighbors are stored in each router. These are the routes being used by the neighbors for forwarding, not every potential route used by the neighbors. This restriction prevents loops.

Many presentations about EIGRP suggest that EIGRP routers contain synchronized copies of the routing tables of their neighbors. Cisco does not release the actual data structures inside the EIGRP code; however, it is significant that there is no command to display the neighbors' tables, although there are commands to display the neighbor and topology tables. It is a useful simplifying assumption, however, to think of the routers as having copies of their neighbors' tables. Because we are concerned here with functionality more than the actual protocol exchanges, this assumption is used in the discussions of EIGRP behavior.

By default, EIGRP hellos are sent every 5 seconds, except on NBMA interfaces with a physical access speed of T1 or slower. In the latter case, the default for hellos is 60 seconds. The hello interval can be set on a per-interface basis with the **ip hello-interval eigrp** command. When comparing EIGRP's convergence time to that of other protocols, you can compare them fairly only when the hello timers are set to the same interval. OSPF, for example, defaults to 10 seconds.

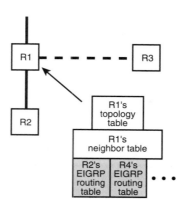

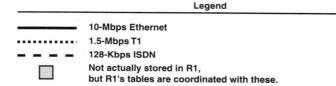

Legend

━━━━━━	10-Mbps Ethernet
··············	1.5-Mbps T1
▬ ▬ ▬ ▬	128-Kbps ISDN
☐	Not actually stored in R1, but R1's tables are coordinated with these.

FIGURE 5.19 *Copies of the routing tables of the discovered neighbors are stored in each router.*

EIGRP continues to exchange hellos with its neighbors, using the hello subprotocol for dead router detection. As long as a neighbor remains alive, a router can assume that neighbor has no new routing information.

Learning About Non-adjacent Routes

As EIGRP learns about routes from its neighbors, it calculates its cost to reach the neighbor to the cost calculated from the metric factors in updates it receives. Like IGRP, the metric is not carried in the update, but the update carries factors from which the metric can be calculated. If the combined cost is lower than the cost of the route currently in use by the receiving router, the newly received route is better and replaces the old. If the costs are equal, the new route is added to the EIGRP routing table as eligible for load balancing. After a route is added to the EIGRP routing table, it is passed to the RIB installation process.

Data structures formed after initial convergence are shown in Figure 5.20. Each router has its own EIGRP routing table and copies of its neighbors' tables.

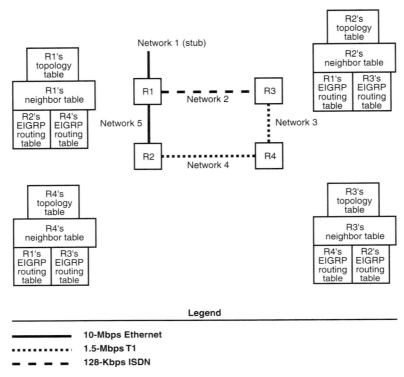

Legend

─────────── **10-Mbps Ethernet**

············· **1.5-Mbps T1**

— — — — **128-Kbps ISDN**

F I G U R E **5.20** *The adjacent routers have found one another. The best path for R4 to send to Network 1 is via the 10 Mbps path through R1. R3 also uses this path to reach Network 1.*

Learning Better Routes

When a feasible successor is found, it is moved from the topology table to the routing table. This changes the routing table, which in turn requires the router to update its neighbors with new routing information.

If the advertisement comes from the router that the receiving router had been using as the next hop, and the new cost is higher than the old, the receiving router checks to see if a lower-cost route exists through a different neighbor.

The receiving router scans through the tables of all its neighbors to see if there is a lower-cost path than the one it just received. Remember that this search is being done in local memory and involves no waiting for updates.

If the neighbor that had been used as the next hop fails to exchange hellos and is assumed dead, the same basic search for alternatives begins by scanning through the local-memory-resident tables of all other neighbors. EIGRP looks for *feasible successors* to the failed route, which is a route with a cost equal to or less than the metric used by the current router for the failed route and is in active use by another router. Failed routes, of course, have infinite cost. Applying the feasibility condition prevents loops.

Imagine this scenario using the topology of Figure 5.20: if R3 had first learned about Network 5 from R2, it would use the slower path R3-R4-R1 to Network 5. Subsequently, R4 would tell R3 of the faster path available to Network 1 via R4 and Network 5. R3 would realize that the R3-R2-R1 path is lower cost and replace the R3-R4-R1 path in R3's active EIGRP routing table.

R3 would also change its own active table to reflect its new cost to reach Network 1. The change in an active route of a routing table causes the following:

1. An update to be sent to R2 and R4.

2. Diffusion toward D to stop because R4 already knows the route.

    R2 to look at the new route and compare it with the cost of its current route to Network 1. Even though the new route uses an additional hop, the cumulative bandwidth is lower, and the new route is lower-cost than the one R2 has been using.

    Over a sufficiently large number of hops, delay becomes a more important metric component than bandwidth. For a small numbers of hops with fast links, delay is not significant.

    R2 updates its own routing table and informs its neighbors it has done so.

3. R3 to change its copy of R2's routing table, but does not change its own routing table. R3 does not propagate the change in R2's table to R3's downstream neighbors, because the change does not affect R3.

When a router receives an EIGRP update from a neighbor, it checks its own table and the tables of its neighbors to see if it already has a working route to the destination.

Failure Recovery

Topology table entries are in one of two states, *active* or *passive*. Think of the active state as one in which the router is searching for a way to reach the destination, because it cannot find a route to the destination from its locally stored information. The router goes into the active state for a specific destination when the router itself does not have a feasible successor to the destination. Passive is the normal case; active is entered only when the router does not have a feasible successor next-hop to one of its destinations.

If a router sees that one of its routes has failed—gone to an infinite cost—it first checks whether one of its neighbors has a feasible route to the destination. When a router is looking for a feasible successor in locally stored tables, the destination is in the *passive* state.

As shown in Figure 5.21, assume that Network 5 goes down. When Network 5 fails, R4 no longer has connectivity to R1. R1 deletes R4's routes from its table and vice versa. R4 has only one neighbor, R3.

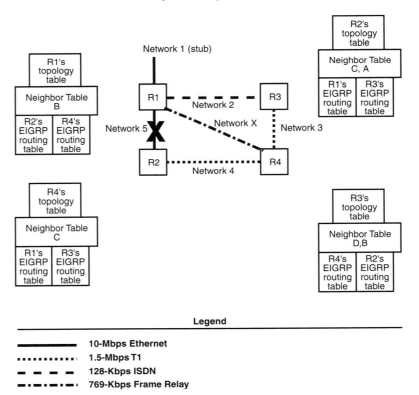

Legend

────────	**10-Mbps Ethernet**
··············	**1.5-Mbps T1**
─ ─ ─ ─	**128-Kbps ISDN**
─·─·─·─·	**769-Kbps Frame Relay**

FIGURE 5.21 *A failure occurs after convergence. EIGRP needs to find new routes. Network X is added to this picture to show alternatives ways to find new paths.*

R4 passively looks at its topology table and sees if it has a feasible successor to reach Network 1. If R4 does not have a feasible successor, it puts its entry for Network 1 into the active state and sends queries to its neighbors. Before getting into details of how R4 determines that R3 does not have a viable alternate path, look at the problem informally.

R3 had connectivity to Network 1, but R3 was forwarding to R4. If R4 forwards traffic destined to Network 1 to R3, a loop would be formed. Loops are not good things.

Case 1: R3 Is a Feasible Successor

If Network X links R3 to R1, R3 is a feasible successor for R2 to reach R1. R2, on detecting a failure of Network 5, examines its copies of its neighbors' tables—in this case, R3 is the only remaining neighbor—and is a feasible successor to R1. The metric in this R3 entry would have a cost to R1 less than the now-infinite cost in R2.

This is a *passive* solution to finding an alternate path. R4 moves the R3 path into its own RIB table and then sends an update to R3.

Case 2: No Network X, Active Resolution Needed

Let's assume there is no Network X, and R3 has been communicating with R1 via R2. This is shown in Figure 5.22.

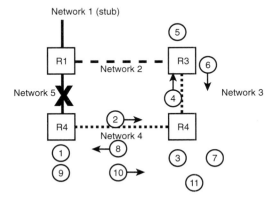

FIGURE 5.22 *In this configuration, R2 must go active to find an alternate path.*

9. R4, remember, has put this route in the active state and is blackholing traffic to it. If R4 has multiple outstanding queries, it has to wait until all of them are received. In this case, there is only one outstanding query. R4 moves the new route from its copy of C's routing table into its own active table.

10. R4 sends R3 a copy of its updated table. R1 is no longer a neighbor of R4, because Network 5 is down.

11. R3 updates its copy of R4's new table and then needs to let R4 know about the updates to R3.

Dynamic Routing Using Link-State Routing Protocols

In link state, also called the *shortest path first (SPF)* algorithm, each node determines which other nodes are adjacent to it and, with this information, sends information about the links to which it is directly connected. Link-state protocols are sometimes called new ARPAnet, in recognition of one of the first implementations. They are also sometimes called Dijkstra routing, after the developer of the main path determination algorithm.

A link is *not* a route. There are two basic types of link, *router links* with directly connected media and *media links* with directly connected router interfaces.

Two link-state protocols have been deployed in a significant number of IP networks, OSPF and IS-IS. Link-state protocols have been used in proprietary DECnet/OSI, IBM, Novell architectures, and also the Private Network-to-Network Interface (PNNI) ATM routing protocol discussed in Chapter 14.

Besides the obvious difference in the addresses used (IP and OSI), IS-IS and OSPF are quite similar. Both use link state algorithms. Both allow multiple levels of default route. Both use designated routers to minimize routing overhead traffic.

OSPF and IS-IS use different terminology for similar concepts. OSPF calls the topology messages it sends out *link-state advertisements* (LSAs), whereas IS-IS calls them *link-state packets* (LSPs). In this book, OSPF terminology is used when not referring specifically to IS-IS.

Not all messages sent out by link-state protocols have link-state information. OSPF and IS-IS both have hello sub-protocols.

EIGRP also has a hello subprotocol. EIGRP's default interval between hello messages is 5 seconds, whereas OSPF's default is 10 seconds. With all other factors being equal, the protocol with the more frequent hellos detects failures faster and, consequently, converges faster. The two protocols show little difference in convergence time when they have their hello interval set to the same value. In some topologies, EIGRP might be faster, and in other topologies, OSPF might be faster. In either protocol, convergence time is quite fast in comparison with RIP and IGRP.

Distance-vector protocols typically use less CPU than do link-state protocols. The CPU usage in distance vector also is spread over time, whereas the usage in LS protocols tends to be bursty and potentially needs more CPU power.

There are theoretical arguments that distance-vector protocols can deal with incorrect routing information better than can link-state protocols. In general, however, neither type can tolerate flatly incorrect information, as might come from buggy router code.

Link-state routers normally do not advertise routes from a routing table. They advertise link states. The algorithm is quick to adapt and does not produce loops, but is resource intensive.

Each router receives link states from all other routers in its OSPF area. An area is a collection of routers and addresses within a hierarchical OSPF routing domain. The underlying propagation process is called *flooding*. The router merges these into a tree of paths/metrics to every destination from its own perspective (that is, with itself as root). It then uses a protocol-specific algorithm to select the best route to each destination, pruning less optimal routes from the tree.

Note

Real implementations do not build the tree and then prune. In the interest of computational efficiency, the modified Dijkstra algorithm used in practical link state begins by building the tree at the root and tests each incremental path to see if it is more expensive than the path already in the tree. If the new information would result in a more expensive tree, it simply is not added. Tony Lauck, then at Digital Equipment Corporation, is credited with the computational improvements over the original algorithm defined by Edgser Dijkstra.

Routers can detect failures of other routers during the process of examining the tree. The router doing the detection notices that another router, which it learned about in a previous LSA, has adjacencies only to media that are known to be down.

In general, link-state protocols converge on a set of routing rules faster than do distance-vector environments, but more computation is required than in distance vector. In most networks, EIGRP probably takes less memory than OSPF, but there are topologies where the reverse might hold. EIGRP could use more memory when the router has a very large number of neighbors for which it must track topology.

Large networks need to be designed hierarchically if they are to scale. Link state is less tolerant of badly designed topologies than are distance-vector protocols, but casually designed large networks using distance vector, even EIGRP, eventually get into scaling problems.

Clueful or Classful?

An eminent routing engineer and I were chatting over drinks at one IETF meeting. We were idly discussing the EIGRP versus OSPF debate, and he made what I consider the definitive comment: "To build large networks, you have to have a clue [hic]. But using EIGRP allows you to stay clueless longer than if you were using OSPF."

Traffic characteristics of LS and third-generation distance vector differ from those of first- and second-generation distance-vector protocols. There is usually a large burst of routing updates when the environment first comes up, and then relatively few on an exception basis. In contrast, distance vector has a steady flow of periodic updates. Over a long term, link state probably produces less traffic.

Any routing protocol that stores alternate route information—information about less preferred routes that might become desirable after a failure— has an increased traffic load at initialization. This applies both to OSPF and EIGRP.

Tip

If your routers are operating near the limit of their CPU capacity, you might be able to control the peak loads somewhat by the order in which you initialize routers. Start at the core of your network and work out to the edges.

Because you rarely have the opportunity to bring up the entire network from the initial state, starting from the core and working outwards is rarely practical in an operational network. Nevertheless, it remains one of the techniques to have in your toolbox to deal with specific situations.

OSPF

OSPF is an interior routing protocol intended to remove some of the limitations of RIP. It is designed to scale for use in very large networks, and it achieves this primarily with numerous mechanisms intended to reduce routing table size and the volume of routing updates. It also does not use the limiting hop count metric, but uses an arbitrary metric defined by the system administrator.

Hop count can be adequate when all links are the same speed, but does not reflect the realities of mixed bandwidth on WANs and LANs.

Generation Gaps Between RIP and OSPF

If you come to OSPF from a RIP background, you might perceive it to be enormously more complex. If you decide to compare the actual standards, you might be appalled to see that the OSPF specification is at least 10 times the size of the RIP specification.

Even the name and the software version are complex. When I first heard the spelled-out name of OSPF, I asked, "Where is this shortest path and how do I open it?" My mentor laughed and told me that *open* meant nonproprietary, and *shortest path first* was just another term for link state.

Several document versions all refer to Version 2 of the protocol. The version level here refers not so much to the version of the standard, but of the version of the data structures used by several generations of the standard. An OSPF Version 1 packet might not be compatible with a Version 2 OSPF router, but a packet generated by an OSPF implementation defined by RFC 1247 is understandable by an RFC 2348 implementation. Both use Version 2 formats.

OSPF Version 6, discussed in Chapter 14, is another matter entirely. The version number here refers to IP version 6. Originally, OSPFv6 was developed for IPv6 routing, not IPv4. Subsequently, it was given the capability to handle IPv4, and indeed arbitrary protocol, addresses. OSPFv6 has technical improvements over OSPFv2 and might indeed be widely adopted when the standard is ready. OSPFv6, for example, has features that make multicast OSPF (MOSPF) more scalable than it is today.

OSPF is more complex than RIP because it does many more complex things. You might find it reassuring, however, to discover that only the first few chapters of the protocol specification need to be read to get a quite good understanding of the protocol. The bulk of the specification is needed only by people implementing OSPF code in routers.

> **Note**
>
> *When looking at any IETF protocol, make a habit of looking first for a document called the Applicability Statement and then reading the Protocol Specification selectively [RFC 2328]. The Applicability Statement sets the context.*

As opposed to RIP and IGRP, OSPF uses a link state algorithm. As routers initialize, they flood the common medium within their area with information about the paths connected to them. If your routers do not summarize to the core, the updates flood into the core, and possibly beyond it depending on whether you define other non-core areas as stub (see discussions of stub areas in Chapter 12). Routers also advertise paths when one goes up or down. Otherwise, updates are relatively infrequent and are sent after many minutes rather than a few seconds.

> **Note**
>
> *OSPF is used in most detailed design examples in this book. For that reason, this discussion is limited. There is an extensive discussion in Chapters 11 and 12 and notes on OSPF in most subsequent chapters.*

OSPF reduces traffic by specializing routers. There are four types of router *functions*, none of which have a complete view of the routing environment, and consequently have a smaller routing table than would be necessary if they had a complete view. All four functions can be in the same physical router box.

There must always be at least one area. If there is more area, one must be an area 0.0.0.0. 0, which is the backbone set of routers through which all inter-area routing flows.

Figure 5.23 shows the four types of routers in OSPF. Routers in area 0.0.0.0 only are called *backbone routers* (BRs). *Autonomous system border routers* (ASBRs) connect to other routing domains. The backbone is linked to non-backbone areas by *area border routers* (ABRs). Routers with interfaces in a single nonzero area only are *interior routers* (IRs).

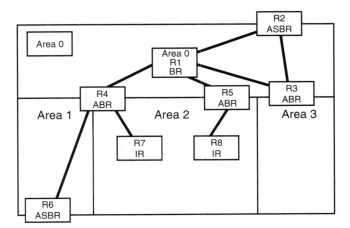

FIGURE 5.23   *An OSPF routing domain has at least one area. The four OSPF router types are defined with respect to areas and the overall routing domain.*

OSPF documents refer to a routing domain as an autonomous system, but in a more modern definition, an autonomous system can contain multiple OSPF routing domains, as well as non-OSPF routing domains.

For small networks, it can be quite reasonable to have a single-area OSPF routing domain. As discussed in Chapter 12, however, you should number that area anything except 0.0.0.0. If you add areas, you have to renumber routers that directly serve user networks, because area 0.0.0.0 should be reserved for inter-area transit and perhaps network management servers.

An ASBR provides a means of exchanging paths to another routing process or to accept static routes for redistribution into OSPF. OSPF itself does not do the routing to other routing domains. An ASBR function most often is in area 0.0.0.0, but can be in nonzero areas if certain configuration restrictions are respected (see Chapter 12).

Areas numbered other than zero contain sets of routers that serve hosts within that area. A given intra-area router only knows how to reach other routers in its area, including the area boundary router that connects the area to the backbone. The internal router can know the router at the boundary of its area that gives the optimal path to a destination outside its area, or it can simply go to the closest area boundary router.

Interior routers have all their interfaces inside a single nonzero area.

The OSPF Protocol Messages

OSPF has a reasonably complex set of protocol messages. To understand them, it is necessary to understand that the LSA is not a unique message, but a standard data structure that can be carried in a variety of OSPF protocol messages. OSPF runs directly over IP. It does not use User Datagram Protocol (UDP) or Transmission Control Protocol (TCP), but does its own retransmission.

The five types of OSPF packets have a common structure as shown in Figure 5.24. All types have a common header in addition to the ordinary 20-byte IP header, shown in Figure 5.25.

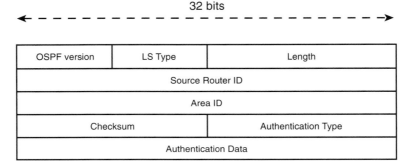

FIGURE 5.24 *All OSPF packets begin with this header.*

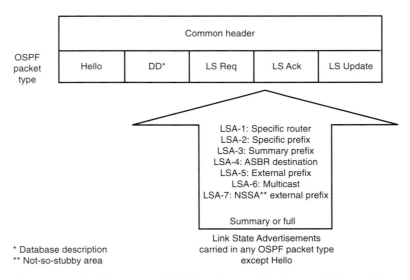

FIGURE 5.25 *Five types of OSPF packets run directly over IP. Four of these types can carry LSAs.*

The OSPF Packet Header

Most OSPF packets have a reserved multicast address as their destination. When these packets are sent, the IP time-to-live (TTL) field in their IP headers are set to one, so they only have link-local scope (that is, the local medium). On various technical mailing lists, I occasionally see a question of "How do I get OSPF packets to go through a firewall?" This is really not a very meaningful question, because the screening routers or bastion hosts of a firewall separate different subnets. An OSPF packet is not intended to go beyond a single subnet.

This address can be **AllSPFRouters** (224.0.0.5) or **AllDRouters** (224.0.0.6). **AllSPFRouters** goes to all OSPF-speaking routers on the medium, whereas **AllDRouters** goes only to the designated router and backup designated router. When a router retransmits an OSPF packet, it sends it to a specific unicast address, that of the router that did not acknowledge a transmission.

Of these five types, the hello packet is used to detect neighbor routers and OSPF router failures. The other four types are involved in database initialization and updating and carry LSAs. See "I Said LSA, Not LSA," later in this section for details of the LSAs.

After OSPF identifies a neighbor with which it wants to synchronize topological database information, it exchanges *database description* (DD) packets. DD packets, and subsequent other packet types, carry LSAs.

An enhancement to OSPF is authentication of routing updates. There are two levels of authentication, cleartext and cryptographic.

Cleartext authentication protects against configuration errors, and cryptographic authentication protects against attacks against the routing system. Neither provides additional security for routed packets, only for the routing information proper.

The IP security (IPsec) architecture, a part of IPv6 and an option for IPv4, provides header authentication, obviating the need for separate OSPF header authentication. OSPFv6, discussed in Chapter 14, eliminates OSPF authentication.

Address and Neighbor Discovery

As an OSPF router initializes, it first determines a unique router ID and then searches for other OSPF routers on the media to which its interfaces connect. The router ID is a 32-bit number displayed in most implementations as an IP address; it is not a true address, but simply is a 32-bit string. Different implementations vary on how the router ID is selected, and the standard has only guidelines. Different ways of selecting the router ID occasionally can result in duplicate router IDs, an annoying problem in multivendor interoperability. See "Configuring OSPF" in Chapter 11 for a discussion of different vendors' methods of determining the router ID.

As OSPF initializes, it builds a variety of data structures, shown in Figure 5.26.

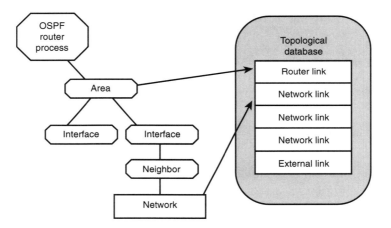

FIGURE 5.26 *A conceptual view of major internal data structures.*

After OSPF establishes interfaces that have been configured, it builds interface state machines for each of its interfaces. The interfaces begin to send out, and listen for, hello messages. When a router hears a hello message on an interface, it copies the router ID it has heard into the next hello packet it sends out. Figure 5.27 shows the basic flow of this process. The hello contains the entire list of routers that have been heard on the interface.

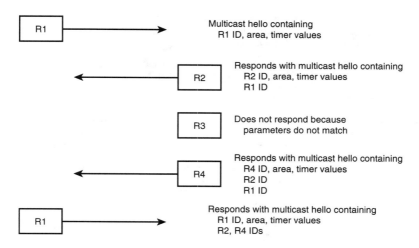

FIGURE 5.27 *In this basic view of the initialization process, in which the initialization progresses in an interface-by-interface manner, R1 has established neighbor relationships with R2 and R4.*

OSPF neighbor discovery is rather like flirting at a bar, where the router searches the room, sends hellos, makes eye contact with a returned hello, and then explores the response to see what sort of relationship it wants to have. The actual hello packet is shown in Figure 5.28.

Where people deciding if they want to date look at humor, physical attractiveness, intelligence, and possibly wallet size as decision factors, OSPF looks at matching area numbers, timer values, stub characteristics (see Chapter 12), and other technical factors. OSPF is far more picky than other protocols, such as EIGRP or IS-IS, on having exact matches of parameters.

When a hello message is received with one's own router ID in it, it goes through a substantial number of validity checks, such as verifying that the timers used by both routers match exactly. The interface state machine goes to a new level indicating a neighbor has been detected and creates a neighbor state machine for that neighbor.

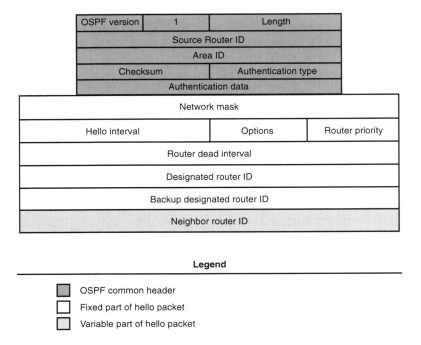

Legend

☐ OSPF common header
☐ Fixed part of hello packet
☐ Variable part of hello packet

FIGURE 5.28   *The OSPF hello is the only OSPF packet that does not contain any LSAs.*

Designated Routers

OSPF defines a designated router function on broadcast multi-access media. The term *designated router* is a little misleading, as it does not refer to a router *box*, but to an interface on a router. There is a designated router interface and a backup designated router interface on each medium. A given physical chassis can be designated for several media.

Designated router election is part of the neighbor/adjacency discovery process. The algorithm is shown in Figure 5.29.

Although it is possible to influence the selection of a designated router if more than one router is contending for the status, it is most common that the first router that initializes becomes the designated router, and the second router that initializes becomes the backup designated router. If a router then joins the medium, and has a higher priority value for designated router status, it does not preempt the existing designated routers.

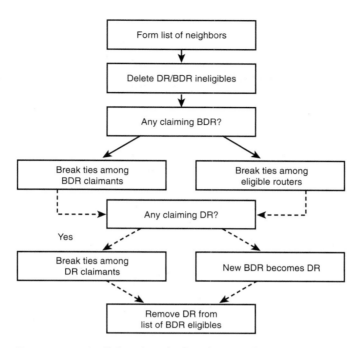

FIGURE 5.29 *If there is no backup designated router, it is elected first. Only after there is a BDR is a DR elected. DR election is shown with dashed lines.*

As a designer, you want to understand this process when sizing the processing power of routers. There is more workload on a designated than a non-designated router, but the only way you can guarantee that a specific router is designated is to make all other routers connected to the same medium ineligible to be DR.

A single DR-eligible router obviously is a single point of failure. You can make more than one eligible to become DR, but when the first one initializes at a random time, it has the highest active priority and thus becomes DR.

The problem of controlling which router is DR tends to be most acute in hub-and-spokes media. It is not unreasonable to make only the hub router eligible for designation, because if it is down, the spoke routers would lose connectivity in any case.

Note

You can find priority mechanisms in a variety of routing features. The features differ on whether a more-preferred router preempts an active router running a given function. In OSPF, for example, the designated router is not preempted by a higher-priority router that joins a running subnet. In HSRP, however, a new higher-priority can preempt an existing one. See Chapter 6 for further details on HSRP.

Be aware that whether high- or low-priority values wins a contest depends on the standard (when one exists) and the vendor implementation.

In practice, OSPF elects a designated router, and there is little reason to adjust the priority. The only plausible reason to set priority is when there are a significant number of low-powered edge routers on a medium and a lesser number of high-powered routers with abundant CPU resources, it can be desirable to keep the heavier CPU load of the designated router function off the edge routers. Also, if you have a highly connected router at a central location, you either want to make sure its CPU is not overloaded or you might to use more than one central and split the DR functions over multiple routers.

The usual practice in such a case is to set priority equal to zero on the edge routers and set nonzero priorities on the distribution routers. Be sure there are enough distribution routers for adequate availability.

If the edge routers are always going to feed the distribution routers, and never communicate directly with one another, it is reasonable to set a zero priority on the edge routers. The situation is more complex when some direct routing might take place between the edge routers. In that case, you want an operational procedure that first initializes the distribution routers and sets a much higher (that is, more preferred) priority value on the distribution router interfaces. If all distribution router interfaces are down, an edge router becomes designated router.

Tip

If there is a significant mismatch in processing power between edge and distribution routers, have a proactive monitoring procedure in place to look for overloaded routers.

After a neighbor is confirmed, the initializing router can route through it. At the singles bar of OSPF, this router has not yet decided if it should enter the higher relationship of *adjacency*, in which it exchanges topological database information with it.

Based on information in the first hello message it receives from a neighbor, the interface goes through the process:

1. Is there an active DR on the medium to which this interface is connected?

2. If not, is there an active BDR? Should it be promoted to DR?

3. If there is neither an active BDR nor DR, a process begins to elect one.

The interface eventually decides if it is the DR, if it is the BDR, or if another interface is the DR. After it makes that decision, the next step in initialization is to exchange topological information with the DR until their topological databases are synchronized. More detail of this process is in Chapter 11.

"I Said LSA, Not LSA"

Several things can be confusing in LSA terminology. First, there are two separate things that can be called an LSA: a link-state acknowledgement packet and a link-state advertisement carried in four kinds of OSPF packets. As a convention for acronyms, one of the packet types that can carry the link-state advertisement (LSA) is the link-state acknowledgement (LSAck). You will deal extensively with Link-State Advertisements in both troubleshooting and performance planning, but the LSAck is primarily of interest to people writing and debugging OSPF router code.

The Link-State Advertisement is best understood in database concepts. An LSA originates in the advertising router. The record, as stored in the advertising router, is the golden copy, which all other copies must mirror. Copies outside the advertising router are *instances* of that record.

Table 5.2 gives an overview of LSA types that either are widely supported or are likely to be in near-term products.

TABLE 5.2 OSPF LINK-STATE ADVERTISEMENT TYPES

LSA type and purpose	Scope	Generated by	Contents
Type 1 (Router)	Area	Any router	Router ID and connected networks
Type 2 (Network)	Area	Any router	Network and connected routers
Type 3 (Summary)	Routing domain[1]	Area border routers	Inter-area route

continues

TABLE 5.2 CONTINUED

LSA type and purpose	Scope	Generated by	Contents
Type 4 (ASBR)	Routing domain[1]	Autonomous system border routers	Route to autonomous system border router
Type 5 (External)	Routing domain[1]	Autonomous system border routers	Route outside routing domain
Type 6 (Multicast)	Routing domain[2]	Multicast-enabled routers	Multicast destination
Type 7 (NSSA) [3]	Routing domain[1]	Autonomous system border routers with NSSA configured	Route outside routing domain; special scope characteristics

[1] *In principle, the scope of LSAs Types 4 and 5 is the entire routing domain. The formal OSPF term for the scope is the AS, but OSPF has an obsolete definition for AS. Routing domain is more correct, because there can be multiple OSPF routing domains within the same AS.*

The propagation of Types 4, 5, and 7 LSA can be further limited by various types of stub area declarations. The various types of stubby areas are discussed in Chapter 12.

[2] *Additional scoping criteria are available. Only multicast-enabled routers accept Type 6 LSAs.*

[3] *Not-so-stubby-areas (NSSA) are discussed in Chapter 12.*

OSPF refers to an LSA describing a specific medium as a *network LSA*. It would probably be more understandable if this were called a subnet, medium, or prefix LSA, but it is not.

All OSPF router types can generate any OSPF packet type. The only message type that does not contain LSA headers or full LSAs is the hello message. In non-hello packets, all router types can generate router LSAs and network LSAs. ABRs generate summary LSAs. ASBRs generate external LSAs (see Figure 5.30).

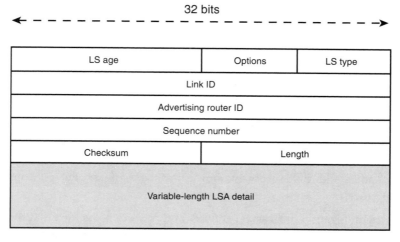

FIGURE 5.30   *LSAs are database records carried inside OSPF packets. They are variable length.*

LSAs, especially Type 1 and Type 2, are relatively large records, larger than EIGRP routing updates. Every OSPF header uniquely identifies its type, the particular link to which it refers, and the router that owns that link information. This unique identifier consists of the following:

- Link-State Advertisement type

- Link-State Advertisement ID

- Advertising Router (that is, the ID of the router that generated the LSA)

These three fields identify the link. The definitive golden copy of the link resides in the topological database of the advertising router, which created the LSA. There certainly can be copies or *instances* of the LSA in transit or in the databases of other routers. Each of those instances contains information on how recent it is, relative to its origination in the advertising router.

- Sequence number

- Age

- Checksum

Although not a true timestamp, the three fields uniquely identify the most recent instance of any LSA.

The variable-length body information varies with the LSA type and the specific configuration. More than one LSA can be packed into a single OSPF packet. Update packets carrying full LSA information, however, typically are several hundred bytes long.

OSPF Database Synchronization

After routers decide they are neighbors, a second decision takes place to determine if they should extend that relationship to adjacency. As a designer, you need to understand this process and how mismatches of parameters can prevent the process.

In the synchronization process, one of the routers needs to be the DR. Point-to-point networks are an exception, in that there is no need for a designated router on a point-to-point medium with only two devices. For purposes of the actual exchange, one router needs to assume the master role and the other needs to assume the slave role. These roles have nothing to do with the designated router status. Role selection takes place in the **ExStart** state of the OSPF state machine. After the roles are agreed to, the routers enter the **Exchange** state and actually exchange database information.

The master begins the process by sending the slave Database Description (DD) records that contain summary information on the contents of the master's topological database. After examining these summary records, the recipient decides if it needs more information, which it requests from the other router. Do not confuse this sort of summarized LSA with a Type 3 LSA that contains information on summarized inter-area routes. DD record summaries are simply identifiers for the information in the database.

As the slave receives data from the master, it considers several factors:

- Do I have better data on this destination than does the master?

- Do I know about this destination but the master's path is better?

- Do I know about destinations that the master does not?

If the master's information is better than the slave's, the slave installs it and acknowledges the LSA. If the slave's information is better, it sends an update to the master, which the master acknowledges.

Eventually, no changes occur in either direction, and the two routers now have synchronized databases.

After databases have been synchronized, the router generates a transient list of routes, sends the generated routes to the RIB installation process, and then settles down to monitor the topology. As each router learns new topological information from new or old neighbors, it *floods* this through the OSPF area using multicasts to the routers to which it is adjacent on each medium.

OSPF Updating

All topological information in an OSPF routing domain is considered to be owned by the router that initially advertises it. LSAs are actually data structures rather than explicit messages, and multiple LSAs can be in a single protocol message.

Updates are sent both to the DR and BDR in a single multicast message; the BDR mirrors the DR passively so it can take over if the DR fails. When an OSPF router receives an LSA flooded to it, or as part of database initialization, it first checks the message and LSA for validity and then analyzes it:

1. Is the LSA ID something that is not in my database? If so, add it.

2. If I already know about this link ID, compare the age information of the two LSAs. The actual age information is derived from the age, sequence number, and checksum in the LSA. The actual algorithm for knowing which is the most recent instance of an LSA is beyond the scope of this text, but it involves several tie-breakers and mechanisms to deal with special values these parameters can assume.

    a. If the arriving LSA is newer than mine, replace the one that I have. Flood the information to downstream neighbors.

    b. If my stored LSA is newer than the arriving one, do not change my database, create an update with my newer information, and send it back to the interface that sent me old information.

    This step always gives me the image of nice versus nasty routers. Nice routers return the newer information with a helpful expression, whereas less courteous routers throw it back with a muttered cry of "Fool!"

    c. If the two LSAs are of the same age, reset the 30-minute timer on my stored LSA.

It's convenient to think of OSPF LSAs as time-stamped, but they do not really have a timestamp synchronized to any real clock. Instead, the moral equivalent of a timestamp is an approximation of relative age since the LSA was created by its advertising router. LSAs are aged both in topological databases and in transit between routers. The exact algorithm is complex and beyond the scope of this discussion, but works nicely.

A common misconception related to OSPF updating is that it refloods the database every 30 minutes, rather like a slower periodic update. First, LSAs are not reflooded in their entirety. Second, individual LSAs are reflooded only after nothing has been heard from them for 30 minutes. If the timers are updated by events listed in the preceding Step 2.c, the LSA might never need to be reflooded.

OSPF path determination triggers whenever the database changes, and only then. The actual updating process is complex, computationally intensive, and quick.

The key part of path determination is the calculation of routes within a single area, building the conceptual routing tree with this router at the root. The actual Dijkstra algorithm that builds this tree runs on data for a single area.

After the tree is built on single-area data, the router examines it and adds new or better paths based on summary or external LSAs. The details of this selection are in Chapters 11 and 12, but the basic rules are as follows:

- Always take the most specific path, the one with the longest matching prefix.

- Between an intra-area and an inter-area route, use inter-area.

- Between an inter-area route and an external route, use inter-area.

- Between Type 1 and Type 2 external routes, use Type 1. A Type 1 metric includes both the internal cost to reach the router that connects to the external route, whereas a Type 2 only includes the external metric.

Initial Convergence Time and the Dijkstra Computation

The discussion of OSPF here is not intended to give the level of detail necessary to design routers, just the level function that you need to design networks.

After the database is initialized, the router is not quite ready to route. An OSPF router now needs to run the Dijkstra algorithm to build the list of OSPF-derived routes.

Properly executed, the Dijkstra algorithm only selects routes that start and end inside the current area. OSPF mechanisms to compute inter-area routes are described in Chapter 12, and mechanisms that compute external routes are also discussed in Chapter 12 (see Figure 5.31).

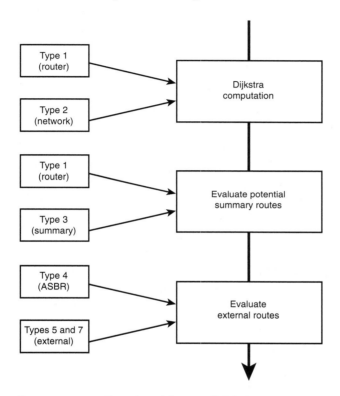

F IGURE 5.31 *Overview of the overall OSPF route computation process, of which the Dijkstra calculation is one component.*

The Dijkstra calculation is only part of the OSPF route calculation process. Algorithms shown here need not be the way the actual router code executes, as long as the same output routes are generated.

Dijkstra computation applies to the path determination for intra-area routes in non-backbone areas. There are two phases to the OSPF Dijkstra calculation, one for non-stub intra-area networks and the second for stub networks.

Although area 0.0.0.0 uses the Dijkstra process to build the shortest-path tree for area 0.0.0.0 internal routes, it uses what is effectively a distance-vector algorithm to manage inter-area routes. Remember that Type 3 LSAs carry routes, not link or router information. When a backbone router receives a Type 3 LSA, it adds its own cost to that route and passes it along to its adjacent routers.

In nonzero areas, inter-area and external routes are examined after the Dijkstra calculation and only are added to the routing table if they can provide connectivity that intra-area routes cannot.

Within an area, the basic Dijkstra algorthm creates a tree with the router doing the computation at the root. There is now a list of candidates to get to various destinations, but not necessarily the lowest-cost path.

In a broad sense, the Dijkstra algorithm looks at candidate routers that can reach a given destination. If the destination is already in the shortest-path tree with a lower cost to it, the new potential path is skipped. If the router being examined offers a lower-cost path to the destination, the old entry in the shortest path is deleted (that is, *pruned*). Equal-cost entries are added to the shortest path tree.

After the basic list of routes for an area is built, OSPF examines the list of non–intra-area routes to see if there are destinations that are not reached by intra-area routes. Inter-area routes are considered first, then external Type 1, then external Type 2.

IS-IS

Like OSPF, IS-IS has different types of routers; no one router has the complete routing table for the network. As opposed to the four types in OSPF, there are two in IS-IS. The IS-IS model is, in most respects, a superset of the model used in DECnet area routing [Perlman, 1992].

IS-IS has been a niche protocol, but is used extensively in some large ISPs. Its proponents say it offers technical advantages over OSPF, and indeed the IETF has started working on standardizing enhancements to IS-IS. At present, however, IS-IS is far less widely implemented than OSPF.

OSPF and IS-IS have different assumptions at the internal design level. Quite frankly, these often fall into the category of engineering art rather than hard science. OSPF and IS-IS both bear the artists' signatures of their principal designers, John Moy for OSPF and Radia Perlman for IS-IS.

As opposed to OSPF and EIGRP (which run directly over IP), RIP (which runs over UDP/IP), and BGP (which runs over TCP/IP), IS-IS runs directly over the data link layer. Proposals are underway in the IETF IS-IS working group to have IS-IS run over IP, as opposed to directly over the data link header. It does not include an IP header. IS-IS messages cannot be routed beyond the local medium. Do remember that they can go through a Layer 2 switch and might leak through to unexpected places in a spanning tree. Given the IS-IS packets do not leave the local subnet, the rationale for running them directly over the data link layer is to avoid the overhead of processing the IP header, and sending 20 bytes of IP header per packet. IS-IS packets are nonroutable, but, in practice, OSPF packets with a TTL of 1 are also nonroutable. Some protocol architects criticize IS-IS for having packets that cannot themselves be routed, but it is difficult to think of a scenario where there is a real reason to do this.

A specialized reason might be to run them through a firewall or network address translator, which I have had clients request. On detailed analysis, these requests always turned out to be unfeasible.

IS-IS constructs a link-state packet (LSP) that contains the current node ID and a list of pairs containing the identifiers of the adjacent pairs, and the costs to reach them. These LSPs are broadcasted, LSPs from other nodes received, and each node then builds its overall routing tables.

The area concept is slightly different in OSPF and IS-IS, with no explicit backbone area. You define user areas. IP addresses do not contain an area number, but OSI NSAP addresses do contain an area value field. IS-IS uses OSI addresses as well as IP addresses to define its addressing structure.

IS-IS intermediate systems are called *Level 1 routers* and *Level 2 routers*. Level 1 routers know the topology within their area, which is a subdivision of the routing domain. The latter is the OSPF model. The backbone is simply the set of interconnections among Level 2 routers (see Figure 5.32).

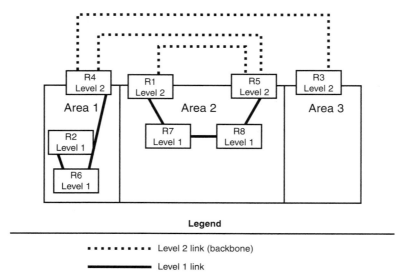

Legend

• • • • • • • • • •   Level 2 link (backbone)

━━━━━━━━━━   Level 1 link

FIGURE 5.32   *IS-IS has Level 1 and Level 2 routers. Only Level 2 routers have knowl-edge of areas other than their own. A given router is in one area at a time; there is not a concept of a boundary router as in OSPF.*

Another difference between OSPF and IS-IS is in the allocation of functions to physical router boxes. A given box is either a Level 1 or Level 2 router; the router function is assigned to the entire box rather than to an interface as in OSPF. A given router is configured only with one area, but if it hears advertise-ments from another area on any of its interfaces, it can automatically become a Level 2 router. Specific implementations can disable the capability of a router to become a Level 2 router.

Proponents of IS-IS point to the way in which an IS-IS router can automatically become Level 2 as an advantage over OSPF, where area border routers and backbone routers must be configured explicitly. IS-IS can repair a partitioned backbone, or create new area border router equivalents, without manual recon-figuration—as long as connectivity exists to repair the problem. OSPF might not use a potential backbone or inter-area link if it is not told that it can.

A Level 1 router, which is an *intermediate system (IS),* knows how to reach all the subnets inside the area. It also knows how to reach Level 2 routers. Level 1 routers communicate indirectly outside their areas, by forwarding all traffic for destinations outside the local area to a Level 2 IS connected to its area.

Level 2 routers know how to reach other Level 2 areas, but do not know the internal topology of the other areas served by the other Level 2 area. A router can combine Level 1 and Level 2 functions so that it knows the topology of its local area as well as the topology of the Level 2 routing structure. Level 2 routers are also the only routers that can communicate with routers outside the routing domain, which are reached by *exterior links*.

IS-IS assumes that the overall network is partitioned into routing domains. Routing domains are bounded by a set of links defined in a network management configuration function to be exterior links. This protocol defines that no intradomain routing information will flow onto an exterior link. An exterior link has a function similar to an OSPF autonomous system boundary router.

NSAP addresses include an area element, built from the initial domain part (IDP) which identifies the NSAP format, and the high-order domain specific part (HO-DSP), which is the equivalent to the prefix in IP. The HO-DSP is itself composed of subfields that can indicate levels of hierarchy. There are different sets of subfields. See *Designing Addressing Architectures for Routing and Switching* [Berkowitz, 1998a] for a discussion of NSAP address formats.

IP addresses do not contain areas, even when you're using an area-supportive protocol such as OSPF. OSPF makes a simplifying inter-area routing assumption by forcing all traffic to go through the backbone, area 0.0.0.0. IS-IS routers do not necessarily need to assume a backbone area, because Level 2 IS-IS routers can maintain maps of routes to other areas.

IS-IS uses OSI addressing principles. OSI network layer addresses are called NSAP addresses. OSI NSAPs, the basic components of which are shown in Figure 5.33, are divided into two main parts, the IDP and the DSP. For routing purposes, the DSP is further divided into an area address part and a part that identifies specific systems and entities.

Because interdomain routing protocols are not sufficiently developed to provide autoconfiguration, exterior links must be configured manually. They are statically configured with the set of address prefixes reachable via that link, and with the method by which they can be reached (such as the DTE address to be dialed to reach that address, or the fact that the DTE address should be extracted from the IDP portion of the NSAP address). The IDP value identifies the structure of the HO-DSP (and the rest of the DSP). Together, the sequence of IDP and HO-DSP form the *area address*. Area addresses are of variable length within a routing domain, because there might be a need to go to other domains using different IDP values and DSP formats. A DSP length is constant within a routing domain.

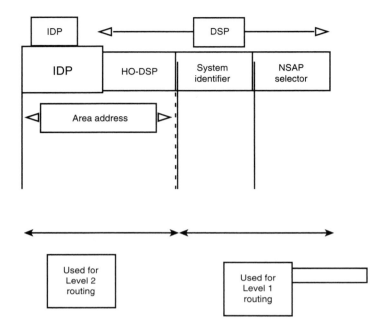

FIGURE 5.33 *OSI NSAP local topologies.*

Area addresses are manually configured into Level 1 routers, but can be learned by Level 2 routers. Routers use the area address to make first-level routing decisions: whether they forward to the Level 2 router or to an intra-area Level 1 router topologically closer to the destination. Level 1 routers forward to the nearest Level 2 router all traffic with area addresses not matching their own.

A Level 1 router, that is configured to stay Level 1, does not a establish adjacency with another router with a different area address. End systems either can be preconfigured with an area address or can learn it from a connected router.

Looking Ahead

Although it's usually wise to plan a router network for substantial growth, there certainly are cases where the nature of the enterprise gives you a fairly firm limit on bandwidth, number of nodes, or both. A dental office, for example, has a fixed number of rooms into which computers can be placed, although imaging applications could create substantial bandwidth growth.

Even in this seemingly fixed physical layout, you should be aware that increasing numbers of healthcare instruments have built-in computers and might need to connect to the office LAN. Still, it is unlikely a three-chair, two-desk office will need hundreds of computers.

Chapter 6 deals with the routing and switching appropriate to such small networks. It also deals with the host issues associated with networks of any size, such as how a host finds its local routers.

CHAPTER 6

Host and Small Network Relaying

I will be small in small things, great among great.
—Pindar

A guest never forgets the host that has treated him kindly.
—Homer

A good edge is good for nothing, if it has nothing to cut.
—Thomas Fuller

Hosts can be passively aware of routing, for simple default gateway location or more complex load sharing. They can also act as routers.

In a small network environment of tens of workstations and two or three servers, almost any combination of switching and routing works. Remember the problem you are trying to solve: relaying packets from host to host, or to external routers. Relaying is the more general concept that includes switching and routing.

In this chapter, we begin by examining the effective use of switching in a small workgroup and show how many configurations might not even need a traditional router. Routers definitely have a place, but you'll want to understand what that place is. There is a widespread tendency to overspecify the routing function in a small environment, due to an incorrect assumption that any host needs full bandwidth to any other host. A more realistic assumption is that access to and from servers needs minimum waiting.

Routing Information Protocol (RIP) design is discussed in this chapter, rather than in the subsequent chapters on routing design (Chapters 11 and 12), because RIP is obsolescent and advisable only in small networks as the primary path determination mechanism.

There is another use for RIP, as a simple signaling mechanism for hosts to find the default gateway router. Your hosts might require RIP to be present for this function, so it is discussed here along with other interactions of hosts with routers. Hosts are rarely, if ever, aware of more advanced routing protocols such as OSPF or EIGRP.

Workgroup Switching

Switches are very good tools for providing fast paths to local servers. Remember that the reason you want a fast path is to reduce latency. The term *guaranteed bandwidth* is misleading, as the value of a switch is to avoid queuing delay waiting for access to a medium and its bandwidth.

Providing raw bandwidth is not the ultimate goal of a network designer. The goal is providing useful bandwidth. You do not want to provide more bandwidth to a server than the server can use. If a particular server is underpowered, it can be dangerous to give it too much bandwidth because it can become overloaded.

Often, it is far less important to give guaranteed bandwidth to the desktop than it is to give guaranteed bandwidth to servers (see Figure 6.1). Not only should bandwidth to servers be free from waits for bandwidth, it should be full-duplex and preferably 100 Mbps.

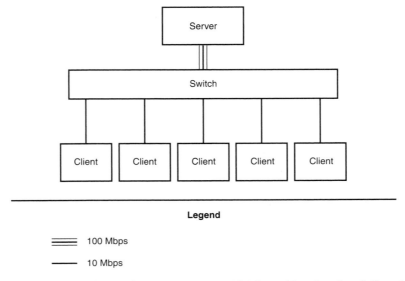

FIGURE 6.1 *Whereas the user ports run at 10 Mbps, either shared or dedicated as a bandwidth domain, the link to the server runs at 100 Mbps.*

Big Companies Can Do It Wrong, Too

A client of mine, a large information technology company, had me evaluate their network. They had perhaps 1500 programmers, a frightening enough thought by itself, who used high-end UNIX workstations. The power of these workstations was applied to compiling and local testing, not to generating large network traffic.

Each workstation was directly connected to a LAN switch port. The switched LANs connected via FDDI links to routers, which, in turn, connected to two server FDDI rings populated with approximately 100 servers. These servers were primarily used for software testing and were thus lightly loaded.

Let's see...*guaranteed bandwidth* of 10 Mbps to 1500 users, for a total of 15 Gbps. Shared bandwidth of 200 Mbps to 100 servers.

In all things, strive for balance. Giving bandwidth to clients, when there will be a bottleneck at the server, doesn't make sense.

There are good and bad reasons to use switches. Some reasons to use them are specific to virtual LANs (VLANs), not generic switches. In small networks, good reasons to use switches include the following:

- Minimizing bandwidth contention on server interfaces. This involves both 100 Mbps interface speed and full-duplex operation.

- Providing fast inter-host paths when there is significant peer-to-peer operation.

VLANs can provide the following additional benefits:

- Broadcast and multicast isolation.

- Some automation of moves and changes within the same user group, requiring significant management tools to do so effectively. Contrary to some vendor claims, implementing VLANs does not instantly give you a plug-and-play environment.

- Cabling flexibility.

An exception to the guideline that user hosts often do not need dedicated bandwidth is when you run collaborative applications, use peer-to-peer applications (for example, AppleTalk file sharing), or service location protocols that need to broadcast to all devices (for example, NetBIOS).

Alternatives to Routers for Inter-subnet Communications

Assuming your destination is in the same subnet as the source, how do you reach it? LAN switches give a fast path to hosts on the same subnet.

If you are in a pure switched environment, how do you reach resources not on your subnet? The classical answer is to go to a router, but do you always need one?

The focus in this section is on using hosts to carry traffic between different subnets. There is some discussion of using switches to complement host-based functions, but detailed discussion of switching systems is deferred to Chapters 8 and 9.

> ### Tip
> Some people try to mix all their servers and clients into a single switched subnet. Although almost any design works with a small number of interconnected computers, this design tends not to be able to scale.
>
> Although some vendors claim router-free, flattened networks are the best of all kinds, there are realistic limitations to how many hosts can be in a single subnet that represents a broadcast domain. Sizing a single subnet in a switched environment can be complex, but 500 hosts is a reasonable rule of thumb for well-behaved IP hosts.
>
> Many factors can reduce this number, often below 250. In carefully designed systems, 1000 or possibly 2000 machines might work, but the designer must work this out carefully.

Application Gateways

It might seem intuitive that hosts need to talk to one another, but in reality, most do not. They talk to local servers, to departmental servers, and so on. A workstation does not send email directly to another workstation, but to a server.

As shown in Figure 6.2, workstations communicate with local print servers, with mail servers, with local application caches and perhaps with a firewall for external access. There is no application requirement for the workgroups to communicate directly with one another.

One of the ways you can avoid routers, or router functions, in a switched network is using application gateways for all inter-subnet communications.

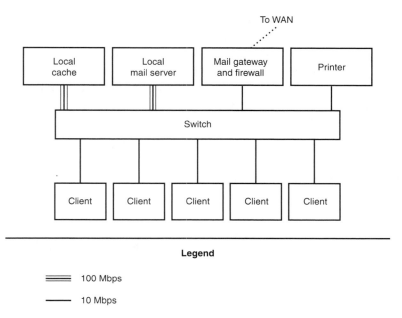

FIGURE 6.2 *Workstation hosts do not have any routine need to communicate with others. They communicate with local servers and with gateway servers that connect both to client links and to distribution-tier, server-to-server links.*

An ideal environment for using application gateways would be an office automation setting, where workers share an office set of files on a local server. There might be a cache of database information on this server, but the server would retrieve it from a higher-level server when needed.

Light-duty firewall requirements would probably work if the firewall had an "inside" interface on each of several user LANs, or if a VLAN-aware interface card was available on the firewall.

Products are coming onto the market that combine some firewall features with a router, such as Bay's Instant Internet or the Cisco 1600 series router. These can be front-ended with a switch, if a switch will help the situation.

Let's look at several representative situations, beginning with one that has no application gateway.

Shared Access to a Printer and a WAN Gateway

At a site remote from the data center, a company has twenty personal computers and two print servers. A customer service application runs on the individual hosts, and, after an order is taken, an application record is created and sent to the WAN gateway. The data center sends back confirmations, but the main database is at the data center. The WAN gateway connects to the data center with a 128-Kbps Frame Relay link.

Relatively small reports are printed on dot-matrix printers preloaded with carbonless forms; the printer servers do spool print output. Figure 6.3 illustrates the configuration for this example.

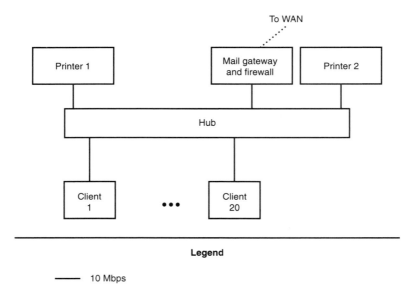

F IGURE 6.3   *A managed hub feeds all LAN-attached devices into the WAN gateway, which can be a router or a router with a separate firewall.*

Switching does not help here. There is no peer-to-peer networking among the local hosts. See the Chapter 10 section "Application Gateways and Switched Network Design" that explains why a switch does not help significantly in this case.

Cached Access to a Printer and a WAN Gateway

Next, vary the application from the previous example so that some of the file lookups normally sent to the data center now can be done on a local cache. There is a backup cache server. These act as application gateways, passing selected traffic to the data center.

The revised configuration is shown in Figure 6.4. In this scenario, a small switch could be useful for speeding access to the critical cache servers. Performance benefits of this switch are discussed in Chapter 10. The ports to these servers could be 100 Mbps full-duplex. Cacheing benefits performance in two ways: those queries that can be answered locally go between client and cache at LAN speed, and the queries that are answered locally do not need to consume WAN bandwidth.

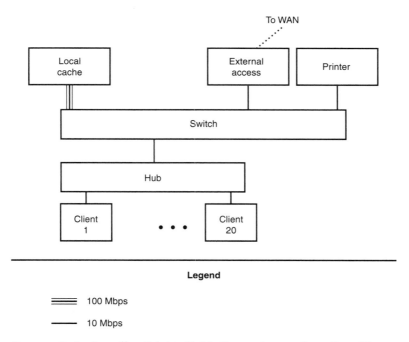

F I G U R E 6.4 *A small switch is added to the previous configuration. All servers are connected to the switch but user hosts connect to the switch via a hub.*

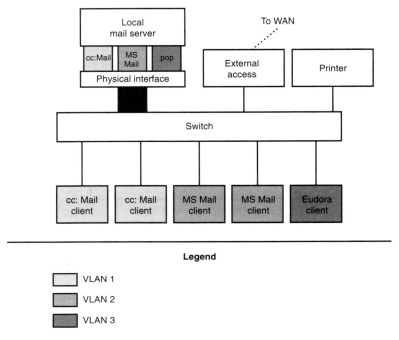

Legend

VLAN 1

VLAN 2

VLAN 3

FIGURE 6.7 *The LAN link to the host runs a VLAN trunk protocol such as ISL, or ATM if the interface card will serve as a LAN emulation client.*

With a VLAN-aware server card, the server appears to be on each VLAN. If clients on the user VLANs only need to communicate to the server, no router is required. If each VLAN uses a different mail protocol, and the VLAN server is a translating gateway, again there is no need for a router. If you have a router, hosts need to be able to locate it.

Tip

If you have a large number of VLANs, and the VLANs have light to medium traffic, a VLAN-aware NIC could be a very good solution. But remember that each VLAN-aware NIC is limited to the trunk bandwidth, normally 100 Mbps.

If you have VLANs with a large amount of traffic, you get a greater amount of bandwidth into the server by having multiple NICs. These NICs can be either VLAN-aware or not. You can spread multiple VLANs over multiple VLAN-aware boards, each with their own 100 Mbps pipe.

Hosts' Involvement in Routing

Hardware platforms intended as general-purpose hosts can be involved in the routing process, or can actually be routers. This section focuses on hosts that use routing information to decide where to send their own traffic not, for example, to PC-based routers. See Chapter 8 for a discussion of host-based routers.

Never forget the original assumption of IP routing, which admittedly does not properly deal with several new technologies. That local versus remote rule assumes that you can reach any destination in the same prefix through Layer 2 mechanisms, whereas you must go to a router to reach other subnets.

One of the resulting challenges is finding the router to which you go for off-subnet routing.

Basic Router Location

To use a default gateway, a host must be able to find it. Several ways have long been used, although they each have certain limitations. Newer methods are building on them, and, as seen in Chapter 14, IPv6 offers new mechanisms for router location. The following are the new mechanisms IPv6 offers:

- Hard-coded default gateways (interactions such as Dynamic Host Configuration Protocol, DHCP, Bay Router Redundancy, Cisco Hot Standby Router Protocol [HSRP], IETF Virtual Router Redundancy Protocol [VRRP])

- Proxy Address Resolution Protocol (ARP)

- Router discovery protocols such as IRDP

- Passive RIP

Hard-Coded Default Gateways

A very common practice is to hard-code the IP address of a specific default gateway into the host configuration. Most commonly, this is a single address, although some implementations can accept a list of default gateway addresses to be tried in sequence.

In its most basic form, this approach has several disadvantages. It requires manual reconfiguration of many hosts if the router address changes. Figure 6.8 shows the next problem. Even if there is a backup router present, a host does not know how to reach it if the IP stack on the host only permits a single default gateway to be coded.

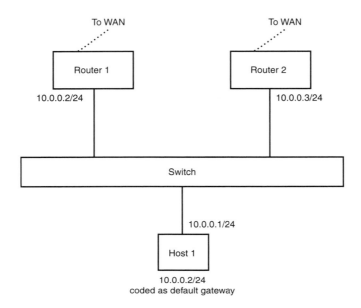

FIGURE 6.8 *Host 1 could use either Router 1 or Router 2, but it is unaware of the existence of Router 2.*

Because DHCP can provide the address of a default router, using DHCP is one way to alleviate the disadvantage of the effort required to reconfigure hosts after a gateway change.

Warning

When depending on DHCP to update default gateway addresses, be sure your specific DHCP clients and servers support setting the default gateway through DHCP. Not all implementations do.

A DHCP-provided default gateway address still does not allow the host to use a backup default gateway. In the absence of dynamic router location mechanisms, the only practical way to provide resilience is for a group of routers to agree that they will collectively act as the default gateway. Within this group, proprietary or standard mechanisms determine which specific router is to act as the active default gateway.

Bay Router Redundancy
Although Bay and Cisco both have a concept of a primary and one or more backup interfaces, the two vendors tend to use the concept in quite different ways when speaking of interface redundancy.

Bay's method emphasizes loss of connectivity on LAN interfaces. You define a group of interfaces that share a common virtual MAC address, that is only active on one router interface at a time. This MAC address is 2*y-yy*-A2-*xx-xx-xx*, where

- 2 indicates that this is a locally administered address.

- *y-yy* indicates the circuit number, which maps to a VLAN identifier.

- A2 is the organizationally unique identifier assigned to Bay.

- *xx-xx-xx* is the unique router identification number.

Bay's router redundancy mechanism really intends that there is a primary router and a backup router, and this backup router has only a standby role— the backup router is only used if the primary router fails.

What Really Breaks?

The idea of a router being only used as backup is not that unreasonable. In my experience, the things that cause failure, in order of probability, are the following:

- Media failures, especially WAN

- Electrical power failures

- Internetworking device software

- Internetworking device interface hardware

- Internetworking device power supplies

- Internetworking device central hardware

So, if you have a limited budget, the most important failures to protect against do not require redundant routers. Router redundancy is important only in the most mission-critical applications. When an application is this critical, dedicating an additional router as a spare can be entirely reasonable and assures that a backup will always be available, not doing other things that would be affected.

Cisco HSRP

Documented in RFC 2281, HSRP is a proprietary protocol used widely. Its basic idea is to define a virtual router address that is active on the primary router of an HSRP group, as shown in Figure 6.9.

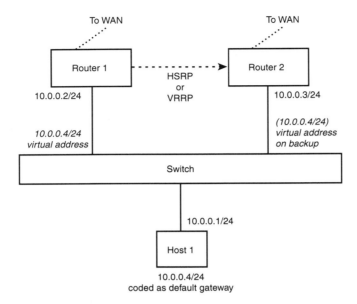

FIGURE 6.9 *In basic HSRP, there is a single virtual router function.*

Within the group, the routers exchange messages in the standby protocol, which runs on top of UDP with UDP port number 1985. Standby packets have a destination address of the multicast address 224.0.0.2, and have their Time To Live (TTL) fields set to one. The TTL value limits their scope to a single broadcast domain. HSRP can be used in fairly complex switched domains, which is discussed in Chapter 9.

An important aspect of HSRP is that not only is there a virtual IP address assigned to each group, but a virtual MAC address as well. Each router interface in the group still maintains its own IP address and MAC address, which is necessary to be able to **ping** interfaces and do other network management functions.

Figure 6.10 shows extensions to the original HSRP that allow a degree of load sharing among default routers. Chapter 10 discusses combining Layer 2 switch fault tolerance mechanisms with HSRP.

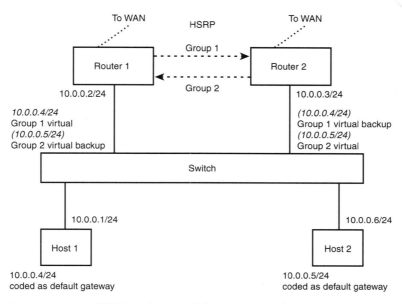

FIGURE 6.10 *HSRP can be extended to have multiple virtual routers.*

Well-known MAC addresses are defined for different LAN technologies. On media other than Token Ring, the MAC address for HSRP Group XX is 0x00-00-00-0C-07-AC-XX. On Token Ring, three functional addresses are defined for Groups 1 through 3: 0xCO-00-00-01-00-00-00, 0xCO-00-00-02-00-00-00, and 0xCO-00-00-04-00-00-00.

HSRP router interfaces always accept packets intended for the configured interface address. They must accept traffic for the virtual address while that router is in the HSRP active state as virtual router, and they must stop accepting that traffic when they leave the active state.

One of the niceties of HSRP and VRRP is that the end hosts are unaware of their existence. Hosts preconfigured with a default gateway address do an initial ARP to the virtual router address, which replies with the virtual MAC address. If the virtual MAC address moves to another physical interface, the host still sends to the same MAC address stored in its ARP cache.

Use caution when combining HSRP with a mixed switched and routed environment. Such mixtures can and do work, but you must ensure that the switch advertises the virtual MAC address in 802.1D hello messages. HSRP can participate in fault-tolerant bridging. Bridges must advertise the virtual group MAC address in its 802.1D hello messages. The bridges involved must be able to keep track of a moving MAC address, which can be difficult in source route bridging.

HSRP works best on Ethernet-family interfaces. Operation on Token Ring can be more difficult because Token Ring management can use some of the same MAC addresses as HSRP. There are workarounds to using HSRP on Token Ring, but they involve manipulating the interface MAC address or MAC filtering.

If you need to change the primary MAC address—the one normally associated with the physical rather than the virtual interface—this can affect non-IP protocols that interact with the MAC address for their network layer addressing. Such protocols include DECnet Phase IV, OSI CLNP, and sometimes Novell and XNS.

IETF VRRP

VRRP is an IETF standards-track protocol that describes itself as similar to HSRP and a Digital Equipment Corporation protocol called IP Standby Protocol [RFC 2338]. Authors of the VRRP standard come from companies including Ascend, Digital, IBM, Microsoft, and Nokia.

Its functionality is very similar to that of HSRP, but is at an earlier stage of deployment.

Proxy ARP

Proxy ARP, illustrated in Figure 6.11, may or may not be enabled on a router; it is only one of several alternatives for an end host to find the next hop address for destinations not on the local network. The main alternative is a hard-coded default route.

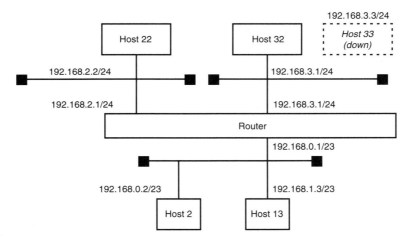

FIGURE 6.11 *Proxy ARP solves many configuration problems, at the expense of increasing broadcasts.*

Router Discovery Protocols

The Internet Router Discovery Protocol (IRDP) has many of the advantages over passive RIP and fewer disadvantages of passive RIP, but has never been widely deployed. Recently, there has been a resurgence of interest in IRDP. Major routers have long supported it, but the problem has been a lack of host client implementations.

Cisco dropped support for an even earlier proprietary mechanism, Gateway Discovery Protocol (GDP), in favor of IRDP.

IRDP is really not a separate protocol, but a set of conventions for using two ICMP message types, *router advertisement* and *router solicitation* [RFC 1256]. Routers periodically multicast router advertisements, so a host can learn of routers simply by listening. If the host wants to learn about routers immediately, it multicasts a router solicitation that triggers immediate advertisements.

Because the default advertising rate is 7 to 10 minutes, the host waits a significant amount of time if it cannot solicit advertisement. This default rate is also too slow for the host to find a new router in the event of router failure.

The protocol is not intended principally for blackhole detection—learning what routers have failed. It is intended to find any available router, which might not be the optimal one to reach a given destination. IRDP expects that if the router found is less than optimal, that router sends an ICMP redirect back to the host. That redirect message tells the host the IP address of a better next hop for the destination.

Although the router does not advertise itself as preferred or not preferred to reach a given destination, the IRDP announcement itself does include a preference level field. If the host hears several routers announce themselves, it should pick the one with the highest preference value as its default gateway.

IRDP advertisements contain a lifetime field with a default value of 30 minutes. After the lifetime expires, hosts should not assume that the router advertisement is still valid.

Passive RIP for Router Location and Other Functions

RIP often runs on non-routing hosts, as shown in Figure 6.12. Most commonly, this is done simply to be able to find a default gateway, so the end hosts only need to hear announcements of the default route.

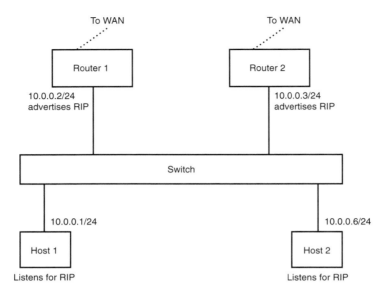

F IGURE 6.12 *Listening to RIP is a common way for hosts to dynamically locate the default router. That router, however, should not listen to any updates generated by the hosts.*

Host behavior varies with their specific implementations. Hosts might only save a single route to a destination, or they might attempt to load share. In the network shown in Figure 6.12, load sharing should be approached with caution. Bandwidth should not be an issue on the LAN, and traffic leaving the LAN will go over two separate paths and be far more likely to arrive out-of-sequence at the destination.

Having the hosts hear more specific routes can be useful in special cases. You might have the router announce a more specific path that is preferred to reach a specific server.

RIP updates are a common means of finding the default gateway in a manner much more flexible than static configuration.

Load Sharing, Load Balancing, and Fault Tolerance

The terms *load sharing, load balancing,* and *fault tolerance,* unfortunately, do not have universal meanings. Figure 6.13 shows several potential ways in which devices can load share or load balance.

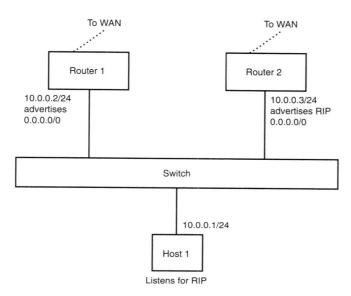

FIGURE 6.13 *Host 1 can load share or load balance either through one or two interfaces to different routers. This is for outgoing traffic from the host.*

A router potentially can balance between multiple hosts on incoming traffic, although this is more characteristic of a load sharing NAT than most commercial routers.

Note

For the case of incoming traffic, it might be very reasonable to use multicasting. A device doing network address translation (NAT), for example, could convert addresses intended for a virtual server to the multicast address of the group that carries out the server function.

Load sharing is a broader term than *load balancing*. Load sharing spreads the load over the shared resources—media, routers, or hosts—in an approximate manner. For example, it might spread a list of destination hosts across multiple interfaces, but not pay attention to the actual amounts of traffic intended for each destination. With a sufficiently large number of hosts, the load tends to level.

Load sharing is a much more tightly controlled mechanism. If Host 1 load balances to Router 1 and Router 2, it sends its first packet to Router 1, the second to Router 2, the third back to Router 1, and so forth. Load balancing is more predictable and controllable than the more general kind of load sharing, but it takes more overhead. The additional overhead comes from the need to choose, explicitly, an outgoing interface for each outbound packet. As opposed to the more general load sharing, the host must remember the state of its interfaces: Which interface was used last?

Having hosts decide how to distribute load to routers is relatively rare. Especially when the hosts are LAN-connected, the media should not be band-width-limited, so there is not a need for absolute bandwidth optimization. Routers usually connect hosts to WANs, and routers have much better facilities for load sharing and balancing than hosts.

Security Exposures

Many end hosts, especially UNIX, depend on receiving RIP updates so they can discover their local router. This is much more robust than a hard-coded default gateway.

In the example shown in Figure 6.14, both hosts on the Ethernet should default to the local router. Successive default routes take traffic to the Internet firewall, which connects to a DS-3 link to the authorized service provider.

Assume, however, that senior management approval is necessary for users to access the Internet through the firewall. Jane has been authorized such access, but John has not.

John urgently needs Web and email access for a legitimate project, but cannot get firewall authorization. In desperation, he buys a modem, sets up an account with a local ISP, and sets up his own connectivity.

What John does not realize is that his workstation, as soon as it has a second active interface, might begin to behave as a RIP router, advertising the Ethernet and possibly all internal routes it hears.

John's workstation running RIP can lead to at least three types of problems. At Point 1, Jane suddenly notices a terrible drop in performance, as her worksta-tion prefers going to John's closer router function…and its 14.4 Kbps access line. Jane's workstation runs RIP, but only passively, for the purpose of finding the default gateway.

At Point 2, John's router learns external routes and advertises them into the corporate network. At Point 3, the external world learns of a back door into the corporate network, bypassing the firewall. The external screening router should accept no routing advertisements from the outside that refer to internal networks.

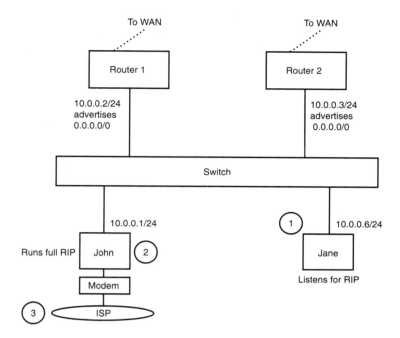

FIGURE 6.14 *Inappropriate activation of RIP can lead to undesired routing and security exposures.*

Warning

Routers that generate RIP updates for purposes of router discovery should only advertise the default route (that is, 0.0.0.0/0) and accept no routing updates from edge networks that should only contain end systems.

Interactions with Microsoft RAS

Figure 6.15 shows a Windows host that either can connect to a default router on its LAN or to a Microsoft Remote Access Server (RAS) through a demand circuit. Normally, host Host 1 goes through Router 1, the LAN default gateway, to reach Server 1 and Server 2.

Before Host 1 connects to the RAS, its host routing table points to Router 1 as default gateway. This routing table shows a metric of 1 to Server 1.

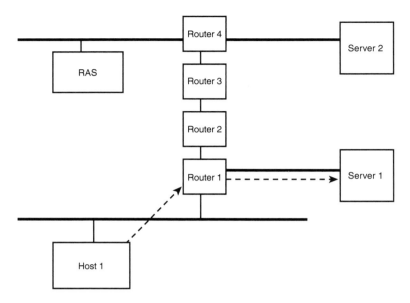

FIGURE 6.15 *As long as John's PC does not have an active RAS connection, it defaults to the LAN-attached router.*

When you connect a Windows host to a Microsoft RAS, as shown in Figure 6.16, the RAS becomes the preferred default gateway even if there is an existing default gateway on a LAN. The end host now defaults to the RAS server and follows the WAN path to Server 1 and Server 2.

Host 1's routing table points to RAS as its default gateway. The RAS changes Host 1's metric to Server 1 to have the value 2.

To avoid unnecessary WAN travel, you need to put static routes to the servers into Host 1, or run a dynamic routing protocol on Host 1.

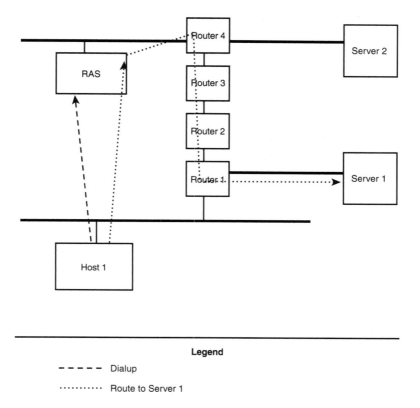

Legend

– – – – – Dialup

⋯⋯⋯⋯⋯ Route to Server 1

FIGURE 6.16 *After John's PC connects to the RAS, the host uses the RAS as its default gateway, not Router 1.*

RIP Workload and Convergence

Of the dynamic routing protocols available to exchange routing information about IP, RIPv1 [RFC 1058] is the oldest that is still used to any significant extent. RIP derives from older protocols developed during early LAN experiments at Xerox. As well as its use in Xerox proprietary protocols, a RIP variant is the basic routing protocol of Novell IPX networking.

As discussed in Chapter 3, RIP is a first-generation distance-vector protocol. It runs over IP and UDP. RIPv1 sends all its updates as broadcasts.

IP headers are 20 bytes long, and UDP headers are 8 bytes long. Illustrated in Figure 6.17, RIP packets have a fixed 4-byte header and 20 bytes per incremental route. A maximum of 25 routes are permitted in a RIP update packet.

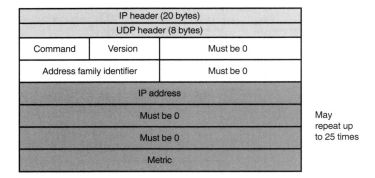

IP header (20 bytes)		
UDP header (8 bytes)		
Command	Version	Must be 0
Address family identifier		Must be 0
IP address		
Must be 0		
Must be 0		
Metric		

May
repeat up
to 25 times

FIGURE 6.17 *The basic RIP header does not contain a subnet mask. The shaded area is repeated for each route.*

RIP Traffic

IP RIP nominally sends its updates at 30-second intervals, producing the following number of bytes:

$$number\ of\ packets = ceil(\#routes/25)$$

$$number\ of\ bytes = (\#packets$$
$$* (frame\_overhead+$$
$$ip\_header+$$
$$udp\_header+$$
$$rip\_header))$$
$$+ (routes \times 20)$$

In practice, several factors affect the interval between routing updates. Many router implementations, if they receive a valid update, incorporate that update and reset their 30-second timer. Several updates spread over time, therefore, can delay a new update from being forwarded.

Because routers are initialized at random times, it would seem that their update timers go off at random 30-second intervals. Although this might seem intuitive, it is incorrect, unless the router implementation has substantial randomization built into it.

Floyd and Jacobson analyzed this situation and established that routers running a periodic update mechanism are weakly coupled [Floyd, 1994]. A weak coupling mechanism means that the updates and delays to process the updates lead to a substantial amount of synchronization among the routers.

Weak synchronization does not lock the router timing together as closely as the Network Time Protocol does. Nevertheless, traffic engineering must assume that all updates are sent at once. Routers go from being unsynchronized to synchronized rather abruptly, so there can be a very sudden increase in routing traffic when the routers synchronize.

RIP Convergence Time

Chapter 4 deals with the general properties of convergence time. This section deals with the specifics of RIP convergence.

Remember that RIP and IGRP only keep track of the routes they are currently using. They do not, as do more modern protocols, store information about potential routes. If RIP or IGRP decide a route has gone down, they must, at a minimum, wait until another router updates them with a new route to the destination.

It would seem that the minimum convergence time is the time to detect a failure, plus the time to get the next update. RIP, however, uses a holddown timer as a protection against looping. The value of the holddown timer is three times the update interval, $3 \times 30 = 90$ seconds.

Due to holddown, after a RIP router has decided a route to a destination is down, it does not accept a newly received update from a router claiming to be able to reach the destination until the holddown timer expires. So, RIP convergence time is the sum of the basic failure detection and the time to get an update, which is instantaneous if it's already in the table, as it would be if there were equal-cost load sharing to the destination. Otherwise, it's failure detection time + holddown + some fraction of update timer (0%–100%).

When and How to Use Routing in Small Networks

RIP is a simple choice for many networks, but it is not always the best choice. Often, static routing is a better choice. If, for example, there is a small number of servers and everything else goes to a single router, static routing might be adequate. If you do need dynamic routing, OSPF and EIGRP have far more functionality than RIP. RIP is adequate for router discovery and very simple topologies. We begin with a simple hub-and-spoke topology and move to distributed topologies, with both equal and unequal costs.

Hub-and-Spoke Topology

Let's begin with the centralized topology of Figure 16.18. All servers are at the data center (that is, the hub). Spoke sites only need to know how to reach the data center, as they do not communicate with other spoke sites.

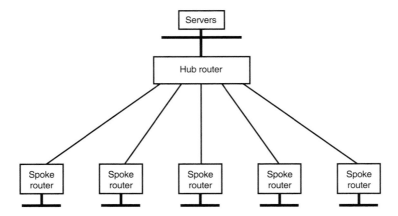

Figure 6.18 *This sort of simple topology can work best with static routing.*

In a straightforward configuration such as this, not complicated with alternate paths or dial restoration, I tend to use static routing.

Note

Don't confuse this usage of hub *as the central router with the use of the term* hub *to describe Layer 1 repeaters.*

Static routing is often criticized as not discovering alternate paths and as being administratively complex to manage. But, in the configuration shown in Figure 6.18, there are no alternate paths.

Administrative complexity can be a concern. Although the spoke routers only need to know the default route, the hub router needs to know the addresses of the remote LANs. People often worry about maintaining the configuration, but I tend to consider this a marginal objection.

If you use a spreadsheet or database for allocating your subnets, it is fairly simple to define a report that generates static route commands. This is most practical when your routers have a native command-line interface, such as Cisco or Livingston. Although Bay routers' primary interface is menu oriented, there is the supplementary, text-oriented Technician Interface. Pure menu interfaces still could be automated with **expect** scripts, but this can require programming beyond the scope of a small end-user organization.

What are the drawbacks of simply using RIP? In fact, RIP can be a reasonable solution, but should not automatically be assumed. The main reasons to be concerned about RIP is the overhead of routing updates, the potential for security exposures as discussed previously, and the limitations of RIP addressing.

Overhead

For small networks, the overhead of RIP is minimal. Figure 6.18 illustrates a requirement for a central server LAN, a client LAN at the data center, five WAN subnets, and five spoke LANs. If split horizon is assumed, a maximum of ten subnets would be advertised to any of the spoke routers. Assuming PPP encapsulation,

number of packets = ceil(10/25)=1

number of bytes = (1

*   * (7+*

*   20+*

*   8+*

*   8))*

*   + (10×20)=243*

At 64 Kbps, it takes 30 milliseconds to send the routing update. This would not be noticeable.

When Is a Network Large? When Is It Complex?

These are questions much like, "How high is up?" Nevertheless, there are some guidelines.

From the perspective of routing, networks with 500 or more routes tend to be beyond what is reasonable in a non-hierarchical network.

In a switching context, addressing and broadcast radiation concerns start appearing at 200 to 250 hosts per subnet. Other scaling factors come into effect between 500 and 1000 hosts.

What if the topology remained simple, but involved many more sites? If there were 250 remote sites,

$$number\ of\ packets = ceil(502/25)=21$$
$$number\ of\ bytes = (21$$
$$* (7+$$
$$20+$$
$$8+$$
$$8))$$
$$+ (502×20)=10943$$

This would require approximately 1.4 seconds every 30 seconds to send the routing update. People can generally perceive differences in delay between 150 and 200 milliseconds; this would be quite noticeable.

Many network architects would consider a 250-site network to be medium to large. Nevertheless, especially when replacing mainframe-based systems, hub-and-spoke topologies are considered small due to their topological simplicity.

Addressing Limitations

Let's return to the simple hub-and-spokes network. The largest LAN needs 10 devices. With a classful routing mechanism such as RIPv1, every subnet needs the same host field size, sufficient to hold 10 hosts and a router address. This fits into a /28.

The smallest classless interdomain routing (CIDR) block that holds the needed 12 subnets is a /24. For this small network, utilization is 10 spoke sites with 11 LAN addresses and 2 WAN addresses equaling 130 hosts, and a central site with 22 LAN and 10 WAN addresses equaling 32, for a total of 162 addresses.

162/254 gives a reasonable utilization ratio of 0.64. Address wastage on the point-to-point lines has not yet become extreme. Looking at a larger number of sites, 250 spoke sites with 11 LAN addresses and 2 WAN addresses equals 3,250 hosts, and a central site with 22 LAN and 250 WAN addresses, for a total of 3,522 host addresses on 502 subnets. In a classful environment, to have 502 /28 subnets, you would need /20 address space, which could be expressed as 16 network numbers in the classical Class C space, or you would need a /16 in the classical Class B space.

Distributed Topology with Equal Cost Paths

Figure 6.19 shows a slightly more complex topology in which all paths are of equal cost. Quasi-static routing can be practical when dealing with a few nodes, but more complex topologies probably need dynamic routing. RIP routing would work here because the primary path to each server farm is to go direct to the WAN hub router that supports that farm. If a spoke link to the hub goes down, the appropriate fallback is to the other hub.

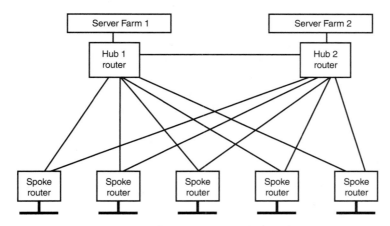

FIGURE 6.19 *Although the topology here is more complex than pure hub and spoke, it remains simple because all paths are of equal cost.*

Warning

Always be aware that when you establish the possibility of alternate paths to increase availability, sooner or later Murphy's Law will cause an alternate path to be taken unexpectedly. Murphy's Law assures this is the most obscure path that can be taken.

This sort of topology has interesting tradeoffs. A single alternate path almost always increases availability. There is a point of diminishing returns in providing alternate paths, in that it becomes harder and harder to find truly independent paths that do not share some common components.

In addition, the more the alternate path topology approaches full mesh, the more overhead it takes to maintain routing convergence. Convergence time for RIP and IGRP increases radically with the amount of meshing because the holddown timer keeps being reset.

Distributed Topology with Unequal Cost Paths

RIP cannot deal effectively with more than the simplest configurations with unequal costs because it is unaware of bandwidth on links. It can only minimize the number of links taken, which can result in taking a slow path that involves a lesser number of links than an alternative with more, but much higher-speed links. Because the largest part of latency is almost always serializing traffic onto inter-router links, which was not the assumption when RIP was designed, minimizing hop count is often undesirable. Bandwidth is a more important optimization criterion.

What if the links to the different hub sites are of different speeds? RIP does not understand bandwidth. Some router implementations do let you artificially increase the RIP hop count to make a route less desirable, but this method is usable in a very limited range of topologies. In Figure 6.20, the normal path for all traffic should be to Hub Router 1. Traffic to Hub Router 2 should follow the longer hop count path over faster lines than connect directly from spoke routers to Hub Router 2. If Hub Router 1 fails, traffic should go to Hub Router 2.

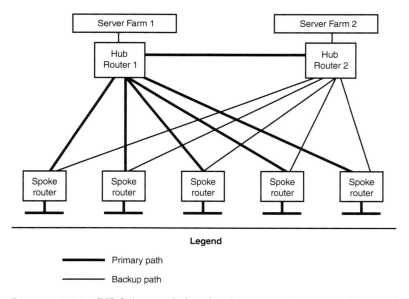

F IGURE 6.20 *RIP, being purely based on hop counts, does not understand the optimal path when links are of equal hop count but different bandwidth.*

If the alternate links are dedicated, a bandwidth-aware dynamic routing protocol such as OSPF or EIGRP works well. Static routes can work if the topology is not too complex, especially when the static routes are to a default route and are activated only when dynamic routing fails. See the section "Multiple Backup Preferences with Defaults and Statics" in Chapter 12.

If RIP is needed by end hosts, routers running OSPF or EIGRP can advertise the RIP default. As discussed in the section "Security Exposures" earlier in this chapter, be careful not to advertise potentially bogus RIP-learned routes into the dynamic routing system.

OSPF does have recently defined mechanisms for handling demand circuits. As discussed in Chapter 10, these do make some essential assumptions about the availability of links, which could lead to blackhole behavior.

Not using demand circuit mechanisms in OSPF or EIGRP can result in significant recomputation if links flap up and down. This can be acceptable, however, when the overall network size is small and a single flapping link insignificant.

RIP Version 2

RIP version 2 (RIPv2) added some additional features to RIP, but did not change the limitations of the first-generation distance vector. The protocol proper is documented in RFC 1723, but the intended usage and limitations are discussed in RFC 1722. RIPv2 fills in several of the reserved fields in RIPv1 packets, as shown in Figure 6.21.

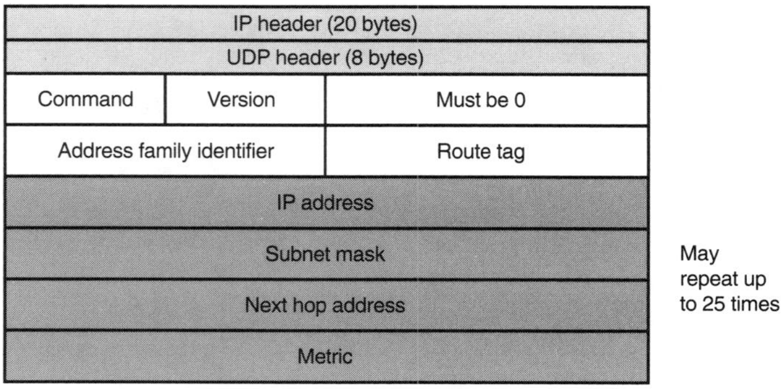

Figure 6.21 *The RIPv2 head fills in RIPv1 reserved fields, including the Subnet Mask field.*

The most obvious change is that RIPv2 sends a subnet mask with each update and thus supports arbitrary length prefixes as needed for variable-length subnet mask (VLSM) and CIDR.

RIPv2 allows implementations to send updates as multicasts rather than broadcasts. If a RIPv2 implementation does use multicasting, and the NICs of non–RIP-aware hosts on a medium are intelligent enough to ignore RIPv2 multicasts, those hosts do not suffer CPU interrupt loads from RIP updates.

Other features introduced in RIPv2 include optional cryptographic authentication of routing updates and support of demand circuits. Demand circuits are usually some sort of dialup medium, but can be extremely low bandwidth circuits where it is desirable to have the absolute minimum of routing traffic [RFC 1582].

RIPv2 still suffers from the scaling limitations of its predecessors. It remains to be seen how widely it will be implemented. True, the major router vendors have implemented it, but it is less clear how widely it will be implemented in hosts that listen to RIP updates.

Looking Ahead

This chapter deals with some design considerations for small networks. Chapter 7 generalizes the choices in selecting routing and switching mechanisms based on user requirements. Subsequent chapters deal with the implementation of the mechanisms chosen.

PART III

Defining an Architecture

CHAPTER 7

Selecting the Routing/Switching Architecture

It's a very sobering feeling to be up in space and realize that one's safety factor was determined by the lowest bidder on a government contract.
—Alan Shepherd

186,000 miles per second. It's not just a good idea. It's the law.
—Seen on a button

If the design of the building be originally bad, the only virtue it can ever possess will be signs of antiquity.
—John Ruskin

Part I discusses defining your requirements at the edge of the network. Part II introduces some of the technologies that underlie interconnecting the edge points.

In this chapter, we begin to unify requirements analysis and networking technologies. Again starting at the network's edge, we will move inward, establishing connectivity and then considering optimizations to the technology. Routing is the most general technology, but appropriate use of Layer 2 techniques provides an overdrive.

In your first passes at defining the enterprise architecture, it's less a question of deciding whether you need switching or routing at a given point than it is of deciding what problem you are trying to solve. I start network designs by deciding the requirements for each community of interest, superimposing the internetwork requirements on the common enterprise network.

Following are the broad steps in creating a design:

1. Define the business requirements—what constitutes success? What constitutes failure?

2. Translate these requirements into quantitative requirements for performance and availability as seen at the user interface to the network.

3. Create a naming structure that identifies the application endpoints—the clients and servers. See Chapter 3 of *Designing Addressing Architectures for Routing and Switching* [Berkowitz, 1998a].

4. Define Layer 3 and Layer 2 addressing that provides appropriate connectivity among the endpoints. Consider external connectivity, security, and network management when you do this. See Chapters 4 through 9 of *Designing Addressing Architectures for Routing and Switching* [Berkowitz, 1998a].

5. Examine host software and other connectivity requirements, and the implementation of name servers. Details are in Chapters 10 and 11 of *Designing Addressing Architectures for Routing and Switching* [Berkowitz, 1998a].

6. Select the internetworking architecture, the major focus of this chapter.

7. Be sure the network is manageable, following concepts in Chapter 8.

8. Design connection-oriented and connectionless Layer 1 and 2 structures, as discussed, respectively, in Chapters 9 and 10. See Chapter 12 of *Designing Addressing Architectures for Routing and Switching* [Berkowitz, 1998a].

9. Design routing, as discussed in Chapters 11 and 12. Detailed addressing and address manipulation features for routers are in Chapters 13 and 14 of *Designing Addressing Architectures for Routing and Switching* [Berkowitz, 1998a].

10. Plan for future technologies, as discussed in Chapters 13 and 14.

Treat these steps as a way of approaching problems rather than a rigid procedure. You will often find that decisions made in one step lead you to revisit an earlier step, because the later analysis helped you better understand the problem or see limitations of a proposed solution. As you gain experience in network design, you will learn when it is time to move to the next step rather than go into infinite level of detail in a given step. I will often consciously move to a next step without having answered every question in an earlier one, because experience has taught me that approaching the problem at a different level of detail often suggests a solution.

Real-World Hierarchical Models

The only way we know how to build networks of appreciable size, that are still scalable and maintainable, is by using hierarchical design. You have seen application-level hierarchy described in Chapter 1. The most common approach is a three-tiered hierarchy (illustrated using the graphic conventions in Figure 7.1), which is composed of the following:

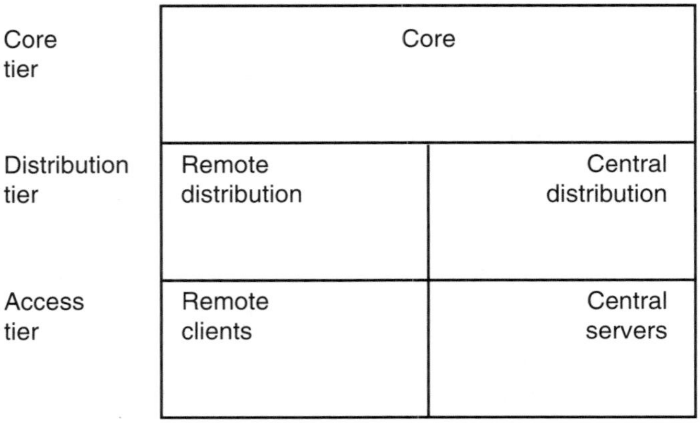

Core tier	Core	
Distribution tier	Remote distribution	Central distribution
Access tier	Remote clients	Central servers

FIGURE 7.1   *These three tiers usefully describe medium-sized enterprise networks. At any given tier, there can be boxes for different applications or network technologies.*

- *Access tier*: Functions that need to be close to the end hosts. Except at large sites, the access function tends to be very cost sensitive. Access tier devices are optimized for minimum cost per site for devices that access dedicated WAN links, for minimum cost per unit of bandwidth within the workgroup, and for minimum cost per on-demand connection.

Small routers are the usual solution for minimizing cost at sites served by dedicated links. Such routers can contain built-in LAN hubs, or hubs or LAN switches can be used to reduce the cost of connecting local devices to them.

Minimizing cost per unit of local bandwidth is the role of workgroup LAN switches. That does not mean minimizing bandwidth; it means providing bandwidth at lower cost per unit than a traditional router could do.

Minimizing connection cost is the role of either small routers (for small but multi-user offices) or, for single users, devices attached to or internal to the workstation. Such devices include analog modems, ISDN terminal adapters and network terminators, and access devices for wireless, cable networks, and xDSL services.

- *Distribution tier*: Concentrates many access paths into efficient paths for connection to the core. Converts protocols and manages bandwidth between access and the core.

Distribution devices most commonly include Layer 3 relaying, either as a traditional router or as a Layer 3 switch. You can also use Layer 2 switches to aggregate bandwidth, especially when using VLANs.

- *Core tier*: Efficient transfer among sites. These might be routers or Layer 2 switches. Although most discussions of the core tier assume that core devices are necessarily high bandwidth, this might not be true when the logical core of the enterprise is distributed over a WAN. The greatest bandwidth might be at the distribution tier within major sites.

Do not put application servers into the core, even if they seem to be the central servers for your organization. The core is intended for network interconnection functions, and the only servers it should possibly contain are network management functions such as DNS, DHCP, TFTP, and SNMP.

Even when servers have a central application function, there almost always are local inter-server communications, or communications with the server by users at the server site. Putting the servers at the distribution tier lets you isolate this local traffic from the core.

Treat this three-tier model as a tool for design, not as a straitjacket, forcing designs that simply don't fit the circumstances. Figure 7.2 shows a common configuration in which the enterprise network architect is responsible for the access and distribution tiers, but the internals of the core are outsourced to a WAN service provider. This arguably can be called a *two-tiered model*, in the sense that the enterprise is responsible for only two tiers.

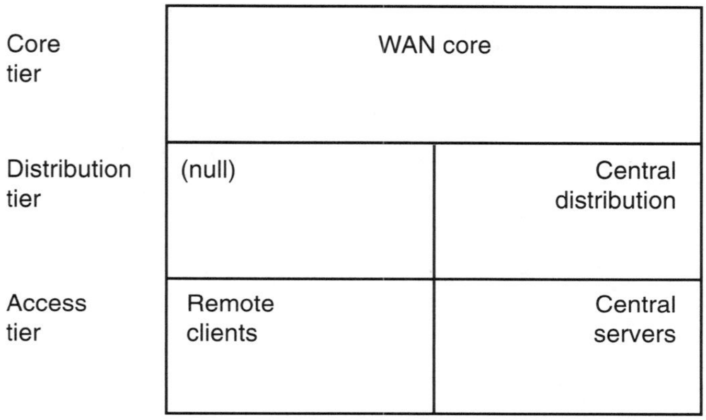

Core tier	WAN core	
Distribution tier	(null)	Central distribution
Access tier	Remote clients	Central servers

FIGURE 7.2 *Not every site needs the same kind of connectivity; you can separate different connectivity types at the same tier.*

A core can be a LAN interconnecting sites on a campus. Figure 7.3 shows a slight variation on Figure 7.1, in which the enterprise is responsible for three tiers. Internet connectivity is treated as one more distribution-tier server connection.

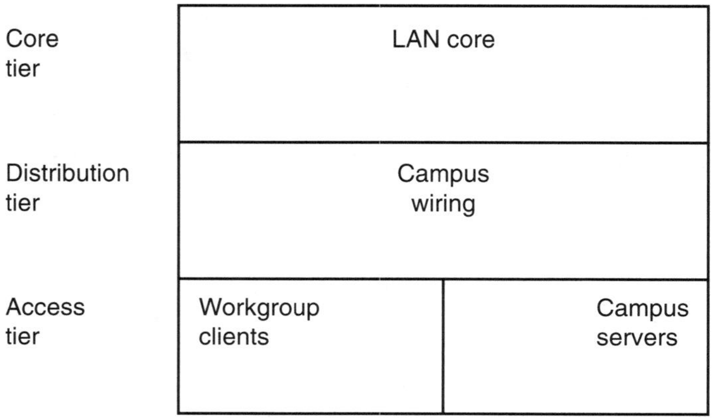

Core tier	LAN core	
Distribution tier	Campus wiring	
Access tier	Workgroup clients	Campus servers

FIGURE 7.3 *When the network is focused on a campus, the backbone can be treated as the core.*

Figure 7.4 shows how a WAN service provider can impose internal structure on a core. Frame Relay increasingly is delivered on T3 facilities, due to the trend of aggregating many spoke sites.

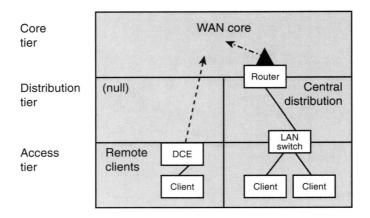

Legend

- - - - -▶ Frame Relay virtual circuit
- · - · - ·▶ Multiple virtual circuits from remote sites on a single physical connection
———— LAN or local cabling connection

FIGURE 7.4 *There can be hierarchical structure within a service provider WAN core.*

Up to this point, the figures have emphasized information flow, not specific components. As your design progresses, you can superimpose component functions onto the relationship diagram (see Figure 7.5). I emphasize *component functions* rather than specific chassis, because many products put multiple component functions, such as hubs, Layer 2 switches, routers, and management processors, into the same physical chassis.

When I explain my design to a consulting customer, I find it helps their understanding to begin with the hierarchical diagram and then build up the component logic on top of it. On a practical basis, I take a presentation graphics package such as PowerPoint, draw the hierarchical diagram as a slide master, and then add slides, a tier or a tier division at a time, showing where the component functions go. Or you can use overhead transparencies, putting the hierarchical diagram on the bottom and layering component functions onto it.

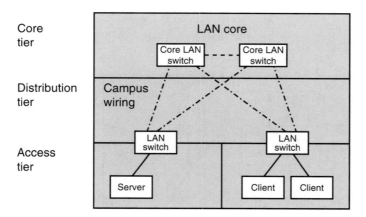

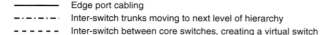

Legend

────────   Edge port cabling
─·─·─·─·   Inter-switch trunks moving to next level of hierarchy
─ ─ ─ ─ ─   Inter-switch between core switches, creating a virtual switch

FIGURE 7.5 *The redundant functions in a core can be shown as you increase the level of detail in a drawing.*

Please don't follow the all-too-common industry practice of trying to fit everything onto one page. Too much visual detail both obscures the logical view and simply is hard to read. One of my mentors, Joe Hunter of the U.S. Department of Labor, used to say, "If you can't cleanly flowchart the problem onto a single page, you don't understand the problem." I've found these to be very wise words, with the understanding that the top-level diagram can be a roadmap to more specific one-page drawings. If the functions in a given box of the drawing become too complex, draw the box as its own slide (see Figure 7.6).

Again, do not let this model overly constrain you. Figure 7.7 is drawn from a consulting client of mine, a worldwide transportation company. It was reasonable to have two levels of core function, one interconnecting sites on a continent, and a higher tier interconnecting the enterprise's continental regions and the Internet.

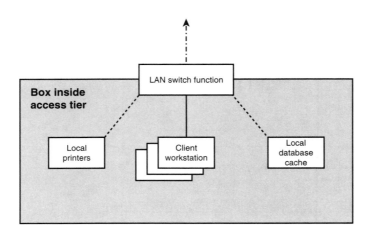

Box inside access tier

LAN switch function

Local printers

Client workstation

Local database cache

Legend

——————— Edge port cabling

— · — · — · — Inter-switch trunks moving to next level of hierarchy

- - - - - - - - Local devices only; traffic does not flow outside box

FIGURE 7.6 *Any of the logical boxes of a high-level hierarchical drawing can be detailed in a separate drawing.*

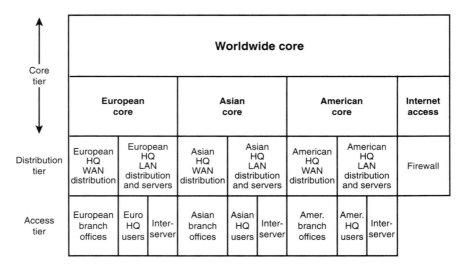

	Worldwide core							
Core tier								
	European core		**Asian core**		**American core**		**Internet access**	
Distribution tier	European HQ WAN distribution	European HQ LAN distribution and servers	Asian HQ WAN distribution	Asian HQ LAN distribution and servers	American HQ WAN distribution	American HQ LAN distribution and servers	Firewall	
Access tier	European branch offices	Euro HQ users	Inter-server	Asian branch offices	Asian HQ users	Inter-server	Amer. branch offices	Amer. HQ users	Inter-server	

FIGURE 7.7 *You can sublayer any tier when it makes sense to do so, such as a sublayered core in this illustration.*

Don't fall into the trap of assuming one monolithic design is necessary. It can be entirely possible to design significant campus or departmental networks, each with a meaningful core function, and then to link these networks with a "core of cores" designed separately. It was reasonable to have two levels of core function, one interconnecting sites on a continent and a higher tier interconnecting the enterprise's continental regions and the Internet. Figure 7.7 shows architectural relationships. Later in this chapter, you learn how specific technologies were used in various parts of this design.

Virtual private networks (VPNs) are a hot industry topic, even though it has been extremely difficult for the IETF to agree on a clear definition of what constitutes a VPN. A basic definition [Berkowitz, 1999b] states that a VPN minimally includes a set of administrative policies that identifies a set of users that need to be connected. Through a set of mapping functions, which can be tunnels, virtual circuits, dialup circuits, or physical media, these user addresses are mapped to a shared transmission system operated by the provider. The VPN can provide optional services for security, quality of service enforcement, multiprotocol support, and so on.

Starting the Routing/Switching Architecture at the Edge

Begin at the user and ask basic questions. As mentioned in Chapter 1, you start with qualitative questions directed at top management and refine them into quantitative requirements for performance and availability at the edge of the network. These basic questions include how users physically interconnect in a workgroup, how the workgroup connects to the next level of the hierarchy, and whether your organization needs to plan for applications with critical quality of service requirements.

There are five major types of users requiring connections:

- *Large office user*. The workstation plugs into a fixed cable plant that runs LANs or possibly ATM. There are multiple LANs at the site. WANs connect the site, not the users directly, to other locations.

- *Small office user*. Typically, there is a single LAN or a very small number of LANs to which the workstations connect. The office is at a fixed location, so it can use WAN facilities with dedicated access media, with services including Frame Relay. There is a single primary point of WAN access, although there might be redundant devices.

Not all small offices need WAN access for their production applications, although some WAN access is almost certainly needed for remote network control. You can have situations where a small office simply needs efficient access among a small group of clients and servers.

- *Telecommuter.* There is either a direct connection between the user device and the WAN or perhaps a very small LAN that might be implemented as a built-in hub in the router. Access might not use a router at all, but instead have an ISDN or analog link to a network access server. The key distinction between a telecommuter and a road warrior or mobile user is that the telecommuter is in a fixed location, so access mechanisms that require prior provisioning are practical. Such mechanisms include Frame Relay, ISDN, xDSL, CATV, and so on.

- *Road warrior.* The classic road warrior is an individual dialing from a laptop in a hotel room to the Internet or his fixed-location computer—as indeed these words are being written. Road warriors call in from different locations, but they stay at one location for the duration of a session. They generally connect with analog modems.

- *Truly mobile user.* Almost always a single user station—if there is a device such as a printer, it attaches to the workstation with a peripheral, not a LAN, interface. There is no fixed location for the user, so facilities that require prior physical provisioning are not feasible. Usable facilities include analog dialup, cellular radio, and possibly very small aperture satellite (VSAT).

These four categories can blur, but are a decent starting point for problem analysis. As an example of blurring, consider a practice increasingly common in large consulting firms, *hotelling*. In this type of business, many workers spend most of their time at client premises, possibly connected to a client LAN and acting as a large site user there, or dialing back to the home office as does a road warrior. Occasionally, however, the consultant returns to his home office to write reports, meet with colleagues, and so on. The home office acts as a hotel in the sense that it provides facilities for transient workers. It has a number of transient worker cubicles or offices, but not as many as the total number of workers. A worker reserves a work area for a time when he will be in the main office, much as you would reserve a hotel room. After the worker is in the office, he connects to the main LAN and his connectivity becomes that of a large LAN user.

Mobile, telecommuter, and small office users' access equipment needs to have their WAN access costs minimized by controlling the cost of equipment at each site and using cheap, on-demand bandwidth when it is adequate for the workload.

Connectivity at the Workgroup Level

Connectionless Layer 2 switching is a means of obtaining large amounts of local bandwidth at low cost. At the access tier, it is primarily appropriate for the large office to provide fast paths between local users and servers. The other three categories rarely need enough bandwidth that an overdrive path makes any sense.

Some small office networks might use a switch as the primary means of interconnection. A decision to use a switch rather than a hub is often driven by management considerations rather than to increase bandwidth. A workgroup switch can provide RMON and other monitoring management functions.

In principle, an SNMP-manageable hub might be an option for small workgroups. In reality, the price difference between manageable hubs and low-end switches is becoming inconsequential.

For the smallest networks, especially when the users have some troubleshooting ability, a non-managed hub might be acceptable. To put it in a personal context, as I write this, I have four Macs, a Windows NT box, a UNIX machine, and a router interconnected through a dumb hub in my home and office. At the moment, I don't have connectivity to one machine and wish that I did have some interface monitoring capability. Then, I remember the hub cost about $60, whereas I would have paid at least several hundred out-of-pocket dollars for a manageable hub. (This really isn't a case of "Do what I say, not what I do." What makes economic sense for me to troubleshoot doesn't apply to a production environment where the users have no networking technical skills.)

Tip

When you want to optimize or enhance an existing network, it can be very useful, even before the real network design is ready, to put workgroup switches in selected representative workgroups. Treat these switches as temporary installations. The switches are there for measurement, not initially for optimizing bandwidth.

Remember there are cases where abruptly replacing a shared medium with a switch might cause problems. The archetype of a situation where you should be careful in introducing a switch is a set of busy clients with one server, the server attached with a 10 Mbps port. Do not ignore the server capacity; it should be matched to the network bandwidth and the client workload.

In large offices, there is no question that connecting users to switches gives significant additional flexibility. One of the major advantages is the capability to move users from one VLAN to another.

Also in a large office, access-level design depends on whether there are non-data applications. Non-data applications probably split usefully into voice (with or without data) and imaging applications.

From a hierarchical standpoint, the access tier can connect directly to a core, or it can go through a distribution tier. Direct core attachment makes sense when the inter-workgroup connectivity is simple and standardized.

Physically Connecting Devices in a Workgroup

Hub-and-spokes hierarchy is the usual physical topology, with user devices connected to a concentrating device. In self-contained workgroups, this device is usually a hub or switch, packaged for an office environment. See Chapter 10 for a discussion of hubs versus workgroup switches.

The cheapest means of connection is a dumb hub without remote management. 10 Mbps workgroup switches with management might be only slightly more expensive than remotely managed hubs, but offer better performance and more management options. Depending on the switch, it might be possible to add remote management after the initial installation, either with a new software image or a plug-in management card.

In larger buildings containing multiple workgroups, you can use a hierarchical building cabling model such as that in Figure 7.8, which contains places for several levels of cable concentration.

The cabling system is the lowest level of detail in most networks. If you are doing a top-down design, you specify cabling at the level after specifying components.

Advanced Technologies for Offices

Whenever I watch *Star Trek*, I feel a sense of loss at how the United Federation of Planets has forgotten so many ancient technologies we know so well, such as seat belts, displays that don't explode, and knowing how to shoot straight when wearing red shirts. Don't lose some key technologies of today when installing network inter-connection devices.

One of those key technologies is Velcro. Many vendors advertise designer-styled hubs and switches as intended for the desktop. The reality is that desks get cluttered, and, if you do not take precautions, said hubs and switches get knocked off a working desktop. Secure them, or put them in a bookcase or on a side table.

continues

continued

If the device does fall off a desk, the RJ45 modular connectors for most wiring tend to stay attached. Most of these small devices, however, have a power cord that uses a slide-on, non-locking connector on the chassis, with the other end sealed into an AC adapter. (*Slide-off* is a more appropriate term when the chassis falls.)

Perhaps a *Star Wars* rather than a *Star Trek* innovation that can secure the power connector, duct tape is very much like the Force. It has a light side, a dark side, and it holds the universe together.

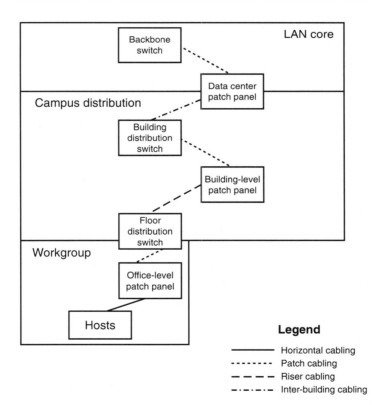

Legend

——————— Horizontal cabling

-------- Patch cabling

— — — Riser cabling

—·—·—· Inter-building cabling

FIGURE 7.8   *In generalized building cable models, end devices connect to wiring closets. Wiring closets concentrate workgroup signals and put them onto a riser medium.*

Assuming you do not have ATM to the desktop, you need a router to connect the local environment to the WAN. When I look at workgroups, I tend to think of local routers effectively as application servers. With the growing trend for small access routers to include proxy and firewall services, this is increasingly valid. The router effectively is an Internet or intranet server. A hub or switch is the main interconnection device.

For more than one or two devices, it is not cost-effective to home-run end-user devices directly into full-capability router ports. That does not mean, however, that the chassis that contains the router function cannot contain hub or switch functions to which the end devices connect.

At the spoke sites, how should the workstations connect to the router function? The lowest-cost solution is to connect the workstations to a 10-Mbps shared-medium, non–SNMP-managed hub. If you have more devices than ports on the hub of choice, you might need to install a system of cascaded hubs.

As you will see in Chapter 10, more intelligent 10-Mbps hubs are only slightly cheaper than workgroup switches. Workgroup switches give more flexibility at only slightly more cost than managed hubs with equivalent port densities. When the user devices connect at 100 Mbps, however, a managed Fast Ethernet hub, for carefully selected traffic patterns, can be more cost-effective than a switch. Switches, however, continue to drop in price, whereas hubs are probably close to their minimum possible cost.

Multiple interconnected hubs, or, as you will see shortly, multiple interconnected workgroup switches, can actually be more useful than a single device. Each device acts as a Layer 1 repeater, so it extends the distance to which you can run cabling. Small switches can also provide a traffic-reducing fast path to small servers such as workgroup printers.

Is It Really That Simple?

In the real world, the model might not be this simple. Even in a small topology, you can find reasons for hierarchy such as improving access to local servers.

Figure 7.6 shows, for an apparently simple network, a situation where it is desirable to have a fast path to some local servers. These servers are part of the network infrastructure, not the primary *golden copy* databases.

Just because you have fast paths available in a local environment, do not immediately rush to make everything 100 Mbps. If the WAN connection is less than 1 Mbps, you will get no performance gain for external connectivity by connecting a simple router port to a switch with Fast Ethernet. If you are doing local inter-LAN or inter-VLAN routing, fast router connectivity might make sense.

Printers rarely accept data faster than a 10 Mbps port can supply. Even though they technically are servers, you do not see performance improvements when typical workgroup printers are attached at 100 Mbps.

If application servers have insufficient processing capacity, putting them on switch ports can make matters worse. A server might be running at 40% CPU utilization, with the number of requests that can reach it on a shared medium. By converting the shared medium to a switched one, you can start delivering traffic to the server at a rate that would drive its CPU utilization to 80%. In most hosts, there is a critical level of utilization at which per-transaction performance gets much worse. If that threshold is 70% for this server, introducing a switch would simply move a problem from the network to the host. The only real way to optimize performance in such a situation is to consider both the host and the network. The better the network designer, the better he or she balances these factors.

High-Workload and QoS-Critical Applications

As voice, video, and other data with quality of service requirements enter the general networking world, designers face the challenge of controlled quality of service at the desktop. There are three fundamental ways to do this:

- Overprovision the LAN or switch to which devices are connected, monitoring utilization and making sure it stays low enough that congestion is unlikely. Because adding LAN bandwidth is inexpensive, this is a reasonable, not overly wasteful, strategy.

- ATM virtual circuits to the desktop, with specific QoS for each call.

- Flow-based reservation systems such as RSVP at the edge, with either QoS routing or ATM beyond the desktop.

Voice is actually a fairly low-bandwidth application that is intolerant of delay. Do your applications consider voice? If so, are you simply providing an alternative to telephones, or are you running an integrated telephony application? An example of the latter is an airline reservation system, where an operator can transfer both a voice call and the associated reservation transaction in progress.

Another argument for voice/data integration is better utilization of WAN bandwidth. WAN bandwidth tends to be the most expensive life cycle cost in most enterprise networks, so if you can avoid duplicating bandwidth for voice, video, and data, your network will be much more cost-effective.

Do you need applications that retrieve document images, or perhaps complex but non-motion graphics such as medical magnetic resonance imaging or computerized tomography scans? Although such applications deal with large image files, they essentially are non-interactive file transfers. They need substantial bandwidth but are tolerant of delay.

Video applications, whether surveillance cameras, videoconferencing, or motion picture editing, are intolerant of delay and need different amounts of bandwidth.

Connectivity at the Individual Level

Cost of connectivity drives access techniques used by telecommuters, road warriors, and mobile users. This cost has two major components: initial capital investment for equipment and software, and recurring costs. The recurring costs can be a fixed monthly amount per user for an Internet account, a limited-access dialup account with a service provider, or the access charge for new local technologies such as cable TV or xDSL. Variable costs can involve a fixed charge per call or a charge for the time connected.

Enterprise-Operated Remote Access

The enterprise, rather than an ISP, can operate modem pools or other on-demand connectivity methods (see Figure 7.9). Enterprise-operated access can be reasonable when users are primarily within local dialing range of a major site within the enterprise. Network access servers combine access ports (for example, modem, ISDN) with routing onto higher-speed media into the core.

Initial costs include the remote access server, modems or other line connection devices (for example, ISDN Network Terminations), and installation costs for the local loops. You might be able to achieve economies of scale by using ISDN Primary Rate Interfaces (PRI) which use a single physical interface to handle 23 (North America and Japan) or 30 connections. You need to check your local provider pricing to determine what is reasonable for your area. In much of Canada, PRI is outrageously expensive. In my home area, even BRI is quite expensive. For my home/office network, I have given up on using ISDN because ADSL and cable are far more cost-effective in my area.

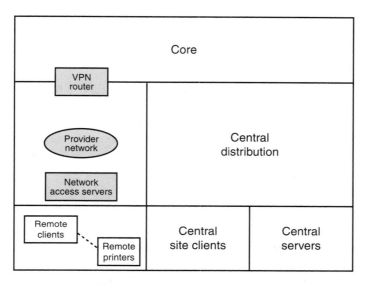

FIGURE 7.9 *When the enterprise runs its own remote access service, the clients are at the access tier and the remote access servers are at the distribution tier.*

Outsourcing Remote Access with Virtual Private Networks

When the user base is distributed over a wide geographic area, or the enterprise does not have the in-house resources to operate modem pools, enterprises increasingly outsource their individual user connectivity using VPNs (see Figure 7.10).

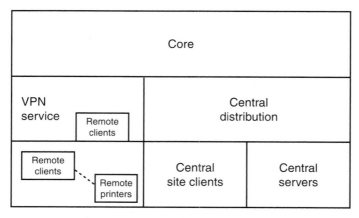

FIGURE 7.10 *Access VPNs outsource individual user access and link it to the enterprise backbone.*

VPN economies usually come from reductions in the recurring access charges, rather than in the initial investment. VPNs are especially attractive when the workforce is highly distributed, so that the enterprise cannot justify its own access servers in a large number of geographic areas.

Most commonly, using an access VPN involves creating ISP accounts for your users and arranging an authenticated tunnel from the ISP to your enterprise. In Figure 7.10, the server farm at the enterprise has a dedicated link to the service provider, over which the user connections are routed. The central-site servers are reached through the central distribution network, which connects to the provider-operated core. Central site users connect locally to servers using the central site distribution function, whereas remote users connect to provider NAS at remote sites, which connect to the central site via the provider network.

Do understand that using a VPN that might employ Internet connectivity is not quite the same as "selling on the Internet." All clients and servers connected by a VPN are defined in advance of their exchanging data. They might be in an intranet or an extranet, but they share some predefined business relationship.

In contrast, a vendor on the Internet does not know the identity of clients before they go to a Web server and read pages or place an order.

A VPN can offer Internet access as one of its services to well-defined users. Certain users can access a VPN through public ISP modem pools, connecting to the VPN only after authentication. Figure 7.11 illustrates a way to conceptualize users with remote access both to the Internet and an intranet.

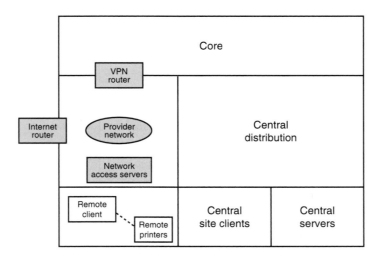

FIGURE 7.11 *Remote site users can use their remote access both for general Internet access and VPN access, as long as security is maintained.*

Complex VPN Relationships

Users can belong to multiple VPNs. You can speak of the scope of a VPN as intranet—controlled by one enterprise—or extranet—control distributed among multiple enterprises. Inside an enterprise, for example, there might be departmental VPNs spanning multiple geographic locations. A human resources information server might be present on each of these intranet VPNs.

For an extranet case, consider a physician's office that belongs to the VPNs of several managed care organizations with which the physician contracts as a service provider. As shown in Figure 7.12, having the various potentially competing managed care organizations, which in turn service the providers, can be much cleaner administratively than requiring all communicating parties to deal with one another through bilateral and multilateral agreements.

Note

One of my clients, a medical transcription firm, uses several sorts of VPNs. It places application-specific servers at customer sites, where the servers must comply with the conventions of the customer's intranet. These servers, however, are also accessed through a router with network address translation, which both translates the customer addresses into that of the transcription network and provides VPN encryption and tunneling back to the transcription data center. Another VPN contains the transcription data center and contract transcribers, who access the data center through on-demand encrypted tunnels from their hosts to the data center, running through arbitrary Internet connections.

In another application area, the Visa and MasterCard credit card authorization networks are operated by service companies owned by their member banks. These banks both cooperate in a common extranet, but are also direct competitors.

Relationships can become even more complex. I worked with one of the major credit card authorization networks, which charges a per-transaction fee to its member banks. Two directly competing banks realized that a large part of their authorization requests went between each other, and the cost of a dedicated line between them was less than the service company's per-transaction charges. Figure 7.13 shows an example of abstracting this sort of relationship.

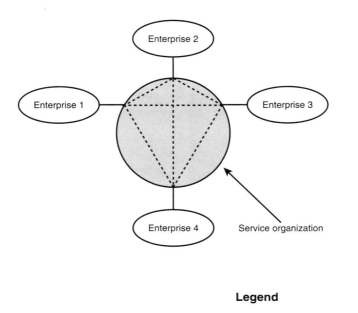

Legend

────────── Connectivity to service organization

- - - - - - - - Tunnels or on-demand
facilities operated by
service organization

FIGURE 7.12   *Having a VPN service provider that competitors can deal with can make administration much simpler.*

Enterprise 1 prefers its direct links to Enterprises 2 and 4 as opposed to going through the service provider. There are many potential variants on the policies here. For example, the bypass links might be backups to a preferred path through the service company. Enterprise 1 negotiated backups because its links to Enterprises 2 and 4 are especially critical.

Bypasses of this sort need not be symmetrical. Although Enterprise 1 might consider the bypass link to Enterprise 2 to be its preferred path, Enterprise 2 might have policies that prefer the service provider as its path to Enterprise 1.

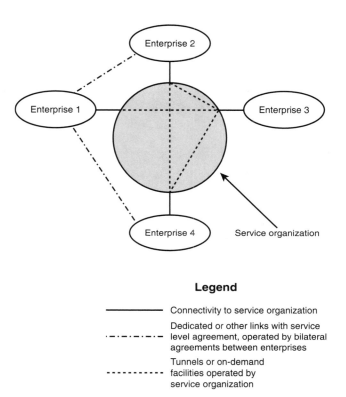

Legend

——————— Connectivity to service organization

·—·—·—·—· Dedicated or other links with service level agreement, operated by bilateral agreements between enterprises

---------- Tunnels or on-demand facilities operated by service organization

FIGURE 7.13 *Separate enterprises can bypass a common service company that operates a VPN.*

This is the opposite of the motivation of many enterprises to use VPNs: getting out of the operational cost of managing WAN facilities. Although VPNs can be quite cost-effective in reducing operational costs for low-volume access, economies of scale are still possible. The term *hybrid VPN* is sometimes used to describe an intranet or extranet that uses some outsourced access services and some dedicated links for high-volume flows, but is managed as one system. A single service provider has engineering responsibility for the entire hybrid network. Figure 7.14 shows an example of this model of responsibility, which differs from that of Figure 7.13.

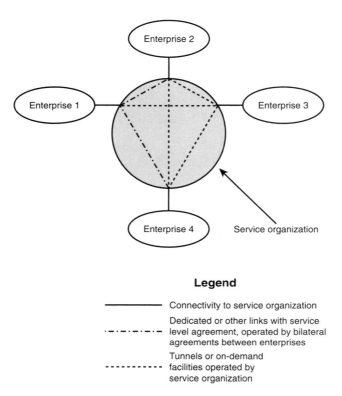

Legend

——————— Connectivity to service organization

·—·—·—·—· Dedicated or other links with service level agreement, operated by bilateral agreements between enterprises

----------- Tunnels or on-demand facilities operated by service organization

FIGURE 7.14 *The enterprises, in this example, put special service level agreements on some paths operated by the service organization.*

In the hybrid case, one organization has operational responsibility for the entire network. In the bypass case, individual enterprises take responsibility for bilateral agreements between each other.

If the service organization charges for traffic, and the enterprises have high volume between one another, it might be cheaper to bypass the service organization for some specific traffic patterns. The enterprises will need additional staff and expertise to manage the links among them.

Do be aware that conventional interior routing might not be appropriate for bypass scenarios. In Figure 7.13, consider what would happen if Enterprise 2 lost its link to the VPN, but all of Enterprise 1 and Enterprise 2's address space was advertised using a conventional interior routing protocol.

Traditional routing would find the service provider to be reachable through Enterprise 1, which might be shocked to find all of its competitor's traffic coming through the Enterprise 1 network to reach the service organization. Extranet connections such as this need static routing, policy filters, or possibly BGP with policy filtering.

Distribution Architecture

After establishing basic edge connectivity, the next step is to build the core and distribution tiers. Often, it is a good idea to move directly to the core, which links major sites, establish its characteristics, and then move to distribution tier design. One of the functions of the distribution tier is to mediate the differences between the core and access tiers.

The Distribution Tier Is the Place You Lie for the Best Reasons

I am a carpenter and cabinetmaker, but I am best known as an outstanding network designer. Nevertheless, I still raise clouds of sawdust in various projects and have learned certain truisms. One of these deals with the case where I have built several shelving units, and my measurements were a little off. Or the measurements seemed slightly off at floor level. But on reaching the top, there was a highly visible gap of over an inch. Worried at first, I evaluated the situation, and then grinned as I realized, "This is why God blessed us with molding." A neat strip of molding covered the gap.

And so it is with the distribution tier. It is the place where you hide the gaps between core and access technologies.

Networks of any reasonable size probably work best when they use a combination of Layer 2 and Layer 3 techniques. The general principle is that Layer 2 LAN switching gives less expensive bandwidth in workgroups and in collapsed backbones. Routing allows more flexible and fault-tolerant topology, clean conversions between media types, and more efficient bandwidth utilization.

Layer 2 WAN switching tends to be more of a carrier service than an enterprise service, when the enterprise network only runs data applications.

Are there situations where a single main WAN technology serves all levels of the hierarchy? Yes. These tend to be either networks restricted to a single large campus or a number of peer sites connected in a WAN. Most campuses are dominated by LAN technologies or a mixture of LAN technologies with ATM.

When there is one main technology, there is no reason to draw one cloud at the middle of your network, obscuring all hierarchy. Instead, draw lines for the virtual circuits that the cloud supports and keep those lines at the correct level of hierarchy.

A key aspect of campus design deals with the number of hosts that can share a broadcast domain. Table 2.2 in Chapter 2 gives general guidance on the number of devices that can share a broadcast domain. This table assumes that the hosts are connected at 10 Mbps and are of moderate speed.

If hosts are Pentium II machines, they potentially can deal with more broadcasts. Connecting such hosts at 100 Mbps or faster, however, might not necessarily increase the number of hosts that can share a broadcast domain. Although a faster host can accept more broadcasts, other fast hosts can generate more broadcasts. 100 Mbps connectivity subjects a host to a potentially larger broadcast load.

There are fundamental limits to the number of devices that can share in a switched system. Often, the practical limit is the sum of the speeds of server interfaces.

Broadcast interrupt load on hosts is another limiting factor. A reasonable upper limit on well-behaved IP hosts is approximately 1000. Well-behaved IP hosts do not generate broadcasts for user applications; they only generate broadcasts for system functions such as DHCP, DNS, and ARP. If the IP hosts generate multicasts and there are hosts in the same broadcast domain that suffer interrupt load from any multicast group—they do not ignore multicasts not meant for them—you cannot treat the IP hosts as well-behaved. Unfortunately, well-behaved IP hosts suffer the unfairness of any collective punishment; the good IP hosts are penalized for the limitations of the bad NIC implementations that do not understand multicasts.

Topological Hierarchy in Layer 2 Switched Networks

Campus networks often qualify as complete switching-based hierarchies, although traditional Layer 2 switching often needs to be complemented with VLAN technologies. A variant on thinking of a campus network as purely switched is that a router function is used only to leave the campus, so the router essentially is treated as a server, not part of the network infrastructure.

When you consider whether a pure switched hierarchy meets most of your needs, the key question often is the distribution of servers. Are some servers, such as printers, used only in a small workgroup, whereas others are departmental or enterprisewide?

You plausibly might have an all-switched hierarchy that gives a fast path to certain local servers. At each level of the hierarchy, there are separate requirements for uplink bandwidth to the next tier, some amount of bandwidth to servers at the same tier. A rule of thumb is to oversubscribe end-user clients by 50%–66%, assuming the nature of the application-level communication is inherently query/response:

Uplink bandwidth = Sum of client (ports/oversubscriptionFactor)

oversubscriptionFactor ranges between a conservative 2 to an often-practical 3 or more.

Client ports are those ports on the switch to which workstations are connected. Do not count ports to which local printers are connected, but include ports that have cache servers or other server functions that need to be refreshed from a distant server.

Enforcing hierarchy can begin at Layer 2 or even Layer 1. There can be hierarchies in one, or in more than one, protocol family. Figure 7.15 shows a hierarchy with LAT kept local to one medium—which doesn't even need to be a VLAN—NetBEUI with a scope of a single broadcast domain implemented with switches and VLAN switches, and IP with a scope of the entire network. In looking at such a hierarchy, it is useful to think of the *scope* of a particular protocol. Is it *link-local* on a single physical or simulated medium? Is it *broadcast-domain-wide*, going through several bridges or switches? Is it *routing-domain-wide*, propagating through every router? Is it *routing-area-wide*, present only in hierarchical parts of the routing domain?

Servers with multiple interfaces can serve as relays, and indeed impose hierarchy. DNS is a good example of application-level relaying.

Another approach uses a thoughtful combination of multiported servers and switches. If you have two largely self-contained departmental networks containing their own application servers, there might be little *application* reason to route between the two. Clients on one of these networks simply do not have an application-specific reason to send packets directly to a server on the other network.

Both departmental networks, however, can have application-level reasons to send application-level messages to one or more common servers. Such common servers can include the enterprise mail server, certainly DNS and DHCP, or an Internet firewall. It is the common servers that you want to have connected to multiple VLANs.

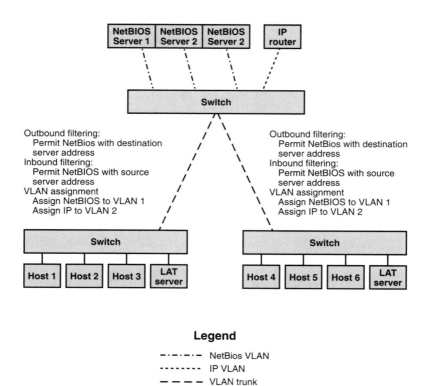

Legend

—·—·—·—   NetBios VLAN

· · · · · · · ·   IP VLAN

— — — —   VLAN trunk

FIGURE 7.15 *LAT is restricted to a single set of switch ports. NetBEUI has a scope of a single broadcast domain, whereas IP can route into other broadcast domains.*

The server-and-switch approach becomes especially strong with VLANs, because multiported servers can act as application-level routers, minimizing or eliminating requirements for network layer routing among VLANs. Such servers should not actually route between VLANs, except possibly for well-defined management traffic such as **ping**s. They can, however, do application-level routing of records between different VLANs. For example, a server might act as a cc:Mail electronic mail server on one VLAN, but forward mail messages as SMTP messages onto another VLAN.

Before deciding only application-level connectivity will suffice, you must consider how you will do network management. Refer to Figure 7.16 and assume that the black box is a common application server. Your most basic question is whether have some way to **ping** all hosts. Can the network manager log in to

the common host and **ping** from there? If so, you have the basis of a manageable network. If not, you might need a small amount of routing capability into
the departmental VLANs, simply for network management.

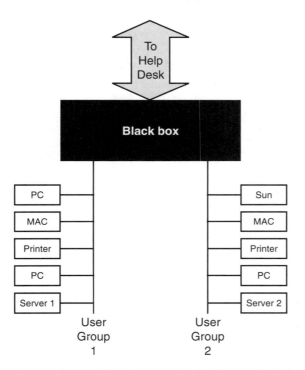

FIGURE 7.16 *There is no routing-level connectivity between 192.168.0.0/23 and
192.168.2.0/23. **Ping**s from the management station cannot reach the user LANs.*

Also, consider how you will do server management on the departmental
servers. Again, just as network layer diagnostics can be done either from a
common host or through routing, you might be able to manage and reload
servers either from the common server or from a remote management station
that needs routing-level connectivity.

The Key to Campus Architecture: Servers on the Same Subnet as Clients?

Assuming that the main application servers are in a central campus location,
the most important architectural decision tends to be whether the clients and
servers can be on the same subnet. Subnets represent broadcast domains, so the
decision on whether or not to put servers in the same subnet usually depends

on the amount of broadcast traffic present and the capability of hosts to tolerate broadcasts. Multicasts can also affect hosts, if the hosts' network interface
cards and associated driver software do not distinguish between multicasts not
destined to them and multicasts they should process.

As shown in Figure 7.17, if you have more clients to connect to the server than
is reasonable to put into a single broadcast domain, you have three main
choices. You can put multiple NICs into the servers. You can route between the
client subnets and the server subnets. You can use VLAN-aware NICs and configure the servers to be on each client subnet.

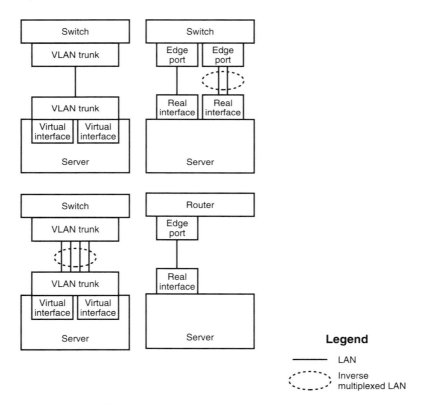

FIGURE 7.17 *There is an assortment of ways servers can connect to switches, with different bandwidth, resiliency, and VLAN awareness. VLAN-aware servers can reduce the
need for routers.*

Bandwidth is apt to be the next factor that determines which choice. Let's say you have 10 client subnets, each with 100 devices connected at 10 Mbps. A reasonable estimate for devices running office applications is they will need 100 Kbps of bandwidth each, so the average bandwidth requirement is 10 Mbps.

Router-on-a-Stick

How much routing is needed between logical subnets, either VLAN or non-VLAN? Often, there is significant inter-application communication among logical networks, but not a major requirement for true routing (refer to Figure 7.16). If the LANs communicate only by email, or through the firewall, is any routing capability needed? Remember that any-to-any connectivity at the application level does not necessarily mean you need any-to-any connectivity at Layer 3 or Layer 2.

Complicating the requirement for routing is the requirements of network management. How does the help desk **ping** Host 2? You might be able to avoid routing between the user subnets if you can log in to the server and **ping** using a server command.

The term *router-on-a-stick* reflects a configuration where the core is a router or set of routers fed by switches. A representative configuration is shown in Figure 7.18. I find the term ridiculous, but it has been popularized by various industry journalists and marketeers. It does describe a meaningful architecture.

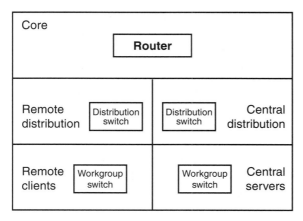

FIGURE 7.18 *All routing takes place in the routing function at the top of the hierarchy. This figure shows a redundant routing function.*

Router-on-a-stick architecture is appropriate when relatively little traffic flows between LANs or VLANs—in other words, when switching is the norm and routing is the exception. Figure 7.19 shows a good application for router-on-a-stick, where the servers are centrally located on different VLANs. This design also is good when the servers are VLAN aware and can connect to multiple VLANs.

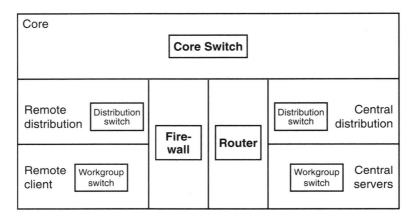

F I G U R E 7 . 1 9 *Routing is a service at the distribution tier.*

In Figure 7.19, the default assumption is that clients reach routers on the same departmental VLAN, going from the local workgroup switch to a distribution switch to a core switch and possibly to another distribution switch that feeds the servers. A small amount of exception traffic goes to other departmental VLANs or via a firewall to the Internet or to extranet partners.

A different way to look at router-on-a-stick is that it assumes there will be an inter-LAN routing service, but inter-LAN traffic will not be the bulk of traffic. See Figure 7.19, where the routers and servers are at the distribution tier. A switch is the true core device. Multiple independent broadcast domains run through the switch; the distribution tier router moves traffic among the domains. Remember the core switching *function* can be implemented with several physical switches for improved resilience.

A complementary technique allows better scalability when routing is a requirement. I am at a loss to understand why it is not called switch-on-a-stick.

Router Cluster

Putting routers at the distribution tier and using a switch in the core is particularly appropriate when you have large volumes of inter-VLAN routing, or frequent requirements for connectivity off the campus. Figure 7.20 shows this architecture, which is a mirror image of router-on-a-stick and is called router cluster.

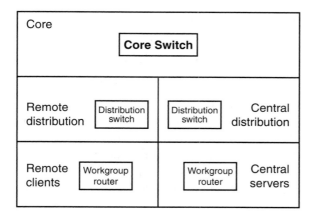

FIGURE 7.20 *In the router cluster architecture, routers separate the access and distribution levels.*

This might seem similar to the topology of Figure 7.18, but there is an important difference. In router cluster, there are multiple router functions, distributed to workgroups. *Router function* implies the distributed device can be primarily a packet forwarding (that is, Layer 3 switching) function that looks at Layer 3 information to make forwarding decisions, but that receives routing tables from a device elsewhere in the network.

See Chapter 14 for what might be the evolution of router cluster, where the edge devices become Layer 3 forwarding engines or use hybrid mechanisms such as *multiprotocol label switching*.

Router cluster organization can also be useful when you want to control broadcast propagation at a low level, and VLANs are not practical. You might not be able to use VLANs if you have a large investment in non-VLAN capable switches, or perhaps have a mixture of vendor switches, each vendor using a proprietary VLAN mechanism. In general, it is far easier to interconnect different vendors' routers than their switches. Routers also are more effective than switches when mixing media, such as Ethernet and Token Ring.

When there is a large amount of routing to be done, it can be easier to add router power incrementally at the distribution tier, rather than requiring a large routing function at the top of the hierarchy.

The Core and Its Connections

Leaving a campus, the network connects to the core. In almost all cases, the device that connects you to the core is a router. ATM switches have a role in certain large WANs, as seen in Chapter 9, but the trend appears to be routing as the core technology.

Core routers differ in two major respects: bandwidth and expected traffic patterns. Traffic patterns divide further into unicast and multicast traffic.

Matching the Router to the Bandwidth

In vendor literature, the term *core router* tends to be applied to high-performance devices that can handle massive bandwidth. Don't fall into the trap of overspecifying a device that logically serves the core function, but does not need high bandwidth. The core is a function, not a bandwidth specification. The core links sites (or major buildings in a campus) and has enough bandwidth to carry the flows among these points.

A consulting client had an enterprise with two major campuses and many small sites. The two main campuses only needed two T1 lines between them, but there was a substantial bandwidth requirement on each campus. The campuses, however, had distribution routers in the moderate performance range, whereas the core routers were lightly loaded with two serial lines and a LAN. The core routers also terminated large numbers of serial lines serving branch offices.

After redesign, the high-bandwidth, relatively low-CPU routers that were then used in the core were reconfigured so they primarily serviced the campuses. Performance improved when the formerly core routers were moved to a distribution-tier campus function, while small WAN routers serviced the T1 lines.

The enterprise increasingly needed compute-intensive services for its branch office connectivity, such as compression and encryption. It also was considering VPN services. To add flexibility in configuring WAN services, additional routers were installed to connect branch offices to the main campuses. These WAN-oriented routers had substantial CPU power, the capability for inserting hardware coprocessors, and a high-speed LAN interface for connecting to the campus network.

From the perspective of the campus, the first constraint on a core router is the number and speed of WAN links to which it connects. If routing to a WAN is a relatively lightweight requirement, you might want to rethink the problem, treating the campus core as a LAN-optimized switch or router and placing the external routing function at the distribution tier. The external routers can connect to a higher-level core, or backbone of backbones.

When it connects to multiple destinations, it is often most cost-effective to use a multiplexed technology such as Frame Relay or ATM. These technologies are more cost-effective because they reduce the cost of router interfaces and of local access lines.

Assume bandwidth charges for a T1 line costs $1000 per month for the local loop, whereas a T3 costs $5,000. More than five T1s obviously are cheaper when the same bandwidth is provisioned over a T3.

But other factors beyond simple line cost need to be considered. To have four T1s, which in principle would cost less than a T3, you need four local loops from the telephone company and four router interfaces.

Matching Forwarding to Traffic Patterns

Traffic tends to follow several models in relation to the core:

- *Case 1*: Most traffic stays within the campus. The core router handles exception traffic.

- *Case 2*: Most traffic from one site goes to one, or a small number, of other sites.

- *Case 3*: Traffic flows fairly equally to all sites. The traffic is primarily unicast. This case further divides into:

    Case 3a: Traffic volume is symmetrical between sites.

    Case 3b: There is significantly more traffic volume in one direction than another.

These three basic cases assume unicast traffic. Efficiently handling large volumes of multicast traffic might need different types of relays. The relays might need to run multicast routing protocols in addition to conventional unicast routing protocols. Alternatively, they might use Layer 2 point-to-multipoint connection-oriented technology, with hardware assistance for data replication:

- *Case 4*: Traffic flows as a multicast from one originating site to some number of other sites.

To understand Case 4, think of the core not so much as an area of high bandwidth, but as a topology that links campuses. The concern is having a device that matches appropriately to the WAN. If the campus network has significantly more bandwidth than the WAN, this device probably needs to do a good deal of bandwidth management. Bandwidth management needs substantial memory for buffering and might need significant CPU resources for categorizing traffic. Alternatively, special processors for traffic management can be extremely useful.

There are other applications for special-purpose hardware. Compression is processor intensive and lends itself to being implemented in coprocessors.

The second case can lend itself to WAN switching as well as routing. When there is a need for resiliency, one of the challenges is having enough link redundancy without overcomplicating the design. Figure 7.21 shows a good design with no single point of failure.

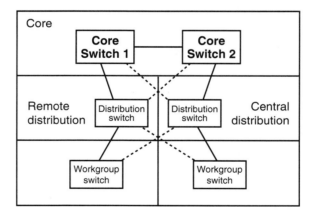

Legend

——————— Primary connectivity using spanning tree
- - - - - - - Backup connectivity using spanning tree and fault-tolerance extensions

FIGURE 7.21 *A redundant collapsed backbone has no central single point of failure.*

Chapter 11 further explores the question of the appropriate degree of meshing in a routed network. In general, meshing beyond a small number of additional sites does little to improve availability and might even decrease it.

When Full Mesh Became a Full Mess

I had a client who obtained Frame Relay service from a service provider that charged a minimal amount for additional virtual circuits from one site to another; the basic charge was for the access line. The client had gotten into the practice of ordering PVCs from each newly added site to all existing ones. They ran dynamic routing.

As the number of sites approached 100, the network was almost impossible to troubleshoot. Small routers were being overwhelmed with memory requirements to buffer all the PVCs involved.

Changing to topology with several hubs improved the performance. The network became more scalable, because the edge access routers only needed to handle a small number of virtual circuits.

The network also became more reliable. Because the Frame Relay circuits were all provisioned by the same provider, there actually was little or no redundancy among them. The new configuration had dialup or ISDN links that were added as backup connections to hub sites. Each spoke site potentially could go to more than one hub site in the event of failures.

Adding more than one backup link did call for more complex routing. With a single backup link to the same hub that services the Frame Relay link, static and default routing is quite adequate. If, however, the edge site can connect to more than one hub router, it is generally necessary to run dynamic routing so the edge router can be found regardless of the hub to which it connects.

Like any networking question, the answer to the optimal design is "it depends." There is a substantial difference between the routing requirements for an enterprise with 500 routes and a default-free Internet service provider with 60,000.

As the number of destinations increases, network architects must consider whether the number of next hops to them increases significantly. A national corporation with which I worked initially had a single Internet firewall and ISP connection, located in the eastern United States. They added a second ISP connection in the western United States.

The question arose, "Should Internet routes be injected into the internal routing system so that the internal routers could pick the best exit route?" This was the intuitive goal of the customer, but, if they did so, the memory requirements for all their routers would grow enormously.

In this case, the cost of absolutely optimal routing was really not worthwhile. One factor that helped convince my client that carrying full routing into the network, or even running internal BGP (see Chapter 12) between them, was not worthwhile was the reality of asymmetrical routing in the Internet.

With two Internet connections to different service providers, it is not uncommon to see 30 to 40% of your traffic behave asymmetrically—queries leaving on one connection but with responses returning on another. There is no current means to enforce the return path.

Large-scale production multicast is in its infancy. The technologies involved are discussed in greater detail in Chapters 13 and 14.

Although many people assume the major application of multimedia is video-conferencing, I find it far more frequently used, in intranets, for distance learning. Remember that multimedia doesn't necessarily imply multicast. Distance learning, however, is a natural application of both multimedia and multicast technologies, with its basic model of a single instructor communicating to multiple students.

Voice over IP clearly is a growing application, but only requires multicasting in audioconferencing uses.

Another growing area for multicasting is fault-tolerant computing, where clients send a query as a multicast to a group of servers. Only one server issue of providing different service levels for different types of traffic. Currently available routing protocols are not QoS-aware, although see Chapter 14 for a review of ongoing work.

To implement QoS, a certain level of manual *traffic engineering* is necessary. RFC 2430 describes traffic engineering as "the ability to move trunks away from the path selected by the ISP's IGP and onto a different path." There is a great emphasis on multiprotocol label switching (MPLS; see Chapter 14 for more information on MPLS) as a means of implementing traffic engineering, but it certainly can be done today with static and/or policy routing, coupled with bandwidth management techniques.

Traffic engineering is relevant both in enterprise networks and for ISPs. For enterprise networks, QoS can be critical for successful deployment of multimedia applications including voice. QoS control plays a lesser role in ensuring appropriate response time for mission-critical interactive applications.

QoS interacts with availability, the combination of which becomes an important aspect of usability. Even though a service might technically be available, if its performance is below acceptable limits, the service is not usable. Keep in mind, however, that your best approach to maintaining usable QoS might not be to use explicit QoS mechanisms, but simply to track resource utilization and add capacity when they become overloaded. QoS mechanisms do add overhead.

In the case of ISPs, Li and Rekhter [RFC 2430] observe that traffic engineering "allows an ISP to route traffic around known points of congestion in its network, thereby making more efficient use of the available bandwidth. In turn, this makes the ISP more competitive within its market by allowing the ISP to pass lower costs and better service on to its customers."

A basic concept in scalable routing systems with different levels of service is the capability to aggregate multiple end-to-end flows into trunks. The worst-case assumption requires a separate trunk for each class of service. If there are N routers entering the backbone and C classes of service, the worst-case assumption would require $N \times (N-1) \times C$ trunks [RFC 2430].

The first approach to reducing the number of physical trunks is to use a multi-plexed Layer 2 technology such as ATM or Frame Relay. An emerging approach, discussed in Chapter 14, is to use label switching to establish virtual paths for classes of service.

A second approach, usable both in label switching and classical routing, is to merge trunks. If two trunks have a common exit point, they can be merged. You determine whether trunks can be merged at the time they are created. When you create the trunk, see if its path would cross that of an existing trunk, of the same service class, going to the same destination.

Trunk merging can reduce the total number of trunks. Label switching automates this process, but the underlying concept applies when setting up static routes for traffic engineering.

Tradeoffs Between Static and Dynamic Routing

You want to use dynamic routing when there are too many alternate paths to specify manually, or you want the ability to discover either alternate paths or failures.

Dynamic interior routing, unless routing information is manipulated, follows a closest exit model. The closest exit might not be optimal for managing quality of service. The desire to do traffic engineering is a major argument for static routes. ATM PNNI does have the capability to consider QoS when it sets up virtual circuits.

The reality is that a model that retains at least some state (rather than classic connectionless, stateless routing) appears necessary, in the near term, to achieve any reasonable control over QoS. ATM SVC setup, RSVP, and MPLS are all stateful to some extent. Traffic engineering extensions to interior routing protocols are not as far along as the various stateful mechanisms, and, even as they develop, they can be used for MPLS path setup rather than classic changing of routing tables.

The basic reason you use dynamic routing protocols is to discover alternate paths. If there are no alternate paths, it might not be necessary to run dynamic routing.

You also can use static routing to enforce traffic engineering policies.

RIP

RIP can be a viable solution for simple networks, preferably ones that do not use low-bandwidth WAN links, have not more than six hops, and ideally have all LAN links of the same bandwidth. Limitations of RIP are detailed in Chapter 6.

Even when you use another routing mechanism, there still might be a need to run RIP because hosts need to hear RIP updates to find routers on their media. Passive RIP, as was discussed in Chapter 6, is not the only way for hosts to discover routers, but it is a popular one. Don't overcomplicate what RIP needs to do to provide end hosts with the information they need to find routers. In most circumstances, all the router needs to advertise is the default route, 0.0.0.0/0.

If all you need to generate is the default route, there might be no reason to import specific routes from the main routing protocol into RIP. You might only need to import a static route to 0.0.0.0 or command the router simply to originate default. On a Cisco router, use the **default-information-originate** command to advertise the default route without the necessity of importing dynamic routes.

OSPF

The good news about OSPF is that it demands a well-thought-out topology and numbering plan to work at its best. The bad news about OSPF is that it demands a well-thought-out topology and numbering plan to work at its best.

One of the advantages claimed for EIGRP is that it is simpler to set up than OSPF. There is truth to that claim, as long as you are dealing with a network of small to moderate size. After your network reaches a point—perhaps when you have 100 or more routers—where address aggregation and other scalability techniques become important, EIGRP can become as complex as OSPF.

> **Note**
>
> *Several colleagues whom I respect consider EIGRP easier to use than OSPF. My feelings remain mixed. Yes, many design considerations that must be examined early in the OSPF design process are not required in EIGRP, but if the network scales to large size and these considerations were not planned for, the EIGRP network can get into trouble.*

Admittedly, I have more experience with OSPF than I do with EIGRP, simply because OSPF has been available for a longer period of time. But in Cisco routers, the only ones that are relevant when comparing OSPF and EIGRP, I find the more advanced configuration commands to be easier to maintain with OSPF than with EIGRP. The OSPF commands controlling aggregation are in a single place in the configuration file, whereas the equivalent EIGRP functions tend to be distributed to the various interface specifications. It's not difficult to miss an interface on a large router with many interfaces.

> **Note**
>
> *A colleague has a lovely analogy for the OSPF (and IS-IS) worldview, as opposed to that of EIGRP. An ideal OSPF network looks like a daisy, with areas surrounding a core. EIGRP, however, looks more like an upside-down head of broccoli, with flowers and sub-branches merging into larger branches and eventually a stalk.*

> **Note**
>
> *When I design a network and need dynamic routing, it is my working assumption that I will use OSPF unless there is strong reason to do otherwise. I like the multivendor flexibility it gives me. I like the level of insight I have into its operation, because its specifications are published [RFC 2328]. It converges quickly and has a well-understood relationship to BGP.*

OSPF has some unique mechanisms that allow you to load share external routes, or enforce a primary/backup policy on external routes. The default route is considered an external route, so OSPF provides mechanisms, discussed in Chapter 12, that can let you set preferred and less preferred defaults. Although you can set different default priorities with static routes, it tends to be more difficult to do this with dynamic routing protocols.

In reasonably configured networks, OSPF has fast convergence time. The main concern is that the Dijkstra computation used to find intra-area routes is CPU intensive. IS-IS uses a similar algorithm and also imposes a significant CPU load. EIGRP generally has a lesser CPU demand than OSPF or IS-IS.

The protocol supports arbitrary length prefixes, as needed for VLSM and CIDR.

IGRP

Cisco's IGRP was, at the time of its introduction, a superior alternative to RIP. The advantages of IGRP, however, have been overtaken by more modern routing protocols such as OSPF and EIGRP. I see no reason to use IGRP in a new network.

IGRP might meet current needs in an existing network. If it does, there is no pressing need to replace it. Incentives to replace IGRP include the following:

- Need for VLSM/CIDR

- Slow convergence

A possible incentive to retain and tune IGRP might be having a large number of old Cisco routers, such as the AGS or MGS models. It might not be possible to upgrade these to an IOS version that runs reliable EIGRP code. Even if this is the case, it can be appropriate to run OSPF, which, having been deployed longer than EIGRP, became stable in earlier IOS releases.

If you need to use IGRP in an existing network where you cannot upgrade to a more modern protocol, the keys to tuning are to make the network hierarchical and minimally meshed and to turn off the holddown timer. Decreasing the value of the update timer can also help.

Another technique that can be useful in tuning IGRP networks is to filter unneeded routes from propagating into lower-level parts of the hierarchy. IGRP can only summarize at classful network boundaries, so you have limited ability to reduce the routing load through summarization.

There are production networks with over 2000 IGRP-speaking routers, so there is no question that the protocol can scale to large size with appropriate tuning. Nevertheless, tuning can take you only so far, before it becomes maintenance intensive. There is no real way to deal with arbitrary length prefixes.

If parts of your network cannot upgrade to IGRP, consider treating them as subordinate routing domains to a backbone with more modern routing. Such a strategy works best if you can keep entire classful prefixes completely in the IGRP domain.

It can be difficult, but not impossible, to handle a major network handled by IGRP but to have certain subnets in OSPF. The key technique is to have more-specific OSPF routes in the backbone and the IGRP as classful and less-specific routes. EIGRP can cope with legacy IGRP routes better than OSPF, but using EIGRP might not always be a perfect solution due to multivendor compatibility issues.

EIGRP

The first decision you must make when considering EIGRP is whether an all-Cisco environment is acceptable. Certainly, with its market share, the likelihood of having Cisco routers everywhere is substantial.

If there is a need to advertise RIP to hosts, this is not a specific argument against EIGRP. Even if OSPF is the main routing protocol, you still need to set up RIP on appropriate edge networks.

Again, if RIP runs at the edge of the current network, redistributing it into EIGRP is a valid approach. Cautions involved in such redistribution are discussed in Chapter 12.

If the existing network is IGRP, EIGRP offers significant ease of migration. EIGRP has automatic compatibility features that support IGRP.

When there is little basis for establishing a hierarchical topology, EIGRP is likely to do better than OSPF, until the sheer network size requires hierarchy for scalability. EIGRP offers distinct advantages when you have a significant amount of Apple and Novell traffic.

For many topologies, the CPU load of EIGRP is less than that of OSPF. If your routers have small CPUs, or are heavily loaded with other processes, EIGRP can be an appropriate choice. Some of my colleagues feel that EIGRP is preferable if a proprietary solution is acceptable. Personally, I go to considerable lengths to avoid proprietary solutions. Unless a capability is only available from one vendor, I'd rather keep my future options available.

Integrated IS-IS

Integrated IS-IS has become a niche protocol, although some routing experts predict its use will become more common. Several large ISPs use it as their interior routing protocol, but historical as well as technical factors had a role in their choice of IS-IS.

In the time period around 1990 to 1991, there was significant interest in the OSI Connectionless Network Layer Protocol (CLNP) as a possible alternative to IP version 4. IS-IS was originally developed as an OSI routing protocol. Integrated IS-IS is an extension that natively supports both OSI and IP routing.

There has been a recent resurgence of interest in IS-IS within the IETF, and extensions are being explored that deal with some of the perceived deficiencies yet exploit the strengths of IS-IS. In general, IS-IS can restore a partitioned backbone more easily than can OSPF.

Note

One of the proposals for IPv6, called TUBA (TCP and UDP over Bigger Addresses), actually replaced IPv4 with CLNP. Although a different proposal was adopted for IPv6, some mechanisms developed in OSI work are part of the larger IPv6 effort. Stateless address autoconfiguration, which lets end hosts dynamically create their own addresses, is very much based on OSI address autoconfiguration.

IS-IS offered flexibility to the ISPs, in that it would have been useful if either IP or OSI became the protocol of the future. In addition, the then-current Cisco OSPF code was much less stable than Cisco's IS-IS code. The OSPF problems have long since been fixed, but by the time these problems were corrected, the ISPs had IS-IS running in production and had no strong reason to change to OSPF.

OSPF and IS-IS are generally comparable protocols, in that they both are link state with a two-level hierarchical structure. There are differences in the details, but the two are of comparable performance. For example, OSPF has a finer-grained metric, whereas IS-IS has a more robust backbone structure. OSPF runs over IP with TTL set to 1, whereas IS-IS runs directly over the data link layer.

Updates to the IS-IS standard are underway in the IETF, which might make it a more common protocol, typically for very large networks.

My advice to an enterprise building a new network, or converting from RIP or IGRP to a more modern protocol, is to consider OSPF or EIGRP as the primary alternatives. Further investigation of IS-IS, however, is worthwhile if

- You use SONET equipment that has OSI management that uses IS-IS.

- Your network is very large (as almost any plausible network containing SONET would be).

If you do have a very large network, it probably is worth keeping track of both vendor implementations and IETF enhancements to the IS-IS standard.

BGP

Large networks have quite successfully used BGP to interconnect regional routing domains into a backbone of backbones. This use of BGP is further discussed in Chapter 13. Obviously, BGP scales to massive size, because it is the fundamental routing protocol of the global Internet. At the time of this writing, a full Internet routing table has approximately 60,000 routes.

BGP can also be appropriate when you need complex connectivity to the Internet. Figure 7.22 shows a refinement of a customer network first described in Figure 7.7. In the refinement, the actual routing and switching mechanisms are added. The European and Asian parts of the network were OSPF routing domains with static routes at the branch level. Data centers in the United States were static routing domains. A BGP backbone interconnected these OSPF domains, other major corporate networks serving the Americas, and provided Internet connectivity.

Even though there are such things as interior BGP (iBGP) and exterior BGP (eBGP), don't assume iBGP is a general alternative to protocols specifically designed as interior routing protocols. The purpose of iBGP, as shown in Figure 7.23, is to help coordinate the activity of BGP-speaking routers that connect to external autonomous systems.

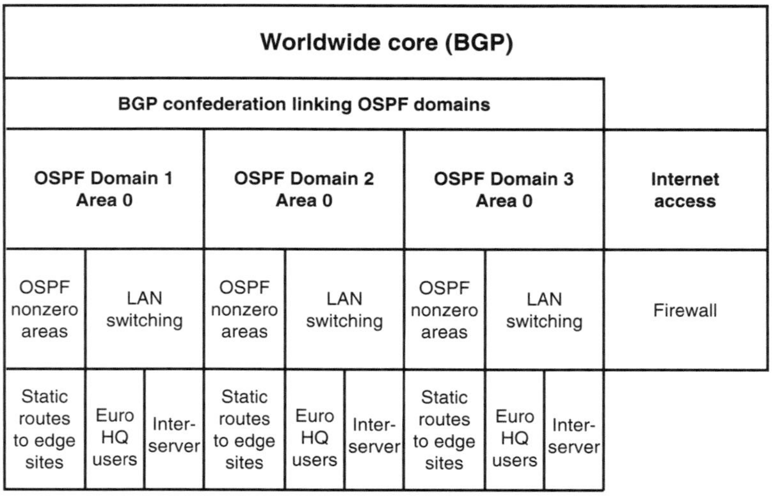

Worldwide core (BGP)
BGP confederation linking OSPF domains
OSPF Domain 1 Area 0
OSPF Domain 2 Area 0
OSPF Domain 3 Area 0
Internet access
OSPF nonzero areas
LAN switching
OSPF nonzero areas
LAN switching
OSPF nonzero areas
LAN switching
Firewall
Static routes to edge sites
Euro HQ users
Inter-server
Static routes to edge sites
Euro HQ users
Inter-server
Static routes to edge sites
Euro HQ users
Inter-server

FIGURE 7.22 *Different types of routing are used at the higher levels of the network. Limited routing is also needed for the WAN access at small sites, and switching is appropriate where there is a high density of users.*

AS 1 Router 1
AS 1 Router 2
AS 1 Router 3
AS 2 Router 1
AS 2 Router 2
Internal BGP
External BGP
Internal BGP

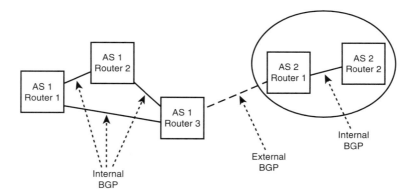

FIGURE 7.23 *eBGP allows the exchange of information on which policy decisions can be made by different AS. iBGP coordinates the views of different BGP speakers within a single AS.*

Some ISPs speak of using iBGP as their interior routing protocol, but these are special applications where the ISP is primarily providing transit service and does not have an extensive internal network.

BGP has a feature especially appropriate for use in enterprise networks, called *confederations* [RFC 1965]. A confederation, as shown in Figure 7.24, allows you to define enterprise routing domains as confederation autonomous systems, so you can define eBGP routing policies among them. The outside world, however, sees your confederation as a single AS.

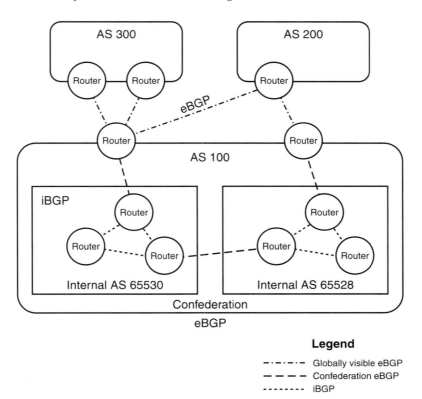

F IGURE 7.24 *Confederations permit the power of BGP within organizations without increasing the number of AS in the global routing system.*

In any but the largest enterprise networks, scaling the iBGP mesh is not a major problem. ISPs, however, face the problem daily. Confederations are not the only way to impose an internal BGP hierarchy that improves scalability. Another method popular among ISPs is to use *route reflectors* [RFC 1966], which build a hierarchy of BGP clients and servers within a single AS, rather than using the multiple AS that confederations do.

IPv6 and OSPv6

OSPFv6 is not the sixth version of OSPF, but is the OSPF that is capable of carrying IPv6 routing information. In the OSPFv6 design effort, which is still ongoing, the opportunity was taken to clean up some internal features of OSPF that were less than ideal. OSPFv6 is not yet commercially available, but might be a better choice than OSPFv2 when it is available, even if you are only running IPv4.

The initial strategy for implementing IPv6 is to tunnel it in IPv4. As IPv6 becomes more widely used, it will be used to carry IPv4 by the reverse sort of tunneling, IPv4 over IPv6.

There are changes that generalize it to run on a per-link rather than a per-subnet basis. These changes eliminate some existing problems with secondary addressing and multicasting.

Authentication has been removed from the OSPF protocol itself, on the assumption that the IPsec Authentication Header and Encapsulating Security Payload will be used when protection is needed. These IPsec features are standard in IPv6 and can be used with IPv4.

Routing Non-IP Protocols

To carry non-IP routing information, you have three basic alternatives. You can run ships-in-the-night routing protocols for the non-IP architectures; you can tunnel the native routing protocols over IP; or you can use a routing protocol that is aware of non-IP routing.

Ships-in-the-Night Routing

In ships-in-the-night routing, multiple routing protocols, especially for different architectures such as DECnet, Apple, and Novell, coexist in a non-interfering manner. Even in a predominantly IP network, you might need to have workgroup routing protocols running on edge networks, because Apple and Novell hosts need to hear routing updates to find routers.

Carrying workgroup protocols over WAN media can be complicated. Apple's native RTMP and Novell's IPX are broadcast-intensive, chatty protocols that can consume excessive bandwidth on WANs. Another issue for WAN connectivity is that Apple RTMP and IPX RIP cannot disable split horizon. Being unable to disable split horizon is a problem for connectivity over NBMA media. Cisco EIGRP can carry Apple and Novell routing information over partial-mesh NBMA media. An alternative to using EIGRP on NBMA media is to declare each virtual circuit as a separate logical network. This means a cable-range in Apple and an IPX network number in Novell. The logical interface model does not scale well for large meshes, because each subinterface needs separate buffers, and a large number of subinterfaces can require excessive memory in edge routers.

Yet another alternative when you are carrying AppleTalk is using Apple Update-Based Routing protocol (AURP), which creates tunnels for AppleTalk routing information. These tunnels run over IP.

DECnet and OSI routing are modern routing protocols and are reasonable to have coexist with pure IP routing. DECnet Phase IV uses DECnet addressing, but DECnet Phase V uses OSI addresses, for which Integrated IS-IS has native support.

Handling Non-Backbone Protocols

You certainly can establish tunnels to carry routed protocols other than IP over an IP network. The disadvantages of doing so are the amount of traffic generated by periodic update protocols such as RTMP and IPX RIP. In addition, tunneling adds approximately 30 bytes per packet.

GRE encapsulation is the most widely supported mechanism for carrying non-IP packets. Several other encapsulations are used for AppleTalk, such as Apple's own Apple Update-Based Routing Protocol (AURP), which is intended to run over IP. Cayman's Gatorbox encapsulation is yet another.

You also can use GRE to carry IP over IP. This is a valuable technique when the host addresses are in the IP private address space, but need to be carried over the Internet.

Layer 2 WAN technologies such as Frame Relay and ATM also have the capability to carry multiprotocol traffic. The basic technique is to use an IEEE 802.2 Logical Link Control/Subnetwork Access Protocol (LLC/SNAP) field in the start of the Layer 2 data field. The SNAP field contains the protocol identifier. RFC 2427 describes the Frame Relay technique, whereas RFC 1483 explains the equivalent method for ATM.

EIGRP has the capability to carry information about AppleTalk and Novell IPX routes as well as IP routes. It does so in a value-added way in comparison with the native routing protocols for those families, Apple Routing Table Maintenance Protocol (RTMP) and Novell RIP. Novell RIP is different from IP RIP. EIGRP also carries the Novell Service Advertising Protocol (SAP), which is the chief source of overhead in Novell networks prior to NetWare 4.x.

EIGRP has several advantages over the native protocols. RTMP and Novell RIP were designed for a LAN environment where bandwidth was not a critical resource. RTMP, RIP, and SAP all transmit the entire routing table—or server table in the case of SAP—at periodic intervals. That interval is every 10 seconds for Apple and every 60 seconds for Novell. When these potentially large tables are sent over WAN links, their size and frequency can have a major performance impact on slow links.

EIGRP reduces this impact by sending not the complete table contents, but only that information that changed as a result of an update message in the native protocol.

You still need to run the native protocols on LANs that have Apple or Novell hosts on them, because these hosts listen for RTMP or RIP to locate routers on their segments. EIGRP, however, automatically redistributes changed information into native protocols. EIGRP can coexist with the native Apple or Novell protocols on a medium that is used for transit as well as for end hosts. You very well may want a configuration where only Apple and Novell routing announcements are heard on edge networks, and EIGRP is the only protocol in the core.

Generic Performance Requirements for Network Interconnection Devices

Look at Figure 7.25. Tell typical users it is the end-to-end path between their client and server and ask them to label the lines and boxes, suggesting that the boxes are the largest part of delay. They will usually mark the boxes as routers and the lines as media.

In reality, they have marked the lines and boxes backward. Most modern routers and switches, except those intended for low-cost, low-speed use, have little difficulty keeping up with their media. Most can forward at wire speed.

As the network designer, you need to ensure that the network performance requirements are met by the sequence of media and interconnection devices along an end-to-end path.

You should begin with an estimate of the user needs for throughput and response time and see if these can be achieved with a particular network design. There is bound to be some refinement of either the requirements or the network capabilities, as budgetary realities force tradeoffs.

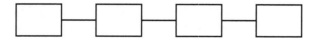

FIGURE 7.25 *Ask your clients to fill in the delay sources.*

The first approximation to delay across the network is to sum up the times it will take a maximum-length (or expected length if you have refined data) to cross the media from source to destination.

Remember that response time involves at least two sets of delays, one from source to destination and the other from destination to source. More complex distributed applications involve multiple information flows.

Characteristics of Media

Selecting internetworking devices such as switches and routers often involves being sure the device is fast enough to handle the speed of the fastest medium to which it will be connected, without paying for unnecessary power. Media speed ranges, for the first approximation, correspond to the speed bands mentioned in Chapter 1:

- Up to 64 Kbps. Typical interconnection devices: ISDN and analog cards in hosts, low-end routers.

- 64 Kbps up to T1/E1. Small routers.

- Up to 16 Mbps. Small routers and workgroup switches.

- Up to 50 Mbps (DS3/E3). High-performance routers when using these speeds in the WAN. Lower-performance routers might have speeds in this range in order to exploit high-speed access media.

- Up to and including 100 Mbps (half-duplex Fast Ethernet and FDDI). High-end workgroup switches, campus switches, high-end routers.

- Up to and including 1 Gbps (ATM OC-3 and OC-12, SONET/SDH, Gigabit Ethernet, Full Duplex FDDI, Inverse Multiplexed Fast Ethernet). ATM switches, top-end routers, WAN switches, high-end campus switches.

- Between 1 and 3 Gbps. (Inverse Multiplexed Gigabit Ethernet, ATM OC-48, SONET/SDH). Bleeding edge technology, such as ATM switches, top-end routers and hybrid switches, and SONET equipment.

- 10 Gigabit range. Primarily a research area for single data streams, although OC-192 SONET is in use. 10xGBE (10 Gigabit Ethernet) is in testing. Even higher data rates are possible with multiple data streams using dense wavelength division multiplexing (DWDM), into the terabit per second range.

Platform designs associated with these speed bands are further discussed in Chapter 3.

Delay Sources and Propagation Time

And so it is that the speed of light is a hard limit to absolute delay. Figure 7.26 shows a thought experiment of a source-to-destination link using two relays of infinite internal speed; they introduce no delay themselves.

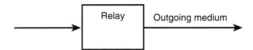

FIGURE 7.26 *Delay with infinitely fast relays.*

If two devices are in a vacuum and signal each other using light, there would still be a delay, which would be a function of distance divided by **c**, the speed of light in a vacuum.

So for physical media, there is a limit imposed by speed-of-light effects in the medium. This means that a signal between two infinitely fast routers still takes measurable time to be delivered.

After a data unit gets on to a medium, a process governed by the basic transmission speed, it then needs to get to its destination. Speed of light issues become involved here.

Geosynchronous satellites tend to produce the longest delay, on the order of 200–300 milliseconds. Terrestrial links vary based on their specific topologies, but still impose delays in the tens of milliseconds over transcontinental links. There can be significantly longer delays, up to 400 milliseconds, on shared media such as cable TV.

Propagation time is defined as

Propagation time=Distance/Transmission velocity

Remember that the oft-quoted 186,000 miles per second, c, is the speed of light in a vacuum. Light, or electronic signals, propagate more slowly in a solid medium. In 10Base5 Ethernet cable, signals propagate at a transmission velocity of 0.67 c, whereas the speed in 10Base2 cable is 0.5 c. Fiber speeds are up to 0.9 c.

Transmission rate is the number of bits per second the medium carries. Electrical and optical signaling methods vary the potential transmission rate on a medium. A T1 line sends individual bits approximately 24 times faster than a 64 Kbps ISDN circuit.

Transmission rate is a physical layer parameter that is the theoretical maximum speed. In practice, it needs to be reduced, or derated, to an effective data link rate for practical purposes. Factors, at the physical and data link layers, that derate the transmission rate include the following:

- Preamble and framing bit overhead. Depending on the data link protocol, there can be from 7 to 20 or more bytes per frame of maximum length.

- Maximum transmission unit size, or frame size. Maximizing the frame size improves efficiency by minimizing the overhead from headers, but it has other negative consequences if IP fragmentation is required. This is discussed in Chapter 3.

- Required gaps between successive frames (for example, Ethernet frames). There is a fixed 9.6 microsecond delay between frames. Some internetworking devices, either due to ambiguities in the standard or an attempt to increase throughput, have tried to reduce the gap below this time. These attempts, however, can prevent end hosts from working.

- Overhead for error detection, such as waits for acknowledgements. At the data link layer, only Logical Link Control, Type 2 (LLC2) acknowledges correctly received frames or retransmits frames that were not acknowledged.

- Queuing delay while waiting for the medium to be available.

Details of the derating are beyond the scope of this text, but are covered in standard data communications texts [Stallings, 1988].

Delay Variability

An assortment of factors makes delays variable. Congestion on the outgoing path is a major issue. There are many proactive and reactive ways for routers and WAN switches to deal with congestion, which are discussed in more detail in the next chapter. LAN switches have little capability to deal intelligently with congestion.

The basic approach when encountering outbound congestion is to either queue or drop the packet. Queuing the packet introduces delay if the packet has to wait for the outgoing line. Dropping data units can make matters far worse. An especially dramatic example comes from ATM. It takes 32 ATM cells to transfer a full-length Ethernet frame. If a single cell is dropped due to ATM congestion, all 32 cells need to be retransmitted. Occasional cell drops, if they fall into different frames, can be catastrophic. For ATM networks, it is better to drop a packet before it enters the ATM cloud rather than drop cells after the packet contents are split into cells and sent into the network.

There are several ways to control traffic so that it does not overrun network capacity. These include the following:

- Traffic policing, usage parameter control or intelligent dropping.

- Traffic shaping. The process of queuing or delaying certain data units so that the rate that they enter the service meets predefined criteria.

- Selective discarding.

- Higher-layer discard.

- Explicit forward congestion notification.

- Available Bit Rate flow control. An ATM concept in which the source varies the rate at which it transmits in response to explicit traffic information sent to the source in Resource Management cells.

Mechanisms that help enforce traffic policies include the following:

- *Connection admission control (CAC)*. The decision, at connection establishment time, if a given connection can be created. This was originated as an ATM concept, but can be generalized to any demand service based on switched circuit setup. It can also be looked at as a criterion of whether or not a flow can be established.

- *Queue prioritization*. The decision, at a router or switch interface, about which traffic is sent first when the interface cannot send all traffic. Traffic that is not sent is queued and, when queues fill, dropped.

Device Characteristics

RFC 1944 is the usual industry definition of the latency of a relaying device. Latency is measured differently for store-and-forward devices, such as routers and bridges, and bit forwarding devices, such as cut-through bridges and time division multiplexers.

The start of the period of device latency, for the former class, begins when the last bit of the input frame reaches the input port and ends when the first bit of the output frame is seen on the output port. For the latter, the time begins at the end of the first bit of the input frame and ends with the start of the first bit of the output frame at the output port.

Tests prescribed in RFC 1944 aim for measuring the internal delay of the device, rather than the effects of line speed or frame length.

Forwarding

Although it is a much-overstated problem, it takes a finite time for a switch or router to move information from an incoming to an outgoing interface, doing necessary processing along the way.

Most modern devices can move information at wire speed. There certainly are cases when other than the latest devices are connected to ATM links, or when general-purpose computers share their CPU for routing and application functions, and the relay itself is the limiting factor.

Typical forwarding speeds in a fast router are under 70 microseconds. This is continuing to drop. Fast switches are slightly faster, but the distinction between routers and switches is blurring anyway.

As you will see in Chapter 10, the major limiting factor in forwarding in LAN environments is not the switch or router, but the speed of the transmission media.

There can be exceptions where the switch or router is the forwarding bottleneck, but this often occurs, not due to the raw forwarding load, but the other tasks that might be competing for the same processing resources. Capabilities of the path determination and forwarding systems of a networking device need to be evaluated separately. You also need to consider the processing load imposed by filtering, accounting, encryption, compression, and bandwidth management functions. In modern high-performance devices, not only are the path determination and forwarding functions on different processors, which do not compete with one another for resources, but also some processor-intensive functions such as encryption and compression are offloaded to special-purpose hardware coprocessors.

Switches and some routers (such as the now discontinued Cisco 7000) may have substantial forwarding capability, but relatively weak CPU performance. Other routers may have a great deal of processing power, but perhaps a slower backplane that does not have a large forwarding capability.

The forwarding delay problem is most apt to be an issue when you're using end-to-end error control protocols without a sliding window, such as Novell systems prior to NetWare 3.12. Forwarding delay also tends to be less of a problem than inbound server contention, or the combination of inbound and outbound congestion when the medium is half duplex.

You will have to estimate the time it takes to forward a data unit, and additional times where the data must wait for the forwarding engine, or for output processing.

Queuing Delay

A data unit might be ready to transmit, but the outgoing transmission medium over which it has to be transmitted might be busy sending a different packet. In Token Ring or FDDI networks, the token might not have been received yet. This is not really a limitation of the router or switch, but more an indication of congestion or high error rates on the medium. See Tanner, page 349, for a discussion of Token Ring performance analysis [Tanner, 1996].

All these conditions represent device queuing, which can be a significant part of overall delay. Queuing delay is often an indication of inadequate bandwidth or too many devices on the medium. Pay close attention to the latter point; increasing bandwidth does not always cure the problem in deterministic systems such as token-passing LANs.

The overall topic of queuing is complex, but a basic understanding is important. We often think of queuing as restricted to waiting for media, but it is a more general concept that encompasses waiting for application servers to respond or for switches and routers to forward data.

Utilization of the resource drives its queuing performance. For a network device, utilization relates to the pattern of arrivals of new work (that is, the *interarrival distribution*) and the work required to process each new unit of work. Queuing theory specialists call this assumption *Little's Result*, "the average number of customers in a queuing system is equal to the average arrival rate of customers to that system, times the average time spent in that system" [Kleinrock, 1975].

For networking devices, a reasonable simplifying assumption is that the processing time is directly related to the number of bits or bytes in each unit of work. This assumption becomes increasingly reliable with the evolution of networking hardware. When I first started working with network device benchmarking, around 1976, vendors loved users that "wanted to hit their devices as hard as possible," and did so by sending large packets. With the technology of the 1970s and 1980s, however, most of the workload for an X.25 packet switch or early router was to process the packet header in software. Looking up addresses was far more processor intensive than moving bytes from input to output port. When I worked for an X.25 network provider, we far preferred test streams of 1024-byte packets to streams of 64-byte packets, because the long packets loaded our processor with far fewer packet headers per unit time. In modern devices, however, address lookup both uses more efficient algorithms and might have hardware-assisted lookup.

When you estimate or actually measure the pattern of workload arrivals, the natural tendency is to take the average (mean) of the interarrival times. As you learn more about network traffic patterns, you often become uncomfortable with using a simple mean for describing traffic that is not smoothly distributed. Little's Result, however, holds independently of the arrival or service patterns.

Most formal discussions use a standard notation for queuing systems, which, for basic application, can be simplified to

ArrivalModel/ServiceModel/numberOfServers

where

ArrivalModel =	M for Markovian
	G for General
	D for Deterministic
ServiceModel =	M for Markovian
	G for General
	D for Deterministic

The Markovian model is a good working assumption for basic queuing models. It assumes that events are randomly distributed, with the times between them following an exponential distribution.

Two very common queuing models are M/M/1 and M/D/1. The first is applicable to systems with variable-length data such as frame or packets, whereas the second is more applicable to fixed-length data as seen with time-division multiplexers and ATM cell switches. These data are called *units of work* in the discussion that follows.

Your first step in using these queuing techniques is to compute the utilization of a communications resource with bandwidth *bps*:

utilization=(unitsOfWork×8)/bps

Your real concern is with the delay experienced by units of work going through the resource. This delay is the sum of *waitingTime* and *serviceTime*, where *waitingTime* is the time spent in queues and the *serviceTime* is the time needed actually to transmit the unit of work.

The number of units of work in an M/M/1 queue is described by [Spohn, 1997]

N=(utililization/(1–utilization)

Increasing the utilization can dramatically increase the time spent in queue. As a rule of thumb, utilization above 0.5 tends to lead to significant delay increases. The average latency experienced by a unit of work, under stable conditions, is

Latency=(serviceTime/(1–utilization)

substituting

Latency=(serviceTime/(1–((unitsOfWork×8)/bps))

This is the latency through a single element—a medium and a buffered output interface to it. To determine end-to-end delay, you have to add the delays through each element in the path.

Selecting Networking Products Part 1: Feeds and Speeds

A rather fundamental concern is plugging the appropriate number—feeds—of media—speeds—into the interconnection device. After you know a chassis can physically connect to the necessary feeds and speeds, you need to look at internal processing. You also need to determine how the component fits into your overall network management strategy, which is the focus of Chapter 8.

The most basic consideration is simple port count. If you have 24 hosts in a workgroup, a 16-port LAN switch alone will not meet your needs. If you had some slower devices in the workgroup, an alternative to buying a larger switch might be to fan out some ports with physical layer hubs. Fanning out into a hub usually decreases your ability down to the device level.

Fanning out router ports into LAN switches often is a good compromise. Switch ports are cheaper than router ports for the same amount of interface bandwidth.

If you have a distribution tier router and an ATM core, the router must have an ATM physical interface even if the router does not need the full bandwidth of the ATM facility. It is actually quite common to put high-speed interfaces on routers that could not handle the full bandwidth that the interface could deliver. This is a rational strategy if you consider that high-speed WAN media come in defined physical speeds over which some number of slower channels can be multiplexed, at the bit (fractional T1/E1/T3/E3), cell (ATM), or frame (Frame Relay) levels.

Designing the most appropriate solution is more than simply counting the required interfaces and searching through a vendor catalog until you find the cheapest box that supports at least that number. Although many customers intuitively believe that "one big box" is always the cheapest solution, this simply is not the case.

The more intelligent a box, the more powerful its internal processing, the more expensive it tends to be. A 10 Mbps port is cheapest on a Layer 1 hub, more expensive on a Layer 2 switch, and most expensive on a Layer 3 router. The more expensive components may or may not give more value for the cost.

There is a significant difference in performance between hubs and LAN switches, at relatively little cost difference. As you will see in Chapter 10, switches give significantly more capability.

If your need is to connect large numbers of LAN-attached devices, however, it is usually a much better practice to connect the devices to LAN switch ports and then connect the aggregate output of the switch to a router port. Depending on your traffic patterns, the switch, or a system of switches, might be able to service a substantial part of your bandwidth requirement. The router, however, is necessary to handle the exception case of going to different IP subnets.

Looking Ahead

As the boundary between Layer 2 and Layer 3 forwarding blurs, there is also interaction between traditional Layer 3 path determination and path determination at Layer 2. Details of evolving techniques in this area are in Chapters 14 and 15.

CHAPTER 8

Component Selection, Fault Tolerance, and Network Management

*The tasks to which they are dedicated seem to be interpretable as embodiments
or incarnations of intrinsic values (rather than as a means to ends outside the
work itself, and rather than as functionally autonomous).*
—*A.H. Maslow*

*What is the difference between a used car salesman and a network sales repre-
sentative? The used car salesman knows he is lying.*
—*Heard at too many trade shows*

Be careful what you sell. It may do exactly what the customer expects.
—*Ferengi Rule of Acquisition 32, from Star Trek: Deep Space 9.*

In Chapter 7, we considered the feeds and speeds needed to connect to inter-
connnection devices. This is not enough. There is a regrettable tendency, in our
industry, for components to be described as plug-compatible, when all that is
really compatible between them is the plugs. Some vendors have excellent,
informative, accurate literature and sales representatives, but others are sufficiently misleading that you need to understand what you are buying.

To make rational selections, you need to consider the performance needed
between the plugs. Methods to establish these requirements, on an end-to-end
basis, are the focus of Chapter 2. In Chapter 3, you looked at how traffic moves
in individual boxes and how each box contributes to overall performance.

After you know the performance characteristics required of network interconnection devices, you can begin to select real-world boxes that meet these requirements. Selecting boxes is not merely a performance issue.

The means available to configure, monitor, and troubleshoot devices can make a major difference in the cost of owning them. You need to choose the appropriate management capabilities in a device. There is no one best vendor management strategy; you need to consider the requirements of your enterprise.

When considering management, be sure you are solving the right problem. It's critical that you consider security and network management as one problem and allocate your components and tools appropriately.

Security, as mentioned in Chapter 1, is the broader problem. Enterprises should have a simple, clear security policy, with the approval of top management, that states who is entitled to use resources.

If the essence of security is ensuring that legitimate users have access to the resources they need to do their jobs, a logical consequence is that anything that keeps users from getting to those resources is a threat. In planning, the most important aspect of a threat is the impact it has on the mission. The cause of the threat is secondary.

Threat events can be divided into three potentially overlapping categories [Ellison, 1997]:

- *Attacks*: Events deliberately caused by an intelligent and unauthorized attacker. You protect against these with a spectrum of security tools, including user authentication, firewalls, host access controls, and so on.

- *Failures*: Events caused by inadvertent malfunctioning of hardware or software components of the threatened system. You protect against these with appropriately redundant components, dynamic mechanisms for reconfiguring around failures, and so on.

- *Accidents*: Events outside the system proper but that affect it, such as hurricanes and earthquakes. Your protections here involve physical facility hardening (for example, backup electrical generators, satellite links, and redundant, diversified facilities).

These categories often overlap. You could consider it an accident when a construction crew fails to check on the location of a buried telecommunications cable, and their backhoe cuts through it, severing 1000 DS-3 circuits belonging to multiple carriers. Your specific WAN link might be a T1 from one of those carriers, so you could look at the backhoe incident as a failure of your specific component, the WAN link.

If a hostile individual rented a backhoe and deliberately dug up the same cable, the event could reasonably be considered an attack. You would respond, however, to the resulting link failure in exactly the same way. There's an old proverb, "Never attribute to malice what can adequately be explained by stupidity." While stupidity is a harsh term, a great many failures come from human errors in configuration.

There is a cost associated with protecting against attacks, failures, and accidents. There is a potential cost of not protecting against attacks, failures, and accidents. As a designer, you need to work with your client and their financial models to arrive at a proper balance between the cost of protection and the potential costs of failures.

Selecting Internetworking Products: Budgets

In Chapter 7, we discussed the first part of component selection. Feeds and speeds characterize the outside of a component, its physical connections to other components. There is a tendency to think of feeds and speeds in relation to initial requirements; you also need to consider growth.

After you have identified the feeds and speeds, you need to think of internal performance among the interfaces. You need to think of the component resources involved, such as memory and processing.

You will sometimes find that the most cost-effective solution involves more than one identical physical box, operating either in parallel or daisy-chained form. Alternatively, you might find that a cost-effective configuration involves several feeder boxes cabled into a higher-performance box. These alternative configurations are shown in Figure 8.1.

Although multiple boxes at a given site can be most effective, many nontechnical managers have the incorrect idea that one large box is always cheaper than several small ones. In this instance, you need to educate and perhaps introduce the idea of budgets.

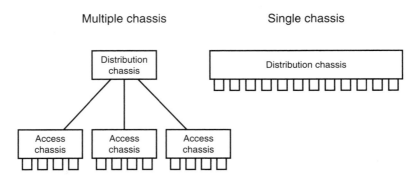

FIGURE 8.1 *Especially if there are distinct CPU-intensive functions at the access and distribution tiers, multiple chassis might be more cost effective than a single one.*

How Many Boxes? More Is Sometimes Cheaper

An example I frequently have used, which deals with some products widely deployed but no longer manufactured, is providing multiple Token Ring interfaces at a given site. The interfaces are there not because there will be extensive communications among the LANs, but to provide access to a router that will tunnel Token Ring frames for WAN access. Tunneling tends to be CPU intensive.

I have had clients that assumed a Cisco 7000 router would be ideal for a configuration requiring four Token Ring interfaces. The 7000, which reached its end of life and has been replaced, had an extremely fast path for inter-LAN communication, but relatively little CPU power. It has a relative CPU speed of 1.0.

Cisco 2500s are not considered terribly fast boxes in terms of CPU performance. Their relative CPU speed is 0.5. If, however, you use four parallel 2500s, you have a combined relative CPU performance of 2.0. Token Ring tunneling is defined with respect to specific interfaces, so it lends itself to parallel processing. The combined cost of these four 2500s is significantly less than that of a single 7000.

If the cost of WAN interfaces and local loops is low, you might simply run a WAN link to each small router. Separate links also have the benefit of avoiding a single point of failure. If WAN costs are high, it still is not an excessive cost to connect the four tunneling routers to a single WAN router. If distribution-tier functions such as prioritization, bandwidth management, and compression are needed, they can go into the distribution router without affecting the performance of the access routers.

Yet another useful multi-chassis solution used a 7000 router, which supports a direct IBM mainframe interface, to connect to the high-speed mainframe channel. SNA tunnels, which require significant CPU power, terminated on a separate fast-CPU box such as a 4700. One or more 100 Mbps interfaces interconnected the 4700 with the 7000, no longer tunneling the traffic but bridging it.

Interface Support

Individual network interconnection devices have real physical interfaces. Fixed-configuration devices are just that; you need to select the particular chassis that has the number and type of interfaces you need now and will need in the near future. If you do not estimate this correctly, the chassis might need to be replaced.

Fixed-configuration devices have a lower cost per interface than modular devices. It might be entirely cost-effective to do forklift upgrades in which you replace the chassis with a larger fixed-configuration or modular box, rather than incur the initial cost of modularity.

> **Note**
>
> *Some enterprises do perfectly well with a policy that migrates fixed-configuration equipment. They might have standardized on a small router configuration that goes in a branch office and a larger configuration that goes in a regional office. If a branch office grows such that it becomes a regional office, it hands down its branch office chassis to a new branch.*
>
> *For smooth operation in such a scenario, if this is the kind of growth you expect, you are wise to have at least one extra branch office chassis. When you are installing the new regional chassis in the same physical location as the previously branch office, leave the old branch office router in place during the conversion. You can even keep the old branch office router on its old WAN link until you are satisfied with the performance of the new regional router.*
>
> *After you are satisfied with the regional router, you can transfer end users to it, which frees up a branch router. Don't reject the idea of keeping the branch router in place and defining the regional router as one to which any branch office router connects, plus any regional-level servers.*
>
> *Install the new branch office router in the new branch office and test its connectivity with the regional router. Before you declare the regional router to be fully operational, you ideally want to verify its performance with at least two branch offices feeding into it.*
>
> *If you do free a branch router, plan on installing it in the second new branch office and connecting the second branch to the newly created region.*

The Forwarding Subsystem

When you need to interconnect high-speed media to a router, you might be able to connect the interfaces but not run them at their full speed. Several factors can prevent full forwarding speed. The interface board itself might be speed-limited, or the forwarding system might be too slow.

Depending on the specific platform, the forwarding system can consist of one or more shared paths and one or more forwarding engines. The highest-speed platforms tend to have a non-shared path.

If the same processor is used both for path determination and packet forwarding, you must pay careful attention to the processor budget. A rule of thumb in the ISP world is that routers using the same processor should not have long-term CPU utilization over 50%–60%, or they might not be able to handle a simultaneous large routing update and their forwarding load. On edge routers that only do static/default routing and do not have other CPU-intensive functions such as traffic prioritization, compression, or encryption, you might be able to get away with a slightly higher long-term utilization. Network traffic remains bursty, however, and it is unwise to overload router processors to the point where a large and unexpected burst can overrun them.

Many of these CPU-intensive features are most likely to be needed on WAN interfaces, where the potential bandwidth savings are far greater, over the system life cycle, than the additional CPU cost to reduce bandwidth. Another tradeoff for the designer and the financial management is to trade off higher initial router cost against reduced life cycle cost for WAN circuits.

Not being able to run the interfaces at full speed is not necessarily wrong. You need to distinguish between the speed of the access medium and the amount of bandwidth you actually need on it. Representative cases where you don't really need full bandwidth include the following:

- DS3 access to Frame Relay

- Microwave or laser short-range wireless communications that have a 10-Mbps Ethernet interface

- FDDI campus backbone

- Fast Ethernet as a VLAN-aware trunking technology with well under 100 Mbps of traffic

The forwarding subsystem can have substantial, and often ignored, memory requirements. If, for example, you have ten Frame Relay PVCs connected to a router, each with its own logical interface, each interface needs its own buffers. The standard Cisco buffer allocation, in process switching, is 40 outbound and 70 inbound buffers. Multiplying this total of 110 buffers by a 1500 byte MTU (ignoring additional bytes actually needed for internal functions), you require 165,000 bytes per interface, or 1.6 MB for buffering for the entire router. Some small routers only have 1 MB available for physical buffers.

The Path Determination Subsystem

Path determination can slow or stop forwarding. The key to avoiding router performance drops is a performance monitoring program, in which you keep track of the utilization of key processors. Before the processor reaches a critical level of utilization, a proper performance measurement program warns you that you need to reduce load on a device or change hardware to get a faster processor.

Memory might be an issue for the path determination subsystem of classical routers, but not as frequently as it is for buffering. You are most likely to see memory problems in central enterprise routers or in routers that accept substantial Internet BGP routes.

Emerging technologies of flow or Layer 4 switching, however, have much greater demands for path determination memory. In a classical router, you might have 100 destinations. If you consider source-destination flows, with 100 user hosts with two windows each, you need 200 lookup table entries for the flows and still might need 100 destination entries for pure routing. Tracking source-destination flows has many advantages for finer-grained control, but can have significant memory impacts.

LAN Switches

Bridges do not forward while recomputing the spanning tree algorithm. Typical recomputation times are on the order of a few seconds, but other events can slow recomputation.

Other processing-independent functions include filtering, either on basic fields such as MAC address or more complex filtering such as rate-limiting broadcasts and multicasts. The same processor does filtering and spanning tree recomputation, or has to respond to complex Simple Network Management Protocol (SNMP) queries while recomputing, the total time needed to recompute may be longer.

Remember that dropped packets are usually retransmitted by their source, depending on the protocol in use. If the bridge or switch defers or drops packets because it is recomputing the spanning tree, there can be a surge of retransmitting traffic just after the recomputation.

Often, the limiting factor to the size of a bridged network is not the usual traffic load, but the capability of the network to deal with burst loads. Retransmissions following drops are one source of unusual loads.

The first budget with which you are concerned is the forwarding bandwidth of the switch. Many switches have adequate bandwidth for all of their ports. Assuming half-duplex operation, if the product of the number of ports times the port speeds does not exceed the switch bandwidth, you will always be within your budget. A 16-port Ethernet switch with one Fast Ethernet uplink cannot exceed its budget as long as the bandwidth is not less than (16 * 10 Mbps) + 100 Mbps, or 260 Mbps.

If some ports are full-duplex, you should double their bandwidth requirement. In the previous example, if the uplink were full-duplex—usually a fine idea— the forwarding budget cannot be exceeded if it is not less than 360 Mbps.

Budgeting on maximum port rate is extremely conservative. In reality, an Ethernet or Fast Ethernet port cannot reach the full port speed, due to required interframe idle times. The actual port speed depends on the frame size.

In Chapter 10, you have a more detailed calculation for bandwidth for uplinks and servers. Much of the time, the limiting factor on throughput is not the switch itself, but performance limitations on servers connected to it. The discussion here gives you a first start.

To begin computing your requirement for bridge throughput, determine the number of ports used for end user workstations. Because applications are usually half-duplex, and the default LAN interface is half-duplex, it is reasonable to budget 30%–50% of the port bandwidth as actual traffic. In other words, if a workstation is connected on a 10-Mbps port, you can assume it needs between 3.3 and 5 Mbps of bus bandwidth.

Ports used for servers and uplinks to other switches or routers should assume full port bandwidth if they are connected with half-duplex links, and double the port bandwidth if they support full-duplex connectivity.

Another consideration is multicast and broadcast frame forwarding. If a frame comes in on one port but is multicast onto four output ports, you need to debit the forwarding budget not simply by the bandwidth of the input port, but four times the bandwidth of the input port.

Some switches might have hardware assistance for handling multicasts, which offloads the impact on the processor. Also, a switch might have multiple paths in its switching fabric, with the ideal being a crossbar design that has a path from every port to every port. If the switch design is such that a multicast packet is copied into the fabric once per output port, the load on the fabric is the input speed multiplied by the number of output ports. If the hardware simply copies the packet at each output port as the frame goes through a common bus, or if a crossbar design is used, the input port speed is all you have to debit from the forwarding budget.

Routers

Routers can stop forwarding if the path determination function runs on the same processor used for forwarding, and a compute-intensive process such as the OSPF Dijkstra calculation has a higher priority than forwarding—which it should. Smaller routers, to keep their price low, often use the same processor for forwarding and path determination. This doesn't mean the router is bad, only that the designer has to be sure it doesn't need to track an excessive number of routes. Edge routers that point toward a network core usually don't need to track more routes than their directly connected interfaces and the default route.

Besides dynamic routing, other functions that have appreciable CPU requirements include the following:

- Filtering
- Traffic categorization and marking
- Selective traffic queuing
- Flow-based routing
- Detailed traffic accounting
- Compression
- Encryption
- Voice encoding

Some routers have coprocessors that offload processing from the CPU. If so, the CPU demands will not be as great. You need to consider tradeoffs between a more expensive, faster main processor and processing power in coprocessors. The coprocessors may very well do the specialized task more efficiently than the main processor. In general, fixed-configuration routers do not have coprocessors, so you might need to consider whether small sites are better off with several small routers or one modular router that accepts special-purpose coprocessors.

In routers that use forwarding caches smaller than the full routing table, there can be a substantial drop in forwarding performance when the cache is being invalidated or refreshed. Depending on the router implementation, either the full cache is invalidated when there is a change, or only the affected entry is refreshed. In general, routers that do not need to keep Internet-sized routing tables invalidate the entire cache but maintain reasonable performance.

Cost Considerations at the Access Tier

Depending on the characteristics of the workgroup, some particular cost factors influence platform choice. You should select internetworking devices that optimize for the chief consideration of a particular workgroup. The chief consideration tends to be the following:

- Optimizing dedicated WAN access cost

- Optimizing cost per unit of bandwidth within the remote site

- Optimizing dialup or other demand WAN access cost

Optimizing Dedicated WAN Access Cost

For small sites, the highest cost tends to be associated with the speed of the access line. You want to investigate whether it is worthwhile to put bandwidth-reducing features on the site's router, such as compression, filtering, and proxy services. Significant bandwidth reductions also can come from using application caches for services including DNS, DHCP, HTTP, and database protocols.

Note

Remember that there are different forms of compression, even on routers. You might not need full packet compression. Especially with small packets, as you will encounter in Telnet or voice over IP, header compression gives substantial benefits without the processing overhead of full payload compression. For VoIP, the analog-to-digital voice conversion process has probably already compressed the payload, and there is no benefit to applying further compression.

For small sites, you want to minimize router costs. Single user workstations, for telecommuters or mobile users, do not need routers. An inexpensive alternative for workstations might be interface cards, even small routers, that plug into the motherboard.

Select small routers for small sites with small LANs. One potential way to minimize costs is to use an internal router card in a workstation, which draws power from the workstation. If multiple workstations are present, this might be less reliable than a free-standing router without user processing loads.

You can have hosts with a single serial interface rather than a LAN interface. Typical devices of this sort include SNA equipment, or other proprietary special-purpose devices such as automatic teller machines. To connect these devices to a WAN, you can use a Frame Relay Access Device (FRAD). A simple FRAD can actually be a small router with two serial interfaces. Alternatively, it can be a Layer 2 tunneling device.

Optimizing Cost per Bandwidth Unit

Switches provide bandwidth at lower cost than routers. The more clients that need to reach local servers, the more important bandwidth becomes. Workgroup switches optimize bandwidth.

Remember that there can be different optimizations of bandwidth to servers local to the workgroup and to servers on the same campus but not local to the workgroup. Switching to a local server, such as a cache or printer, not only gives a fast path between client and server, but avoids using bandwidth on switched trunks at higher levels of the hierarchy.

Optimizing Dialup or Other Demand WAN Access Cost

For small or single-user sites, it might not be cost-effective to install a dedicated physical link to the next layer of the hierarchy. For mobile users, it is impossible. Optimizing costs for this sort of user means cost-effective client dialup equipment and appropriate network access servers at the distribution tier.

Much more than with dedicated access, you need to consider the interactions of access tier and distribution tier functions—typically the dialing and dialed devices. When your users are widely distributed, you should also consider the role of outsourced VPN access in your enterprise. If users need to make long-distance calls, or are calling from random locations, VPN access might both be cheaper and more reliable.

Cost-effectiveness in the client includes tradeoffs between transmission speed and the cost of transmission equipment. For example, if you are being charged for connection time, the faster the transmission rate, the better—if you are concerned with non-interactive applications, where you can download and then disconnect. If the applications are interactive, higher speed may or may not lead to greater productivity. For generic Web browsing, higher speed can lead to searching faster and then disconnecting. Higher speed, however, can encourage additional browsing and not reduce connect time.

The transmission equipment, at the client end, can increase speed by using compression, faster modulations on analog links (for example, 56 Kbps), parallel links (for example, multiple analog channels or B channels on ISDN), or new media such as xDSL and IP over cable TV.

At the network access server end, the equipment should be sized appropriately for the expected demand. There are small servers and routers with eight or fewer interfaces, or you might need larger network access servers with 16 to 64 single-user interfaces per chassis. There are network access servers that accept high-speed access links from the local access carrier, such as primary rate ISDN. There are stackable network access servers that can accept hundreds or thousands of users.

Selecting Internetworking Products 3: Fault Tolerance

Earlier in this chapter, we looked at the broad context of fault events, which can be caused by attacks, accidents, or failures. Before you can plan for response to failures, you must understand the way failures can take place. The effect of a failure can be more important than its cause. Failures can be simplistically categorized in the following three ways:

- *Sane* failures: The component recognizes it is malfunctioning and shuts down in a manner intended to cause the least impact. In a graceful shutdown, the component sends appropriate alarms to a management function.

- *Dead* failures: The component abruptly stops operating without generating an alarm. The first indications of its malfunction come either from other components that depend on it or from monitoring functions.

- *Crazy* failures: The component either stops or continues normal operation, but sends inappropriate signals or messages into the rest of the system. Crazy failures can become apparent because a device depending on the failing component does not receive appropriate information, or a monitoring function detects inappropriate behavior. Crazy failures, however, can cause cascades of failures if the specific inappropriate behavior causes other components to fail.

In the real world, you might have the frustrating special healing case of any of these failure modes, in which a failing device suddenly returned to normal. There is a delicate balance in giving systems time to fix themselves. In routing classes, where 24 novice administrators are simultaneously trying to make routers work by typing yet another configuration command, I have been known to advise the class to use a special troubleshooting technique: Go to lunch. Especially with AppleTalk, and some old OSPF implementations, the routers would fix themselves when no one was changing their configurations and they had time to converge.

In other cases, the decision of a device to fix itself comes closer to Clarke's Second Law: "Any sufficiently advanced technology is indistinguishable from magic." Or Crowley's Corollary to Clarke's Second Law: "Any sufficiently advanced magic is indistinguishable from technology." Or, in our industry, Murphy's Corollary to Clarke's Second Law: "Any sufficiently advanced technology is indistinguishable from a rigged demo." Regardless of the cause, you should plan on several functions that respond to fault events:

- Fault detection and filtering

- Fault reporting

- Fault circumvention

- Fault diagnosis

- Fault correction

- Future fault avoidance

Fault Detection and Filtering

Fault detection services find faults, either in specific components or in delivery of a service. Network managers often first learn of a problem through a user report. The user knows that the desired service is not working properly, but usually does not know why service is not being provided. The process of fault isolation examines the problem and determines which component or components are causing the service to fail.

Some software or hardware components both provide a processing function and an error detection function. For example, routing protocols give the information necessary to forward data, but they also detect router and link faults. Routing protocols can route around faults, circumventing the fault, and send alarms that a given resource has gone down.

Other fault detection comes from pure monitoring functions. Such functions detect statistical trends.

> *Tip*
>
> *You will find it worthwhile to separate the concepts of how faults are detected from the way in which you process the notification of the fault.*

There are a number of useful techniques on the border between detection and reporting, which reduce the number of false notifications. Assume, for example, you have some number of sites interconnected in a hub and spoke topology. The spoke sites have some way of reporting faults back to the central site. If the hub goes down, all of the spokes time out. If your management software understands the relationships among these sites, after it knows the hub has failed, it suppresses reports that the spokes have timed out.

Of course, if the spokes have automatic backup capabilities, you want to ensure that the alarm filtering does not prevent the backups from detecting a failure and starting the backup operation. Even more intelligent filtering, however, might detect the hub failure, then look for the backups to trigger and only report on backups that do not trigger.

Fault Reporting

Think of a general function of notifying an operator that a problem has occurred. As a second step, think of this operator either as an automated or a human operator.

Automated operators can be purpose-built software that directly receives and processes SNMP traps and other alarms, or they can be computer scripts that simulate a human being at a console. Software such as **expect** and **tcl** is widely used to simulate operators. See the section "Human Interfaces" later in this chapter for a discussion of the various management system interfaces to which scripts might need to respond.

Although there is an intuitive desire to display all faults graphically, be aware that it is very easy to overload operators with so much visual information that they lose what fighter pilots call situational awareness. When you use graphic displays, it's best to leave them at a high-level view of the network and allow the human operator to zoom in on detailed topology when he begins to analyze a specific fault.

"If the Blob Moves, Shoot It"

I once saw a failed experiment in which an Army commander asked for a display of the status of every communications device in his division, which had thousands of devices. He asked for the status to be shown in red, yellow, or green. If the display was set to a sufficiently high viewpoint to show every device, it showed nothing but a pulsing brown blob.

Unfortunately, it is far too common for people to try to put too much information into network displays, to a point where they are so busy that problems are missed and structure cannot be discerned. Do not give in to the temptation of trying to fit your entire network drawing on a single screen or piece of paper, if the resulting picture is hard to follow. Draw the network on a series of screens or pages, adding detail as you move lower in the hierarchy.

Fault Circumvention

After you know there is a problem, *fault recovery* services come into play. Fault recovery can be a temporary *problem circumvention*, or a definitive repair. Fault recovery can be automatic (for example, a redundant component taking over) or can require human intervention.

It might not be possible to restore full service function or performance at once, but some service can be returned using the principle of *graceful degradation*. System responses to failure exhibit graceful degradation when performance slows but does not drop below unacceptable limits.

Automatic fault recovery is usually what people have in mind when they speak of fault tolerance. People often are confused, however, by what really is involved in fault tolerance.

Do not equate fault tolerance redundancy. Component redundancy *might* provide improved availability, but there are many cases where apparently redundant components are not, or where redundancy imposes an additional workload that actually decreases availability or so complicates the network that real-world operators cannot fix it if something breaks.

A common error is obtaining WAN circuits from several different providers, with the hope of getting completely separate facilities. For reasons discussed in the "Grooming" section in Chapter 9, all the carriers involved might lease capacity from an additional carrier not known to you, producing a single point of failure. Table 8.1 shows fault tolerance mechanisms and where they are discussed in more detail in this book.

TABLE 8.1 FAULT TOLERANCE MECHANISMS

Component	Mechanism	Additional Discussion
Single dedicated WAN link	Dial backup, including ISDN and other demand media	Chapter 12
WAN link with available alternate dedicated paths	Alternate routing	Chapter 11
LAN link	Alternate media found via spanning tree, inverse multiplexing	Chapter 10
Workstation	Dual NIC; spanning tree-aware workstation, application level NIC selection or application that sends duplicate data and understands multiple responses	Chapter 10
Hub	No inherent redundancy; consider dual NIC	
Component power	Load-sharing power supplies internal or external to chassis. External uninterruptible power supplies (UPS).	
LAN switch interface	Inverse multiplexing	Chapter 10
LAN switch	Alternate switch via spanning tree, fast recovery techniques using controlled spanning tree violations	Chapter 10
Router	Dynamic routing	Chapters 11 and 12

Component	Mechanism	Additional Discussion
Default router (from host perspective)	VRRP/HSRP, Bay router redundancy, dynamic router discovery, special ARP techniques	Chapter 6
Router CPU	Hot standby CPU, multiple routers	
Router forwarding processor	Inverse multiplexing, multiple routers	

Who's Watching the Automatic Safeguards?

Automatic circumvention is usually a good idea, but don't let it hide the information you need to set up scheduled repairs. In the early 1980s, I worked for a national packet-switching service provider. When a line between our packet switches failed, the switch could automatically select one of up to eight backup lines. Unfortunately, the switch did not notify the network operations center when it did so; the general concept was to rely on routine maintenance to repair failed lines. On one memorable occasion, however, we lost all connectivity between New York and Washington, D.C., because a series of lines failed, and we had no advanced warning that we were running on the last backup line. When the last backups failed on two separate switches, the network crashed.

A major telephone failure, whose effects included jeopardizing major airports, came from a chain of events, as many failures do. During an especially hot summer week, the electrical utility in a very large city asked if organizations with their own backup generators could run from their own generators, reducing the overloaded municipal power system. One major telecommunications provider did so.

Recent cost reductions, however, left a given telephone office manned only during the business day. During the night, the generator failed, and there was no one to hear the alarm. Still, there was no immediate interruption in service, because the large batteries of the office took over the load.

Unfortunately, the regular staff did not come in at the start of business. Instead, they went to a scheduled seminar on improving network reliability. But by the time they returned to their control centers, the batteries had been drained, and no one was there to switch them back to utility power.

Fault Diagnosis

Components can fail in several ways. One informal but useful taxonomy of failures divides them into the three categories discussed earlier in this chapter: sane, dead, and crazy.

Sane failures are easily diagnosed. It is more difficult to identify the other two categories. Useful methods include *component substitution* and *loopbacks*.

There's an old story of how a classical field engineer approaches component substitution: "How many <name of vendor> engineers does it take to change a light bulb? Answer: It depends on how many burnt-out bulbs they have to swap before they find the bulb that works." Nevertheless, swapping a known good component with a suspected bad one, and checking if the problem moved with the bad component, remains a useful method.

Loopback tests are most associated with physical and possibly data link layer failure testing. They are the ancestors of **ping** and **traceroute** tests at Layer 3. Appropriate graphic displays form the next generation for connectivity diagnosis at all layers (see Figure 8.2).

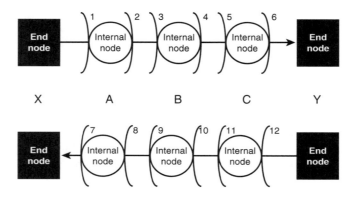

FIGURE 8.2 *Loopbacks originated in physical layer testing and are the ancestors of* **ping***.*

In the example shown in Figure 8.2, assume each intermediate node, A through C, has the capability to loopback data at its input and output in each direction. At loopback Point 1 on Node X, for example, a testing device can loopback to the Node X receiver the signals received from Transmitter X.

If no signal is received at X when Loopback 1 is activated, the transmission facility connecting X and A is likely to be the problem. An alternative explanation could be that the Node X transmitter is not actually putting signals into the medium.

In the example, the actual failure is the transmitter on the Y side of Node B. Successively looping at points from near to far from Node X shows normal operation up to Loopback 4. Looping from the Y direction up to a failure at Loopback 10 isolates the problem.

Fault Correction

Although you can circumvent a failing component, you eventually need to repair or replace it. Especially when some circumventing mechanism provides a backup service, you might be able to correct the problem without interfering with user service. It is most likely, however, that there might be some service interruption when the failed component returns to service and the user traffic no longer flows through the mechanism used to circumvent the fault.

Your planning for fault recovery should consider the ways in which you will schedule fault correction and how you will inform users of any service interruption. You might choose to correct faults only outside of working hours, which, of course, is impossible if you have 24x7 operations. The longer the period of time for which you defer definitive correction, the more backup resources you might need. As the time to repair increases, the likelihood that another component will fail also increases.

Future Fault Avoidance

You need a long-term monitoring program to decide on the appropriate backup component level and to decide if a particular component type is causing an unacceptable number of problems.

The Management Architecture

Real platform and network components do not magically appear and begin to exchange protocol information. They must be installed and related to one another within an overall configuration structure. They will break. There must be usable mechanisms to detect failures and correct them.

Network management architectures require that networks be built from real resources, such as modems, wires, computers, and relays. Although real resources share general attributes, the specific characteristics of real resources is implementation-dependent.

At the next level of detail, several different views of the management problem have to be taken to build practical management systems. Several technical models cooperate to define the design of the management support system, whereas a final model defines the operational relationship of the management system to the organization as a whole.

To allow an implementation- and vendor-independent view of network resource management, models for abstraction allow separation of implementation-dependent and implementation-independent characteristics of resources. Network management standards prescribe means of operating on generic abstractions of resources, much as virtual terminal protocols map from a real terminal implementation to an abstract representation of a terminal. A useful set of models includes the following:

- The functional model asks this question: What are the technical functions needed in management? A framework for analyzing functional requirements for management. Each component of this framework is called a system management functional area (SMFA).

- The information model asks this: What are the resources to be managed? Most modern information models provide a standard means of describing abstractions of network resources to be managed, a means of defining product-independent operations on those abstractions, and principles for mapping from the abstractions to specific real resources.

- Function distribution models and communications models are really intertwined pieces of the same thing. They define the logical groupings of abstract resources and the things that operate on them, and the means of computer-to-computer communications among these groupings.

- Finally, the organizational model defines what kinds of users and operational staff will be needed. What is their work flow? This is less a technical matter than one of the organizational requirements discussed in Chapter 1.

These standards alone are insufficient for building management systems. Other important components, potentially subject to standardization by groups outside the OSI and Internet management efforts, include the following:

- Operator interface, including command languages and standard presentations of alarms

- Policies for defining names and addresses

- Security policies

- Performance objectives

- Means of mapping between managed objects and real realizations

The Functional Model

The Chapter 6 sidebar, "What Really Breaks," introduced my ranking of the most common sources of failures:

- Media failures, especially WAN

- Electrical power failures

- Internetworking device software

- Internetworking device interface hardware

- Internetworking device power supplies

- Internetworking device central hardware

The emphasis of Chapter 6 is on small networks. In larger networks, more advanced redundancy techniques become easier to cost justify.

In network and system management, span of control is formalized in *management domains*. There are many reasons for establishing domains:

- Scalability

- Security

- Reliability/firewalls

- Administrative

Domains can be nested within another, as in a previous example where both the higher-level departmental naming and lower-level personal naming functions are in the same corporation. Domains can also be separate but cooperating, in the sense of interdomain, policy-based routing defined in Chapter 6.

ISO's SMFAs represent requirements more than implementation techniques. Another set of categories, the system management functions (SMFs), is oriented toward implementation rather than requirements. In requirements analysis and design, this set is matrixed against the SMFAs. The list of SMFs includes the following:

- Object management function

- State management function

- Alarm reporting function

- Event reporting function

- Log control function

- Security alarm reporting function

- Security audit trail function

- Workload monitoring function

- Test management function

- Summarization function

IBM, in its System Network Architecture (SNA), defined a different but interesting set of functions. The underlying functions are fairly similar to those covered by the ISO SMFA definitions, but have more of a real-world operations focus [Rose, 1988]:

- Problem management

  - Determination

  - Diagnosis

  - Bypass and recovery

  - Resolution

  - Tracking and control

- Configuration management

- Performance and accounting management

- Operations management

It is a slippery slope to delve too far into application management when discussing network management. Certainly, there are MIBs defined for many application-related functions.

Protection Against Media Failures

Your major concern with failures of media will be with WAN media. Analog or ISDN on-demand circuits can provide a reasonable level of protection against dedicated circuit failures.

One common means of backing up WAN media is to create a dialup link when the primary dedicated link fails. Dedicated link failure can be detected with physical layer events, Layer 2 keepalives, or Layer 3 routing protocol hellos. When both ends of a dedicated medium can detect a failure, be sure that they have different timer values to wait before initiating the call. If they try to dial at the same time, you can have a *call collision* that causes both to sense a busy signal at the other end.

Other than for quite large bandwidth requirements, routers are the interconnection device to the WAN. Does the router under consideration have appropriate interfaces and enough of them? An ISDN basic rate interface fully backs up a 128-Kbps Frame Relay virtual circuit, but provides only half the speed of a 256 Kbps and one-twelfth the speed of a T1. You might want to have multiple ISDN backups. Your final decision comes only after you have analyzed the pricing for PRI and BRI available to you in a given geographical area.

Alternatively, you might have one or more analog modem backups. Current modem technology limits connectivity to 53 Kbps per telephone line, a speed that often is not attainable. Speeds of 30 Kbps or so might be more realistic.

Remote Management After Media Failures

User traffic is not the only reason to have dialup connectivity to an interconnection device. All user communications are local to the campus. Nevertheless, there are no local technical support personnel. For diagnostics to be run, staff at the network management center needs a control channel that lets them communicate with the remote consoles, SNMP agents, and so on in the switches, see Figure 8.3.

There might be a management station at the local site for use when service personnel are present. Such a station might routinely provide DNS, DHCP, TFTP, or related services needed at the site. It also can run scripts to automate operator functions.

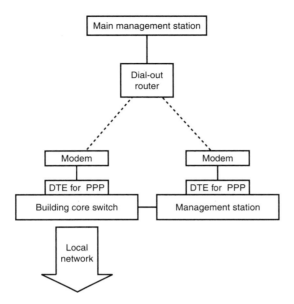

FIGURE 8.3 *Dial connectivity can go either directly to the managed devices or to a management station at the unattended site.*

Reverse Telnet in Management

A related method for controlling devices at a site without technical support staff is to use reverse telnet to manage devices that only have local asynchronous terminal consoles. This is also a useful method for controlling remote development or network training laboratories.

Figure 8.4 shows some of the ways in which **telnet** windows or physical terminals can control devices at a remote site. Remember that you can have electromechanical interface switches at the remote site, which lets you remotely reconfigure the physical relationships among interfaces. You also might be able to reconfigure the remote site by redefining port assignments to VLANs.

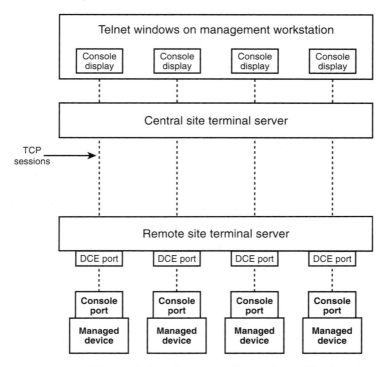

Figure 8.4 *The terminal sessions at the client end can either be real terminals or, more commonly, **telnet** windows on a workstation.*

Protection Against Power Failures

Power failures affect two areas: the actual source of electrical power and the power supplies themselves. If your budget is limited, it is usually far more cost-effective to be sure the internetworking device receives its electricity from an uninterruptible power supply (UPS). In even more critical installations, you might want to consider multiple utility power feeds or your own generators. Major disasters—and strange disasters—can bring down any power system.

Yes, We Planned for Everything…We Thought

One of the major national Internet service providers has a point of presence in the computer science building of a West Coast university. The provider is extremely concerned with availability and tried to handle every contingency in an earthquake-prone area.

Two separate utility power feeders come to the computer science building. These heavy electrical cables are carefully routed from substations at opposite sides of the campus. In addition, there is a diesel generator at the building.

The power feeders and the generator output come into a straightforward electromechanical power transfer switch, which feeds the selected power source into the battery chargers of a large UPS.

In the darkest hours of the night, a loud explosion was heard near the power room. Operators rushing to investigate found a gap of several feet in the high-power electrical cables to and from the transfer switch, and a smoking hole where the switch had been. There was a smell of burning meat in the air.

On investigation, it was found that a love-struck pair of rats had nested inside the power transfer switch. Their frolics caused them to put a literally dead short across the power feeder. The resulting sparks and arcs sent pieces of switch and well-done rat-burger over the immediate area.

It's rather hard to find an electrician capable of splicing heavy utility cable at 3 a.m. The UPS did take over as long as its batteries lasted, but eventually they ran down. Power was available from the utility and the diesel, but it couldn't physically get to the UPS charger.

Even the most critical military command posts hardened for nuclear war cannot protect against every threat. The military strategy to maintain command and control in a hot nuclear war is to diversify facilities, including making them mobile. No level of backup facilities at a single site is proof against a sufficient number of nuclear explosions over a period of time.

Note

There is such a thing as having too much physical security, as suggested in a favorite science fiction novel, Martin Caidin's The God Machine [Caidin, 1989]. If you decide to set up a nuclear reactor as your UPS, repeat after me: "I will not give the computer the authority to shoot at anyone it thinks might be trying to pull its plug."

When planning for redundant power, it's more important to have the internetworking device connected to a UPS than it is to have dual power supplies connected to utility power.

Do you need dual power supplies? They do provide an additional level of reliability. If you do use them, especially if they are only connected to utility power, please be sure they are on circuits connected to different circuit breakers.

Another real-world caution in using dual power supplies is to be sure a failed power supply can be removed from the internetworking device without having to disconnect either the power cord of the other supply or any data interface cables. Large routers and switches, when filled with electronics, are heavy. There is a natural tendency to take the electronics out when lifting the devices into a rack, then replace the power supply modules, then plug in the interface cards, and finally connect the interface and power cabling. In the process of installing a large number of interface cables, it is quite easy to position a large cable bundle so that it blocks a power supply from sliding fully out of the chassis. Please avoid doing this!

The Information Model

The broad definition of most management is done through the SNMP specification. Current network management specifications are written as Management Information Bases (MIBs), which are abstract descriptions of various timers, counters, and so on, that are relevant to protocol operation. The abstractions of the MIB are mapped by implementation-specific software into the actual memory locations, hardware switches, and so on of the managed devices.

You build an SNMP management system from one or more *manager* nodes and one or more *agent* functions for managing network resources. SNMP is the protocol that communicates between managers and agents and, in the more recent versions of SNMP, between managers and other managers (see Figure 8.5).

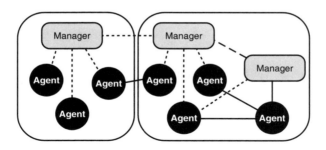

Legend

- - - - - - - -   Manager-to-manager communication is not available in SNMPv1

FIGURE 8.5   *Within management domains, managers control, and can coordinate with, other managers in the later versions of SNMP.*

Note

I have a personal law of protocol naming: Anything that has the word simple in it isn't. SNMP was conceived partially as a response to the perceived complexity of the ISO Common Management Information Protocol (CMIP).

A key moment in the maturation process is the first time you recognize you are sounding exactly like one of your parents. There's a parallel with management protocols. CMIP proper has largely fallen out of use, yet the newer versions of SNMP have many of the capabilities of CMIP.

Agents and managers can have different levels of capability. Nodes can contain both manager and agent functions.

A major enhancement in SNMPv3 is adding sufficiently strong security that the architecture can be used both for management and control. Unless the SNMP **SET** command, which changes values in agents, can be trusted, an SNMP management system can provide no more than monitoring. There needs to be authentication of the source, unitary and sequential integrity of SNMP messages, and possibly some confidentiality of messages.

The SNMP architecture has a core set of MIB objects, to which numerous technology-specific standard MIBs are chained. There are also vendor-specific MIB extensions.

Figure 8.6 shows the SNMP MIB and the OSI management model within the extremely broad hierarchy of ISO network object names. Each node on the tree, such as ISO or DoD, has a numeric value. A general MIB browser can traverse this tree and find arbitrary objects, but there is no question this takes substantial operator knowledge. Management applications usually provide a graphics-oriented view of the MIB tree.

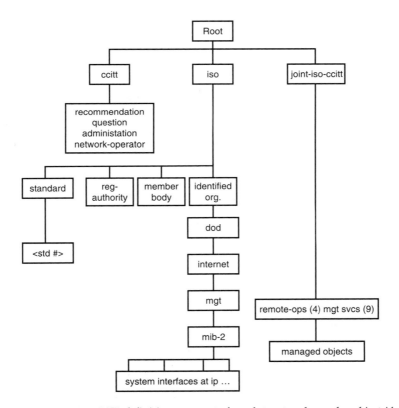

FIGURE 8.6 *MIB definitions are part of an abstract and complex object identifier system defined by ISO.*

Vendor-specific MIB objects are necessary to monitor vendor-dependent features such as processor utilization and buffer counts. All major vendor management applications let you examine their specific private MIB objects. Bay has made extensive use of the MIB tree in its management features, and Bay does allow you to script references to the MIB tree from its control consoles.

Original MIB Goals

The basic list of managed objects is meant to be the minimum necessary set of objects. Every implementation is expected to support all of the objects. Three mechanisms exist for extending the MIB:

- Adding new standard objects through the definitions of new versions of the MIB

- Adding widely available but non-standard objects through the multilateral subtree

- Adding private objects through the enterprises subtree

A number of criteria were used to define the initial MIB:

- An object needed to be essential for either fault or configuration management. Subsequent versions introduced objects needed for performance, accounting, and security management.

- Only weak control objects were permitted (by *weak*, it is meant that tampering with them can do only limited damage). This criterion reflects the fact that the original management protocols are not sufficiently secure to do more powerful control operations. SNMPv2 and SNMPv3 relax this requirement because they have much stronger security.

- Evidence of current use and utility was required.

- An attempt was made to limit the number of objects to about 100 to make it easier for vendors to fully instrument their software.

- To avoid redundant variables, it was required that no object be included that can be derived from others in the MIB.

- Implementation specific objects (for example, for BSD UNIX) were excluded.

- It was agreed to avoid heavily instrumenting critical sections of code. The general guideline was one counter per critical section per layer.

MIB Evolution

The core MIB itself has evolved over time. At the time the basic MIBs were defined, IP addressing was classful. As of mid-1999, RFC 2096 is the most recent evolution of the forwarding table. This RFC specifies additional semantics that allow routing table entries to be defined as CIDR prefixes.

A managed device has at least one IP address with which device-level information is associated. This IP address is associated with an interface, but the managed object can have more than one interface. The common MIB elements do have a field for a system identifier, which could be a DNS name. As address assignment becomes more and more dynamic, it makes more and more sense to track devices by a unique identifier other than an IP address.

The original MIB model assumed a one-to-one correspondence between interfaces and IP addresses. As networking evolved, this assumption no longer applied to many types of interfaces.

In Layer 2 virtual circuit services such as Frame Relay, X.25, and ATM, there can be many logical interfaces, each with their own IP address, per physical interface. Multiple logical addresses can map to a single physical interface, using what the Cisco IOS calls secondary addresses and Bay RS calls multinet addresses.

The mirror image of many-to-one is one-to-many. Multilink PPP, for example, is one inverse multiplexing service where an IP address is associated with the bundled output of several physical interfaces.

Just to complicate things, both one-to-many and many-to-one might both apply. Multiple logical interfaces also can be imposed on a physical interface using Layer 1 multiplexing, such as fractional T1. A physical T1 interface might have two or more data streams, each with their own IP address, that are made up of multiple DS0 64 Kbps channels inverse multiplexed together.

**Redundant Management
Mechanisms Can Be a Good Thing**

Some monitored products, including Cisco IOS routers, have a MIB view of counters and timers, but also have an additional local view. On a Cisco router, the statistics displayed with **show** commands reflect different internal counters than those retrieved with SNMP **Get** commands. You use command language **clear** commands to reset the counters used for **show** commands, but use SNMP **PUT** commands to reset MIB counters.

You can use the existence of two sets of counters to your operational advantage. Plan your long-term statistical analysis as based on MIB statistics. When troubleshooting, clear the relevant counters before making a change. Make the change and see if the counters reflecting the error increase.

Function Distribution and Communications Models

SNMP carries MIB-defined commands to SNMP agents on managed devices and collects MIB information from them. These commands are issued by an SNMP manager. Managed devices can also send SNMP **TRAP** messages to the manager at any time when the **TRAP**-triggering condition exists on the managed device.

Any processing of the information received by the manager, however, goes to a higher-level mechanism not specified by the SNMP architecture, the *management application* (see Figure 8.7).

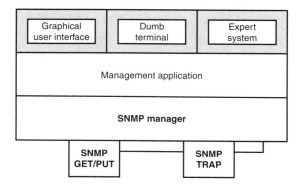

F IGURE 8.7   *Functions in an SNMP management station.*

Most major internetwork vendors have their own management applications: Bay's Optivity, Cabletron's Spectrum, Cisco's CiscoWorks, or 3Com's Transcend. These run on top of a workstation-specific SNMP manager such as Hewlett-Packard's Open View, Sun's Network Manager, or IBM's NetView.

The network managers provide an operator interface and a general means of manipulating standard MIBs on managed devices. They generally also have a MIB browser function that lets you examine vendor-specific MIBs, but they do not have the graphic front-ends to these extensions that the internetwork vendor products do. To work with an arbitrary MIB, you need a substantial knowledge of the SNMP architecture's Structure of Management Information (SMI) [RFC 2578], including the subset of the ASN.1 notation used in the MIBs.

The internetwork vendor software typically has software not simply for simplified extensions to vendor MIB extensions, but an assortment of tools for working with them. These tools include both textual and graphic reports, data reduction that allows alarms to be generated on trends or on passing specific limits, configuration file managers for all routers and switches, and so on.

Although different internetwork vendor applications run on the major network managers, it sometimes can be a challenge to make more than one application run on the same workstation. The human interface to these packages also varies among manufacturers.

The two major cost factors in most enterprise networks are the long-term cost of WAN links and the people cost of configuration changes and troubleshooting. WAN costs are the largest factor.

Network management tools can reduce the latter cost factor, although they can require a greater initial investment. This initial investment includes not only equipment and software, but the cost of training your personnel to use the tools effectively. Network management tools can indirectly reduce WAN cost by giving you the capability to fine-tune the WAN resources you need.

Differing human interfaces bring up a sometimes overlooked cost of operations: the need to train operations staff in several different systems if you want to run a multivendor environment making use of all vendor-specific tools. In smaller enterprises, you might want to examine seriously the cost of owning multiple vendor solutions. Sometimes, the different vendor capabilities justify the complexity. In an academic environment, the operations staff might have extra technical knowledge that helps them work with different packages.

There are two principal aspects to management: the capabilities in the managed devices and the capabilities of the management station and associated tools. These capabilities complement one another. If the managed devices do not collect information, the management station cannot make decisions based on it. In turn, the capabilities of the management station dictates the range of operations that can be performed on the managed devices.

To put this in context, unless a switch or router collects port-level statistics, you cannot detect a network problem caused by excessive traffic at the port. If the management station cannot send a reset or stop command to the port, you cannot remotely clear the problem. You might not be able to send the command either because the management station cannot generate it, or because there is no secure and trusted control channel between the manager and the managed device.

You need communications among the managers and managed objects for planned statistics gathering, for updating system software and configuration files, and for ad hoc debugging. SNMP is the main communications method for automated statistics collection, although there are applications for automated operator functions that simulate interaction between a human and a device's console function. Simulating the human interface can be more or less difficult depending on whether the device interface is command-oriented or graphics-oriented.

Human Interfaces

Different vendors have evolved different styles of configuring the systems. Many of the differences derive from single engineering decisions made early in the product life cycle.

In the mid-1980s, as commercial routers were introduced, an early decision was how to store executable router code. Cisco's choice was to put this information in read-only memory (ROM), so changes initially meant that chips needed to be replaced. Because chips of the time had limited capacity, a text-oriented configuration language was chosen because it took less memory.

Cisco was also concerned about reliability. Wellfleet's (later Bay's) alternative, a floppy disk drive, had moving parts, so it was bound to be more reliable than solid-state components. By implementing floppy disks, however, Bay had much more storage, which let them build a more powerful, menu-based, user interface. Having removable media also made software upgrades easier to install.

GateD's ancestry is in UNIX systems, so there was little question about deciding to use a command-line interface.

With today's platforms, the availability of flash memory removes most storage restrictions. Router operating systems continue to evolve in the basic forms of their original interfaces. Both Bay and Cisco are adopting add-on features reminiscent of the competitors' style.

In general, menu systems such as Bay/Wellfleet original interface are faster to learn. Command-line interfaces, as Cisco originally used, can be faster to use for a skilled operator.

My own thinking about human interfaces has evolved, as new technologies emerge and have new management requirements. As a programmer, I have always liked command-oriented interfaces. I realized the learning curve might be less for some menu-based and graphic user interfaces, but have found such interfaces cumbersome if I have to configure many devices.

As this realization matured, I began to understand the first of several distinctions among human interfaces: user-friendliness versus expert-friendliness. A new operator, doing minimal configuration on a simple device, does not know the expectations of the device, and the interface should help her. As the operator does increasingly complex things, it is hard to make such things work if the operator does not have an abstract model of the problem in her head, and eventually a GUI or menu gets in the way of the mental model. Command interfaces let you tell the device being managed exactly what you want it to do, as opposed to filtering your desires through the conceptual model of the interface.

An additional realization came when I began to work with complex global Internet routing, virtual LANs, and virtual private networks. Although I am quite capable of reading routing tables, VLAN spanning tree status, and VPN tunnel information, it can be a time-consuming process to work out which potential paths are active. I've found that graphic interfaces should be used in troubleshooting, not configuration. The useful graphic interfaces here are those that analyze tables and show active or failed paths, with an adequate level of detail available.

An emerging area of technology, which for many years was not practical, is a graphic interface to let end users specify requirements—which end hosts need to talk to which servers. There are some relatively straightforward tools for configuring small networks of 20 hosts or so. As networks grow, these techniques will continue to be useful only if they permit abstraction and aggregation of user requirements into classes. If you try to draw every host in a network with thousands of hosts, the visual model becomes incomprehensible. If the configuration tool lets you work on a site and then abstract its connectivity to services outside the site, you have a fighting chance!

On the other hand, visual interfaces can be extremely helpful in troubleshooting. They are especially useful when you use technologies that overlay multiple logical structures onto an infrastructure, such as VLANs or VPNs. It can be very time-consuming (and require significant expertise) to trace out the paths your data is taking if, for example, you have to display the spanning tree status of each switch in a VLAN. A graphic network management tool can obtain the status information, analyze it, and present the information in a manner that helps you see the failure.

Automated Operator and File Transfer Interfaces
Command-line interfaces lend themselves to scripting and automation of the user interface.

Although Bay now has a command quite able to handle scripting, its earlier menu systems used SNMP to control remote devices. SNMP traffic was not easily scriptable, although it could be done using an ASN.1 compiler. ASN.1 describes SNMP messages, but is a complex notation.

Products vary as how commands are sent to managed remote devices. Depending on the product, you might have one of the following:

Interaction	Configuration File Is Text	Configuration File Is ASN.1
Interactive	Telnet, http	SNMP
Batch	TFTP	TFTP

You can script various tasks.

With an interactive configuration editor, you can set up an internetworking device. There will always be a need, however, to transfer binary files to the device, files that contain the executable code of the operating system. In managing networks of any appreciable size, however, you also need to be able to manage configuration files as files and transfer them to your internetworking devices from an appropriate server. Most commercial products use the Trivial File Transfer Protocol (TFTP) to transfer files, a requirement discussed in the next section, "Configuration Management."

Configuration Management

Perhaps the most basic configuration management requirement is agreement on the identifiers of the objects to be managed. After that is done, managed objects can be created and deleted by object management.

In addition to simple existence, configuration management considers relationships among managed objects. Developing a static routing table is a basic example of configuration relationships, based on the relations *adjacent* and *reachable*.

Effective configuration management requires effective change control. Changes should be made by appropriate authorities that, for purposes of change, have exclusive control of the resources affected. Audit trails of configuration changes can be of great help in learning when a problem first occurred.

Configuration management has administrative, as well as topological, aspects. Installation, repair, and removal of resources all must be scheduled. It must be possible to identify resources under repair, their backups if alternative service is being provided, the disposition of the backup when the primary resource returns to service, and so on.

The IEEE POSIX architecture considers distributed authentication, naming services, time services, and client/server relationships to be part of configuration management. Software installation and version control is part of both local and distributed management; it can be difficult to separate true networking software from application software. Remember that users are concerned with obtaining service, not the internal allocation of resources.

Users themselves, from the standpoint of configuration management, are configurable. Services for managing the configuration of users consist of the capability to do the following:

- Create a new user or group of users

- Delete a user or group of users

- Allocate system resources to a user or a group of users

Beyond any minimal level of complexity, you need to configure routers and switches. Before configuration can begin, the router or switch needs an executable image of its operating system. Your first concern is being sure that a given new chassis has an image loaded into it.

If there is no image in a device, and it does not have a full image in local mass storage, the device has to obtain an image from a remote server. Obtaining this configuration can be a two-step process, in which the device initializes with a minimal image stored in ROM, which gives just enough running code to download a full image from a remote server. *Bootstrapping* is the process by which a router or switch starts with a minimal capability that it uses to get a more comprehensive file.

How Do Configurations Get into the Device?

Assuming you are physically at the device, you can log in to a local console port of an internetworking device and configure it. Many devices have some form of memory that retains its contents when the chassis is not connected to external power; so preconfiguring and testing devices at a central site, and then shipping them to a remote site, can be a perfectly reasonable practice.

If you are not going to configure a device using the local console, the device must obtain a configuration from a remote server. Just as you might need to bootstrap an executable image into a device, you might need to bootstrap the configuration with a two-step process. The device first obtains a minimal configuration that lets it communicate with the remote server, then obtains the full configuration.

Most vendors do the actual file transfer with TFTP, although SNMP can be used. When the internetworking device is actually a general-purpose UNIX or Windows host, you can use FTP to transfer files.

TFTP is a stripped-down version of FTP. It was originally designed for booting diskless workstations and had the firm constraint that code for TFTP and supporting protocols had to fit into a relatively small ROM. TFTP runs over UDP and IP. UDP is used because it is far simpler than TCP. Because UDP does not do retransmissions, TFTP has to do its own retransmissions with a simple algorithm. TFTP file transfers are not extremely efficient, but efficiency is not the major concern. TFTP lacks security features, and so it needs to be used in a well-controlled manner. Block TFTP access to or from external addresses.

Minimal bootstrapping monitors need to know the IP address or DNS name of the TFTP server. They also need to know a filename.

Tip

When you specify a filename in TFTP, you usually need to specify the fully qualified name rather than a name relative to a current directory. TFTP does not know about relative names.

IP Address Management and Renumbering

Managing your IP addresses is a critical part of configuration management. Although the IP address really should not be thought of as more than a potentially transient identifier of an interface involved in routing, its meaning has been overloaded such that it is assumed to be an endpoint or a device identifier.

Although there is not yet a perfect endpoint identifier, DNS names are much more appropriate for that purpose than IP addresses. Nevertheless, various network management and application functions depend on the IP address.

Thomas Paine said, "The tree of liberty periodically has to be watered with the blood of patriots." The reality of modern networks, especially those with Internet connectivity, is that addresses are likely to change. When you do have to renumber, be aware that it is not simply a matter of changing host addresses. IP addresses can be embedded in network management functions, in routers, in switches, and so on. Renumbering is not trivial! See RFC 2072 for a detailed discussion of renumbering considerations applicable to routers.

A good general strategy is to think of your DNS as the core of your thoroughly integrated naming and addressing system. In complex networks, you might want a more powerful database system at the core, with contents that map to DNS.

The overall address plan of a large enterprise is beyond the scope of this text, but is the principal focus of *Designing Addressing Architectures for Routing and Switching*. [Berkowitz, 1998a]. In general, you want an inventory of everything that IP regards as a host: user workstations and servers, router interface addresses, and management interfaces in switches.

To the maximum extent possible, define end host addresses in DHCP servers. DHCP servers have three modes of operation:

- Assign a fixed IP address for a specific host identifier, which is usually a MAC address

- Assign an IP address from a pool, with an infinite lease time on the assigned address

- Assign an IP address with a limited lease time

The first DHCP mode is, of course, the most controllable, but also requires you either to have locally administered MAC addresses, track changes in MAC addresses, or have the host use a different host identifier in its DHCP requests. In a Microsoft environment, an alternative is to use a NetBIOS name as the host identifier, understanding that this might not scale if you need the same NetBIOS name in different domains. If the specific host supports using it in DHCP, a DNS name might make a very good host identifier.

The second mode is quite reasonable for servers, if there is linkage between DHCP and DNS. When the server gets an address assignment, DNS should automatically be updated. If you do not have a linkage between DHCP and DNS, it is still reasonable to use DHCP to assign host addresses, but you should assign fixed addresses based on predefined host identifiers.

General workstations should get dynamically assigned addresses. On a LAN, they can get this directly from DHCP. On a WAN connection, PPP has the capability to assign addresses, which can come from local address pools on the access server, on an authentication server, or from a DHCP server reached by a proxy function on an access or authentication server. After any address is dynamically assigned, it should be stored in the DNS.

Routers and switches generally cannot use DHCP for their address assignments, but you still can automate some of their addressing. The router and
switch configurations can be stored on a server, most often TFTP. You can use
programming tools such as macro processors to substitute host-specific
addresses into a configuration template.

Accounting Management

Accounting management is not simply a financial process, but a more general
way to understand the use of resources. Depending on the organization's
requirements, accounting management may or may not include cost analysis
and financial chargeback mechanisms.

Because off-the-shelf network and host components can produce vast amounts
of resource usage data, these data usually need to be filtered to produce manageable amounts of useful data. Filtering is part of the general process of the
event management function described earlier. The original Internet management architecture does not support filtering as a basic architectural element;
this is a major difference between OSI and Internet management that changed
with the Remote Monitoring (RMON) feature of the Internet architecture.

Accounting logs can be a significant contribution to security management. One
of the computer security books that made the *New York Times* bestseller list is
Cliff Stoll's *The Cuckoo's Egg* [Stoll], which describes an international search for
crackers that began when he became suspicious of a 75-cent discrepancy in
accounting records.

As voice services integrate with data, there will be a significant accounting
requirement to reconcile telephone company charges with network usage.
Nevertheless, such reconciliation will become increasingly important due to
the trend to see data network demands increase while data network budgets
have minimal growth. Voice budgets, however, have typically remained constant with relatively constant growth. If some of the voice budget can provide
data services as well, the overall enterprise budget grows at a lower rate.

The goal of slowing budget growth is one of the major motivations for VoX or
Voice over X technologies, which include Voice over IP (VoIP), Voice over
Frame Relay (VoFR), and Voice over ATM (VoATM). In these technologies, both
voice and data can be carried over common transmission systems, reducing
duplication and cost.

Performance Management

Performance management includes defining performance objectives, measuring to see that they are met or not met, and acting to change capacity or tune network components as appropriate to meet objectives. Remember that excessive resources can be devoted to assuring unnecessary levels of performance. The buzzword *rightsizing* has come into currency as the process of assuring that the appropriate resources are devoted to problems.

Performance management services include passive measurement, active workload simulation, and performance adjustment. Measurement includes standard, implementation-specific, and user-specific parameters. In addition to measuring standard performance parameters such as those defined by ANSI X3.102, there are practical needs to measure implementation-specific things such as memory utilization. User-specific measurements include workload and user-visible performance (for example, interactive response time and non-interactive message delivery delay).

Performance information is used both for short-term tuning and longer-term *capacity management*. Tuning can include the following:

- Reconfiguring to balance workloads

- Splitting subnetworks into multiple networks, each with fewer users

- Rescheduling batch processing and maintenance activities (for example, backups) for minimum interference with performance-critical activities

- Considering performance in application design

Capacity management makes sense only as a long-term activity. Realistic capacity planning includes keeping long-term statistics about both workload and observed performance, as well as the relationship of observed performance to service level agreements or goals.

Don't forget that application scheduling can be an important part of performance management. An often overlooked way to improve performance is to change selected activities to batch operation. If a large job can be run during idle time at night, it can return significant processing capability and network bandwidth for interactive jobs during the day. This sort of scheduling must assure that jobs are complete at the time their results are needed, and that jobs run without operator supervision do not interfere with one another's resource needs.

An interesting problem in budgeting for network monitoring is balancing the cost of monitoring versus the cost of wrong decision making. This is a fairly standard statistical problem, when stated as the test of a hypothesis: "The ISP is not giving me proper service."

The decision matrix for this hypothesis test can be shown as follows:

	Truth if Total Population Measured	Inference from Measurement
Decision	**Provider meets objective**	**Provider fails objective**
Provider meets objective	Correct choice	Subscriber risk
Provider fails objective	Provider risk	Correct choice

As the sample size approaches the size of the true population measurement, the chance of error grows ever smaller. The more samples taken, however, the more expensive it is to measure. Measurement itself can have a performance impact on the measured system.

The challenge in developing a monitoring program is to decide the right sample size.

VLANs: Real Benefits Versus Marketing Hype

Path determination in VLAN trunks is not terribly complex. The complexity comes in the network management of VLANs, particularly the assignment of edge MAC addresses to VLANs, and, above all, the movement of edge MAC addresses from one VLAN to another.

The difficulty of understanding VLANs comes mostly from the conflicting, sometimes flatly wrong, sales and press literature that permeates the industry. An unfortunately large number of network customers want to believe that VLANs will greatly simplify their operations and performance. VLANs have been much oversold based on belief. VLANs are excellent tools for appropriately selected parts of a network, but neither VLANs nor routers nor LAN switching nor ATM switching is a panacea.

Another irony of VLANs comes with multivendor interoperability. At this stage of the industry, I would not want to stake my reputation on different vendors' products inter-operating using the "standard" 802.1Q protocol. Ironically, there is a better chance of interoperation between different vendors, all of whom have licensed Cisco or Bay or Cabletron or other well-defined proprietary protocol, with tighter specifications and some oversight by the vendor.

LANE has been demonstrated to work well in multivendor environments, as long as you take care to avoid proprietary extensions. You might need to have more than one vendor's management station to configure LANE devices or to use vendor-specific troubleshooting tools.

Security Mechanisms and Security Management

Every enterprise has a different security requirement. After the security policy exists, you create a security plan to implement it.

Firewalls, encryption, authentication, and audits are all components of a security solution. Increasingly, they interact. On a boat, safety features include fire extinguishers and life jackets. Although both are appropriate for their intended tasks, it would be unfortunate if one depended on a fire extinguisher for flotation or used a plastic life jacket to snuff a gasoline fire. In like manner, different security features complement one another in networks. These various features often operate at different OSI layers. Routers provide security at the network layer. Bastion hosts are application routers that provide security at the network layer. Encryption devices can operate at the data link or network layers.

Security management is the set of functions that controls security services such as encryption and firewalling, rather than the services themselves.

Encryption, for example, requires key information before it can lock and unlock data. How these keys are managed, including their creation, distribution, verification, and revocation, is a complex and essential part of network design. The actual encryption is a security mechanism, whereas key distribution is a security management mechanism.

You will have budget tradeoffs among the placement of security functions. A router can run many firewall functions, but potentially with a significant CPU impact. Is it more cost-effective to put firewall functions on a separate host, to put the more real-time, less CPU-dependent functions on routers, and put more specialized ones on security servers?

Encryption

Encryption can be between pairs of physical interfaces, between network layer entities such as routers and encrypting firewalls, and at an application layer between end hosts or between a trusted application layer gateway and a host.

Encryption, even more than compression, can make very heavy demands on a relay's CPU. Again as in compression, it is best to offload encryption processing onto a hardware coprocessor.

Warning

Don't try to compress traffic after it has been encrypted. Encryption algorithms remove the redundancy on which compression depends. If you need both compression and encryption, compress and then encrypt.

Firewalls and encryption usually are complementary, but you can use both functions on a firewall bastion host that is trusted with cryptographic information. The IPsec architecture, discussed further in Chapter 12, calls an encrypting relay a *security gateway*.

As shown in Figure 8.8, you can encrypt between pairs of interfaces at the physical/data link level, between security gateways at the network/transport layers, and between hosts at the application layer. The figure is only a starting point for creative configurations.

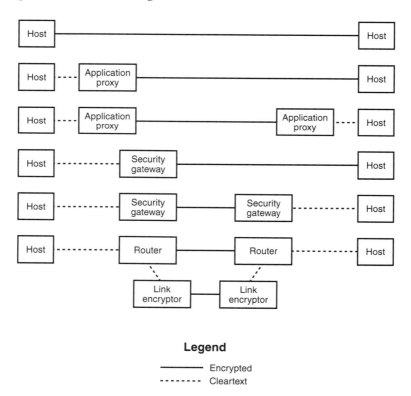

Legend

——— Encrypted
------- Cleartext

FIGURE 8.8 *Solid lines are encrypted, whereas dotted lines are cleartext.*

Link-level encryption effectively authenticates addresses, if it can be assumed that the sender on the link has a valid encryption key.

Cryptography: A Brief Review

An encryption algorithm takes understandable plaintext, manipulates it based on the value of a key, and produces unintelligible ciphertext. Decryption reverses the process by applying a key to ciphertext and producing plaintext.

The combination of an algorithm, the platform it runs on, and the keys form a cryptosystem. Administrative procedures, especially involved in key distribution, are enormously complex issues in security systems.

Either the same key can be used for both encryption and decryption or two related keys can be used, one for encryption and one for decryption. When the same key is used for encryption and decryption, the cryptosystem is called *symmetrical*. The key forms a *shared secret* between sender and receiver.

Asymmetrical cryptosystems use different keys for encrypting and decrypting. In a public key system, either the encrypting or the decrypting key is made widely available, depending on the application of cryptography.

When the goal is confidentiality, the protection of information from disclosure to unauthorized users, a public key is used to encrypt sensitive information, and a private key is used to decrypt it. Separate public/private key pairs are needed for each direction of transmission.

When the goal is authentication, to verify that the information is coming from a known source, well-known information such as a signature is encrypted with a private key and decrypted with a public key.

Confidentiality

James Bond and other spy thriller movies often show parties communicating using codebooks taken from a safe, or a typewriter-like cipher machine into which a secret key was set. This is the classic model of shared secret cryptography.

Shared secret mechanisms can provide both confidentiality—prevention of disclosure of message contents—and authentication. Authentication is implicit in the assumption that only authorized parties possess the keys. For shared secret to be useful in communications, the parties need to be known to one another so they can agree on a key to use. Shared secret has the administrative complexity that the keys must be distributed before they can be used.

When public key encryption is being used to provide confidentiality, the sender uses a public key to encrypt information that needs to be protected. In other words, the plaintext is secret, as is the decrypting key. There is a mathematical relationship between the encrypting key and the decrypting key that allows only the authorized receiver to decrypt the ciphertext.

Authentication

In digital signature applications, where the concern is that the sender's identity is verified, the sender encrypts public information, such as his name, with a secret encrypting key. The decrypting key is public. If a receiver can retrieve the public information using the decrypting key, the sender's identity is validated.

Note

An increasing number of digital signature applications can be expected to be seen within the global Internet addressing and routing structure. To cope with the problem of organizations advertising addresses not assigned to them, there is active research on how address assignment authorities can sign allocations, and the organizations that actually advertise these can sign the signature as well. Secure DNS uses digital signatures.

When DNS information can be authenticated, it can be useful for basic checks on the source of an address. Double DNS lookup is a method that has long been used to validate the source of requests, a method that becomes much stronger when digital signatures prevent tampering with DNS databases.

In double DNS lookup, an application server extracts the source address from a request packet and does a reverse lookup of that address, obtaining a domain name. This domain name is then looked up, and the resulting address range should include the received source address. If the reverse lookup does not work, or the addresses from forward and reverse lookup do not match, the packet is suspect.

Firewalls

Perhaps the most popular buzzword in security technology is *firewall*. Properly, a firewall is a set of security components that sits between the protected inside network and outside users. These users can access the network through dialup links, the Internet, and so on.

Routers are an important component of firewall solutions, but are not the only mechanism in a comprehensive firewall. In selected environments, simple router-based filtering can provide appropriate security, but limitations must be understood.

Cheswick and Bellovin describe the firewall as "a hard crunchy shell around a soft chewy center" [Cheswick, 1994]. The soft chewy center is the set of resources the firewall protects. This analogy deals with a simple black-and-white view of the world: things are either trusted and inside the firewall, or untrusted and outside it.

I find a more complex, if somewhat mixed, metaphor to be useful in dealing with more complex firewalling. At the first level of metaphor enhancement, think of a hard crunchy shell surrounding an onion, with each level of the onion being a different level of sensitivity. Some services in a company are intended to be available to the public, but in a controlled way. Other services are never to be available to the outside world.

Sometimes, when cutting into a real onion, the chef finds that it is not a single symmetrical set of layers surrounding a core, but made up of two or more cloves, each with a set of layers. In many network environments, access to certain selected resources must be restricted inside the organization. By only slightly strained analogy, both the moderately and highly sensitive resources are protected by the outer skin of the onion, but the different communities are separated inside. This separation is invisible from the outside.

Major firewall components include the following:

- Screening routers that use filtering logic to permit or deny network-layer packets to flow through the firewall.

  Routers typically are the fastest devices in a firewall system. They do not maintain information on user connections to applications, which is more the job of the slower bastion host.

- Authentication challenge servers, such as RADIUS or TACACS+.

- Personal identification devices used as authenticators. These include one-time password generators such as products from Security Dynamics and Enigma Logic, biometric devices that check fingerprints or other personal characteristics, and individually generated paper lists of one-time passwords using S/Key.

- Accounting and audit trail mechanisms, which can be trusted disks or even printers.

- Bastion hosts, such as the public domain **ftwk** or commercial-grade Gauntlet from Trusted Information Systems, Firewall/1 from Checkpoint, and so on. Some routers do support true bastion host functions, such as the Content-Based Access Control of Cisco's Firewall Feature Set.

Routers with access control features are sometimes called firewalls, but that is a simplification. Figure 8.9 shows an idealized architecture in which routers screen the bastion host, an internal screening router between the dual-homed bastion host and public networks, and an external screening router between the bastion host and the protected inside network. The external screening router has a physical connection to the outside, to the bastion host, and to the demilitarized zone network. A secure perimeter network connects the bastion host with the internal screening router.

Note

In traditional firewall systems, the public hosts (for example, WWW, FTP) are on a LAN between the external router and the bastion host. This is called the demilitarized zone (DMZ).

Bastion hosts can be dual homed, separating the DMZ and perimeter networks, or a single-homed traffic cop on the DMZ. Single homing, also called screened host, is less secure than the dual-homed screened subnet method [Chapman, 1995]. Newer bastion hosts can have more than two interfaces and put public hosts on a LAN interface that is reachable only through the bastion, allowing much greater control over access to public hosts.

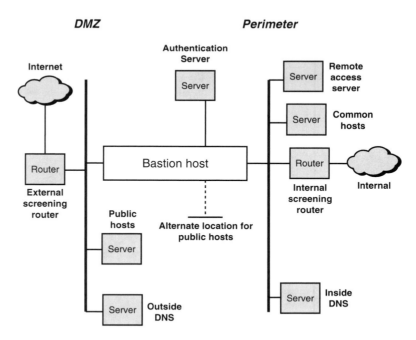

FIGURE 8.9 *Not all components here need to be in separate boxes; this is an idealized architectural view of a full-featured, screened-subnet, dual-homed firewall.*

> *Note*
>
> *Although it is most common to see public hosts such as Web servers on the DMZ, an increasing number of bastion hosts support three or more interfaces. In such configurations, public hosts are on their own medium. The traditional DMZ, between the external screening router and the bastion host, might contain a DNS or no servers at all.*

It can be a reasonable economy, when the risks are understood, to use a single router (with enough interfaces) as the interior and exterior screening router functions; the bastion host is still desirable in this scenario. Alternatively, there can be additional screening routers inside the protected network to give extra protection to specific projects or organizations.

Screening routers are sensitive parts of the firewall. Many organizations disable the virtual terminal login into such routers and use secure modems on the auxiliary console port if remote access is needed. Screening routers complement bastion hosts, protecting them from attacks including denial of service attempts based on flooding the network layer. They can also help in protecting against TCP sequence prediction attacks that hijack existing connections. There are many other protocol threats they can help protect against, such the smurf attack, which floods a target subnet with ICMP requests directed to the subnet-specific directed broadcast address, causing a huge number of responses.

New threats constantly emerge, and it is impossible to detail or anticipate all of them here. An authoritative source of information on threats is the CERT Coordination Center at **www.cert.org**. Obviously, if the router vendor doesn't support a protection measure, you can't use it. Keep track of your vendor's security announcement. Major router vendors usually are highly responsive to identified threats.

Key Management

Key management procedures depend on whether you use symmetric or asymmetric cryptography. Symmetric keys are secret and need to be transmitted in a secure way. Historically, military organizations locked keys in a briefcase chained to the wrist of an armed courier. Organizations with less stringent security requirements might send printed or machine-readable keys in a tamper-resistant form through registered mail or other commercial services. There is an excellent discussion of practical means for making keys tamper-resistant in *Internet Cryptography* [Smith, 1997].

Another alternative is to establish an especially strong cryptosystem that is used only to exchange master keys. This is quite common with shared secret keys, in which a single key can be used for part or all of a network. If common keys are widely used, you want an emergency revocation mechanism that lets you change keys as soon as you learn a key has been compromised.

In asymmetric cryptography, private keys also need to be distributed securely. Public keys can also be distributed to each recipient, but, because you need a separate key for each direction of communications with each destination, key distribution becomes a much larger challenge.

A more scalable approach for key management in an asymmetrical cryptography environment is to obtain keys from a directory service (for example, DNS, LDAP) associated with a *certificate authority*. The system of obtaining public keys is called a *public key infrastructure (PKI)*, and an IETF working group is dealing with standards for networked PKI.

In PKI, you look up a destination name in a directory service and obtain both the address and a public key for the name associated with that destination. The public key should be countersigned with an authenticating digital signature from the certificate authority so you can validate that the key is authentic.

Authentication, Identification, and Auditing

Perhaps the most fundamental requirements for a security system to work are to be able to identify users and track their behavior: *authentication* and *auditing*. In many environments, the process of user identification is closely associated with assigning addresses to them, especially in dialup access.

After the address is assigned, it is often used as a primary identifier for the user. This works in environments where there is no security threat, but IPv4 packets have no built-in method to authenticate the validity of addresses. The IPsec security mechanisms, which were developed as part of IPv6 work and retrofitted to IPv4, do provide address authentication. See Chapter 12 for a discussion of IPsec.

If you obtain the address from a PKI server, you do know the original address is authentic, but you have no protection against subsequent spoofing of the IP address. Nevertheless, this can be adequate security in a network without Internet connectivity.

There are many circumstances, however, in which it is dangerous to trust an address. Yet, many mechanisms, such as SNMPv1 network management, often rely only on addresses as identifiers. Without stronger identification, these mechanisms cannot be fully trusted. New versions of SNMP contain their own cryptographic authentication mechanisms.

Another issue where security and addressing can conflict is that IP addresses are assumed to have end-to-end significance. If these addresses are changed by network address translation devices or firewalls, which are invisible to upper layer protocols, upper layer mechanisms that depend on IP addresses can break.

Firewalls themselves might assume that the source address of any IP packets arriving at the firewall is the true source address. This assumption does not work with various tunneling mechanisms, both for security and those that carry IP traffic with hidden addresses. See the discussion of IPsec tunnels in Chapter 12.

It is quite easy to counterfeit IP addresses, and you should avoid using them as critical identifiers. Some basic filtering techniques, shown in Figure 8.10, will help protect your enterprise on Internet connections.

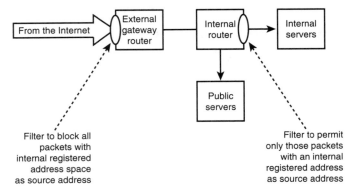

FIGURE 8.10 *When your enterprise is connected to the Internet, never accept a packet from an external source that has one of your internal registered addresses as its source.*

Be careful in depending on security mechanisms that use IP addresses as end-point identifiers. If you renumber without keeping router and firewall filters consistent with your addressing plan, you can either open holes in your security or cause existing functions to fail.

Serious security includes per-user authentication coupled with access controls to resources. When routers participate in security processes such as encryption, they need to be authenticated as trusted devices.

Routing protocols can have header authentication. There are two levels of authentication, a cleartext password and a cryptographic hash code. Cleartext passwords protect against configuration errors, whereas cryptographic hash codes protect against denial of service attacks directed at the routing system itself. Neither level gives protection to user data flowing through the routers. See Chapter 11 for additional discussion.

Looking Ahead

With the information in this and the preceding chapter, you should have a reasonable idea of the technologies you want to use in your network. Chapters 9 through 12 discuss the detailed design of various current switching and routing technologies, whereas Chapters 13 and 14 explain emerging routing and switching technologies for which you might want to plan.

Details that you find in these chapters might lead you to alter the architecture you defined here. If you find you need to change architectural details, you are on your way to becoming an experienced network architect, not letting theory overwhelm reality. You might need to refine your architecture.

After your architectural design is complete, use Chapters 9 through 12 for final component selection and planning your implementation.

PART IV

Deployment

CHAPTER 9

Connection-Oriented Switching

Good things, when short, are twice as good.
—Baltasar Gracian

A thing in itself never expresses anything. It is the relation between things
that gives meaning and that formulates a thought.
—Hans Hoffman

Oh if in my lagging lines you miss/The roll, the rise, the creation.
—Gerard Manley Hopkins

The term *switching* has many meanings in networking. The most common industry usage is connectionless relaying—bridging—at OSI reference model Layer 2, which is discussed in Chapter 10. There is a broad family of switching functions that rely on a connection-oriented model, although these have tended to be associated with internal telephony applications.

I could call these connectionless functions Layer 1 and Layer 2 connection-oriented switching, but that can be somewhat misleading. When learning about many of the newer technologies, do not fall into the trap of forcing their functions into the OSI model. The various technologies do operate on layered models, but the layers are not necessarily the OSI layers. An ATM, ISDN, or Frame Relay stack, much less some of the emerging technologies, does provide the equivalent of an OSI Layer 2 interface to higher OSI layers. That does not mean the stack only has two layers in it. It has its own meaningful sets of layers.

Above all, don't fall into the trap of some people that come from LAN backgrounds and assume connection-oriented switching is an inflexible technique loved only by telephone bureaucracies. Connection-oriented Layer 2 switches primarily are used for WAN applications, but definitely have a role in campus environments. The use of connection-oriented Layer 2 services to the desktop is more controversial, but can be justified when non-data services are involved.

Connection-oriented switching, both at Layer 1 and Layer 2, needs to be considered in wide-area applications that need either very small or very large bandwidth. At the extremes of the speed range, there are more connection-oriented options than connectionless ones. Connectionless techniques, however, tend to be easier to configure and quite adequate for the normal performance range.

Modern connection-oriented switching systems do more than simple port-to-port switching. Some areas to examine to see if a connection-oriented solution fits include the following:

- Needs for multimedia, either IP or Layer 2

- Telephony integration

- Mission-critical applications with critical quality of service (QoS)

- Access to large servers that support direct ATM connectivity, such as mainframes with extremely large databases, and image retrieval systems

- Access to Internet and extranet partners

Distinctions between switches and routers, of course, are blurring rapidly. This chapter deals with forwarding decisions that are made on connection-oriented identifiers stored in the forwarding table. Such identifiers for connections include Frame Relay data-link connection identifiers (DLCIs), Asynchronous Transfer Mode (ATM) virtual path identifiers (VPIs) and virtual channel identifiers (VCIs), Integrated Services Digital Network (ISDN) terminal endpoint identifiers (TEIs), and so on.

A given product can have both connectionless and connection-oriented features for routing, as you will see in the case study later in this chapter, "Nortel Passport Routing." Some prefer to split switches into WAN and LAN varieties, but if you do so, are ATM switches WAN or LAN? The WAN versus LAN question is often asked, but it really is rhetorical. The WAN versus LAN distinction simply is not meaningful in today's high-speed transmission systems. ATM can be either.

Architectures and Planes

Layer 2 connection-oriented switching is, in many respects, the evolution of Layer 1 switching that forms the basis of the digital telephone network, which is, in turn, based on analog circuit switching. For this reason, you want a good understanding of ISDN circuit switching before moving into the more recent ATM and Frame Relay switching methods [Goldstein, 1992].

These more recent methods are built on techniques developed in the main narrowband ISDN effort, and in the less visible *Broadband ISDN* (BISDN) standards work. Originally, the intention was that ATM would be an intercarrier standard only, with ISDN access at the low-speed end, Frame Relay at medium speed, and a BISDN interface at the high user rates. The ATM Forum's work in establishing *User-Network Interfaces* (UNIs) effectively superceded BISDN.

Useful architectural techniques were shared among these standards development efforts that were born in the telecommunications industry. If the underlying protocol is connection-oriented, a connection has to be created before data can be transferred, much as you cannot have a useful telephone conversation without first picking up the phone, getting a dial tone, dialing, and having the called party pick up his telephone.

A rather useful product of ISDN and other telephony-oriented communications is an extended protocol reference model, which extends the two-dimensional OSI layered architectural model to three dimensions, shown in Figure 9.1. ISDN also has a functional model that shows protocol exchanges, shown in Figure 9.2. The OSI model was designed to describe user applications that begin at the top of Layer 7 and exit at the bottom of Layer 1. It really is application-oriented and becomes awkward for describing the infrastructural protocols that operate only inside a layer, such as routing or call setup. Planes, described slightly later in this section, help explain that infrastructure.

Traditional two-dimensional OSI layering. Infrastructure protocols either mix with user protocols or are ignored.

Three-dimensional ISDN model. Infrastructure protocols are in a clear relationship to user protocols.

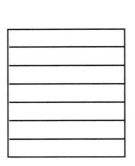

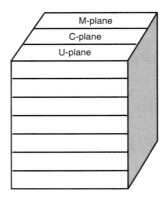

FIGURE 9.1 *The OSI versus ISDN models. Control and management functions are conceptually hidden behind user information.*

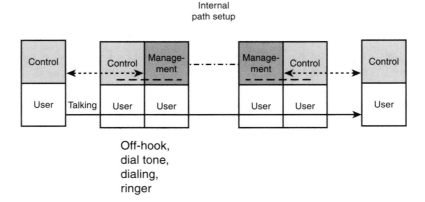

FIGURE 9.2 *The ISDN functional model, showing protocol exchanges among the planes at a given layer.*

With the introduction of the Internal Organization and IEEE LAN models, as well as sublayering at layers above those of interest to us in this lower layer discussion, to say the OSI model truly has seven layers is a bit superficial. When you think of these two- versus three-dimensional models, do not assume they have to apply to any specific number of layers. The ISDN and ATM reference models certainly are layered, but they do not have seven layers.

The three-dimensional model builds a cube, shown in Figure 9.1, as opposed to the traditional OSI apartment house. The additional dimension of information comes from the following three protocol planes:

- *User-plane (U-plane)*. U-plane protocols carry user data from end to end. Most protocols shown in the OSI Reference Model belong to the U-plane. The telephone analogy would be the conversation between users.

- *Control-plane (C-plane)*. C-plane protocols interact between the end system and the ingress or egress device entering the transmission system. The telephone analogy would be obtaining dial tone, dialing, and ringing.

- *Management-plane (M-plane)*. M-plane communications are internal to the transmission system. In the telephone network, the analogy is setting up the end-to-end path through a sequence of telephone switches.

A three-dimensional model helps me conceptualize what is happening in a given protocol environment, in the sense that the C- and M-planes underlie the main user communication. U-plane communications are the reason a particular protocol stack exists. C- and M-plane protocols, however, are necessary for that stack to work. The U-plane is in front. I can describe user services with the understanding that the infrastructure protocols, at the C- and M-planes, are hidden underneath.

Don't restrict the idea of signaling (C-plane) protocols to telephony, because the ideas of host-to-edge and edge-to-edge protocol interactions are increasingly important in the IP world. Even though the protocols involved might be connectionless, there are still needs for an end host to signal to other end hosts, or to ingress switches or routers, before user data flow can begin. One C-plane mechanism is determining the transmission system address that should be used to forward to a given logical address. This is the process of address resolution, which works differently in detail on various types of transmission media.

Figure 9.2 reinforces the idea that user communication cannot happen without C- and M-plane mechanisms.

Connection-Oriented WAN Switching and the Enterprise Network

In the industry as a whole, connection-oriented Layer 2 switching is a major technique for telecommunications service providers and large Internet service providers (ISPs). See Chapter 14 for a discussion of the Layer 3 onto Layer 2 overlay model. Providers often use Layer 2 virtual circuits in their core networks.

This is not to say that Layer 2 switched *services* are not extremely common in enterprise networks, but Layer 2 *switches* tend to be more common in service provider environments than in user networks. There are definite enterprise network applications for switches, but these tend to be in large enterprises or those with special needs, such as video production.

There is an industry trend, however, to mix Layer 2 and Layer 3 functions. This can be seen in devices for campuses that need significant bandwidth.

Evolving from Time Division Multiplexed Networks

The telecommunications network originated with circuit switched and dedicated facilities, first analog and then digital. Telecommunications carriers traditionally provided dedicated lines through Layer 1 time division multiplexing (TDM). As shown in Figure 9.3, basic multiplexing is a means of combining multiple user data streams onto a faster trunk medium. The complementary technique of *inverse multiplexing* allows high user data rates to be provisioned using multiple slower, but available, trunks.

Multiplexers can be split into at least two useful categories, although the constant advance of technology can blur the two classes.

The first class is *fixed* or *time-division*. In this class, a given payload always is mapped to the same time slot in the higher-speed trunk, whether or not there is any traffic to send. Multiplexers in this class can be simpler than the next class, although they are not trivial in design. The first challenge in such a multiplexer is maintaining the timing relationship between payload and delivery streams. These streams can be bits or groups of bits (bytes). Mappings of the payload streams to trunk time slots are either fixed—the model in the basic analog channel bank—or programmable. If programmable, the mappings typically are sent as table updates, rather than real-time labels that occupy bandwidth in the main data stream.

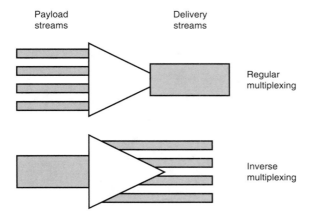

Payload streams

Delivery streams

Regular multiplexing

Inverse multiplexing

FIGURE 9.3 *Multiplexing methods match user speeds to the available transmission speeds.*

The second class is *intelligent* or *statistical time-division*. Such a multiplexer does not maintain a constant relationship between input streams and time slots in the trunk. If a given input stream has no data to send, the trunk bandwidth that would be used for the silent input stream is made available for other input streams. Because most applications, especially voice, have silent periods, statistical multiplexing allows the available trunk bandwidth to be less than the sum of payload stream bandwidths.

Intelligent multiplexing requires some M-plane interaction among the multiplexers, so a receiving multiplexer knows how to assign incoming bits to a receiving payload stream. M-plane interaction conveys some sort of labeling information for individual payloads.

Basic Telephony Multiplexing

Analog telephones were integrated into the digital telephone system using *channel banks*, shown in Figure 9.4. A channel bank is a combination of analog-to-digital conversion and digital multiplexing functions. Each analog channel is converted to a 64-Kbps DS0 bit stream. The digitizing algorithms differ in different parts of the world. Canada, the United States, and Japan use μ-*law*; Europe uses *A-law*; and there are a few other algorithms such as K-law used in Mexico. A converter is needed for pairs of voice algorithms. Although the details of these algorithms are beyond the scope of this text, the significant point is that a demultiplexed stream might need additional protocol conversion before it is usable.

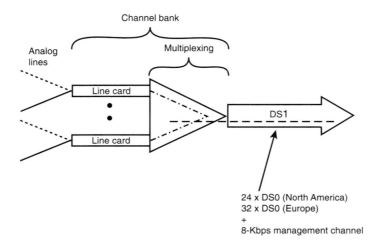

Legend

——————— U-plane analog information

— · — · — 64-Kbps DS0 streams combining U-plane and C-plane

- - - - - - - C-plane ringing, dialing, etc.

— — — — M-plane diagnostics and synchronization

FIGURE 9.4 *Basic channel banks convert analog telephone channels to 64-Kbps DS0 bit streams and combine those streams into a 1.544-Mbps DS1.*

Basic telephony multiplexing is fixed rather than statistical. North American channel banks combine 24 DS0 signals into a DS1 signal. Technically, DS1 is a signal format, and T1 is a specific transmission system that carries DS1 signals over twisted copper pairs, but the terms are interchangeable in practice. The CCITT/ITU version, used in Europe, is the E1 signal.

Basic digital voice services are provided with a combination of analog-to-digital converters and multiplexers called *channel banks*, as shown in Figure 9.4. A North American channel bank converts 24 analog channels to a single DS1 stream.

Figure 9.5 looks at the channel bank from an architectural standpoint. The 24 DS0 channels take 1.536 Mbps of bandwidth, and the remaining 8 Kbps of the DS1 channel is used for synchronization and diagnostics between the multiplexers; thus, it is M-plane information. User-level information, such as dialing, is also carried within the digital streams, but the details of carrying it are beyond the scope of this discussion.

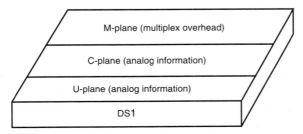

FIGURE 9.5 *Telephone signals include U-plane (the actual voice signal) and C-plane (dialing, ringing, and so on). M-plane signals provide synchronization and control between multiplexers.*

As an example, in North America, the digital hierarchy built from 64 Kbps at the edge, to a variety of multiplexed facilities shown in Table 9.1. This is sometimes called the *plesiochronous digital hierarchy*, mercifully referred to by the abbreviation PDH.

TABLE 9.1 THE NORTH AMERICAN AND JAPANESE DIGITAL HIERARCHY

Level	Speed	Voice Channels
DS0	64 Kbps	1
DS1	1.544 Mbps	24
DS1C	3.152 Mbps	48
DS2	6.312 Mbps	96
DS3	44.736 Mbps	672
DS4	274.176 Mbps	4032

In Europe and much of the world outside North America and Japan, a different hierarchy emerged, still based on multiples of 64 Kbps. Japan uses the DS1 and DS2 rates, but has a different hierarchy above the DS2 level. It is worth noting that 64 Kbps is the basic rate at which a single voice call is digitized. Table 9.2 shows the European hierarchy defined by the Conference of European Postal and Telecommunications Administrations (CEPT).

TABLE 9.2 THE CEPT DIGITAL HIERARCHY

Level	Speed	Voice Channels
E0	64 Kbps	1
E1	2.032 Mbps	32
E2	8.448 Mbps	120
E3	34.368 Mbps	480
E4	139.268 Mbps	1920
E5	565.148 Mbps	7680

In further discussions, I speak of the T or DS hierarchy, but the concepts work the same with the E hierarchy.

Fractional T1 services were an extension of this multiplexing to the user premises. The T1 physical facility remained the main way of providing bandwidth to the customer premise. On Cisco routers, the MultiChannel Interface Processor (MIP) is used as the physical interface for both primary rate ISDN and fractional T1 services, demultiplexing them into 64-Kbps channels.

Refinements of Digital Telecommunications Multiplexing

DS0, DS1, and DS3 services often are provisioned with a digital cross-connect (DCS) device, also called a digital access cross-connect system (DACS), as shown in Figure 9.6. A DCS combines several multiplexers with a switching matrix.

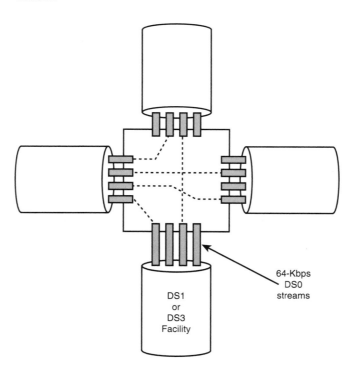

FIGURE 9.6 *Digital cross-connect systems combine multiplexers with switching of bit streams.*

In a fractional T1 service, the DCS is connected physically to a set of trunks—the arrow in Figure 9.6. The individual (that is, subrate) DS0 channels are demultiplexed and mapped, by the DCS, to time slots in another trunk. Trunks are multiplexed DS1 or DS3 channels. The figure shows a one-to-one relationship between incoming and outgoing channels, but more sophisticated DCS can combine subrate channels. A given site, for example, might be able to use 384 Kbps of a T1 line. This site would be assigned six DS0 channels, which would be switched as a unit to the destination. 384-Kbps streams are quite useful for videoconferencing.

Fractional T1 services are Layer 1 multiplexing services, as opposed to Layer 2 multiplexing services such as Frame Relay. In Frame Relay, the individual circuits can transmit at the full speed of the trunk. It is possible, indeed, to provision Frame Relay over a fractional T1 service. In such a case, you might have a circuit with a Frame Relay committed information rate (CIR) of 128 Kbps provisioned over a 256-Kbps fractional T1 link. Here, the Frame Relay could burst at up to 256 Kbps. Even though the physical medium runs at T1 rate, the DCS would drop any data over 256 Kbps.

Modern switched services are capable of acting as replacements for dedicated lines or TDM networks. They can provide the guaranteed bandwidth of real-world dedicated lines, but also can provide less stringently controlled bandwidths at much lower cost.

Emerging Access Technologies

There may well be a distinct niche for specialized devices that connect new last mile technologies at the edge. DSx technologies are certainly not the only ones that are viable contenders for the local loop.

Some of the newer technologies for the local loop include a variety of *digital subscriber loop* technologies generically called *xDSL*, cable TV-based data transmission, *fiber optics to the home* (FTTH) and *fiber optics to the curb* (FTTC), and wireless access. See George Abe's *Residential Broadband* from Macmillan Technical Publishing for details of these technologies [Abe, 1997]. Our concern here is not with the electronic and optical mechanisms of these transmission systems, but simply that their support is desirable in edge switches.

Figure 9.7 shows a representative central office device for DSL technologies, the DSL access multiplexer (DSLAM). A DSLAM is similar to a DCS, but accepts DSL links from the customer site as well as DSx links to other network components. A key deployment issue is the amount of bandwidth available from the DSLAM to an ISP. I have seen 7-Mbps customer links that connect to 384-Kbps links from the end office to the ISP. Obviously, such a 7-megabit link is, at best, no more than 384 Kbps.

Actual DSL connectivity involves devices at the customer premises and can include splitters for analog voice service. Because the intention here is to show how a DSLAM is an evolution of a DCS, analog facilities are not shown. The specific example shown in Figure 9.7 is for asymmetric DSL (ADSL). The *ADSL transmission unit-central office* (ATU-C) components are similar to line cards in a voice channel bank.

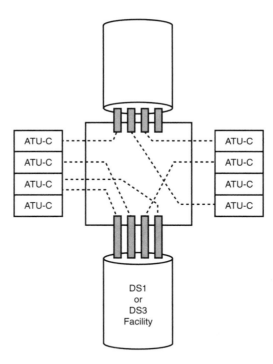

FIGURE 9.7 *A DSLAM combines the functions of xDSL line cards and digital cross-connection. In this example, the data streams from several customers might be distributed to two different ISPs over DS1 or DS3 trunks.*

Although these services can be dedicated bit streams that are handled by TDMs, virtual circuits can be set up over them. They can be concentrated into ISDN, Frame Relay, and ATM circuits.

SONET, PPP over SONET, and DWDM

At its higher speeds, starting with OC-3 at 155 Mbps, ATM is actually transmitted over optical transmission systems in the Synchronous Optical Network (SONET) or Synchronous Digital Hierarchy in Europe. SONET is an intelligent multiplexing system with substantial management capabilities. Figure 9.8 shows the SONET physical architecture for which management capabilities are defined.

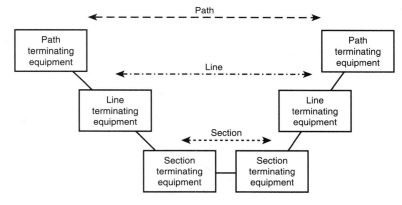

FIGURE 9.8 *Paths are end-to-end connections between SONET end equipment. Lines are multiplexed physical medium. Sections interconnect regenerators on media.*

Between the path, line, and section endpoints, SONET has its own layered architecture, as shown in Figure 9.9.

SONET *paths* are logical connections between an entry point and an exit point for digital frames. Typical *path terminating equipment* would be a central office switch or a router with a SONET interface.

Line terminating equipment terminates a physical SONET transmission facility. Devices with LTE functionality include digital cross-connects and add-and-drop multiplexers (ADM). A digital cross-connect essentially is a solid-state patch panel for bit streams. ADMs, shown in Figure 9.10, accept a high-speed trunk and insert a slower-speed digital channel. ADMs are used for a wide range of transmission systems, not only SONET.

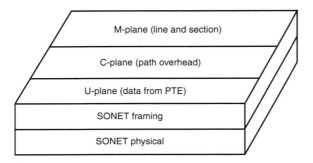

FIGURE 9.9 *SONET has a layered architecture whose layers do not map to OSI layers. It can operate over various kinds of optical fiber, either natively or using dense wavelength division multiplexing.*

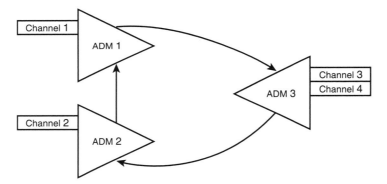

FIGURE 9.10 *ADMs provide access to a high-speed medium interconnecting multiple locations.*

LTE can connect to a primary and backup SONET medium. The specific SONET terminology used is the *working* and *protection* ring. Statically routed ATM does not heal itself, whereas dynamically routed ATM may or may not be able to reroute calls in progress if a trunk fails. ATM's capability to reroute depends on the dynamic routing mechanism selected and its implementation. ATM over SONET, when the SONET has protection switching, does have a reroute-on-failure capability that can operate in milliseconds.

Remember that ATM is connection-oriented, so if an ATM circuit fails, it needs to be re-established. If that ATM circuit can be rerouted over a SONET protection ring, the ATM circuit does not go down.

The basic SONET self-healing capability assumes a fully redundant backup ring, with the associated expense. Simply because you are on SONET does not mean you are on redundant facilities. Alternatives that involve 1:M sparing, where a backup ring provides backup to M primary rings, have been developed. Figure 9.11 shows a fault-tolerant arrangement.

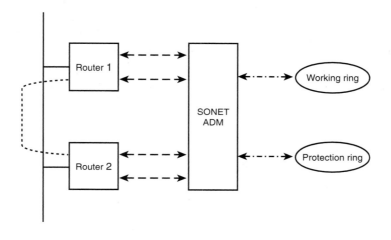

Legend

⬅ – – ➤ Path interface
⬅ ·–·– ·➤ Line interface
——————— LAN
- - - - - - - - - APS Protect Group Protocol

FIGURE 9.11 *This fault-tolerant system is protected against failures of either router and either SONET ring.*

There are a variety of fault tolerance mechanisms, but the example in Figure 9.11 is a Bellcore-defined architecture for 1:1 sparing with automatic protection switching (APS). A UDP-based protocol, APS Protect Group Protocol, senses the failure and switches interfaces from the working to the protection ring.

The protection ring, in 1:1 sparing, is not idle; the same signals are sent over both the working and protection rings. Receivers use M-plane information in the SONET stream to know which is the active interface.

SONET Speed Hierarchy

The SONET speeds in Table 9.3 are described as the physical medium speed. Some of this bandwidth is taken by SONET path, line, and section management and is not available for user traffic. Some misleading comparisons have been drawn between IP being sent as packet-over-SONET (POS) and over ATM. There is no question that POS has less overhead than IP over ATM, because POS does not consume the overhead of cell headers. Nevertheless, neither POS nor ATM over an OC-3 facility makes the entire 155-Mbps bandwidth available for user data. Table 9.6 shows the benefits of POS for throughput. It can give up to 19% better throughput than ATM/AAL, assuming 1500-byte payload frames.

TABLE 9.3   SONET HIERARCHY

OC Level	Speed
OC-1	51.84 Mbps
OC-3	155.52 Mbps
OC-9	466.56 Mbps
OC-12	622.08 Mbps
OC-18	933.12 Mbps
OC-24	1.244 Gbps
OC-36	1.866 Gbps
OC-48	2.488 Gbps
OC-96	4.976 Gbps
OC-192	9.953 Gbps

As you can see, the 51.84-Mbps rate is the basic building block of SONET. It is slightly faster than a DS3 line, so the various speeds at DS3 and below can be multiplexed into an STS-1 channel. In general, the slower rates are called *virtual tributaries* (VTs). The exact mechanics of multiplexing involves complex synchronization and is beyond the scope of this text, but, in general, the various types of service multiplexed into an STS-1 are shown in Table 9.4.

TABLE 9.4   MULTIPLEXING INTO AN STS-1 BIT STREAM

Service	Speed	Carries
VT 1.5	1.728 Mbps	DS1
VT 2	2.304 Mbps	CEPT1/E1
VT 3	3.456 Mbps	DS1C
VT 6	6.912 Mbps	DS2
VT 6-Nc	$N\times$6.912 Mbps	$N\times$DS2
Async DS3	44.736 Mbps	DS3

SONET is by no means the highest-speed emerging core technology. Dense wavelength division multiplexing (DWDM) can carry multiple digital streams over the same fiber used for a single SONET physical link. DWDM currently is being used to carry 160 OC-192 streams over a fiber.

One of the issues of classical SONET is that the protection ring is not used other than as a backup. Both carriers and research networks are evaluating whether Layer 3 routing, used with the massive capacity of DWDM links, can be as fault-tolerant as physical SONET. Because many real-world carrier SONET implementations do not use 1:1 protection switching, but use M:1, routing with excess capacity might turn out to be even more fault-tolerant than affordable SONET. In M:1 protection, M active rings are backed up by a single protection ring.

Enterprise Applications of PPP over SONET Connectivity

Running the Point-to-Point Protocol (PPP) over SONET (POS) [Simpson, 1998] has greater bandwidth efficiency than ATM, because it does not require the minimum 5 bytes of cell header overhead for every 48 bytes of payload. When you send 1500 bytes of user information over ATM, this amount of information takes 32 cells to transmit. 32×5 is 160 bytes of overhead.

In contrast, sending the same information over PPP requires 7 bytes of header overhead. ATM, of course, allows you to have multiple virtual circuits running through the same physical facility. ATM also lets you define QoS on a per-virtual-circuit basis. With the advent of MPLS, ATM may or may not be the preferred means of implementing QoS (see Chapter 13).

If your application is inherently point-to-point, it is reasonable to argue that ATM does not give any advantages over PPP over SONET.

The first applications of PPP over SONET were internal to large ISPs and for inter-carrier links. It is reasonable to use PPP over SONET for high-bandwidth inter-campus links that use the full 155-Mbps bandwidth (less the SONET management overhead). Another application would be connecting Web servers at your facility to a major interconnect point, again assuming you can justify the full 155-Mbps bandwidth.

SONET's fault tolerance is attractive for mission-critical applications. If you have routing, as you probably would if using POS, routing might give you the necessary alternate path selection rather than requiring protection rings that are idle much of the time. In the event of a failure, however, SONET ring fallover with dual rings takes milliseconds. Rerouting at Layer 3 can take seconds.

ATM Architecture

Originally intended purely as a core technology, ATM has also become a widely used access technique for high-bandwidth user connectivity to WANs, and for selected desktop and campus environments. Although Gigabit Ethernet potentially is a lower-cost campus technology, ATM products are operational today.

ATM has its own layered architecture, as shown in Figure 9.12. There are a great many alternatives in the protocol stack, and I cannot emphasize strongly enough that any kind of practical end protocol runs over the ATM Adaption Layer (AAL), not the raw ATM cells. Devices see the AAL interface either as Layer 2 frames, in AAL3/4 or AAL5, or as a continuous bit stream in AAL1.

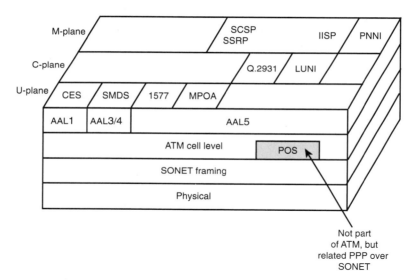

FIGURE 9.12 *ATM has its own multilayered protocol architecture. Its layers do not directly correspond to OSI layers, although the top of the ATM stack is generally equivalent to an interface to OSI Layer 2, the data link layer.*

Figure 9.13 illustrates the broad context of ATM and SONET. It shows that there can be multiple ways ATM supports LAN services, and that there can be ways to use SONET without ATM. ATM virtual circuits can simply provide pipes among LAN switches that run VLAN trunking protocols over ATM facilities, or LAN emulation (LANE) can be provided through ATM. Do remember that LANE is effectively an application to the lower layers of ATM.

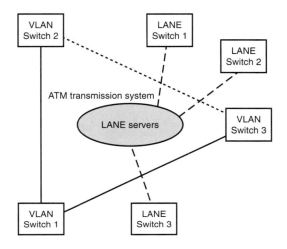

Legend

——————— Virtual circuit uplink for VLAN (active in spanning tree)
- - - - - - - - Virtual circuit uplink for VLAN (blocked in spanning tree)
— — — — LANE client-to-server-system virtual circuit

FIGURE 9.13 *ATM can provide connectivity among LAN switches, or the LAN emulation service can provide a LAN environment. The ATM cell layer is unaware of LANs.*

LANE server functions do not usually run on actual ATM switches, but on dedicated physical router platforms, special processor boards in edge devices, and so on. The server functions need to be inside the cloud so they can be reached by all the LAN Emulation Clients, but they do not actually have to run on the switching nodes.

ATM Physical and Framing Layers

The most widely implemented physical interfaces in North America are DS3, TAXI, and OC-3. OC-12 is becoming increasingly common, and OC-48 is starting to be deployed in bleeding-edge products (as of 1998). Lower-speed interfaces, such as 25 Mbps and T1, have not been widely deployed. In Europe, 2-Mbps and 34-Mbps E3 also are common.

Although it would be unlikely that individual enterprises would today need that much bandwidth, remember that ATM can be multiplexed into higher-bandwidth facilities, such as SONET OC-192, at nearly 10 Gbps. Carriers and research networks are using DWDM to go to even higher bandwidths; there are operational research networks that are sending 160 OC-192 signals over a single fiber.

The ATM Cell Layer

The ATM layer proper defines the actual cell exchange among ATM devices. Cells are 53 bytes long, with a 5-byte header and 48-byte payload. Bytes are called octets in telephony- and ATM-speak. Figure 9.14 shows the cell header structure.

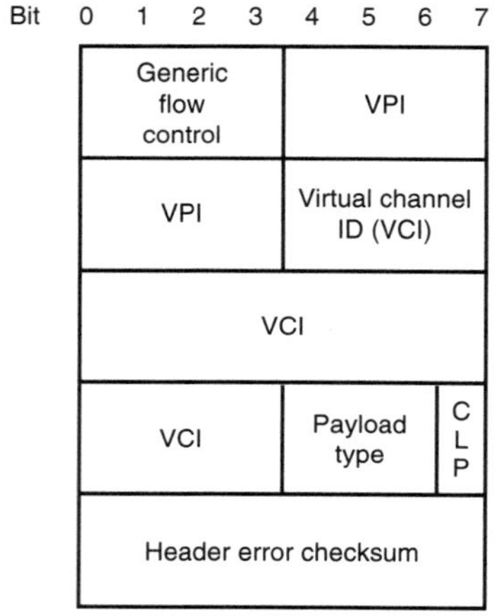

FIGURE 9.14 *The 5-byte header precedes a 48-byte payload.*

For every 48 bytes of raw ATM payload, there are 5 bytes of header overhead. Approximately 10% of the total bandwidth, this overhead is often called the *cell tax*. ATM advocates say this overhead is trivial at the speeds of ATM. PPP over SONET advocates, however, say every bit counts. The exact overhead difference depends on the ATM adaptation layer in use and its contribution to the overhead beyond that of the cell header (see Table 9.5).

TABLE 9.5 OVERHEAD AT CELL LEVEL

AAL type	Bytes of AAL	Octets of payload overhead per cell	Per-cell overhead of combined cell header and AAL
AAL1tb	1	47	12%
AAL3/4	4	44	17%
AAL5	0	48	9%

To send a 1500-byte frame with AAL5, you need 32 cells, each with its own header. 32×53 means 1696 bytes are necessary to send that frame over the most efficient ATM adaptation layer. In contrast, a PPP header is 5 bytes long, with a 2-byte trailer (see Table 9.6).

TABLE 9.6 OVERHEAD FOR FULL FRAME TRANSMISSION

Transmission	Total bytes to send 1500 data bytes	Overhead bytes	Overhead
AAL1	1696	196	12%
AAL3/4	1855	355	19%
AAL5	1696	196	12%
POS	1507	7	Well under 1%

The Generic Flow Control field is not used in basic ATM. The next two fields, VPI and VCI, are used together in routing the cells at each ATM switch. In private ATM networks, the VPI value is zero. It can be used to select carriers when going to a public network, or possibly to aggregate virtual circuits with a common quality of service requirement. The VCI, however, is used in making the next hop forwarding decision within an enterprise network. Carrier-oriented switches, or switches for very large enterprises, can make decisions based on VPI. As shown in Figure 9.15, the combination of VPI and VCI uniquely identifies a virtual circuit link between ATM devices.

ATM permanent virtual circuits are configured hop-by-hop, from physical interface to physical interface. In contrast to switched virtual circuit (SVC) setup, endpoint addresses are not used. SVC setup dynamically assigns the VPI/VCI values on each ATM hop from one destination to another. Endpoints in ATM are identified with one of several formats, generally called a Network

Service Access Point (NSAP) address in private ATM networks. The path between endpoints is made up of a sequence of link-local VPI/VCI pairs. You can learn more about ATM address structures in *Designing Address Architectures for Routing and Switching*, also from Macmillan Technical Publishing.

Not all ATM cells carry user data. The Payload Type field allows certain cells to be identified as *operation, administration, and maintenance* (OAM). OAM cells are used for diagnostics and similar functions; the amount of OAM overhead is implementation-specific.

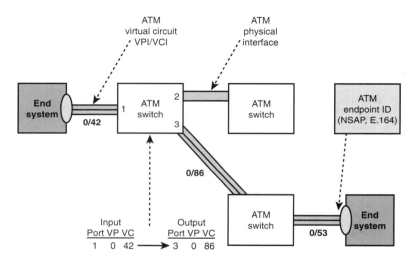

FIGURE 9.15   *VPI/VCI information is redefined for each connection and at each physical link. NSAP addresses are the phone numbers that identify interfaces and persist between calls.*

ATM Adaptation Layer (AAL)

AAL is used at the endpoints and provides a mapping between cells and the format expected by end equipment. In AAL1, this is the circuit emulation service (CES) that looks like a DS1 or faster dedicated bit stream. The CES has 1 byte of overhead in the payload.

AAL3/4 and AAL5 are used in data applications. Most applications other than Switched Multimegabit Data Service (SMDS) use AAL5, which has no overhead in the payload field.

The ATM Upper Layers

RFC 1577 prescribes a means of encapsulating IP packets for transmission over ATM. It is IP-specific, as opposed to a method called *Multiprotocol over ATM* (MPOA) [RFC 1483].

Unfortunately, the meaning of MPOA has gone beyond the original definition in RFC 1483. The original specification simply provided a way of encapsulating any Layer 3 information for transmission over ATM, using IEEE 802.2 Logical Link Control/Subnetwork Access Control (LLC/SNAP) identifiers to indicate to the receiver what protocol type was contained in the frame. This usage of MPOA remains valid.

Table 9.7, drawn from private suggestions from my colleague Galina Pildush, summarizes the options.

TABLE 9.7   SUMMARY OF TECHNOLOGIES FOR CARRYING DATA OVER ATM

Technology	Protocols Redundancy	L2/L3 mapping	Other features
RFC 1483 MPOA	Any L2/3 None	Manual	
RFC 1577/2225	IP Proprietary only	Dynamic ARP	Inter-operability over multiple LIS; multicasting
LANEv1	Layer 2 Proprietary only	Manual	SVC setup
LANEv2	Layer 2 SCSP	Manual	QoS support, selective multicast
ATM Forum MPOA NHRP and MARS	Layer 2 and 3 plus cut-through	Dynamic ARP	

The ATM Forum, however, extended the meaning of MPOA to include extensions to LANE that allow mixed Layer 2/3 forwarding. This meaning of MPOA, which is discussed in Chapter 14, is a very promising technique. I simply wish the Forum had defined another term for this mechanism, which is vastly more complex than mere protocol identification.

Integrating Existing Voice Equipment

In an enterprise network where you are building an ATM backbone, you might want to connect your existing PBX devices, which expect a T1 or E1 interface. With ATM, you provide a constant bit rate service as an equivalent to the dedicated service. See the section "Constant Bit Rate" later in this chapter for more information. Figure 9.16 illustrates the potential issue of compatibility between existing PBXs and new ways of carrying voice: VoX, which encompasses Voice over Frame Relay (VoFR), voice over ATM (VoATM), and voice over IP (VoIP). Rather than having a VoX interface, the PBX is most likely to have a T1 or E1 interface, and the ATM switch you use for this, of course, needs to have a physical interface compatible with T1 or E1.

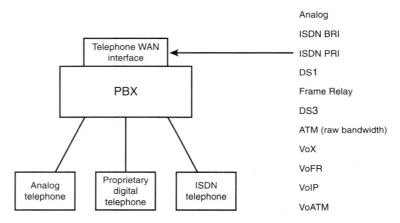

Figure 9.16 *Trunk interfaces on installed PBXs might not support newer technologies. To preserve PBX investment, you might need external protocol converters.*

Although VoX services are a hot industry topic, the question remains of how to best integrate them with existing voice equipment. The reality is that all analog voice equipment, and much digital voice equipment, does not understand voice over IP. It still can be perfectly reasonable to use the newer voice technology, but you need to plan for protocol conversion for PBX compatibility. Some organizations are using Y2K compatibility concerns with their existing PBX to replace it with a Y2K- and VoX-compatible new unit.

Domains

In dealing with switching, or Layer 2 relaying, you need to think of several levels of domain. For both WAN and LAN switching, there is a meaningful idea of a *management domain*, or the set of lower-level domains that can be controlled as a single unit or from a single management station.

The next level down differs in connection-oriented (CO) and connectionless (CL) switches. In LAN switches, the underlying medium model is a broadcast one. The next domain level in a CL switch is the broadcast domain: the set of devices that can hear one another's non-unicast frames.

The underlying medium model in WAN switches is either point-to-point or point-to-multipoint. This can be considered the multiplexing domain, the set of Layer 2 circuits that share a common trunk medium. It might be useful to think of a level above the multiplexing level, which describes the set of physical interfaces on a switch.

WAN switches are most likely to be manually configured, although ATM switches can have a dynamic setup mechanism. ATM is also involved in WAN switching, and the lower-speed feed to ATM usually is Frame Relay. There are some proprietary dynamic setup mechanisms for Frame Relay switches.

With the apparent dominance of LAN switches in campus data networks, why use connection-oriented switches? There are several reasons.

First, not all networks, including user networks, carry only data. There is an increasing demand for voice, image, and video services over a common network. CO switches were originally developed for voice, and support it well. Their capabilities include quality of service enforcement and detailed accounting.

Connection orientation is not the only way to achieve controlled quality of service. There are IP mechanisms as well, including Resource Reservation Protocol (RSVP).

A different strategy is to overprovision campus facilities so congestion does not occur. Campus bandwidth is sufficiently cheap that implementing much higher than expected capacity might be of minimal cost when compared to the greater complexity of CO equipment.

Second, the telephony origins of CO switching means that it fits well into wide area networks. Without routers, LANs simply do not scale beyond metropolitan size.

Some argue that CO switches have more growth capability than LAN switches, but this is much less clear-cut. True, the switching fabrics of high-end CO switches go into the tens of gigabits, and, when paralleled, into the hundreds of gigabits. LAN switches more typically have switching fabrics with speeds well below 10 Gbps. It is hard to make a clear-cut distinction between the switch types, because an increasing number of high-end campus switches can use cell-based switching fabrics.

CO Switch Management Domains

Connection-oriented switching systems evolved from telephony switches and follow the ISDN/ATM reference model with U-, C-, and M-plane protocols.

Above Layer 2, there can be Layer 3 routing domains. Various cut-through schemes based on flows can have their own sorts of Layer 4 routing domains.

The management domain is most general and consists of one or more broadcast domains. Management domains are especially important when VLANs are in use, because the management domain defines the assignment of end system addresses to VLANs.

In any practical switch, there is a configuration management function by a local or remote terminal, or through SNMP, HTTP, or other IP-based protocols. Alternatively, some telephone-oriented switches use the OSI Common Management Information Protocol (CMIP), which might expect OSI routing using the Connectionless Network Layer Protocol (CLNP) and the Intermediate System to Intermediate System (IS-IS) routing protocol. For remote management, it is necessary to assign one or more IP addresses to the chassis itself, simply to access it for management. The switch also needs to know one or more IP addresses of network management servers.

> ### Note
>
> From the perspective of management, a chassis is an IP host. As such, it needs to know the things any IP host does—its address, the address of a DNS server, the address of its SNMP trap server, the address of a **syslog** server, and so on. It either must learn a default gateway address or participate, at least passively, in routing.

A WAN switch usually has a combination of edge and trunk ports. Edge ports present a DCE interface to user equipment. In ATM, the edge function is called the UNI. ATM draws a distinction between public and private network UNIs. Public network UNIs follow public addressing conventions for the global ISDN numbering space.

Trunk ports can be a DTE or DCE but, in the more intelligent protocols, run a *Network-to-Network Interface* (NNI). Properly, NNI is used in single public or private domains. When the interface is between multiple public service providers, the function is called the *Broadband Intercarrier Interface* (B-ICI) in ATM documents.

Physical and Multiplexing Domains

The set of physical interfaces on a WAN switch is a meaningful domain. It is common practice to multiplex bit streams from one interface to another.

Inverse Multiplexing

In practice, there can be a level of aggregation above physical bit streams, in which multiple physical links are combined into single bit or byte streams. The term *bundle* increasingly is used to describe the aggregate of streams used in inverse multiplexing. Such combination is called *inverse multiplexing*. For one example of physical layer inverse multiplexing, see the discussion of the Topology Manager in the later section "Nortel Passport Routing."

Other inverse multiplexing techniques operate at OSI Layers 2 and 3. See the section "Load Sharing" in Chapter 11 for a discussion of inverse multiplexing at Layer 3.

At Layer 2, both PPP and LAP-B have *multilink* modes, in which frames are sent over multiple links, typically in round-robin order, and reassembled into the proper sequence at the receiving end.

Multilink PPP is very useful when you need more bandwidth, but cannot get faster links. A very common application for multilink PPP is combining pairs of ISDN B channels into a 128-Kbps stream. Where ISDN is not available, an increasing number of commercial products offer multilink PPP on analog circuits. Multiple links also increase availability, because the failure of one link does not cause a Layer 3 subnet mapped on top of the bundle to go down.

Do not confuse multilink PPP with *bonding*, a different inverse multiplexing technique. Bonding interleaves bits, not frames, and is intended for videoconferencing, not data, applications. It is most commonly used to bundle six ISDN B channels into a 384-Kbps videoconferencing channel.

LAP-B inverse multiplexing tends to be used as much to increase availability as to gain more bandwidth. Because LAP-B retransmits frames in error, there can be significant link-level overhead and delay if the error rate is substantial and LAP-B has to retransmit. Nevertheless, multilink LAP-B can make good sense for critical communications. If one of the links fails, the network layer is not aware of the failure and you can avoid rerouting.

Yet another connection-oriented inverse multiplexing technique is used with critical telephony infrastructure applications, as well as management channels for ATM call setup. The protocol is Service Specific Convergence Protocol (SSCOP), which you can think of as a LAP-B variant designed for even higher availability. When SSCOP is used in a multilink manner, neither link should ever be loaded more than 50%. Given two active SSCOP links, the same frame is sent over both links. If the frame is received in error on one link, the other link is checked to see if the same frame has been received without error. If an error-free frame is available on the other link, there is no need to retransmit. If a redundant link fails or if there is only one physical link, all traffic runs over the single link and conventional retransmission is used.

Layer 2 inverse multiplexing also is widely used in connectionless campus applications. See "Inverse Multiplexed Parallel Paths" in Chapter 10.

Inverse multiplexing will remain a viable alternative to new last mile technologies such as xDSL, because these new technologies will not be available in all areas. In general, service providers will be more concerned with the support of large numbers of xDSL or cable TV-based technologies, but they remain alternatives for specific user environments where end users are distributed over wider distances than LANs can go.

Grooming

Another reason for customers to want to use switches is to avoid excessive *grooming*. Although, as I write these words, I admit I am in need of a haircut, I do not refer here to the appearance of networking staff. Grooming is a telecommunications term for a process intended to get the most efficient use of bandwidth in large carrier trunk facilities, especially those they lease from other providers.

It might not be the fault of the carrier if you lose the diversity you thought your circuits had. Do *not* assume using multiple carriers automatically will assure facility diversity, due to widespread cross-leasing of facilities. Part of the service you think is coming from Sprint and GTE might actually run over a common Worldcom facility in which Sprint and GTE both independently lease capacity. These specific carrier examples are hypothetical, and I make no predictions about which carrier has bought which other carriers after the time of this writing.

Grooming is a normal part of what the telephone industry calls OAMP: operations, administration, maintenance, and provisioning. Provisioning is the telecommunications term for selecting and installing the carrier circuits and multiplexer channels that underlie a customer-ordered service. Grooming is a perfectly reasonable economy measure that can impact on fault tolerance unless carefully managed. An initial situation in which grooming can cause a problem is shown, from the customer perspective, in Figure 9.17.

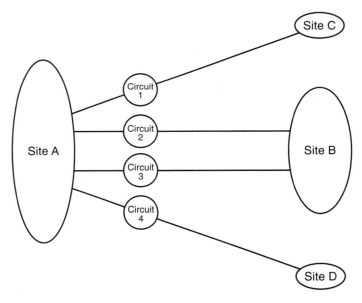

FIGURE 9.17 *Customer view in which grooming is invisible.*

Your enterprise at Site A orders four circuits, 1 through 4. Circuits 2 and 3 go to a critical destination, B. B might be another campus of your enterprises, a business partner, or an ISP. Circuits 1 and 4 go to important but less critical destinations, C and D. When users order circuits in the usual manner, they specify endpoints but are unaware of the actual trunks used in the carrier's implementation. Figure 9.17 shows this basic customer view of provisioning.

Circuits 1 and 2 go over Trunk 1. Trunk 1 is owned and operated by your carrier, but they lease Trunk 2 from another carrier. Your carrier runs Circuits 3 and 4 over Trunk 2. Your carrier is not sure if they need to build their own facilities over the path taken by Trunk 2. Figure 9.18 shows the initial way your carrier provisions the circuits.

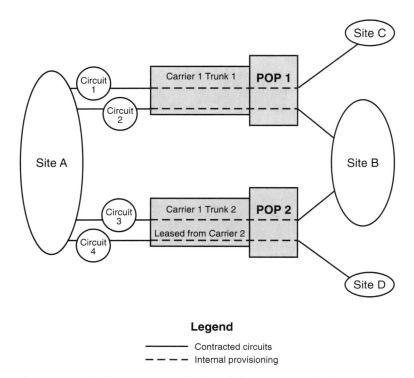

Legend

—————— Contracted circuits
– – – – Internal provisioning

FIGURE 9.18 *The initial provisioning of the four circuits indeed has diversity on the critical paths.*

Assume that your carrier decides it needs more bandwidth in the path taken by Trunk 1, and it upgrades Trunk 1. After this new bandwidth is in place, it is normal operational practice to try to use it efficiently. The grooming process searches for circuits that can be moved onto Trunk 1, possibly eliminating the need for Trunk 2. Your carrier is willing to build new local loops from POP1 to Sites B and C.

Circuit 4 can indeed be groomed onto Trunk 1. When a carrier engineer looks at the requirements for Circuits 3 and 4, it seems, superficially, that Circuit 3 can be groomed onto the new Trunk 1. The new layout is shown in Figure 9.19.

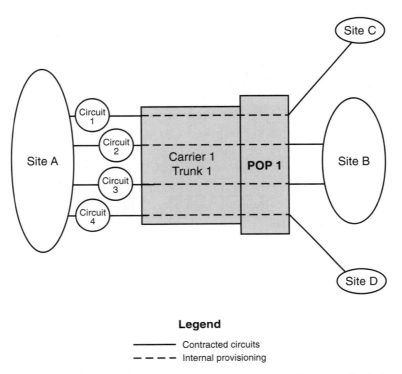

Legend

—————— Contracted circuits

– – – – Internal provisioning

FIGURE 9.19 *Grooming actions that inadvertently break diverse physical routing.*

Putting Circuit 4 onto Trunk 1, however, violates the diverse routing specified in the contract. Unfortunately, well-intentioned grooming engineers do not always read the contract.

What if your enterprise leases large facilities, as in Figure 9.20, so you can institute your own controls to be sure that diversely routed paths stay diverse? You still need to be sure carriers do not groom the larger paths into even larger ones, but managing your own slower paths can simplify the task of coordinating with the carrier. The enterprise is responsible for engineering user access.

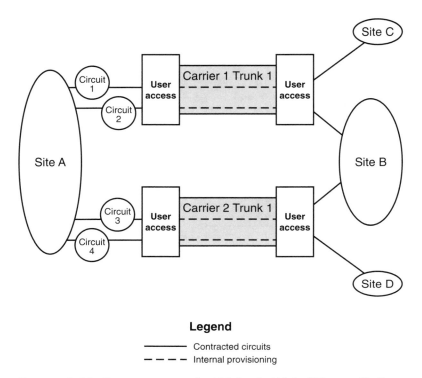

Legend

—————— Contracted circuits

— — — — Internal provisioning

FIGURE 9.20 *Large users can order high-bandwidth facilities, specify diverse routing, and provision bandwidth themselves.*

Even if you specify diverse routing, it is a good idea to write into your contract a provision that lets you audit the data circuit layout record (DCLR) for the circuits you pay to have routed diversely. Most carriers do use the term DCLR, or slight variants of it. You do want to ensure that the carrier provides their internal working document, whatever its name. Under normal circumstances, you might want to do this about every 60 days. Industry mergers also can cause combining of facilities you thought diversely routed; always audit your routing after any of your carriers merge or are acquired. Some carriers might claim this is proprietary information. If you are in a country that has telecommunications competition, simply tell the carrier that if its competitor will give you the information, the carrier refusing the information might just have lost your business.

Connection-Oriented Switch Types

One argument for using CO switches is that they tend to have greater capability to scale the switching fabric speed. The line between routers and switches certainly is blurring; routers in the gigabit range routinely use a crossbar switch as the forwarding engine, as do ATM switches. The router crossbar switch can operate on packets or cells.

Routers are necessary to send packets between subnets. There are several alternative ways to provide routing services, even before marketing-speak confuses the situation. In *Animal Farm*, George Orwell had his revolutionary pigs chanting "four legs good, two legs bad." Irresponsible vendor and trade press comments have equally and incorrectly polarized many people into believing the function of routing is obsolete.

In this section, we concentrate on an approximate taxonomy for categorizing CO switch products. Many of these products can contain a Layer 3 routing function, without even beginning to consider the hybrid Layer 2/3 functions discussed in Part V.

Most CO switches are modular chassis, into which you plug various interface cards. Some workgroup-level switches have a fixed or semi-fixed design. Some of these modular chassis allow redundant management processors for fault tolerance.

WAN Concentrators

A WAN concentrator, such as the Cisco 3810 or the Cisco MGX 8220 (formerly the AXIS) edge concentrator or shelf, has many low- to medium-speed interfaces and one or more high-speed uplinks. Like the 3800, it can have Layer 3 routing capabilities, but, if it has ATM interfaces, it does not have the capability to switch cells from ATM interface to ATM interface.

The term *shelf* tends to describe a device primarily designed to be located next to the main switch. Increasingly, concentrators might be remotely located and connect to the main switch through a DS3 or ATM/SONET link.

Concentrators intended for installation at telephone facilities might very well have -48 volt DC power supplies.

WAN concentrators can be surprisingly useful in organizations where there are large numbers of T1 links coming into a site. Although it might be advantageous to have these multiplexed into a fractional T3 or ATM service, such service might not be available in a given area. In Chapter 10, you will see that it can be quite cost-effective to fan out high-speed router ports with LAN switches. As shown in Figure 9.21, it can also be cost-effective to fan out expensive router ports with WAN concentrators.

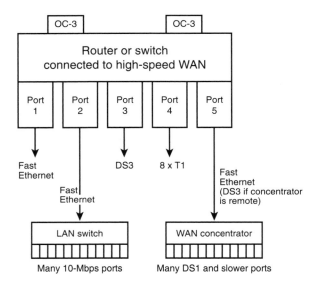

FIGURE 9.21 *WAN concentration for port fan-out.*

A given slot on a Cisco 7500 router, for example, can take an eight-port serial card. This same port can take an OC-3 card. If you need to bring in 100 T1 circuits, you would need 13 ports, more than is available on a single 7513 router.

LAN Switches with CO Uplink

A LAN switch with an ATM uplink, shown in Figure 9.22, has many similarities to a WAN concentrator. Arguably, ATM is a WAN technology, but equally reasonable arguments can be made that ATM is a LAN technology as well. So, if you are WAN oriented, feel free to call this device a WAN concentrator!

By whatever name, a LAN switch with an ATM uplink does not switch cells among its local interfaces, but uses a high-speed link to connect an edge device to a core. LAN switches with ATM uplinks do not have to run LANE, although many do.

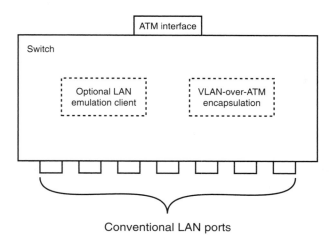

FIGURE 9.22 *LAN switches with ATM uplinks do not have end-user ATM interfaces.*

Just to confuse the terminology further, several vendors' switches have ATM uplinks, but can have an optional module that does full cell switching. A chassis designed as a LAN switch, however, usually does not have the range of WAN interfaces (for example, DS1) available on a workgroup ATM switch.

Workgroup/Campus CO Switches

If a device in the workgroup/campus CO switch category has ATM interfaces, it has the capability to switch cells from port to port. Typically, devices in this category have an internal switching fabric with speeds in the 1 to 5 Gbps range. Figure 9.23 shows a representative switch architecture.

Switches in this category are moderately fault-tolerant in that they can have redundant power supplies, but do not have hot-standby management processors. Examples of such switches include the Cisco LS1010 and Bay Centillion 100.

In my consulting practice, I find ATM quite common in medical applications. Several factors drive this use. First, large medical organizations frequently must interconnect buildings in a campus separated by public streets, or multiple campuses in a region. They cannot rely on a high-speed technology that cannot be provided by a common carrier.

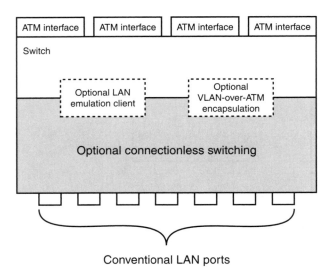

FIGURE 9.23 *An ATM switch has ATM interfaces among which it can switch cells. Typically, it also has modular WAN interfaces and might have LAN interfaces.*

A second medical driver for ATM is not so much ATM to the desktop, which has largely been replaced by Fast Ethernet to the desktop, but ATM to the special-purpose host. Medical imaging equipment, such as computerized axial tomography, magnetic resonance imaging, single photon emission computed tomography, and so on, often has an ATM interface on its control computer. These interfaces are used to transfer the very large image files created by the medical device.

Another application area that often has ATM interfaces on special-purpose hosts is video production. Video camera, editing machine, and special effects hosts also work with very large files and have ATM interfaces on the host.

Universities, which used to be the only things we thought of when we spoke of campus networks, often have more than one campus and have the same need to interconnect them as do medical organizations.

Corporate mergers also can have good justification for using common-carrier-provided ATM among several campuses.

An insurance firm is a good example of the use of campus switches. After several mergers, a company found its operations scattered into several buildings in a radius of perhaps 100 miles. The corporate headquarters was overcrowded. The firm decided to consolidate operations into two of the cities, eventually moving headquarters operations to a suburban location. Services needed to continue to operate during the transition.

The firm also wanted to prepare for high-bandwidth applications, which are not the first thing one thinks of in relation to presumably text-based insurance firms. Insurance firms, however, deal with huge amounts of paper, and they increase productivity by digitizing paper documents and using image retrieval and transfer systems. Such imaging systems are bandwidth intensive.

Enterprise CO Switches

An enterprise switch is generally faster than a campus switch, with a switching fabric in the 10 to 20 Gbps range. It has both narrowband and broadband (DS3 and faster) interfaces, although it can use concentrating shelves for more cost-effective fan-out of the lower-speed circuits.

It is inherently a more reliable system than a campus switch, typically with hot standby management processors. Examples here include the Cisco IGX 8400, formerly the Stratacom IGX.

Intuitively, it would seem that a switch with complete internal redundancy is more reliable than a single campus-class switch. But consider the situation in Figure 9.24. A critical financial application has fully redundant risers and server rooms in a New York skyscraper.

In a large building, there can be substantial physical separation between the risers. What if there is a fire in one of the risers? No matter what the reliability of a single switch, if there is only a single switch in the main computer room, this switch can be destroyed.

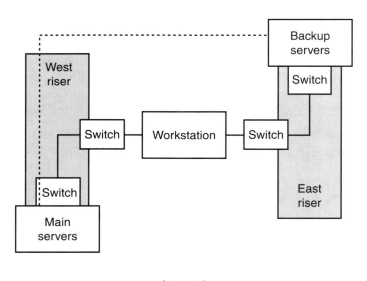

Legend

—————— ATM connectivity

- - - - - - - - Application backup and/or synchronization

FIGURE 9.24 *A highly redundant switch is still a single point of failure. Two less internally redundant switches can give higher total availability, especially when you are concerned with recovering from major disasters.*

Carrier CO Switches

A carrier-class switch often is made up of parallel switching fabrics from enterprise class switches. Examples here include the Cisco BPX, Fujitsu FETEX-150,
and GDC Strobos. Bay Networks, prior to its merger with Nortel, used the
BNX switch as a feeder to the Fujitsu switch.

A carrier-class switch is likely to have only SONET/SDH interfaces on the
switch proper, because it does not connect directly to narrowband end users.
Typical speeds for connecting to edge switches are OC-3/STM-1 and faster and
higher speeds, at least OC-12/STM-4, to connect to other core switches. The
switch relies on concentrators, often mounted in shelves in the same set of
racks, for lower-speed connectivity.

Carrier CO switches are meant for installation in carrier facilities and usually
have -48 volt DC power supplies.

The Relationship of Switches to Routers

When connectionless or connection-oriented switching is a major technology in a network, you find various applications for a device: the *single-armed route, router on a stick, or one-armed router,* shown in Figure 9.25. Do you see arms in Figure 9.25? I don't, but I am not shocked because I am used to strange marketing terminology. You could as easily call it a single-legged router, but always remember that Abraham Lincoln once asked, "If you call a horse's tail a leg, how many legs does the horse have?" He answered himself, "Four. Calling a tail a leg does not make it one." I digress here, but it is important not to become excessively concerned with the meaning of the words in some technologies. The words are merely a name.

Single-armed routers have useful applications as what might be called service processors or management servers. In Cisco's original LANE implementation, a router platform (typically a 4700) with a fast CP and a single ATM interface is dedicated to LANE support. It connects to an ATM switch and provides the CPU-intensive broadcast and multicast replication function. LES, BUS, and LECS functions run on this platform, which is not used for general routing. Newer Cisco implementations have LANE support boards, with their own processors, which plug into 5000 series switches.

An additional router or routers would be used for actual routing.

Cisco also uses a single-armed router to offload the segmentation and reassembly functions in large stacks of network access servers.

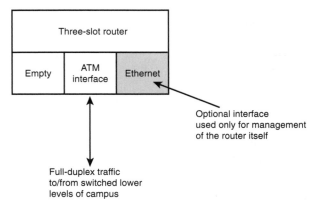

FIGURE 9.25 *Routers with a single interface—single-arm routers—have numerous applications in switched networks.*

Figure 9.26 details the usage of the rather silly term *router-on-a-stick*. I suppose it is no sillier than many other terms that describe useful functions. The developers of the major public domain Web caching tool, **squid**, commented that they named the tool **squid** because all the other good acronyms had been taken.

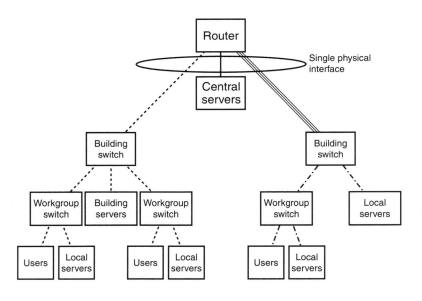

FIGURE 9.26 *Router-on-a-stick is an optimization for the flow pattern where most traffic stays on a single subnet.*

Editorial onsiderations aside, the idea of router on a stick is that most traffic stays internal to the network, and indeed most traffic stays on its own VLAN/ELAN.

Cisco uses the term *router cluster* to describe a configuration (see Figure 9.27) where a switch is at the top of the hierarchy, with routers at the distribution tier.

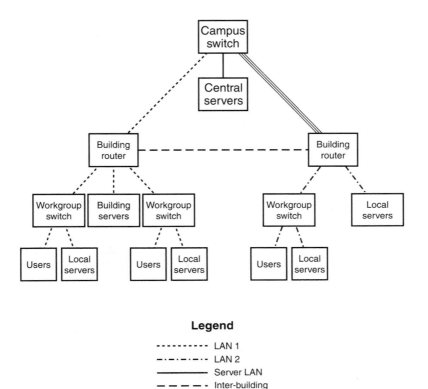

Legend

- - - - - - - - - LAN 1
— · — · — · — · · LAN 2
——————— Server LAN
— — — — · Inter-building

FIGURE 9.27 *Router cluster is an optimization for the flow pattern where clients and servers are on different subnets.*

In practice, the distribution layer routers are often implemented on multilayer switch platforms that can both switch and route. These switches support LANE, VLAN, or both and can route among these virtual subnets. Arrangements of this type offer more potential when there is substantial routing between different VLAN/ELAN subnets. (See Figure 9.28.)

You need to know your application traffic patterns before you can decide if the router on a stick or the router cluster design is more appropriate for your enterprise. Many other factors affect this choice.

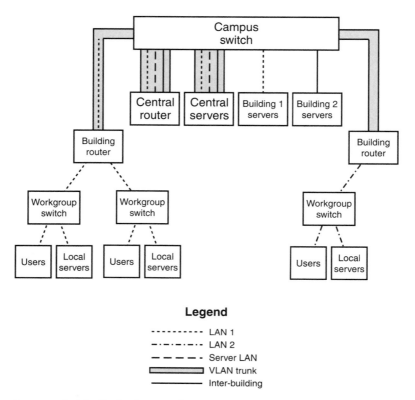

FIGURE 9.28 *Evolved router cluster uses VLAN/ELAN-aware routers at the distribution tier; these routers also have a switch function for high-speed relaying within the same virtual subnet.*

If, for example, you have a set of campuses linked by ATM circuits, it makes sense to have a switch at the top of your campus hierarchy—if the bulk of traffic goes to other ATM-linked sites. If the bulk of your traffic goes to other sites linked by other media, you want a router at the top of your campus hierarchy.

Because routers do more complex processing than switches, it's easier to have a router run out of CPU power than it is a switch. When a router is the core of your network, be sure to monitor its utilization regularly and add capacity before you have a crisis.

Emerging technologies, such as MPOA (see Chapter 14), distribute the packet forwarding part of routing into hardware. If you can distribute some of the forwarding functions to lower levels of the network, you can reduce the processing load for the central router.

Virtual Circuit Setup

There are three types of virtual circuits; of these three, a call setup procedure is needed for the second and third:

- *Permanent virtual circuits (PVCs).* These are logical equivalents of dedicated lines. Another term for PVC is a *nailed-up connection*. PVCs are manually configured.

- *Switched virtual circuits (SVCs).* Analogous to dial circuits in the telephone system, these are paths that are set up dynamically by the carrier cloud on receiving a call request.

- *Soft PVC.* A PVC that is set up using the dialing mechanisms of an SVC, but that is never disconnected. Using SVC setup simplifies the process of configuration because the switched setup service finds the path, rather than requiring you to configure it explicitly.

Both the ATM and Frame Relay SVC setup protocols are descendants of Q.931, the ISDN call setup protocol.

The same network or carrier service can use both PVCs and SVCs. Assuming that both are available, the application-level choice to use one or the other is largely an economic decision. If there is a need for application-specified QoS, you want to use SVCs so the application can request a particular QoS.

SVCs are attractive when the carrier's pricing gives an incentive to use a virtual circuit only on an as-needed basis. In private networks, they work better with switch interfaces that support only a limited number of concurrent connections.

There are functional as well as economic reasons to use SVCs. When there is a need to charge internally for network services, records are far easier to generate at call setup and termination time than it is to do continuous usage monitoring.

It is generally simpler to set up SVC services than PVCs. A manually configured full mesh, the extreme case, needs $(N \times (N-1))/2$ PVCs to set up.

ISDN

ISDN uses the Q.931 protocol for call setup. The setup protocol for Frame Relay SVCs is also a derivative of Q.931.

ISDN and Frame Relay are access protocols rather than end-to-end services. For a call to be created, the end host must learn a connection identifier for the call. Think of the ISDN called number as the telephone number you are dialing on a five-button phone, with one button for each line on the phone. The ISDN terminal endpoint identifier (TEI) connection identifier is a transient identifier that tells you which device identifier you are using for this particular call. TEIs can be preconfigured or dynamically assigned.

The basic Q.931 call setup mechanism mirrors the process of dialing a telephone. It begins when the end host sends a **SETUP** message. At its most basic, this message conveys the desired number to call. The protocol, however, allows information elements (IEs) to be attached to the basic **SETUP**. In telephony, IEs could contain features such as reverse charging or a credit card number.

ATM

It is no accident that ATM's call setup protocol is called Q.2931, because Q.2931 is derived from Q.931. ATM end devices send connection setup requests to the ingress switch using the Q.2931 protocol. That switch, in turn, uses a proprietary mechanism or, with increasing likelihood, a standard M-plane protocol to determine if the desired circuit can be set up.

As in ISDN, a **SETUP** message is sent from the end equipment to the ingress switch. At a minimum, the **SETUP** message conveys the desired called ATM endpoint address, but it can carry supplemental IE as in ISDN.

Standard M-plane protocols are the Interim Inter-Switch Protocol (IISP) and the Private Network-to-Network Interface (PNNI) routing protocol. IISP, which was once called PNNI-0 but is not related to modern PNNI, is discussed in this chapter, whereas PNNI is covered in Chapter 14. Because PNNI derives some of its design from OSPF, it is easier to understand after OSPF has been discussed.

Frame Relay

Frame Relay was introduced as a PVC service. PVC setup is generally specific to a vendor. It can use a proprietary switch setup protocol or can set up virtual circuits using IP routing to find the paths. SVCs are a relatively recent enhancement to Frame Relay. They have various applications, a significant one being VoFR. VoFR is a member of the VoX class.

Frame Relay is normally provided over a dedicated physical access line, over which both PVCs and SVCs are multiplexed at the data link layer. When provided in this manner, you pay a fixed rate for the access line. PVCs are usually also charged at a fixed rate associated with their committed information rate, but charging sometimes depends on traffic. Practical SVCs are billed on connection time.

Early commercial services have prioritized SVC over PVC traffic, primarily for Voice over Frame Relay applications. Videoconferencing is another application. There is a subtle way to simplify the quality of service problem if the carrier assumes all SVCs are prioritized over all PVCs.

When pricing is appropriate, SVCs can be a more cost-effective means of telecommuter access than ISDN. ISDN provides two 64-Kbps channels, but is not available in all areas. SVCs can run over a plain DS0 facility, which might be available where ISDN is not. 64 Kbps, however, is marginally faster than current modems. SVCs might be more attractive when the local loop is DS1, because the per-bit transfer time is faster at 1.544 Mbps than 128 Kbps.

Sizing Switch Throughput

Before you know whether you have adequate switching capacity, you must know the load that will be imposed on the switch. Most commercial numbers for switch performance tend to portray the ideal input-port-to-output-port throughput of a switch. You need to look at the potentially concurrent flows, as well as potential output blocking.

General Benchmarking Parameters for Network Interconnection Devices

In characterizing workload, the basic concern is the intended load [RFC 2285]. Additional load—the true *offered load*—can be less than the intended load. It is the total numbers of frames per second that can be observed to be forwarded to a device or system under test (DUT/SUT) for forwarding. Congestion avoidance and control mechanisms, such as waiting for tokens, waiting for half-duplex media to become quiet, or resolving collisions, can reduce the intended load. In addition, spanning tree maintenance activities also generate traffic that can reduce the available bandwidth.

As a consequence, throughput measurements for devices really need to be done with unidirectional communications between a single test load and a single SUT/DUT. After multiple devices are involved, you have to compensate for the delays and lower transfer rates caused by other devices. Data unit counts on interfaces can exceed the rate at which the source device sends to the SUT/DUT, due to the presence of management information. These include OAM cells in ATM, frames destined to the local management interface (LMI) in Frame Relay, and 802.1D BPDU frames in LAN environments.

RFC 1944 treats these additional loads as *modifiers* and recommends that benchmarks should contain many of these conditions as well as results without the modifiers. The modifiers include the following:

- Broadcast frames

- Management frames

- Frames carrying routing updates

RFC 1944 recommends adding 1% broadcast frames to the test data stream, evenly distributing these among the unicast traffic. This 1% guideline provides a target for filtering mechanisms that attempt to restrict excessive broadcasts. One percent is considered high, but an appropriate challenge to see if the system under test can deal with real-world problems. A management workload of one SNMP frame in each second, sent as the first frame, is suggested. This RFC also suggests evaluating traffic flow with filters in place, using 1-filter and 25-filter test cases.

The *forwarding rate* is a measure of the number of frames the switch can successfully transmit to the correct destination interface under a specified offered load. Because this measurement does not explicitly consider frame loss, you must specify an offered load with it. If the offered load is greater than the forwarding rate, the switch might be dropping, or queuing, frames. Alternatively, the switch might exert congestion control on the incoming interface.

The forwarding rate at maximum offered load (FRMOL) is the forwarding rate with the greatest offered load that is tested. The forwarding rate of a switch can vary with the load presented. It might seem counterintuitive, but the forwarding rate can decrease when the maximum load is presented at a given interface. Maximum forwarding rate (MFR) can be less than maximum forwarding rate under maximum offered load (MFROL). It is the latter rate that is more important for operational planning.

Broadcast and Multicast Replication by CO Switches

If a host connected to a connection-oriented switch sends a broadcast or a multicast, how does that information reach the other hosts? Either the host must copy it to all other virtual circuits or there must be some hidden replication mechanism underlying the connectivity.

Depending on the switch, there might be additional hardware support for copying these broadcasts, or this might be a load for the management processor in the switch. Alternatively, the host might need to send to an explicitly defined multicast server. For ATM networks, one mechanism for the latter is called the *Multicast Address Resolution Server* (MARS) [RFC 2022]. MARS is a part of the MPOA architecture.

A challenge in ATM broadcast replication, when a single device replicates for all virtual circuits, is avoiding out-of-sequence non-unicast frame delivery. The problem is that cells arrive at the replication node not necessarily in the order they belong in frames, but in fairly random order. Realistically, the replication node has to reassemble the frames and then replicate them onto each virtual circuit, breaking the frame back into cells.

The problem of order takes place if there is a single ATM device that copies multicast cells. This device is an endpoint of multiple connections from the frame generating sources. Although it has a point-to-multipoint virtual circuit to the devices receiving the multicasts, cells can be arriving simultaneously on different interfaces. Let's say the multicast replication device is receiving a sequence of 32 cells on Interface 1 and Interface 2 and will transmit the multicast cells on a point-to-multipoint VC from Interface 3.

The multicasting device cannot simply accept an incoming cell and switch it to the point-to-multipoint VC. To do so is to risk interspersing cells belonging to the stream being received on Interface 1 with the stream arriving on Interface 2. AAL5, the most bandwidth-efficient form of AAL for data applications, assumes that cells on a VC are in order, from first cell of frame to last frame of cell.

To be able to mix cells from different frames, you have to use AAL3/4, which imposes much more overhead. So, a real-world multicasting engine reassembles the cells on each VC into frames in its internal memory, and only after it knows it has a complete frame does it segment it back into cells that are copied onto the point-to-multipoint VC. The two steps of segmentation and reassembly introduce delay.

ATM-Specific Parameters

Cell transfer delay is the time between a cell exiting the measured device at the source and the cell entering the destination at the destination measurement point. For an ATM network, the source measurement point is the source UNI, and the destination measurement point is the destination UNI.

ATM parameters fall into two general categories:

- Traffic

  - Peak Cell Rate (PCR)

  - Sustained Cell Rate (SCR)

  - Measured Bucket Size (MBS)

- QoS

  - Cell Transfer Delay (CTD)

  - Cell Delay Variation (CDV)

  - Cell Loss Rate (CLR)

  - Cell Error Rate (CER)

  - Cell Misinsertion Rate (CMR)

Measured in seconds—in practice milliseconds or microseconds—CTD is the sum of the time for transmission between nodes and the processing time in nodes.

Cell delay variation (CDV) is the variation of cell transfer delay under a given workload. CDV is the result of integrating the delays encountered by the number of data units measured for some specified interval. CDV is the difference between maximum and minimum CTD during this interval. Again, it is expressed in seconds or fractional seconds.

Cells can arrive at a destination but have an incorrect header checksum. The rate at which this happens is measured by the cell error ratio (CER), which is calculated and expressed much as is CLR. CER should be extremely low in ATM networks, much lower than CLR. It is expressed as a dimensionless number, in the range 10^{-1} to 10^{-15} or as **unspecified**.

Another dimensionless number is the ratio between cells dropped in transit errors and all cells, Cell Loss Rate (CLR).

Cell Misinsertion Rate (CMR) is another ratio that measures an unsuccessful transfer. In this case, it measures the ratio of the cells received that were not sent by the source.

ATM in a Metropolitan Extranet

Animation and movie special effects demand huge amounts of bandwidth. Although graphics files sometimes can be transferred on tape, there is no time to do this during show production.

Several studios began using FDDI for their internal networks, but 100 Mbps was too slow as requirements grew. They converted servers and graphics workstations to use ATM interfaces and connected them to a building-level switch.

Studios and production facilities tend to cluster in geographic areas. Hollywood, of course, is well known, but there are clusters of advertising agencies in New York. Another cluster is in London's Soho district, where an ATM switch was installed at London's largest cable company, and single-mode fibers were run to several post-production houses that used ATM in their in-house networks.

The network began by connecting four production facilities, but is growing to connect to advertising agencies, pre-press facilities, and movie studios in the UK, Europe, and eventually in Hollywood.

Establishing a LANE Infrastructure

This section deals with establishing the virtual circuits among LANE components. The "LANE Operation" section of Chapter 10 discusses the way in which connectionless frames move through these virtual circuits.

There is no question that multivendor interoperability is practical with LANE. Do distinguish between protocol-level interoperability and network management; the configuration and diagnostic applications of different vendors often talk only to their own products.

ATM Forum LANE uses ATM virtual circuits to interconnect a variety of functions. LAN emulation clients (LECs) are the functional units that connect LANE-unaware devices to ATM trunking of LANE.

Complementing LECs, LANE has three service functions, which in basic LANE are single points of failure. The server functions are as follows:

- LAN emulation configuration server (LECS)

- LAN emulation server (LES)

- Broadcast and unknown server (BUS)

Devices using MAC addresses do not see changes in the underlying ATM topology. From a system administration standpoint, the MAC-addressed devices can move from one emulated LAN (ELAN) to another, much as devices move from one physical segment to another. Functionally, ELANs and VLANs are the same thing; they are simply names developed by different standards groups. ELANs are VLANs that run over an ATM virtual circuit service.

In LANE Version 1, illustrated in Figure 9.29, there is one LECS per system of ELANs, and one LES and one BUS per ELAN.

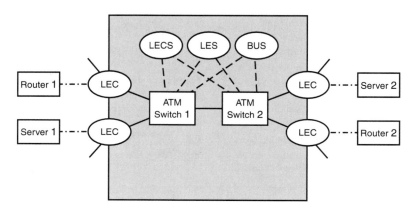

Legend

—·—·—·   Emulated LAN (outside LANE cloud)
————————   Data VC (inside LANE cloud)
— — — —   Control VC (inside LANE cloud)

Figure 9.29   *Basic LANE Version 1 has single points of failure.*

As Figure 9.30 shows, there is an assortment of control and data flow virtual circuits among LANE clients and servers.

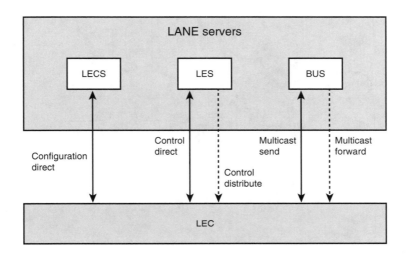

Legend

→ Bidirectional point-to-point
- - - - ▶ Unidirectional point-to-multipoint

FIGURE 9.30 *Unidirectional point-to-multipoint and bidirectional point-to-point virtual circuits interconnect LANE components.*

There are extensions that allow backup servers, the IETF Server Cache Synchronization Protocol (SCSP) [RFC 2334], Cisco's Simple Server Redundancy Protocol; and the emerging simple cache allows multiple LECS, BUS, and LES. Figure 9.31 shows how these extensions allow redundant servers. LANE version 2 (LANEv2) natively supports multiple LECS, BUS, and LES.

According to the ATM Forum specifications, a LEC can belong to multiple ELANs. In common vendor implementation, a LEC belongs to one ELAN, although there can be more than one LEC function on a physical platform. When a router does serve as a LEC for several ELANs, it can route packets between them.

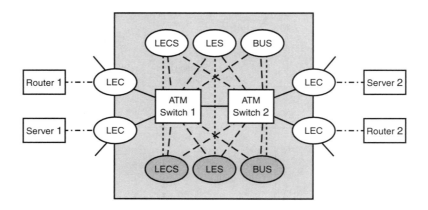

Legend

- - - - - - - -   IETF SCSP or Cisco SSRP
- ·- ·- ·-·   Emulated LAN (outside LANE cloud)
————————   Data VC (inside LANE cloud)
— — — —   Control VC (inside LANE cloud)

FIGURE 9.31   *LANE version 1 extensions add reliability.*

LES and especially the BUS functions are CPU intensive. In practice, the LES, BUS, and LECS run on the same chassis. For this reason, the usual practice is to put them on a separate processor, with a fast CPU, that does not provide direct user services. Different vendors implement these functions in different places. One vendor might use them in a workstation; another might use a special-purpose processor inside an ATM switch chassis; and yet another might use a single-armed router with a fast CPU and a single ATM interface.

Remember that the LECS is a service for the entire LANE system. If you have many emulated LANs, it might make sense for the LECS service to reside on a management workstation or other separate host. The LECS service is not nearly as CPU intensive as the BUS or LES services.

The LAN Emulation Client function in switch S1 now queries the LECS to determine which ELAN the address belongs to. Assuming the LECS recognizes the address, it returns the address of the LAN Emulation Server that services that specific ELAN. Most commercial LEC functions are preconfigured with the knowledge of the ELAN to which they belong and can skip this step.

ARP maps logical addresses onto MAC addresses. LANE uses a further level of indirection, in which it maps MAC addresses onto ATM virtual connections using the LE-ARP function. This additional level of indirection is invisible to devices using MAC protocols, allowing the benefits of ATM to be used with existing LAN equipment.

LAN-based devices speak as they do today to routers and switches. Routers and switches implementing LANE, however, contain a function called the LEC that does the mapping of real MAC addresses into ATM addresses. Workstations and servers can also have LEC functionality, which gives them the impression of connecting to multiple LANs.

Most of the complexity of LANE comes from how the LEC determines which LAN address to which a given destination address is mapped and how the LEC forwards frames until the destination MAC address is resolved to a specific ATM address. Additional complexity comes from supporting multicast and broadcast MAC addressing.

LANE is a complex technology, and the discussion here does not attempt to get into the fine details of the internal protocols [ATMForum AF-LANE-0084-000].

Each emulated LAN corresponds to one bridged system. This can have one or more logical addresses mapped onto it by Layer 3-aware devices or can appear to be purely a MAC-address level bridging system. Basic LANE is not aware of Layer 3 addressing, although the MPOA extensions to it are.

LANEv2 natively supports redundant infrastructure servers, illustrated in Figure 9.32.

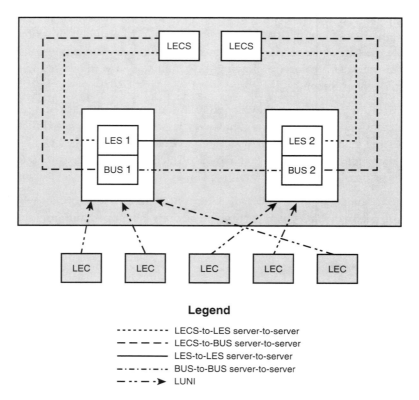

Legend

- - - - - - - - - LECS-to-LES server-to-server
— — — — - LECS-to-BUS server-to-server
——————— LES-to-LES server-to-server
—·—·—·· BUS-to-BUS server-to-server
— ·· — ·➤ LUNI

Figure 9.32 *LANEv2 is designed to have LANE service-to-service connections for redundancy and load-sharing.*

LECS Configuration: Defining Components of an ELAN

Strictly speaking, the LECS is not necessary as long as there is only one ELAN. Architecturally, the LECS can contain four kinds of entries in its database:

- Emulated LAN name—the ATM address of LANE server pairs

- LANE client MAC address/emulated LAN name pairs

- LANE client ATM template/emulated LAN name pairs

- Default emulated LAN name

LEC Initialization

A LEC is the point at which conventional MAC-addressed devices interface to the LANE system. On initialization, each LEC connects to a LECS and requests the ATM address of the LES that services the ELAN to which the LEC belongs. If the LEC belongs to more than one ELAN, it repeats the process for each. For the same reasons that a port on a VLAN switch should not belong to more than one VLAN, having a LEC belong to multiple ELANs is rarely a good idea (see Chapter 10).

Practical limitations to the number of ELANs in which a given physical device can belong include the number of VCs that its ATM interface supports and the bandwidth of that interface.

The LEC Configuration Phase

LANE clients have several possible ways to find the LECS. The specific mode selected is an implementer choice from the following list, which runs from most to least preferred:

- Locally configured ATM address

- Integrated LMI

- Fixed address defined by the ATM Forum

- PVC 0/17 (that is, Virtual Path Identifier 0, Virtual Channel 17)

After the LEC contacts the LECS, the LECS returns the name of the ELAN that will service the LEC. It's worth emphasizing that the LECS service is global to all the ELANs and is the directory assistance function that finds all numbers.

The LEC Join Phase

A virtual circuit for carrying control information is set up between the LEC and its LES. The LES also adds the LEC to its point-to-multipoint virtual circuit to the set of its LECs.

In its tradition of confusing terminology, such as the LECS being different from more than one LEC, LANE has its own ARP mechanism: LAN emulation ARP (**LE_ARP**) does *not* replace the ARP mechanism that binds a logical address to a transmission system address.

Remember that LANE appears as a bridging system to conventional MAC-addressed LAN devices on the LANs serviced by LECs. The **LE_ARP** is internal to the LANE environment and binds a MAC address at the LEC to an internal ATM address in the trunking system that provides the connectivity among components of the LANE environment.

Initial Registration by the LEC

The LEC establishes connectivity with the BUS by sending an **LE_ARP** request to the LES, asking the LES to resolve the ATM address associated with the MAC broadcast address FF-FF-FF-FF-FF-FF. The LES returns the BUS address, and the LEC creates a VC from the LEC to the BUS.

When the LEC first registers with the LES, it identifies itself either as a proxy or non-proxy device. If it chooses to be a proxy, it simply responds to ARP requests. If it chooses to be a non-proxy LEC, it actively registers all MAC addresses for which it wants to receive traffic. These addresses can be multicast as well as unicast. The LEC can subsequently withdraw registrations of specific addresses, and the registrations do have a lifetime, usually in minutes.

Figure 9.33 shows the relationship among components before user data flow begins but after registration.

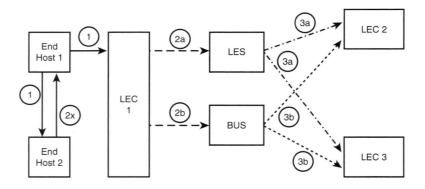

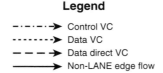

Legend

—·—·—▶ Control VC
·········▶ Data VC
— — —▶ Data direct VC
————▶ Non-LANE edge flow

FIGURE 9.33 *Virtual circuits among LANE components need to be set up before user data can flow.*

Several design choices in LANE version 1 limit its use to small to medium LANE environments. These include the single-point-of-failure among servers and the computational demands on the BUS. LANEv2 introduces a LANE Emulation Network-to-Network Protocol (LNNI) that lets you have redundant servers, including multiple active BUSes in the same ELAN.

The BUS

The BUS function is the most computationally intense server function in LANE. Effectively, it is the device most responsible for making the connection-oriented ATM transmission structure look like a connectionless network to the end hosts. The bus is responsible for distributing, in a form that results in meaningful edge frames:

- Data with the broadcast address FF-FF-FF-FF-FF-FF

- Data with multicast addresses, including group addresses and the functional addresses primarily used in Token Ring

- Data from Token Ring end hosts, that expects to be delivered using source routing determined from explorers

- Data whose MAC address has not yet been associated with an ATM virtual circuit

These functions are computationally intensive, and the BUS function usually is implemented on a processor separate from the main ATM switching fabric. Such a processor can be in the ATM switch chassis, on a single-armed router, or a management workstation.

The rationale for flooding information to potentially unknown, or even nonexistent, destinations is that the LEC to which the destination will be connected has not had time to learn about a certain MAC address that will be reached through the LEC. Perhaps the MAC address is on the distant side of a conventional bridge from the LEC, or the LEC is simply in the process of updating tables when it receives the **LE_ARP**.

Of course, frames destined to multicast or broadcast MAC addresses should be flooded. The BUS does this flooding for such frames, using the same point-to-multipoint virtual circuits it uses for unknown traffic.

Multicast and QoS in LANEv2

In LANEv2, the workload of handling multicast traffic can be distributed onto multiple selective multicast servers (SMSs) rather than a single BUS. With this mode of operation, LAN Emulation Clients (LECs) register with the SMS as well as the LES when they initialize. A separate VC is created from the LEC to the SMS, over which traffic flows for that specific multicast group. Of course, there needs to be an implementation-specific mechanism for the LEC to know that edge hosts connected to it want to be in specific multicast groups.

LANEv2 provides the capability of having up to eight sets of QoS parameters per LEC and allowing up to eight virtual circuits between LE clients, each with a distinct QoS. Mechanisms for deciding when to use which QoS are outside the scope of the specification. The most obvious way to do this is to use Layer 3 signaling mechanisms such as the IP precedence bits or the RSVP protocol. See Chapter 13 for a further discussion of these end-host-to-ingress-device signaling mechanisms.

The Component Relationships in LANE

LANEv2 extends the original LAN model in several ways. Perhaps the most significant is that it has the capability of moving beyond LANE version 1's single point of failure structure. LANEv2 also has improvements in multicast handling and ATM VC utilization, the latter by using SNAP encapsulation to allow multiple protocols to be handled. LANEv2 also supports QoS.

In both versions of LANE, there is a sequence of seven steps:

1. Initial state

2. Configuration state

3. Join state

4. LECS connect phase

5. Initial registration

6. Connecting to the BUS

7. Operational

Failures in any state except the Operational cause a reset back to the initial state. In the Operational state, a loss of connectivity to the BUS drops back to the Connecting to the BUS state.

The Initial State

A device is in the Initial state before any LANE protocol activities. In this state, however, it must be preconfigured with such parameters as ELAN names, ATM addresses, frame sizes, and so on. The mechanism of such configuration is specific to each implementation.

ELAN Configuration Checklist

❑ ELAN name assigned to each ELAN the LEC wants to join?

❑ Frame size set on LEC?

❑ Method of LECS location specified?

The LECS Connect Phase

As each LEC joins the LANE system, it creates a *Configuration Direct* virtual circuit to the LECS. The first problem in this process, of course, is knowing the address of the LEC. A LEC can obtain this information in several ways, as follows:

- Be manually preconfigured with the ATM address of the LECS.

- Use the SNMP application protocol (that is, LANE does not use SNMP over IP) to retrieve the LECS address from the Interim Local Management MIB.

- In LANE Version 1 *only*, default to the reserved LECS address 47-00-79-00-00-00-00-00-00-00-00-00-00-00-A0-3E-00-00-01-00.

LANE Management Checklist

❑ Is this a LANEv2 system? If so, does SNMP connectivity exist between the LEC and the ILMI, or is the LEC preconfigured with the LECS address?

When the LEC sends its LANE configuration request, it can include an MPOA field, which informs the LECS that the requesting client is MPOA aware. MPOA is an extension of LANE and is discussed in Chapter 13. MPOA extensions consider routing as well as switching.

Configuration Phase

After the LECS Connect phase, the LEC knows how to find the LECS, assuming a LECS exists. If there is no LECS, the LEC needs to be preconfigured with the LES address.

LANE Configuration Checklist

❑ Do you have only one emulated LAN? If so, is the LES address preconfigured in each LEC?

The Join Phase

After the LEC learns the address of the LES, it needs to set up the connections of control VCs to the LES. After the LEC connects to the LES, the LES assigns a unique LEC identifier (LECID) to the LEC. The LES also tells the LEC its LAN type assumed by the LES (that is, 802.3, 802.5, and so on) and the maximum frame size supported.

During this process, the LEC also registers with the LES if it is a *proxy LEC* or a *non-proxy LEC*. Non-proxy devices must explicitly register every MAC address for which they want to receive traffic. The LES optionally can store this full list. If a LEC registers as proxy, it does not register the addresses, but responds to ARP requests for them.

Maximum frame sizes in LANEv2 can be larger than in LANE version 1, due to the need to carry the additional header information. Because the frames are segmented into cells to transmit among the LANE devices, problems are not likely to occur inside the ATM infrastructure.

LANE-aware end hosts might be more likely to have a problem. If a LANE host driver expects a maximum frame size of 1500 bytes and the LLC header is delivered to the destination host, it might be 1512 bytes long. A conflict exists here, hopefully one that will not require IP fragmentation.

Initial Registration

After the LEC completes the Join phase, it can tell the LANE system the MAC addresses for which it wants to receive frames. This phase is deliberately separate from the full Operational phase, to give the LEC an opportunity to be sure its MAC addresses are unique within its emulated LAN.

Do remember that some host stacks, especially non-IP, often have duplicate MAC addresses. This tends not to be an operational problem because the MAC addresses are often on different broadcast domains and thus are unique in each broadcast domain. DECnet, for example, sets each interface of a router or multi-interface host to the same MAC address. The DECnet MAC address is derived from the DECnet logical address.

Connecting to the BUS

The last step before full operation is establishing the virtual circuit between the LEC and its BUS. From the perspective of the LEC, this is a semi-passive process. The LEC sends to the LES an **LE_ARP** with the broadcast address FF-FF-FF-FF-FF-FF. On receiving this, the BUS creates the Multicast Forward virtual circuit to the LEC.

After the multicast forward circuit is established, LANE is operational on the LEC. Establishing the LEC to BUS connection is the last connection-oriented step in LANE. Detailed operation appears connectionless to the edge hosts.

Interim Approaches to Providing Quality of Service

A major reason to use connection-oriented Layer 2 switching is its capabilities to enforce quality of service, which are currently in advance of those provided by Layer 3 routing and LAN switching. Using Layer 2 switching is not a panacea for quality of service. LAN-attached devices still have no means of requesting the quality of service they need.

Setting up quality of service on connection-oriented Layer 2 switches remains an essentially manual process. Although it is true that ATM end hosts can request a given QoS if they initiate ATM connections, most applications are unaware of the need to request a specific QoS. ATM workstation network interface cards (NICs) remain far more expensive than Fast Ethernet NICs. See Chapter 13 for a discussion of the overall process of requesting QoS.

Remember that ATM-connected workstations still need to establish virtual circuits to an ingress ATM switch. Switch interfaces might not be able to handle large numbers of virtual circuits.

The dominant role of connection-oriented Layer 2 switching is as a technology to interconnect switches and routers. It remains more cost-effective to connect workstations and most servers using LAN technology to their ingress switch or router and then interconnect the switches and routers using connection-oriented technology. Even in this case, it might be appropriate to route, rather than switch, among ingress devices and the backbone.

Requirements for significant video traffic, as might be required on a workstation that does television editing, might be a valid reason for direct ATM connectivity.

Servers are most often connected to LANs, and load considerations for that case are discussed in Chapter 10. It is also plausible that some servers will be directly connected either to native ATM or to ATM facilities using ELAN-aware network interface cards.

Emerging technologies discussed in Part V modify but do not destroy this approach. When workstations are able to request the traffic characteristics they need using RSVP, their ingress devices more intelligently can decide whether to switch or route to the backbone. RSVP, however, has a fundamental scaling problem: It specifies the requirements of individual flows. Individual flows, however, are too fine-grained to be practical in a reasonably sized backbone. As a consequence, the *differentiated services* model has emerged as a means of aggregating flows for greater backbone scalability. The differentiated services model sets precedence bits in the IP header to establish seven classes of service internal to the network.

End hosts could signal QoS requirements either using RSVP or differentiated services marking. These are, of course, Layer 3 mechanisms. The edge network interconnection device makes the Layer 2 versus Layer 3 decision. Alternatively, the end host can make a QoS request if it is directly connected to an ATM device or a Frame Relay device capable of accepting different QoS requests in SVCs.

Neither traditional Layer 2 nor Layer 3 techniques are quite the answer. The long-term solution is probably to use Layer 3 decision making to build tables of labels, which are used for decision making on a hop-by-hop basis [Bernet, 1998].

Ingress devices, which will probably look like extensions of present-day LAN switches, will use NHRP or MPOA to decide whether to switch or route to end destinations. NHRP can be used in other than LANE or MPOA environments. RSVP is intended only for signaling between end hosts and ingress devices; quality of service routing will be used among devices in the backbone. Label switching, as being developed by the IETF MPLS working group, is yet another hybrid of Layer 2 and Layer 3 technologies. Several vendors, including Cisco, Ipsilon, and Nortel, have implemented proprietary equivalents to label switching in their products.

Most of these vendors regard their implementations as pre-standard and actively participate in MPLS. Ipsilon is a significant exception, understandably because its products were first to market and had a competitive advantage. Ipsilon products did run into some scaling limitations, although they definitely work well in certain environments. Ipsilon has been acquired by Nokia and is no longer a significant independent player.

What QoS Problem Are You Trying to Solve?

Throughput is a basic requirement of applications. If they cannot transfer enough data, the link is useless. In both WAN Layer 2 switched services and RSVP, there are several basic parameters for expressing average and burst bandwidth requirements. Table 9.8 shows QoS design considerations and terminology for different media and measurement specifications. See Chapter 2 for a discussion of X3.102.

TABLE 9.8   QoS CHOICES

General	ATM	Frame Relay	X3.102
Average transfer rate.	Sustainable cell rate.	Committed information rate.	User information transfer rate.
Burst capability.	Peak cell rate.	Committed burst rate.	Not defined; Absolute delay is a function of pure transmission, of queuing in switches and congestion effects on lines.

Delay variability is associated with congestion and workload, when workload causes variation in switch times. The ATM parameter that describes delay variability is CDV.

Specifying QoS in ATM

ATM specifications divide services into two general categories, guaranteed service (GS) and best-effort (BE). Life itself, much less data networks, is not truly guaranteed, so the GS category needs to be understood in perspective. Switches distinguish between GS and BE, on a practical basis, by dropping BE cells before, in the presence of congestion, they drop GS cells.

The basic GS type is constant bit rate (CBR), used in the circuit emulation service (CES) that appears as a DS1 or DS3 dedicated circuit. Also in the GS category are variable bit rate (VBR) services intended for voice and video with strict latency limits. CBR has an underlying assumption that the information being transferred is a continuous stream, whereas VBR assumes the information can be grouped into bursts.

BE services include available bit rate (ABR) and unspecified bit rate (UBR). BE services are tolerant both of reasonable delay and cell loss. The difference between the two is that ABR includes a flow control mechanism, whereas UBR is a shoot and pray service, much like UDP at Layer 4.

Constant Bit Rate

CBR service is most commonly nailed up and given dedicated bandwidth in an ATM system. Conventional voice and video services are the mail CBR application. These applications need a constant bandwidth and minimal delay variability.

Cell loss should be low in these services, because bit loss is low on the circuits that CBR emulates. Nevertheless, some applications that are not tolerant of variable delay, such as uncompressed voice, can be somewhat tolerant of cell loss. When such tolerance is known, some type of VBR service might be more appropriate than CBR.

In an enterprise, you are most likely to use CBR when connecting existing voice equipment that expects a T1 interface. As you gain experience with the characteristics of your network, you might be able to redefine these connections to use real-time VBR, if the end equipment does not depend on constant bit rate to obtain its clocking (that is, bit timing information).

Variable Bit Rate

VBR service splits into two categories, *real time VBR* (rt-VBR) and *non–real-time VBR* (nrt-VBR). VBR remains a guaranteed service.

rt-VBR is appropriate when the application can handle small variations in both the bit rate and the cell loss ratio. Compressed voice and video are typical applications.

nrt-VBR is more intended for data applications that need tighter control on loss than is possible with BE services. VBR of both types is cheaper to implement than CBR. Special services for IBM SNA applications, which were designed for dedicated lines, are a good example. DEC's Local Area Transport (LAT), which was designed for single Ethernets, is really not intended for WAN use at all, but might be much more reliable on nrt-VBR.

Unspecified Bit Rate

The simplest ATM performance category, this is a BE service. The sender has no guarantee of delivery. ATM provides no quality of service guarantee to the sender, although higher-level protocols such as MPLS might do so. The sender simply transmits bits, and they either arrive at the destination or fail to arrive. If error and flow control are needed, they are done at a higher protocol layer than ATM.

Given the low error rates in modern networks, UBR is appropriate for most data applications, where TCP handles error and flow control when reliable delivery is needed. UBR also works well when UDP is the transport, and either the application tolerates loss or an even higher-level protocol, such as remote-procedure call (RPC), takes responsibility for delivery. RPC is the reliability mechanism that underlies transaction services such as the Network File System (NFS).

Available Bit Rate

In ABR, there is a feedback mechanism from the network to the source that lets the source know how much bandwidth is available at call setup. If the required capacity is not present when the call is requested, the call request is denied. There are parallels to TCP's flow control mechanism, but ABR is not a TCP replacement. It does not use the windowing scheme that TCP uses.

When using ABR, an additional performance parameter is used, the *minimum cell rate*. This is the rate at which the source is always allowed to send. This is still a best-effort service, so cell delay variation is not controlled.

Controlling QoS

There are an assortment of ways to control QoS in switched networks. In practice, they are used primarily by manually configured edge devices, until more applications are aware of the need to request a particular QoS.

QoS enforcement mechanisms vary on whether they are applied at connection establishment time or after the connection has been established. *Connection admission control* (CAC) is the ATM term for deciding whether or not a particular connection is permitted, based on a determination that the resources are or are not available to meet the requested QoS. The decision to admit the call or not is made in each switch along the path, during call setup.

Other mechanisms apply after the virtual circuit is set up. Applicability of these mechanisms depends on the type of service requested. *Selective cell discarding*, for example, discards cells marked with cell loss priority of 1 in preference to those with CLP of 0. CLP is set to 1 in cells belonging to best effort service, whereas CLP of 0 is associated with cells belonging to guaranteed services.

Traffic shaping, also called traffic pacing, is a buffering technique that smooths bursts of traffic into a steady stream the network is prepared to support. Buffering traffic, of course, delays it. When the amount of buffering needed depends on unpredictable network traffic, the delay is also variable. Traffic shaping, therefore, is not appropriate for CBR service.

Explicit forward congestion indicator (EFCI) and generic flow control (GFC) are intended for use with ABR.

ATM Forum Standard Routing: IISP

The Interim Inter-Switch Protocol (IISP), as its name suggests, is an interim ATM call setup mechanism with slightly more capability than simple static routing. It is a simple protocol that extends the call setup procedure of ATM to include the capability to route through multiple switches. Switch routing tables are populated manually, in a vendor-specific way, but IISP can dynamically select next hops to route around failures using predefined alternate static routes. IISP does not dynamically discover routes; it selects among predefined ones.

ATM addresses used for switched virtual circuit in private networks are 20 bytes long. Alternative formats, based on the ISDN telephone number standard, E.164, are used in public ATM networks. See *Designing Addressing Architectures for Routing and Switching*, also from Macmillan Technical Publishing, for further details of ATM addresses (see Figure 9.34).

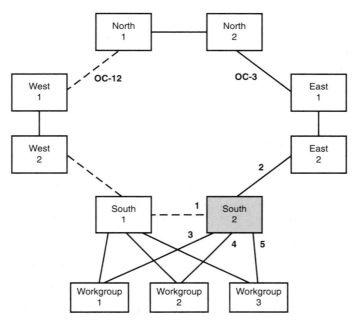

FIGURE 9.34 *A simple network for which Table 9.9 shows the routing table.*

TABLE 9.9 SOUTH 2'S IISP ROUTING TABLE

Destination	Outgoing Port on South 2 Switch
South WG1	3 Primary 1 Backup
South WG2	4 Primary 1 Backup
South WG3	5 Primary 1 Backup
Any West	1 Primary 2 Backup
Any North	1 Primary 2 Backup
Any East	2 Primary 1 Backup

IISP sets up paths by making hop-by-hop decisions. At each switch, it examines the next hop table to see if it can find the destination ATM address. Table 9.9 shows the representative routing table for switch South 2. This table assumes an addressing convention of *site.workgroup*. The switch knows the primary and backup ports to reach its local workgroup and also knows the primary and backup ports to reach any workgroup at another site.

If the routing table contains no match for the destination, the IISP process signals a **RELEASE COMPLETE** message with the cause code **no route to destination**.

IISP might be able to match the destination, but not complete the call for one of two main reasons. The outgoing interface might not be available for routing additional calls, either because it is inactive or there is no available capacity. If the outgoing interface is inactive, IISP returns a **RELEASE COMPLETE** message with the cause code **network out of order**. If, after the call is set up, the interface goes down, IISP specifies that SVCs routed through it should be cleared.

There could be more than one equal-cost path to the destination. The IISP standard is silent on how to select the appropriate path; it merely says the implementation shall do so. This decision might consider the traffic requirements of the call, such as sustainable cell rate and peak cell rate. It is also a responsibility of the person doing manual configuration to be sure the alternate route is loop-free. There is no dynamic routing protocol to check for looping.

SCR, PCR, and other parameters optionally can be considered, if the ingress switch supports CAC. IISP CAC does not guarantee end-to-end QoS, but only that the local switch believes it can or cannot provide the appropriate QoS.

If, at any point in the call setup, there is a rejection due to CAC, the **RELEASE COMPLETE** message should include an appropriate code, such as **user cell rate unavailable** or **quality of service unavailable**.

Representative Systems

Major vendors in WAN switching had proprietary Layer 2 routing architectures before ATM routing was developed. There have been a great many mergers and acquisitions in this area, so the organization that originally developed the technology might have been absorbed. Stratacom was acquired by Cisco. Cascade was acquired by Ascend, which in turn was acquired by

Lucent. Northern Telecom became Nortel Networks in a merger with Bay Networks. These proprietary methods include techniques for minimizing latency using small cells or by being able to interrupt a packet stream, and you certainly may encounter them.

Nortel Passport Routing

Nortel's Passport family supports multiple types of routing [Northern Telecom, 1998]. It's important to distinguish among the means of path determination and forwarding in these various options. There are blends of connectionless and connection-oriented services, and these further differentiate as the internal mechanisms versus the end-user service is seen. For example, the *dynamic packet routing system* (DPRS) provides a connection-oriented virtual circuit service to end users, such as Frame Relay, but internally uses connectionless forwarding. Nortel's routing techniques include the following:

- DPRS, a connectionless service that provides the internal support for Frame Relay, IBM APPN and SNA DLR services, and internetworking with Nortel DPN-100 devices. DPRS was formerly called DPN routing and RID/MID routing.

- InterLAN Switching (ILS), another connectionless service that sets up path for IP, IPX, and IEEE 802 bridging, and the closely related virtual networking system (VNS) that extends ILS to operate over WANs. ILS is a true Layer 3 routing system and is not further discussed in this chapter.

- Path-Oriented Routing System (PORS), providing connectionless support for voice, bit transparent data services, and AAL1 Circuit Emulation Service. PORS can consider cost and delay in selecting paths.

- ATM Routing System providing connection-oriented routing for ATM bearer service, ATM multiprotocol encapsulation, and Frame Relay to ATM interworking. This uses ATM Forum IISP.

Layer 2 path selection between Passport nodes uses either proprietary unacknowledged (UNACK) HDLC-based or ATM media over which proprietary paths are routed.

UNACK trunks are used on non-ATM media from 9.6 Kbps to 44.736 Mbps. These trunks operate in one of two modes, depending on whether the transmitted units are frames or bits. HDLC mode UNACK is intended for frame services only, whereas interrupted mode UNACK minimizes the latency for bit-oriented traffic such as circuit emulation or voice.

Nortel distinguishes between *base routing* and DPRS, PORS, and VNS. Base routing keeps track of the trunk topology. The *transport resource manager* tracks all physical links connected to a Passport node and builds higher-level structures from them such as inverse multiplexed *link groups* and *topology regions*. Topology regions are a means of enhancing scalability by keeping some topology information localized, much as OSPF areas do, but at Layer 2.

Layered on top of the transport resource manager is the *Topology Manager*. The Topology Manager uses an OSPF variant to find paths to other nodes, passes this information to DPRS and VNS, and builds a database that is accessed by PORS.

Any large networking system needs to be hierarchical, and the Passport is no exception. It can establish a two-level hierarchy of up to 126 topology regions, each of which can have up to 1000 Passport nodes.

DPRS sets up permanent or switched virtual circuits for Frame Relay, IBM protocols, X.25, and other user protocols. It provides both PVCs and SVCs, in the flavors of *full-weight* and *light-weight*. A full-weight VC is a guaranteed service in the ATM sense, but also does end-to-end acknowledgement for error control. This is appropriate for replacing error-intolerant networks for IBM services and is also used to interconnect Nortel switches.

The Topology Manager creates link groups of multiple physical paths. Multipath traffic balancing creates paths through different link groups between source and destination, whereas the multilink facility shares traffic among multiple physical paths inside a single link group.

At each Passport hop, the packet is forwarded based on using routing tables built by DPRS. DPRS can pick a best route or both loadspread or loadshare across multiple paths. Loadspreading can either be multipath or multilink, whereas loadsharing is always multilink. The significant point to consider about DPRS in the context of this chapter is that it presents a Layer 2 switched interface to end hosts, but internally uses Layer 3 routing. This is a perfectly reasonable approach, and it helps you, the reader, understand that real-world systems need not explicitly be Layer 2 or Layer 3.

In contrast with DPRS, Nortel PORS is internally Layer 2 switched. One of the advantages of PORS is that it can run over non-ATM trunking, which can be the dominant transmission type in an older or smaller network. PORS can run over ATM trunks when they are available.

PORS is intended for connection-oriented end services, such as dedicated data lines, voice, and AAL1 CES.

The administrator manually defines the trunks in the network. The view of trunks comes from the proprietary OSPF-based routing protocol used internally. Again, here is an example of mixed Layer 2 and Layer 3 technology— Layer 3 dynamic routing is used to discover potential trunks over which PORS can be configured. When administering trunks, you set cost, bandwidth, and delay attributes of the trunks. Subsequently, PORS selects paths based on cost and delay values when it sets up virtual circuits.

Cisco/Stratacom

Stratacom introduced a proprietary cell relay format in 1986, long before the development of ATM. As ATM developed, Stratacom added ATM routing.

Before ATM, however, Stratacom had routing mechanisms including the Credit Manager and ForeSight.

Stratacom topological concepts include two types of Frame Relay connections between the same two nodes. *Bundles* are circuits that run on the same Frame Relay card, and *grouped connections* are sets of up to 16 virtual circuits that can be on any card in a node. These are aggregation concepts, because they are treated as a single physical circuit within the node's logic. Without bundling or grouping, a node is limited to 252 virtual circuits. By grouping up to 16 circuits in up to 255 groups, a node can support up to 1024 circuits.

Path Determination

The system maintains a model of the network topology and the traffic on it. It tracks the number and type of all connections on each trunk and the utilization limits for trunks. Utilization defaults to 40% for voice trunks with silence suppression and 100% for Frame Relay.

When a connection is created, the calling node determines the bandwidth requirement. Delay is not explicitly specified, but trunks can be marked terrestrial or satellite, and the routing search can be restricted to terrestrial-only.

The intention is to load balance on a per-connection basis.

If a specific route has been specified, the routing mechanism attempts to use it. If the directed route cannot be satisfied, the connection is cleared.

If there is no preferred route, the list of available trunks directly connected to the node is searched; as soon as a trunk is found that has adequate bandwidth and the destination is at the other end of that trunk, the search is terminated and the call is routed through that trunk. If no directly connected trunk terminates at the destination, the search is widened to see if the destination is reachable by any node that is two hops away. There must be a trunk to the two-hop node to the master, originating node, which has sufficient bandwidth for the connection requirement.

If the destination is not connected to a node two hops away, the search is expanded, one hop at a time, until the destination is reached or it is determined the destination is unreachable.

After a connection is set up, it is not rerouted unless the trunk or other component fails, the reserve bandwidth on the trunk is exhausted, or the connection has been preempted by a higher-priority connection.

Traffic Management

Traffic is categorized into the following:

- Bursty A

- Bursty B

- Non-timestamped

- Timestamped

- Voice

- High priority

The Credit Manager is always present, as opposed to ForeSight, which is activated when required. It allows a short burst to be sent from any queue, up to a limit of *credits* given to the by the Credit Manager, which allocates credits at a rate associated with the Frame Relay CIR. Short bursts are intended to fit within the credit, but after credits are spent, no more than the CIR can be sent.

Different credit types are defined for voice, timestamped, and non-timestamped traffic.

Frame Relay Interworking

Frame Relay is a midrange technology, less expensive than ATM but more expensive than analog and ISDN demand circuits. As a consequence, interworking that complements Frame Relay has emerged: ISDN access as a lower-cost way to access Frame Relay, and Frame Relay as a lower-cost way to access ATM.

ISDN Access to Frame Relay

ISDN is a potentially lower-cost way to access Frame Relay services than using the usual dedicated local access line. Most commonly, Frame Relay over ISDN is seen outside North America, in areas where dedicated local loops are prohibitively expensive at low speed. Indeed, in some of those locations, the ISDN connection is kept up permanently, rather than being billed on a time-of-connection basis.

On a worldwide basis, however, Frame Relay over ISDN has the potential of offering switched backup to dedicated Frame Relay. If the Frame Relay end equipment and the carrier both support the A bit signal in the LMI signaling to notify that a PVC has gone down, the ISDN backup can trigger to restore the virtual circuit.

Frame Relay to ATM

Frame Relay was originated as a means of low- to medium-speed access to broadband ISDN. Broadband ISDN has never come into wide use, but essentially was a user interface to ATM. Today, Frame Relay is a means of connecting to ATM backbones. Specifications for such connections come from the Frame Relay Forum, which prescribes two modes of Frame Relay to ATM interworking.

FRF.5 describes network interworking, which connects two Frame Relay end devices over an ATM backbone. The end devices are unaware of the ATM backbone; the Frame Relay service provider does the mapping from Frame Relay to ATM.

In FRF.8, the Frame Relay Forum specifies service internetworking, which allows native Frame Relay end devices to connect to ATM, running the Frame Relay service over an ATM virtual circuit. Service interworking need not be at both ends of the virtual circuit, so it is entirely plausible to connect spoke devices to native Frame Relay, but to bring their PVCs into a data center over an ATM access facility.

Looking Ahead

In this chapter, we have looked at one of the two major strategies for switching—connection-oriented switching at OSI Layers 1 and 2. In Chapter 10, we will look at the other Layer 2 alternative—connectionless switching.

Chapters 11 and 12 examine the current best practice and routing, whereas Part V, Chapters 13 and 14, looks at evolving hybrids between routing and switching.

CHAPTER 10

Connectionless LAN Switching

Don't cross that bridge until you come to it.
—Folk saying

Beginning of the teaching for life/The instructions for well-being…Knowing
how to answer one who speaks/To reply to one who sends a message.
—Amenemope

The good things in life are not to be had singly, but come to us with
a mixture; like a schoolboy's holiday, with a task at the end of it.
—Charles Lamb

Chapter 9 deals with forwarding devices that make decisions based on Layer 2 information. This chapter also deals with Layer 2 forwarding, but uses a connectionless model that does not require circuit setup before communicating.

Layer 1 repeaters—that is, and/or hubs—present end hosts with shared bandwidth and broadcast domains. Traditional bridges reduce the sharing of bandwidth, but still present a shared broadcast domain. Switches largely can eliminate sharing of bandwidth. Although bridges and switches are connectionless, they can be joined either with connectionless or connection-oriented media.

In this chapter, we deal with LAN switches, which are sometimes likened to bridges on steroids. There is an assortment of marketing terms, such as *Layer 3 switch*, *IP switch*, and *multilayer switch* that really are not pure Layer 2 switches in the sense used in this chapter. Such enhanced switches are really distributed routers, with a Layer 3 path determination function in one device and Layer 3 forwarding in one or more forwarding engines. Layer 3 switches are discussed in the next chapter, the focus of which is routing. Evolving techniques that mix Layer 2 and Layer 3 forwarding are discussed in Chapter 13.

> **Note**
>
> *Don't fall into the trap of calling everything a switch, (some vendors avoid using the term* router *because of a perception that routers are slow). If it quacks using Layer 3 information, if it swims using Layer 3 information, and you configure it with Layer 3 information, it's a duck…I mean, a* router.
>
> *A Layer 3 switch does routing functions, but there often is an implication that actual forwarding is hardware assisted.*

To return to the tradition of bridging and Layer 2 switching, see Figure 10.1.

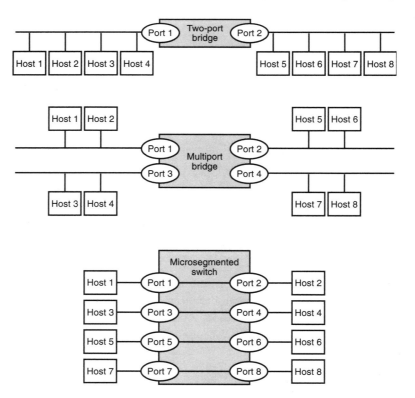

FIGURE 10.1 *Two-port bridges improve bandwidth availability; multiport bridges improve bandwidth with better scalability; and microsegmented switches minimize contention for bandwidth.*

Traditional bridges began as two-port devices that *segmented* two bandwidth domains. Bridges evolved to a learning model, where they could also reduce traffic by keeping traffic that was local to a segment from propagating beyond that segment. Learning involved creating a table—a *station cache*—of source MAC addresses and the bridge interface on which they were first seen.

Note

There is a certain moment when you really feel adult: when you realize you are sounding just like your mother or father. For years, there has been a trend to replace bridges with routers. There are now arguments to replace routers with evolved bridges, which, so they sound like something new, we tend to call switches. In reality, modern networks should be a mixture of Layer 2 and Layer 3 devices. All have their roles.

Layer 2 functions, such as VLANs and microsegmentation, allow control not previously available in bridges. Nevertheless, that Layer 3 devices do some things better, such as complex topologies and bandwidth management.

Just as in Chapter 9, we examine Layer 1 devices, but in this case, we examine hubs—that is, multiport repeaters—used on LANs. Although the emphasis of the chapter is on Layer 2 techniques, there are some niches where hubs still are an appropriate technology. In addition, hubs are extremely common in current networks, and they might be doing a perfectly good job and not need to be replaced.

The Role of Hubs

Hubs are Layer 1 devices that can overlap Layer 2 devices. Commercial switches often include multiport Layer 1 repeater (hub) functions. In general, however, the role of hubs is decreasing as the cost of switches continues to drop. Sometimes, though, using hubs remains a reasonable choice.

To borrow an analogy from construction, it's far more likely that you will remodel operational networks than build networks that have never before existed. In those operational networks, another construction analogy applies, the First Law of Plumbing: "If it don't leak, doesn't fix it."

And so it is with 10-Mbps hubs: If some users are now connected to them and are not having performance problems, and if you don't foresee significant traffic growth for these users, they don't leak. Replace them only if you need better management capabilities.

Even dumb, or non-SNMP manageable, hubs can have basic diagnostics. In my home office, I use such a hub, which still has useful indicator lights. I don't need remote management for a hub that rests on top of my monitor. Admittedly, some techniques for home office debugging do have subtleties: If I note that a connection light has gone out, I might tug on the cable to see if it has become loose. On occasion, the cable pulls back at me, and I discover my feline assistant, Clifford, is under the table playing with the other end. Mouse problems are common in large and small offices, but cat problems are more rare in giant enterprises.

Note

When you use desktop connectivity products, whether hubs, small switches, or access routers, consider some technologies that can be important for reliability. Velcro is one of them, in that it can prevent small devices from being knocked off desks. Although modular cables snap into place, the power cords of most small devices usually have sliding fits and easily can come loose. Duct tape has its role in anchoring power cords!

Velcro appears to be a stiff cloth tape that sticks to other Velcro. More specifically, it comes as two pieces or tapes, each with an adhesive backing, and a front with either hook or eye material that sticks to its counterpart, but can be pulled away. Think of Velcro as a distributed zipper.

The cost difference between 10- and 100-Mbps NICs is minimal. There also might be a role for 100-Mbps hubs. 100-Mbps hubs might give better cost performance than 10-Mbps switches when any of the following conditions are present:

- All stations go to a single server
- User traffic load is bursty
- There are relatively long times between client requests
- There is a large volume of requests/responses

A good application for a fast hub might be a group of graphic artists who occasionally upload and download files from a single server, but do this infrequently.

Switches tend to be more effective than hubs when there are multiple servers. Of course, 100-Mbps switches are higher in performance than 100-Mbps hubs. When the traffic pattern fits the performance envelope of 100-Mbps hubs, however, the fast hubs can outperform 10-Mbps switches.

Bridges and Multiport Bridges

Traditional two-port bridges evolved to multiport bridges. In a multiport bridge, the station cache knows the interfaces where source addresses live and knows more than two such interfaces. Given that the internal forwarding fabric of a bridge is inside its chassis and can use faster media than would be economical on a LAN, the bridge can send an incoming frame to an outgoing interface faster than the frame could be sent across the LAN medium.

End hosts do not know they are going through a switching fabric. Fast switching fabrics are wonderful examples of the constructive untruths in networking, as opposed to the sadly more common sales untruths. These fabrics allow the end hosts to be fooled, but in the best interest of your network.

> **Note**
>
> *Examples in this chapter illustrate the speed benefits of various technologies, but do use some simplified statistical assumptions. In the examples, frames are assumed to arrive at a uniform rate. In reality, frame interarrival rates follow an exponential or fractal distribution function.*
>
> *The statistical simplifications illustrate the principles involved, but might not represent the actual numbers you would see on a real switch.*

How does a fast fabric give the illusion of instantaneous transfer among several ports? A full-length 802.3 frame, on the medium, has an 8-byte preamble and 1518 bytes of Layer 2 information. This takes approximately 1200 microseconds to transmit at 10 Mbps. There is a mandatory inter-frame gap of 9.6 microseconds, so after a frame begins to enter a port, a new frame cannot arrive for 1210 microseconds. *Wire-speed forwarding* means you can forward full-length frames in less than 1210 microseconds.

If the internal speed of the fabric is 1 Gbps, the fabric can forward the 1518 bytes of Layer 2 information—the preamble is not needed after the frame begins to arrive in the port—in 12 microseconds. In a high-performance switch, destination address lookup is done in hardware and adds very little delay.

Refer to the 8-port switch in Figure 10.1. Assume that the ports are half-duplex and each input port sends to a unique output port. If the bridge can deliver a frame from Port 1 to Port 2 in fewer than 1200 microseconds, the switch gives the illusion that it is not present.

With a 1 Gbps fabric, the bridge sends the frame between ports in 12 microseconds. The output port actually forwards the frame onto the medium, which should be easy to do at wire speed. Now that the switching fabric has delivered the frame, the fabric knows that Port 1 cannot have another frame ready for 1188 microseconds. If there were no other ports, the fabric could bask in the warmth of its power supply, working on its suntan for over a millisecond.

But our fabric is afflicted with the work ethic, and, after sending the frame from Port 1, it moves on to check Port 3. Aha! Another frame to send! The fabric spends 12 microseconds to forward the frame to Port 4, leaving 1176 microseconds before Port 1 again needs to be checked.

Readers who are football fans will see that the fabric operates much as a quarterback does in a no-huddle offense in the last two minutes of a game, grinding out plays with minimal delay. Perhaps with a grunt, the fabric now moves to Port 5 and sends its frame to Port 6. There remain 1164 microseconds before Port 1 can need service. The fabric now can move to Port 7 and send a frame to Port 8.

Now, the fabric can relax for a leisurely 1152 microseconds. Think of a juggler who keeps five balls moving. At most, only two balls are being touched at any given instant; the remaining balls are in the air. A multiport bridge is a juggler of frames.

But what if the frames are short and arrive faster? A minimum length 802.3 frame has 8 bytes of preamble, 14 bytes of header, 64 bytes of data, and 4 bytes of frame checking information, for a total of 90 bytes. At 10 Mbps, it takes approximately 72 microseconds to transmit this frame at wire speed. Add the 9.6 microseconds of inter-frame delay, and you have approximately 82 microseconds between frames.

The fabric can transfer a minimum-length frame—remember that the preamble does not need to be transferred—in approximately 0.66 microseconds. There are still about 81 microseconds before Port 1 can possibly have another frame ready for forwarding. If the fabric now has to service a maximum length frame on Ports 3, 5, and 7, the fabric still has 45 microseconds left before Port 1 can need service, plenty of time left to take several sips of Layer 2 coffee.

Not all bridges, of course, have 1 Gbps fabrics. But speeds of hundreds of megabits are common. Not all ports of a bridge have the maximum loads described in these examples.

Campus Traffic Aggregation

In fashion, the length of ladies' skirts varies through cycles. There have been frequent attempts to correlate hemlines with various phenomena, such as stock prices. The fundamental fallacy of that particular correlation was demonstrated in the 1970s, when skirts could physically get no shorter, but the stock market continued to rise [Malkiel, 1996].

Nevertheless, the idea of fashion is an important one in many fields. In information technology, there are fashions in the physical location of servers. We began with centralized mainframes, distributed functions to departmental minicomputers, exploded to the desktop, and have been returning to centralized campus server rooms. Much of the popularity of server rooms lies in the capability to have them in more secure locations, both from the perspective of physical access control as well as support mechanisms, such as redundant power and air conditioning.

For many years, the *80/20 rule* was the byword of distributed computing: 80% of processing should stay local, and 20% go to a remote site. In modern campus networks, however, that ratio often reverses: 80% or more of the computing is done in the server room.

In my experience, much of the effort involved in the moves and changes that affect the network has to do with server placement, more than moving users. Very frequently, end users might move to other cubicles, but their computers might not go with them, or at least the wall plate from the computer to the wiring closet is not recabled.

With the movement to centralized server farms, often on a different floor or in a different building of a campus, there is an increasing need for large amounts of bandwidth between user and server locations.

When compared to classical Layer 1 hubs, bridges and switches have a major advantage for campuses. Their ports need not be at the same speed. User workstations can connect at 10 Mbps, whereas servers can connect to the same switch at 100 Mbps or faster. The configuration on the left side of Figure 10.2 shows how different speeds can be configured on a single switch. The configuration in the center shows how machines in different groups can have different speeds. The configuration on the right reminds you that high speed to local caches is desirable, but high speed connections to a WAN router rarely add value, because the router is limited by the speed of the WAN.

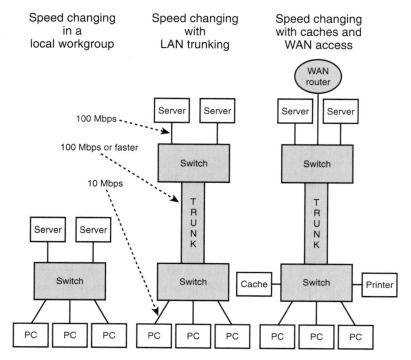

FIGURE 10.2 *There are many applications of the speed-changing capability of switches when connecting to servers and to other switches.*

Even more important in campuses, switches can interconnect to one another at speeds greater than any of their user ports. High-speed inter-switch trunking is shown in the center of Figure 10.2. Inter-switch trunking can be implemented with fiber optics, giving increased cabling range. It can use even higher-speed facilities, such as Gigabit Ethernet.

Techniques described later in this chapter allow you to inverse multiplex several physical facilities into one load-shared, resilient trunk. This ability lets you put expensive high-bandwidth facilities in wiring closets or a building communications room and lets users share the facility capacity.

As I mentioned, fashions change over time. Today's fashion backs slightly away from the 20/80 model that was the fashion that briefly replaced the traditional 80/20, using application caching to develop a model that might be 20/20/40/20: 20% on the workstation, 20% on local cache servers, 40% in the server farm, and 20% on facilities reached through a WAN.

The right part of Figure 10.2 shows how you can use a system of switches to optimize access both to local servers and servers in the central room. Users have fast paths through their local switch to the printer and an application cache, but go through the switched trunk to reach the server room.

Figure 10.2 shows homogeneous switching systems with a common broadcast domain among all devices. As we will see later in this chapter, virtual LANs (VLANs) allow multiple user communities of interest to share common trunk facilities.

Switches: The Next Evolution of Bridging

Traditional two-port bridges reduced medium contention for two media. Each of these media forms what is variously called a *segment, bandwidth domain,* or a *collision domain.* I prefer the term *bandwidth domain* because collisions do not occur on Token Ring or FDDI. In addition, the term *bandwidth domain* recognizes that collisions are not the only factor that limits bandwidth, even on an Ethernet. Well-behaved hosts defer their transmission when they sense traffic on the medium, avoiding a collision but again reducing bandwidth.

Where two-port bridges split a LAN into two segments, each of which can be shared among several devices but in a smaller-bandwidth domain, switches evolved to a model where each device was in its own bandwidth domain. Putting each host in a separate bandwidth domain is called *microsegmentation.* Even when this is done, there still might be restrictions on the availability unless the switched medium is full-duplex.

Being in its own bandwidth domain does not totally free a station to transmit whenever it desires to do so, unless its interface is full-duplex. When the port is half-duplex, a client still has to wait for bandwidth while its server is sending its response.

Half-duplex operation is one of the fallacies of the glib "switches guarantee bandwidth" heard so often in the trade press and in sales presentations. It is true that switches guarantee bandwidth not affected by other peers attempting to send in the same direction at the same time.

The earlier example of how a bridge gives the illusion of not being there really used a model of a switch, because only one device was on each port. If this model were of a more traditional bridge, the devices sharing each bridge port would have to wait for other devices' traffic and/or collisions.

So bridges reduce contention for bandwidth by reducing the size of collision domains, whereas ideal switches are evolved bridges that reduce contention even further by putting each device in its own bandwidth domain.

Another glib marketing concept is that switches are inherently faster than routers. This simply is not true; there are many routers that are faster than workgroup switches. The situation becomes even more confused with marketing terms, such as multilayer switching or Layer 3 switching, which, if they mean anything, mean that the Layer 3 packet forwarding process is moved to one or more hardware-assisted forwarding engines.

Limitations of Bridges and Switches

Switches provide bandwidth at lower cost than routers, but without the flexibility of routing. They also have potential scaling problems, principally caused by the following:

- Spanning tree issues, such as the inability to forward while the tree is being recomputed

- Unknown MAC address flooding for unicast frames

- Broadcast and multicast flooding

If your network were no more complicated than a single switch chassis that interconnected a few hosts with two servers, your switching design would be simple. As a network designer, you can be more comfortable in knowing that most real-world designs are more complex and more challenging. As with any other network, the only way for it to be scalable is to introduce hierarchy. Figure 10.3 shows some hierarchical levels typical of pure switched networks. The hierarchy has bandwidth at the lowest level and broadcast at the next level. These two levels actually affect traffic flow.

In large campus networks, however, you must consider the additional hierarchical level of the management domain. Depending on the vendor, you might be limited to hundreds or thousands of VLANs per management station. This is not a practical limit for most enterprises, but you should bear it in mind, especially if you plan on having a central network management center for multiple campuses.

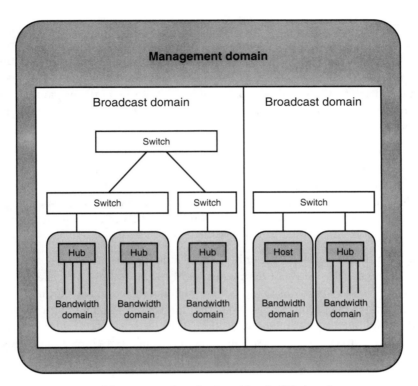

FIGURE 10.3 *Management, broadcast, and bandwidth domains.*

Issues Associated with the Spanning Tree

We first talked of the spanning tree mechanism in Chapter 2. Remember that it is less a process of specifying where to forward than of specifying where not to forward. It is principally a technology to avoid loop formation, and avoiding loops is more important than forwarding speed. During the period when the spanning tree is being recomputed, no frames can be forwarded.

The spanning tree algorithm operates, in a system of multiple bridges, to put certain bridge ports into a blocking state. When a port is in the blocking state, a bridge will not forward to it. Blocking does not mean, however, that devices on the medium associated with the blocked port are isolated. Blocking simply means that the blocked bridge does not forward onto that medium, but the spanning tree algorithm ensures some other bridge is responsible for doing so.

As part of the process in which a bridge learns about other bridges, the spanning tree algorithm might block some of the bridge's ports, because forwarding onto them would cause a loop. When a bridge receives a frame whose destination address is not in the current station address table, the bridge copies that frame and sends it out all of its ports that are not blocked by the spanning tree algorithm. It still floods the frame out locally connected ports on which there are no other active bridges.

The spanning tree algorithm first causes a root bridge to be elected. From the perspective of this algorithm, only one path can be active between any two bridges. Some vendors provide proprietary extensions that allow parallel physical links between pairs of bridges to be treated as one path by the spanning tree algorithm. See the section "Inverse Multiplexed Parallel Paths" later in this chapter.

Inverse multiplexing is not the only useful vendor extension to the spanning tree. (Perhaps *extension* is not the perfect word, because some very useful features involve selectively disabling parts of the more general algorithm.) Figure 10.4 illustrates the problem that some other modifications solve. With a standard spanning tree, a complete re-election of the root has to take place before the backup path can be used. Although the root is being re-elected, a process that takes at least 30 seconds, no frames can be forwarded.

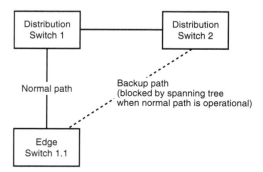

FIGURE 10.4 *For the edge switch to find the alternate path, you must either wait a significant time for the spanning tree algorithm to draw a new map or use vendor-specific variations on the algorithm.*

It's worth noting that routers, as opposed to Layer 2 bridges and switches, do not stop all forwarding when they are recomputing their routing tables. They might discard packets intended for specific yet unreachable destinations while a new path to that destination is being found. Also, recomputing the routing table can cause a high-speed cache or forwarding information base to be invalidated, so the forwarding speed of the router can drop during reconvergence.

For more detail on spanning tree special cases, see the section "Minimizing Delays for Finding Alternate Next-Level Switches" later in this chapter.

Minimizing Delays for Initial Host Connectivity

When you connect a host to an edge port of a switch, if that port strictly follows 802.1D, there is a delay of about 30 seconds before the host can start forwarding traffic through the port. During this time, the port is acting like a royal investigator in *Cinderella*, wondering if the newly connected device has a foot that fits the glass slipper. In this metaphor, the port hopes that the new device is eligible to become root bridge, replacing the existing one.

Alas, few hosts are called to be the root. Although the switch administrator might be considered one of the evil stepsisters to do so, it can be very good practice to configure edge ports so that the glass slipper is never tried on the arriving hosts. In less fanciful terms, if you know that a port will be used only for end hosts, you can prevent the delay of the port searching for a bridge that simply will never be present on a port. You can either disable the spanning tree algorithm on that port or enable it in a modified way that causes the delay for root searches to be skipped.

Root election is not the only reason for initial delays when connecting, although it makes a much better metaphor. There is an assumption in IEEE 802.1D that isn't unreasonable for bridges connecting shared media segments, but isn't really needed on microsegmented switch ports.

That assumption is that it is highly desirable for a port to enter the listening state at first, so it has the maximum possible knowledge of MAC addresses that are local and should not be forwarded. If you are microsegmenting, there is only one address per port, so the idea of blocking the forwarding of traffic destined to local destinations is irrelevant. In a microsegmented switch, every frame at least needs to enter the local switch.

Skipping the learning state in the spanning tree algorithm is perfectly reasonable for microsegmented switch ports. You do need to be careful, when disabling root election or local address learning, that your end users will never install a hub or bridge at their end of the port cable. In real life, users do such things as install hubs when they are out of ports on star-wired wall plates that connect them to the wiring closet. I'm not suggesting that this will be catastrophic, but it does mean, for example, that local address destination filtering will not be enabled, at first, on the now-shared segment. The switch should eventually learn about these addresses and begin blocking them.

Issues of Unknown MAC Address Flooding

Spanning tree algorithm information about the tree structure is not the only factor in decisions on where to forward frames. Bridges also learn what MAC addresses are present on which media.

Keeping traffic for local destinations on a segment, and flooding to all segments, are the extreme cases. Forwarding to a specific segment does not waste bandwidth.

Another issue in LAN switching is the degree to which bridges propagate unicast frames whose destinations are not yet known. When a single bridge, unconnected to any other bridges, receives a frame whose address does not appear in its station address table, it copies that frame and floods it out all its ports. This process, called *unknown MAC address flooding*, can have a significant performance impact on a bridge with a large number of ports. The more unblocked ports, the more frames that must be copied.

If the switch has not yet learned where Host 9 is connected, a frame generated by Host 1 has to flood onto Ports 2, 3, and 4. That flooded frame occupies bandwidth on the segments associated with Ports 2, 3, and 4, but hosts (other than Host 9) on those receiving segments do not experience CPU interrupts from the flooded frame because it is a unicast not addressed to them. In addition to the bandwidth consumed on the segments that receive the frame destined for Host 9, the bridge has to copy the frame to flood it. Although high-performance bridges might have hardware to assist in copying, if the same processor is responsible for both copying and flooding, frames with unknown unicast destinations can affect the forwarding capacity of the bridge.

Switches microsegment to reduce competition for bandwidth. Although microsegmented switches still avoid collisions, unknown address flooding defeats the capability of microsegmentation to improve port-level bandwidth utilization. In an ideal microsegmented environment, a host connected to a port sees only those unicasts intended for that host. On that port, the only bandwidth consumed is for those desired unicasts. With unknown address flooding, the available bandwidth is reduced by the volume of unicasts whose destination is not known, and which must be flooded onto ports.

Keep in mind that flooding of unicast frames whose destinations are unknown can have as much impact on bandwidth as non-unicast frame flooding. Non-unicast frames, however, can impose additional workload on hosts and can increase the workload on bridges/switches.

Also realize that a bridge might not know the destination of a unicast frame for two reasons. The most basic reason is that it is a host that has just been connected. A less obvious reason, however, is that there might be too many MAC addresses to be held in the bridge station cache. Typically, if there are too many addresses for the cache, the least recently used are discarded and need to be relearned.

In early bridges, caches could be quite small. I remember old bridges that had only 64 memory slots for MAC addresses. The basic MAC address table size when running bridging on a Cisco router holds 300 entries, although the software allocates additional 300-entry tables when needed.

More modern bridges have much larger tables, but cache size can become a problem especially when upgrading your network. Bay switches dedicate a 1024 slot memory to each port. Cisco switches have a single cache per chassis, ranging from 1K to 16K slots.

If you are converting from a badly engineered bridged network that has more than 1024 active devices, the Bay cache can overflow and the excess addresses flood. Cisco's solution, however, can have problems as well. If you put 48 ports into a switch and assign each port to a different LAN, 16384/48 would give you approximately 341 MAC addresses per LAN, with even distribution. Although an excess of 250 addresses per LAN should often be viewed with caution, you could easily create a situation where you overrun the shared cache on a large Cisco switch. There is no perfect solution. With both Bay and Cisco designs, you need to be aware of how many MAC addresses you have and on which spanning trees and physical ports they appear.

Helping the cache sizing problem, and confusing it, is that not all MAC addresses are likely to be active at once. Nevertheless, it is far more likely that most MAC addresses on a campus will be active at once than in a routed WAN network where you might be able to take advantage of time zone variations.

Issues of Broadcast and Multicast Flooding

In principle, individual spanning trees, whether defined physically or with VLANs, represent single broadcast domains. Broadcasts and multicasts propagate throughout a broadcast domain, which can have negative effects on host performance. An assortment of vendor extensions is available to help control broadcasts.

When hosts use workgroup protocols, such as those of Apple, NetBIOS, and Novell, there historically has been a high volume of non-unicast packets generated for the process of clients and servers finding one another. These protocol families were developed for relatively small networks—low hundreds of devices—in an all-LAN environment in which bandwidth was essentially free. IP hosts, with significant exceptions, tend to generate far fewer numbers of non-multicast frames. Well-behaved IP workstations do initial broadcasts to get their addresses and other parameters from DHCP servers and then query DNS servers to find the IP addresses for specific hosts. After those host addresses are found, however, the workstation issues an ARP request broadcast, caching the response. ARP caches do have a lifetime after which entries need to be refreshed with new broadcasts.

Newer workgroup protocols, such as Novell 4.x protocols, are moving to a directory model similar to the one used by IP. Such a model greatly reduces bandwidth requirements. Nevertheless, the industry trend is to move to native IP support. Novell NetWare 5.x and Microsoft Windows 2000 are IP native.

A common assumption in the industry is that "broadcasts take up lots of bandwidth." Like many such assumptions, this one is oversimplified. Non-unicast frames—multicasts or broadcasts—take up exactly the same amount of bandwidth on a medium as does a unicast frame. Where non-unicast frames affect bandwidth is in a broadcast domain that is segmented or microsegmented, because the frame needs to be copied onto each segment. Unicast frames for which there is no destination in the station cache also need to be flooded onto each medium. So, the original common assumption might be rephrased as "unicast frames with known destinations only consume bandwidth on source, transit, and destination segments."

Aside from the bandwidth they consume, broadcast and multicast frames also can have a direct and negative effect on hosts. Hosts suffer from broadcasts and multicasts in two ways. The better-known way occurs when broadcasts replicate through broadcast storms, sloppy host implementations, and so on, and simply occupy a great deal of bandwidth.

The lesser-known effect is the interrupt load presented to hosts by broadcasts and sometimes multicasts. Cisco calls this broadcast radiation and considers it a matter of concern. Other vendors, such as Cabletron, consider it much less of a problem as CPUs become faster. The key question, of course, is whether increases in CPU speed mean more broadcasts will be generated per unit of time.

Broadcast traffic can be a load on CPUs more because of the interrupt load it produces, rather than the pure bandwidth it takes up. The effect of interrupt load depends on the following:

- CPU power

- Current CPU load

- NIC/driver differentiation between multicasts and broadcasts, when both are present

Broadcasts must be processed by every host that receives them, and, depending on the NIC and driver implementation, multicasts might also need processing by every host. In a sufficiently large broadcast domain, or where one or more hosts generate an inordinate amount of broadcasts (a *broadcast storm*) in response to a real or perceived error, non-unicast processing can consume significant host resources. Broadcast storms can consume enough resources to cause some hosts to crash or to degrade their performance to unacceptable levels. Switch vendors do not agree on the impact of broadcasts on hosts. Cisco cites tests of a Sparcstation 2 with SunOS 4.1.3 (without the multicast kernel), on which 100 broadcasts per second imposed 3% CPU load, 1000 broadcasts per second caused a 25% load, and 3800 broadcasts per second caused the host to crash [Cisco CID]. Sparcstation 2s are relatively old and slow machines, but the principle holds: An excessive number of broadcasts can have significant CPU impact depending on CPU power.

In an excellent white paper dealing with many aspects of capacity, Cabletron points out that more modern hosts have faster processors that can handle higher rates of broadcasts [Cabletron, 1999]. I agree with this premise, but I also observe that more modern hosts can *generate* greater numbers of broadcasts with a result of correspondingly heavier loads.

A 10-Mbps Ethernet can transfer roughly 14,000 short frames per second, and broadcasts are mostly short frames. If a new host is connected to a 10-Mbps port and is 10 times faster than the Sparcstation 2 that crashed at 3800 frames per second, the port cannot generate enough frames to cause a hypothetical failure at 38,000 frames per second. The 1000 broadcast per second load on a faster processor might result in more of a 2% additional load, which probably is insignificant.

What if that same host is connected to a 100-Mbps Fast Ethernet port, which can deliver 140,000 short frames per second? Making generous assumptions, that faster port is quite capable of transferring enough broadcasts to crash the workstation. Faster devices connected elsewhere might be able to generate that amount of traffic during an error condition.

So, more modern workstations connected to 10-Mbps switched ports might be immune to crashes due to broadcast storms and might suffer minimal performance degradation. Workstations and servers connected to faster media, however, might still be susceptible to severe problems induced by broadcast storms. Motivations remain to control broadcasting.

Several vendors have proprietary schemes for intelligent control of multicasting in a single broadcast domain. These schemes mirror the function of the Internet Group Management Protocol (IGMP) at Layer 3. IGMP allows hosts to enter and leave multicast groups.

IGMP informs routers that individual hosts, potentially on different subnets, want to be in a multicast group that can span multiple routers. IGMP information flows directly from end host to edge routers. The edge routers use multicast routing protocols, not IGMP, to communicate this information across the routed network.

In the real world of networking, end hosts still issue Layer 3 IGMP **JOIN** commands. When the IGMP receiver sees them, however, it can send back a CGMP (or other vendor equivalent) command back to the switch port to which the end host is connected, telling it to listen to the multicast MAC address that corresponds to the group joined with IGMP.

Protocols to establish membership in Layer 2 multicast groups have been introduced as vendor specific. The IEEE 802 committee is developing a mechanism for controlling the propagation of multicasts, the GARP Attribute Registration Protocol (GMRP). If your switch permits it, you can block traffic to specific multicast addresses at individual ports.

The significant operational issue with multicast management on switches is the administrative workload. Early vendor protocols needed a specific list of MAC addresses to include in a multicast group. Later mechanisms allowed dynamic joining and leaving groups.

Other methods, such as Cisco's Cisco Group Management Protocol (CGMP), also called *IGMP Snooping*, actually mix Layer 2 and Layer 3 functionality. I had trouble understanding, at first, how these methods worked, until I came up with an analogy.

For example, assume you are planning a long weekend in front of a TV set, flipping from football game to football game. (If this idea appalls you personally, think of someone who *would* do this.) In preparation for the channel flipping, you buy a new, high-end remote controller.

This remote controller has the normal black buttons that let you select an arbitrary channel. It also has a red, blue, and green button that can be programmed to jump immediately to a certain channel.

Pressing the black buttons is equivalent to issuing an IGMP **JOIN** command for an arbitrary multicast group. The programming function that sets the colored buttons to jump directly to a channel—a multicast group—are equivalent to CGMP.

Occasional broadcasts and multicasts are harmless. The danger is the dreaded broadcast storm, the data link layer equivalent of the feedback squeal of an abused public address system.

Large volumes of broadcasts can result from poorly designed protocol stacks, or from outright software failures. There are several ways to protect against the negative effects of non-multicast storms:

- Migrate hosts to use less bandwidth-intensive protocol stacks, such as Microsoft NetBIOS over TCP (NBT) rather than non-routable NetBEUI.

- Per-port filters limit the number of broadcasts that can be sent in a given period.

- Per-port filters restrict the propagation of protocol types especially prone to high broadcast volume. For example, you might localize NetBEUI but allow IP and Apple to pass a filter. With VLANs, you might also direct the Apple and IP traffic to different VLANs, each an independent broadcast domain.

- VLANs reduce the size of broadcasts. If the sales and engineering departments are split into different VLANs, sales broadcasts will not affect engineering and vice versa.

- Separate broadcast domains with routers.

VLANs as an Extension to Basic Switching

Basic bridging reduces contention for shared bandwidth, and microsegmentation is the ultimate in minimizing bandwidth contention. Neither bridging nor switching, however, reduces the load imposed by broadcasts and multicasts.

VLANs, among their other useful properties, do reduce the various loads imposed by broadcasts. These loads include host processor interrupts and bandwidth taken up on switched ports by replicated multicasts.

VLANs extend the basic switching (bridging) model by superimposing a multiplexing model onto connections among bridges/switches. That multiplexing model involves associating ordinary frames arriving at a VLAN-aware switch port with a VLAN identifier. In the VLAN techniques other than ATM LAN emulation (LANE), this identifier is a field added to frames sent over the VLAN-aware ports of the switch. In LANE, the identifier is implicit rather than explicit—the virtual circuit over which frames are sent provides the identification; the frames themselves are unchanged. Figure 10.5 gives an overview of the process of VLAN tagging, in which frames arriving on edge ports are in the native LAN format of that port, such as IEEE 802.3. The tagging process associates VLAN identifiers with the edge frames and delivers tagged frames to VLAN-aware ports. The switch delivers non–VLAN-tagged frames to ports belonging to the appropriate VLAN.

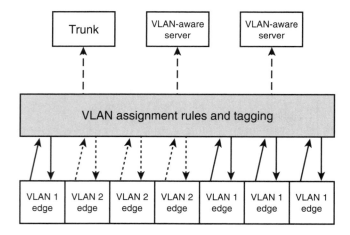

FIGURE 10.5 *The VLAN tagging process.*

VLANs are used primarily in Layer 2 multiplexing, which is invisible to devices at the edge of the VLAN. Think of the basic time-division multiplexing (TDM) techniques introduced in Chapter 9.

Hosts that belong to a VLAN need not attach to the same physical switch. They are closer to the add-and-drop multiplexers shown in Figure 9.10 in Chapter 9, although their trunk interconnections need to follow spanning tree conventions. ATM-based LANE can have more complex interconnection topologies. In the statistical multiplexing extension of TDM, the sum of user interface speeds is greater than the capacity of the trunks interconnecting multiplexers. Statistical TDM, which is the direct ancestor of packet switching and routing, works because not all user interfaces are active at once. Because the user transmissions on the trunk no longer are in a fixed time-slot relationship, statistical TDM must tag the individual user transmissions so they can be assigned to the correct port at the destination.

If you understand statistical TDM, you are well on your way to understanding VLANs. Traffic entering a VLAN switch is tagged with a VLAN identifier. The switch forwards tagged frames to ports on the switch, or on an inter-switch trunk to another switch. At the destination port(s), the VLAN tagging information is stripped and the frame is delivered to the edge port.

VLAN tags are assigned most commonly based on port configuration. They also can be assigned based on filtering criteria. Layer 2 filters are used to control traffic on non-VLAN switched systems. Their use is detailed later in the chapter, in the section "Port Filtering."

VLANs help the three problems of non-unicast flooding, unknown address flooding, and spanning tree instability by separating large connectionless switched environments into multiple virtual switched networks, each a broadcast domain. With VLANs, the scope of the problem is limited to a smaller virtual LAN. Many of these problems are acceptable with hundreds or even a few thousands of devices, but do not scale into the tens of thousands or more. The scaling limit of a VLAN is highly dependent on the upper-layer protocols in use, because it is these protocols that define the rate of broadcasts.

Traffic on one VLAN does not propagate onto other VLANs, thus isolating non-unicast traffic on one VLAN from affecting other VLANs. VLANs thus become an alternative to routers for preventing the propagation of broadcasts. They split the large broadcast domain into multiple smaller ones based on communities of interest.

The original intention of VLANs, in IEEE 802.10, was to provide Layer 2 security. 802.10 creates a header that can contain information necessary to manage encrypted communications at Layer 2. In addition, VLAN tags can be used to direct traffic only to selected ports.

Operational Benefits of VLANs

In operational practice, VLANs have been especially attractive because they can lower the workload in configuration: moves, adds, and changes. Although they legitimately can be helpful here, some vendors have oversold the benefits of VLANs in reducing network management workload. The industry is constantly enhancing the management capabilities of VLANs, and over time VLANs will become more and more significant as *pieces* of the management solution. VLANs alone do not solve the configuration problem, but provide additional capabilities that a management application can make use of.

At present, however, you can trust a VLAN to provide a virtual patch panel, as shown in Figure 10.6, where a software command moves Host 2 to a new VLAN 5 and reassigns Host 5 to VLAN 1. Patch panels allow you to change the cabling relationships between ports. They are commonly found in wiring closets, where patch cables interconnect the cable from an end host's wallplate to a port on the ingress network interconnection device—the first hub, switch, or router port touched by the host.

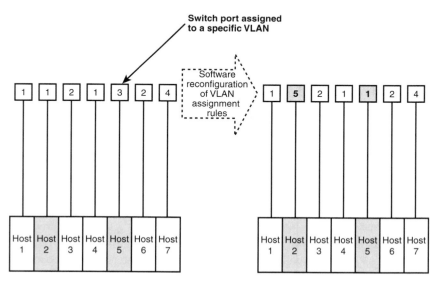

F IGURE 10.6 *A VLAN can act as a virtual patch panel.*

Software commands change port assignment rules, allowing a given device to be moved to a different VLAN, or new VLANs to be created. The operational advantage of such commands is that they can be sent rapidly from a remote location.

VLANs and Traffic Aggregation

Traffic passing through trunk ports is in the VLAN frame format—the first MAC header is that of the delivery protocol. As shown in Figure 10.7, all, some, or none of the ports of a particular switch can be VLAN aware. To have ports dedicated to specific spanning trees, a switch might not need full VLAN support, but simply the capability to assign ports to different spanning trees.

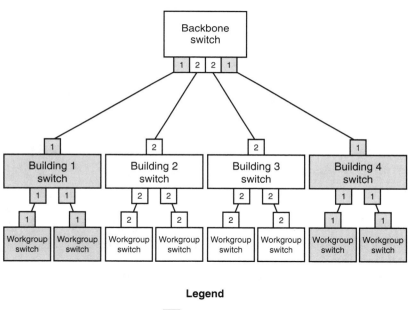

FIGURE 10.7 *Only the backbone switch sees the multiple spanning trees, yet there is a hierarchy in each building.*

Most commonly, trunk ports go to other switches or routers. Increasingly, there is a trend toward having VLAN-aware servers. Applications for VLAN-aware workstations are less common, but do exist.

Chassis Usage

Commercial switch products have different capabilities, depending on their planned usage. The lowest-cost switches have fixed physical configurations and limited memory for address tables. Switches intended for use higher in the hierarchy are increasingly likely to have modular interface cards, increased address memory, and faster internal switching fabrics. Switches tend to be designed for the following hierarchical levels:

- *Campus/data center.* Modular. Can include full ATM cell switching. Needs to know about all MAC addresses.

- *Wiring Closet.* Often modular or stack. Needs to know about MAC addresses in the wiring closet and in its subordinate workgroups.

- *Workgroup.* Usually fixed configuration. Ethernet/Token Ring or perhaps 10/100 speed-sensing Ethernet edge ports. Usually single fixed trunk port. If this is ATM, it will be a LAN emulation client (LEC).

Addressing and management are the factors that define the independence of modules in a chassis. Full multi-chassis topologies are loosely coupled, in the sense that each chassis has an independent management processor. The simplest multi-chassis topologies form a broadcast domain. More complex topologies include VLANs, each a broadcast domain.

A term for one common means of interconnecting chassis is called a *collapsed backbone*. Although this sounds more like an orthopedic emergency than a network design technique, it is quite common and actually is a convenient design. Another term is *backbone-in-a-box*, which most often refers to a single-chassis network. Forgive me if I need to pause here to reflect on who comes up with industry terms such as backbone-in-a-box. Jack the Ripper?

A collapsed backbone is a tree-structured arrangement of chassis, as shown in Figure 10.8. The root of the tree is physically inside the topmost chassis. In the most pure collapsed backbone, either all the root chassis ports are connected to other ports or, in the backbone-in-a-box case, all end hosts connect to the common chassis.

A pure backbone switch connects only to other switches, but a common variant connects central servers to the backbone switch. Figure 10.8 shows such a variant configuration, with servers connected to the switch, and provisions for out-of-band management.

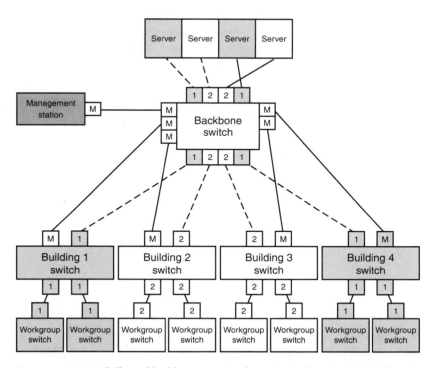

FIGURE 10.8 *Collapsed backbones can involve a single chassis—the backbone-in-a-box—or a tree-structured hierarchy of chassis.*

Out-of-band management involves having separate connections for the management interfaces of managed components, such as switches, and to the management station. You need a management station somewhere in the switched network. In Figure 10.8, management interfaces on workgroup switches are not shown for reasons of clarity. Workgroup switches, however, might actually not have their own management interfaces to lower their cost. In such low-cost configurations, you rely on the management capabilities of the next switch level to diagnose workgroup problems.

The trunks can either all belong to a single broadcast domain or carry VLANs. The switch at the top of the hierarchy does not have any edge ports and is called a *backbone switch*.

Obviously, a collapsed backbone switch is a single point of failure. You can have redundant backbone switches, as shown in Figure 10.9. Keep in mind that the spanning tree algorithm prevents the backup switch from forwarding any traffic, as long as the primary switch is active. If the primary switch fails, there is a pause in forwarding, typically 30–90 seconds, while the spanning tree rebuilds. Vendor-specific modifications to the spanning tree, intended for fast recovery, can drop the cutover time to a few seconds.

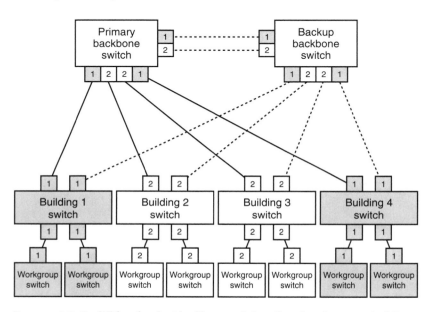

FIGURE 10.9 *With redundant backbone switches, there is only one root of the spanning tree at any given time.*

You might need to work with switch hardware from several vendors. For example, your enterprise might merge with another that owns switches from a vendor different than yours. The first general rule of LAN switch interoperability is there is a good chance of interoperability among devices as long as VLANs are not involved. In Figure 10.4, if the switches for Building 1 and 4 were from one vendor, Buildings 2 and 3 from another, and the backbone switch from a third, interoperability would be likely as long as Buildings 1 and 4 form one 802.1D spanning tree and Buildings 2 and 3 form a different 802.1D spanning tree.

Interoperability refers to the capability of the switches to pass data. It is probable that you will need a separate management station, or at least management function on a common workstation, to configure and monitor each vendor's products.

The IEEE 802.1D protocol used to maintain single spanning trees is relatively likely to interoperate among the chassis of multiple vendors, but VLAN trunking protocols are generally vendor specific. The emerging IEEE 801.1Q protocol is becoming the solution for multivendor interoperability with VLANs.

Even with a multivendor trunking protocol, there still are apt to be vendor-specific extensions and configuration tools. Proprietary trunking protocols might have useful features that are not in 802.1Q, so you might want to keep islands of proprietary protocols and link them with 802.1Q, accepting that some features will not carry across the 802.1Q link. Another issue in mixing trunking protocols is that you might need multiple management applications to make use of vendor-specific features.

Practical wiring considerations affect the distance between edge devices and switches, and between switches (see Table 10.1).

TABLE 10.1   MAXIMUM DISTANCES FOR MEDIA

Medium	Distance
10BaseT	100 meters without repeaters on twisted pair.
FDDI	Tens of kilometers, depending on fiber type.
100BaseTX	100 meters.
100BaseT4	100 meters.
100BaseFX	2000 meters with full-duplex, 412 meters with half-duplex.
ATM	Tens of kilometers between repeaters, depending on the underlying SONET or other physical medium. Using repeaters or new DWDM techniques can extend the distance to thousands of kilometers.

Extended LANs

Extended LANs are Layer 2 systems with a range beyond a single campus. They are flattened alternatives to extending sites with router-based links. LANE can be an extended LAN and, indeed, is probably the preferred technique for extending LANs due to the range possible with ATM trunks. Remember that using ATM trunking, however, does not strictly require LANE. You can run VLAN trunks over ATM virtual circuits.

Extended LANs suffer the same scaling limitations as any other Layer 2 LAN. In addition, speed of light delay might become an issue. The longest-range LANE system with which I have operational experience is a Canadian provincial telecommunications carrier's internal consultant network, which has maximum distances in the low hundreds of kilometers. I find the idea of reliable extended LANs over continental distances to be rather dubious. As a favorite button says, "186,000 miles per second. It's not just a good idea; it's the law." Until the speed of light is repealed, there are physical limits to the size of a broadcast domain where there is any concern with timing. See the section "What Latency Problem Are You Trying to Solve?" later in this chapter.

If campus LANs or VLANs are interconnected by routers, you no longer have an extended LAN. You also might have a more flexible and reliable system, because the routers can deal with more complex topologies than can switches.

For relatively simple topologies, as shown in Figure 10.10, you might use encapsulated bridging between sites. At appreciable speeds, the sort of commercial products that do encapsulated bridging tend to be platforms that can run routing, so there are no cost savings from not using routing. The major motivation for encapsulated bridging is that you need to run non-routable protocols such as DEC Local Area Transport, IBM Logical Link Control type 2, or NetBEUI.

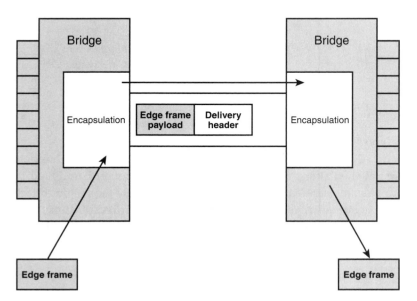

FIGURE 10.10 *Encapsulated or remote bridging simply establishes a virtual bridge between pairs of sites, not a complex tree.*

Figure 10.10 is deliberately drawn in a non-hierarchical manner, as individual encapsulating tunnels are point-to-point. You can build up a hierarchy of them, but the individual tunnels are unaware of their role in a hierarchy. In this figure, the delivery encapsulation is assumed to be another data link protocol, such as FDDI or PPP. Frame Relay and ATM also are used as encapsulating tunnels, with extensions of the delivery protocol that identify the type of the passenger protocol.

Data link protocols are not the only ones used to encapsulate Layer 2 edge protocols. For carrying IBM edge protocols, such as SDLC or LLC-2, it is extremely common to run tunnels over IP networks as well as Layer 2 networks. Although the devices used for such Layer 3 encapsulations usually are branded routers, this application is sufficiently identified with Layer 2 connectivity that it is shown in Figure 10.11. The multivendor technique for such encapsulation is data link switching (DLSW). Cisco's earlier techniques are called remote source-route bridging (RSRB) and serial tunneling (STUN). DLSW always runs over TCP/IP, but RSRB and STUN can run over Layer 2 connectivity as well.

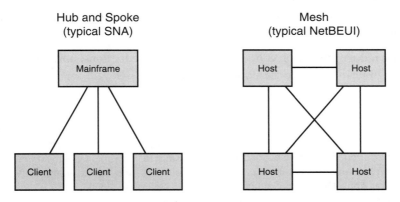

FIGURE 10.11 *When establishing tunnels where data will flow, do not establish full mesh unless the application requires it.*

Figure 10.11 shows two kinds of topological relationships: hub-and-spoke and full mesh. Both are built from point-to-point tunnels. The hub-and-spoke topology is commonly used for client-to-mainframe applications, whereas full mesh is more common for NetBIOS client/server applications. A basic rule in configuring encapsulated bridging is not to define tunnels between hosts where you do not expect data to flow. TCP tunneling is the encapsulation most commonly used, but imposes fairly significant overhead on the tunneling device. Large tunneled networks often require that groups of end devices be concentrated at distribution-tier sites, and a backbone be connected among the distribution devices.

TCP tunnels impose an appreciable processing load on routers. The multivendor data link switching group came to the consensus that 200 to 300 tunnels was the practical limit for current routers, even with fast processors. Cisco developed enhancements to data link switching that work around this limitation by establishing a two-level hierarchy of tunneling routers, radically reducing the number of tunnels required in comparison with full mesh. Another Cisco enhancement was to allow on-demand peering, for cases in which a given router might need to connect to large numbers of peers but only would need to connect simultaneously to a subset of those peers.

Bandwidth

Many vendor documents speak of switching as offering guaranteed bandwidth, but this is a misleading term. The bandwidth on an Ethernet hub or switch remains 10 Mbps. The value of a switch is that it reduces the latency in accessing that bandwidth.

Switches reduce latency on congested media. Such reductions, however, might not be significant when considering other sources of delay.

Late Collisions

If you start seeing late collision Ethernet errors after implementing a device that supports full-duplex, be sure you don't have a configuration with full-duplex at one end and half-duplex at the other.

Charles Spurgeon put full-duplex in real world terms when he explained, "Full duplex basically translates to 'shut off the CSMA/CD protocol and send whenever you like.' So the full duplex end sends whenever it likes and if it happens to transmit while the half duplex end is sending a frame then the half duplex end says 'Hey! Somebody transmitted in the middle of my frame transmission and caused a late collision.'" [Spurgeon, 1998]

He makes the real-world observation that "mismatched links will typically 'work OK' until the load gets high enough that the late collisions become frequent enough to be a noticeable problem."

Other problems that can lead to late collisions include cables that are too long or failing or poorly implemented NICs.

The value of a switch is that it reduces the latency in accessing the bandwidth of a conceptually shared path. In general, bandwidth on a switch is cheaper than bandwidth on a router. Switches reduce latency on congested media. Such reductions, however, might not be significant when considering other sources of delay. The fastest switch in the world will not help if the problem is a slow server.

What Latency Problem Are You Trying to Solve?

Remember that there are multiple dimensions to latency. You need to consider both your requirements for latency and the way in which you will monitor the network to see if it meets these requirements.

The absolute value of latency affects throughput in windowed protocols and end-to-end acknowledgment. Delay variability is more important to voice and video applications.

Some critical timers to be aware of include those shown in Table 10.2.

TABLE 10.2 SIGNIFICANT TIME VALUES

Time value	Event
20 milliseconds	Approximate speed of light in vacuum delay to go 2500 miles
40 milliseconds	Approximate speed of light in 10Base2 cable to go 2500 miles
80 milliseconds	LAT polling timer
200 milliseconds	Approximate low end of human perception of response time
1.5 seconds	Token Ring LLC2 T1 acknowledgment timer

Will Switching Help in This Environment?

Twenty PCs are on an 802.3 LAN, which has an application server. Assuming no collisions and retransmission, the maximum latency that a given station would experience, given equal-length input and output transmission, is the time it would take all other stations to transmit their frames.

A standard 802.3 frame is 1518 bytes long and takes approximately 1201 microseconds to transmit. There is a mandatory 9.6 microsecond idle time between successive frames, which can be rounded to 1210 microseconds.

If a client must wait for 19 other stations to exchange frames with the server, the delay would be $2 \times 19 \times 1210$, or approximately 460 milliseconds. Nearly half a second of delay is perceptible to users of interactive sessions.

Full-duplex connectivity cuts in half the delay in waiting for the server. It

continues

continued

does not improve the performance of individual workstations, because interactive applications are inherently half-duplex.

Will adding a switch cause a dramatic effect in performance? True, making the server connection full-duplex will help, assuming the server can receive one request while simultaneously sending a response. Adding a switch means there will not be a wait for the medium to clear, although there will still be approximately 1200 microsec-

onds to transfer the frame into the switch, and the internal switching time on the order of 50–60 microseconds.

All 20 stations are still contending for the server. Ideal conditions would have the server on a 100-Mbps interface, so a transfer from the switch to the server would take 120 microseconds. Assuming the switch has a full-duplex interface, a given station still would have to wait for up to 19 other frames to traverse the switch: $19 \times (120+50) =$ approximately 3200 microseconds.

Switches help some, but not all, application traffic patterns. Switches are apt to help when the following conditions are met:

- A single server on a subnet can accept traffic at a higher speed than its clients (for example, 10-Mbps Ethernet clients and a Fast Ethernet server).

- There are multiple servers so there can be the effect of concurrent client/server transfers on the same subnet.

- There are significant peer-to-peer communications.

Switches also can reduce the physical cost of interfaces when combined with routing, especially VLAN routing.

Do not rush into replacing everything with Fast Ethernet. It is true that the cost difference between Ethernet and Fast Ethernet NICs is minimal. In most cases, it does make sense to put 10/100-Mbps cards into new end hosts. It might not make good economic sense, however, to replace existing 10-Mbps NICs. Unless there is a specific reason to replace 10-Mbps NICs now used with a shared medium, the cheapest upgrade path is usually to keep the 10-Mbps cards, but connect them individually to 10-Mbps ports on a switch.

Although 100-Mbps NICs are almost the same cost as 10 Mbps, the same cannot be said about switch ports. 100-Mbps edge ports, or 10/100-Mbps speed-sensing edge ports, still are more expensive than pure 10-Mbps ports. Although vendors continue to improve products, a fair number of allegedly autosensing 10/100-Mbps ports fail to autosense and might need manual configuration to run at the correct speed. You should use nothing slower than 100 Mbps to interconnect switches, whether you run VLANs or not. Any modern switch has a 100 Mbps or faster uplink; and with switches, you do not have the danger of overloading as you do with hosts.

For equivalent bandwidth, ports on routers tend to be more expensive than ports on switches, assuming you are comparing ports of the same speed. It can be less clear whether ports on Layer 1 hubs are less expensive than ports on switches. It is true that ports on dumb hubs without SNMP management are significantly cheaper than ports on switches. The cost difference between smart SNMP-managed hubs and workgroup switches tends to be minimal, and the operational advantages of switches improves the life cycle cost.

Figure 6.3 shows a topology in which switching would be of minimal help, and conceivably might make matters worse if the workstations overloaded the server. If the server is adequately sized, switching might give a marginal improvement in performance and definitely would give improved management capability in comparison with a non-managed hub. Management capabilities of a workgroup switch are often slightly better than those of an SNMP-managed hub and offer more potential for growth at only slightly more expense. In this example, where there is no peer-to-peer computing among the workstations, the main way the switch can help is to provide effectively concurrent transfers to the application server and the printer. Assuming that the servers are linked to the LAN with 100-Mbps full-duplex ports, these transfers are both concurrent and at a higher speed relative to the 10-Mbps workstation connections.

There is a slight improvement in transfers among the workstations and the router, assuming that the router is also on a 100-Mbps full-duplex port. This improvement is not noticeable due to the bottleneck of the 128-Kbps WAN port, but the LAN is slightly less busy because the transfers to the router are faster.

If the hosts ran a peer-to-peer protocol, such as AppleTalk or NetBIOS, switches would likely be quite helpful by providing the effect of concurrent transfers among host pairs.

If the hosts communicate with multicasts or broadcasts, a switch might help, if it has hardware features that help with multicast handling. A switch has much less capability to help when there are large numbers of broadcasts. The best a switch can do with broadcasts is to have a rate-limiting feature that drops broadcast frames that are transmitted more frequently than some predefined limit. Such a limit would be intended to protect against malfunctioning devices that are causing broadcast storms, rather than for ordinary traffic conditions.

Sizing Uplink Bandwidth

To make a switched network theoretically nonblocking, you need to be sure the sum of the bandwidth on edge ports does not exceed the bandwidth of the uplink to the next hierarchical switch level. This is not out of the question with 10-Mbps edge ports, but becomes much more difficult when you have 100-Mbps edge ports.

To accomplish this nonblocking state, you almost certainly need inverse multiplexed Fast Ethernet, Gigabit Ethernet, or one or more ATM links. Consider a switch with 16 edge ports, which certainly is not a large number for a switch. Such a device needs 160 Mbps of uplink speed to be nonblocking, which requires at least two inverse multiplexed 100-Mbps uplink media. You can see how shared FDDI would rapidly become exhausted as a backbone technology, because it is not commonly inverse multiplexed.

A common industry guideline is to accept 50% oversubscription on the edge ports. A switch with 16 ports, therefore, needs 80-Mbps uplink bandwidth, which could be delivered with a 100-Mbps Fast Ethernet.

It is true that a given medium does not deliver the theoretical bandwidth, but these are approximate guidelines. The uplink bandwidths given so far are half-duplex. Full-duplex theoretically doubles the bandwidth.

In Figure 10.12, assume that you have 10 workgroups, each with a 16-edge-port switch. These ports link to a building switch.

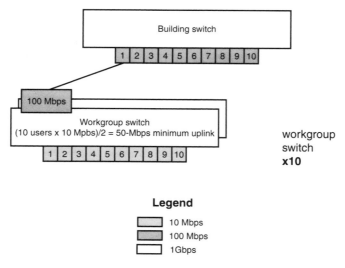

FIGURE 10.12 *Sizing workgroup switch uplink bandwidth depends on how much traffic stays local to the workgroup and how much traffic is generated by each host.*

If the building switch forms a collapsed backbone, it is reasonable to think of its switching fabric as the bandwidth requirement. A reasonable guideline here suggests not oversubscribing the ports of the building switch, but ensuring it has enough bandwidth to connect the sum of the uplinks connected to it. Ten 100-Mbps uplinks to the building switch require 1-Gbps bandwidth, which is quite achievable with commercial products.

Remember that those 100-Mbps uplinks are not completely filled by the edge switches; they have 80 Mbps each, assuming half-duplex operation. So, the actual load feeding into the building switch, assuming the trunks are full-duplex, might be closer to 400 Mbps than 1 Gbps.

But what about the campus as a whole? To continue the nonblocking assumption, you could have Gigabit Ethernet links from the building switches to a campus backbone switch. A 10-Gbps switching speed is available with high-end switches. Figure 10.13 shows a campus configuration with a single backbone switch. A reasonable worst-case assumption is the backbone switch is located at a data center that contains all non-workgroup application servers.

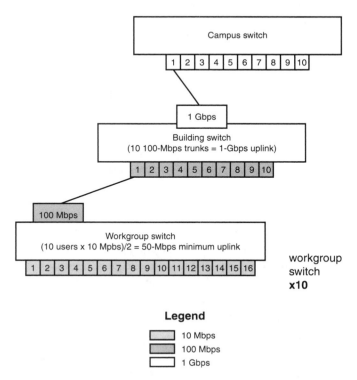

FIGURE 10.13 *Multiple gigabit uplinks quickly push the available state-of-the-art in campus switches.*

There is a point at which the cost of staying nonblocking cannot be justified. In the extreme case discussed here, there is an implicit assumption that every endpoint needs to be able to have full nonblocking bandwidth to every other endpoint.

Another point to consider in the scalability of a backbone device is whether to introduce routing functions to separate broadcast domains and provide queueing and prioritization between switched domains. ATM switches also can be a more scalable way to expand large campus networks, because ATM has admission control that prevents traffic from entering an overloaded network. IEEE 802.1P prioritization has no admission control, although you can obtain admission control with Layer 3 functions, such as RSVP. See Chapter 13 for further discussion of 802.1P and RSVP.

Most small to medium sized building networks, however, can work perfectly well with LAN switches linked by single or parallel Fast Ethernet.

Return to the workgroup described earlier, with a 16-port workgroup switch. If a printer assigned to the workgroup is connected to one of the switch ports, traffic between workstations and the printer does not need to traverse the uplink. With 50% oversubscription, there are 15 devices that conceivably could use the uplink, for a total bandwidth of 45 Mbps.

Excluding local printers from the uplink bandwidth requirements is a fairly trivial case of looking at application and server characteristics in determining your bandwidth requirements. Server issues interact with both switching fabric and uplink bandwidth requirements.

Server Issues

In well-designed networks, there is a balance among switching fabric speeds, uplink speeds, and the speed of server ports. VLANs add complexity; see the section "VLAN-Aware Hosts" later in this chapter.

Before you know whether you have adequate switching capacity, you must know the load that will be imposed on the switch. Most commercial numbers for switch performance tend to portray the ideal input-port-to-output-port throughput of a switch. You need to look at the potentially concurrent flows, as well as potential output blocking. Remember that flows can be between ports of the same switch, but might also need to traverse inter-switch trunks.

In existing 10-Mbps networks, switches can help when a server can process more data than its port allows it to receive. A switch can provide a cheap speed-shifting capability to let you connect a server at 100 Mbps.

Switches help most when there are multiple servers and multiple clients. In Switch 1 in Figure 10.14, there is only one server. The maximum throughput for the switch is limited by the speed of the server port. In this specific example, the maximum combined traffic rate of all the client ports is the same as the server port speed, so the switch is perfectly balanced.

In the Switch 2 configuration, assuming no server-to-server transfer, the peak transfer rate through the switch is limited by the combined speed of the client ports. Any client can get to Server 1 or Server 4, which have 100-Mbps ports, with no blocking. Only one client at a time can access Server 2 or Server 3, which are connected at 10 Mbps. The Switch 3 configuration in Figure 10.14 shows an unusual configuration that can be encountered when the server can have multiple connections on the same subnet. If 100-Mbps connectivity is not available, using multiple 10-Mbps ports, either inverse multiplexed or load-shared with different addresses, can increase available bandwidth to the switch. I've seen this done most frequently with Novell networks.

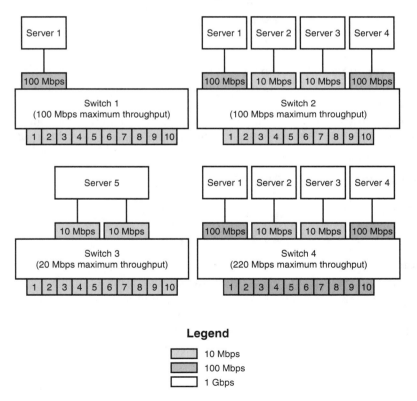

FIGURE 10.14   *The effective throughput of a switch might be more related to the number of server ports than their speed.*

The Switch 4 configuration allows the greatest throughput of the four configurations. Although all the client ports now run at 100 Mbps, there is output port blocking if all the client ports are active because the combined output bandwidth is 220 Mbps.

Let's look at some simplified examples of best-case throughput. Real switching networks are more complex in their statistical properties than these examples, but the examples will show some general principles. For greater precision, you need modeling tools that consider more sophisticated queueing algorithms than the uniform distributions described here.

No matter how fast the switch might be, the effective bandwidth to the server and the throughput of the entire switch can be no faster than the speeds shown in Table 10.3.

TABLE 10.3   THROUGHPUT LIMITED BY DERVER BOTTLENECK

Throughput	Server Port	Duplex
5 Mbps	10 Mbps	Half
10 Mbps	10 Mbps	Full
100 Mbps	100 Mbps	Full

In the configuration shown on the right in Figure 10.10, individual servers still are limited, as shown in Table 10.3. If the clients distribute their load equally over the servers, however, we can assume that there are effectively concurrent transfers to each server. With four servers, even though no server obtains more bandwidth than in Table 10.3, the total throughput is shown in Table 10.4.

TABLE 10.4   THROUGHPUT IMPROVES WITH CONCURRENT TRANSFERS

Throughput	Server Port	Duplex
20 Mbps	10 Mbps	Half
40 Mbps	10 Mbps	Full
400 Mbps	100 Mbps	Full

Adding servers seems to be making better and better use of the switch. Other limits, however, come into play. If the switching fabric of the switch is 1 Gbps, you can use Table 10.5 to find the switch throughput in a 16-server switched domain. As you see, you have reached a point of diminishing returns. You now need to start investigating the actual server utilization. The limits described are being reached with continuously utilized servers, which might not mirror real-world experience.

TABLE 10.5   THROUGHPUT LIMITED BY SWITCHING FABRIC BOTTLENECK

Throughput	Server Port	Duplex
320 Mbps	10 Mbps	Half
640 Mbps	10 Mbps	Full
1000 Mbps	100 Mbps	Full

Even if a switch repeals the speed of light and has instantaneous transfer among ports, it can forward traffic no faster than its ports can accept or transmit frames. Port speed limitations are especially significant in topologies with multiple interconnected switches. In Figure 10.15, although the effective port-to-port speed between Ports 1 and 2 is 1 Gbps, the effective speed between Ports 1 and 3 is 100 Mbps.

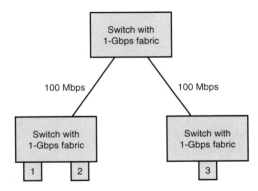

FIGURE 10.15   *In a single switch, throughput is limited by port and switching fabric speeds. Multiple interconnected switches also are limited by uplinks.*

Switches are not the only way to solve the limitations of throughput caused by server ports, as illustrated in Figure 10.16, which shows the common problem of backups causing performance problems. If backups are generating excessive traffic on a client/server network, an often overlooked technique for reducing traffic is very simple: Move the server-to-server backup traffic to its own network. To create such a network, add a second NIC to each server and connect these NICs to their own switch ports. Designate the set of switch ports to which the second NICs connect as a second spanning tree.

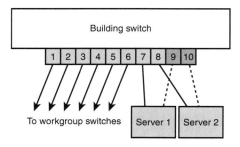

Legend

→ ▭ Broadcast Domain 1
- - - - - ▬ Broadcast Domain 2

FIGURE 10.16 *Additional server interfaces, used for inter-server communications, can connect to the same switch as clients. They form a different broadcast domain.*

Backup requirements can be subtle. It's easy to say, "Do them on the night shift," but that assumes that operators are physically present at night. It's easy to say, "Do unattended backups at night," but what if the backup volume is large enough to require changing disks or tapes?

If backups can run at the same time as application processing, a second interface on servers can relieve congestion. Just because a port can physically deliver traffic to a server does not mean the server can process it at the speed of the interface.

Another consideration is that data arrives at a port in bursts. When you buffer traffic, you are likely to have to buffer an entire burst. How large will a burst be?

Burstiness and Buffering

When hosts transfer data using a windowed protocol, they tend to send bursts of packets that contain a full window size. A TCP window consists of 65536 bytes. An 802.3 frame with 802.2/SNAP encapsulation splits this into 1495 byte pieces (that is, the 1500-byte data 802.3 data field less 5 bytes for 802.2/SNAP headers), or approximately 44 frames.

Traffic loading tends to be large bursts from non-interactive applications and small bursts from interactive ones.

So, realistic buffer sizes, either at input or output ports, should be able to hold at least one expected burst. Buffering too many bursts, without careful consideration of the latency that will be added, can create major performance problems.

Remember that TCP decreases its window size—the size of its bursts—if it senses congestion. It senses mild congestion from an increase in the round trip time of acknowledgement and senses severe congestion when it fails to receive acknowledgements. Providing enough buffering that TCP packets are never dropped can have the unexpected consequence of causing the burst size to increase and congestion to get worse.

A more refined strategy, which is supported by the IEEE 802.1P draft standard, is to mark frames with a priority value and have multiple queues at output interfaces. These multiple queues are serviced in the order of priority set in the priority field of appropriately marked frames. If applications are 802.1P aware, they can set the bits. Otherwise, the ingress switch needs to do so.

Having the ingress switch mark frames can be challenging (see the section "IEEE 802.1P" in Chapter 13).

Port Filtering

Of course, if a frame never enters a medium, it does not need bandwidth on that medium. Port filtering is another way to limit traffic. As a frame enters a port, the switch can apply an assortment of tests to decide whether the frame is to be forwarded or discarded. Depending on the switch, some or all of these tests also can be used to assign frames to VLANs (which is discussed in the next section). These tests are beyond the basic learning bridge traffic reduction.

Some of the Layer 2 information on which you can filter includes the following:

- Broadcast/multicast

- MAC address

- Ethertype/Vendor code

Some switches offer the capability to filter on L3 protocols by using the protocol field in the L2 frame or flow identifier. In my opinion, when such filtering criteria are used, the devices are no longer pure Layer 2 switches but have added routing or Layer 4 routing capabilities. This is not at all a bad thing, but things become extremely confusing if we call everything a *switch*.

Figure 10.17 shows the architecture of basic filtering. In filtering, you specify rules that apply some matching rule to frames and, based on whether the rule is matched or not, either forwards or discards the frame.

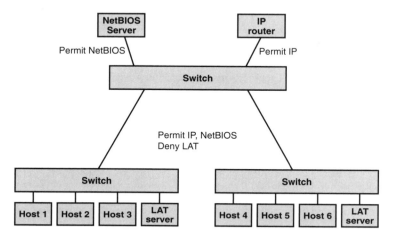

FIGURE 10.17   *Basic permit/deny filtering is available on most commercial switches.*

Matching rules also can be used to assign frames to specific VLANs. The most common criterion to assign frames to a VLAN, however, is not filtering but simply the port to which the host is connected. VLAN assignment rules and port filtering can complement one another.

Figure 10.17 shows an example of how port filtering can be used to reduce traffic in a cascaded-switch environment. This example would probably work even better with VLANs, but assume VLANs are not available.

LAT was designed for use on a single physical Ethernet between a terminal server and a DEC VAX host. It is perfectly reasonable to extend the idea of a single physical segment, of course, to a switch. LAT has a critical 80 millisecond timer and is not intended to go over wide areas.

In this example, assume the connected hosts can speak LAT, NetBIOS/NetBEUI, or both. Only the NetBEUI traffic propagates beyond the local switch.

Mixed Media Issues

When end hosts create frames that are too large for downstream media, a wide range of performance and reliability problems emerge. These problems are most common when you mix Layer 2 media that have different bit orderings or maximum frame sizes. Various translational bridging schemes exist, but are cumbersome.

When designing switched systems, you need to decide how you will deal with the potential of mismatched MTU sizes among different media types. The simplest and usually best solution is not to use Layer 2 connectivity between media of a different type, such as FDDI and Ethernet. It is better to route between them and let routing deal with medium conversions. Token Ring and Ethernet are even more difficult to join. Route, do not bridge, between Token Ring and Ethernet if at all possible. Data Link Switching is preferable to translational bridging.

Medium conversion by fragmentation, however, tends to be quite inefficient. Again, I recommend routing between different media types, because frame size is not the only issue. Other issues include bit ordering in addresses and the need to handle overhead frames unique to each medium type. For example, how should 802.1 BPDUs be translated onto 802.5? Nevertheless, if you do need to switch between media types, it is a good idea to implement MTU path discovery, so the hosts do not generate packets that need to be fragmented.

Another problem with frame length, which is *not* an IP MTU size problem, can occur on VLANs, such as Cisco Inter-Switch Link (ISL), that prepend the edge frame with a VLAN header. The combined length of the delivery header and the payload frame might be longer than the data link protocol allows. See "Small Giants Roam the Trunks" later in this chapter.

Fault Tolerance in Non-VLAN Switched Networks

Media will fail. Switches will fail. How can the effects of failures be minimized?

The fundamental mechanism of fault tolerance is automatic rerouting by the spanning tree algorithm (see Figure 10.18) if the link between Bridge 2 and Root Bridge 3 goes down. Prior to the failure, there are unused links between Bridge 2 and Bridge 4 and between Bridge 1 and Bridge 5. These links were disabled by the spanning tree algorithm to avoid loops.

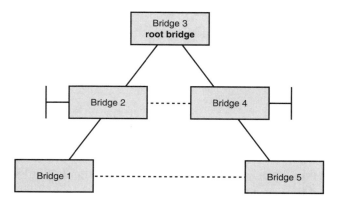

FIGURE 10.18 *Idle paths (dashed) in a spanning tree topology remain available for backup.*

Remember that the cost of having additional paths is the cost of the media and of the unused ports on switches, not large monthly costs for WAN links.

There are some caveats to router superiority in fault tolerance: Routing can slow significantly if a cache needs to be invalidated and refreshed, and if the same processor is used for forwarding and routing table computation, that processor might not be able to do both simultaneously.

Network congestion can cause false recomputations, if 802.1D hello messages are delayed too long in reaching another bridge. Not hearing hello messages from another bridge indicates that connectivity has been lost to that bridge, or that the bridge has failed.

Inverse Multiplexed Parallel Paths

Although the spanning tree algorithm is only allowed to see a single active path between two bridges, this path can be implemented over parallel physical paths that are inverse multiplexed into a single Layer 2–visible path. Inverse multiplexing has been common in the past on WAN links between two half-bridges. The term *half-bridge* originated in IBM Token Ring networking and referred to a pair of bridges linked by a point-to-point WAN circuit. Each bridge has a LAN interface and a WAN interface.

Other terms for bridges linked by a medium other than the basic LAN include *encapsulated bridges* and *remote bridges*. To get more bandwidth, some of these WAN-oriented bridges used parallel point-to-point circuits. Frames received on the various physical interfaces were recombined into a single stream before the bridging software saw them. The motivation for developing these techniques was principally to make more bandwidth available, but inverse multiplexed paths can also add reliability.

Implementation techniques for inverse multiplexing have been vendor specific, but IEEE has begun the 802.3AD committee to develop a standard multiplexing method. Cabletron's term is *port trunking*, whereas Cisco's, which came from the acquisition of Grand Junction, is *Fast EtherChannel*. Bay and 3Com also do inverse multiplexing between certain switch types.

Regardless of the name, you must remember that the inter-chassis trunks need to comply with spanning tree rules.

You have to configure explicitly the relationship between physical and spanning-tree–visible paths, through the interconnection of cards, software commands, or both.

In the example in Figure 10.19, the bundle of two physical paths between Bridge 2 and Bridge 3, and the bundle of three paths between Bridge 4 and Bridge 5, are treated as a single path from the perspective of spanning tree.

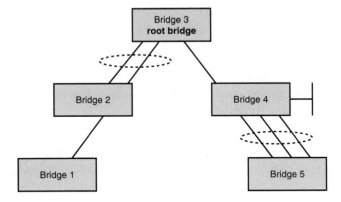

FIGURE 10.19 *A limited exception to spanning tree really doesn't violate the algorithm, because the multiple physical paths are hidden from the algorithm. The ellipses show the bundles of multiple physical links.*

Non–VLAN-Aware Fault-Tolerant Workstations

Figure 10.20 gives a rather high-level, application-oriented view of the placement of a workstation in a critical application, such as money trading. Each
workstation has two interfaces.

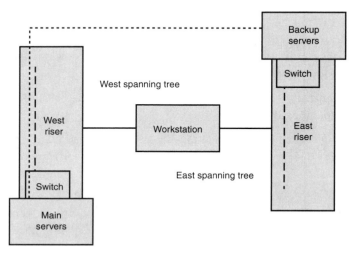

Figure 10.20   *Simply connecting a workstation to different switched domains does not
guarantee fault tolerance. The dashed line shows potential backup, but the host needs to be
aware of it.*

You really cannot evaluate fault tolerance here without understanding the
application. Does the application speak concurrently to both sets of servers, or
is the application aware one is in standby?

It is reasonable to assume that the two sets of servers are interconnected, as
shown in Figure 10.20. The mirroring protocol between them could contain a
go to sleep message sent from the primary server to the secondary. As long as
the secondary server receives this message, it does not respond to the client
requests.

The application on the workstation has to have the intelligence to decide how
to process server responses. Does it accept the first response received? Does it
have a preference and only accept a response from the backup server if a workstation timer expires?

If a server response is intended to replace data on the workstation, it can be perfectly reasonable to accept responses from any server and apply them to workstation databases. If the response does something like add a number to the database, the workstation must apply the transaction more than once.

Again, the application determines whether the client should only accept the first response it receives, or if it can apply any response it receives. If the response is of the form "add 1 to a record," it can only safely act on the first response. If the response is of the form "replace this record," and it can be assumed both servers send the same record, that simplifies the problem.

After you understand the application requirements, you can design the network for resiliency. Figure 10.21 shows the first step in understanding connectivity from the workstation.

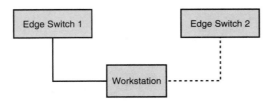

FIGURE 10.21 *A fault-tolerant workstation can connect to two separate ingress switches.*

Assuming the workstation and both ingress switches are in the same spanning tree, access to one switch is blocked (represented by the dashed line) as long as the other switch is operational. Such a workstation needs to include a bridging function to know which port to block.

Vendor extensions to the spanning tree, such as Cisco's PortFast, reduce the time needed for a host to be recognized by the bridging system. Bridges make the default assumption that any host that connects to a bridge port might be a bridge, and indeed might become root. Typically, there is a 30-second delay before the system determines that the new device is an end host and traffic can be forwarded to it. Mechanisms like PortFast force the port into an immediate forwarding state, skipping root election and learning. In most cases where you are attaching an end host, this is a reasonable assumption.

For such cases as the fault-tolerant host, you must allow the host to go through the learning process. You must not use features such as PortFast, or the host cannot learn which interface to use.

Figure 10.22 shows a bit more of the configuration. The ingress switch connects to a distribution tier switch. How are you protected against failures of individual links or interfaces?

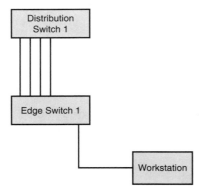

FIGURE 10.22 *Inverse multiplexing, implemented invisibly to the spanning tree algorithm, provides more bandwidth and greater resiliency in the event of link failures.*

In Figure 10.22, there are inverse multiplexed links between the ingress and distribution switch. If a link or link interface fails, the inverse multiplexing mechanism spreads the load over the remaining operational links. The spanning tree algorithm is not aware that there are multiple physical links; the bundle of real physical links appears to the spanning tree algorithm as if it were a single path.

As a designer, you need to consider if the two switches should be completely separate. To get parallel operation, it probably makes sense to have two separate spanning trees. Otherwise, in the event of a failure, using the standard spanning tree algorithm, you have to wait for the spanning tree to reconstitute. The time that a spanning tree takes to rebuild might be less than it takes the workstation application to realize it needs to send on the backup LAN, if the workstation has to make the decision on where to send traffic.

Minimizing Delays for Finding Alternate Next-Level Switches

Another variant on the spanning tree algorithm reduces the time for an edge switch to find an alternate switch in the event of a failure of the next higher-level switch in a hierarchy. This variant requires a disciplined, but very reasonable, topology such as that in Figure 10.23. More complex variants are shown later in this chapter.

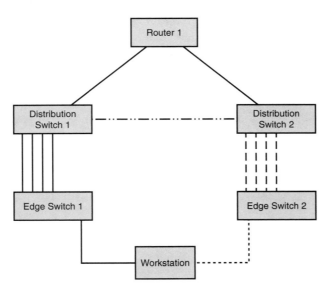

FIGURE 10.23 *The basic topology for a resilient uplink in a hierarchical switched network involves designated primary and backup links to primary and backup switches at the next hierarchical level.*

Edge Switch 1 is configured with the information that Distribution Switch 1 is its primary uplink (that is, the path to the next hierarchical level), and Distribution Switch 2 is its backup next-level switch. If Edge Switch 1 decides that Distribution Switch 1 is down because the edge switch no longer hears BPDU hellos from Switch 1, the edge switch would normally discard its station MAC address cache and recompute its spanning tree.

If the full spanning tree needed to be recomputed, it would normally take at least 30 seconds for Edge Switch 1 to learn before forwarding to Distribution Switch 2. While the recomputation is in progress, Edge Switch 1 would do no forwarding. If the variant on the spanning tree discussed here is used, there is still a brief period where frames are black-holed while the failure of Switch 1 is being recognized. After the failure is recognized, which takes a low number of seconds, forwarding quickly changes to use the backup link to Switch 2.

By preconfiguring Switch 1 with explicit information indicating "Switch 2 is your backup," Switch 1 would not go through a full spanning tree recomputation after losing connectivity with Switch 1. (Cisco's Fast Uplink is an implementation of such a capability.) During that time, Edge Switch 1 would forward no frames.

The next step in resiliency concerns how you leave the switching domain. At this point in the design, the router is a single point of failure. Figure 10.24 shows how you can have redundant routers while keeping the basic design straightforward.

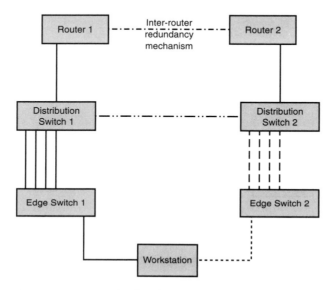

FIGURE 10.24   *The distribution switches connect to a subnet on which they can reach primary and backup routers.*

These routers are linked by a router resiliency mechanism that makes one router primary and one router backup, but with only one address seen as the default router address.

In Figure 10.24, each distribution switch is connected to a router on the same subnet. Some type of redundancy mechanism, such as the IETF Virtual Router Redundancy Protocol, Cisco Hot Standby Routing Protocol, or Bay Router Redundancy, runs between them.

Although the router interfaces have unique addresses, they have an additional shared virtual address. This virtual address is active only on the active router of the pair. When the primary router fails, the backup router begins to respond with both the virtual IP address and an associated virtual MAC address. The end hosts do not know that the MAC address has changed.

There is likely to be a short period of confusion during such a cutover to the backup router. Although the end hosts do not see the change, the switches have cached the virtual MAC address on one port, so the station address caches at the time of the failure become inaccurate until they learn the new position of the MAC address. A plausible vendor extension for redundant router protocols is to send out a message (gratuitous ARP) to switches at the time of cutover, forcing a cache change. This avoids 30 seconds or so of relearning. Making single changes to caches, however, rather than invalidating and rebuilding the entire cache, can be a complex problem in switch implementation.

VLANs

VLANs have several roles. They were originally conceived as a means of security isolation, hiding the traffic from one VLAN to another. Aside from the security aspects, this has the effect of hiding broadcasts and multicasts on one VLAN from another. If the only reason to insert a router into a given configuration is to control multicasts, VLANs connected to an application server can be a viable alternative.

A VLAN can be created by using switch software to isolate (or provide connectivity between) specific devices. Devices belonging to a VLAN are not required to be part of the same workgroup nor must they be connected to the same physical switch. VLANs can, for example, temporarily combine members of different workgroups into a taskforce working on a special project.

The number of VLANs per system is primarily a management limitation, whereas the number of devices per VLAN tends to be a performance limitation (see Table 2.2).

Legacy 802.3 or 802.5 equipment is unaware that it is connected through a VLAN and only sees its native LAN. It is possible to make end equipment VLAN aware, which can be quite useful for servers. VLAN awareness involves specific configuration and software support.

It is probably true that VLANs make it easier to move hosts within the same "color" VLAN, no matter where the device is located in a campus. Moving a workstation onto a different VLAN, and thus a different IP subnet, is much more complex. To automate the move and to change the process to any real extent, you need a well-engineered infrastructure, including VLAN management workstations and linked DNS/DHCP servers. It is true that a VLAN provides high-speed connectivity between devices on the same subnet at a lower cost per unit of bandwidth than does a router. A broadcast or multicast on one VLAN is not visible to another, making VLANs a technique for stopping broadcast radiation problems.

Remember that broadcasts and multicasts are real frames and occupy bandwidth. A broadcast storm, especially one that affects several VLANs simultaneously, can eat up bandwidth on VLAN trunks.

Wherever possible, use multicasts rather than broadcasts. LANE version 2 can be selective as to the dissemination of multicasts and can use different BUS platforms to replicate traffic for different multicast groups.

From the perspective of ordinary end hosts, the VLAN is simply the broadcast domain to which they connect. The internal implementation of VLANs includes the following:

- VLAN-aware switches that perform VLAN tagging

- VLAN trunking

- VLAN management

- VLAN-aware hosts

VLANs provide mechanisms that, when properly used, can alleviate some of the principal problems of traditional LANs: traffic loading from non-unicast traffic, flooding by frames with unknown unicast addresses, and spanning tree problems caused when congestion delays the delivery of hello messages. The basic way in which VLANs solve these problems is to provide a flexible way to divide broadcast domains into smaller, more reliable ones, while still allowing the overall Layer 2 structure to be managed as a unit.

VLAN Tagging

Mechanisms at edge ports apply various criteria—either the physical port or various criteria used in filtering—to assign frames to specific VLANs.

After traffic is assigned, it must be tagged or otherwise identified so that traffic belonging to different VLANs can be differentiated on shared trunk media.

Per-Port/Physical Assignment to VLANs

The most common way to assign hosts to VLANs is to assume a single host per port and to assign individual hosts each to their own ports (see Figure 10.25).

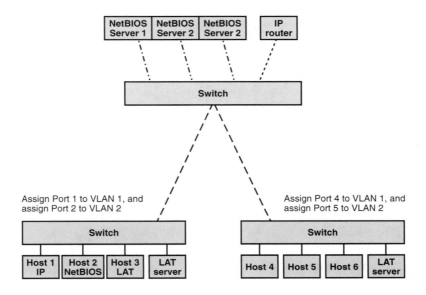

Legend

– · – · – NetBios VLAN

- - - - - - - IP VLAN

– – – – VLAN trunk

FIGURE 10.25 *Per-port configuration is the most common way to assign traffic to VLANs; many filtering criteria can be used to assign frames.*

On some switches, you can filter traffic before it is tagged for a given VLAN, which is illustrated in Figure 10.26.

If your goal is to control traffic, you can do it by assigning certain traffic to specific VLANs, or you can do it by preventing other traffic from entering various trunks. The latter does not require VLAN support.

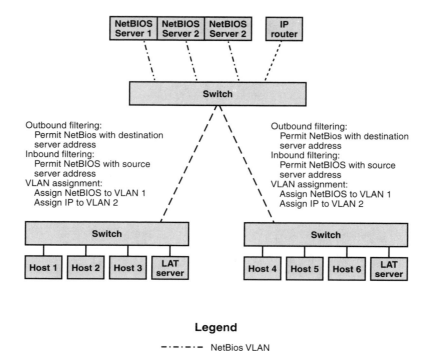

Legend

– · – · – NetBios VLAN

········ IP VLAN

– – – – VLAN trunk

FIGURE 10.26 *Filtering criteria can prevent undesired traffic from entering LANs. This is not the same as assignment by protocol type; it is blocking by protocol type.*

VLAN Assignment by Layer 2 Information

There are two ways you can assign traffic to VLANs based on Layer 2 information. You can use the MAC address field or the Protocol Type field. Remember that the Protocol Type field in 802.3 frames is inside the 802.3 Data field and is part of the 802.2 LLC header. Only Ethernet II frames have a protocol type in the main frame header, and not all switch ports support Ethernet II. Also remember that there is a special frame type used by Novell, which has an 802.3 header but contains no LLC information.

If your VLAN tagging mechanism supports filtering *and* tagging by protocol type, as found in an Ethernet II type field or in an LLC DSAP or SNAP field, you can have considerable and useful control over the propagation of workgroup traffic.

VLAN Assignment Based on the Layer 2 Address

Many VLAN switches support assigning hosts to VLANs by MAC address. VLAN assignment by MAC address tends to be either a niche application or closely coupled to network management tools. The network management tools that support this capability usually are proprietary.

Most commonly, the source MAC address is used to assign traffic to VLANs. This is a bit puzzling because it could be perfectly reasonable to assign traffic to VLANs based on the destination MAC address. The destination MAC address, with respect to clients, would identify the server and go a long way to establishing application-based VLANs.

Of course, the servers would need to know how to return responses to the host. But simply returning the frame on the edge host on which it arrived, or using VLAN awareness if the server has a VLAN-aware NIC, should suffice. In the extreme case, the server would need to know the VLAN to which each source MAC address belongs, but only if the server port has multiple VLANs present.

The fundamental problem with this technique is knowing the MAC address associated with a specific host. Because changing the NIC on a host changes its burned-in MAC address, if you are to avoid a massive manual administrative task on networks of appreciable size, you must have some means of automating the configuration of MAC address to VLAN mapping tables.

Networks that use IBM or some other software that manually administers MAC addresses can much more plausibly use VLAN assignment by MAC address. There are other applications where the MAC address might be in user-specific software, such as set-top IP boxes for cable TV systems.

Only Part of the Address Might Be Useful

Remember that IEEE 802 addresses have a bit that indicates whether they are globally or locally assigned. Globally assigned addresses have 24 bits of vendor ID and 24 bits of station ID assigned by that vendor.

If your particular switch allows you to do filtering or address-based VLAN assignment on certain bits of the MAC address, it might be perfectly plausible to direct all locally administered MAC addresses to one VLAN, on the assumption that they are IBM devices that require local administration.

To complement this assignment, you then might assign hosts with a Silicon Graphics or Sun vendor code to a VLAN

continues

continued

intended for UNIX boxes, an Apple vendor code to an AppleTalk network, and all others to a default VLAN assumed to be PC IP.

Note that selecting machines with an Apple vendor code does not mean they actually are running AppleTalk. Only protocol type fields on specific packets can tell if a given Mac-generated frame is AppleTalk, IP, or indeed NetBEUI or Novell.

If your goal is to automate your configuration as much as possible, you might make use of assignment by MAC address. This particularly makes sense for the initial VLAN configuration for an existing network. On the first day of operation, assume the workgroups are meaningful. Let the switch capture the MAC addresses it detects on the port and store them in a file. You now have a list of MAC addresses by port, and if you have an inventory of what devices are plugged into which port, you have the basis of a database of assignments. Vendors that can assign hosts to VLANs based on MAC address include 3Com, Agile, Cabletron, Cisco, and Xylan.

Assigning Traffic by Protocol Type

As shown in Figure 10.27, you can go beyond simply keeping LAT local and isolating IP and NetBIOS broadcasts from one another. You can allow the LAT to go between the two switches, but not beyond them.

In Figure 10.27, LAT is intended as a small workgroup protocol. Traffic to LAT server L1 does not leave Switch 1. Traffic to L2 does appear on Switch 2. This control is done using VLANs. Only LAT edge ports and the trunks between Switch 1 and Switch 2 permit the LAT VLAN.

NetBIOS/NetBEUI traffic can go more broadly into the switched system. The network administrator has chosen to defeat the mechanism by which NetBIOS confirms a host's name is unique. This mechanism causes a host, at initialization time, to send out a burst of broadcast or multicast name queries, trying to determine if any other host will respond to the name the initializing host wants to use.

By filtering NetBIOS inbound to client-only ports, you force name queries to go only to servers. NetBIOS frames are assigned to VLAN 1. IP should be able to go anywhere. The VLAN assignment criteria mark frames with an IP protocol type for VLAN 2.

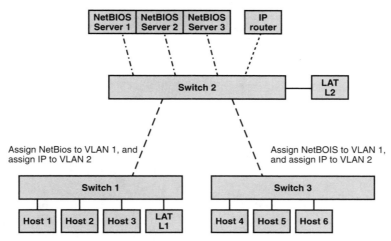

Hosts 1 through 6 speak IP, NetBIOS/NetBEUI, and LAT

FIGURE 10.27 *Assignment by protocol type is more general than filtering by protocol type, although you can use both methods.*

Not all vendors support assignment to VLANs by protocol type. At the time of this writing in November 1998, Cisco and Bay/Nortel did not support this assignment, but tests by *Data Communications* magazine showed various capabilities for VLAN protocol assignment from 3Com, Agile, Cabletron, Newbridge, and Xylan.

The argument for assigning traffic to VLANs by protocol type is that it gives you the ability to manage each protocol separately. You restrict broadcasts to devices of the same kind, which is more general than controlling the propagation of multicast groups. The counter-argument of several major vendors is that the world is rapidly moving away from non-IP protocols, and the customer would be better served if the vendors were to concentrate their development resources on IP VLANs.

Multiple VLANs per Edge Port
Generally, edge ports of switches are assigned to a single VLAN. There are exceptions, such as 3Com, which considers it a desirable feature that a given port can be assigned to more than one VLAN. As in most networking features, there are advantages and disadvantages to this feature.

Tread very carefully when establishing multiple VLANs per edge port. A good application of the technology is that shown in Figure 10.28, where different paths are used for different protocols by a workstation that is undergoing transition from NetBEUI to NBT. LAT is also used for access to the local printer only.

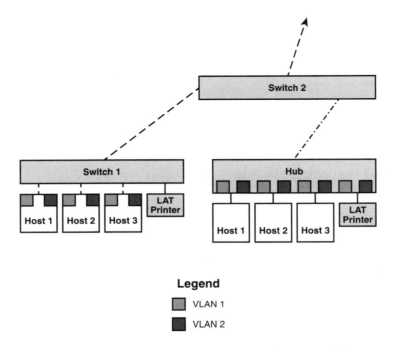

Legend

VLAN 1

VLAN 2

FIGURE 10.28 *There can be different reasons to have devices belonging to different VLANs connected to the same edge port.*

Some advocates of using multiple VLANs per edge port suggest that it simplifies configuration for IP, which I consider a potentially dangerous method. This technique is *not* the same as a VLAN-aware edge host connected to a switch port, as shown in Figure 10.29.

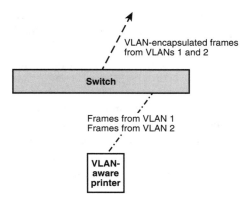

FIGURE 10.29 *If the VLANs use routable protocols, the printer needs an address in each. If the VLANs are separate NetBIOS broadcast domains, as long as the printer's name is unique, this works.*

In Figure 10.29, a non–VLAN-aware printer exists on two VLANs. Potential problems with this technique, above all, involve broadcasts. Practical hardware replicates all received broadcasts onto all broadcast domains at the port.

For any of a number of reasons, it might be impossible to change the users from the hubs in the short term, or even in the long term. Having devices on multiple VLANs share a common broadcast port isn't necessarily a bad approach but you need to understand its limitations. The most significant limitation is that there is no way, at the port level, to protect members of one community of interest from non-unicast or unknown-destination-unicast meant for a different COI.

Look at Figure 10.29 and focus on where broadcasts do and do not propagate. The port to which the printer connects is *not* VLAN aware. Any broadcast arriving on either VLAN must be sent to the printer; any broadcast generated by the printer must be sent to both VLANs.

Multicast storms might not be as much of a threat, if the switch is smart enough to know that some multicast groups only are present on certain VLANs and distribute them appropriately. If a Layer 2 multicast management mechanism such as IGMP snooping, CGMP, and so on is available, multicasts can be handled more selectively than broadcasts. Only those multicast frames for which the printer has subscribed to their multicast group need to be delivered.

What if the end host suffers a failure that makes it send continuous broadcasts? These go onto all connected VLANs. The only real way to protect against a serious broadcast storm is to have a broadcast rate limit on the switch port, limiting the number of broadcasts per unit time the host can send into the ports.

In a routable network, there are additional configuration questions that do not apply to a Layer 2 protocol such as NetBEUI. Does the end host support secondary addresses? If so, it is interrupted by broadcasts on any and all of the connected subnets. Probably the best application of this technique is putting a uniquely named printer on segmented NetBIOS broadcast domains.

Note

I confess to being a bit conservative in network design. VLANs were first designed architecturally to isolate things, not to make resources available to many users. Whenever a feature diverges from the original architectural intent, it's worth examining very carefully, lest there be unintended effects of the change.

The ideal case for having a port belonging to more than one VLAN is a shared printer or other server. Having it appear on multiple VLANs means you don't need workgroup servers for each separate VLAN.

My first question, however, is, "How do clients on each VLAN reach the shared device?" In IP, the normal case is that a client ARPs to find the server. If the server is on the same subnet, the client finds it. If the server is on a different subnet, the client sends to a default gateway router to reach the server. But this solution was being advocated to avoid having routers!

3Com, in particular, has advocated the idea of assigning multiple VLANs to a port to share a common device such as the printer in Figure 10.29.

This approach strikes me as superficially reasonable, but questionable in practice for IP networks. It might make sense for a nonroutable protocol environment such as NetBEUI, but it becomes much more questionable for IP. NetBEUI devices are found with broadcasts in a flat address space. You need to assign an IP host an address in each IP subnet in which you want it to be reached. Many IP hosts, especially ones you might use for a printer or other shared resources, do not support multiple addresses on an interface.

If there are three NetBEUI networks all accessing the printer, broadcasts can be isolated to each of the user networks. The printer is still affected by the broadcasts on each network. It has the potential, if it fails, to cause broadcast storms on each network. Broadcast throttling can protect the networks.

For IP, however, the printer has to have an address in each subnet. Many IP stacks can support only a single host address, a single default router address, and so on. So the idea of sharing a device among several IP subnets can first be challenged by asking if the host supports multiple addresses. If it does, how are these configured? Remember that our goal is to reduce configuration.

The next question to ask is how that host gets the multiple addresses. Basic DHCP assumes that a client will issue a broadcast request with all zeros in the host IP address field. But if secondary addresses are needed, can either the DHCP server provide them in the first response or must the workstation issue—and understand what it is issuing—multiple DHCP requests?

Assigning to VLANs by Layer 3 and 4 Information

There are several vendor-specific schemes for assigning frames to VLANs based on information carried in the data field of frames at the edge. Several of these techniques have potential, but none are quite as simple as sales information would have you believe.

These methods all have the reasonable assumption that because there is usually a one-to-one mapping between IP prefix (that is, subnet identifier) and VLAN, if the switch knows the subnet, it automatically knows and can assign to the VLAN.

Secondary addressing, a term used by Cisco and several other vendors, involves assigning multiple subnets to the same physical or virtual medium. (Bay also does this, but calls it *multinetting*.) In the real world, secondary addresses are common, and multiple IP subnets can be assigned to the same VLAN. This is common, for example, when there is more than one DHCP server on the same VLAN, each server maintained by a different organization. Any automatic assignment scheme based on Layer 3 information either needs to handle secondary addressing or clearly indicate that it does not support secondary addressing.

The real challenge for any of these schemes is identifying the subnet associated with the incoming packet. This is a problem because an ordinary IP packet does not carry a subnet mask or a length field telling how many bits of the source address form the subnet prefix. Potential ways the switch could learn this critical information include the following:

- Prefix lengths could be manually configured on each port.

- The switch could passively participate in a classless routing protocol such as OSPF, RIPv2, or EIGRP and dynamically learn prefix lengths.

- A router path determination function on a different chassis could download a forwarding information base, which contains prefix length information, to the switch.

The first approach is limiting because the whole point of assigning by Layer 3 address is to minimize configuration.

The argument against the second method is that it takes a substantial amount of memory and processing to understand a routing protocol, even when the chassis itself does not do packet forwarding on Layer 3 information. One of the main reasons to use switches is to have devices that can forward at a lower cost per unit of bandwidth than do conventional routers.

Note

I once worked as a product architect in a company where I gave technical presentations to customers and prospects. The vice-president of sales often would tell me how wonderful I was at sales-related things and how I should transfer to sales.

"Jerry," I would always answer, "if I wanted to be in sales, I would already have transferred." And so it is with switches that want full understanding of routing. If they had wanted to do that, they should have been routers!

You should guard against believing sales propaganda that refers to everything as a switch, which is a code word for a vendor strategy that presents routers as slow devices.

The third approach is probably the most reasonable. When you place this much Layer 3 intelligence in a switch, you effectively have built a Layer 3 switch, and you might as well call it that!

Of course, other vendors delight in calling everything a hub, whether it is a shared medium, a switching device, or a router. Vendor terminology confusion motivates the question, "What is the difference between a used car salesman and a network salesman? The used car salesman knows when he is lying."

Several vendors have autoconfiguration schemes where the switch port establishes a table of source IP addresses that appear as incoming packets on an edge port. The switch extracts the IP address and its subnet.

At least some configuration is necessary so that the switch knows the prefix length, unless it participates in a classless routing protocol such as OSPF. For its learning, Cabletron requires that you send packets to a specific default router address.

The argument is made by several vendors that, after the switch knows which addresses are associated with which port, it can do Layer 2 switching between those ports in the same subnet using a faster Layer 2 switching path internal to the chassis.

With subnet knowledge, it can propagate broadcasts based on Layer 3 information—it knows which nodes are in a broadcast group. There is no equivalent to IGMP for joining broadcast, as opposed to the more restrictive multicast, groups. Controlling broadcasts is one of the more attractive reasons for a switch to have Layer 3 awareness.

VLAN Trunking

After traffic is accepted for a VLAN, it must be prepared for transfer over the shared VLAN trunk, as shown conceptually in Figure 10.30.

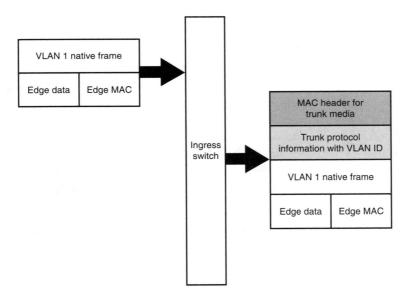

FIGURE 10.30   *The ingress switch tags edge frames with a VLAN identifier, then prepares them for transmission over the trunk.*

Protocols used to carry VLAN traffic between switches include the following:

- IEEE 802.1Q

- IEEE 802.10 Secure Data Exchange (SDE)

- Bay LattisSpan, a variant of 802.1D

- Cabletron SecureFast, a virtual circuit technology

- Cisco ISL

Some of these protocols prepend a VLAN header to an existing frame, and others manipulate existing headers. Prepending approaches tend to be more flexible in carrying different edge frame types, but they are not architecturally clean from the IEEE 802 architecture. Prepending also can create extra-long frames that are not carried properly by networking devices not aware of the VLAN protocol.

LANE provides comparable functionality, but does not tag frames. Rather, it identifies the virtual circuit that goes to a destination or set of destinations. Think of this as implicit rather than explicit tagging.

Many of these methods have subtle compatibility problems. The basic 802.10, for example, assumes that an IEEE 802.2 LLC field will be present in the edge frame. Ethernet II frames, which do not contain LLC, are not compatible with this VLAN technique. It cannot flatly be said that IEEE 802.3 is compatible with 802.10, because there are Novell variants that use the 802.3 MAC frame format but do not use LLC.

Another potential compatibility problem is shown in Figure 10.31. ISL, and any protocol that prepends a VLAN tag header to payload frames, can have problems with maximum-length 802.3 frames. A tagged delivery frame with a 64-byte VLAN header, if the native frame is longer than 1454 bytes, violates the 802.3 frame length specification. Although many repeaters accept this format, some do not. As shown in Figure 10.31, there can be vendor compatibility issues when intermediate protocols are not VLAN aware, simply because they don't understand that the tagged frames legitimately can be slightly longer than permitted by 802.3.

The IEEE 802.1Q committee recognizes the problem and has been working on the idea of controlled violations of the 802.3 length rules. In general 802.3, a frame of excessive length is called a *giant*. IEEE working groups have joined the ranks of those who came up with the oxymorons jumbo shrimp, civil war, and working vacation, by coining the term small giant. A *small giant* is a valid 802.3 frame with a valid VLAN header and trunk MAC header. 802.1Q-aware interfaces should have no problem with small giants. Cisco ISL interfaces deal properly with small giants of the length created by ISL and so on.

The danger comes when you might run the trunks through a repeater or switch that is not small-giant-aware. In Figure 10.31, several VLANs run over a Fast Ethernet medium. These media, and other non-VLAN Fast Ethernets, run to the campus switch.

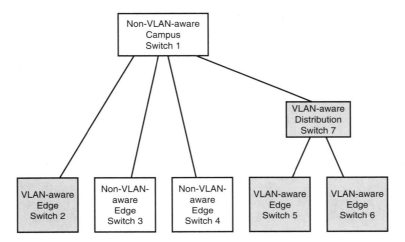

FIGURE 10.31 *All devices in the path through which a VLAN trunk runs must support small giants, or some frames cannot be transmitted.*

There is full connectivity among Switches 5, 6, and 7. If the campus switch, Switch 1, is not VLAN trunking aware, it might discard small giants that are perfectly valid from the perspective of the VLAN switches, but invalid to a device that is not aware of the need for small giants. Switch 2, therefore, would not have full connectivity with Switches 5, 6, and 7.

Small Giants Roam the Trunks

The 802.3AC committee is modifying the 802.3 standard to help support VLANs, but the problem of maximum length edge frames that break the standard with a VLAN header remains. IEEE refers to them as baby giants or small giants.

Here is the problem: What if you have a full-length 1500-byte frame at the edge of the network, but you need to tag the header with additional VLAN identification. You now have a frame that has become illegal by a strict interpretation of the 802.3 standard, as its total length exceeds the specification.

To make things more complex, not all frames will be affected by VLAN tagging, only those that are near or at the maximum length.

The 802.3AC work is modifying the standard to make small giants legal. Even when its work is done, however, there are likely to be very large numbers of deployed devices that do not understand small giants.

A VLAN-aware device, however, must understand small giants, so the practical answer is to be sure that all switches (and possibly repeaters) in the path are VLAN aware.

VLAN Management Domains

There are architectural limits to the number of VLANs in a given enterprise system, but they are quite high and unlikely to be a major limitation. These limits are primarily seen by management systems, and, if there is a need for extremely large numbers of VLANs, it is reasonable to have multiple management domains. Because VLANs are usually limited to a campus, it is perfectly reasonable to have a separate management domain per campus.

Assuming a single VLAN per port, the maximum number of VLANs on a campus is limited to the number of edge ports. This is an almost completely absurd limit, as a set of single-device VLANs can do no useful work.

A switch can have software or hardware limits in the number of VLANs it can support. For example, there could very well be a maximum hardware table size for VLAN tags.

Bandwidth of the inter-switch trunks is not a limit on the number of VLANs in the system, but on the amount of traffic, including overhead, in the set of all VLANs that traverse the trunk.

The enterprise-wide limit to VLAN technology is not related to hard numbers like bandwidth of links or raw traffic generated, but is related to the VLAN capabilities of the individual components that make up the network topology.

Some vendors place a limit on the number of VLANs that can be carried by an inter-switch connection. Cisco Systems, for example, places a limit of 1000 VLANs per inter-switch connection.

If routers are participating in the VLAN topology, one logical interface must be dedicated to each VLAN active on a physical interface. The number of logical interfaces that can be defined is limited to the capabilities of the router operating system. Cisco defines a maximum of 256 subinterfaces for each router, although large increases in this number might be in IOS Release 12.0. This limit means that no more than 256 VLANs can connect to a given router. In practice, the limit should not be a terribly onerous one.

Both VLAN control information and user data flow between VLAN switches. Before user data can go onto VLAN trunks, it must be marked so the switching system knows which VLAN each frame belongs to and use that membership information in replicating the frames onto each port assigned to the VLAN.

Protocols used to carry VLAN configuration information among switches include Cabletron policy protocols and Cisco Virtual Trunk Protocol. Cisco's VTP has a somewhat different function from VLAN tagging protocols.

In LANE, frames—or the cells into which they are segmented—are not tagged. Rather, their destination is defined by the virtual circuit over which they are traveling.

The relationship among MAC addresses and ELANs is defined in the LAN emulation server (LES) database. There can be cached versions of this information on LAN emulation clients.

How Much Multivendor Interoperability with VLANs?

Do not expect any level of compatibility among different vendors' proprietary VLAN protocols. IEEE 802.1Q does offer the potential of a deployable standard, but there remains room for interpretation. Most major vendors have implemented 802.1Q, although their initial releases might have been built from different and possible non-interoperable drafts of the standard.

I see the biggest problem due to the reality that 802.1Q does not have as rich a set of features as some proprietary VLANs. Even if you were interconnecting two "islands" of the same vendor through 802.1Q, you would lose some of the functionality of either island when it communicates with the other. The problem becomes even more acute when you try to interconnect multiple vendors' proprietary VLANs, each of which might have features that the other does not.

It is probably most reasonable, at least in the near term, to assume that VLAN switching domains are single vendor. If you have a requirement for multivendor switching, use routing between VLAN systems. You are apt to need different network management systems for each vendor VLAN.

Although it is still an emerging technology, there is a much better chance of multivendor interoperability among ATM LANE products that comply with recent ATM Forum specifications. Again, be cautious and be aware that each vendor has a different network management system. You need to be extremely careful that all vendors have built their products against the same version of the standard.

VLAN-Aware Hosts

Many servers need to be visible on many user subnets. Such servers include infrastructure functions such as DHCP and DNS; Internet and extranet access such as mail gateways, firewalls, and central Web caches; and application databases. The industry trend has been to centralize servers, other than perhaps local printers and caches. If you assume that switching is more cost-effective than routing within the campus, you want each user subnet to contain the central servers.

If large numbers of subnets are to appear on a given server, that server either must have multiple network interface cards or one or more VLAN-aware interface cards.

A VLAN-aware NIC essentially is a limited capability switch on a card, which recognizes VLAN-tagged frames intended for the host containing the VLAN-aware NIC. Non–VLAN-aware Fast Ethernet NICs cost about $100, whereas Fast Ethernet VLAN-aware NICs cost approximately $500. Ignoring bandwidth issues, the VLAN-aware NIC is certainly more cost-effective when five or more subnets need to connect to a server. Because there is a cost for slots into which NICs can be connected, and multiple NICs need to be cabled to multiple switch ports, the number of VLANs that make a VLAN-aware NIC cost-effective is often significantly less than five.

If you need only two light-traffic VLANs connected to a server, it might be more cost-effective to use two 10-Mbps NICs. Again, remember that each one of the NICs needs a switch port and cabling, so the savings might be minimal.

The various VLANs appear to host software as directly connected interfaces, whereas the NIC appears as a switch to other switches (or as a LEC to other LANE devices).

Nothing is free. The good news about a VLAN-aware card is that it presents a single physical interface for all VLANs to which it belongs. The bad news about a VLAN-aware NIC is that it presents a single physical interface for all VLANs to which it belongs. The bad news issue is that a Fast Ethernet (for example) VLAN-aware NIC offers a total of 100-Mbps bandwidth to be shared among all VLANs. If the sum of traffic on the separate VLANs is greater than 100 Mbps, you have a capacity problem.

There are several workarounds to a capacity limitation. Assume that you have four VLANs, each with 50 Mbps of traffic. In that case, as long as the server can support them, you can insert two VLAN-aware NICs and assign two VLANs to each.

If you have six VLANs, four of which have 10 Mbps of bandwidth each but two of which need 80 Mbps each, you could insert one VLAN-aware NIC into the server and connect the other two VLANs directly to edge switch ports.

Inverse multiplexing is another way around bandwidth limitations. A number of server and NIC vendors have licensed Fast EtherChannel from Cisco, which bundles together up to four Fast or Gigabit Ethernet links into one VLAN trunk.

The Number of Devices per VLAN

In practice, there are no architectural limits on the number of devices in a VLAN. There are many limits that derive from the specific VLAN protocol, the implementation of that protocol, the extent of broadcasts and multicasts, and the addressing capabilities of hosts. See Table 2.2 in Chapter 2 for a summary of such limits.

Implementation limits on the number of devices in a VLAN include the size of tables that map MAC addresses to VLANs. Bay and Cisco, for example, structure their tables differently, but a limit applies in both cases. Bay dedicates a 1024 slot address table to each switch port, whereas Cisco shares a table among all ports. The Cisco table, on high-end switches, has a maximum size of 16 K or 32 K slots.

VLAN trunking protocols have several functions. Before they can carry user traffic, they must establish connectivity among the interconnected switches.

Fault Tolerance in Switched Networks with VLANs

Fault tolerance in switched networks is dominated by the requirements of the spanning tree algorithm [Perlman, 1999]. The key restriction comes from the prohibition of more than one active bridge between any two LANs.

This is slightly different than having more than one active medium between two media, if the bridges use inverse multiplexing to hide the multiple media.

In general, spanning tree allows you to have an active path and one or more standby paths between different media. Load sharing is not as rich as with routed systems. Counter-balancing the restrictions of spanning tree switches is the reality that switches are used primarily in LAN environments, where bandwidth is cheap. The key function of load sharing is optimizing bandwidth use, which is appropriate when bandwidth is expensive.

Techniques such as HSRP and VRRP, which you learned about in Chapter 6, are principally concerned with routing. They work when switches are present but you need to be aware of potential interactions.

We can extend the fault tolerance model that has been presented with non-VLAN switched networks. The extensions, shown in Figure 10.32, allow load sharing of the different VLANs over the different components. If this were a single spanning tree, non-VLAN environment, half the switches and routers would be in hot standby.

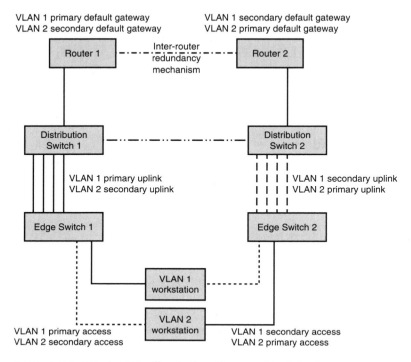

FIGURE 10.32 *VLANs allow both resilience and load sharing.*

In this configuration, however, VLAN 1 traffic normally uses the equipment on the left, whereas VLAN 2 traffic usually uses the traffic on the right. If there is a failure in either the left or right stacks, the network automatically reconfigures to put the traffic of both VLANs on a single stack.

Although this configuration is highly resilient, equipment failures can cause brief losses of connectivity while failures are being detected, caches are being built, and so on. True total redundancy requires the workstations to be connected to two completely independent switching systems, with the workstations or servers responsible for dealing with duplicate records.

LANE Operation

LANE is available in real products. It is especially attractive for situations where there is a need for connectivity among campuses. Until IEEE 802.1Q is more widely deployed, LANE probably offers the best chance of multivendor interoperability of various VLAN technologies.

LANE continues to evolve. The first LANE specification from the ATM Forum was version 1, which in many respects was an interim standard. Version 2 is now available and is the version against which most new products are being built. Multiprotocol over ATM (MPOA) is yet a newer generation that includes both Layer 2 and Layer 3 functions. MPOA is discussed in Chapter 13.

Formally, LANE supports emulated LANs (ELANs) rather than virtual LANs (VLANs). In practice, these are functionally equivalent.

LANE involves an infrastructure consisting of LAN Emulation Clients (LECs), LAN Emulation Configuration Servers (LECS), LAN emulation servers (LESs), and Broadcast and Unknown Servers (BUSes). Chapter 8, "Component Selection, Fault Tolerance, and Network Management," discusses the initialization of virtual circuits that interconnect these functions, as well as extensions for the interconnection of redundant functions.

Local configuration policies determine which ELAN a single LEC belongs to. It is an implementation matter in the LEC for it to determine which MAC addresses belong to its LANE.

Basic LANE Operation

When a frame arrives at a LANE client, the client looks up the destination address to see if it is local to the physically attached LAN. In Figure 10.33, MAC addresses 1 through 3 are local to LEC 1, which contains an LEC function. It is possible for LEC 1 to belong to more to one VLAN/ELAN, but the immediate discussion is concerned with the single VLAN/ELAN case.

In its tradition of confusing terminology, such as the LECS being different from more than one LEC, LANE has its own ARP mechanism. **LE_ARP** does *not* replace the ARP mechanism that binds a logical address to a transmission system address. **LE_ARP** binds a MAC address to the ATM address of an LEC.

Remember that LANE appears as a bridging system to conventional MAC-addressed LAN devices on the LANs serviced by LECs. The **LE_ARP** is internal to the LANE environment and binds a MAC address at the LEC to an internal ATM address in the trunking system that provides the connectivity among components of the LANE environment.

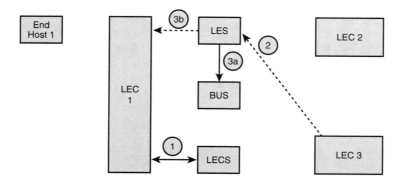

Legend

——————— Control VC

- - - - - - - Data VC

FIGURE 10.33 *Major steps LE_ARP resolution. The BUS multicasts the frame until the MAC to LANE correspondence is known—omitted from the figure.*

Each LEC has a LANE ARP cache. This cache can be populated with manually configured static entries, with dynamic information learned from the **LE_ARP** mechanism, or both. When an LEC becomes active in a LANE system, it has no dynamically learned information. When no local information is available, the process to resolve the MAC address involves the following steps:

1. The LEC establishes a Configuration Direct VC to an LECS and determines the LES address (Point 1).

2. The LEC sends the **LE_ARP_Request** to the LES for its ELAN, over the point-to-point control VC between LEC and LES (Point 2).

3a. Assuming that the LES has no local cache information about the destination MAC address, the BUS forwards the payload to all other LECs in the ELAN, using the unidirectional point-to-multipoint VC from the LES to all of its clients.

   Each LEC receives the request and checks its local tables to see if it connects the MAC address. If so, the LEC informs the LES of the ATM address that will reach the MAC address (Point 3).

3b. The LES caches the MAC-ATM correspondence and sends it back to the LEC that originated the **LE_ARP** (Point 4).

4. The originating LEC now creates a bidirectional VC to the ATM address where the destination MAC address can be reached and starts passing the data to that LEC for delivery to the destination MAC address. The flow after resolution is shown in Figure 10.34.

Although the LEC does not know the ATM address for the destination, it forwards the user data to the BUS, which floods the data to all other LECs.

A frame from MAC Address 4 arrives at Server 1, and Server 1 learns that Address 4 is local, just as any transparent bridge would do.

Assume that the destination MAC address is Address 5, which does not appear in Server 1's local cache. Server 1 has previously learned which LANE server is associated with the ELAN. Server 1 now sends a query to LES 1 to resolve the ATM address associated with the destination MAC address. This query is called an **LE_ARP**. If LES 1 already knows the ATM address associated with the destination, it replies directly to Server 1 with that address. If LES 1 does not know the ATM address, it forwards a query to all other LE clients in the ELAN, asking if they know the MAC address.

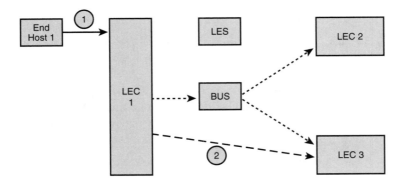

Legend

------- Multicast flow
— — — Unicast flow
——— Non-Lane edge flow

FIGURE **10.34** *After resolution, data flows directly between LECs. The LES is not involved after resolution; the BUS is involved only for multicasts.*

When using a LANE technique—or indeed any VLAN technique—that caches the location of MAC addresses, be careful when working with existing fault-tolerant source-route-bridging networks. Such networks are common with IBM mainframes.

Several IBM approaches for fault tolerance employ redundant front-end processors (FEPs), as shown in Figure 10.35. A given MAC address is active on only one front-end processor at a time, but, if an FEP fails, the address activates on a different FEP on a different Token Ring.

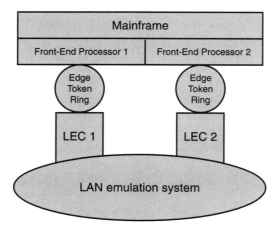

FIGURE 10.35 *If a MAC address moves, there will be some delay for caches and virtual circuits to reflect its new location.*

If the new Token Ring is connected to a different LEC, the virtual circuit that previously carried traffic to the MAC address is now pointing to the wrong LEC. There will be a delay before a VC can be constructed that goes to the correct LEC.

You can work around this problem, but you need to think about how to do so. The problem would not take place if both Token Rings connected to the same LEC, or both front-end processors were connected to the same Token Ring. These workarounds, of course, introduce one or more single points of failure.

Unknown and Non-Unicast Traffic

Although the LEC does not know the ATM address for the destination, it forwards the user data to the BUS, which floods the data to all other LECs. This is computationally intensive, and the BUS function usually is implemented on a processor separate from the main ATM switching fabric. The rationale for flooding information to potentially unknown or even nonexistent destinations, is that the LEC to which the destination will be connected has not had time to learn about a certain MAC address that will be reached through the LEC. Perhaps the MAC address is on the distant side of a conventional bridge from the LEC, or the LEC is simply in the process of updating tables when it receives the **LE_ARP**.

Of course, frames destined to multicast or broadcast MAC addresses should be flooded. The BUS does this flooding for such frames, using the same point-to-multipoint VCs it uses for unknown traffic.

The BUS might be the limiting factor to the scalability of an ELAN, due to its computationally intensive task. All the scaling problems of non-unicast traffic in LANs apply to LANE, but the additional challenge is the capacity of the BUS to forward frames. Remember, however, that there is one BUS per LANEv1 ELAN.

An additional constraint on the BUS is that it must reassemble all frames from their constituent cells before they can be transmitted. Not to do this creates a risk of out-of-order frame delivery.

The registration of an LEC with an LES is distinct from the function by which a LEC can register specific MAC addresses with the LES. LE Clients can register their MAC addresses with the LES that services their ELAN. By doing so, the client is saying it wants to receive traffic destined for the addresses it registers. The client can also register to receive frames destined for specific multicast groups.

The failure of a LANE infrastructure server has serious consequences. The LECS is the directory service function needed to set up no calls. An LECS failure means no further LE Clients can join the system. An LES failure means no new addresses can join the system, and a BUS failure stops the propagation of non-unicast frames.

Workarounds to these limitations include mechanisms that support primary/backup server relationships, as distinct from load-sharing servers. Load-sharing servers are a feature of LANE version 2. The IETF has a Server Cache Synchronization Protocol (SCSP), which was operationally preceded by Cisco's SSRP.

LANE Version 2

LANEv2 is intended to improve the scalability of LANE. A major enhancement allows you to work around the limits of LES/BUS performance by supporting more than one LES/BUS per ELAN. There are two LANEv2 protocols: LANE User-to-Network Interface (LUNI) that manages the interactions of an LE Client and a server and the LANE Network-to-Network Interface (LNNI) that coordinates the work of several servers.

Inter-server communications with LNNI works around the single point of failure problems of LANE version 1. Another way in which LANE version 2 is more scalable is that it permits the establishment of multiple BUSes in a single ELANE, with different multicast group replication assigned to different BUS platforms.

Although a single processor can handle the workloads of multiple ELANs, you can apply more CPU power to the BUS function by having multiple BUSes. Additional BUS devices, of course, add cost, but it might be necessary to implement more than one BUS to get the necessary performance. In all cases, you want a proactive monitoring program that tracks CPU usage on the BUS as a function of non-unicast traffic. If the CPU usage goes above a manufacturer-defined threshold, you need to either split the ELANs so they can use different BUSes or obtain a more powerful BUS platform if such is available. A major change is the capability to multiplex traffic on the Data Direct VCs that run between LE clients. The frames sent over these VCs use LLC to identify the ELAN number. Adding the LLC control field to a maximum-length frame can make it longer than the 802.3 limit, much as can Cisco's ISL header prepending discussed earlier.

Contrast the LANE header, shown in Table 10.6, with the LANE version 2 header in Table 10.7.

Table 10.6   The LANEv1 header

Offset	Length	Field
0	2 bytes	LANE header
2	6 bytes	Destination MAC address
8	6 bytes	Source MAC address
14	2 bytes	Type/length
16	Variable	Information

LANE version 2 builds on the LANE header, but precedes it with an 802.2 LLC/SNAP header and a LANE identifier.

Table 10.7   The LANEv2 header.

Offset	Length	Field
0	3 bytes	LLC DSAP 0xAAAA03
3	3 bytes	LLC/SNAP 0x00A03E
6	2 bytes	LLC/SNAP frame type
8	4 bytes	LANE identifier
12	2 bytes	LANE header
14	6 bytes	Destination MAC address
20	6 bytes	Source MAC address
26	2 bytes	Type/length
28	Variable	Information

Among the benefits of LANEv2 multiplexing is the capability to have a lesser number of virtual circuits on a given interface. Real ATM interfaces have physical characteristics of buffers or other system memory that limit the number of concurrent active VCs.

Quality of Service in LANE and VLANs

LANE version 2 allows multiple ATM addresses that can reach a destination, each associated with a different quality of service. Because LANE operates among LAN Emulation Clients, not directly between the end hosts, the LANE implementation has to have some mechanism for knowing when different qualities of service are needed.

We've seen that pattern matching, in the form of frame filters, can be used to select frames for filtering or for assignment to VLANs. The same sorts of decisions can be made to distinguish traffic intended for LANE VCs with a specified quality of service.

For connectionless VLANs, the emerging IEEE 802.1P specifications allow setting of priority fields rather than VLAN assignments. 802.1P and LANE version 2 prioritization have similar functions.

Prioritization, in either connectionless or connection-oriented systems, adds complexity. Always remember that an alternative in campus networks might be to overprovision bandwidth. Quality of service control becomes increasingly necessary when contending for limited bandwidth, as in trunk facilities or especially in WANs.

Switched Network Design and Interconnection Devices Above Layer 2

You can interconnect LANs and VLANs either at the network layer or at the application layer. There are several ways to provide routing services, even before marketing-speak confuses the situation. In *Animal Farm*, George Orwell had his revolutionary pigs chanting, "Four legs good, two legs bad." Irresponsible vendor and trade press comments have incorrectly polarized many people into believing that the function of routing is obsolete.

In reality, both routing and bridging are viable and complementary techniques. Many commercial products offer bridge (that is, switch) and router functions in the same chassis. The degree to which these functions are integrated varies widely. The functions might share no more than a common power supply and be configured in complete separation. The router might provide WAN access for a single LAN or VLAN.

Layer 2 bridging and Layer 3 routing, however, might not be the only technique appropriate for your particular network. There is a distinct role for application gateways, which operate at OSI Layer 7.

Do You Need Layer 3 Routing?

In *Monty Python and the Meaning of Life,* the narrator asks, "What is the most important machine in the hospital?" Several demented doctors respond, "The machine that goes *ping!*" In another example of applying British comedy to network architecture, whenever I do a complex design, I always use The Machine that Goes Ping as a reality test.

Given the current network design, if a user calls the help desk and complains she cannot connect to the network, the fundamental questions are the following:

- Do you know a unique IP address that can be used as the argument to the **ping** command?

- Do you have Layer 3 connectivity from the help desk to the workstation, such that you could deliver a **ping** if the network were operating properly?

If you need the ability to send a packet unchanged among user subnets, with a source on one of the user subnets, you need true routing. If you need the ability to send a packet with a source address on a network management subnet, you need true routing.

If you need the ability to send an application record among user subnets, or the ability to send a higher-level request (for example, **ping**) from a management workstation, but not necessarily true packets, you might have alternatives other than routing.

Figure 10.36 shows two user groups. Each has a local server and printer and needs to communicate with a mail server. Each user group is physically connected to a black box, which might be a router or a server.

You need to look at applications carefully to see that packet-level transmission between subnets is truly required. If the only servers used by each workgroup are the local server, local printer, and corporate mail server, there really is no reason for User Group 1 to send packets directly to User Group 2. The only direct communications between the user groups go through the mail server.

It might seem that if the black box were the mail server, there would be no need for a router. Routing functions are necessary when sending packets directly between subnets, and it would first appear you are not doing so in this configuration.

Again, the wisdom of Monty Python applies: "What is the most important machine in the hospital? The machine that goes *ping*!" If the black box in Figure 10.36 is a server, there is no direct Layer 3 connectivity between the interface to the help desk and the user subnets. Without Layer 3 connectivity, the help desk cannot *directly* **ping** the user devices to check connectivity.

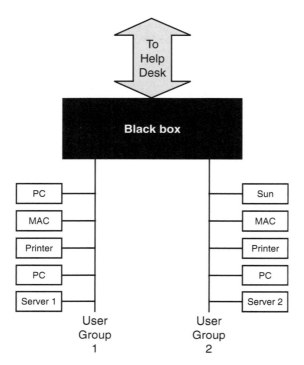

FIGURE 10.36 *How will you do diagnostics on the user subnets?*

If you do not use routing, it is important to consider how you will troubleshoot the network. In Figure 10.36, you can avoid the need to route between the user subnets if you can log in to the server and issue **ping** or other diagnostics from the server onto the user subnets.

If you use a multiported server, you also need to consider how you can remotely maintain the local servers. Again, this might be part of the server software.

Figure 10.37 reinforces the way in which an application gateway can replace a router. VLAN 4 is the backbone that connects VLANs 1, 2, and 3 to the rest of the network. The server does application-level relaying to VLAN 4, and a VLAN 4 port on the switch goes to the next level of hierarchy.

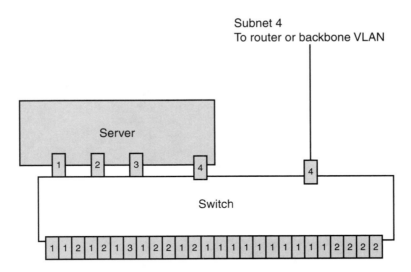

FIGURE 10.37   *Subnet 4 is the uplink to which outgoing packets on Subnets 1 through 3 are routed, after application processing.*

Connecting Switches and Routers

Depending on your bandwidth requirements, you can have multiple physical interfaces or VLAN-aware interfaces, as discussed earlier in the section "VLAN-Aware Hosts." The left side of Figure 10.38 shows a VLAN-aware connection between a switch and a single-armed router. You use this configuration when you are only routing between VLANs. This is perfectly reasonable if, for example, one of the VLANs connects to a firewall. The single-armed router, in such an application, is at the distribution tier.

The right side of Figure 10.38 shows a configuration where you use a VLAN-aware interface for access to the switch, but where the router also has connections to a WAN and to a server subnet.

Where bandwidth is an issue, the same considerations apply when connecting servers to routers. You can use a VLAN-aware interface, as shown in the left side of Figure 10.39.

The middle configuration in Figure 10.39 is useful at both extremes of the bandwidth spectrum. When there is little inter-VLAN routing, as would be typical when workgroups have their own servers and the only routing to them is for network management, you don't need much routing power. It can be quite cost-effective to connect the switch to the router with a 10-Mbps edge port for each VLAN.

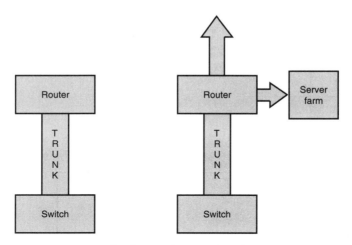

FIGURE 10.38   *Single-armed routers do only inter-VLAN routing.*

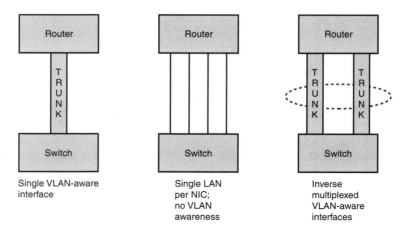

FIGURE 10.39   *You can fine-tune the physical connectivity between routers and switches to have the appropriate amount of bandwidth.*

High-end switches often have a routing function on an optional card. Cards that plug in to high-end switches often are called *blades* rather than *cards*. Blade seems an odd term to me, unless it is the explanation of how the backbone-in-a-box was extracted from its original body.

Shaking my head to return from the strangeness of terminology in this industry, I observe that internal routing cards often offer fairly high performance and are consequently expensive. An external router of lower performance, placed next to the switch and linked to it by VLAN-unaware or VLAN-aware ports, can be considerably less expensive. VLAN-unaware routers are the cheapest and might be adequate when the main routing load comes from network management rather than application traffic.

When you need high bandwidth into a router, for large amounts of inter-VLAN traffic, you can use inverse multiplexing on a VLAN trunk. Alternatively, internal router cards with direct access to the internal switching fabric might give even higher bandwidth. The choice here often centers on the routing functions available on an internal card rather than a full-featured standalone router. See Chapter 14 for a discussion of multilayer routing relationships between internal packet forwarding engines and internal or external route servers.

Application Gateways and Switched Network Design

When using application gateways, introduced in Chapter 6, one of your most important goals is matching the bandwidth available to servers with their processing capacity. Let's examine several scenarios with different application characteristics.

Access to Printer and WAN Gateway

Figure 10.40 shows a simple configuration with a local printer and a WAN gateway. All application information comes from the mainframe reached across the LAN. The individual workstations have their screen formats preloaded onto their hard drives. All devices connect to a 10-Mbps non–SNMP-managed hub.

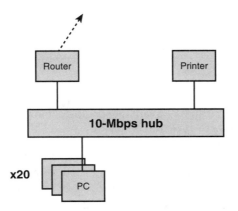

FIGURE 10.40 *Twenty PCs are on a LAN, which has a local printer. The router is connected to the WAN with a 128-Kbps Frame Relay link.*

For this configuration, a switch does not help performance. Your performance is limited by the speed of the WAN link. Although the printer is LAN attached, it is a sufficiently slow device that faster access to it will not make any difference in its printing rate.

The only real justifications for a switch, ignoring future requirements, are improved management and a cheaper fan-out of the router LAN interface.

Cached Access to Printer and WAN Gateway

Now, vary the application shown in Figure 10.40 so that some of the file lookups normally sent to the data center now can be done on a local cache. There is a backup cache server. These act as application gateways, passing selected traffic to the data center.

The revised configuration is shown in Figure 10.41. In this scenario, a small switch can be useful for speeding access to the critical cache servers. The ports to these servers could be 100-Mbps full-duplex.

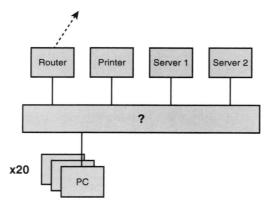

FIGURE 10.41 *The presence of a server suggests that a switch, or possibly a 100-Mbps hub, might improve performance.*

If there is a single cache server, it might be worth considering upgrading the hub and the NICs to 100 Mbps. For this to be advantageous, the clients should transmit infrequently and transfer large bursts when they do so.

With multiple servers, however, switching makes more sense. If the servers are true caches, they only contain transient data and there is no need for a separate backup subnet between them. If the servers also have the function of storing form definitions or other information distributed from a master copy, again no backup is required.

Looking Ahead

You should regard switching as an overdrive to Layer 3 routing. Routing and switching are complementary technologies. The next two chapters deal with routing architectures, first in a relatively flat topology and then in a formally hierarchical one.

Remember, when introducing switching into a routing system, you might not always need VLANs. If you do, both VLANs and LANE work. As with any technology, there are strengths and weaknesses with each.

Chapters 11 and 12 deal with conventional routing. Chapters 13 and 14 show new methods that merge routing and switching.

CHAPTER 11

Routing in a Single Area

The principle of equality does not destroy the imagination, but lowers its
flight to the level of the earth.
—Alexis de Tocqueville

We shape our buildings; thereafter they shape us.
—Winston Churchill

Those who expect to reap the benefits of freedom must, like men, undergo the
fatigues of supporting it.
—Thomas Paine

This chapter sets the broad stage of hierarchical routing, discussing elements from the global Internet down to groups of subnet prefixes in part of an enterprise. In this chapter, you learn how to design a homogeneous routing domain based on OSPF or on static routing. The pros and cons of the major dynamic routing mechanisms, OSPF and EIGRP, are compared in Chapter 7. This chapter assumes that you have chosen the routing protocol, and, unless mentioned otherwise, it is assumed that you have chosen OSPF.

Note

There are definite reasons that you might choose EIGRP, and EIGRP examples are given where appropriate in this and subsequent chapters. OSPF lends itself to being used for examples, and there is no reason to keep repeating the same design process for both protocols.

Why route rather than switch, anyway? Aren't switches faster than routers? A good way to answer these questions is to think of switching and routing as complementary technologies. Switching is an "overdrive" that you can apply in parts of your network, after routing has gotten them to "highway speed."

An even better way to think about these questions is to recognize that *routing* and *switching* are imprecise and, arguably, obsolete terms. It's better to think in terms of Layer 2 and Layer 3 path determination and Layer 2 and Layer 3 forwarding. A classical router does Layer 3 path determination and Layer 3 forwarding. A classical switch does Layer 2 path determination and Layer 2 forwarding. Emerging multilayer and cut-through techniques, discussed in Chapter 14, "New Methods in the Enterprise Core," both combine and distribute these functions. As you saw in Chapter 3, "How Do Switches and Routers Forward?" modern routers can distribute the forwarding function onto multiple processors.

What's a Router Anyway?

A few years ago, I taught a Cisco routing class at Advantis, which was then a joint venture of IBM and Sears Roebuck. My students kept laughing at me, saying they had much better routers than Cisco. At first, they wouldn't tell me the brand of these routers.

Eventually, they admitted they had Craftsman routers in mind. I sighed. Yes, I have a Craftsman router in my house—in my woodworking shop, where it belongs.

Woodworking routers actually have some parallels to modern networking routers. There are two main kinds of routers: conventional and plunge. A conventional router has a fixed motor with a chuck that holds a high-speed cutting bit. The conventional router is cheaper and simpler than the alternative, the plunge router. Conventional routers are more rigidly constructed

and are actually better for such things as edge-trimming kitchen countertops.

Plunge routers, however, have a motor housing that can move downward, like a miniature drill press. They are far superior when routing a hole in the middle of a board, because they can smoothly cut straight down. A conventional router has to be tilted gently down into the middle of a board, and—believe me—it can spin out of control when doing so.

Conventional routers, whether for networks or for wood, are cheaper, simpler, and more stable at the edges of their work. Plunge and cut-through routers give better price-performance in the center of the work, be that work wood or net. Cut-through network routers are also appropriate for high-density sites at the edge of the network.

You can create much more complex topologies with routers than with switches. With a few exceptions, connectionless switches forward within the constraints of a spanning tree. Only one path can be active between two switches, from the perspective of the spanning tree algorithm. Inverse multiplexing hides multiple links from the spanning tree algorithm.

When a link goes down in a standard switched system, the remaining switches go into a recomputation of the spanning tree. Although the spanning tree is being recomputed, which takes at least 30 seconds using standard timers, no traffic is forwarded over backup links. In contrast, when a link fails in a routed network, traffic continues to be forwarded to the remaining links.

The Context for Single Area Routing

Beyond the small routing systems described in Chapter 6, "Host and Small Network Relaying," practical routing systems are hierarchical. On a practical basis, there are several levels of hierarchy, shown in Figure 11.1:

- Global routing systems

- Autonomous systems

- Enterprises

- Routing domains

- Areas

- Intra-area routing

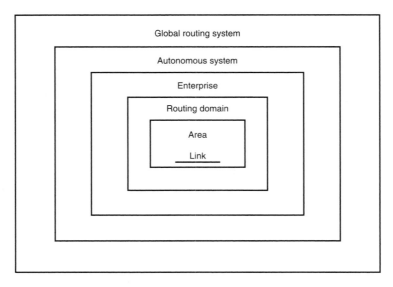

FIGURE 11.1 *The larger a routing system, the more levels of hierarchy it might need. Not all levels are present in every enterprise.*

Global Routing Systems

The most common global routing system is the general Internet, but it is not the only one. Remember that the Internet's predecessor, ARPAnet, was the first multiuser routing network, and its funding came from the U.S. military. Military networks have long used complex routing, but, for security reasons, do not connect to the general Internet.

There are many other multi-organizational networks that do not connect to the general Internet, such as inter-bank and credit card networks, supplier networks in the automotive industry, and so on. Any of these networks can divide their components into autonomous systems. These can use the same interorganizational routing techniques as the general Internet. These separate systems do need to have distinct administrative authorities to manage allocation of autonomous system numbers and addresses. Autonomous systems are the base units of global routing. Border Gateway Protocol, version 4, (BGPv4) transmits information on the reachability of autonomous systems and only secondarily—but critically—on the reachability of address blocks contained in the autonomous systems.

Autonomous Systems

An *autonomous system* is a superset of a routing domain. It is a set of routers and addresses that might be under one or more administrative authorities [RFC 1930]. The various administrative authorities cooperate, but only one authority controls the way in which routing information is advertised to, and accepted from, an Internet.

In this context, the Internet can be the general global Internet or a routing system containing multiple organizations that interconnect to one another. Examples of the latter type of routing system include military networks containing security-classified data, inter-bank networks, networks among stock brokerages, and so on. Private internets can use static routing between enterprises. If they use dynamic routing, BGPv4 gives a level of control that interior routing protocols do not. Advertisements propagate with BGPv4.

You also can use BGP to establish an intra-enterprise backbone of backbones, which is discussed in Chapter 12 "Special and Hierarchical Routing Topologies."

Enterprises

Because enterprises define business functions, which are driven by end hosts running applications, you should think of the enterprise first as a domain of unique names. You then map addresses to those names and define routing among those addresses. Using names as the basis of enterprise design allows you far more flexibility in using private or registered addresses, or in changing ISPs when your address space is lent by the ISP.

The key to defining an enterprise network is that there is some central authority that assigns addresses and names, even though the detailed maintenance of address and name space can be delegated to departmental network administrators. A concept under development in the IETF is that of a VPN identifier, which uniquely identifies an enterprise network provisioned over a set of service providers.

Enterprises might have one or more routing domains. Mergers and acquisitions can force the joining of separately designed routing domains. You also might want multiple routing domains for different geographic or administrative regions.

All but the smallest enterprises have at least some links they do not completely control, the WAN links provided by carriers. They might also have connectivity to the Internet.

Routing Domains

Routing domains are sets of routers and addresses that implement a consistent set of routing mechanisms, such as dynamic routing protocols, assumptions about metrics, and complementary static routing. A simple example is an enterprise that does all its dynamic routing with OSPF, EIGRP, RIP, or IS-IS. All routers have the same routing code implementation and use the same values for metrics.

An example of multiple routing domains can have two OSPF routing systems, one using 3Com defaults for metric and another using Wellfleet/Bay defaults. 3Com defaults to a bandwidth-based metric, whereas Bay defaults to hop count. Mixing the two can cause unpredictable and generally weird routing.

Inside routing domains, there can be one or more areas. If the routing domains have multiple areas, there is some sort of hierarchical relationship among the areas.

A large enterprise often contains multiple routing domains, for any of a number of reasons. Different divisions of a large firm often run their own networks, but a corporate change of direction can force them to connect to a corporate-level backbone. Mergers and acquisitions can put wildly dissimilar networks together, with a top-level mandate to make it all work.

Areas

Area is an OSPF term for a part of a routing domain in which local routing information is contained. In other words, change propagation inside the area is at least partially hidden from the rest of the routing domain. Only selected changes leak out, and there might be restrictions on the external routes allowed into the area.

An area contains a set of cooperating routers that share a synchronized and distributed topological database. Routers connected to multiple areas have multiple databases. Even though this example has a strongly hierarchical topology and addressing plan, the number of routes is sufficiently small for which-summarization is not required.

An area is a basic element of calculating the load on a router. For a link state protocol such as OSPF, in Area K, the workload is based on the following:

- The product of the number of intra-area routes in Area K and the logarithm of the number of routers in Area K

- The number of summarized or explicit inter-area routes seen in Area K

- The number of routes external to the routing domain seen in Area K

The capability to hide details of areas from other areas makes a significant reduction in routing traffic possible. Additional refinements are possible, further hiding the details of knowledge about areas outside the local area.

In this chapter, the term *area* is used for any area of restricted routing. An area must have the following:

- One or more routers

- A set of address ranges, which can be contiguous, noncontiguous, or fall into several contiguous groups

An area can have the following:

- One or more router interfaces to another area, routing domain, or autonomous system

- In OSPF, an area identifier

Inside an area, it is perfectly reasonable to have hierarchy. OSPF does not allow address summarization inside an area, although EIGRP, with its less strict model of areas, does.

In any case, address summarization is not the only way to impose hierarchy. The edge routers in Figure 11.2 can be relatively small devices with limited processing power and memory because they do not participate in dynamic routing.

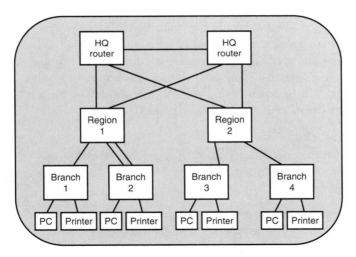

FIGURE 11.2 *A hierarchy of branch offices with local print servers, regional offices with regional servers, and a data center. There are parallel paths but no complex alternate paths.*

There are fewer routers at the next level within the area: the routing domain, autonomous system, or global routing system.

Media and Routing Constructs

Underlying all of the preceding routing abstractions are transmission media— or what appear to be transmission media. It is said that a noted physicist was giving a public lecture on the origins of the universe, after which a determined English dowager came up to him and said, "Young man, I don't believe in all this Big Bang nonsense. The ancient Chinese understood things properly, and they taught that the world stands on the back of a giant tortoise." The physicist, being no fool, responded, "And what, madam, does the tortoise stand on?" She said, "Another tortoise." Hawking thought he saw the opening to regaining control. "Madam, then on what does that tortoise stand?" She gave him a withering look. "Oh, I'm ahead of you, young man. It's tortoises all the way down."

And so it is with most networks of any size. They do not follow the classical OSI layering, but are layered. The conventional wisdom is that Frame Relay is a Layer 2 service. Yet if you obtain a Frame Relay connection of T1 or slower speed from at least one major carrier, the first provider device to which you connect is a Wellfleet/Bay/Nortel Networks BNX router. This device runs OSPF and encapsulates your frames in IP for delivery over the best available path to an ATM switch.

Security tunnels can be a shim between Layer 3 and 4 (one of the options of IP security [IPsec]) or a Layer 2 protocol over Layer 3 (such as PPTP). To get components to interoperate, you might be forced to do things that seem ugly from a purist standpoint of layering. I can only try to soothe you with Samuel Johnson's remark, "The important thing about a dog walking on his hind legs is not how well he does it, but that he does it at all."

Virtual Private Networks

VPNs are administrative definitions rather than strictly technological ones. You might define the routing for an area, a routing domain, or an enterprise to run over VPN connectivity.

There is not yet a generally accepted industry consensus definition of VPNs. In a proposal made to the IETF [Berkowitz, 1999b], I've described what I find to be useful in designing with VPNs: I have found the only way I've been able to grasp VPNs is to think of a core set of services, which are not terribly useful in and of themselves. The basic core service is the capability to establish, by administrative criteria, a set of members of the VPN. The *membership function* is the fundamental core service provided by a VPN. Not all IP-addressable nodes in an enterprise need to be in a VPN; there might be more than one VPN in an enterprise. Extranets, involving multiple enterprises, can be defined as VPNs.

Another core service might be associating a VPN identifier with each VPN. This identifier is not necessarily transmitted with packets; it might be there simply for management functions.

To this core set are added more interesting user services such as security, non-IP protocol handling, quality of service, and address translation. After the set of user services is defined, it needs to be mapped to one or more underlying transport services.

The connectivity services can be routed IP or a set of tunnels. As shown in Figure 11.3, they can be provisioned over one or more transport systems. As you can see, that which the VPN system perceives as a routed IP transport actually maps to a lower level of transport. This lower level is invisible to the end user and shows the flexibility possible with a routed or MPLS infrastructure—the transport provider can change transport media as operational realities make necessary.

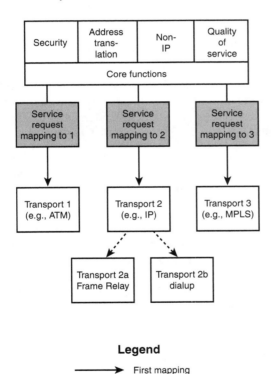

FIGURE 11.3 *VPN tunnels map to actual transport facilities run by an external service provider(s).*

For details of mapping the user-perceived VPN to the underlying transport, see the section "Tunneling" in Chapter 12.

Components of Areas

Areas, at the least, contain address ranges and routers. In link-state protocols, there are explicit identifiers for the area itself and for routers inside it. EIGRP allows you to configure the equivalent of areas, but does not have a concept of an area identifier. RIP and IGRP really do not support areas, although you can introduce some hierarchy with filtering. See "Pseudo-summarization with RIP and IGRP" in Chapter 12.

Areas can be manually configured using static routing. When you configure areas either for static or dynamic routing, you need to consider the appropriate degree of meshing within the area. When the area is dynamically routed, you need to consider the number of routers and links.

Static Area Structures

Many applications, especially those that are mainframe-based, are inherently hierarchical. If there are no alternate physical paths, you have a good candidate for static routing.

Route lookup is fast in modern routers. Other than in the largest enterprises, the true speed of lookup is not the limiting factor. Rather, having a small routing table in each router makes the routing system more understandable for maintenance and troubleshooting.

Although route lookup rarely is a performance limit in enterprises, bandwidth occupied by routing updates can be. Static routing can actually outperform dynamic routing if bandwidth is scarce, because you do not incur the overhead of routing updates.

Modern routing protocols, such as OSPF and EIGRP, impose minimal overhead when running. They tend to have an increased load at initialization in comparison with earlier protocols such as RIP and IGRP, as they build their initial routing tables. EIGRP generally has lower CPU utilization than OSPF, but has the disadvantage of being proprietary. See Chapter 7 for some of the issues of the choice between OSPF, EIGRP, and IS-IS.

Warning

Don't assume that static routing completely removes all overhead on links. If you have any sort of failure notification or automatic backup, you need some sort of keepalive mechanism to inform you when a link fails.

In dynamic routing, routers generate routes inside areas. Distance-vector protocols propagate routes inside the area, although both their advertising and installation into Routing Information Bases (RIB) can be restricted by acceptance policies implemented with route filters. See "Hierarchy with Inter-Area Dynamic Route Summarization" in Chapter 12.

With link-state protocols, topological information about all media and routers inside the area is propagated to everyone else, but configuration options might be available for preventing some from being installed in the RIBs of specific routers. The lack of capability to restrict flooding of topological information is not necessarily a problem, because link-state protocols (as well as EIGRP) only transmit changes after the databases are established. The need to restrict flooding is related to area size. In large networks, you want a hierarchical structure that lets you summarize at area boundaries.

Figure 11.4 illustrates flooding inside an area structure. There is no need to flood to the branch routers, because they are statically routed. Routers in the area can pass summaries to the next hierarchical level. In some cases, you want to pass specific routes to the next level; see "OSPF Internal Summarization" in Chapter 12.

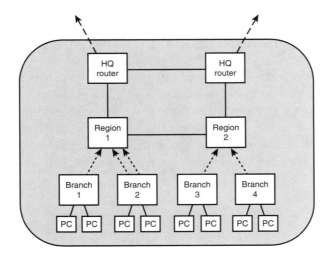

Legend

—————— Dynamic intra-area
-------> Static routed
— — —> Summaries to higher level

FIGURE 11.4 *Routers inside a dynamically routed area flood routing information to their neighbors, which pass on information according to the rules of the routing protocol.*

Routers at the edges of areas propagate topological information to the backbone. The information sent to and from the backbone usually is at a higher level of detail than is propagated inside the area.

How Much Meshing Is Enough?

Within an area, there is always a question of how much to interconnect routers. This section deals with connectivity in the overall area topology and complements the later section, "How Many Neighbors Should a Router Have?" which deals with the topology from a perspective of a single router.

Following are the two main arguments for a high level of meshing:

- Increasing the number of alternate paths, presumably increasing availability

- Reducing latency between two endpoints by reducing transfers through intermediate hops

Increasing the number of paths might increase availability at first, but suffers from diminishing returns. A key factor is that you really might not be creating independently redundant paths when you add circuits. In Figure 11.5, there might appear to be multiple paths between Sites 1 and 3, but, in reality, there is only one local loop for each site. Having multiple physical circuit identifiers from the carrier does not guarantee that the circuits will go through independent physical facilities that cannot be taken out by the same failure. The carrier backbone easily might provision both circuits through a common path; see the section "Grooming" in Chapter 9.

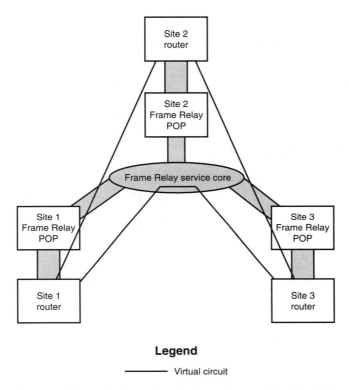

Legend

——————— Virtual circuit

FIGURE 11.5   *Is there real redundancy between Sites 1 and 3?*

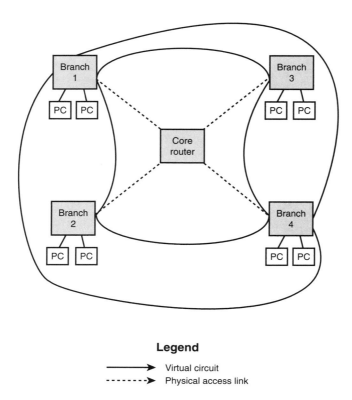

Legend

⟶ Virtual circuit

- - - ⟶ Physical access link

FIGURE 11.6 *Latency requirements need to be balanced against ease of maintenance.*

Latency is a more complex issue. In Figure 11.6, a Frame Relay carrier would have a typical internal delay of 65 milliseconds. *Internal delay* is the delay encountered after traversing the local loop. Purely from the transmission rate standpoint, a 1500-byte packet takes 225 milliseconds to traverse a 64 Kbps local loop, 9 milliseconds to traverse a T1, and 0.32 milliseconds to traverse a T3.

So, the direct path between Site 1 and Site 3, assuming that each site has a 64-Kbps local loop, is 515 milliseconds. If a core router is established as a hub and has a T1 access, the delays the traffic would encounter in the mesh and hub-and-spokes configurations are the following:

Delay Element	Mesh	Hub and spoke (ms)
Site 1 local loop	225	225
Site 2 local loop	225	225
First hop network delay	65	65
Site 2 local loop		
In		9
Out		9
Second hop network delay		65
Total	515	598

It might appear that there is little cost difference between mesh and hub and spoke. But increasing the number of virtual circuits on an interface is not free for many carriers. Figure 11.7 illustrates the alternative of treating one virtual circuit to the hub site as the default route.

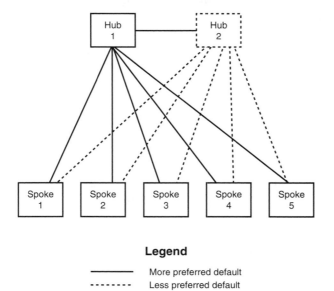

Legend

——————   More preferred default

- - - - - - -   Less preferred default

FIGURE 11.7 *You can build fault-tolerant hub-and-spoke networks. Hub 1 and Hub 2 could be at the same or different sites.*

By adding the next hop, you add about 16% to the delay. Is this significant in a WAN environment? You need to trade this off against other costs, which include the following:

- Incremental costs, initial and recurring, of the additional circuits, be they real or virtual.

- Additional maintenance cost to configure static routes for the full mesh, assuming all-static routing.

- Lack of a central point for measurement. The carrier might provide adequate measurement, making this a non-issue.

- Additional memory on the router for handling buffers for each virtual circuit.

- Additional router processing load imposed by scanning through a longer list of data link connection identifiers (DLCIs).

- Additional router processing time to maintain neighbor relationships, if dynamic routing is used.

- More complex troubleshooting.

The percentage differences of meshing are more dramatic in a LAN environment, but the absolute values are less:

Delay Element	Mesh	Hub and Spoke (ms)
Site 1 local loop	1.2	1.2
Site 2 local loop	1.2	1.2
First hop network delay	1.2	1.2
Site 2 local loop		
In		1.2
Out		1.2
Second hop network delay		1.2
Total 3.6	7.2	

There is a much more fundamental problem in excessive meshing. Increasing redundancy does not always increase availability and might actually decrease it.

This seemingly counterintuitive point comes from the research of Radia Perlman [Perlman, 1992]. She discusses a concept from formal reliability called the Byzantine Corruption Problem. Essentially, this problem deals with system failures that are caused by corruption of control information, not component outages. If inaccurate information enters a control system, increasing redundancy tends to propagate the wrong information more quickly.

Unfortunately, dynamic routing protocols are just the sort of control systems she describes. Routing protocol designers have searched for various ways of making their software more robust in response to information errors caused by misconfiguration or bugs in the routing code. There is no general solution to this problem.

Hierarchical design with address summarization helps protect against bad information, because detailed information that might contain errors is hidden from routers outside the immediate area. Another issue, long a matter of religious war among routing designers, is the robustness of different routing algorithms when presented with incorrect information.

Arguments can be made that advanced distance-vector protocols are more robust than link-state protocols, because an error in a link-state database propagates to all routers. All the routers in a link-state area, therefore, base their computation on the same wrong data. Advocates of distance-vector mechanisms suggest that the incremental computation done by distance vector gives an opportunity to catch errors before they propagate everywhere. In practice, modern link-state and distance-vector protocols are fairly free from errors, but this area of discussion remains a challenging one for protocol architects interested in designing routing protocols for ever-larger networks.

The Basics of Dynamically Routed Area Sizing

You need to consider both application requirements and router performance capabilities in determining how many routers can go into an area. From the application perspective, your goal is defining areas that hold complete communities of interest: sets of clients and servers that primarily communicate with one another.

From the platform capabilities standpoint, the goal is keeping the size of the area sufficiently small that a burst of routing changes, which propagate through the entire area, do not overwhelm the memory and route processor of the routers in the area. Numbers between 50 and 200 routers often are mentioned, but need to be taken in perspective.

When considering the number of routers in an area, count only those that run dynamic routing protocols. Many edge routers use static and default routing to reach the next higher level of hierarchy, and thus never generate a burst of routes nor have to process one.

Consider the CPU power of routers. When the 50 to 200 router guideline was written, a high-end router had a relatively modest CPU. Fast RISC processors on commercial routers can handle much more activity, as long as you keep in mind that additional software features tend to be loaded onto newer routers. With "feature creep" not all the power of the router processor is necessarily available for pure routing. Cisco still recommends a target of 50 routers per area, but other vendors build areas of 500 or more. Cisco's limit is very conservative.

There are reasons other than performance to limit the number of routers in an area. The more routers, the more likely it is that there will be configuration errors. Smaller areas have smaller configuration files and tend to localize the effect of configuration errors. Smaller areas have smaller routing tables, which are easier to troubleshoot than large ones.

If you run multiple vendor implementations of OSPF, a conservative engineering approach suggests that you try to keep the routers in a single area to be all from the same vendor and ideally of the same operating system version. If there are compatibility problems, you can focus your troubleshooting on the area border routers rather than having to look everywhere.

Area Sizing Considerations

Assuming that there will be multiple areas, the backbone area 0.0.0.0 should be reserved for transit traffic and network management servers. See "Considerations for Area 0.0.0.0" in Chapter 12 for details of special concerns in designing area 0.

To decide which subnets and routers should go into a specific non-backbone area, here are some basic guidelines:

- Examine a list of communities of interest. (You can find details of defining communities of interest in Chapter 3 of *Designing Architectures for Routing and Switching*, also from Macmillan Technical Publishing.)

- Does a given community of interest need fewer than the vendor limit of routers that speak a dynamic routing protocol, allowing reasonable growth? On Cisco, a conservative limit is 50, although it can be exceeded with routers with more than minimally powerful CPUs.

- Is there reason to believe some of the routes will be unstable, because they run over poor lines or are dialups? Consider using a demand routing protocol or making these static or blackhole routes. See "Blackhole Routes" in Chapter 12 for additional detail. If you cannot reduce the number of unstable routes, be very careful with the size of the area. Definitely keep it under 50 routers, and you might want to have 10–20.

If there is reason to believe some of the routes will be unstable, make it a preliminary area. If there is not, go back to Step 1 and consider whether there are natural geographic boundaries to the area (for example, Eastern versus Western Sales). If there is a set of servers common to geographically separated client groupings, you might have defined a need for hierarchical structure.

When Does a Single-Area OSPF Make Sense?

It isn't always necessary to set up a multiple-area hierarchy to get the benefits of OSPF. You certainly can get its advantages of fast convergence and variable-length subnet mask (VLSM) support with a single area.

Even in a single area, it still is worth being hierarchical as much as is practical. See Figure 11.2 for an example of topological hierarchy within a single area. Topological hierarchy does not let you summarize, but, if you do not have too many routes, this is not a major problem.

When you use OSPF in a single area, do not succumb to the sometimes "intuitive" idea of making it area 0.0.0.0. A good design guideline, discussed further in Chapter 12, is that no application servers should be in area 0.0.0.0. If your network grows to a point where multiple areas make sense, user routers need to be renumbered out of area 0.0.0.0.

If the routers do not group into a reasonable area, it might even be appropriate to think of setting them up as more than one routing domain, a technique discussed in Chapter 12.

An alternative to a single-area OSPF routing domain is to use EIGRP. EIGRP is easier to configure in a topology that does not lend itself to hierarchical organization, although EIGRP also supports fully hierarchical topology.

Configuring OSPF

OSPF needs far more configuration than RIP or IGRP. My experience is that it is best to go beyond the minimum configuration, if you want it to be easy to extend and troubleshoot.

OSPF router initialization begins by selecting a router ID and building data structures for its locally connected interfaces, and then begins transmitting hello messages to find other routers.

OSPF requires an explicit identifier for a router itself, as distinct from any of its links. Most router vendors have a convention that uses some physical interface IP address as the router ID, but you should avoid this in the interest of stability.

Different OSPF implementations have different defaults for the router ID; the OSPF standard is silent on the subject. The default mechanisms might come into conflict; using the loopback or equivalents on other vendors (for example, circuitless interface on Bay) lets you know what everyone will do. 3Com, for example, has a default that uses part of the MAC address.

On any vendor's router, it is quite useful to be able to set the router ID explicitly rather than rely on some software-defined or hardware-defined default. Many vendors are implementing this capability, but have been very slow to do so. See "An Identity Crisis among OSPF Routers" later in this chapter for an example of the problems that can come from allowing the router ID to default. Virtual links, described in Chapter 12, are another OSPF feature that can become very confused if router ID selection is not tightly controlled.

Different vendors have different commands for starting OSPF. Bay enables it with an interface-oriented command, whereas Cisco has global configuration statements.

Basic Setup

For any OSPF process to initialize, it must be able to define a router ID for the entire OSPF process. After the router-wide data structures are built, it is then necessary to define the networks that the router will advertise and the area numbers into which these networks will be advertised.

The OSPF Management Information Base (MIB) [RFC 1850] suggests a set of assumptions that can be used to automatically configure a simple OSPF configuration. **GateD** comes the closest to being able to autoconfigure OSPF. Remember that autoconfiguration can be a dangerous oversimplification in a network of any real complexity.

Assuming that IP is already up and running and the MIB constructs for each interface are configured, a minimal set of assumptions for OSPF autoconfiguration are the following:

- Driver code on the router automatically obtains the interface bandwidth.

- The OSPF code automatically discovers all interfaces in the router and generates matching OSPF interface tables.

- Type of service (TOS) is either not used or is used as Type 0 with all metrics automatically determined.

- OSPF automatically determines the areas that will be required. In practice, this tends to mean that autoconfiguration is limited to a single area.

In principle, doing an SNMP **SET** of **ospfAdminStat := enabled** causes this autoconfiguration to take place, resulting in an OSPF configuration with attributes including the following:

- The RouterID is one of the IP addresses of the router (the specific address selected is vendor specific).

- The router does not provide either area border or autonomous system border functions.

- Every IP-capable interface of the router runs OSPF.

- Every interface is in Area 0.

- Broadcast and point-to-point interfaces are enabled, but NBMA interfaces require the manual configuration of at least one neighbor.

- All timer values are set to the defaults recommended by the MIB specification:

Timer	Default Value
Hello Interval	10 seconds
Dead Timeout	40 seconds
Retransmission	5 seconds
Transit Delay	1 second
Poll Interval	120 seconds

- None of the following options are used:

    Address summarization

Authentication

Stub links to hosts

Virtual links

- Interface costs are set automatically using the MIB recommendation of 10^8/bandwidth.

Bay RS Router Setup

With the Bay RS command interface, you begin by navigating to a defined IP interface, and enter the following command:

ospf area {*area-id*}

If you do not configure an explicit router identifier on a Bay router, it defaults to using the IP address of the first interface configured to run OSPF. You can set an explicit router ID with the following command:

router-id {*ip-address-value*}

Cisco Router Setup

Cisco OSPF initialization begins with selecting, as the router ID, the numerically highest IP address configured on a loopback interface, if one or more loopback interfaces exist. If no loopback interfaces are defined, the OSPF process uses the numerically highest IP address value on an active physical interface. If no physical interfaces are active and configured with an IP address, the OSPF code does not initialize. In recent IOS versions, the router issues an error message if it cannot find a router ID. Older versions simply do not initialize OSPF.

Note

Numerically highest IP address value means the value of the IP address configured on the interface, not the number of the interface itself. If you have Ethernet 0 with an address of 172.16.1.1 and Ethernet 1 with an address of 10.0.1.1, the highest address would be 172.16.1.1.

On Cisco routers, you enter a global **router** command followed by parameters that control the interfaces on which OSPF will run:

```
! first OSPF process
router ospf process-id
network  <prefix-to-advertise>
              w.w.w.w
         area
         <area for prefix>
```

```
! second OSPF process (if you use multiple processes)
router ospf process-id
network statements...
```

The **router** major command creates an OSPF process. *process-id* is a local value used to identify multiple OSPF routing domains on the same physical routers. Not all vendors support multiple OSPF domains on the same chassis, so this might be confusing. *process-id* is *not* propagated outside the router. It is *not* an autonomous system number. A given OSPF interface belongs to one process only. See Figure 11.8.

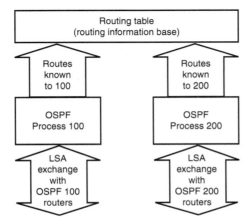

FIGURE 11.8 *The routing table contains information from both processes, but the processes are unaware of one another.*

OSPF 100 is not aware of OSPF 200, and vice versa. Only with explicit redistribution, discussed in Chapter 12, do they exchange any information. Routes from both OSPF 100 and OSPF 200 appear in the routing table of this router. The process ID numbers do not propagate outside the router; they are only used to separate processes inside the router.

Having multiple routing processes can be quite useful in consolidating networks and in creating another level of hierarchy in a large enterprise or an enterprise with a tricky physical topology. See "Multiple OSPF Processes" in Chapter 12 for more information.

network subcommands of **router ospf** cause routing advertisement if the corresponding interface is initialized. Although you can create network statements that refer to multiple physical interfaces, I do not recommend doing so, I find that the additional work of writing one network statement for each physical interface pays major dividends in subsequent maintenance and troubleshooting. The area parameters of network statements help define the router type and the inter-area topology. **area** parameters of network statements define router type and define topology. Network statements are detailed later in the section "Address Advertising Inside Areas."

An Identity Crisis Among OSPF Routers

Consider the following scenario of Cisco routers that do not use loopbacks. Cisco is used for illustration here, but the problem is relevant to most implementations.

Routers R1 and R2 are connected over their e1 interfaces. Someone configures R1 with the following configuration, which has an error on e1:

```
hostname R1
int e0
ip addr 192.168.0.2 255.255.255.0
int e1
ip addr 192.168.255.1 255.255.255.0  ! mistyped...should have
been .255.2
int e2
ip addr 192.168.1.2 255.255.255.0
router ospf 1
network 192.168.0.0 0.0.0.255 area 1
network 192.168.1.0 0.0.0.255 area 1
network 192.168.255.0 0.0.0.255 area 1
```

The router comes up with router ID 192.168.255.1. It happily is routing on e0 and e2; e1 is a stub for now. e1 is working perfectly well on a single router, but is misconfigured for the overall routing system.

Now, an administrator adds another router, with the correct configuration:

```
hostname R2
int e0
ip addr 192.168.2.1 255.255.255.0
int e1
ip addr 192.168.255.1 255.255.255.0  ! this is correct
int e2
ip addr 192.168.3.1 255.255.255.0
router ospf 1
network 192.168.2.0 0.0.0.255 area 1
network 192.168.3.0 0.0.0.255 area 1
network 192.168.255.0 0.0.0.255 area 1
```

> R2 comes up with the router ID 192.168.255.1. The hello initialization fails because R2 hears a duplicate router ID from R1.
>
> Our Hero, the network administrator, troubleshoots and discovers R1/e1 was misconfigured. He fixes the *ip address* statement.
>
> But R1 still thinks it's 192.168.255.1. The only way to get the router ID to become the correct 192.168.255.2 is to restart OSPF or reboot. But that will disrupt service on e0 and e2.

Most OSPF commands that are not specific to interfaces go under the **router** command. These include commands that set the following:

- Global import policy (called redistribution by Cisco. See "Importing, Exporting, and Controlling External Routes" in Chapter 12)

- Global export policy to the routing table

- Global authentication

- Area-specific default cost

- Area-specific stub mode (see Chapter 12)

- Area-specific demand capability

GateD Router Setup

GateD, whose publicly available code is the basis of many router vendor implementations, runs over UNIX and uses a command language. The global setup command for OSPF includes the following:

```
ospf yes ¦ no ¦ on ¦ off [ {
    defaults {
        preference preference ;
        cost cost ;
        tag [ as ] tag ;
        type 1 ¦ 2 ;
        router-prio ;
        ospfarea [backbone ¦ area-id]  ;
    } ;
    exportlimit routes ;
    exportinterval time ;
    traceoptions trace_options ;
    monitorauthkey authkey ;
    monitorauth none ¦ ( [ simple ¦ md5 ] authkey ) ;
    stubhosts {
            host cost cost ;
        } ;
```

```
        interface interface_list; [cost cost ] {
            interface_parameters
        } ;
        interface interface_list nonbroadcast [cost cost ] {
            pollinterval time ;
            routers {
                gateway [ eligible ] ;
            } ;
            interface_parameters
        } ;
        Backbone only:
        virtuallink neighborid router_id transitarea area {
            interface_parameters
        } ;
    } ;
} ] ;
```

Address Advertising Inside Areas

Routers inside areas advertise blocks of addresses. In link-state protocols, all addresses must be advertised. Distance-vector protocols allow selective advertisement. You need to tell the routing protocol which prefixes to advertise and either let the protocol select its default metric or provide a per-interface metric.

You need to configure the router according to which prefixes it is to advertise. For OSPF and IS-IS, you also need to assign the addresses to areas. Different vendor implementations vary in how addresses are assigned to areas.

By using a classless protocol such as OSPF, IS-IS, EIGRP (with **no auto-summary** configured), or RIP-2, the discontiguous network problem really does not exist if you use classless routing, because there is no inappropriate summarization of addresses at classful network boundaries. All subnets are advertised, so there is no lack of information.

The advertisement of all subnets, however, can lead to excessive overhead. It is not that you never want to summarize; it is that you want to control the summarization better than a classful protocol will do.

Summarization is detailed in Chapter 12. At this point, you should assume that all subnets will propagate throughout an OSPF area. EIGRP allows summarization at arbitrary points in a topology and does not impose a strict area structure.

Wellfleet/Bay RS Addressing Inside Areas

On a Bay router, you activate OSPF on a per-interface basis, so the subnet mask for the advertisement is that of the interface. As part of the interface-level configuration, you specify an **area** *area-id* command to associate the interface prefix with an area.

It's probably a matter of style, but I find the Bay technique to be less error-prone on initial setup, but Cisco's to be more maintainable in the long run, especially on routers with many interfaces. Both methods work.

In maintaining a Bay configuration, you can miss an interface while changing things on a large router. You can foul things up equally on Cisco, however, by using **network** statements that wildcard addresses and pick up addresses you do not mean to advertise in a given area. One of the most common configuration errors in Cisco OSPF is putting **network** statements in the wrong order.

Cisco Addressing Inside Areas

On Cisco routers, you define OSPF advertising rules on a global **router** command for the router chassis. You should specify a **network** statement for each link you want to advertise, although other factors become involved before actual advertising takes place. As I have mentioned before, it is possible to have a single **network** statement that covers multiple interfaces, but I strongly advise you not to do so.

In the context of using a single **network** statement per interface, the **network** commands have masks that specify the length of the prefix to advertise.

Simply coding the **network** statement does not cause the associated address to be advertised. A physical interface with an address inside the address range specified with the address and mask on the **network** statement must be active and running OSPF before advertising will take place.

It can be very easy to make coding errors that assign addresses to areas other than the ones you intend. My practice is to make the assignments as specific as possible, minimizing the chances of inadvertent error. When you make the assignments more specific, you find it is much easier to make changes to the configuration without unforeseen effects.

Figure 11.9 illustrates how, on a Cisco router, **network** subcommands of **router** statements define the advertisements for which a given router originates advertisements.

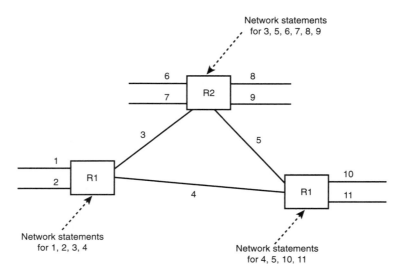

FIGURE 11.9 *Cisco uses network commands for all its routing protocols. In this picture, all numbered networks become known, but you only specify networks that are directly connected.*

network statements with classful addresses only are used for classful routing protocols such as RIP and IGRP, and EIGRP in classful compatibility mode.

Various OSPF configuration statements use masks to show prefix length. Not all statements use the same kind of mask.

Network statements use *wildcard masks*. A wildcard mask has a zero bit in every position of the prefix—the part on which we want to make routing decisions. This is the opposite convention of the more common subnet masks. Table 11.1 shows various network statements, some of which are in a form I do not recommend.

TABLE 11.1 EXAMPLES OF NETWORK STATEMENTS

Address	Subnet Mask	Wildcard Mask	Description
0.0.0.0/0	255.255.255.255	0.0.0.0	Any network—but don't do this!
10.1.0.0/16	255.255.0.0	0.0.255.255	A subnet
10.1.0.1/16	255.255.255.255	0.0.0.0	A specific router interface
172.31.1.0/24	255.255.255.0	0.0.0.255	A subnet
172.31.1.1/24	255.255.255.255	0.0.0.0	A specific router interface

Address	Subnet Mask	Wildcard Mask	Description
192.198.24.32/28	255.255.255.240	0.0.0.15	A subnet
192.168.24.32/27	255.255.255.255	0.0.0.0	A specific router interface
172.31.18.100/32	255.255.255.255	0.0.0.0	A single host route
172.20.3.53/23	255.255.254.0	0.0.1.255	A subnet
172.20.3.53/23	255.255.255.255	0.0.0.0	A specific router interface

Wildcard masks are also used in Cisco access lists. Be careful not to use wild-card masks on Cisco OSPF summarization commands, which use subnet masks. The format of the network command, which uses wildcard masks, is the following:

network *prefix wildcard-mask* **area** *area-number*

Tip

When specifying the wildcard mask on a Cisco router, the subnet and wildcard byte mask values should add up to 255. In tabular form, the rules for the relationship between subnet and wildcard mask octet is this:

If the Octet in the Subnet Mask Is	The Corresponding Wildcard Mask Octet Is
255	0
254	1
252	3
248	7
240	15
224	31
192	63
128	127
0	255

Cisco's algorithm for assigning interfaces to routing protocols sometimes is subtle, especially with OSPF. It is order dependent, so the first rule that matches an address is the rule that applies, even though a more specific rule might follow in the list. This logic is the same as in Cisco access lists.

Subnet masks on each interface of the router are logically ANDed with the interface address, producing a prefix associated with the interface. This prefix is then compared with each prefix defined by a **network** subcommand of each **router** command. If the prefixes match, the routing protocol specified by the **router** statement activates on that interface.

OSPF router statements use a wildcard mask to tell how many bits of the address in the **network** statement should be considered.

Tip

*Use one network statement for the prefix of each interface of each router. This means more writing, but makes them easier to troubleshoot. Consider offline editing for complex configurations. For OSPF process 999, begin the new configuration with **no router ospf 999** followed by **router ospf 999** and the new set of network statements.*

Remember order dependency. As soon as a rule is matched, the corresponding action occurs, even if there is a better match later in the list.

GateD Addressing Inside Areas

The simplest way to specify area membership in **GateD** is to use the *simple default case,* which is intended to activate OSPF for all current interfaces. All that is needed is the command **ospfarea {backbone | area-id}**. This command is usable only for cases when all interfaces go in the same area.

In the more general case, you explicitly set the area number. You are not allowed to set the value 0.0.0.0, but must use the **backbone** keyword.

A list of **network** statements defines the address ranges to be advertised. Intra-area routes that fall into one of these ranges are not advertised outside the area, which makes GateD more automated than other implementations in generating summary ranges.

Stub hosts, which are directly connected routers, are explicitly configured with **stubhost** commands. You also configure the loopback interface with a **stubhost** command. The loopback interface address, as on Cisco routers, is used as the router ID.

Metrics

When OSPF was designed, the working group consciously did not specify a particular metric. This was intentionally left to be an implementer or network administrator choice to maximize design flexibility. Although a bandwidth-based metric is generally most appropriate, the working group recognized that there might be situations, for example, where a monetary cost might be associated with going through particular interfaces. The OSPF protocol proper simply defines a per-interface cost, and the route metric for inter-area routes is the sum of interface costs along the path. Additional factors become involved in calculating inter-area routes and external routes; these are discussed in Chapter 12.

The OSPF MIB specification suggests a bandwidth-based interface cost of 10^8/bandwidth. This is the most common default value for OSPF interface cost. 3Com and Cisco use it as their default. Bay recommends manually configuring 10^8/bandwidth, but uses a different interface cost default of 1. **GateD** defaults to an interface cost of 1.

Given the different vendor defaults, I strongly recommend manually setting explicit interface costs whenever you have a multivendor OSPF environment.

Bay RS and GateD Metrics

Bay's default was selected for non-obvious but rather creative reasons. On the assumption that an organization is converting from RIP to OSPF, Bay's default is an interface cost of 1. By using this cost, the routing metric becomes hop count and is consistent with RIP. The idea is that the paths will stay the same during conversion, a reasonable idea that helps in troubleshooting.

When configuring **GateD**, you specify interface costs with **interface** *interface_list* [**cost** *cost*] commands.

Cisco Metrics

Be careful with the default on Cisco serial interfaces. If you do not explicitly configure the **interface bandwidth** value, the Cisco IOS software assumes the interface cost is that of a T1 interface on serial lines.

The 10^8/bandwidth default works up to 100 Mbps. Because the metric is internally an integer, a speed faster than 100 Mbps has an undefined metric of 1. Newer Cisco releases allow you to change the scaling factor to be other than 10^8. If you have a network with an extremely wide range of speeds, such as the U.S. Coast Guard network with both 2.4-Kbps radio links to ships and 100-Mbps LANs, the simple convention of dividing a constant by a bandwidth does not cover the entire range of interface costs. In such cases, you need to develop a system of interface preference values that produce a metric that reflects your policies.

Media Issues

Routing mechanisms are most comfortable with broadcast multiaccess media, such as LANs, and with point-to-point media. But these are not the only kinds of media, and you should be aware that several types need special handling, as discussed in Chapter 12. Special media types or attributes, which might need to be considered in routing protocols other than OSPF, include the following:

- Passive.

- Simplex and unidirectional.

- Nonbroadcast multiaccess (NBMA), including both point-to-point and point-to-multipoint. There are both vendor-specific and IETF-defined means of handling point-to-multipoint NBMA.

- Demand.

OSPF interfaces have a maximum transmission unit (MTU) size. Packets sent to an interface that are longer than the MTU for that interface are rejected, so be careful that all the interfaces connected to a multiaccess medium have the same MTU.

Note that Bay uses a default of 1200 bytes for PPP synchronous interfaces. With Cisco's default of 1500, this is often a reason for interoperability failures. Be sure the MTUs at both ends of a PPP link are compatible.

Specific MTU sizes also affect Frame Relay. On a physical interface, the number of Frame Relay virtual circuits—that is, data link circuit identifiers (DLCIs—is limited by the size of the status message you can send on the local management interface (LMI). To find this limit, subtract the 20 bytes of fixed header from the MTU and determine how many 5-byte DLCI status messages will fit into the frame:

```
MaxDLCI = (MTU-20) / 5
```

Passive Routing

Simplex routing involves transmitting routing updates from one end of a link to a receiver at the other end. Passive routing is not the same as simplex routing, although there are similarities. In passive routing, the source of the updates heard by the receiver can itself listen to routing updates. In pure simplex routing, the transmitter does not listen to updates.

Passive routing is used in situations where a router wants to listen to routing but not participate in it. Applications of passive routing include the following:

- Having a central gateway learn about all routes (see Chapter 12) without using active interaction among routing processes

- Preventing leaks of a routing protocol, typically classless, onto an ISP network

- Allowing routers to learn the default route

When a router interface is passive, OSPF cannot successfully exchange hellos with it, so neighbor relationships are never built. The passive interface still hears announcements sent to the multicast address **AllSPFRouters**, so it can learn about routes but not generate them.

Simplex and Unidirectional Routing

There are two seemingly similar but substantially different functions on some routers: simplex interfaces and unidirectional routing. A simplex interface transmits in one direction, but pairs of simplex interfaces, one for each direction, can be used with conventional routing. Unidirectional routing, however, is truly one way.

Applications for simplex interfaces include the following:

- Supporting full-duplex Ethernet on routers that have two physical interfaces that only support half-duplex operation

- Bulk data transfer over a high-speed link, such as a satellite, with only acknowledgements and other control messages in the other direction

For the first case (shown on the left side of Figure 11.10), you define one interface as passive and the other as active, pairing the two with a Y-cable. On a Cisco router, the transmitting interface must be configured as passive, which means routing messages are not generated on the interface.

Conventional routing protocols assume that symmetrical links are used, with at least the capability to transmit in both directions if not the same metric in both. Current dynamic routing does not fit the model of true unidirectional routing, as with a satellite sending to numerous earth stations. You need to use static routing for unidirectional operation until new routing protocols emerge. See the right side of Figure 11.10 for a sample of such a configuration.

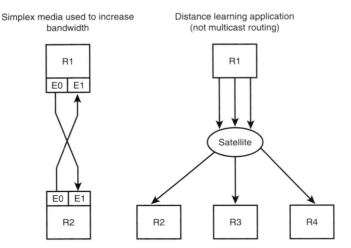

Simplex media used to increase bandwidth

Distance learning application (not multicast routing)

FIGURE 11.10   *Applications of simplex interfaces.*

For dynamic routing to work, there needs to be a mechanism for the routers to exchange identity and routing information. To see current work in this area, consult the IETF Unidirectional Link Routing (UDLR) working group page at www.ietf.org.

Unidirectional routing is very useful when most of the transfer is in one direction. I am working with an application in which multi-gigabyte medical imaging files are transmitted over a satellite to major medical centers for second opinions. The reverse direction only carries acknowledgements and text reports. Unidirectional routing is also useful in multicast distance learning applications.

OSPF NBMA Networks

Routing issues with NBMA media include both concerns inside NBMA subnets and with the local-versus-remote decision in leaving the subnet. In the first case, IP assumes that there is full Layer 2 connectivity among hosts in the same subnet. In the second, a host needs to be able to reach the default gateway router.

Routing-specific issues include establishing neighbor relationships among routers. OSPF hellos are multicast. In a partial mesh network as shown in Figure 11.11, how do R1 and R2 reach the designated router, DR? How are neighbors found? How will the designated router, R1, be found? Do the non-designated routers have any way to determine if there is a backup designated router? With a partial mesh network such as the one in Figure 11.11, the non-designated routers cannot consistently answer these questions.

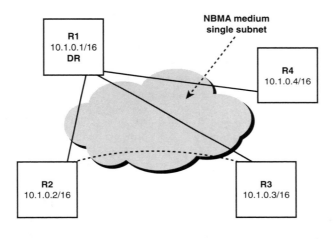

Legend

———————— Virtual circuit

- - - - - - - - - - Layer 2 connectivity incorrectly inferred from IP local versus remote assumption

FIGURE 11.11 *NBMA media are partial mesh subnets, which violate the basic IP model of full Layer 2 connectivity within a subnet.*

There are several ways to deal with this problem. Manual configuration is the most straightforward but also the most labor intensive and error prone. The OSPF specification now includes a point-to-multipoint mode, which describes the set of PVCs as a set of point-to-point networks known internally to OSPF. A third but vendor-dependent method is to use subinterfaces.

One of the issues you face in deciding on the appropriate method is the need to support older routers and software. Not all provide, for example, automatic learning of neighbors.

In OSPF, all traffic in a broadcast multiaccess medium goes to the designated router and backup designated router. A good point-to-multipoint NBMA emphasizes the hub-and-spoke topology, in which the hub is the designated router. The hub has a router priority greater than 0, whereas each spoke has a priority of 0. Setting the priority in this manner prevents the spokes from becoming designated routers.

A timer used for NBMA networks is the *poll interval*. This timer has a value significantly greater than the hello timer and is used to check send hellos to a virtual circuit that is down. Down is defined as having occurred when the local router has not heard a hello from a router in **deadInterval**. RFC 2328 recommends 120 seconds as a typical value for X.25 networks, but does not require a specific value. Routers with different **pollInterval** values still interoperate, in contrast to routers with different **helloInterval** values.

Think about the potential frequency of learning about new circuits in Frame Relay. You certainly will not learn that a PVC has come up faster than the next status inquiry/status exchange on the LMI. If inverse ARP or other dynamic discovery mechanisms are supported, a plausible implementation choice is not to poll at all, but to wait to start sending hellos until an inverse ARP arrives from the previously down router. When a router is eligible to become DR, it must periodically send hellos to any of its neighbors that also are eligible to become DR. If the router already is DR or BDR, it must send periodic hellos to all its neighbors. Remember that each of these hellos must be sent as a separate packet, so the hello workload is substantially greater for NBMA than it is for other medium times.

Good design minimizes the number of potential DRs on an NBMA network. This isn't a practical limitation on reliability, because a spoke router in a hub-and-spoke topology does not have the PVC connectivity to be a useful DR.

The more spokes, the more workload on the hub router, both for designated router functions and relaying to other spokes. You might want to use a router as the hub with greater CPU power than at any spoke.

What about the backup designated router? If there is a well-connected BDR candidate, there should be a PVC between the DR and BDR. If the network is truly hub and spoke, there might only be one router that reasonably can serve as DR, and it might be a rational choice to have no BDR. You implement this by having a priority of zero on all but the hub router.

Bay RS NBMA

Bay has especially rich support for Frame Relay, based on the idea of a *service record* that links multiple virtual circuits. These virtual circuits can be on more than one physical interface and include both PVCs and switched virtual circuits. Bay has a proprietary *multiline* load-sharing mechanism for Frame Relay, which allows you to pair two physical Frame Relay access lines.

Multiline creates a superinterface that combines multiple service records. When using multiline, the DLCI in each physical Frame Relay interface must have the same value if they go to the same destination. In other words, if the Philadelphia router has two physical interfaces, each with a PVC that goes to Madrid, they both need to be DLCI 42 (or whatever value, as long it is the same on both interfaces).

Network layer addresses are defined for the service records, not for specific interfaces or PVCs. More than one service record can map to a given physical interface. You can set up multiple service records for different network layer protocols, separating their broadcasts. By configuring Frame Relay encapsulation, you automatically create a *default service record*. Any VCs that are not explicitly assigned to another service record are associated with the default service record. VCs learned on the LMI are automatically configured onto the default service record.

To create a service record, you navigate to a Frame-Relay prompt and enter the **service** command with the name of the service record to be created:

service *service-name*

After you have established the service context, you add individual PVCs or ranges of PVCs:

pvc *pvc-number*

There are three modes of operation with service records: group, direct, and hybrid. Group mode service records describe point-to-multipoint topologies. A single network layer address is assigned to each Frame Relay interface.

Direct access mode treats each PVC as a separate point-to-point connection. Broadcasts sent to the Frame Relay interface propagate only onto this PVC. Hybrid access mode is intended for mixed bridging and routing applications.

Cisco NBMA

The subinterface model defines a separate subnet for each PVC. See Chapter 13 of *Designing Addressing Architectures for Routing and Switching*, also from Macmillan Technical Publishing. This usually works quite well in a pure Cisco environment, but can introduce multivendor compatibility problems.

On Cisco routers, there might be restrictions on the maximum number of subinterfaces the IOS version supports. In releases prior to 12.0, this number has been limited to 256, except for a special ISP release with 1024. This number is tied to the number of interface descriptor blocks (IDBs), an internal data structure of the IOS. Large numbers of subinterfaces also can cause excessive memory consumption when buffers are dedicated to each subinterface.

You define a Cisco subinterface as point-to-point or point-to-multipoint. Most commonly, you define them as point-to-point with a /30 prefix (that is, subnet mask 255.255.255.252), as shown in Figure 11.12. Point-to-multipoint subinterfaces are primarily used when there is a resource constraint on the router, such as buffer space for subinterfaces or the number of internal IDBs.

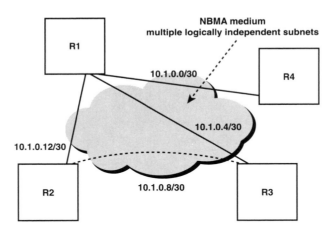

FIGURE 11.12 *Using the subinterface model, each virtual circuit is treated as a separate subnet.*

This is different from defining an interface as point-to-multipoint in OSPF, which is done with the **ip ospf network point-to-multipoint** subcommand. Using the OSPF command creates multiple host routes (/32 prefix, 255.255.255.255 mask).

To propagate hellos onto all media, you code **ip ospf network point-to-multipoint broadcast**. Adding the broadcast keyword allows dynamic neighbor discovery on NBMA partial mesh media (for example, Frame Relay, ATM).

To use the OSPF point-to-multipoint mechanism, go to an interface and enter **ip ospf network point-to-multipoint**. Alternatively, when you want to treat the entire interface as point-to-multipoint, with the interface simulating broadcast, go to an **interface** command and enter the subcommand **ip ospf network point-to-multipoint non-broadcast**.

Next, go to an OSPF process and specify a cost for each neighbor that you do *not* want to assume the default cost. Explicit neighbor costs were added to the Cisco IOS in Release 11.3. The default cost either is derived from the **bandwidth** or explicitly configured with an **ip ospf cost** command. Configure non-default NBMA neighbor costs with the **router** subcommand **neighbor** *ip-address* **cost** *number*.

A Cisco-specific issue of multivendor interoperability exists on Frame Relay interfaces. Cisco defaults to a proprietary encapsulation of packets in frames. To ensure multivendor interoperability, be sure to code the **ietf** keyword on the **encapsulation frame-relay ietf** command. I make this my routine practice unless I know there is a Cisco router configured with the Cisco encapsulation at the other end.

Cisco also has an optional proprietary protocol type identification method used on X.25 virtual circuits.

OSPF Demand Networks

Demand network support was introduced as a RIP standard and has been extended to OSPF. Although it is usually associated with dial circuits, it actually is relevant to any medium where bandwidth is expensive, such as ship-to-shore radio links that run at 2400 bps.

The fundamental assumption in demand network support is what is called the *presumption of reachability*. This means that the hello mechanism for verifying neighbor reachability is not used. It is assumed that unless an interface is explicitly disabled, it is reachable.

In Figure 11.13, all the routers must support demand circuits, even though not all of them actually have demand links. Different applications of demand media are shown. R4 and R8 have backup links to core routers, for which the interface costs need to be higher than those of the dedicated media. R2 polls R5, R6, and R7 as needed by applications routed through R2. You define the demand circuits at the hub, R2, of the point-to-multipoint circuit. Note that R7 has a dedicated link to R11, which is not affected by the demand circuits.

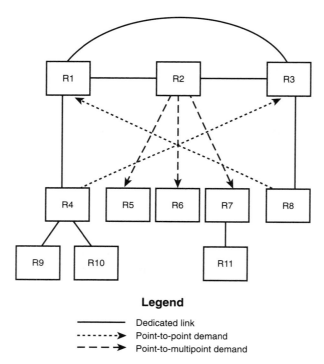

Legend

—————— Dedicated link
·······► Point-to-point demand
— — —► Point-to-multipoint demand

FIGURE 11.13 *All OSPF routers in an area must understand demand routing, although demand links are enabled on specific interfaces.*

Only significant link-state advertisements (LSAs) are sent over demand media. *Significant LSAs* are those that actually change the topology, rather than those that simply refresh entries in the topological database. This is a recent extension to the OSPF protocol, and there is not a huge amount of operational experience with it. It might be very useful in the right circumstances, but do think through how you will troubleshoot it.

Every router in an area must have the code to understand demand circuits. You actually enable the demand feature at one end of a circuit. If you are configuring the demand feature on a point-to-multipoint circuit, you enable it on the hub end, not on each spoke end.

Demand Backup for Multiplexed Channels

Routers use single physical interfaces to multiplexed services or NBMA media. Until now, we have assumed that if a medium goes down, the associated physical interface is down. This is not true when circuits are multiplexed onto a single physical interface, at OSI Layers 1, 2, or 2.5. With fractional T1/T3 services, bit streams are multiplexed at Layer 1. Frame Relay and ATM multiplex at a reasonably strict Layer 2, and X.25 multiplexes at Layer 2.5. See the "Path Determination versus Forwarding" section of Chapter 3. In principle, Frame Relay should give a failure indication on the LMI. In practice, you might not always receive such an indication. It tends to be a fundamental problem of the way the service is implemented rather than due to an intermittent problem, so you might be able to set up a reliable backup that depends on such notification.

If the LMI failure notification is reliable, it's usually simple to set up a less-preferred static route that serves as backup. For an assortment of reasons, however, you might need to use dynamic routing to detect the failure. In Figure 11.14, routing runs over the dotted lines, the PVCs.

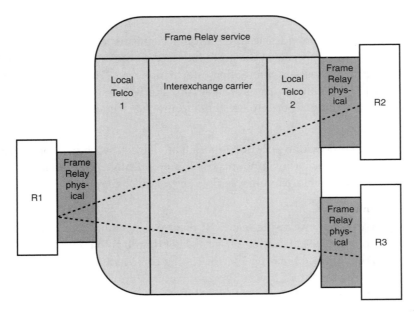

FIGURE 11.14 *End-to-end routing is one way to invoke dial or ISDN backup if an individual PVC fails and you cannot use the status change on the LMI.*

If failure notification from the LMI is not reliable, your only alternative is running full routing between the endpoint routers and defining the demand backup to be invoked when the dynamic route is lost. When you use routing more as a keepalive mechanism rather than a mechanism for finding alternate paths, you definitely want a protocol, such as OSPF, EIGRP, or IS-IS, that has a low-overhead hello mechanism rather than a periodic update protocol such as RIP.

The most common reason for LMI status information is shown in the way in which the PVCs are provisioned by multiple vendors, as illustrated in Figure 11.14. If any of the local or long-distance providers do not implement the Frame Relay Network-to-Network Interface (NNI) to a neighboring carrier, a notification generated by one carrier does not propagate to its neighboring carrier and does not reach the end user interface. There are some obscure failures that LMI information might not reveal, such as loss of a specific virtual circuit at the remote site while the remote Frame Relay interface stays up.

IP Feature Issues

Routing is complicated by Layer 1 and 2 issues. Use of extended IP features at Layer 3, such as route filtering, load sharing, fragmentation, and tunneling, also complicate things.

Filtering

Any modern router provides access control mechanisms for permitting or denying the flow of packets at the input interface, at the output interface, or to and from such processes as the routing information base. The basic characteristics of access control mechanisms are a set of patterns to match, and actions to be taken on matching. Conceptually, these techniques were introduced in Chapter 3.

Filtering takes processor overhead, although advanced distributed forwarding processors can do increasing amounts of filtering. Ideally, core routers should filter as little as possible, leaving the filtering task to edge routers.

Filter Placement

Filtering takes some processing overhead on any router, although it can be distributed into interface hardware. A basic rule of thumb is to minimize the execution of filters. Implementation-specific tuning considerations can affect where you place the filters, but minimization of execution is a good first rule. Figure 11.15 shows a broad view of filtering, which shows input, output, and interprocess filters.

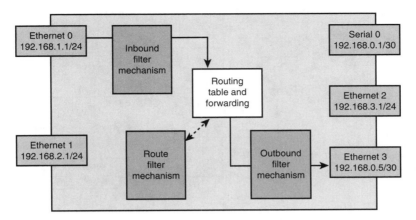

FIGURE 11.15 *There are at least three places filtering can be applied: at input interfaces, between internal router processes, and at output interfaces.*

In Figure 11.16, the majority of packets stay on the LAN. A small set goes to interface Ethernet 1. To minimize load on the router, it is ideal to filter packets at Ethernet 0, discarding packets that will not be forwarded. Only the packets that will actually go through the forwarding process enter the router.

There are a great many applications for filtering. The most common sort of filtering applies to user traffic, but it can also apply to routing updates. Filtering can be applied at input or output interfaces.

Assuming that no fundamental forwarding path differences result from input versus output filter placement, the basic rule of filter placement is to minimize the number of packets that need to go through filters. Filtering often adds overhead.

If a filter rule needs to be applied to most or all packets entering a router, putting the filter on the input interface makes the most sense.

If, however, only some packets need to be filtered, such as those going to your ISP, it makes sense to let the routing process be applied to all packets and only filter those packets that go to the relevant output interface.

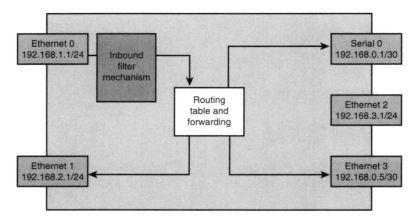

FIGURE 11.16 *The ideal application for input filtering is a traffic pattern where you can deny most packets from entering the router.*

We introduced input filtering in the Chapter 3 section, "Input Actions in Layer 3 Forwarding." You need to know the effect on the forwarding path of your specific routing implementation of putting filters on the input or output interfaces.

Be sure that input filtering does not have a major performance impact on your router. When Cisco first implemented input filtering, turning on input filtering on any interface put the entire chassis into the slowest forwarding mode, process switching. At the next step of IOS evolution, only the specific interface where you enabled input filtering would go to process switching. Further improvements put input filtering into faster paths, such as fast or silicon switching. You really have to configure the filter and check the forwarding mode before you can be certain of the performance effect of filtering, because there are far too many variations of configuration, IOS version, and hardware platform to cite definitive rules.

Figure 11.17 shows a different traffic pattern, where packets subject to filtering go to Serial 0. No filtering is needed for Ethernet 1.

Often, you will find that the minimal performance impact on a Cisco router comes when you put filters on outbound serial interfaces. Such interfaces are often process switched anyway, for the greater buffering provided by process switching or because you use such IOS features as priority or custom queuing. Newer releases move some of these features to faster switching paths, but you certainly might see process switching in legacy routers.

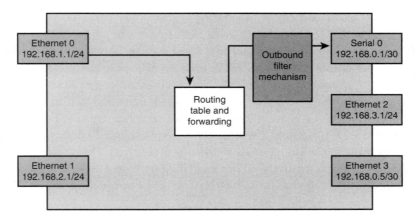

FIGURE 11.17   *Output filtering is best when filtering needs only to be applied to a sub-set of forwarded packets.*

You can filter routes and even manipulate fields within them. Applications of this technique, shown in Figure 11.18, are discussed in Chapter 12.

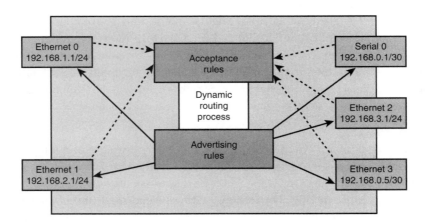

Legend

———————▶ Outgoing routing updates

– – – – – –▶ Incoming routing updates

FIGURE 11.18   *Route filters can control import of routes into the routing table for routes generated by all protocols. They can control the export of distance-vector routes, as well as link-state inter-area and external routes.*

Static Routes as an Alternative to Filtering

One technique that can improve filtering performance, in selected cases, is using static routes to a null interface to discard packets with specified destination addresses but any source address. Common reasons to do this include blocking inappropriate packets to a service provider. As you have seen in Chapter 3, Cisco routers have an especially wide range of forwarding modes. Whether this technique is useful depends significantly on the specific router platform and its IOS version. The real motivation is to avoid knocking an interface into a slower forwarding mode by adding access lists. This is particularly important where you are in the silicon switching path on a 7000, or the autonomous switching path on a 7000 or AGS, or the optimum path of a 7500.

More recent IOS versions tend to be better about access list performance. Originally, you could not do silicon switching for any access lists. IOS version 10 allowed silicon switching for standard, but not extended, IP access lists. Standard access lists define filtering on the source IP only. Later versions of both the IOS and switching engine firmware let you do more and more filtering in the switching engine.

Frankly, there are so many permutations of features, versions, and switching modes that I hesitate to say how a particular interface in a particular configuration will switch—until I configure it and try a **show ip interface** command. Before you add an extended access list that matches any source address (the only thing the null interface technique does), display the interface switching mode. Add the **access-group** statement and check the switching mode again. If the mode changes to a slower one, use the null interface technique.

Static Load Sharing

Load sharing is a far more complex subject than many people expect it to be. This discussion deals with the most widely used methods at Layer 3; see "Dynamic Load Sharing" in Chapter 14 for a discussion of evolving methods. You need to think carefully about why you want to load share, rather than let the routing system pick the best path. Reasons to load-share include the following:

- Optimizing the use of bandwidth on low-bandwidth lines

- Inverse multiplexing

- Speeding convergence time

Routing is not the only way to achieve some of these goals. Physical layer inverse multiplexers exist. At the data link layer, there are multilink PPP and LAP-B, discussed in the section "Inverse Multiplexing" in Chapter 9.

In equal-cost IP load sharing, Bay can load share groups of up to five interfaces, whereas Cisco, as of IOS 11.0, can load share groups up to six interfaces. Cisco automatically load shares up to four interfaces; you must explicitly configure maximum paths of six. Bay also has a technique called *multiline* that allows load sharing over multiple Frame Relay PVCs.

To enable equal-cost load sharing on physical interfaces on a Bay router, you enable the feature on a router-by-router basis with the command

```
ecmp-method [disabled ¦ roundRobin ¦ srcDestHash ¦ destinationHash]
```

At the single router level, three main methods have been used [Villamizor, 1998]. True dynamic load sharing is more a future technology than a feature of any current commercial router implementation. Emerging protocols, such as OSPF-OMP discussed in the Chapter 14 section "Dynamic Load Sharing," advertise the actual utilization on links so the routing algorithms can consider end-to-end congestion.

Even though current link-state protocols advertise the state of each router in the routing domain, they typically advertise an interface cost based on a statically configured bandwidth. IGRP and EIGRP do have a metric factor that considers utilization, but only from the perspective of directly connected links.

All three of the preceding methods—round robin with equal costs, per-destination, and source-destination hash—suffer from the problem that "equal" load sharing, based on the information available to a single router, does not always give the best end-to-end path. In Figure 11.19, although one decision is appropriate based on local information, the best end-to-end path is not the best local one.

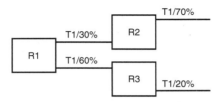

FIGURE 11.19 *Available load sharing modes all suffer from the limitation of the perspective of a single router only.*

Round Robin with Equal Costs

Seemingly the most straightforward method is called *round-robin* or *deterministic* load sharing. See Figures 3.6 through 3.9 for illustrations of load sharing principles. Cisco calls this method *per-packet*; Bay refers to it as *round robin*, or, when referring to the multiline load sharing technique for Frame Relay, *random distribution*.

In this method, some set of interfaces 1 to n is known to be able to reach some destination IP address, such as 1.2.3.4. The first packet to 1.2.3.4 goes out the first interface, the second packet out the second interface, and so on up to the nth packet going out interface n. Packet $n+1$ goes out interface 1, and the cycle repeats. This method assumes that each interface is of equal cost.

One limitation of this mode is often one of implementation. The router must remember which interface it used to send the last packet, so it can select the next interface to use. It must be able to cope with the failures of individual interfaces within a load balancing group. To do all this, a reasonably large amount of CPU and memory must be devoted to managing the load sharing process. On a Cisco router, this generally means that interfaces that do per-packet load balancing are put into the slow but intelligent process-switching path discussed in Chapter 3. If the Cisco router has Versatile Interface Processors (VIP) and uses Distributed Cisco Express Forwarding (DCEF), it can do this sort of load balancing without significant CPU involvement. VIP and DCEF are available only on high-end routers, admittedly the routers that most need high performance.

Another limitation is that strict round-robin load sharing sends packets to the same destination over multiple paths. This can lead to out-of-sequence packet arrival at the destination. Depending on the upper-layer protocols in use, out-of-sequence delivery can cause high overhead, retransmission, or outright failures.

Round Robin with Unequal Costs

As part of its IGRP, Cisco introduced a method of unequal cost load balancing. This does work, but its applicability is not as wide as had been originally thought. The limiting factor is that delay becomes a significant factor, but the algorithm used by IGRP and EIGRP considers only bandwidth.

Bandwidth Isn't Always Enough

On most media, delay can be approximated as 1/bandwidth. When dealing with multiple media in a routing path, this no longer can be used.

One basic method of approximating delay is to use *ping*. This method has significant limitations, depending on the specific routers in use. There are ways to work around these limitations.

First, the initial *ping* to a destination is apt to be inaccurate if there must first be an ARP exchange to find the medium address associated with sending to that destination.

Specific implementations, such as Cisco, prioritize ICMP responses lower than other routed traffic. This is a conscious design decision and helps protect the router against denial of service attacks based on *ping* flooding. The presence of user traffic artificially inflates *ping* times.

It might seem intuitively obvious that dividing the *ping* time in half will give one-way network delay, but this often is an inaccurate assumption.

Dividing the round trip time by two can be reasonable in the telephone network, or in enterprise networks where the paths are likely to be symmetrical. In the Internet, however, asymmetrical routing is quite likely; the response comes down a different path than the request. Estimates of asymmetrical routing in the Internet range from 30% to 50%.

If you can synchronize the router clocks (as with the network time protocol), log each arriving ICMP request (for example, with Cisco *debug* and send *ping*s from both routers), you can get some accurate timestamps and derive delay from that. The low prioritization of ICMP refers to the response, not the arrival, of the request.

Cisco's approach is to introduce a **variance** parameter. When the ratio of IGRP or EIGRP metrics is less than or equal to the variance, the two media are treated as equal for the purpose of equal-cost load sharing.

Assume that a 128-Kbps and a 256-Kbps medium are being considered for unequal-cost load sharing, and **variance** is set to 2. Under these circumstances, the Cisco feature considers them equal cost, although it sends twice as many packets out the link that is twice as fast.

I have used this feature successfully in private time division multiplexed networks. In these networks, it was not as easy simply to increase the speed of a single channel as it would have been in a commercial Frame Relay service.

The limitation of this feature comes from the delay being distinctly unequal on links of different bandwidth. Ignoring long-delay media such as satellite links or congested cable television systems, delay is generally equal to **1/bandwidth**. For example, the delay of a 128-Kbps link is twice that of a 256-Kbps link.

When the delay ratio between two lines becomes excessive, TCP performance can suffer. The detailed behavior varies with the specific TCP stacks in use, but the basic problem is that when out-of-sequence packets arrive, TCP retransmits them as a means of resequencing. Retransmission, in turn, keeps the TCP window size small and inefficient. Maximum delay ratios between 2 [Cisco CID] and 3 [Villamizar, 1998] have been recommended. Consider that a 600-byte packet takes approximately 3000 microseconds to transfer to or from a medium at 1.544 Mbps. At the 44.736-Mbps DS-3 rate, the same packet transfers in under 100 microseconds. At OC-12, it transfers in less than 7 microseconds.

A different IGRP feature uses dynamic load as a factor in computing the metric. In practice, this and other dynamic approaches have not proved useful, because they lead to oscillation.

Destination Cache

Another approach to load sharing, shown in Figure 3.8, is to distribute the interfaces by destination address. This has the advantages of being compatible with cache-based forwarding and requiring minimal CPU resources.

The level of load balancing actually achieved, however, can be questionable. Often, from any given location, most traffic goes to the same destination. The link chosen that goes to that destination might be overloaded, while capacity remains on the other links.

Destination caching can work reasonably well when there are a large number of destinations, many of which receive a non-trivial amount of traffic.

Source-Destination Hash

Source-destination hashing was used in the original T3 NSFNET, a predecessor of today's Internet, and is supported on Bay routers. Load sharing based on flow identifiers is a related method. Bay calls it *address-based distribution* when used with Frame Relay. The technique is illustrated in Figure 3.9. Source-destination hashing, incidentally, is used in most LAN inverse multiplexing methods. See the section "Inverse Multiplexed Parallel Paths" in Chapter 10. In the NSFNET method, a 16-bit value is computed from the combined 32-bit source and 32-bit destination addresses. This value, in turn, is looked up in a specialized routing table, which can be implemented in hardware.

Flow-based hashes derive a value from the combination of the source address, IP protocol type, source TCP or UDP port, destination address, and destination port type. Flow implementations might have wildcards that match any address or port in a certain position. One reasonable flow wildcard, for example, would accept any source address or port destined to port 80—the Web server—at a specific destination address. You might generalize the destination to any Web server on a server subnet.

Source-destination hash tends to give a smoother distribution than either round-robin or destination hash. It has the advantage over round robin that all packets to a given destination take the same path, as long as the path is up. Consistently taking the same path avoids overhead caused by out-of-sequence packets.

Fragmentation

When the data field of a packet is larger than the specified MTU of an outgoing interface, it must be fragmented or dropped.

On Cisco routers, when packets need to be fragmented, they go through the process-switching path, unless it is already present as it might be on a WAN interface. Avoid the need for fragmentation, wherever possible, by using MTU path discovery on hosts.

One area where MTU path discovery might fail is when tunnels are present. Tunnels can create a special problem of fragmentation. If you have a perfectly valid maximum-length packet that does not need to be fragmented, what happens when it hits a tunnel that goes through an interface with the same MTU?

Tunnels add overhead bytes to outgoing packets and can create unexpected requirements for fragmentation.

Router Relationships

Routers are something like people, in that they need to get to know one another before they can work together. Routers need to find one another and then, like people, form different sorts of relationships. They might simply use one another for forwarding or exchange meaningful information. They also can back up one another.

As opposed to what people do in all-too-frequent destructive relationships, you can assume that routers form relationships with the best possible intentions. If a router receives a routing update that will do damage, it is either due to a failure in another router, misconfiguration, or malicious cracking. For the latter two problems, we have route authentication mechanisms.

Hello Protocols and Interface Initialization

OSPF and EIGRP multicast hello messages on interfaces as they initialize. OSPF progresses from a down condition to its initial transmission of hello messages to recognizing other routers.

Hello protocol advertises from only the primary interface on the same medium. Additional IP addresses on the same interface, called multinet by Bay and secondary by Cisco, do not form neighbor or adjacency relationships.

OSPF expects neighbors to be in the same area. If the area declarations on two interfaces connected to the same medium are different, no neighbor relationship can form.

There definitely are occasions when you do not want neighbor relationships to form between routers in the same area. You might have, for example, two default gateway routers connected to the same stub medium. The two routers are there to back up one another, and the routers should never send transit traffic to one another across the stub medium.

There are some transient states in which OSPF is deciding whether to recognize a neighbor and recognizing or creating a designated router. When initialized, each interface should be in the following operational states on broadcast and NBMA media declared as broadcast:

- **DR.** This interface is the designated router for the medium.

- **BDR.** This interface is the backup designated router for the medium.

- **DR-OTHER.** This interface has recognized other interfaces as designated router and backup designated router for the medium.

And each interface should be in the following operational state on point-to-point or point-to-multipoint media:

- **POINT-TO-POINT**

If the hello timer values do not match between two routers, they will not form any relationships. The OSPF standard specifies a default of 10 seconds. Cisco uses this as its default, as does Bay.

Bay, however, recommends using alternate values on interfaces to media not of the broadcast type:

Medium type	Bay default
Default value and broadcast media	10 seconds
Point-to-point media	15 seconds
NBMA media	20 seconds
Point-to-multipoint interfaces	15 seconds

These might be perfectly reasonable tuning values, but do remember them as part of multivendor interoperability. If you are connecting non-Bay routers to Bay routers, and the administrator of the Bay routers has read the Bay documentation, he might have used Bay's tuning recommendations to create a configuration that does not interoperate with yours. I leave it to you to assess the likelihood, in your enterprise, of the administrator (1) having read the documentation and (2) having followed it.

Another timer that Bay recommends tuning is the dead timer:

Medium type	Bay default
Default value and broadcast media	40 seconds
Point-to-point media	60 seconds
NBMA media	80 seconds
Point-to-multipoint interfaces	60 seconds

The dead timer needs to have the same setting for all routers connected to a common medium.

Neighbor and Adjacency Relationships

In general terms, a neighbor router is any router that the local router recognizes as one it can route through. In most routing protocols, neighbors exchange routing information.

To recognize a router as a neighbor, key parameters in the hello packet must match exactly. These include the area identifier and various timers, such as the hello interval. Other parameters that must match, discussed in Chapter 12, include the stubbiness of the area.

OSPF makes the finer distinction that a router can forward to a neighbor, but only exchanges routing information with those neighbors with which it has also established an adjacency relationship (see Figure 11.20).

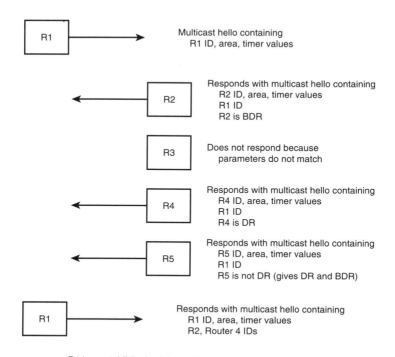

R1 → Multicast hello containing
R1 ID, area, timer values

R2 ← Responds with multicast hello containing
R2 ID, area, timer values
R1 ID
R2 is BDR

R3 Does not respond because
parameters do not match

R4 ← Responds with multicast hello containing
R4 ID, area, timer values
R1 ID
R4 is DR

R5 ← Responds with multicast hello containing
R5 ID, area, timer values
R1 ID
R5 is not DR (gives DR and BDR)

R1 → Responds with multicast hello containing
R1 ID, area, timer values
R2, Router 4 IDs

R1 has established neighbor relationships with R2, R4, and R5
R1 is adjacent to R2 (and implicitly R4)

FIGURE 11.20 *R1 has no relationship with R3 because R2 has a different area number. R1 has neighbor relationships with R3 through R5, but is adjacent only to R5.*

The hello handshake must be correct, and one of the participants should be the designated router. If there is a backup designated router, it also hears the updates, which are sent to the **AllDRouters** multicast address, the scope of which is limited to the local medium. OSPF packets also have their IP time-to-live field set to 1, which causes them to be discarded if they are routed beyond the local medium.

In the presence of secondary addressing on a subnet, both OSPF and EIGRP only exchange hellos between routers on the primary subnet.

Warning

When you have multiple router interfaces with secondary addresses connected to a common medium, make sure the same subnet interface is primary on each. Also, be sure that the secondary subnets appear in the same order on each interface. Do not declare the secondaries in the order, for example, .2/.3/.4 on one interface and .4/.2/.3 on another.

This is one of those little things that may or may not be important on a specific platform, software version, or vendor implementation, but never hurts. When an implementation is sensitive to this ordering, ARP caches might not work properly, and you might be unable to delete some addresses without clearing all.

How Many Neighbors Should a Router Have?

How many neighbors should a router have? This depends on why you want to go to a neighbor. Figure 11.21 shows a good reason to have large numbers of neighbors. This figure shows alternate, presumably dialup, connectivity to a backup hub. See Chapter 12 for a discussion of core area design, which goes further into how much redundancy is enough.

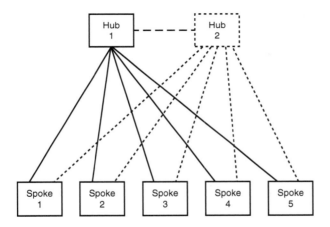

Legend

FIGURE 11.21 *When the application date flow is inherently hub and spoke, large numbers of neighbors are appropriate. Often, static routing is all that is needed for such configurations.*

Figure 11.22 depicts a method of getting even greater availability in a hub-and-spokes topology, while retaining simple configuration. Parallel, usually load-shared links go from edge routers toward the core.

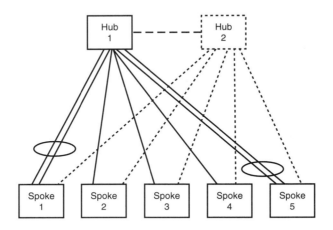

Legend

—————— Lower metric

- - - - - - - - Higher metric

— — — — Minimum metric (sum of minimum metric
and lower metric must be less than higher metric)

◯ Load-shared Links

FIGURE 11.22 *Load shared parallel links are a simple way to add more reliability.*

Figure 11.23 is an all-too-common configuration, which is done for the wrong reasons. Remember that excessive meshing can degrade availability rather than improve it. Even if an edge router can handle the routing recomputation load common with excessive meshing, meshing makes the router's configuration more complex and more difficult to troubleshoot. In almost every case, the right way to improve availability is to increase redundancy toward the backbone.

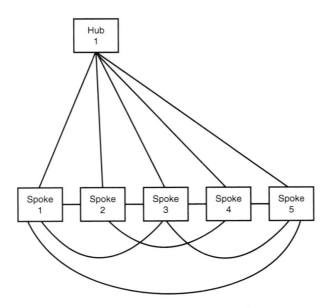

FIGURE 11.23 *Without careful design, randomly linking edge routers can increase costs without improving availability.*

The argument in favor of the Figure 11.23 configuration is "Well, if something goes down, the routers can find an alternate path." But if the router is overwhelmed by the workload of maintaining neighbor relationships, those paths might not be usable.

Statistical Independence?

There are several problems with the assumption that simply adding links and relays will improve availability. Pure statistical approaches assume that the lines and routers have independent chances of failure. Unless you design quite carefully and enforce engineering specifications on your WAN carriers, WAN links are apt to have at least some common components, such as the physical cable between your location and the local telephone office.

Routing makes matters more complex. In my experience, the most common thing that causes a router to fail is software. Pure human error in the router configuration is the most common source of software failure.

How independent is the process by which you configure two allegedly independent routers? When the same administrator configures both, if she doesn't understand some facet of the requirements, she might make the same error in both configurations. When different administrators configure the two routers, they might disagree on techniques and come up with incompatible configurations.

Although commercial router software is quite reliable, it is complex and does have bugs. I sometimes think of keepalives as saying, "I am a router. Trust me. Nothing can go wrong…can go wrong…can go wrong…"

If you are running the same version of native code on two different routers, do you have real redundancy? Arguably, the two routers might have different traffic mixes, which means that at a given instant, their internal state might be slightly different. A timing bug might be affected in one but not the other. But timing-independent bugs can crash both routers.

Two independent routers running the same code are hardly independent from common software failures. Some designers suggest that the ultimate in router redundancy comes from using multiple vendor implementations, but I find the chance of multivendor interoperability problems tends to be greater than the chance of critical software bugs.

I have seen very critical applications where the enterprise deliberately used routers from two different vendors, on the hope that the same configuration error could not be made on both, and the same system software error also could not happen to both. Of course, if you do this, you need to make sure that the second vendor's router is not using licensed code from the first vendor. Also, if the person doing the configuration doesn't understand a concept, they could cheerfully misconfigure the commands in both routers.

Even if the software is reliable, the degree of redundancy you need is not a simple decision. Yes, lines do fail, and WAN failure is probably the most common cause of lost connectivity. But there is a large incremental cost with adding lines and the associated router interface, cabling, DSU/CSU, and so on. What is the cost of downtime? How does this cost compare to the cost of the additional resources?

Many inexpensive routers have one or two serial interfaces. Adding another line might require you to replace the entire router.

What Statistics Are Appropriate?

Another problem is with the statistics themselves. A single parameter, such as percent availability or mean time between failures (MTBF), is never sufficient to characterize real-world availability. In the real world, errors are not smoothly distributed over the period of availability. They occur in bursts.

Mean time to repair (MTTR) might be the key additional parameter in planning redundancy. If your application is a critical money-trading one, where the money traders can make or lose $1 million per second, it's trivial to provide an additional line costing $1000 per month if the expected MTTR is 3 hours. This is an application where downtime is not acceptable.

Now, consider a home user who pays $20 per month for a telephone line used for Internet access. The Internet access is used for recreation and minor applications such as billpaying, and nothing done over the Internet link cannot wait for 24 hours. If the local telephone company has a next-day repair commitment, and, if the modem fails, one can be bought at the office supply store down the street, on-site backup doesn't make economic sense.

As a professional working in a home office, I have partial backup. Although I have one telephone line dedicated to dialup access, I have another line primarily used for facsimile, but available for data use. I have a backup modem in my laptop. When I finally can get reasonable ISDN, cable, or ADSL access, I will still keep analog backup.

More complex statistical models of availability can be relevant, but take significant statistical background and also need good availability information. In general, you probably want to use a network modeling tool rather than try to deal yourself with the complexities of probability theory.

OSPF Internals Relevant to Network Design

OSPF runs directly over IP, with IP protocol number 89. It does not use UDP or TCP, but does its own retransmission.

The five types of OSPF packets, which were detailed in Figure 5.24, run directly over IP, which were detailed in Figure 5.25. All types have a common header, in addition to the 20-byte IP header. As the destination address in this header, most OSPF packets have a reserved multicast address as their destination. This address might be **AllSPFRouters** (224.0.0.5) or **AllDRouters** (224.0.0.6). When a router retransmits an OSPF packet, it sends it to a specific unicast address.

If you use switches that control multicast traffic with IGMP snooping or CGMP, you must ensure that these do not inadvertently block routing updates (see Figure 11.24). OSPF uses two well-known multicast group addresses, but does not issue an IGMP **Membership Report**.

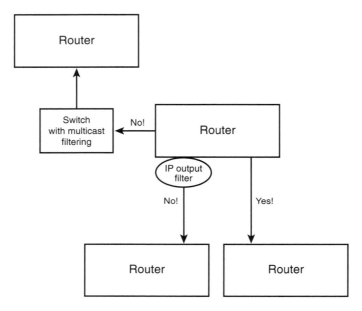

FIGURE 11.24 *You must allow LSAs to propagate everywhere in an area.*

Note

I've always been surprised to see how often the question is asked, "How can I make OSPF go through a firewall?" This doesn't make a great deal of sense, because the scope of OSPF announcements is limited to a single link. Firewalls go between links.

Hello Considerations

Of these five types of OSPF packets, the hello packet is used to detect neighbor routers and OSPF router failures. The other four types are involved in database initialization and updating, and they carry link-state advertisements (LSAs). Figure 11.25 reviews the relationship between OSPF packets and LSAs, emphasizing that LSAs are carried inside OSPF packets.

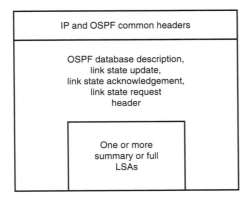

FIGURE 11.25 *LSAs are database records carried inside OSPF packets.*

Hello packets carry timer values that must match if two routers are to form a neighbor relationship. The OSPF standard calls for a 10-second value, but some vendors either have different default hello timers or recommend a different value be manually configured in certain circumstances. These variations are not done capriciously; the vendors do have reasons for what they are doing.

It is characteristic that vendors really believe their equipment will be the only type operating in a given domain. Multivendor interoperability is rarely the first goal.

For example, IBM 6611 routers have often defaulted to a hello timer value of 3 seconds, along with other timer values that minimize convergence time. This value is perfectly reasonable when convergence time is critical. When running LLC-2 with standard timers and no local acknowledgement, SNA sessions drop after 14 seconds. To tune a routing network to have a convergence time less than 14 seconds, reducing the hello timer is one of several essential changes.

In an all-IBM environment, there is no problem. If you mix Cisco with IBM routers, however, they cannot route to one another if their hello timer values do not match.

If you are running SNA over IP in this manner, you probably want to manually set the Cisco routers in an area to have a hello timer of 3 seconds. It might even be necessary to reduce the hello interval on all routers below 3 seconds. You incur additional bandwidth overhead and CPU load for these more frequent hellos, but the alternative is having frequent session loss.

If you have no SNA and no other especially critical convergence requirements, it probably makes more sense to change the IBM hello timers to 10 seconds.

Authentication

An enhancement to OSPF is authentication of routing updates. There are two levels of authentication: cleartext and cryptographic. There is a place for each one, or not authenticating at all.

Neither authentication mode provides additional security for routed packets, only for the routing information proper. In formal security terms, they are protecting against denial of service, but provide no authentication or confidentiality for user information.

It's easy to get sniffer software for most hosts. Given that reality, cleartext passwords provide no real protection against bad guys on your local network. So what is the value of cleartext passwords?

There's an old proverb, "Never attribute to malice that which can adequately be explained by stupidity." When merging multiple existing OSPF routing domains, it's not difficult to forget to reconfigure some small number of routers. Picture situations where you are merging two domains that have used the same private address space or simply have assigned certain addresses to different areas.

When you go through the configurations and update them to the new architecture, the last step in configuring can be to set a cleartext password. After you do that, routers only accept routing information from routers that have been reconfigured with the password. They ignore information from routers that have not yet been reconfigured.

Cryptographic authentication can do everything that cleartext passwords can do, but imposes a heavier CPU load on the router. This method is appropriate when there is a reasonable expectation of actual malice, such as a university network where there might be hackers with entirely too much spare time.

In Chapter 14, we will look briefly at OSPF version 6, which assumes that routing information flows either in IPv6 packets with built-in IPsec or over IPv4 with optional IPsec. Because IPsec provides authentication, OSPF version 6 eliminates OSPF authentication.

Database Initialization

After routers decide they are neighbors, a second decision takes place to determine if they should extend that relationship to adjacency. One of the routers needs to be the DR or BDR if the medium is broadcast capable.

After OSPF identifies a neighbor with which it wants to synchronize topological database information, it exchanges database description (DD) packets. DD packets, and subsequent other packet types, carry link-state advertisements (LSAs). Table 5.3 gives an overview of LSA types that either are widely supported or are likely to be in near-term products.

Designated Routers

OSPF defines a designated router function on multi-access media. The term *designated router* is a little misleading, as it does not refer to a router box, but to an interface on a router. As shown in Figure 5.8, there is a designated router interface and a backup designated router interface on each medium that either is broadcast capable or declared as broadcast.

I find the term designated router a bit confusing. It is best to think not of a designated router as a box, but as a designated router interface for a medium.

Although it is possible to influence the selection of a designated router if more than one router is contending for the status, it is most common that the first router that initializes becomes the designated router, and the second router that initializes becomes the backup designated router. If a router then joins the medium and has a higher priority value for designated router status, it does not preempt the existing designated routers.

Note

You can find priority mechanisms in a variety of routing features. The features differ on whether a more-preferred router preempts an active router running a given function. In OSPF, for example, the designated router is not preempted by a higher-priority router that joins a running subnet. In Hot Standby Routing Protocol (HSRP), however, a new higher-priority router can preempt an existing one.

Be aware that whether high- or low-priority values win a contest depends on the standard (when one exists) and the vendor implementation.

In practice, OSPF elects a designated router, and there is little reason to adjust the priority. The only plausible reason to set priority is when there are a significant number of low-powered edge routers on a medium, especially a point-to-multipoint medium, and a lesser number of high-powered routers with abundant CPU resources. It can be desirable to keep the heavier CPU load of the designated router function off the edge routers. The designated router would be the hub in a hub-and-spokes topology.

The usual practice in such a case is to set priority equal to zero on the edge routers and nonzero priorities on the distribution routers. Be sure that there are enough distribution routers for adequate availability.

If the edge routers are always going to feed the distribution routers, and never communicate directly with one another, it is reasonable to set a zero priority on the edge routers. The situation is more complex when some direct routing might take place between the edge routers. In that case, you want an operational procedure that first initializes the distribution routers and sets a much higher (that is, more preferred) priority value on the distribution router interfaces. If all distribution router interfaces are down, an edge router becomes designated router.

> **Warning**
>
> *If there is a significant mismatch in processing power between edge and distribution routers, have a proactive monitoring procedure in place to look for overloaded routers.*

Propagating Topology Changes

It is important to distinguish between the processes of updating, where a router on a shared medium tells its DR and BDR of new or changed information, and flooding, where the router sends new or changed information to neighboring routers on media other than where the information was first reported.

When a new router or network initializes, other routers need to be told of its existence. When an existing router or network fails, other routers also need to know. Detecting that failure is discussed later in this chapter.

When a router receives an **LS Update** containing new or changed information, it performs a number of consistency checks. After basic consistency is validated, the router considers the following:

- Is this LS identifier in my topological database? If not, add it to the database and schedule flooding.

- Is this LS update newer than the LSA instance currently in my database? If so, replace my current instance and schedule flooding.

- Does the age of this LSA update exactly equal the age of the instance in my database? If so, update timers in the database.

- If the LSA in the update is older than the one in my database, do not change my database. Send an update back to the originator of the just-received update, containing the newer information in the receiving router's database.

Details of the age comparison are beyond the scope of this text; simply assume that the router is able to tell which LSA instance is older. For details, consult RFC 2328 or *Anatomy of an Internet Routing Protocol* [Moy, 1998].

In Figure 11.26, R1 detects a change in network N1. R1 transmits an LSA update onto N2 (1). That update is transmitted to the well-known multicast address, **AllDRouters**, so that both the DR and BDR hear it (2).

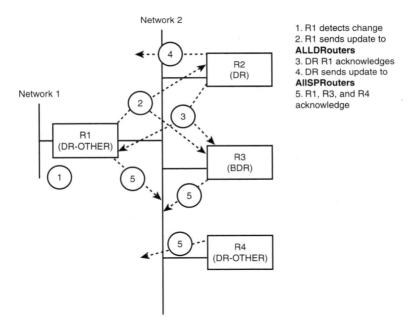

FIGURE 11.26 *Updating involves several routers on a shared multiaccess medium.*

Mark Twain wrote, "Conscience is the still, small voice that tells you someone is watching." R3, the BDR, is the conscience for the DR, R2. If R3 does not hear an LS acknowledgement (3) issued by R2 for the update from R1, before a timer expires, R3 assumes that R2 is dead.

"The DR is dead; long live the DR." In the event that R3 does not hear the acknowledgement, R3 promotes itself to DR and responds as the DR.

The acknowledgement was sent as a multicast to **AllSPFRouters**, so only a single packet is needed for both R1 and R3 to hear R2 acknowledge the new information. OSPF allows and encourages the DR to acknowledge multiple updates with a single acknowledgement. If R4 had sent an update at the same time that R1 did so, or within a short time interval of R1 sending its update, acknowledgements for R1 and R4 could be multicast into the same packet.

In the OSPF flooding procedure, a router transmits new or changed LSAs that it has validated to downstream routers. Figure 11.27 shows the relationships involved.

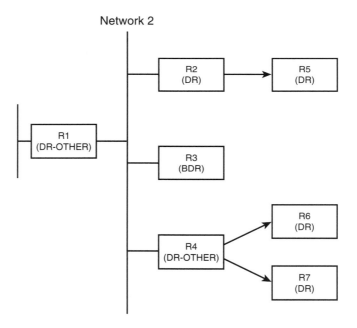

FIGURE 11.27 *Flooding is the process of sending changed or new LSA information to routers not on the same medium upon which the information was first heard.*

The flooded LSAs travel in **LS Update** packets and must be acknowledged. Acknowledgements can be explicit or implicit. Explicit acknowledgements are signaled with **LS Ack** packets. Routers implicitly acknowledge by sending the same update to one another.

OSPF implementations can batch several LSAs in the same **LS Update**. Batching reduces the overhead of sending LSAs. So, implementations can defer immediately flooding valid LSAs, in the hope that more will be coming in a short interval, and can be included in the same packet. Typical delays are 5 seconds.

It might be possible to infer acknowledgement and not require an **LS Ack** packet to be sent. If your router receives an update for a given LSA, and you just sent an update for that LSA, the other router has given you an *implicit acknowledgement*. In any link direction, for a given LSA, only one acknowledgement or one update should be sent.

OSPF also tries to avoid route flap by setting a **MinLSInterval**, or the minimum time in which an update will be accepted for the same LSA. The protocol has a default of 5 seconds for **MinLSInterval**. Cisco implements a holddown mechanism that increases **MinLSInterval** to 10 seconds when apparent flapping is detected. Both the basic and holddown values are configurable.

Flooding can be limited or unlimited in scope. The most common scope is inside the current area, but scope can be link local, areawide, or global within the routing domain. Global inter-area flooding is discussed in Chapter 12. Link-local flooding is a relatively new idea in OSPF.

Although OSPF must propagate all link-state information inside an area, that does not preclude OSPF from filtering the routes it generates, preventing some of them from entering the routing table of the local router. Of course, boundary routers, whether on an area boundary or a routing domain/autonomous system border, can filter or summarize.

Stub Networks and Host Routes

A stub network is a medium that is never used to reach another medium. There might be more than one router connected to a stub network, but the routers are there to share load or provide redundancy in reaching end hosts on the network, not to talk to one another.

In OSPF, stub networks are advertised as host routes. There are other applications for host routes, all of which require VLSM support as provided by OSPF, EIGRP, or IS-IS.

One Cisco-specific technique is called *host mobility*. When you enable host mobility on an interface, as shown in Figure 11.28, the interface learns about host addresses on its local medium that are not part of the subnet configured for the interface. Cisco's host mobility was implemented to solve a problem that is dealt with more generally with an emerging standard; see "IP Mobility" in Chapter 13.

Mobility methods can be useful, but also can have a severe impact on network scalability if they are overused. Mobility generally defeats all attempts at address aggregation to reduce routing table size. It can jeopardize security and certainly makes troubleshooting more of a challenge.

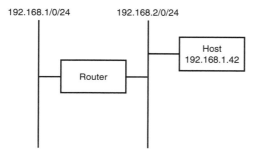

FIGURE 11.28 *Cisco host mobility deals with hosts that cannot acquire an address from DHCP.*

There's an old saying in the U.S. Army, "You only need a pistol when you need it very, very, very much, as in the enemy is too close to call in artillery!" Host mobility is one of those things; it solves specific problems but introduces operational liability. Shall we say, "Viewer discretion is advised?" This mechanism was introduced to solve a specific customer problem, in the absence of standards. The problem was caused by portable hosts that had no DHCP client. In the long term, better approaches involve IETF mobile IP and PPTP.

When the interface learns about a foreign host such as 192.168.1.42, the router generates a host route to 192.168.1.42/32 and propagates it into the routing system. Because a /32 route is the most specific possible route, traffic destined to 192.168.1.42/32 goes to R2, whereas all other traffic to 192.168.1.0/24 goes to R1.

If host mobility were used for every host, you would lose all the scaling advantages of routing over switching. If someone on 192.168.2.0/24 accidentally misconfigured a host as 192.168.1.42, traffic would be diverted from the real 192.168.1.42.

Other problems apply to the host itself. What does it use as a default gateway? In the example described here of a non-DHCP host, if the host has a hard-coded default gateway address, that gateway would be on its home subnet, not where it is connected. Proxy ARP is one alternative, but you need to think how the foreign host will communicate off the guest subnet. Proxy ARP also helps the foreign host deal with reaching addresses that the foreign host thinks are on its own subnet, but are actually remote. IRDP is another way to discover the gateway, although it's not likely that a TCP/IP stack that is too stupid to know how to be a DHCP client will support IRDP.

There is no intention to criticize Cisco's host mobility feature. It is an interim technique to solve a specific problem, and I cite it here as an example of the many ways in which extensions that violate the basic IP architecture can be difficult to support. Newer, standard mobility techniques are discussed in Chapter 13.

Fault Tolerance in Routed Networks

In Chapter 6, you saw various redundant techniques for reaching the default router, such as HSRP and Virtual Router Redundancy Protocol (VRRP). Let's look at them from the router perspective.

One of the first concerns is that the host can locate its default gateway. Dynamic mechanisms for router discovery include IRDP and passive RIP. The most common mechanism, however, remains hard-coding configuration of a default gateway address, either manually or through DHCP.

Cisco's HSRP and IETF VRRP are router-to-router mechanisms for creating a virtual router address to which workstations default. HSRP is described in informational RFC 2281, and the VRRP specification is coauthored by engineers from Ascend, Digital, IBM, Ipsilon, and Microsoft [RFC 2338]. In the event of a physical failure, both the IP and MAC virtual router addresses activate on a backup router. Because the MAC address will be the same, the ARP caches of end hosts are not affected and will not be aware of the change to a different physical router.

From the router perspective, the active router generates go to sleep messages to the backup router(s). When the active router goes down, a timer expires on the backup router, which activates the virtual MAC address and IP address.

Convergence Time After Changes

Conceptually, reconvergence starts after a change is detected. In actuality, reconvergence can only begin after a failure has been detected, or it has been recognized that a new link has been added to the topological database.

Changes received as LSA updates from other OSPF routers first must be consistency checked. After they are validated and it is determined they update the topological database, a recomputation of the routing table is scheduled and the change is flooded to other downstream routers.

Detecting a failure on one of the current router's own interfaces causes an LSA to be generated. Failure detection time depends on the nature of the failing component.

Failure Detection on the Local Router

Interface-level failure detection time depends on whether the interface type gives a hardware-specific indication of failure. In the case of Token Ring or FDDI, loss of the token causes a data link level **beacon** event in less than 1 second. When the carrier detect signal or clock is monitored on a serial interface, this also can trigger a failure notification within a second.

If there is no hardware level failure detection mechanism, OSPF relies on declaring a neighbor down after three successive hellos from that neighbor are missed. With the default hello timer value of 10 seconds, this means failure detection takes between 20 and 30 seconds.

After a failure is detected, the routing table can be recomputed. In commercial routers, this recomputation takes less than 1 second.

Resources needed to recompute routes do not vary greatly with the number of routes that change, because the most CPU-intensive part of the computation, the Dijkstra algorithm, must evaluate all Type 1 and Type 2 LSAs in the database. This is not to say that it does not take more resources to recompute after receiving a large number of new LSAs; it certainly does.

But the amount of resources needed to recompute after receiving 1 or 10 LSA changes is not significantly different; it is doing the recomputation that is CPU intensive. Commercial implementations, therefore, often use a holddown timer to delay immediate recomputation after receiving a change. This is done in the hope that additional changes will be received in a short interval, and the same recomputation can account for all of the changes. The holddown timer also minimizes the effect of links that are flapping—rapidly cycling between up and down.

Bay's default holddown value is 1 second. Cisco's basic default holddown is 5 seconds, although a second threshold is at 10 seconds if the link appears to be flapping. If a medium is flapping up and down, a slight delay allows it to be ignored or its changes to be minimized.

So, the basic single-router convergence time is the sum of the following:

Failure detection time

+   Holddown time

+   Routing table recomputation

Change Propagation

For each router connected to the router that detects the change, there is additional convergence time of the following:

Time to transmit the LSA reliably to the next router

+   Holddown time

+   Routing table recomputation

OSPF attempts to batch LSAs into one announcement, so there is at least a retransmission timer. The default is 5 seconds. Bay recommends changing it by medium type:

Medium type	Bay timer recommendation
Broadcast interfaces (default)	5 seconds
Point-to-point interfaces	10 seconds
NBMA interfaces	10 seconds
Point-to-multipoint interfaces	10 seconds

Looking Ahead

Chapter 12 extends the design techniques here to include routing information from heterogeneous sources, such as including static, RIP, and BGP information in an OSPF routing domain. Chapter 12 also discusses creating backbones of backbones with multiple OSPF domains.

Although Chapter 12 deals with widely implemented mechanisms, Chapters 13 and 14 introduce new mechanisms that you are apt to see introduced into products in the near term.

CHAPTER 12

Special and Hierarchical Routing Topologies

There are no elements so diverse that they cannot be joined in the heart of a man.
—Jean Giradoux

Pray that success will not come any faster than you are able to endure it.
—Elbert Hubbard

Every area of trouble gives out a ray of hope, and the one unchangeable
certainty is that nothing is certain or unchangeable.
—John F. Kennedy

In Chapter 11, we looked at routing as it can work in a small- to medium-sized enterprise. In a "flat" single-area routing domain, all routers have information on the same set of routes. As the number of routes increases, workload on routers increases both for path determination and route lookup in the packet forwarding process. As the number of routes increases without additional structure, it becomes more and more difficult to troubleshoot the network, to predict its need for additional resources, and to plan for increasing its capacity.

The solution is to impose hierarchy on the routing system. At the simplest level, you can impose hierarchy with a combination of physical topology with static and default routing. As complexity grows, manually configured static routing becomes too much of an administrative load, and dynamic routing becomes necessary. Practical networks often mix static and dynamic routing.

You impose hierarchy on a dynamic routing system by hiding more detailed addresses from routers that do not need the detailed information. Several techniques provide mechanisms for hiding; the most notable is address summarization.

Open Shortest Path First (OSPF) has a very formal structure for summarization, which makes it a good model for demonstrating how the process works. OSPF defines a backbone area that is always designated area 0.0.0.0.

Considerations for Area 0.0.0.0

Area 0.0.0.0 should be used only for transit between other areas. It should have a simple structure, with enough redundancy to avoid single points of failure, but without so much redundancy that neighbor maintenance becomes a substantial source of overhead.

To keep traffic flow in your network understandable, do not put application servers in area 0.0.0.0. You may put key network management servers, such as your Simple Network Management Protocol (SNMP) manager, primary Domain Name Service (DNS), and Trivial File Transfer Protocol (TFTP) functions into the backbone, because they generate little traffic and need to be highly connected to all areas.

Even if your applications servers are highly centralized, as in a mainframe data center, I prefer to put them into their own area. There will almost certainly be inter-server and operations traffic that should stay local to the data center area. Traditional data centers also tend to have user devices that access the mainframe directly, and it would be silly to congest area 0.0.0.0 with their traffic.

Let's consider an example, where your initial network deployment will need 10 routers, and you plan to use OSPF on Cisco routers.

Cisco makes a conservative recommendation, which works with the slowest routers, that there should not be more than 50 routers per OSPF area. Your 10 routers clearly could all go into the same area and still meet this rule. But a single order of magnitude projection would take you to 100 routers—too many for a single area.

You could put your 10 routers in area 0.0.0.0, and it would initially work. But if you were to grow to more than 50 routers, you would want more than one area. It's generally unwise to put user router functions in area 0.0.0.0; you should leave that for inter-area communications only. So, if you were to grow to 100 routers interconnected by area 0.0.0.0, you would need to reconfigure half the routers into area 1 and half into area 2.

One scalable approach would have been to put your initial 10 routers into area 1, and, as growth took place, create a backbone area 0.0.0.0 and an area 2, with routers 51 and up going into area 2. Alternatively, you could start with 5 routers in areas 1 and 2. The latter is especially attractive if communities of interest or geographic boundaries reasonably suggest some routers will send data primarily to a subset of the total set of routers.

> **Note**
>
> *Throughout this chapter, keep in mind that what most people regard as routing is really packet forwarding. As long as packets arrive on a router that has the proper information to forward them, it doesn't matter if this information was locally configured or learned through some dynamic mechanism.*
>
> *Many valid designs used in hierarchical routing may not advertise, among routers, the precise information that will actually be used to forward traffic. Instead, the advertised information is enough to tell other routers that they should send certain traffic to it. The advertised router is not sharing everything it knows, and may have considerable information it hides. For example, a router used in a transition from RIP to OSPF may know all information known to RIP and a substantial amount of what OSPF knows, but will tell RIP very little other than the default route.*

Hierarchy with Static and Default Routes

Proverbs say that your home is the place you will always be accepted. Default routes, therefore, must be the true homes of wandering IP packets, because they always accept them. Like parents of teenagers, however, they are also the last resort, tried only after all more specific routes have been exhausted. Default routes are inherently hierarchical, providing a path from a lower level of a hierarchy to a higher one.

In OSPF, RIP, and BGP, the convention to represent the default route is 0.0.0.0/0. It's reasonable to always consider the default route to be external.

Let's trace some applications of default routes, first from the perspective of going from a lower to a higher hierarchical level. Figure 12.1 shows the most basic use of default routing on edge router 1. Distribution router 2, to which it connects, needs to know the prefixes to which R1 is connected, if R2 is to correctly send traffic in the reverse direction. Assume for the moment that R2 knows the subnets on R1 as well as its own directly connected prefixes. R2, in turn, defaults to core router R3 when R2 doesn't know where a specific destination is located. There is a very key idea here: Different routers in a hierarchy do not have to have the same default. R1 defaults to R2, but R2 defaults to R3.

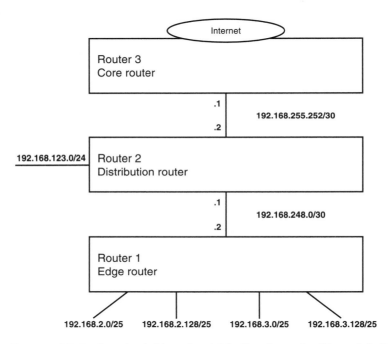

FIGURE 12.1 *In a simple hierarchy of defaults, edge router R1 can default to distribution router R2, while R2 defaults to core router R3.*

R1 has four local interfaces to /25 subnets. The addresses of these subnets are in fact contiguous, but treat them as independent for the early part of this discussion. The next hop address for R1's default route is 192.168.248.1/30. R2 defaults to an interface on R3: 192.168.255.253/30. R3 defaults to an interface in the ISP's address space.

Warning

A real-world caution is to set up a filter or blackhole (see "Blackhole Routes and Dynamic Routing" later in this chapter) on routers that connect to the Internet, which prevents them from looking for your internal registered address space on the insecure Internet. If you lack this filter or blackhole and one of your systems has a coding error, or is hacked, and sends a packet to an undefined subnet in your address space, this packet could be forwarded on to the general Internet. After it is on the Internet, the packet might wind up at a hacker site, which is advertising part of your address space. Because you would not normally send to this unknown address, you are unlikely to know it is out there.

In like manner, you should filter out packets arriving from the Internet that have source addresses from your internal registered space.

Using a default route is perhaps the simplest way to connect to the Internet. Contrary to some "conventional wisdom," it is quite practical, in many cases, to have multiple Internet connections with enterprise routing based on defaults. ISPs may also be reluctant to accept BGP advertisements from organizations that do not have frequent operational experience with this complex protocol.

The Complementary Static Path

Figure 12.2 shows the information that the higher-level routers need to know, and that can be configured with static routes.

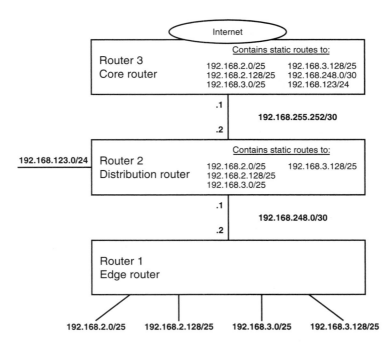

FIGURE 12.2 *In a simple hierarchy of defaults, edge router R1 can default to distribution router R2, while R2 defaults to core router R3.*

R1 knows how to reach its directly connected routes and defaults everywhere else.

R2 knows how to reach its directly connected routes and needs to know how to reach the local routes of R1.

R3 defaults to an ISP but needs to know how to reach directly connected routes on R1 and R2. Like any route, a static route must contain, at the least, a prefix and a length specification (for example, a subnet mask), and a specification of the next hop. The next hop conceptually can be a reachable IP address on a distant router, or an outgoing interface on the current router.

The destination address in a static route may be a specific subnet, as shown in Figures 12.1 and 12.2, or may be a summary route, as shown in Figure 12.3.

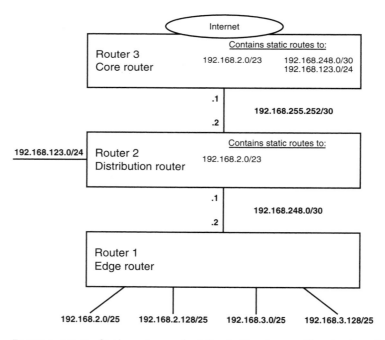

FIGURE 12.3 *Static routes can be defined either for specific subnets or for summarized blocks of addresses.*

Bay RS static routes have the basic form

```
static-route address destination mask destinationMask
    next-hop-address nextHopAddress [mask nextHopMask]
```

Supplemental parameters that can be specified either in the Site Manager menu, or with BCC subcommands, include cost and preference. *Cost* is a hop count, such as the RIP metric, and is used to pick the best static route to a destination or to recognize multiple static routes as equal-cost and eligible for load sharing. *Preference* is an administrative criterion for picking the best route or identifying equal-paths. Preference is independent of hop count.

Cisco static routes are of one of two forms:

```
ip route destination destinationMask nextHopIP [AD]
```

where *nextHopIP* is a reachable IP address, and *AD* is the administrative distance between 1 and 255.

or

```
ip route destination destinationMask interface-name
```

where *interface-name* is an interface on the current router.

Assume that a route of the first type is considered the best path, using the criteria in Chapter 4, based on information in the current router's routing table. In other words, the next hop needs to be something learned from dynamic routing, from another active static route, or from a local interface that is in an up condition. Static routes of the *nextHopIP* form are not automatically advertised by dynamic routing protocols. Only static routes of the *nextHopIP* form can have different AD values and be considered in order of preference.

The other form stays in the routing table as long as the associated interface is in an up condition, regardless of the status of the next hop. Dynamic routing protocols running on the local router treat static routes of the interface-name format as directly connected interfaces, and advertise them to their peers automatically.

There is a danger that multiple levels of defaults could form routing loops. The *blackhole route* technique, involving a special kind of static route, can help prevent such loops.

Blackhole Routes

A special static route—the blackhole route—has many applications. A blackhole route is a static route that, if traffic were actually sent to its next hop, would cause the traffic to be discarded. In practice, however, the purpose of a blackhole route is to advertise reachability to a supernet of addresses, with the advertisement coming from a router normally expected to have non-advertised but more specific information on reaching the destinations.

In Bay RS, you configure a blackhole route as a static route with a special sub-net mask and next-hop address:

```
static-route address destination mask destinationMask
    next-hop-address 255.255.255.255 mask 255.255.255.255
```

Cisco's convention is to configure a blackhole route as a route whose next hop is defined as the null interface:

```
ip route destination destinationMask null0
```

Cisco has an explicit software-defined null interface. GateD uses the loopback interface for blackholing. An additional address can be assigned to the GateD loopback interface to set the OSPF or BGP router IDs.

Applications for null interfaces vary considerably. The most common applica-tion is probably using the null interface as an "anchor" for a summary route, as shown in Figure 12.4. A router using this technique advertises that it can reach the summary, but has more specific, more preferred, internal routes that are used for actual forwarding of packets that arrive at the router. If all of these more specific routes are down, the router has an additional default, local to this router only, that can be used.

If the default is down, the blackhole route causes the incoming packets to be discarded with no ICMP Destination Unreachable being generated. Not generat-ing ICMP reduces traffic in failures. You can still diagnose problems, because a **traceroute** to the ultimate destination will stop in the router with the blackhole.

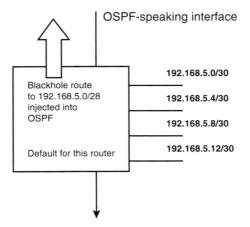

FIGURE 12.4 *The less-specific summary route is advertised into the routing system, but the more specific static routes over dial interfaces are visible only inside the router. The router also has a local default.*

Another technique is an alternative for the specific packet filtering requirement of discarding certain packets based solely on their destination address. The subtle rationale for this technique is that routers are optimized to forward traffic rather than to filter it. Routers may have caches or other hardware assistance for forwarding, but may need to do filtering in a slower general-purpose CPU.

To illustrate this principle, the following Cisco static route commands provide the fastest way to discard packets destined to private address space:

```
ip route    10.0.0.0      255.0.0.0      null0
ip route    172.16.0.0    255.240.0.0    null0
ip route    192.168.0.0   255.255.0.0    null0
```

(See Chapter 14 for the specific format of Cisco static route and access list commands.) Setting up routes that discard traffic destined to the private address space would be a very reasonable thing to do on a router acting as the default gateway to the Internet.

Load Balancing Among Static and Default Routes

Static and default routes of the same preference (see "Installing Routes in the RIB: Administrative Preference Factors" in Chapter 4) can be load-shared using the particular implementation's load-sharing capabilities. Bay RS can load-share over up to 12 equal-cost paths, and Cisco can load-share over up to 6 paths. In general, static routes do not have metrics (Bay RS is an exception), so the choice between routes of the same prefix length is based on preference.

As discussed in the section "Static Load Sharing" in Chapter 11, load sharing is not free. Round-robin load sharing increases the probability of out-of-order packet delivery, which may increase processing load on the destination host. Per-destination load sharing may or may not evenly distribute load. Even source-destination load sharing, probably the best method available to a router making decisions on local information, is unaware of distant congestion and may take a suboptimal path.

Nevertheless, the technique is quite useful. For a Cisco router with two T1 interfaces, as shown in Figure 12.5, you could code the following:

```
interface s0
ip address 192.168.1.1 255.255.255.252
no ip route-cache    ! sets process switching for IP
interface s1
ip address 192.168.1.5 255.255.255.252
no ip route-cache    ! sets process switching for IP
!
ip route 0.0.0.0 0.0.0.0 192.168.1.2    1
ip route 0.0.0.0 0.0.0.0 192.168.1.6    1
```

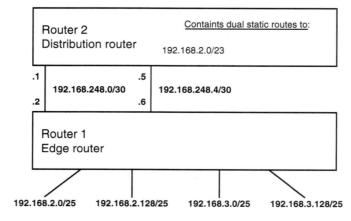

FIGURE 12.5 *Default routes on the edge routers are mirrored by static routes in the distribution router.*

The default administrative distance for a static route of the *nextHopIP* form is 1, but the *AD* is shown explicitly so you can see the routes are of equal preference. On a Cisco router, to set per-packet round-robin load balancing, the interfaces need to be in the process switching mode. On Bay RS, you explicitly enable load sharing.

Multiple Backup Preferences with Defaults and Statics

What if you want to extend the example in Figure 12.6 to include ISDN backup if both T1s go down? You can extend the configuration to include a dial-on-demand route less preferred than either T1.

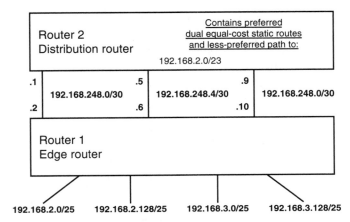

FIGURE 12.6 *The edge router has two preferred equal-cost routes and a less preferred backup. The distribution router has static routes to mirror these default routes.*

With this configuration (Figure 12.6) the behavior would be:

- Both T1s up: Load balance

- One T1 up: all traffic over that interface

- Both T1s down: ISDN comes up and provides the default.

When either T1 comes back up after a failure, it becomes a more preferred path than the ISDN path. Traffic moves to the T1 path, and the ISDN path eventually disconnects due to inactivity. You need to be sure that no network management traffic, routing updates, or keepalives run on the ISDN path, or it will never disconnect. The extended configuration would be:

```
interface s0
ip address 192.168.1.1 255.255.255.252
no ip route-cache    ! sets process switching
interface s1
ip address 192.168.1.5 255.255.255.252
no ip route-cache    ! sets process switching
interface bri0
ip address 192.168.1.9 255.255.255.252
! dial-on-demand code omitted
!
ip route 0.0.0.0 0.0.0.0 192.168.1.2    1
ip route 0.0.0.0 0.0.0.0 192.168.1.6    1
ip route 0.0.0.0 0.0.0.0 192.168.1.10   40
```

Finding a Backup Router on Multiaccess Media

The two preceding examples assume that the media between the core and distribution routers are point-to-point. Point-to-point media can give specific failure indications when the link is down. It is also much more clear that a remote router is down, if the physical link is up but no hellos or routing updates are being received.

On multiaccess media, however, the situation is not as clear. Especially on Ethernets where there is not a hardware-level indication of link failure, it can be hard to tell whether there is a connectivity problem or a router is down. In general, on a multiaccess medium, it is best that the routers lower in the hierarchy learn the default dynamically, as shown in Figure 12.7.

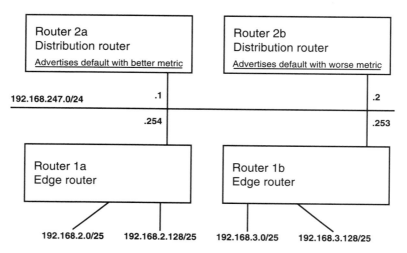

FIGURE 12.7 *Routers on a multiaccess medium can find routers dynamically.*

As discussed in Chapter 6, hosts also can discover hosts dynamically. Alternatively, hosts may default to a default address defined in their fixed configuration or by DHCP, and this address may actually be a virtual router running HSRP, Bay Router Redundancy, or VRRP.

Hierarchy with Inter-Area Dynamic Route Summarization

The OSPF standard specifies two kinds of boundary routers: area border routers (ABRs) and autonomous system border routers (ASBRs). ABRs summarize routes inside a routing domain, creating summaries between the backbone area 0.0.0.0 and nonzero areas.

ASBRs inject routing information from outside the routing domain. The information they inject may be imported from other routing domains, or may be created with local configuration information on the ASBR.

OSPF Internal Summarization

Inside an OSPF routing domain, you explicitly configure summarization at the ABRs between area 0.0.0.0 and nonzero areas. OSPF does not support summarization at arbitrary points within an area, although there are practical ways to impose hierarchy within an area, using topology rather than addressing, or using static routes imported into OSPF.

When configuring real routers, you explicitly describe the summaries you want to advertise. These are not the same advertisements as the router makes of its locally connected networks, and the distinction can be confusing. It would be difficult to auto-generate summaries, because the summary reflects the addresses on interfaces of all routers in the areas. The summary should include addresses on interfaces in the area whether the interface is active or not, and whether or not the associated router is generating specific intra-area LSAs for it.

Bay RS routers generate a summary for each explicit **summary network** command you code with the BCC, or insert in the equivalent Site Manager menu.

The syntax of the command is

```
summary network ip-address subnet-mask
```

where the subnet mask defines the prefix length for the summary. You would code 255.255.252.0, for example, to advertise a /22 summary block.

On a Cisco router, you specify OSPF ABR summarization with the **area...range** subcommand of the **router ospf** major command. It's quite easy to make errors in specifying this command, because although it uses a conventional subnet mask to specify the prefix length at which to summarize, the **network** subcommands adjacent to it use less conventional wildcard masks.

You write a separate **area...range** statement for each summary address you want the ABR to generate:

```
hostname r1
interface e0
ip address 172.16.1.1 255.255.255.0
interface e1
ip address 172.17.1.1 255.255.255.0
interface e2
ip address 172.17.2.1 255.255.255.0
interface s0
ip address 192.168.1.5 255.255.255.252
router ospf 1
network 192.168.1.4 0.0.0.3   area 0
network 172.16.1.0  0.0.0.255 area 1
network 172.17.1.0  0.0.0.255 area 1
network 172.17.2.0  0.0.0.255 area 1
area 1 range 172.16.0.0 255.255.0.0
area 1 range 172.17.0.0 255.255.0.0
```

Note

This particular configuration is written for ease of understanding. There are several variants, some of which I personally would not use and some that I would.

In the specific lines here, the **network** statements identify the subnets that this router will advertise, assuming that it has active interface addresses that fall into these subnets. R1 has only two subnets on it, but R1 is the ABR for Area 1 and needs to announce summaries that include all addresses in the area. The summaries generated by the two **area...range** commands define different address ranges than the specific **network** commands.

172.16.0.0/16 and 172.17.0.0 are contiguous blocks, and actually could be advertised as 172.16.0.0/15. To generate this summary, replace the two **area...range** statements with:

```
area 1 range 172.16.0.0 255.254.0.0
```

In principle, however, you could reduce the number of **network** statements by writing one broader statement that picks up both subnets of 172.17.0.0:

```
network 172.17.0.0  0.0.255.255 area 1
```

I do not recommend this practice because I find it harder to maintain and troubleshoot. It's easiest to check a configuration when you can map each **interface** statement to a corresponding **network** statement. In the Cisco configuration language, the order of **network** statements is critical.

When you look at the **area...range** statements, think of them as representing the set of **network** statements for the area on all routers in the area. If you want to advertise some more specific, nonsummarized routes, they are not covered by the summary explicitly generated by the ABR.

Advertising Holes

Your enterprise has long been organized on major divisional lines, with Sales Division sites assigned to 172.16.0.0/16 in Area 1, Service Division sites assigned to 172.17.0.0/16 in Area 2, and corporate facilities in 172.31.0.0/16 (see Figure 12.8) in Area 3. The corporate network backbone, area 0.0.0.0, has been in 192.16.255.0/24. Until now, the corporate network has been small, and contained the executive offices, a data center, and the research laboratory. Assume you are running OSPF with summarization at classful boundaries. This simple summarization is adequate to reduce traffic leaving a division. The section "RIP to OSPF Transition," later in this chapter, discusses a more real-world and complex situation where the reorganization and transition to a new routing architecture are simultaneous.

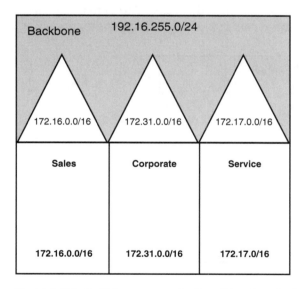

FIGURE 12.8 *Before a reorganization, this enterprise has been able to rely on classful summarization.*

A corporate reorganization intended to reduce costs, however, has moved to take certain apparently duplicated functions out of the divisions and move them into the corporate network. Typically, the budget-cutters select one of two groups, its computers and users, and transfers it to corporate. In the case we are about to discuss, the former Accounts Payable group in the Service Division, which had been on 172.17.42.0/24, is being transferred to corporate. If the Service Division advertises 172.17.0.0/16, how can you ensure that traffic to this group, now in Area 3, goes to Area 3? Do you have to break summarization in Area 2?

This problem is often described as a requirement to advertise a *hole* in a larger supernet. In practice, the actual hole is not advertised by dynamic routing protocols, but the effect is the same as if they advertised "don't go to" some address.

Your problem is solved by the fundamental longest-match rule of IP routing. A router always uses the most specific route available to select the next hop toward a destination. Area 2 should continue to announce 172.17.0.0/16 into the backbone. Area 3, however, should add 172.17.42.0/24 to its announcement into the backbone (see Figure 12.9).

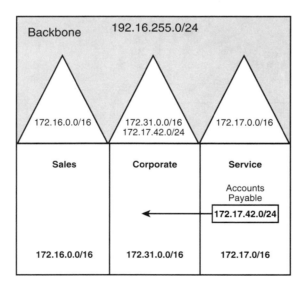

FIGURE 12.9 *After the reorganization starts, this enterprise minimizes the routing impact by advertising a more specific route from the area to which a subnet moved.*

Multiple ABRs

Obviously, a single ABR is a single point of failure. An area certainly can have multiple ABRs. Remember that it is interfaces that are in an area, not router chassis. Figure 12.10 shows several potential configurations for ABRs.

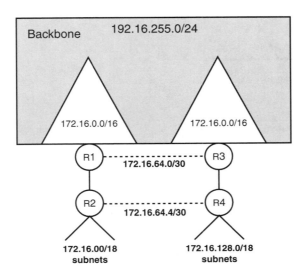

FIGURE 12.10 *Multiple ABRs usually generate the same summary addresses.*

In a regular area, as opposed to a stubby one, traffic to a given destination outside the area leaves by the ABR that gives the lowest end-to-end metric. The end-to-end metric considers both the sum of costs from the current router to the ABR, and the cost of the inter-area or external route injected from area 0.

The default route injected into an area has a fixed cost, so if you are sending to a destination outside the area, for which you have no better information than the default route, you take the lowest-path cost from the sum of intra-area costs and the default cost. Unless you explicitly specify different default costs on different ABRs, the normal case is that you take the closest exit from your nonzero area into area 0.

Because ABRs are manually configured with the summary to advertise, the usual practice is that all ABRs advertise the same summary routes. In configurations such as that of Figure 12.11, this can lead to apparently strange behavior after certain failures. For example, a packet might reach R1 and need to get to 172.16.128.0. Although R1 is advertising a summary that contains 172.16.128.0, it does not actually know how to reach that address and would drop the packet.

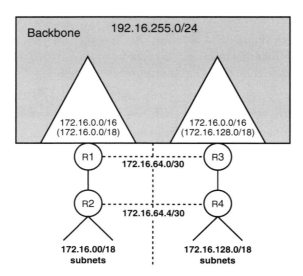

FIGURE 12.11 *After a failure, multiple ABRs advertise the same summaries, even though some of those addresses may no longer be reachable through a specific ABR.*

Summarization and Pseudo-Summarization in RIP and IGRP

Within a major classful network (see Table 12.1), RIP and IGRP advertise all subnets. Other than in RIPv2, there can be only one prefix length. RIPv1 and IGRP do not advertise subnets of one major network across an interface belonging to a different classful major network. These protocols cannot usefully advertise the subnets to a different major network, because they do not transmit subnet masks. Table 12.1 shows the rules used to define classful major networks.

TABLE 12.1 CLASSFUL ADDRESSES

Binary starting value of actual 32-bit address	Decimal range for first octet of address as written	Class of traditional classful major network in dotted decimal	CIDR prefix to which advertisements are to be auto-summarized
0	1–126	A	/8
10	128–191	B	/16
110	192–223	C	/24

Instead, RIPv1 and IGRP *auto-summarize* the subnet announcements to a single major network announcement. In Figure 12.12, router R1 knows all subnets of 172.16.0.0/16 and 172.17.0.0/16. R1 advertises the 172.16.0.0 subnets only on interfaces 2 through 4 whose address is in 172.16.0.0, and advertises the 172.17.0.0 subnets only on interfaces 5 through 6 with addresses belonging to 172.17.0.0. R1 advertises 172.16.0.0/16 and 172.17.0.0/16 on interface 1. It summarizes 192.168.1.32/28 to 192.168.1.0/24 and advertises that on interfaces 2 through 7.

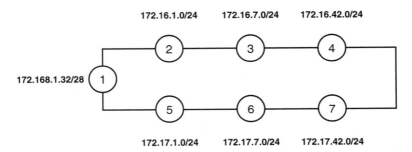

FIGURE 12.12 *Classful protocols automatically summarize at interfaces belonging to a different major network.*

When the interface address does not match the address of a subnet, the router generates a summary announcement at the classful level. On 172.16.0.0 interfaces, it announces the 172.16.0.0 subnets and also a summary: 172.17.0.0/16. R1 does not mark 172.17.0.0/16 as a summary route, and does not send the prefix length in RIPv1 and IGRP.

EIGRP and RIPv2 can be set up either to auto-summarize or to use manually configured classless summarization. This is a feature, not a bug, that is useful in converting IGRP to EIGRP and RIPv1 to RIPv2. With auto-summary enabled, the more capable EIGRP or RIPv2 does not generate routes that IGRP or RIPv1 cannot understand, such as routes with different prefix lengths inside the same major network.

If you have a large classless network using RIPv2 or EIGRP, with a few legacy RIPv1 or IGRP domains, it may be awkward to restrict the bulk of the network to classful behavior. The simplest way to deal with this problem is to export the detailed routes into the more capable protocol, but to import only the default route to the less capable protocol.

EIGRP

EIGRP is more flexible in summarization than OSPF, because it is not restricted to summarizing on formal area boundaries. Before you do any significant classless summarization in EIGRP, disable classful summarization with the **no auto-summary** subcommand of **router eigrp**.

Although I find it useful to think in terms of areas even when designing EIGRP, you can summarize within an EIGRP area, as shown in Figure 12.13.

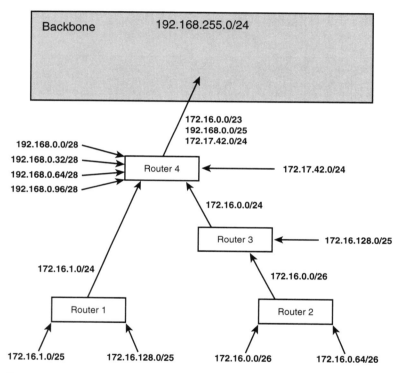

FIGURE 12.13   *In contrast with the OSPF summary in Figure 12.12, you can summarize at multiple levels within an EIGRP "area."*

R4 is the EIGRP equivalent of an ABR. R1 and R3 summarize before they advertise routes to R4, which cannot be done with OSPF intra-area routes. R2 summarizes the routes it advertises to R3.

You configure EIGRP summarization on a per-interface basis:

```
hostname r1
interface e0
ip address 172.16.1.1 255.255.255.0
interface e1
ip address 172.17.1.1 255.255.255.0
interface e2
ip address 172.17.2.1 255.255.255.0
interface s0
ip address 192.168.1.5 255.255.255.252
ip summary-address eigrp 1      172.16.0.0 255.255.0.0
ip summary-address eigrp 1      172.17.0.0 255.255.0.0
router eigrp 1
no auto-summary
network 172.16.0.0
network 172.17.0.0
network 192.168.1.0
```

The important thing to understand about the **ip summary-address** command is that you place it on the interface from which the summary is to be generated, rather than under the router commands as is done with OSPF. On a large router with many interfaces, it is easy to miss applying or removing an interface-level summary command when the topology changes. Check very carefully when you do this on a critical router, and it is not at all a bad idea to have a colleague cross-check your configuration. Cisco's NETSYS product can check the reachability of a particular configuration.

This configuration emphasizes ease of understanding rather than greatest efficiency. You could generate a single supernet summary by replacing the two **ip summary-address** commands on s0 with:

```
ip summary-address eigrp 1      172.16.0.0 255.254.0.0
```

Pseudo-Summarization with RIP and IGRP

If your real problem is the overhead of RIP or IGRP, your long-term solution should be to transition to a more modern routing protocol. In some networks, an interim solution can involve using route filtering to block routes from being advertised to routers that you, as the network architect, never need to see.

Route filtering is a last-resort step, because the process of filtering can impose significant processor overhead. Route filtering of this sort is probably most appropriate when the limiting factor is due more to very slow links than to slow processors, and static and default routing are infeasible.

As shown in Figure 12.14, branches and districts don't send directly to one another, because the purpose of the network is to send inventory data to the data center. Both districts do need connectivity to the support center, and prefer to connect through their direct link to it. The districts, however, do have an alternate path to the support center via the data center.

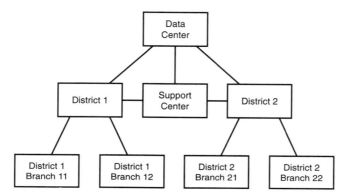

FIGURE 12.14 *If you have too much routing traffic with a classful protocol and a strict hierarchy, you can reduce traffic with route filters.*

Assume all routers are in the same classful network. The data center and support center routers know all subnets.

To reduce traffic, however, you filter out all District 1 information on the data center interface to District 2. You filter out all District 2 routes on the data center router interface to District 1. The data center router advertises default to both districts.

Filters are needed on the support center router as well as the data center router, to ensure that the support center does not advertise the more specific routes it knows.

If you do not want the districts to use the support center router as an alternate path to the data center, filter out the data center route advertisement on the link to the districts.

At the district level, the district level routers only advertise default to the branch offices, filtering out more specific routes if necessary.

This sort of selective route filtering, incidentally, is the fundamental technique used to enforce policy in BGP—the combination of route advertising and route acceptance filters.

Importing, Exporting, and Controlling External Routes

Chapter 5 introduces the idea of exporting and importing information among routing processes. See the section "Sharing Information Among Routing Sources."

Do distinguish between what goes into the routing table (that is, the RIB), and what goes into an OSPF topological database (see Figure 12.15).

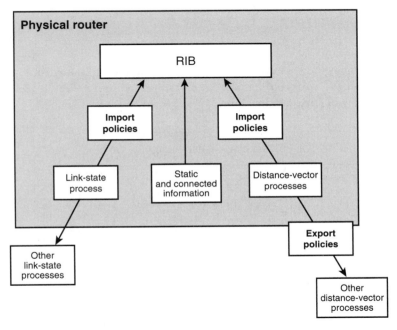

FIGURE 12.15   *The RIB on the router is aware of all routes found by all routing processes, unless you explicitly filter between a process and the RIB.*

You can filter routes generated by a link-state routing protocol such as OSPF or IS-IS before they reach the RIB, but you must not filter out the exporting of intra-area LSAs. You can filter both incoming and outgoing route advertisements from distance vector protocols such as RIP, IGRP, and EIGRP.

Understanding Cisco's Use of Redistribution

Cisco's term for importing is *redistribution*. First, redistribution refers not to the outward transmission of routes, but to the redistribution of external information into a specific routing process. On a Cisco router, the redistribute commands specify an import policy:

```
router ospf 1
network 192.168.1.0 0.0.0.255 area 1
redistribute rip subnets
default-metric 100
```

An *external route*, to generalize beyond the OSPF definition, is any route that is generated outside your routing domain and imported into it. Figure 12.16 gives a general view of such relationships.

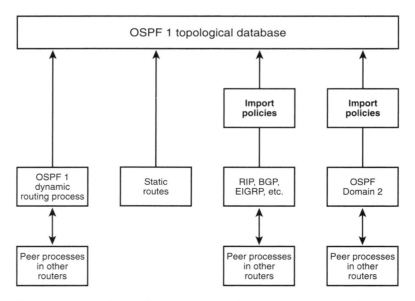

FIGURE 12.16 *External routes can come from many sources, and do not need to involve dynamic importing.*

In Figure 12.16, from the perspective of OSPF Routing Domain 1, routes learned from routing domain 2 are external. Pay close attention to the relationship between your own domain and another OSPF domain: You receive LSAs from other routers in your own domain, but receive external routes from routers in other OSPF domains. These external routes are then converted to Type 5 or Type 7 external LSAs in your domain.

You can import static routes, especially the default route. Remember that the purpose of an advertised route is to announce that your router offers routing services to that destination. Your router is not claiming to have current dynamic information of the actual destination, and may simply pass the packets it receives to its own default.

From OSPF's viewpoint, all static routes are externals, because they were not generated by OSPF. The default route is specified manually, so the default is always treated as external.

External routes can be aggregated into summaries, much as internal routes are. The ultimate summary, of course, is the default route, 0.0.0.0/0. Let's begin looking at the behavior of externals with the idea of summarization in mind.

You might have a situation such as that illustrated in Figure 12.17, where you have a single external router that advertises a classful RIP network into your routing domain. That router actually has interfaces to two subnets of the RIP domain, but your domain really doesn't need to know that level of detail. No matter how detailed the level of information the external router may have, as long as an address is contained in the classful network it advertises, the rest of your domain will send to the external router.

If you try to import the RIP subnets into your routing domain, you add no value and increase overhead. The trick shown in Figure 12.17 is not to import the actual dynamic RIP updates, but to declare a summary that covers all the RIP routes and imports only that summary.

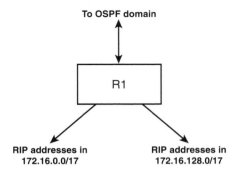

FIGURE 12.17 *You can import a statically declared external summary rather than importing many dynamically announced subnets, thus reducing overhead.*

Hierarchical Versus Mutual Importing and Exporting

Router vendors' advanced routing courses tend to focus on complex importing and exporting scenarios, scenarios that tend more to show how to exploit the router command set, and explore odd hardware configurations implicit in a teaching lab setup, than real-world scenarios. For some obscure reason, there is relatively little focus on very practical importing strategies. In most real-world situations, you can avoid complex loop prevention filtering by doing hierarchical (see Figure 12.18).

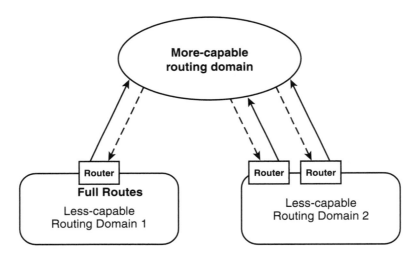

FIGURE 12.18 *In the real world, a way to simplify many protocol coexistence and migration scenarios is simply to advertise all routes from the less capable to the more capable protocol, and advertise default from more capable to less capable.*

The alternative to hierarchical route exchange among different routing domains is much more complex (see Figure 12.19).

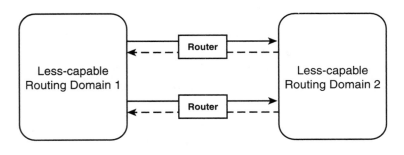

Legend

——————▶ Routes originating in Domain 1 only
— — — ▶ Routes originating in Domain 2 only

FIGURE 12.19 *Mutual importing and exporting needs much more complex configuration to avoid loops.*

This isn't to say there cannot be perfectly legitimate reasons to import and export between multiple domains using the same routing protocol. See the section "Complex RIP to OSPF Transition" later in this chapter. It is still necessary to be extremely careful to avoid routing loop formation. Explicit filters still are often necessary.

You should be especially careful about causing routing loops with improperly exchanged default routes. It never makes sense for two domains to default at one another!

Routing information exchange between multiple instances of similar protocols is somewhat simpler because the metrics are compatible. Potentially, doing so enables you to exchange meaningful metrics among routing domains. It may or may not be useful, however, to exchange metrics.

Blackhole Routes and Dynamic Routing

In the first application of blackhole routes discussed in this chapter, the blackhole route did not leave the router. It was purely local information to terminate loops. A quite different application involves deliberately advertising a blackhole route. This application is powerful but subtle. Advertising is a particularly appropriate word to describe it, because the purpose of commercial advertising, in daily life, is to get people to buy products—without necessarily first looking inside the product's package.

In the case of blackhole route advertising, the router advertises reachability to a block of destinations. The real purpose of attracting traffic to this router is to enable the router to decide what it actually wants to do with it. The router advertising the blackhole has more specific routing information that it does not advertise, and it intends to delete any traffic for which it does not have a more specific route.

The advertising router rarely really intends to blackhole all the packets sent to it. It might do exactly that if all hierarchically subordinate routes, however, were unreachable. In large networks, especially the Internet, this is desirable behavior on the part of the router advertising the blackhole. By advertising a blackhole for which the router takes responsibility for dropping packets, the advertising router relieves other routers from a potentially substantial work-load. This workload involves recomputing routing tables whenever a subordi-nate route in the blackhole range goes down—or back up. Frequent up-down changes are called *route flap*, and are a serious problem in global BGP routing. Containing the effect of route flaps is a strong motivation for hierarchical design in enterprise networks, especially those that use link-state protocols.

When connecting to the Internet, it is usually far more robust to define black-hole route(s) that cover your address space, and advertise these to the ISP, rather than exporting your internal routing table into BGP. Uncontrolled exporting of the internal table is bad enough when it causes unnecessary growth of the size of the global routing table, but it is worse when it causes flapping in the global table.

Remember that your BGP router has more specific routes from your IGP or sta-tic routes. When an external packet arrives at the router, if the sub-block is down, the router returns ICMP destination unreachable. If the sub-block is up, the router routes to it because a more specific route to the sub-block is already in your routing table. You never actually route to the null interface unless the packet is to a sub-block you don't have defined.

OSPF External Route Summarization

Much as you explicitly declare inter-area summarized routes, you can summa-rize external routes. In practice, the most common summarization is to the ulti-mate level: the default route.

You might, however, want to create explicit summaries when you know a given router has more than one connection to another routing domain, but only one connection to the OSPF routing domain. In Figure 12.19, R1 needs to know the subnets of the RIP network so that it can pick the appropriate outgoing interface to destinations it learns from RIP.

R1, therefore, *must* learn specific subnets of the RIP network. There is no reason to advertise these more specific subnets into the OSPF network, because OSPF sends to R1 to reach any destination in the range.

In like manner, when R1 terminates a block of statically routed edge sites, and the static routes form a contiguous block, you should advertise a summary external route for the block of static routes, rather than importing the static routes into OSPF:

```
hostname r1
int e0  ! this is the only path from R1 into the OSPF domain
ip addr 192.168.255.1 255.255.255.0
int s0  ! this is one of two interfaces to the RIP domain
ip addr 10.1.0.1 255.255.0.0
int s1  ! this is the other interface to RIP
ip addr 10.128.0.1 255.255.0.0
int s2  ! this is the first statically routed interface
ip addr 192.168.0.1 255.255.255.252
int s3  ! the second static routed interface
ip addr 192.168.0.5 255.255.255.252

ip route 192.168.2.0 255.255.255.0 192.168.0.2
ip route 192.168.3.0 255.255.255.0 192.168.0.6

router rip
network 10.0.0.0

router ospf 1
! r1 will only speak OSPF on the Ethernet
network 192.168.255.0 0.0.0.255 area 1
summary-address 10.0.0.0 255.0.0.0
summary-address 192.168.2.0 255.255.254.0
redistribute rip metric 1000 subnets
```

Following Cisco defaults, the two summary addresses are advertised as Type 2 external routes.

Multiple OSPF Processes

Some vendors, such as Cisco, allow you to configure multiple independent OSPF processes on the same physical router. An obvious application for this technique is merging multiple separately implemented OSPF domains, as might result from a merger, when the eventual goal is to merge the domains.

Another reason to use multiple OSPF processes is to create an additional level of summarization among them, when you do not need the complexity of a full backbone of backbones.

IGRP-to-EIGRP Transition

EIGRP is intended to ease migration from IGRP. It is upwardly compatible with IGRP, although EIGRP does not directly accept IGRP routing updates. The rule for automatic route learning is what IGRP and EIGRP call the autonomous system number:

```
router igrp as-number
router eigrp as-number
```

IGRP 100 and EIGRP 100, on the same physical router, learn routes from one another without explicit redistribution statements. IGRP 100 and EIGRP 200, however, do not learn automatically, although you can explicitly redistribute between them. You might want to have two separate (E)IGRP domains for different parts of an enterprise, or, even more likely, during a migration from IGRP to EIGRP in one part of your enterprise while new routes are added in a separate EIGRP domain. EIGRP does have the capability to mark routes as external, but not with the flexibility of OSPF type 1 and type 2 externals. If I need to control external routes between EIGRP domains, I've found it more realistic to use BGP.

The router prefers EIGRP-generated routes over IGRP-generated routes, unless you change the default administrative distances, which are 90 for EIGRP and 100 for IGRP.

Figure 12.20 shows a configuration in which router R1 learns IGRP 100 routes automatically, and propagates them into EIGRP 100. EIGRP 200, however, does not learn routes from IGRP 100. R1 can forward to both 100 and 200 because both those (E)IGRP AS populate its RIB. R2 speaks only IGRP while R3 and R4 speak only EIGRP.

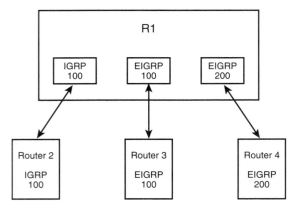

FIGURE 12.20 *Automatic redistribution features can help in IGRP-to-EIGRP migration.*

During the migration from IGRP to EIGRP, it is a good idea to accept the EIGRP default classful behavior. Doing so prevents EIGRP from propagating a classless route into IGRP, which IGRP does not understand. When the migration is complete, use the EIGRP **no auto-summary** command to invoke classless behavior, and manually create a summarization hierarchy.

Controlling Route Propagation with Stubby Areas

The path determination workload of an OSPF area is influenced most strongly by the number of network, summary, and external LSAs involved in the routing computation. The various stub area schemes—stub, not-so-stubby (NSSA), and the vendor-specific totally stubby—all help when a large number of externals would be injected into an area.

In medicine, there is a classic piece of advice from a physician to a patient who complains that some odd movement of his arm hurts: If that hurts, don't do it. If the nature of a routing environment is such that large numbers of externals do not exist, then there is no benefit to exploring stub area techniques to control the propagation of externals.

Most beginners tend to think of floods of externals into OSPF being primarily due to Internet connectivity. They imagine nearly 50,000 routes of a current Internet default-free routing table overwhelming their routers. In practice, injecting such a table into the OSPF routing system is not likely to offer any significant benefit. In most cases, no more than a default route needs to be injected to achieve connectivity. Even if preferential exits for certain exterior destinations are desired, that is more likely to be an interior BGP problem than an OSPF one.

In practice, a great number of external routes can come from one's own enterprise, as part of a migration from RIP or IGRP, or from static/default routes used to connect edge routers to the main routing system. Another way to think of this is that large numbers of external routes can come from other routing domains in your own organization. Declaring nonzero areas as stubby keeps non-summarized—specific—external routes from entering the nonzero areas.

External route aggregation in area 0.0.0.0 thus complements stubbiness. Stubbiness reduces the number of externals in nonzero areas, whereas route aggregation reduces the number of routes in area 0.

Declaring an area as stubby in any way restricts what you can do in it. Virtual links cannot go through a stub area. All routers in the area must agree on the type of stubbiness.

Other than in NSSA areas, you cannot have ASBRs in a stubby area. Although many people assume they do not need ASBRs because they have no Internet connectivity from an area, there is a logical trap of forgetting that if you import static, RIP, or IGRP routes, the router doing the importing becomes an ASBR.

If the intra-organizational external routes are injected into OSPF through ASBRs connected to area 0.0.0.0, stub techniques may be effective in controlling the number of externals that impose workload on nonzero areas. Even in this case, summarize the externals as much as possible.

Basic Stub Areas

A basic stub area accepts some or all of the inter-area routes from area 0.0.0.0, but does not accept external routes other than the default route. If there is a significant number of external routes in area 0.0.0.0, preventing them from entering a stub area may considerably reduce resource requirements in the stub area.

Stub areas are appropriate when the only way to leave the area is in the direction of area 0.0.0.0, through one or more ABRs. You cannot have an ASBR in a stub area.

Stub areas are most useful when all ASBRs connect only to area 0. Without stubby areas, OSPF's standard behavior would be that shown in Figure 12.21. The nonzero areas have to send their traffic to area 0.0.0.0 to leave the OSPF routing domain.

There is little value for the nonzero areas to know specific external routes if the traffic is simply going to go to area 0.0.0.0 in any case. Declaring areas 1 and 2 as stubby, as shown in Figure 12.22, prevents the external routes from entering areas 1 and 2, where they add no useful information. Area 0.0.0.0 knows the specific exit router to choose for a specific route, if a choice exists.

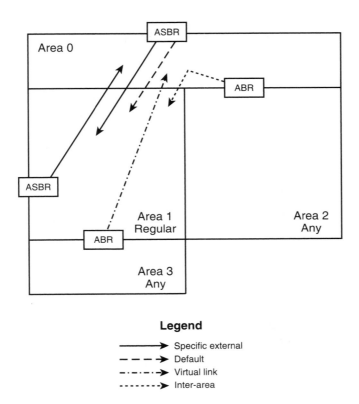

Legend

→ Specific external
- - → Default
-·-·-· → Virtual link
········› Inter-area

FIGURE 12.21 *Without stubby areas, all external routes propagate into every nonzero area.*

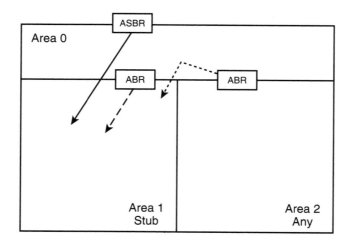

Legend

⟶ Specific external

--- ⟶ Default

------ ⟶ Inter-area

FIGURE 12.22 *After declaring areas 1 and 2 stub, the RIP routes do not enter the stub areas.*

Totally Stubby Areas and Closest Exit Routing

Cisco extended the idea of the stubby area to its logical extreme, the *totally stubby area*. In totally stubby areas, as shown in Figure 12.23, the ABRs only inject the default route. Inter-area routes are suppressed.

The ABRs do advertise full routes, or whatever summaries you configure, into area 0. Routers inside the totally stubby area strictly follow closest exit routing to area 0.0.0.0, if there is more than one ABR.

Routers must agree on their stubbiness on a given interface if they are to become neighbors. You cannot run virtual links through a totally stubby area.

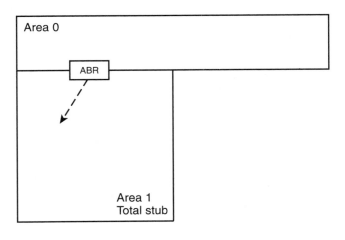

Legend

– – – ➤ Default

FIGURE 12.23 *Totally stubby areas only inject the default route into the nonzero area. Externals and inter-area routes are suppressed.*

Not-So-Stubby Areas

NSSAs are a relatively recent and useful extension to the OSPF standard (see Figure 12.24).

More challenging situations arise when the intra-organizational routes come in at the edge of a nonzero area. Assume, for example, that an organization has a large number of small offices, each with a single frame relay PVC that carries its traffic to the next level of the corporate routing hierarchy. Each of the small edge routers needs a default route toward the next level.

The next level, however, is composed of OSPF-speaking routers. Even though they are in a nonzero area, they are still ASBRs. Because these routers do not speak OSPF to the edge routers, these second-level routers need to have static routes that point to these edge subnets, and then the static routing information needs to be advertised as external routes into OSPF. Remember that these externals can be summarized on the ASBR.

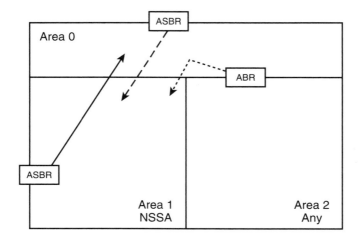

Legend

FIGURE 12.24 *Not-so-stubby areas enable you to accept external information needed by area 0.0.0.0 without having to flood unnecessary externals to other nonzero areas.*

You can make an area both totally stubby and not-so-stubby, if you are willing to accept a rather silly-sounding name. Figure 12.25 shows this configuration. It is actually a potentially useful configuration, in which an external router in the nonzero area is closest to another routing domain, but the nonzero area has a simple path into area 0.

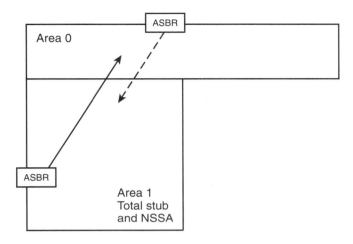

Legend

——————▶ Specific external

– – – ▶ Default

FIGURE 12.25 *Not-so-stubby and totally stubby attributes can be combined.*

Basic RIP-to-OSPF Transition

A key question is whether to do a complete or incremental conversion between RIP and OSPF. Another part of the question is whether you are concerned with knowing the dynamic structure of the RIP network, or are more concerned with its reachability.

Bay RS has a default interface cost of 1, as opposed to the 10^8/bandwidth default used by most other vendors. Bay, however, recommends using 10^8/bandwidth after an all-OSPF network is running. Using a default cost of 1, however, results in hop count becoming the effective metric. If you were converting a RIP network completely to OSPF, the paths would remain the same in OSPF as RIP.

If your routers do not support NSSA, you probably want to try to connect a set of RIP routers to area 0. See Figure 12.26, in which the nonzero areas can be stubby since they only reach the RIP destinations through area 0. The stub ABRs generate default into the nonzero areas, while ASBR 2 connects to an ISP and generates default for area 0. It would be wise to filter so that a RIP-generated default cannot enter area 0.

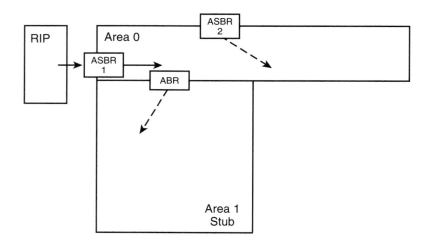

FIGURE 12.26   *Adding RIP to an OSPF domain, when the RIP domain can connect to area 0.0.0.0, is fairly easy.*

The physical topology may not lend itself to connecting the RIP domain to area 0.

If there is one ASBR that connects the RIP domain to OSPF, as shown in Figure 12.27, it may not be necessary to import full RIP routes during a transition. You can simply generate a summary address on the ASBR, advertising the prefix(es) associated with RIP. As long as the router containing the ASBR function has the specific RIP routes in its routing table, it will send the traffic correctly to the RIP destination.

It is true that if the RIP destination were unreachable in RIP, you might form a routing loop because the router would send the RIP unreachable traffic back to the default route on the ASBR. You can break such loops by putting in a blackhole route describing the RIP network.

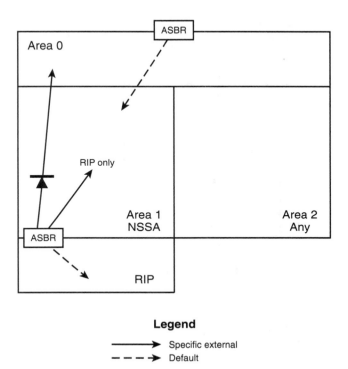

Legend

——————→ Specific external

– – – → Default

FIGURE 12.27 *Cases where the RIP domain cannot connect to area 0.0.0.0, but connects to a single nonzero area, are excellent NSSA applications.*

Complex RIP-to-OSPF Transition

Figure 12.28 shows a more complex topology, which you might see during a phased transition. A colleague who looked at this topology commented it reminded her of the Bermuda Triangle. Ships still have to sail into the Bermuda Triangle, and at times, you still have to deal with ugly topologies in real-world networks.

Although both RIP routing domains advertise routes into an OSPF area, the two RIP address ranges are aware of one another. The best route for a packet from RIP 1 to RIP 2 may not be through OSPF, but through the RIP router connecting RIP 1 and RIP 2. In like manner, the OSPF areas need to be regular and import all RIP routes, so the OSPF routers can decide whether the better path is through the backbone or directly via RIP.

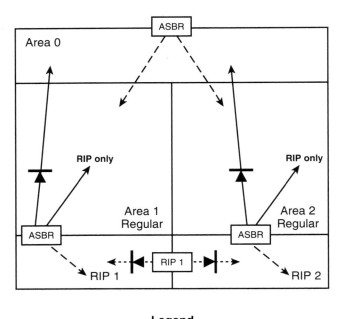

FIGURE 12.28 *More complex topologies may preclude the use of stub areas, increasing the workload in each area because the areas see a much larger number of external routes.*

Breaking Hierarchy

During the Napoleonic period, there was a high decoration, for commanders only, known as the Order of Maria-Theresa. It could be awarded only to commanders who won battles by disobeying orders. Of course, if they lost battles by disobeying orders, they were shot.

You can break hierarchy when you do it for the right reasons and have a better network as a result. You may not be shot for the consequences of breaking hierarchy for the wrong reasons and having an enterprise network collapse, but you may suffer the corporate equivalent.

Right reasons for breaking hierarchy can include handling large traffic volumes, or traffic with special quality of service requirements. Wrong reasons include greater meshing on the assumption that it increases reliability.

Traffic Engineering

Figure 12.29 shows a case in which a static route violates hierarchy for a good reason: traffic engineering. In this example, there are high-volume flows between Client 1 and Server 1. The two endpoints are in different OSPF areas. For this specific application, a set of dedicated lines link the two endpoints, but do not go through the core.

R1 has a static route to R4, with a next hop on R2. The link between R2 and R3 runs through two different areas, so it must not be described to OSPF. R3 has a static route to R4.

None of these static routes should be imported into OSPF, because they are intended for only specific traffic.

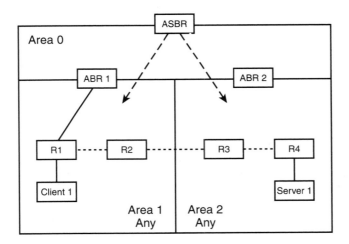

Legend

Specific external
Default
Static route

FIGURE 12.29 *Specific traffic patterns may justify well controlled violations of hierarchy.*

On a Cisco router, you would configure, in each router along the path, a static route with an administrative distance less (that is, more preferred) than OSPF's 110. You must not allow this route to be imported—redistributed—into OSPF, but simply designate it as the preferred route in the RIB of each router along the path. If this route goes down, a dynamic OSPF route that traverses the backbone will automatically replace it, as long as you have described both host interfaces to OSPF.

This technique, although useful, should be used only if absolutely necessary. When a customer tells me he needs many such traffic engineering bypasses in his network, I often find such a statement to be a clue that he needs to reexamine the structure of his core. It may be appropriate to put some of the proposed nonzero-area-to-nonzero-area links into area 0.0.0.0. Alternatively, he may need more than two levels of hierarchy, as discussed later in this chapter in the section "Backbones of Backbones."

Bay does not have the capability to declare a static route that is more preferred than OSPF, so this specific technique does not work on a Bay router. A direct-connected route is preferred to the most preferred intra-area OSPF routes, so one alternative might be to establish a Frame Relay or ATM PVC between the two endpoints, which would be treated as a directly connected interface.

Alternatively, the two OSPF areas could be put into different OSPF routing domains, and a BGP policy set up that gives first preference to the direct route and the second through what previously was the OSPF backbone.

Tunneling

Large organizations' mail rooms send out large quantities of postal mail and express shipments. Each individual envelope has a label of its own, giving source and destination.

The shipping clerk, however, packages the multiple envelopes together in a mail bag or tray, which is used to transfer the aggregate of envelopes to the post office or express carrier. Effectively, there is the "bag" label with a set of "envelope" labels inside. Rules for handling the bags are the rules of the *delivery protocol*, and rules for handling the individual envelopes are the *payload protocol*.

This analogy holds well for tunneling. The tunnel is analogous to the service relationship between the mailroom and the post office. It is invisible to the end user. See Figure 12.30 for the relationships between payload and delivery information. The different shadings in this figure refer to different protocol headers, the flow of which is shown in Figure 12.31.

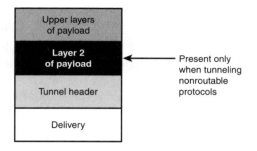

FIGURE 12.30 *Header relationships in tunnels.*

Table 12.2 lists a wide variety of tunneling mechanisms used, some of which carry legacy protocols and are not detailed further in this book. It is assumed that the mechanisms that use IP as their delivery protocol are running over Internet facilities, which require registered addresses. Obviously, if the underlying IP facilities are private, they simply need to be unique.

You will see that you cannot simply assume everything runs over IP. A legitimate, admittedly controversial, argument can be made that Frame Relay and ATM are tunneling mechanisms.

TABLE 12.2 COMMON TUNNELING MECHANISMS

Tunnel Mechanism	Payload Tunnel	Endpoint Addresses	Payload Endpoint	Security
GRE	Any	Registered IP	Any	None
IPsec Tunnel	IP	Registered IP	Any IP	Integrity, confidentiality
IPsec Transport	IP	Registered IP	Registered IP	Integrity, confidentiality
L2TP/L2F/PPTP	Any PPP encapsulated	Registered IP	Any	Access
RFC 1504 AURP	AppleTalk routing updates	Registered IP	AppleTalk	None
RFC 1001	NetBIOS records	Registered IP	NetBIOS name	None
RFC 1234	IPX packets	Registered IP	IPX	None
RFC 1613 XOT	X.25 packets	Registered IP	X.121	None
RFC 2427	Any	Frame relay	Any	None
RFC 1483 MPOA	Any	ATM	Any	None

In routers, tunneling depends on a mechanism called *recursive route lookup* (see Figure 12.31). In normal, non-tunneled routing, when the destination of an outgoing packet is found in the routing table, the routing table points to an outgoing interface. When the packet is forwarded to the code associated with the outgoing interface, that code wraps the Layer 3 packet in an appropriate Layer 2 frame, containing the Layer 2 addresses of the outgoing interface and the next-hop destination.

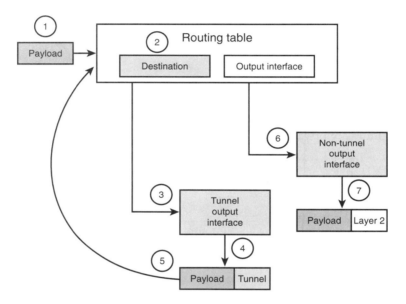

FIGURE 12.31   *Normally, the destination of a packet entering the router is looked up once. A tunneled packet requires at least two lookups.*

After a packet enters a tunnel, its payload is not examined until it reaches the other end of the tunnel. In tunneling, when a packet arrives at the input interface (point 1), its destination is still found in the routing table (point 2). The next hop in the routing table takes it to a tunnel interface (point 3). At a tunnel interface, the processing differs from a real interface—the outgoing packet is not encapsulated in a layer 3 packet. The tunnel interface code wraps the outgoing payload packet in a Layer 3 or Layer 4 packet (point 4), and puts the tunnel destination address into the destination address field of the delivery packet containing the payload packet. A tunneling protocol header goes into the delivery packet, immediately following the delivery packet header and before the payload packet header.

The tunnel interface code then sends the delivery packet back to the main routing process (point 5). This triggers the recursive lookup, where the delivery destination address is now looked up, and an output interface is again selected. The output interface selected is normally a real interface, the code for which wraps the delivery packet in a Layer 2 frame (point 6) and sends it out the interface to the next hop (point 7). It is possible, however, to have multiple levels of tunneling, where the output interface selected by the first tunnel interface lookup is itself a tunnel.

The delivery mechanism acts as an envelope to carry the payload data through some routing system that is unaware of the delivery part's contents.

Tunnels form the basis for VPNs. As discussed earlier in the chapter, the term *VPN* may have replaced *switch* as the industry buzzword that is applied to the most situations.

IP-over-IP tunneling is one technique for carrying IP through an arbitrary medium. Routing sees the tunnel as a point-to-point line.

OSPF has a method for tunneling routing information through areas called *virtual links*. Virtual links are routing tunnels with at least one end in Area 0. You could use Generic Route Encapsulation (GRE) tunnels to combine two discontiguous sets of routers and links into the same OSPF area.

Troubleshooting with tunnels, to put it mildly, can be interesting. Consider what happens when you **traceroute** through a tunnel, as shown in Figure 12.32. The endpoints show in the **traceroute** log, but none of the intermediate nodes do. Further complicating the situation is that you may not even know you are going through a tunnel, if part of your network is outsourced.

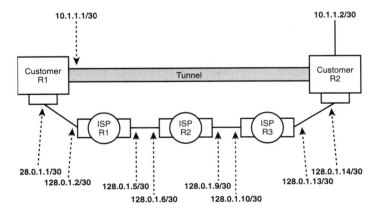

FIGURE 12.32 *traceroute from a host with a payload interface does not show the tunnel. **traceroute** from a host with a delivery interface does not show the endpoints.*

GRE

GRE has a wide variety of applications, including:

- Healing discontiguous networks

- Providing VPNs

- Allowing discontiguous parts of OSPF areas

- Handling bogus IP addresses and private IP addresses over a public core

- Carrying non-IP traffic

The general protocol is described in RFC 1701, with IP-specific aspects in RFC 1702. Although the protocol was developed by Cisco, it is supported by most major vendors.

A completed GRE packet has a delivery header, a GRE header, and the original IP header. The general structure of a GRE packet is shown in Figure 12.33.

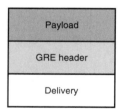

Protocol type 47
for IP delivery

FIGURE 12.33 *GRE has a delivery header, tunneling information, and a payload header, shown in the same shading as appeared in Figure 12.30. This three-part structure is characteristic of most tunneling mechanisms.*

Most commonly, GRE runs over IP [RFC 1702]. An IP protocol identifier number of 47 identifies GRE-containing packets.

On Cisco routers, GRE is the default tunnel encapsulation, but it is shown explicitly here for clarity:

```
interface tunnel 0
tunnel mode gre
tunnel source serial 0
tunnel destination 172.16.1.2
ip address 192.168.1.1 255.255.255.0
ipx network 2000
```

This example illustrates how you can run multiple protocol types on the same tunnel. Without further configuration, this tunnel can carry all IPX periodic broadcasts of SAP and IPX RIP packets, as well as IPX data packets. You can use EIGRP to send SAP and IPX RIP changes only, which represents a major reduction of traffic. If you are running NetWare 4.x, however, the hosts send only SAP and IPX RIP changes, so the motivation to use EIGRP as a means of reducing traffic disappears.

You can use GRE to come up with some unusual single-area OSPF configurations. In Figure 12.34, for example, two campuses are made part of the same area when GRE tunnels are placed between them. Another application for GRE tunneling is healing discontiguous networks if you are running a classful routing protocol.

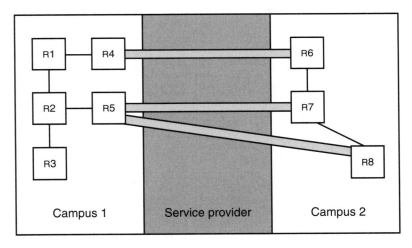

FIGURE 12.34   *GRE for bonding links.*

Why not connect the two campuses to a common backbone? In many circumstances, that is the appropriate technique. Small networks, however, may benefit from the simplicity of a single area. You might have some small routers that might not support inter-area functions, or that use autoconfiguration and are limited to operating in a single area.

IPsec

IPsec is the common name for the IP Security architecture defined in RFC 2401. Figure 12.35 shows an assortment of ways in which secure tunnels can be defined with IPsec or with lower-layer security protocols. Formally, it is not one protocol, but a set of architectural specifications, protocols, and protocol options:

- Security protocols—Authentication Header (AH) and Encapsulating Security Payload (ESP)

- Security associations

- Key management—manual and automatic (The Internet Key Exchange [IKE])

- Algorithms for authentication and encryption

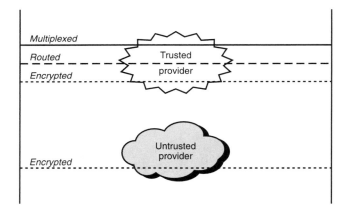

FIGURE 12.35   *Basic secure tunnels go between end hosts. Firewalls are not aware of their existence.*

IPsec includes the AH and ESP headers that actually go in secure packets, but also includes a wide range of key management mechanisms. IPsec security mechanisms, originally developed for IPv6, have been adapted to be usable both with IPv6 and IPv4. These mechanisms run at "Layer 3.5," in that they are connectionless and passed as option fields in IP packets, but are originated and primarily evaluated at endpoints.

Most cryptographic systems to date have aimed at producing confidentiality, and, by extension, authentication. Some systems are specifically intended for authentication only. IPsec's designers consciously separated the authentication and confidentiality capabilities in an effort to make the techniques available on a worldwide basis.

For a variety of reasons beyond the scope of this text, governments tend to be uncomfortable with cryptography in general. When pressed, they tend to accept the need for authentication.

IPsec sets up one-way *security associations* between trusted endpoints. Shown graphically in Figure 12.36, endpoint relationships can be:

- Host to host

- Host to security gateway

- Security gateway to security gateway

Administering key information is simplest when cryptographic information needs to be distributed to the fewest number of computers, as is the case when only the gateways contain keying information. If the gateways are not trusted by end users, cryptographic information needs to be distributed to the end hosts.

Figure 12.36 shows some of the potential relationships in IPsec. IPsec may provide end-to-end, client-to-server secure communications, or it may be implemented between gateways or between hosts and gateways. A real-world alternative may be using IPsec to implement trusted VPNs between security gateways. Most commonly, a security gateway runs on a router, preferably with hardware encryption.

In such a model, there is no longer true host-to-host trust. The trust is from host to security gateway, from security gateway to security gateway, and from security gateway to destination host.

In transport mode, IPsec assumes end-to-end significance of IP addresses. If an organization truly wants to use only host-to-host trust, it cannot use private address space for its secure hosts and still communicate across the Internet.

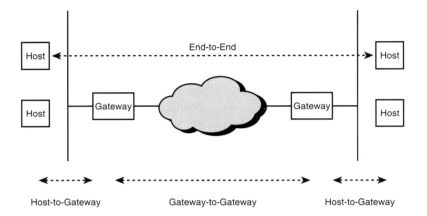

FIGURE 12.36 *The scope of trust in IPsec may be between end processes in hosts, between hosts, or between trusted gateways.*

Note

Widespread use of host-to-host IPsec has enormous implications for the global address space. Host-to-host IPsec modes that do not trust an intermediate gateway/firewall cannot use private addresses that are then translated, on a many-to-one basis, between private and public addresses.

This potential address demand might be alleviated in multi-organizational private networks that obtain registered address space that explicitly is not globally routable. Such organizations can still use address translation and proxies for selective Internet access.

From the addressing aspect, there are two IPsec modes, shown in Figure 12.37. *Tunnel mode* creates an encrypted tunnel between two hosts. These hosts may be end hosts or security gateways. When the tunnel is between two gateways, it provides a proxy service for hosts in the trusted domain.

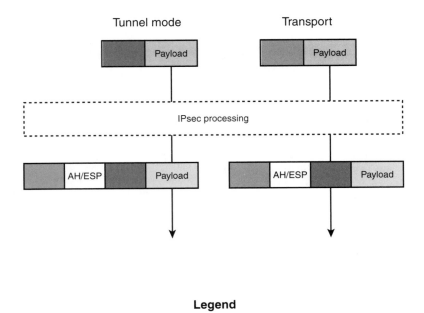

FIGURE 12.37 *Tunnel mode increases the size of each packet, but accommodates more flexible addressing than transport mode.*

Addressing Implications of IPsec Modes

When tunnel mode is used between security gateways, it can conserve addresses if those security gateways also have a NAT function. Transport mode will need registered addresses to function across the Internet. Although transport mode does not conserve addresses, its advocates prefer the trust model that puts the sensitive parts of cryptography onto end hosts, rather than onto gateways.

Cryptography is CPU-intensive. The burden for a single host's traffic may not be great, but when a router needs to do the cryptographic processing for many hosts, that can impact router performance. Host-resident cryptographic processing reduces load on the router.

Widespread use of transport mode could very well reduce the trend of lessened registered address require-

continues

continued

ments for enterprise networks. This trend has arisen with widespread address translation on firewalls with NAT functionality. If the firewalls can no longer translate, the address space requirement will jump.

Growth in requirements for unique end host identifiers would be likely to accelerate demand for IP version 6. Although IPv6 addressing strategies have not yet been standardized

beyond the basic 128-bit address size, it is likely that addresses will be dynamically assigned, and will have a part that uniquely identifies the end host and a part that gives global information on how to route to that end host. It is the latter part that would go into global routing tables, so that using the larger IP version 6 address does not necessarily impose a significant load on global routing resources.

Tunnel mode ESP preserves the IP address of the originating host, as the source address in a packet that is completely enclosed in the encrypted field of an ESP data unit. The ESP is placed in another packet with its own IP header, and this header and its addresses are actually used to route the information end-to-end. No relationship needs to exist between the unencrypted carrier packet addresses and the addresses in the encapsulated packet inside the encrypted ESP.

In some applications it is desirable to conceal not only what is being said, but who is saying it. The technique of obtaining information from knowledge of traffic patterns is called *traffic analysis*. Military intelligence organizations make extensive use of traffic analysis, because it can be almost as important to know that the aircraft carrier *USS Abraham Lincoln* is transmitting from a location near you as it is to know the contents of its messages.

Traffic Analysis Can Deceive as Well

Military history is full of examples where one side generated dummy traffic to mislead traffic analysts on the other side. Before the D-Day invasion of Normandy, the Allies created a dummy First U.S. Army Group invasion force under General Patton, with extensive traffic generated to convince the Germans that the main invasion was a sideshow.

Traffic analysis errors are not limited to one side. In World War I, a British admiral asked where a particular radio call sign was currently located, and was

told, correctly, it was moored in a harbor. Unfortunately, the admiral did not ask the right question: "Where is the call sign currently associated with the German High Seas Fleet?" The German Navy had recently moved some of its call signs to new ships. Although the call sign remained in harbor, the flagship was at sea, approaching unsuspecting British ships. I mention this to remind that the theme of Chapter 1, "What Is the Problem You Are Trying to Solve?" can be rephrased as "What Is the Question You Are Trying to Ask?"

Concern with traffic analysis is not limited to the military. Consider the value of knowing that a sudden burst of traffic is coming from a minerals prospector to a home office, which may mean gold has been found—and perhaps an eavesdropper can file a claim before the prospector can do so. Sudden surges in financial information among banks or stock exchanges might be useful in predicting market trends.

Transport mode does not preserve the original host header. Instead, it inserts the ESP into the IP packet just before the IP data field. Appropriate headers are re-created at the receiver.

Virtual Links

In OSPF, a virtual link is a tunnel that has at least one end in area 0. It does not necessarily carry traffic in tunneled form, but carries routing information from an arbitrary area into area 0. Virtual links (VLs) are a mechanism that can be used within OSPF to handle certain connectivity patterns. The standard is a bit "soft" on their applications, and support engineers have seen a variety of VL applications. For some of the problems being raised, it appears better OSPF solutions may exist.

A matter of particular interest is the potential advantage of NSSAs over some of the VL solutions in bringing in a new "community of interest." See the following discussion of VL applicability in other than backbone robustness.

The perception of virtual links' utility seems to be as a means of accommodating special connectivity requirements "inside" a single "OSPF domain," the latter defined as a set of an Area 0.0.0.0 and some number of nonzero areas.

In some of these requirements, virtual links may be completely appropriate, one of several potential solutions, or definitely not an appropriate solution.

Some designers may use virtual links to avoid other mechanisms that they do not like, such as defining the enterprise's network with multiple interconnected OSPF domains.

Virtual links are not necessarily the appropriate solution, but cases have been seen where they are used for

- Protecting against area 0.0.0.0 partitioning. Appropriate physical topology with redundant links inside area 0.0.0.0 is a much better way to protect against its partitioning.

- Making one area 0.0.0.0 following the merger of two enterprises, both of which previously ran independent OSPF.

- Providing connectivity to a separately engineered routing domain (for example, a corporate acquisition) whose best connectivity is to a router in a nonzero area of the acquiring enterprise.

Figure 12.38 shows how one heals a backbone partition with a virtual link. The partition is caused by the failure of the direct link between the two backbone-only routers, Backbone R1 and Backbone R2.

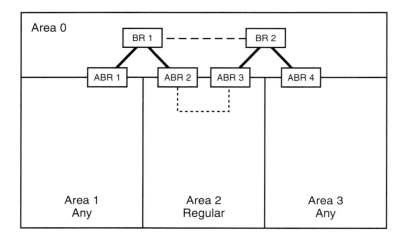

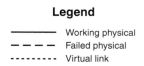

Legend

——————— Working physical
— — — —   Failed physical
· · · · · · · · · Virtual link

FIGURE 12.38   *Virtual links can be used to heal backbone partitions.*

The virtual link through area 2 is logically part of area 0.0.0.0, and heals the partition. Area 2 must not be stubby in any way if a VL is to traverse it.

In general, it is better to provide adequate link and router redundancy in the backbone than it is to use virtual links. Virtual links restrict your use of stubbiness, tend to be hard to configure, and may impose significant processing loads on the routers using them.

Figure 12.38 illustrates the use of a VL to connect a noncontiguous, nonzero area.

Healing Backbone Partitions Across a Non-OSPF Domain

If you have an OSPF domain with private addressing, and your enterprise chooses to outsource part of the WAN supporting area 0.0.0.0, one potential workaround is to use GRE tunnels to link two or more pieces that otherwise would be partitioned (see Figure 12.39).

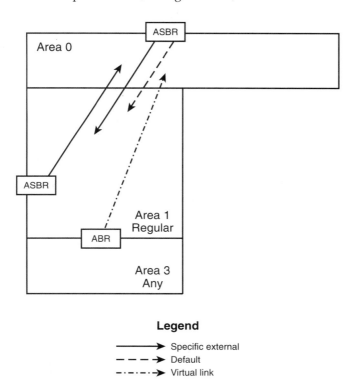

Legend

———————▶ Specific external
— — — ▶ Default
—·—·—·▶ Virtual link

FIGURE 12.39   *GRE tunnels can be used to link, through an ISP, parts of an OSPF domain that uses private addressing.*

It can be entirely reasonable to manage a small number of GRE tunnels across arbitrary service providers. When a large number of tunnels across WANs are needed, it may be more productive to define the system of tunnels as a VPN and outsource its operation.

Overlay Networks and VPNs

Proprietary definitions of virtual private networks proliferate in the marketplace, to the confusion of end users. Each vendor seems to have its own definition of VPN, and equipment vendor definitions do not necessarily agree with service provider definitions. Service providers often describe their Frame Relay or ATM services as VPNs, and a case can be made for doing so. Nevertheless, part of the politics of defining VPNs in the IETF is closely associated with the marketing concerns of service providers that do not want to be in the position of "defending" Frame Relay or ATM services, that do a perfectly good job, from "new and improved" VPNs.

In the IETF, there is a certain sentiment that the industry understands perfectly well how to provide Frame Relay and ATM services and understands they are quite appropriate for many applications. Equipment vendors have focused more on VPNs that provide either IP or PPP interfaces to user equipment, on the assumption that it is these technologies that are not yet well understood, and where standards may help. IETF working papers on VPNs [Gleeson, Muthukrishnan, Rosen] have dealt with fairly specific models where specific underlying technologies are considered at length.

The discussion here does not focus on the internal VPN technologies, which are more the concern of service providers rather than the enterprise-oriented reader. Drawn from "Requirements Taxonomy for Virtual Private Networks" [Berkowitz vpn tax], it focuses on user requirements to be conveyed to service providers.

Any VPN has a minimal set of core capabilities, which, alone, are unlikely to satisfy any real-world user requirements. The taxonomy discussed here provides a systematic way for extending the core capabilities to meet those requirements. It also provides a way to describe requirements for the shared infrastructure over which the VPN runs. A description of a specific VPN requirement will state the core capabilities, optional user services, and the administrative model. A response to this requirement will state the infrastructure technologies and how the user requirements will map to them.

The taxonomy consists of:

- Core capabilities

- Optional capabilities

- Administrative model

- Mapping of user services to different infrastructures

- Infrastructures

For a VPN to work, it must be possible to map the user services to corresponding capabilities in the infrastructure. Mechanisms for these mappings are outside the scope of this taxonomy. A quality of service user requirement, for example, could map to ATM QOS facilities, to RSVP or differentiated services in an IP network, or to priorities in an 802.1p LAN.

The keel of a yacht may not be very interesting, but all the luxurious structures of a yacht eventually connect to the keel. VPN definitions have their own keel or minimal set of functions on which you build other capabilities.

To define a VPN, it is necessary to be able to define an administrative mechanism for designating membership in the VPN. The administrative rules in defining the VPN should closely coordinate with the enterprise security policy.

A given host may belong to one or more VPNs, as well as have connectivity to the global Internet. If there are security requirements for the VPN, the owning enterprise should define a security policy that states the allowable connectivity over multiple VPNs and public networks.

The set of members of a VPN will have an identifier [Fox], although that identifier might be null.

Optional Capabilities

This is the point at which your technical specification of a VPN becomes complex. Not every VPN needs all the capabilities in this section, but most plausible VPNs need at least one and usually more of them. These capabilities include:

- QoS
- Security
- Addressing and load sharing
- Frame sequencing and MTU management
- Non-IP protocol support
- Multicast support
- High availability services

QoS support is a hot industry topic, but overspecifying it may greatly increase your costs or limit your options for providing the VPN service. You might specify a single QoS for the entire service, or define different QoS classes for different applications or user communities.

When you define different classes, you must be able to identify traffic belonging to each class. Traffic characterization is most commonly done at edge rather than backbone routers, but one of the administrative decisions to be made in VPN services is whether to characterize in end hosts, on the customer router closest to the hosts, or on the provider ingress router. The VPN may accept QoS requests from end users signaled with RSVP, IP precedence bits, and so forth, or may internally assign quality of service requirements to be mapped to the transmission infrastructure. For quality of service to be effective, the infrastructure either must support explicit quality of service requests, or there must be a high level of confidence that the infrastructure consistently provides adequate QoS. Assumptions about QoS need to be stated as part of any VPN design.

User connectivity may be defined to include security using a variety of security mechanisms, including IPsec, L2TP, and so on. Security may be requested on a discretionary basis by end user hosts, or the VPN may enforce a mandatory security policy. Cryptographic protections may be under the control of the enterprise, using host-to-host or host-to-security gateway methods, or the infrastructure may be trusted to provide encryption. The responsibilities for encryption must be specified as part of the design of any practical VPN.

The VPN may provide address assignment, presumably with DHCP. It also may provide network address translation (NAT), network address and port translation (NAPT), and load-shared network address translation (LSNAT). DNS services may be associated with the VPN, and operated by the enterprise or the service provider. Although VPNs can appear as a single IP prefix (that is, a single user domain), single prefixes do not scale to large size. The provider may set up multiple prefixes to serve user connectivity requirements. If there are multiple prefixes, the provider must specify whether routing among them is an enterprise or provider responsibility.

There may be requirements to deliver frames or packets in sequence. In addition, there may be a requirement to support, efficiently, larger MTUs that the provider might normally handle.

Although the emphasis of this taxonomy is on VPNs that support IP, the VPN may provide mechanisms for encapsulating non-IP protocols for transmission over an IP infrastructure. See Chapter 8 of *Designing Addressing Architectures for Routing and Switching* [Berkowitz, 1998a] for a discussion of the general issues of supporting non-IP protocols. For specific protocol handling, see RFCs for NetBIOS over TCP [RFC 1001/1002], IPX over IP [RFC 1234], GRE [RFC 1702], and so forth.

The IP VPN, as seen by end users, may support broadcast or multicast addressing. Estimates of the multicast traffic are important in provisioning.

The enterprise may specify availability requirements for the infrastructure and for VPN gateway services. If redundancy of links or components is needed to provide the desired level of redundancy, these redundant components may either be visible to, or hidden from, the using enterprise.

The enterprise may need to be able to signal to the provider that new sites and/or users (especially dial users) have been added to the VPN. Although it should generally be transparent to the VPN if new users are added to VPNs at existing sites, security requirements may make it necessary to inform the VPN, securely, that a new user has been added or an old user deleted.

The Administrative Model

Several administrative issues apply in VPN deployment: whether the enterprise is responsible for any customer premises equipment (CPE) that intelligently interoperates with components of the shared infrastructure, whether a service provider is contracted to operate the WAN infrastructure, and how any VPN client software in user hosts is managed and operated. A service provider may place service provider-operated equipment at a customer site, and present a LAN or serial interface to the customer.

Anything beyond the provider device is contractually a provider responsibility, but it cannot be directly controlled by the customer. There are two basic models of the administration and management of VPNs, although subcategories are perfectly viable. In the first category, the end user organization designs and operates the VPN, often with end user access through the public dial network. In the second, a service provider has contractual responsibility for designing and operating the VPN in response to specified user requirements.

Another aspect of the model is whether clients are aware of the VPN, and whether provider access components are aware of it. In principle, a client could attach to a generic ISP, establish an encrypted tunnel to a destination host, and operate transparently to the ISP. The VPN provider may be the ISP. In such cases, the VPN provider responsibility is to provide logins and connectivity. The login might specify a class of service to be used in the provider network.

In an alternative model, the clients do not contain encryption software. Clients connect natively to the provider's access device through an administratively trusted link such as the dial telephone network. The client authenticates with the access device, and the access device(s) provide cryptographic services.

Yet another model is traffic driven. Routers at customer sites sense when end user devices wish to send across the VPN, and either route them to predefined tunnels over dedicated infrastructure, or create appropriate dial calls to carry the traffic, encrypting if necessary.

Mapping to the Infrastructure

The specific means by which end user views of the VPN are mapped onto the shared infrastructure generally involves tunneling, virtual circuit setup, or the establishment of a set of labels. When tunnels are used, they may provide no security (GRE), authentication (L2TP, L2F, and PPTP), or a wide range of security services (IPsec).

Security services may also be provided by hosts, and a less secure tunnel mechanism used to carry host-encrypted data.

Alternatively, the mapping of IP connectivity may be to virtual circuits using Frame Relay or ATM, or to real circuits with ISDN or analog dial. When the VPN seen by the user appears to be multicast-capable, but the infrastructure is connection-oriented, provisions need to be made for supporting multicast. Techniques here might involve point-to-multipoint circuits, or the use of multicast replication servers.

Infrastructure Capabilities

When different kinds of VPN infrastructure are proposed, the main requirement is for the infrastructure provider to take responsibility that all relevant user capabilities have matching capabilities in the infrastructure. The actual mappings are technology-specific and outside the scope of this document.

In this section, the emphasis is not on the shared infrastructure, but rather on the capabilities that may be needed if a user capability is to be mapped successfully into one or more infrastructures. Specific VPNs may well be provisioned over one or more infrastructure types. In such cases, the designer needs to ensure the user capabilities map into each of the infrastructures. Major infrastructures are similar to, but not identical to, the list of optional capabilities:

- Quality of service
- Security
- Addressing and load sharing
- Frame sequencing and MTU management
- Non-IP protocol support
- Multicast support

- High availability services

- Interprovider provisioning and connectivity

When the user or the enterprise can request explicit QoS, either the infrastructure must be able to understand the explicit requests, or it must consistently supply a QoS that meets the most stringent user requirement.

Users may be responsible for cryptographic security, transparently to the provider. Alternatively, the VPN provider may offer encryption. If the user operates firewalls, VPN tunnels typically terminate at the firewall. If the firewall is operated by the service provider, or if the user has stringent security requirements requiring end-to-end encryption, there may be compatibility issues for authenticated firewall traversal.

Providers can use registered or RFC 1918 addresses internally in their networks. These may or may not be visible to the enterprise. When they are not, there should be a well-defined operational procedure that allows the user to request **traceroute**s through IP infrastructures. When the provider uses VPN identifiers to distinguish between routing tables for different VPNs, the same addresses, especially from the private address space, may be reused.

Commonly, the enterprise provides the tunneling necessary to carry non-IP protocols over the enterprise. When the VPN is offered as a service, however, the provider may offer appropriate encapsulation services. If the infrastructure is Layer 2 and supports a protocol type field, it may be appropriate for the provider to encapsulate non-IP traffic with explicit protocol identification.

When a specific availability requirement is defined for the enterprise VPN, it is a provider responsibility to ensure the infrastructure has the component reliability, diversity, and so forth, to meet these needs. It can be useful to distinguish between availability in the access part of a VPN, such as modem pools, and the backbone that carries the tunnels over the long-haul shared infrastructure.

It may be necessary to provision the VPN infrastructure through multiple service providers. In such cases, the providers need inter-provider provisioning and VPN identification.

Much as a BGP confederation presents a single AS number to the outside but contains multiple internal ASNs, a multiprovider VPN identifier may map to a set of publicly visible ASNs. Although BGP may be used to convey VPN reachability information among providers, the actual destinations may be prefixed with VPN IDs, and carried using the BGP-4 Multiprotocol Extensions. When

VPN IDs are used in this manner, the routes carried need not be visible on the global Internet, but simply used to exchange information between ISPs with bilateral agreements.

Route Filtering

Most router implementations give you the capability to filter routing information. Figure 12.15 shows where filters relate to learning routes on the local router, and in propagating routing information. As you can see, there is a significant difference between distance vector and link state protocol filtering. You must not filter OSPF link state information within an area, although you can filter it from entering the RIB of a specific router.

Although hierarchical design is the usual goal, there can be good reasons to break it. A large corporate client of mine was consolidating its business unit network, as shown in Figure 12.40.

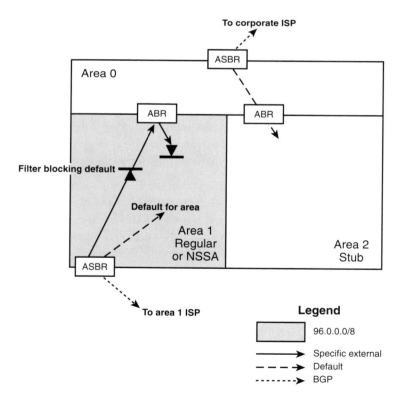

FIGURE 12.40 *Many enterprises have a corporate single point of Internet access, but there are often special cases when different points are needed.*

The research arm of the company had been one of the pioneers of the Internet, and had its own connectivity. As an Internet research center, it had long had ATM connectivity. Although the corporation as a whole had the address block 192.0.0.0/14, the research arm, one of the original Internet participants, had 96.0.0.0/8.

In this example, assume OSPF interior routing, because OSPF can distinguish between type 1 and type 2 external metrics. The main default for the enterprise comes from one or more ASBRs in area 0.0.0.0, all routing to the same ISP. One or more organizations brought into the corporate network have pre-existing Internet access agreements with an ISP other than the corporate ISP, and wish to continue using this for their "divisional" Internet access.

This situation is frequent when a corporation decides to have general Internet access, but its research arm has long had its own Internet connectivity.

Mergers and acquisitions also produce this case, where the acquired firms have Internet connectivity in place, perhaps under long-term contract.

In this situation, an additional ASBR(s) is placed in the OSPF area associated with the special case, and this ASBR advertises default. Filters at the Area Border Router block the divisional ASBR's default from being advertised into area 0.0.0.0, and the corporate default from being advertised into the division. Note that these filters do not block OSPF LSAs, but instead block the local propagation of selected default and external routes into the Routing Information Base (that is, main routing table) of a specific router.

Because it was not part of the organization's security policy to let internal routers attempt to reach pieces of the enterprise address space via the Internet, the ABRs injected summary routes for the enterprise's major address blocks into the nonzero area. Doing so ensured there was always a more specific route than the area 1 default to the enterprise address block.

Multihoming to External Providers

A simple default route to an ISP is no more complex than the simplest external route handling. As the Internet connectivity requirement becomes more critical, however, multihoming requirements become more important.

Single-Homed Multihoming

A large proportion of enterprises have a single ISP that provides all their Internet connectivity. Under the definition of "autonomous system" from RFC 1930, the enterprise does not have its own Internet routing policy, but all its routing is subject to the routing policy of its provider. The enterprise is thus part of the provider's autonomous system.

Such an enterprise is primarily concerned with protecting against link or router failures, rather than failures in the ISP routing system. It may have one or more physical links to the provider, which in turn may connect to one or more ISP routers. There are several variations on this theme.

The simplest case involves a single active data link between the customer and provider. A slight variation would include switched backup over analog or ISDN services. Another alternative might be use of alternate frame relay or other PVCs to an alternate ISP POP, with the frame relay provider responsible for rerouting.

This isn't a complex configuration, and the default route is sufficient. We will build on this to satisfy more complex requirements.

In OSPF, you would advertise the default route from the ASBR that connects to the ISP. When only a single default is advertised, it really makes little difference whether it is advertised as type 1 or type 2. If you plan to upgrade the connectivity to primary/backup, which uses type 2, or load-shared, which uses type 1, you might as well use that type initially.

Single-Homed, Parallel Link Multihoming

In this configuration, multiple parallel data links exist from a single customer router to a router (see Figure 12.41). This protects against link failures, but not against failures of the entire router.

The single customer router constraint allows this router to do round-robin packet-level load balancing across the multiple links, for resiliency and possibly additional bandwidth. The capability of a router to do such load-balancing is implementation-specific, and may be a significant drain on the router's processor.

If the router uses a cache as the forwarding information base, parallel, round-robin load balancing leads to faster reconvergence after failures. The speed of reconvergence comes from obviating the need to repopulate the cache. When you do round-robin load balancing, the FIB already contains all routes leading to the common destination.

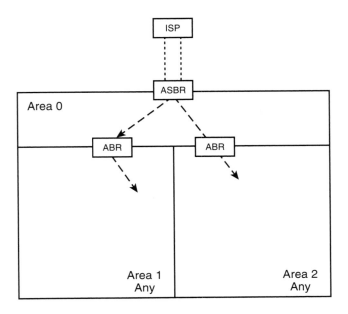

Legend

– – –▶   Default

······▶   Static

FIGURE 12.41 *Parallel links between a pair of routers give more bandwidth and protect against single link failure.*

Single-Homed, Multi-Link Multihoming

Figure 12.42 shows separate paths from multiple customer routers to multiple routers of the same at different POPs. Default routes generated at each of the customer gateways are injected into the enterprise routing system, and the combination internal and external metrics are considered by internal routers in selecting the external gateway.

This configuration is often attractive for enterprises that want resiliency but want to avoid the complexity of BGP. It has no single point of failure in terms of routers or links, but does not protect against a major ISP routing system failure.

If you advertise the default route as an OSPF type 1 metric from both routers, using the same interface metric on both, you will share the outgoing load. There is no real way for you to control sharing load on incoming paths to you, although this to some extent can be controlled by the ISP.

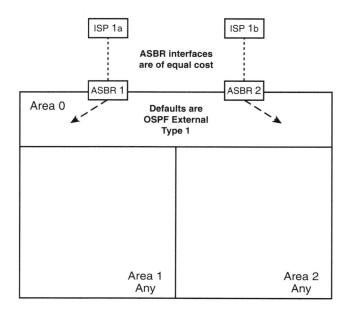

Legend

− − −▶ Default
∙∙∙∙∙∙∙▶ Static

FIGURE 12.42 *This configuration has a single ISP responsible for connectivity at multiple points of presence, which can reduce finger-pointing.*

Special Cases

Although the customer in this configuration is still single-homed, an AS upstream from the ISP has a routing policy that makes it necessary to distinguish routes originating in the customer from those originating in the ISP. In such cases, the enterprise may need to run BGP, or have the ISP run it on its behalf, to generate advertisements of the needed specificity.

Probably the best way to do this is to arrange for the ISP to add an appropriate community attribute to customer-generated routes [RFC 1998]. This involves more administrative coordination, but offers the advantage of leaving complex BGP routing to professionals.

Tagging routes with the community attribute works best if the customer has provider-independent address space, or at least a separate block used by the customer alone. The problem here is one of addressing rather than the protocol proper. If the customer address space is assigned by the provider from a larger provider allocation, the provider normally advertises only the larger address block, aggregating the customer routes into it. The aggregate can either carry the same community attribute for all its addresses in the block, which is incorrect, or drop the aggregate, which loses the customer-specific information.

Multihomed Routing

In multihomed routing, the enterprise connects to more than one ISP, and desires to protect against problems in the ISP routing system. It accepts additional complexity and router requirements to get this. The enterprise may also have differing service agreements for Internet access for different divisions.

The simplest way to multihome is to designate one ISP as the primary and the other as the backup. This has the potential advantage of protecting against a failure in the routing system of either ISP, although it leaves one link unused.

OSPF has two ways of evaluating the cost of external routes. Type 1 considers the combination of internal cost to reach the ASBR plus the external interface cost on the ASBR. Type 2 considers only the external interface cost. Both types have distinct and useful applications.

Primary/Secondary ISP Backup

It's often simplest to set up external connectivity with a primary and secondary ISP, or even a primary and secondary link to the same ISP. You might do this if the backup link is significantly slower than the primary.

Using type 2 externals makes this is quite easy to do in OSPF (see Figure 12.43). The idea is that the less preferred path has a lower external interface cost.

You can also do this with static routes, but both the primary and secondary static route usually need to be on the same physical router. If they are on different routers, the problem becomes much more complex, because with pure static routing, there is no way for the secondary router to know whether the primary router has gone down.

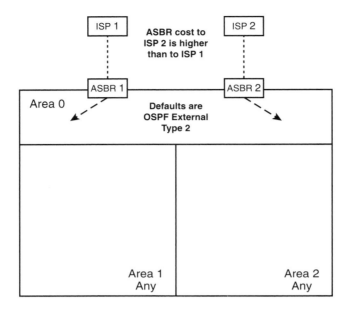

ISP 1   ISP 2

ASBR cost to
ISP 2 is higher
than to ISP 1

ASBR 1   ASBR 2

Area 0   Defaults are
              OSPF External
              Type 2

Area 1   Area 2
Any   Any

Legend

– – – ▶   Default
‧‧‧‧‧‧‧‧▶   Static

FIGURE 12.43 *In primary/secondary backup, you always make the backup less preferred than the primary.*

A common concern of enterprise financial managers is that multihoming strategies involve expensive links to ISPs, but, in some of these scenarios, alternate links are used only as backups, idle much of the time. Detailed analysis may reveal that the cost of forcing these links to be used at all times, however, exceeds the potential savings.

The intention here is to focus on requirements rather than specifics of the routing implementation, several approaches to which are discussed in RFC 1998. Exterior routing policies can be described with the Routing Policy Specification Language [RFC 2280].

Operational as well as technical considerations apply here. Although the Border Gateway Protocol can convey certain information between user and provider, many ISPs are unwilling to risk the operational integrity of their global routing by making the user network part of their internal BGP routing systems.

More Complex Load Sharing

Even with a primary and backup policy, you can attempt to make active use of both the primary and backup providers. Understanding the detailed mechanisms involved requires a knowledge of BGP beyond the scope of this text, so the functions are described more conceptually.

Separate mechanisms are required to influence both the outgoing path from your enterprise to multiple ISPs, and the path traffic takes to reach your enterprise through different ISPs. The word "influence" is chosen carefully here, because you cannot control the policy of an AS with which you have no business relationship.

The simplest way to loadshare incoming traffic, shown in Figure 12.44, is to take partial BGP routes from your backup ISP. These partial routes identify destinations that are either in the backup provider's AS, or perhaps directly connected to that AS. For all other destinations, the primary provider is the preferred default. A less preferred default is defined to the second ISP, but this default is advertised generally only if connectivity is lost to the primary ISP.

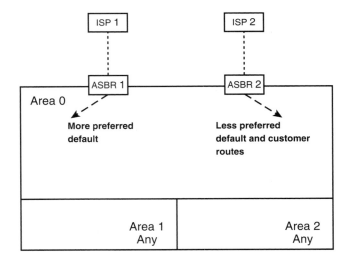

Legend

------→ Default

·······→ BGP

FIGURE 12.44 *Partial routes can significantly loadshare the paths taken by outgoing paths. It does not affect how incoming traffic comes to you.*

This technique controls which exit point the enterprise is to use. It does not affect the way in which external ISPs see the enterprise; other techniques are used there. Asymmetrical routing behavior is common; some guidelines suggest that 30% to 40% of the queries leaving on one path will have responses return on the other.

Controlling how other ASs see yours is more complex. One method in common use is called *AS path prepending*. As opposed to sharing your outbound traffic to two ISPs by preferring directly connected routes of the backup provider, AS path prepending influences the path incoming traffic from different ISPs takes to you.

Figure 12.45 is an introduction of how BGP sends routing information. The originating AS, AS1, announces a block of addresses, and perhaps supplementary attributes such as communities. As the routing information traverses additional ASs on the way to the destination, their AS numbers are prepended to the update.

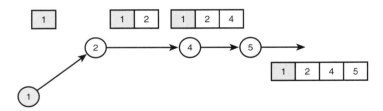

FIGURE 12.45 *BGP sends routing information including an address range, attributes of that range, and the sequence of ASs through which that address range can be reached.*

AS path prepending (see Figure 12.46) is done by the originator to make a path less desirable. In the figure, R0 prepends its own AS number to the path being advertised to R1, making it a longer and conceptually less desirable path.

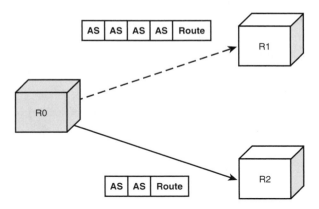

FIGURE 12.46

As shown in Figure 12.47, the prepending may have no significant effect on path length after the path reaches distant AS. You have no control over the interconnections of other ASs, and the exit path you prefer actually may have many more intermediate ASs between you and the destination than does your less-preferred path.

Nevertheless, AS path prepending will help control your traffic.

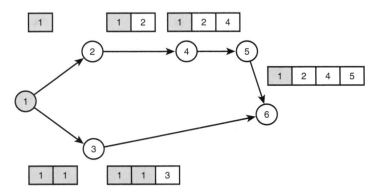

FIGURE 12.47   *You cannot control the length of the AS path seen by the destination; you can only influence it.*

Backbones of Backbones

A single routing domain normally has some sort of backbone, whether an OSPF area 0.0.0.0 or a medium at the highest level of summarization in EIGRP. Scaling to a larger network size may involve creating a higher-level transit structure that interconnects the backbones.

From the perspective of lower levels of a hierarchy, the top-level structure may simply be the highest-level default for these regions.

There are four general ways to find paths within a backbone:

- Static routing
- Interior BGP
- Exterior BGP
- Exterior BGP with confederations

Static Routing

Static routing is appropriate and convenient when you have a well-defined addressing structure and not many backbone routes. It can be especially convenient when you have dialup routes and do not use an interior routing protocol that supports demand routing.

Figure 12.48 shows a basic version of an enterprise with a statically routed backbone of backbones. Each region has a separate address range. Each region has static routes to the address blocks in the other two regions, and defaults to the firewall for external access.

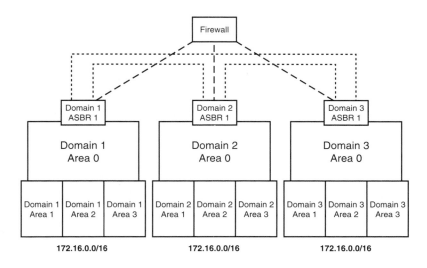

Legend

-------- Explicit static

— — — Default

FIGURE 12.48 *Static routing can be adequate for a highly structured hierarchy with cleanly assigned addresses.*

Figure 12.49 is a simplified version of the network of one of my consulting clients, an international pharmaceutical company. Meaningful communities of interest are in each continental region, and between the regions and the corporate headquarters. Very little traffic travels directly between the regions, so it can reasonably be forwarded through the corporate core. It is important to have reliable communications from regions to the core.

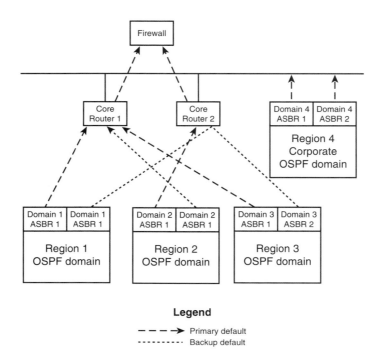

FIGURE 12.49 *Static routes run from each region to a corporate collapsed backbone. (Note that the static routes from the core downward are not shown.)*

Each region is a single OSPF routing domain with a unique block of addresses. The two ASBRs in area 0.0.0.0 of that area originate a type 2 default and advertise it into the OSPF routing system. One ASBR has a dedicated line and originates default with a metric of 50. It has the Cisco **default-information-originate** command without the **always** keyword, which means the default is advertised only when the router can actually reach the default.

The second ASBR originates default with a metric of 200. Be sure to understand the effect of the Cisco **default-information-originate always** command. A router always originates default even when it does not have an active default route. In this case, packets go to ASBR 2 only if the ASBR 1 default, of a lower Type 2 metric, is no longer being advertised.

After packets arrive at ASBR 2, and the routing process decides they need to go onto the default route, the ISDN backup link is brought up by dial-on-demand routing. In other words, the advertised default lures packets to ASBR2 only if ASBR 1 no longer advertises the default route. When those packets arrive at ASBR 2, it quickly creates the default path.

At the corporate site, the regional links terminate in two core routers. From any region, the primary link terminates on one router and the backup terminates on a different router. Inter-region communications, and communications to the corporate region, traverse this backbone, which is a redundant LAN switch. The core routers, in turn, default to the corporate firewall.

Interior BGP

Another technique for linking routing domains is to define the set of routing domains as a single AS, and use interior BGP to distribute routes selectively into them.

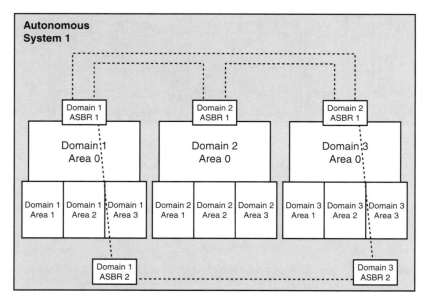

FIGURE 12.50 *When the enterprise backbone is iBGP, all routers are in the same AS. If you connect to an ISP, you are logically part of its AS.*

An interior BGP backbone can be useful if you have multiple internal regions, and multiple connections to the same ISP. The connection to the ISP, however, will be eBGP. iBGP allows you to select which ASBR is best to leave a given domain, without flooding all external routes into the OSPF domain. If you have complex policies, however, eBGP is usually more powerful in enabling you to define them.

Exterior BGP

Exterior BGP gives you more powerful filtering capabilities than iBGP. If you have no Internet connectivity, you can define multiple AS numbers inside your enterprise and run eBGP among them (see Figure 12.51).

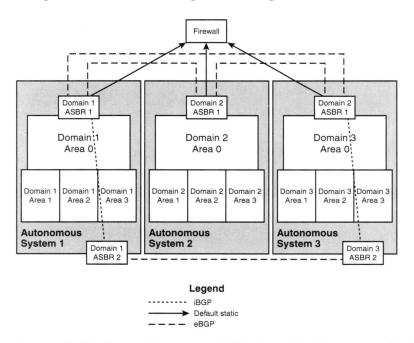

FIGURE 12.51 *You can have a pure eBGP backbone of backbones, especially when you do not connect to the Internet.*

Because registered AS numbers are a limited resource, they are not issued for internal connectivity requirements. A block of AS numbers is defined for internal use, much like the private address space defined in RFC 1918. If you want to use eBGP inside the enterprise, but also need Internet connectivity, confederations are yet another option.

Exterior BGP with Confederations

Confederations (see Figure 12.52) allow you to have multiple ASs interconnected with eBGP inside your organization, but also to connect to the Internet. Current practice is to use private AS numbers for the internal AS, and to have a single registered AS number for advertising routes to the general Internet.

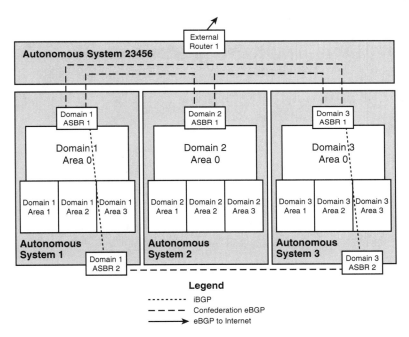

FIGURE 12.52 *Confederations allow you to have a complex internal backbone of backbones without advertising your internal AS or routes to the global Internet.*

ISPs that need to scale their iBGP systems beyond the capabilities of full mesh use both confederations and route reflectors. Route reflectors tend to be used almost exclusively by ISPs, but confederations are used in both enterprise and ISP environments.

Looking Ahead

The discussions in this chapter conclude a look at current practices in routing in switching. Chapters 13 and 14 consider new methods likely to be available in products in the near term.

PART V

Near-Term Futures for Routing and Switching

CHAPTER 13

New Methods at the Enterprise Edge

> *"This way to the egress."*
> —P. T. Barnum

> *"We run carelessly to the precipice, after we have put
> something before us to prevent us seeing it."*
> —Blaise Pascal

> *"In every organization there are limits on the span of control;
> increasing amounts of power go to decreasing numbers of people.
> The slopes of the pyramid become steeper the higher up you look."*
> —Judith M. Bardwick

One of the definite trends in relaying is not to treat all routers alike, but to make a distinction between edge and core devices. One of the advantages in this distinction is a model that distributes processor-intensive computing to a large number of edge devices, and allows the core devices to be optimized for hardware-enabled forwarding.

In contrast with the OSI model, the distinction between edge and core has always been clearer in the ISDN architecture, with its distinction among control, user, and management protocols, shown in Figure 13.1.

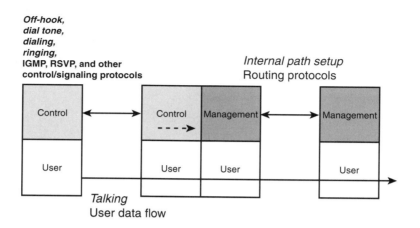

FIGURE 13.1 *User plane protocols run end-to-end. Control plane protocols run between an end device and an ingress or egress relay. Management plane protocols run between relays.*

Signaling deals with the contribution of edge devices to routing based on multicast and quality of service. Signaling also is involved in setting up access tunnels for mobile users.

Many, if not most, of the new technologies for edge devices can be thought of as control plane protocols as defined by the ISDN and ATM functional architectures. They involve signaling between end hosts and an ingress router or switch.

Other edge mechanisms operate in ingress or egress routers and Layer 2 switches. Some of these mechanisms, such as the Next Hop Resolution Protocol (NHRP) or Multiprotocol over ATM (MPOA) are "cut-through" techniques that blur the boundary between Layer 3 and Layer 2 forwarding. Cut-through techniques are most often implemented on ingress routers, but they could run on hosts. Certainly, they are more edge than core functions and thus are discussed in this chapter.

New paradigms are emerging. New paradigms also are being stated in very confusing ways, perhaps due to complexity, perhaps due to marketing pressures, and perhaps due to misunderstanding. A reasonable approach to the new paradigms is to think of them as:

- Route everywhere (in other words, make all decisions and all forwarding at Layer 3) . This covers classical routing, with speed improvements.

- Route once and then switch (in other words, make subsequent forwarding information at either Layer 2 or an intermediate Layer 2-Layer 3 label). This is the model in distributed multilayer switching, such as Cisco distributed NetFlow and Express forwarding, and in label switching.

- Route when you must, switch when you can.

- Switch everywhere.

As these paradigms evolve, they tend to have distinct features at the edge of the network, where end hosts connect to it, and in the core of the network. This chapter deals with the edge features.

Ingress, Egress, and Forwarding Equivalence Classes

Many of the techniques in this chapter operate on ingress routers or switches. Some, however, involve the egress device.

Shirish Sathaye of Alteon made some illuminating comments at the January 1999 NANOG meeting:

> You can't switch at Layer 4 *but* you can use Layer 4 information to make switching decisions! The term "Layer 4 Switching" is too confusing. It usually means one of two things:
>
> 1. Layer 4 information is used to prioritize and queue traffic (routers have done this for years).
>
> 2. Layer 4 information is used to direct application sessions to different servers (next generation load balancing).
>
> Though the term may be meaningless, the idea and value of L4 switching is valid. [Sathaye, 1999]

Many products that claim to be doing Layer 4 or higher-layer switching, for-warding, or whatever term their marketers create, actually make their forward-ing decisions at Layer 2 or Layer 3, and use Layer 4 or higher information to refine the prioritization of traffic. Another way to look at these mechanisms, which also applies to multicast routing, is that reasonably traditional Layer 2 or Layer 3 mechanisms are used to direct traffic to the egress router, which then uses specialized mechanisms to control traffic on the egress subnet. Such spe-cialized mechanisms include multicast group filtering (see the section "IGMP Overdrives: Snooping and CGMP" later in this chapter), load sharing network address translation [RFC 2391], prioritization on the output interface, and so forth.

Some of the functions in "higher-layer switching" are more characteristic of a proxy or NAT server than a true relaying device. See Chapter 6 of *Designing Addressing Architectures for Routing and Switching* [Berkowitz, 1998a]. Sathaye defined Layer 4 switching as "session aware." Layer 2 forwarding can be used to obtain high bandwidth, but the Layer 4 function integrates egress device traffic analysis at Layer 4 coupled with end system functions such as Web caches and redirectors, firewalls, DNS redirectors, and so on.

Forwarding Equivalence Classes

The idea of Forwarding Equivalence Classes (FECs) originated in label switch-ing work, but can simplify a great many of the newer mechanisms. In Figure 13.2, how many ways are there to leave R1 from the perspective of the enter-prise? Even if R1 exchanges full Border Gateway Protocol (BGP) routing of 60,000 routes with the two ISP routers, R1 still actually forwards in only two ways: to ISP 1 or to ISP 2.

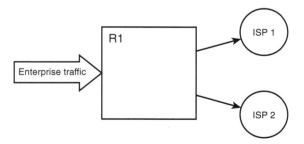

F IGURE 1 3 . 2   *FECs greatly simplify the view of what a router actually is doing.*

If you introduce three levels of traffic prioritization—high, medium, and low—
to both ISPs, as shown in Figure 13.3, there are now six possible ways traffic
can leave R1: three classes of service times two interfaces.

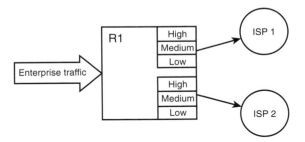

F I G U R E 1 3 . 3 *Even adding classes of service usually keeps the number of FECs low when
compared to the number of destination routes.*

According to the Multiprotocol Label Switching (MPLS) architecture, an FEC is
"a group of IP packets which are forwarded in the same manner (e.g., over the
same path, with the same forwarding treatment)." From the perspective of the
enterprise, R1 has two FECs in Figure 13.2 and six FECs in Figure 13.3.

Deployment Issues and Router Alerts

One trend in modern routing is to add new functions to existing protocols,
either through host-to-router signaling or by adding new information to router-
to-router (that is, management-plane) protocols.

A function can only assume that another router knows a next hop to a destination, not that it has supplemental information, such as a topological database,
traffic loads, or state. There is a challenge to deploying new features when they
cannot be implemented simultaneously in every router in a large enterprise.
How is a router to know which of its neighbors supports a new function?

One FEC might be to the set of routers implementing the function. You would forward only to those routers that do. Unfortunately, there is a dearth of mechanisms
for routers to exchange information about their capabilities. Traditional unicast
routing, which is aware only of next hops and metrics, cannot assume any more
knowledge than that an adjacent router offers routing to some destination.

Resource Reservation Protocol (RSVP) routers are expected to be proactive, examining each packet they carry to see whether it contains RSVP information. Routers that do not support RSVP do not look for RSVP information, so simply serve as points in a conceptual tunnel between RSVP routers. But this requirement can impose a major performance penalty on the main router performance path, especially if the majority of traffic is non-RSVP, because every packet still needs to be examined. In the main router path, adding even a single instruction can drop overall forwarding by hundreds of packets per second. As new protocol mechanisms are deployed in an existing set of routers, how do we deal with the problem of routers that do not understand the mechanism? Indeed, it may not be important for many routers to understand a mechanism. Given the strong trend to have specializations at the edge and in the core, a core router may have no particular need to understand an edge-oriented function, and vice versa.

One approach to ensuring that routers do the minimum yet sufficient amount of new protocol mechanism processing is the Router Alert option, which is required by new mechanisms, such as Internet Group Management Protocol Version 2 (IGMPv2) or RSVP. It allows packets that need special handling to be treated as exception conditions, keeping normal packets and options that the router supports with high speed in the optimized main forwarding path. Special cases of packets that either are unsupported or need special handling are generically designated by the Router Alert option.

Multicast Signaling

If it's not too painful, think of broadcast television. Many stations broadcast their information streams through the air or onto cable. Premium cable and pay-per-view services send to subsets of users on the television medium. For you to listen to a specific station, you must select its channel.

This discussion, as is appropriate given the title of this book, deals with enterprise-wide multicasting, not multicasting in the Internet as a whole. A complex set of technical and non-technical obstacles must still be overcome before general Internet multicasting is practical.

Major nontechnical obstacles include billing and access control. Dave Meyer raises the questions "Do you bill for the transport or for the application service?" [Meyer, 1998].

Some issues are both technical and non-technical. Who commits the resources to replicate? Do you optimize for closest exit or best exit in terms of multicast replication? What about security, both denial of service and unauthorized access?

In digital networking, you need to perform a similar function to listen to a particular multicast stream or streams. Rather than passively selecting a channel on a television set, you need to signal to your local router that you want to "tune in" on a given multicast stream. The signaling mechanism used for this is a C plane protocol, IGMP.

IGMP is a host-to-router protocol, which has been deployed in three versions of increasing power. IGMPv1 was the first widely deployed version. IGMPv2 is intended to reduce the latency for a multicast router to learn there are no members of a multicast group still on an interface. IGMPv3, still in Internet Draft, adds support for address-based filtering within multicast groups.

IGMP does not directly specify the behavior of a receiving router with respect to other routers. Information conveyed to the router, however, is used to add or prune branches from the multicast routing tree(s) maintained by multicast routing protocols such as Protocol Independent Multicast (PIM), Distance Vector Multicast Routing Protocol (DVMRP), and so forth. See Chapter 14 for a discussion of multicast routing.

Hosts use IGMP to join and leave *host groups*, also called *multicast groups*. A given host may belong to any number of multicast groups. Multicast groups are identified with a Class D IP address, which may be:

- Well-known (that is, permanent)

- Link-local

- Administratively scoped [RFC 2365]

Note

See ***ftp.isi.edu/in-notes/iana/assignments/multicast-addresses*** for the most current list of multicast assignments.

Permanent groups may have zero or more members at any given time, but their address is reserved. Transient group addresses are significant only when there are members in them. Table 13.1 shows the assignment policy for IPv4 multicast.

Table 13.1   Multicast Address Assignments

Usage Policy	Type of Hosts	Address Range
Well-known, link local	All systems	224.0.0.1—224.0.0.255
	All routers	224.0.0.2
	All SPF routers	224.0.0.5
	All designated routers	224.0.0.6
Administratively scoped	Enterprisewide or less	239.0.0.0—239.255.255.255
Organization local scope	Enterprise-defined restricted area	239.192.0.0—239.195.255.255
Local scope	Single medium	239.255.0.0—239.255.255.255

Membership in a multicast group means that a host wants to receive multicast traffic addressed to that group. Any host can send to a multicast address, and need not be a member of that group.

Routers will forward multicast datagrams with an IP time-to-live (TTL) value greater than 1, so creating multicast packets with a TTL of 1 effectively makes them link-local. OSPF packets, for example, are kept link-local because they are created with a TTL of 1.

> **Note**
>
> *For further information, see the IETF Inter-Domain Multicast Routing (IDMR) working group page at* **www.ietf.org/html.charters/idmr-charter.html**.

IGMPv1: Soft State

Formally, a client requests a service and a server provides it. TCP uses a hard state mechanism, in which the requesting entity explicitly requests a connection and either terminates it or accepts an explicit termination from the called host.

In soft state mechanisms, a client closes a connection indirectly by ceasing to respond to polls sent to it by the server. After failing to receive a response for some predefined period, the server terminates the connection.

Soft state mechanisms require less client overhead than hard state. Servers, however, may maintain state longer than they need to do so.

RFC 1112 introduced IGMPv1, in which hosts explicitly join multicast groups by sending Membership Report messages to a local router. That router accepts the signals and sends appropriate multicast routing information to other routers, using a multicast routing protocol. IGMP does not propagate beyond the ingress router.

IP hosts use IGMP to report their host group memberships to any multicast routers on the same subnet. IGMP is an asymmetric signaling protocol in its most common use, from a client host to a server router.

Version 1 has two basic protocol messages: host membership **Query** and host membership **Report**. Routers send the **Query** message, which is sent to the well-known All-Hosts multicast address, 224.0.0.1, and have a TTL of 1. Hosts join groups and respond to **Query** messages by sending **Report** messages.

Routers only begin sending **Query** messages after there is at least one member of a multicast group, so the first multicast traffic you see on a given subnet is the initial **Report** message. IGMPv1 recommends that the initial **Report** be repeated once or twice at the time of joining a group, to guard against lost packets.

Query messages are normally sent at a low rate, such as once a minute, to reduce overhead. When an IGMP router initializes, however, it may send these messages at a higher rate, to build up its knowledge of multicast groups that are present on the interface.

One of the disadvantages of the server—the ingress router—maintaining soft state is that the resource impact of retaining state is not limited to the single router. When the first host connected to an ingress router joins a multicast group, the router uses a multicast routing protocol to join the multicast tree. Data in a multicast tree now flows to the router.

When additional hosts connected to the same router join the multicast flow, no additional flows go to the router. When the last host leaves the flow, the router can signal other routers that it no longer wants to receive the flow, and thus reduce its workload.

Soft state mechanisms, however, cause the router to receive the flow longer than it needs to. Specifically, the router—and possibly other routers in the path—participates in the flow for an interval between the points when the last subscribing host loses interest in the flow and the soft state timer in the router expires.

IGMPv2: Explicit Leaves

A major motivation for IGMPv2 was the latency implicit in soft state. State of any sort is maintained on the router that issues queries, which is called the *querier* in IGMPv2 and IGMPv3. IGMPv2 adds a new protocol message, **Leave Group**, and changes the meaning of some IGMPv3 fields in a compatible manner.

Although the mechanism is now standardized, it is entirely possible that an IGMPv2 router may have to coexist with an IGMPv1 router on the same sub-net—a router with a different query mechanism. If the IGMPv2 router connects to an IGMPv1 network, the IGMPv2 router needs to maintain compatibility by setting options in a manner compatible with IGPMv1: Max Response Time set to zero in all queries, and ignoring Leave Group messages.

An IGMPv2 router initializes as a querier and listens for other IGMPv2 routers issuing queries. If there is another router, the conflict is resolved by the router with the higher IP address deferring to the router with the lower IP address. The lower the router IP address on a subnet, the higher the probability the router will become querier. Note that this rule is the opposite of OSPF desig-nated router election for routers with the same priority, where the higher-num-bered router becomes DR.

The querier election mechanism is fault-tolerant, because non-querier routers maintain a timer, Other Querier Present Interval. If this timer expires without the IGMPv2 router hearing a **Query** message, it makes itself the querier.

IGMPv2 extends the **Query** to allow group-specific queries. After a host leaves, for example, the router can send an immediate query to the group the host left so that it can decide quickly whether there are any remaining hosts in the group.

When an IGMPv2 router receives a **Report** for a new group, it creates a timer for that group with the value **Group Membership Interval**. The router periodi-cally sends a query at that interval, and if no hosts respond with a **Report** for that group, the router can assume no members of that group present on the subnet are attached to its interface.

If you have any existing IGMPv1 routers, you can still put IGMPv2 routers on the same subnet. Just as we have the router alert feature because we have no way to know the capabilities of a given router, we have no real way to know whether IGMPv1 or IGMPv2 is configured on a specific router.

On a practical basis, the people configuring enterprise level multicasting should talk to one another. Even if multiple routers are connected to a corpo-rate backbone and have different administrators, these administrators should be aware of one another, and need to coordinate their efforts.

IGMPv2 [RFC 2236] requires that routers default to IGMPv2 unless IGMPv1 is explicitly configured. If a router is capable of both IGMPv1 and IGMPv2, it must, while in IGMPv1 mode, send Periodic Queries with the Max Response Time set to 0, and it must ignore Leave Group messages.

IGMPv1 routers that hear IGMPv2 queries and IGMPv2 routers that hear IGMPv1 queries should issue warning messages. Such warning messages must be rate limited, because it is quite likely that a considerable period of time may pass before a human can change the configuration, if indeed the configuration is to be changed. In the time before change, there could be a huge number of warnings unless the rate of their generation is controlled. Nevertheless, administrators should make a practice, during IGMPv2 implementation, to search logs to find a neglected router that is configured for the wrong version of IGMP.

IGMPv3: Source Filtering

IGMPv3 fills me with regret that it doesn't have a real-world counterpart that I could use at certain meetings I attend. Have you ever been at a meeting where most people have something useful to say, but certain individuals are in love with the sounds of their own voices? IGMPv3 allows a host to specify that it either listens to only designated source addresses within a multicast group, or listens to everyone *but* a list of source addresses in the group.

IGMP Overdrives: Snooping and CGMP

Several vendors have implemented proprietary "overdrive" mechanisms that reduce the amount of bandwidth consumed by irrelevant multicasts on microsegmented ports of LAN switches. The vendor approaches differ on whether the intelligence is implemented on the switch or on the ingress multicast router.

In contrast, older switches do not know the difference between a broadcast and a multicast. When such switches are used, multicasts consume the same amount of port-level bandwidth as multicasts do.

In IGMP snooping, used by 3Com, Bay, Cisco, and Extreme, the ingress switch has enough IP awareness to recognize IP packets that carry IGMP, and to select those packets and extract IGMP information from them. After the snooping function recognizes that an IGMP **Report** has been issued by a host attached to a port, the snooping function permits traffic from the requested multicast group to flow from the switch fabric to the port.

IGMP snooping requires a significant but not overwhelming additional capability on the switch. Ideally, at least the IGMP packet recognition function will be implemented in an application-specific integrated circuit (ASIC). Such implementation is reasonable because the IP protocol type is in a fixed position in the IP header, which makes protocol type recognition a candidate for ASIC processing.

Cisco also uses the Cisco Group Management Protocol (CGMP). When a switch-attached host joins a multicast group, the message is passed transparently to the ingress router. That ingress router sends a CGMP message to the switch, telling it to allow traffic belonging to the multicast group (as defined by MAC address) to begin flowing onto the port on which the host requested membership. Up to that point, if CGMP is enabled on the switch, the port receives no multicast traffic.

A third approach to limiting unneeded multicast traffic on individual ports is the IEEE 802.1P Generic Attribute Registration Protocol (GARP) , which allows multicast joins at Layer 2. This technique is applicable whether or not IP multicast is used, and is especially appropriate for "flattened" switched networks.

Yet another approach is proposed as the IGMP Multicast Router Discovery Protocol. This mechanism is intended to enable bridges to discover the existence of multicast routers. Multicast router advertisements can contain timer values for different multicast groups.

Although it might seem that this approach duplicates the function of ICMP Router Discovery discussed in Chapter 6, there are important differences. Unicast and multicast topologies may not be the same, and the two protocols would have different coverage. Filtering and recognition are made easier when there is a recognizable link-local address associated with multicasting. Multicast router discovery does parallel ICMP router discovery, with its two protocol messages: Multicast Router Solicitation and Multicast Router Advertisement.

This protocol also provides an extensible base for signaling from multicast routers to end hosts, as new requirements evolve. New multicast routing techniques continue to evolve, and decoupling the router-to-host signaling mechanism will prevent a large number of multicast routing protocol-specific mechanisms from proliferating.

Devices such as Layer 2 switches, which do not normally participate in IP, could send multicast router solicitations to obtain multicast information.

Quality of Service Signaling

Quality of service (QoS), in the broad sense, means giving some level of control of performance parameters to different types of traffic. The major parameter types controlled are loss probability and latency. QOS needs to be specified with respect to a workload.

Like any technology, the more complex a service, the more difficult it is to maintain. Although there can be a very broad range of quality of service parameters applications ideally might like to obtain, a more realistic view establishes a relatively small set of service classes. At the edge of the network, traffic entering it will be assigned to this manageable number of classes.

Airline Quality of Service?

I'm a frequent flyer. I can cope with coach, business, and first class. I can deal with domestic first class being equivalent to international business. I can even deal with the concept in many airlines that if I buy full-fare domestic coach, I am automatically upgraded to first class. But when it gets to the explanation that "you can't upgrade a B-06 discounted coach class to a first class with a 2500 MX frequent flyer award; you have to use 10,000 mile RX awards unless you are flying through Cincinnati on an even-numbered day with a Saturday night stay in Portland."

So think of a limited number of classes of service you rationally need to support:

- Critical network management, routing updates, and so on
- Voice and other traffic that is extremely sensitive to delay variability
- Mission-critical transaction processing
- General interactive applications
- Non-interactive bulk data transfer

These different services may need guaranteed service, controlled load, or best effort with different priority levels. Because TCP flows are far more responsive than UDP to congestion, it's reasonable to prioritize them over UDP.

There are several approaches to ensuring quality of service. The simplest, but practical only in campus networks, is to overprovision bandwidth. Overprovisioning is not a true controlled method of controlling QoS, and it needs continued monitoring to determine when more bandwidth may be needed. Still, it may be a perfectly viable means of providing QoS on a campus. It is especially appropriate when using a Fast or Gigabit Ethernet backbone, because these media do not provide controlled QoS. Even when 802.1P prioritization is readily available, 802.1P provides relative prioritization among frames. 802.1P will still admit traffic to a congested network.

On WANs, however, bandwidth is too expensive to overprovision in every case. The more practical methods there are to reserve bandwidth for guaranteed service and controlled load traffic, and prioritize within the remaining bandwidth for best effort traffic. Remember that the best effort traffic shares a bandwidth that is not reserved, so the highest-priority traffic can always get some bandwidth, although it may be delayed, by a predictable amount, by reserved bandwidth.

Be careful in reserving bandwidth for data applications, because end-to-end flow control may suffice to avoid congestion. Typically, the applications most appropriate for reserved bandwidth are multimedia: voice and video. Application-level server synchronization is a data application that might well justify reserved bandwidth. Only the most critical user data traffic should receive reserved bandwidth. It is generally much better to assign critical user data to a high best effort priority than it is to guarantee service.

If you have worked with time-division multiplexing, consider that using reservations is much like giving an application its own channel, which nothing else can use. You must ask yourself the question "Does this application warrant the cost of giving it reserved bandwidth?" before you use RSVP or other methods to reserve bandwidth.

To manage the QoS for best-effort traffic, you need to select methods consistent with a QoS policy. There are two broad technologies for QoS control for best-effort services: the traditional reactive responses to congestion, and the newer proactive congestion avoidance methods.

Reactive methods prioritize outgoing traffic in the presence of congestion. Proactive methods either limit transmission rates within a well-designed traffic engineering model, so critical network elements cannot be congested, or impose implicit flow control on TCP transmitters.

Do consider that while you might guarantee part of the bandwidth, as long as some bandwidth is allocated to best-effort functions, the highest-priority best effort should get through. Figure 13.4 shows how bandwidth is shared between guaranteed and controlled-load reserved flows, and best-effort (BE) flows. The figure shows the traditional military precedences for traffic marked with IP precedence bits, and more common civilian applications for those precedences. The current usage of IP precedence for differentiated services is discussed in the section "Differentiated Services" later in this chapter.

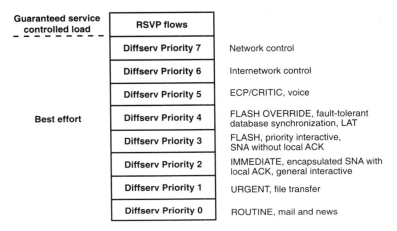

Guaranteed service controlled load	RSVP flows	
	Diffserv Priority 7	Network control
	Diffserv Priority 6	Internetwork control
	Diffserv Priority 5	ECP/CRITIC, voice
Best effort	Diffserv Priority 4	FLASH OVERRIDE, fault-tolerant database synchronization, LAT
	Diffserv Priority 3	FLASH, priority interactive, SNA without local ACK
	Diffserv Priority 2	IMMEDIATE, encapsulated SNA with local ACK, general interactive
	Diffserv Priority 1	URGENT, file transfer
	Diffserv Priority 0	ROUTINE, mail and news

FIGURE 13.4 *Reservation methods for guaranteed and control load services should not take up all the bandwidth, leaving some for best-effort services. The highest-priority BE service always gets through.*

At the network edge, you need to mark the traffic in a manner that tells core devices how to handle it. The basic approach is to mark it so that it is recognizable as belonging to a class. You can do this in the host or in the ingress device.

Marking in the ingress device is generally easier to implement, because there are far fewer ingress devices to upgrade with marking capabilities than there are hosts. In the long term, host-based marking makes a great deal of sense, assuming the hosts are trusted to mark traffic appropriately. Such trust is a much more reasonable assumption in an enterprise than in the general Internet.

A considerably more advanced approach is to describe quantitative types of traffic, and obtain a flow label or Layer 2 service contract. Even here, the practical realization in the core needs to be mapped to a manageable number of classes.

Admission control may be combined with marking, or serve a similar purpose without marking. With admission control, traffic is not allowed to enter the network if the network is at or above its capacity.

Hosts, as well as ingress devices, may set QoS parameters such as the IP precedence bits. In an enterprise, letting the hosts set these parameters often is reasonable, because a central administrator can enforce policies. In a public environment, or in a less-controlled enterprise such as a university, the ingress relay should either check to see whether host-set parameters are allowed, or simply override them with its own settings.

Marking Traffic on Ingress Relays

Before you can give differentiated service to different kinds of traffic, you need to be able to identify that traffic. A very practical means of doing so is to sort the traffic into broad service classes, and then set the IP precedence bits in the Type of Service field of the IP header. 802.1P defines similar class of service bits at Layer 2.

After these bits are set by the ingress relay, they can be used to affect the per-hop behavior (PHB) at each subsequent relay. Behavior beyond the first hop is discussed in Chapter 14.

Setting the precedence bits is an example of the general concept of *marking*. First-hop routers or source hosts may mark packets and perform other *traffic conditioning* functions, including metering, policing, and shaping. First-hop routers also may perform admission control.

Differentiated Services

The differentiated services architecture (diffserv) allows an enterprise network or a service provider to offer a range of classes of service, each with a different quality of service. Whereas practical use of differentiated services in the general Internet requires economic incentives and disincentives to setting a preferred class of service, differentiated service is even more practical in an enterprise where there is a single policy authority.

In an enterprise, even though the network utility does not have pricing as an incentive, there is still a strong motivation for differentiated services. Separating the traffic marking function from the forwarding function makes it possible to simplify core relays and improve their cost performance. When the core devices need only understand service classes, rather than track individual flows, they can focus their attention on forwarding.

If QoS is used at all, you should reserve classes for network management. Multimedia applications are likely to take the next priority, followed by interactive data applications. Non-interactive data applications are at the next level.

IEEE 802.1P

IEEE 802.1P defines quality of service and marking criteria that can be used at Layer 2. The actual signaling of this mechanism uses Tagged Frames as defined in IEEE 802.1Q. Tag Control Information (TCI) includes the following:

- User Priority. Frames have a three-bit user priority field.

- Canonical Format Indicator (CFI). This type of information is used in Token Ring and FDDI to indicate the bit format of the information in the encapsulated frame, and, in 802.3, to signal the presence of or absence of source routing information and the bit order of addresses in the encapsulated frame.

- VLAN identifier (VID).

ATM LANEv2 also makes use of the 802.1p conventions.

This priority is used in two ways:

- Internally within a bridge, to select the order in which queued frames of different priorities are to be transmitted on an output interface

- After the frame is at the head of the transmission queue, selecting medium access in MAC protocols that support multiple priority levels

When you use 802.1P, you have to consider the nontrivial decision of where the user priority bits are set. Is the host aware of 802.1P, so that the end host can set the bits? If so, are applications in that host also aware of being able to request priority? Today's applications may not know how to request QoS, although an increasing number do. Microsoft, for example, has released RSVP support in an upgrade of NT 4, and will make strong use of RSVP and other QoS mechanisms in Windows 2000. Sun and other UNIX vendors also support host QoS.

For an ingress switch to be aware of specific traffic that needs a specific priority, it is likely that the switch will need Layer 3 or Layer 4 awareness. Such awareness will complicate the switch and add cost. A more likely strategy is for the first hop router to categorize the traffic and send a message back to the ingress switch that matches a source-destination MAC address pair to a particular priority.

There is a potential security vulnerability, probably acceptable in enterprise networks, that a host might obtain a priority to reach some host based on initial Layer 3 or 4 criteria, and then change to a different application that does not deserve the same priority.

Of course, having these mechanisms in the operating system is only half of the host problem. Multimedia applications such as NetMeeting, however, often know how to request QoS. They are more likely to request RSVP services than 802.1P, simply because RSVP has been available for a longer time.

If you set 802.1P user priority bits on an ingress switch, how does the switch decide what to prioritize, if hosts do not set these bits? Remember, most application traffic that needs priority will be identified by Layer 3 or higher layer information, of which a classic switch is not aware. Either the switch needs some higher-level awareness, which will increase its complexity, or the ingress router needs to detect the traffic type and send priority-setting rules to the ingress switch.

LANE v2 QoS

One of the enhancements in LANEv2 is the permission given administrators to assign up to eight classes of service on each LAN Emulation Client. Each LEC can establish up to eight VCs to other VCs with which it shares a class of service.

Each VC corresponds to a class of service defined for the ELAN. It is assigned to one of the basic ATM service types: CBR, VBR, ABR, or UBR, with appropriate traffic contract parameters.

Note

See the work of the Integrated Services over Specific Link Layers (ISSLL) working group of the IETF: **www.ietf.org/html.charters/issll-charter.html**, *as well as the ATM Forum.*

Using QoS in LANEv2 is an alternative to 802.1P prioritization in VLANs. A scalability limit on QoS in LANE is the number of VCs that a given LEC can handle, because it potentially requires eight times the number of VCs required with a non-QoS architecture.

Several factors may tend to reduce the actual number of VCs, but that number still may be substantial. QoS may not be required to all other LAN Emulation Clients.

If QoS is used at all, you should reserve classes for network management. Multimedia applications should probably take the next priority, followed by interactive data applications. Non-interactive data applications are at the next level.

Resource Reservations: Requirements, Realities, and the Future

IP precedence bits can be set by either hosts or relays; in early implementation practice it appears that diffserv will be router-driven. The thrust of differentiated service is to simplify, to reduce a large range of requirements into a small set of classes of service.

RSVP has the potential of giving much finer granularity than diffserv. This is both a strength and a weakness. Finer granularity, and RSVP's concept of reservations rather than arbitrating among preferences, could give applications a higher probability of obtaining exactly the service they need. On the other hand, the additional state that has to be maintained for the finer granularity requires much more tracking by routers, and is less scalable than diffserv. RSVP systems should be limited in scope to a single enterprise, or a routing domain within it.

Note

See the ongoing work of the Resource Reservation Protocol working group of the IETF: **www.ietf.org/html.charters/rsvp-charter.html**.

RSVP tends to be host driven, although it can be used to reserve resources on a hop-by-hop basis. RSVP hosts send a message to a RSVP server that they are interested in receiving information on a particular flow.

RSVP was originally developed for multicast flows, which are best-effort and one-directional. Support for point-to-point flows was an add-on to the protocol. Although multicast routing is covered in more detail in the next chapter, assume that the topology in Figure 13.5 has magically been constructed, and we will explore how RSVP behaves in that topology.

Don't try to find "connections" in RSVP, because it uses a soft state model. RSVP messages are sent over UDP, and need to be retransmitted periodically to ensure state is maintained. You may want to prioritize UDP packets that contain RSVP information.

Much as hosts join multicast groups with IGMPv1 but leave with an implicit timeout, RSVP state information on an RSVP interface flushes after timers expire, if periodic RSVP messages do not arrive to reset the *cleanup timeout* timer. The protocol does support explicit clearing with a **Teardown** message. When a participant in RSVP wants to change the reserved paths, it simply sends new **Path** or **Resv** messages containing the changed information. The new paths change either because the soft state expires, or because the participant sends an explicit teardown.

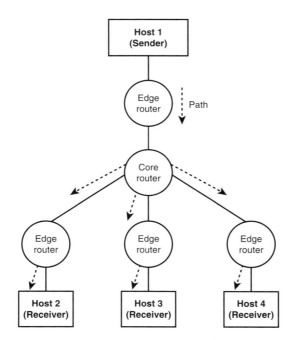

F IGURE 1 3.5 *RSVP is easier to understand when looking at its original objective: controlling resources in a multicast tree.*

RSVP Conceptual Function

From the multicast perspective, a potentially sending host advertises it with **Path** messages. As receivers hear these messages, and want to listen to that flow, they send **Resv** messages from the receiver to the sender to reserve bandwidth along the receiver-to-sender path. In Figure 13.6, a sender announces the existence of a flow and multicast receivers selectively decide whether they want to receive it. In the **Resv** message, multicast senders can be explicitly specified, or selected with a wildcard.

Resource allocation is receiver-oriented, which can be confusing if you are used to an application client requesting service and a server providing it. When an end host, usually an application client, is interested in a flow from a server, the end host asks RSVP to listen to a flow from the server. If the network (and potentially server) resources exist between the application server and client, access to the flow is granted.

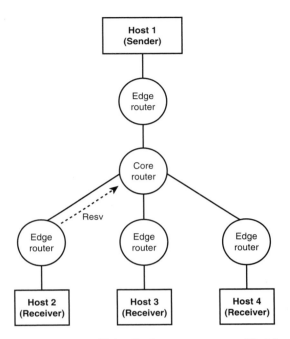

FIGURE 13.6 *Using* **Path** *messages, source Host 1 announces a flow over the multicast tree. If receivers desire to listen to it, they send* **Resv** *messages.*

RSVP is smart enough to merge reservations. In Figure 13.7, the first receiver, Host 2, reserves bandwidth all the way back to Host 1. When the next receiver, Host 4, joins the multicast flow, bandwidth is reserved between Host 4's ingress router and the core router, but no additional bandwidth is needed between the core router and Host 1. No additional bandwidth is needed there because bandwidth has already been allocated. On the link between the core router and Host 1, the bandwidth allocations for Host 2 and Host 4 have been merged.

You can see that flow merging essentially enables an unlimited number of receivers to share the same bandwidth.

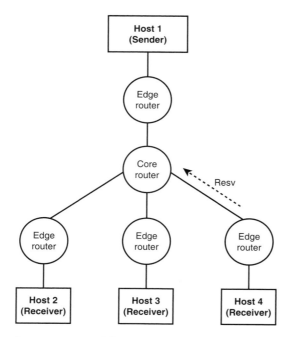

FIGURE 13.7 *RSVP merging avoids allocating unneeded bandwidth when multiple receivers need access to a common flow.*

Be sure not to confuse RSVP with a QoS routing protocol. Examine Figure 13.8 to see where it runs.

RSVP is not QoS aware. Routers passing along RSVP messages have no standard way of selecting a path based on load. Future developments in QoS routing will make RSVP much more intelligent, but currently, implementations tend to use RSVP as a means of locking up the highest-priority bandwidth, so non-RSVP flows experience any congestion.

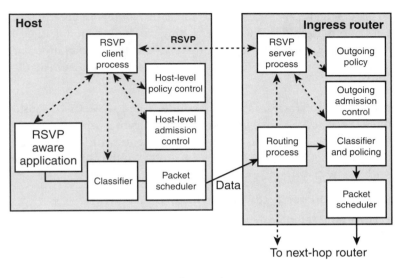

Legend

——————— Data path
- - - - - - - - Control path

FIGURE 13.8   *RSVP components are both in end hosts and in routers.*

RSVP Setup in Commercial Products

Bay RS and Cisco IOS both support RSVP in recent releases. Bay RS separates the RSVP function from its Line Resource Manager (LRM), which actually reserves the bandwidth. When a Bay RS router receives a **Resv** message, it passes the flowspec from that message to LRM. It is the LRM that actually allocates the bandwidth or refuses the request. Non-RSVP mechanisms also can call upon LRM. You configure the RSVP and LRM functions separately.

RSVP is enabled by default. You can set non-default timer values through Site Manager RSVP screens.

You set the amount of bandwidth available to RSVP in the Edit Line Resources window of Site Manager. First, you set estimated bandwidth for the medium as a whole, which usually is the full bandwidth on a point-to-point medium, but some smaller value for a shared medium. You then set reservable bandwidth as the maximum amount that can be reserved by RSVP.

You also need to decide whether you want a policy of using best effort for all traffic, or if you want reserved traffic scheduled before non-RSVP traffic.

Cisco considers the RSVP mechanism as the basic bandwidth control mechanism. On Cisco routers, RSVP works by setting bandwidth limits rather than the full IntServ parameters. By default, up to 75% of the bandwidth on an interface can be reserved by RSVP, and any single flow can reserve all the bandwidth.

When you use subinterfaces, as with Frame Relay and ATM, Cisco considers both subinterface and physical interface bandwidths in reserving capacity. If the physical bandwidth is 1.536 Mbps, the sum of bandwidth reserved by all subinterfaces cannot exceed 1.536 Mbps, regardless of the CIR on the subinterfaces.

The command to reserve bandwidth on interfaces is:

```
ip rsvp bandwidth interface-Kbps [single-flow-Kbps]
```

Note

I would hesitate to say that Bay and Cisco are not interoperable, because I think of interoperability as a matter of protocols. More informally, their defaults and granularity are different.

Cisco, for example, automatically prioritizes RSVP traffic over best-effort in WRED and WFQ. Bay's default is to treat reserved and BE traffic alike, although precedence for reserved can be configured.

RSVP Full Setup

In the most general implementation of RSVP, fully conformant with the integrated services architecture, senders who offer traffic send **Path** messages in the direction of receivers.

A receiver interested in a particular flow sends a **Resv** message upstream. The message contains a *flow descriptor,* consisting of a *filter spec* defining the flow and a *flowspec* consisting of a TSpec and an RSpec. See the "Integrated Service Requests" section of this chapter for further details on TSpecs and RSpecs. **Resv** messages follow a path opposite the one that the desired data is expected to take, which might be a real challenge if routing is asymmetrical.

This request is either accepted or rejected by each router on the path to the destination. These routers establish soft state for the flow reservation. If the request reaches the sender, a flow ID is created. IPv4 packets belonging to flows are described in filters, although a flow ID is part of the IPv6 header.

RSVP documents do not specify the values or policies for quality of service; RSVP is a mechanism for passing this information opaquely, in that it does not itself understand the information but knows how to deliver it to entities that do. QoS parameters themselves are defined by the IETF Integrated Services Working Group.

RSVP requests go to two modules: admission and policy control. The admission and policy checks can proceed in parallel, but the requester can have access to an RSVP flow only if both checks succeed. Admission control checks to see whether resources are available to fulfill the QoS requirement in the RSVP request, whereas policy control checks to see whether the user has the administrative permissions to be granted these resources.

Although the protocol gives a model for requesting a quality of service based on a peak and average rate, practical implementations reserve bandwidth on a hop-by-hop basis.

Marking Traffic on Hosts

Hosts can mark traffic as well as ingress devices, assuming the hosts have the appropriate software. A practical concern is that the hosts both need marking capability at the NIC/driver level, but applications need to be aware that they can request different classes of service.

As a player in both the internetworking device and NIC markets, it is not surprising 3Com has taken an aggressive early position in host-based marking with its DynamicAccess LAN software.

3Com's Fast IP is one proprietary solution that brought NHRP awareness to the end host. It can use NHRP with either VLANs using IEEE 802.1P and 802.1Q, or ATM ELANs. In comparison with many NHRP systems where the NHS is in the ingress relay, or in which the ingress relay forwards to the NHS, the NHS function is in the destination host.

In the default mode of MPOA operation, a host does not immediately issue an NHRP request. As in MPOA, the NHRP request is triggered after a certain number of packets are sent to a destination host not on the same subnet.

The initial NHRP request follows the "route once" model, although packets sent before the traffic trigger level may all have been routed. Routers on the path to the destination may apply traditional filters and other controls. One way of forcing a given host not to cut through is to have an access list that blocks the NHRP request from going to the destination host, although routed data packets might be permitted.

Assuming the destination host is running Fast IP, it acts as an NHRP server, and returns the NHRP response to the MAC address of the originating host, an address that is contained in the NHRP request.

If the originating host hears the NHRP response, it knows there is a Layer 2 connection between itself and the destination. If that is the case, the originator now sends frames to the MAC address of the destination end system, rather than the MAC address of its ingress router.

If there is no switched connectivity between the two hosts, the originating host continues to send to the MAC address of the ingress router.

How do cut-throughs come into existence? When the underlying infrastructure is an IEEE 802.1Q VLAN, the requesting end host may include its VLAN ID in its NHRP request. The response is addressed to the requester's VLAN ID and MAC address, and the subsequent traffic uses 802.1Q tagging, which the trunk switches know how to route.

When the underlying infrastructure is ATM LANE, with end stations on different subnets, these subnets are mapped to the same ELAN. Basic LANE address discovery establishes an appropriate VC.

Fast IP also can work with MPOA. MPOA dynamically creates cut-throughs based on traffic.

Integrated Service Requests

RSVP is a setup protocol that carries QoS requirements from edge hosts to routers and between routers. But what information does it carry? The Integrated Service architecture defines two forms of information to request: Traffic Specifications (TSpec) and Service Request Specifications (RSpec).

TSpecs define the traffic the endpoint will offer when a contract to provide a particular service is requested. RSpecs describe the service requested. When a host violates the terms of the traffic contract defined by the TSpec, the network is no longer obligated to provide service of the requested type. The network is allowed to *police* the traffic so that it comes under the prior TSpec agreement.

As an example, a TSpec might describe the peak rate at which a host will transmit, whereas an RSpec would describe the bandwidth to be allocated, the expected maximum loss rate, or the expected maximum delay.

RSVP is not the only setup protocol. At ATM Layer 2, the Q.2931 protocol has the equivalent function.

The major types of integrated service are:

- Guaranteed service

- Controlled load service

- Best effort service

Guaranteed Service

Guaranteed service is a class of service that promises that packets will arrive in a time less than or equal to the guaranteed delivery time specified in the RSpec, and will not be discarded due to congestion, as long as the traffic load stays within the TSpec.

This class of service is appropriate for applications such as audio and video, where the packet is useless if it arrives after some period of time. For example, if the packet arrives after other packets have been delivered to a human output device, they are meaningless.

The maximum delay is exactly that: a maximum. In most real systems, the actual delay is less, but the maximum delay should be specified to limit the maximum queuing delay. In fact, most packets arrive sooner than the maximum delay and need to be buffered.

Guaranteed service does not attempt to control jitter. Jitter should be minimized by buffering before the final destination.

To specify guaranteed service, you must be able to specify (or accept product defaults) for five components:

- A floating-point rate r, measured in bytes per second, with an accuracy of at least 0.1%.

- A floating-point bucket size b.

- A floating-point peak rate p, measured in bytes per second. It is the maximum rate at which the source, and any traffic shaping relays along the path, can inject into the network. p must be greater than or equal to r.

- An integer minimum policed unit (that is, packet size) m.

- An integer maximum policed unit M.

Setting these parameters establishes a maximum end-to-end queueing delay, which must be added to the path propagation delay to find the true maximum delay. The parameters do not control minimum or average delay.

Packets must not be fragmented along the path. This requirement, of course, suggests that MTU path discovery, or setting end hosts to a prudent minimum MTU, is appropriate. Consider any potential tunneling when deciding on the MTU.

An RSpec for guaranteed service consists of:

- A rate **R**, which must be greater than or equal to the TSpec rate **r**. The rate is represented as a bucket and a peak rate.

- A slack term **S**, measured in microseconds, that is the difference between the desired delay and the delay obtainable with reservation of rate **R**.

The RSpec rate can be larger than the TSpec delay, because increasing the RSpec rate reduces queuing delay.

Controlled-Load Service

Controlled-load service is equivalent to the best-effort service that a network provides when unloaded (that is, under no significant load, as distinct from no load). Such a service has the following characteristics:

- There is a very low probability of packet loss, on the order of the error rate of the underlying transmission medium. In other words, it will be unlikely for packets to be dropped due to congestion.

- The great majority of packets do not experience more transit delay than is inherent in the medium propagation times and fixed processing times in relays.

For the network elements to deliver this high-grade service, the end hosts must provide an accurate TSpec defining the traffic they will impose. If the traffic offered by a host exceeds this TSpec, the network may provide a QoS characteristic of a highly overloaded network, such as long delays and high packet loss rates.

The effectiveness of a controlled-load service depends on three factors:

- The short-term burstiness of the traffic stream.

- The degree to which the load changes, over a significant period of time, while staying within the TSpec.

- The ratio of controlled-load traffic to all other traffic at a given relay.

Best Effort Services

Even when controlled QoS is supported, a substantial amount of traffic is best effort. BE services make especially good sense when diffserv is applied to them.

Real-world implementations of RSVP allow you to configure how much bandwidth is to be available for RSVP flows on a particular interface. Cisco's default, for example, sets 75% of the bandwidth available for RSVP. The remaining 25% is for BE traffic.

Within the BE traffic, however, you can set differentiated services priorities. If 25% of the bandwidth on an interface is not subject to RSVP, then the highest priority BE traffic always gets through. Remember that the highest priorities in IP precedence are for network control and internetwork control.

Mobility

QoS mechanisms are not the only evolving edge technology. In Chapter 1, we categorized users as:

- Telecommuters: single users at fixed distributed sites

- Small office users: small groups of users at fixed distributed sites, with bandwidth requirements possibly low enough to be served by on-demand media

- Users at large sites, who need dedicated access facilities and relaying internal to the site

- Road warriors, or single users who dial in from multiple access points, but use a single access point for the duration of a session

- Mobile users, who connect to multiple access points during the length of a session

Our focus here is the road warrior, who needs remote access to home networks using dialup connectivity, and the mobile user, who most commonly connects to some sort of wireless medium.

In Chapter 12, we discussed the Layer 2 tunneling protocol (L2TP) from the perspective of tunneling routers, but did not go into the details of its application. L2TP, and its ancestors L2F and PPTP, deal with requirements that tend to be associated with the telecommuter and small office: users that operate from a fixed location, but frequently use the on-demand facilities of a VPN. L2TP also applies to road warriors: users who dial in from various locations, typically to the modem pool of a local ISP. The road warrior maintains a constant relationship between an IP address and a Layer 2 PPP port for the duration of a connection.

Historically, one of the fundamental assumptions about IPv4 is that its IP address is associated with a persistent local address on its medium. Even when IP runs over a virtual circuit service such as Frame Relay, X.25, or ATM, there is a long-term association with an identifier such as the Data Link Connection Identifier (DLCI), X.121 address, or NSAP address. There may be a level of indirection between a small connection identifier and the persistent address, such as the Logical Channel Number to the X.121 address, and the VPI/VCI to the NSAP.

Truly mobile users employ wireless access techniques such as cellular and satellite radio. Although the more familiar communications satellites have been in geosynchronous orbit, fixed in relation to a position on the Earth, newer commercial systems include low-earth orbit (LEO) satellite "clouds," with changing relationships between a user and multiple satellites during the duration of a connection.

Cellular radio, of course, also involves a changing relationship between the IP address and the geographic cell in which the user is located. A user in a car goes through multiple cells during a conversation, hopefully paying attention to his or her driving during the conversation.

Protocols for wireless media face other challenges. Bandwidth is often lower than on wired media, and the error rate may be higher. Mobile nodes also may have limited electrical power available, either from batteries or the onboard power supply of a vehicle. All these factors combine to require that mobile protocols should transmit as little as possible, avoiding unneeded overhead messages.

To guard against denial of service and masquerade attempts, all mobile communications need to be authenticated.

There are two potential ways to deal with the problem of an actively mobile user: at the data link layer or at the network layer. Data link layer mobility mechanisms change the data link address but hold the network layer address constant, while network layer mobility mechanisms change a local IP address as the user moves through different IP subnets. The local address, however, is mapped to a *mobile node address* on the user's home network using tunneling mechanisms.

IP mobility goes beyond L2TP to deal with situations where the relationship between IP address and transmission system address changes frequently during a connection.

L2TP

L2TP provides tunnels for PPP connections originating at an L2TP Access Concentrator (LAC) to one or more L2TP network servers (LNSs) (see Figure 13.9). A LAC has analog, ISDN, or other media that support PPP operation. Each tunnel runs between one LAC and one LNS, as one might suspect given that it carries the point-to-point protocol, not the point-to-multipoint protocol. Although the tunnels run only between LAC/LNS pairs, a single tunnel can have multiple PPP sessions multiplexed onto it. Extensions also allow the tunneling process to emulate multilink PPP.

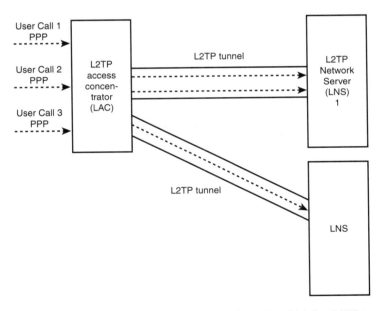

FIGURE 13.9 *Real PPP users connect to the LAC, which has L2TP tunnels to one or more LNS. Multiple users can go through the same L2TP tunnel to the same LNS.*

L2TP can be considered a proxy mechanism that allows users at arbitrary dial-in points, typically provided by ISPs, to connect to home networks as if they were connecting to a dial-in network access server physically attached to a LAN at the enterprise network. In fact, they are connecting to a virtual dial-in server. Although the user goes through an initial authentication process at the remote dial-in point, the final decision on access comes from a CHAP or PAP authentication function in the enterprise network. L2TP itself does not provide data security, only per-user authentication. Figure 13.10 shows how IPsec can be used in conjunction with L2TP to provide data authentication and/or confidentiality.

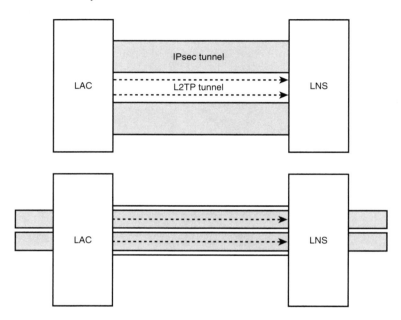

FIGURE 13.10 *Host-to-host, transport mode IPsec can run through L2TP tunnels. Alternatively, you can protect L2TP tunnels by tunneling them in IPsec between routers.*

At the ISP, a given user may or may not connect to the enterprise. The user could create a conventional PPP connection, and, for example, be assigned a dynamic IP address in the provider's address space, and communicate normally on the Internet. Alternatively, the particular user ID that the user enters may be predefined to force the user to tunnel to the LNS.

If access to the virtual dial-in service is indicated, the LAC creates an L2TP tunnel to the desired LNS if no tunnel exists. If a tunnel to the destination is already in place, the new session is multiplexed onto it with a unique call ID. The LAC then passes a connection request to the LNS, which can include the user identifier and other authentication information that the ISP's dial-in server used to authenticate the original dialup. Such information includes a CHAP username, challenge, and response, or a cleartext username and password.

Alternatively, the LNS can strip the L2TP tunneling information and pass raw PPP frames to the virtual dial-in service, and go through an enterprise-specific PPP validation using CHAP or PAP. PPP Link Control Protocol (LCP) negotiation with the LAC can pass to the LNS, or the LNS may require a new negotiation.

L2TP actually can support any protocol that runs over PPP. The focus here, however, is on IP. When the user frames pass to the LNS, the LNS goes through normal PPP address assignment, either accepting a static IP address proposed by the client, or dynamically assigning an address.

After the PPP setup to the LNS is complete, frames pass to it from the LAC as if they were locally attached to the LNS, with the caveat that framing, frame checking, and transparency bytes used on the client-to-LAC connection are not passed to the LNS. The LNS can do authorization, filtering, and so forth, as if the client were connected locally.

Because L2TP provides a PPP interface, it can provide PPP functions such as multilink. As shown in Figure 13.11, you can have multiple tunnels between a LAC and an LNS, reassembling the PPP frames at a designated LNS.

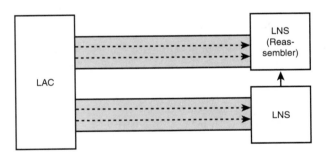

FIGURE 13.11 *Multiple L2TP tunnels can be used to provide virtual multilink PPP.*

The advantage of virtual multilink PPP is fault tolerance. If one tunnel fails, the PPP stream continues to be delivered. The disadvantage is that any multilink PPP is processor-intensive.

Mobile IP

Mobile IP is intended as an answer to one of two mobility problems, the "macro" one in which the user moves from one IP subnet to another, changing not more frequently than once per second [RFC 2002, RFC 2005]. The "micro" problem where the node moves among different points in the same subnet, as, for example, in a wireless LAN, is considered a different problem. Micro-level mobility is more appropriately solved with data link layer mobility technology.

> **Note**
>
> See the ongoing work of the IP Routing for Wireless/Mobile Hosts working group of the IETF: www.ietf.org/html.charters/mobileip-charter.html.

Mobile nodes are the core idea of mobile IP. Conventional IP hosts communicate normally with them, and are unaware of any special characteristics imposed by mobility. The home address associated with the mobile node is treated as a conventional address on the home network, and indeed can operate on its home network without being mobile.

Only when the mobile node leaves its home network do mobility mechanisms come into play. At that time, a *home agent* manages a "care-of" address associated with the mobile node. The home agent is a router with the capability to tunnel to different *foreign agents*, which are routers at the *visited network* where the mobile node is located at a given moment.

Foreign agents manage the mobile end of the tunnel back to the home agent, and can serve as default routers on the visited network.

Two kinds of advertisement need to take place in mobile IP. Agents need to become aware of one another, which they do by listening for **Agent Advertisement** messages generated by host and foreign agents.

Mobile nodes can passively listen for **Agent Advertisements**, or send **Agent Solicitation** messages. Mobile nodes use information in **Agent Advertisements** they hear to decide whether they are on their home networks or visiting a foreign network.

Mobile nodes may operate with or without mobility services. They would not use mobility services when on their home networks. On return to the home network, a mobile node deregisters from its home agent, through an exchange of **Registration Request** and **Registration Reply** messages.

The first step for a mobile node that finds itself on a foreign network is to obtain a care-of address that it is to send back to its home agent, again through an exchange of **Registration Request** and **Registration Reply** messages. These messages may move through a foreign agent. The care-of address comes from a mechanism specific to the foreign network, and might involve listening to advertisements from the foreign agent or using DHCP.

After the mobile node is registered with its home agent, the home agent sends traffic intended for the mobile node to its present foreign location. The home agent uses a tunnel to the foreign agent.

Tunnels from the home agent are needed for traffic sent to the mobile node, but not for traffic sent from the mobile node. The mobile node usually sends traffic using general IP routing services available on the foreign network, placing its home network address in the source address field of IP headers.

Using different mechanisms for sending and receiving causes significant asymmetry in the paths taken by data. **traceroute** from the mobile node and to it will show significantly different paths.

You should also ensure that routers and firewalls at the foreign network will accept packets with a source address other than one within the foreign network. Always remember that tunnels may be incompatible with firewalls using proxy mechanisms.

Mobility mechanisms let users float from one edge location to another. Other emerging mechanisms optimize the connectivity between specific edge locations and the core, selectively breaking the traditional routing model to "cut through" to the destination using Layer 2 mechanisms.

Cut-Through and Label Switching Mechanisms

The traditional methods of relaying from the edge of a network are switching and routing. Although LAN switching is often optimal within workgroups, there are other scaling issues for large "flattened" networks.

VLANs and ELANs do deal with the issues of broadcast and multicast control, but they also cause a logical flattening of the network that can complicate troubleshooting and security. Flattened networks may seem simple answers, but they may not be the right ones for large enterprises.

Switches make extensive use of ASICs, and can have very substantial forwarding bandwidth. If the network has substantial inter-VLAN communications, and VLAN-aware servers cannot meet all requirements, you need to route among the VLANs and physical LANs. The same switching bandwidth traditionally is more expensive on routers than on switches, but, also traditionally, routers are more intelligent than switches and can deal with more complex topologies.

There are two broad approaches to speeding the forwarding of packets: increasing the performance of routers, or to use some form of hybrid forwarding. As you saw in Chapter 3, a thin line separates a high-performance router with multiple processors and a hybrid forwarding method.

High-performance routing uses crossbar matrices or shared memory architectures to improve forwarding performance among input and output interface processors. They have distributed forwarding engines with high-speed forwarding information bases. Devices in this class include the Cisco 12000, Ascend GRF, Bay BN, and Juniper M40.

An assortment of new forwarding mechanisms have a common goal: establish a mapping between destination Layer 2 addresses and Layer 3 destination addresses:

- Server-based, usually NHRP. NHRP may run on a router or a true server.

- Multiprotocol over ATM.

- Peer-to-peer multilayer mapping of network layer addresses to MAC addresses or ATM VPI/VCI addresses.

- Label and tag switching.

NHRP and MPOA provide cut-through services on virtual circuit transmission systems that allow hosts and edge routers connected to NBMA media to avoid multiple routing hops and use virtual circuits to connect directly to a destination. NHRP can operate with a variety of NBMA media, while MPOA is intended, as its name would suggest, to operate over ATM. MPOA does, in fact, call upon NHRP for certain information.

Proprietary cut-through LAN switching techniques associate a destination IP address with a destination MAC address to which the switch can directly forward traffic. These are examples of the "route once, switch thereafter" paradigm.

MPLS generalizes this paradigm even further by inserting labels between Layer 2 and Layer 3 headers. Labels can have much stronger semantics than Layer 2 headers, yet have the same high-speed hardware-assisted lookup of simple, fixed fields.

Many proprietary methods, including Ascend/Cascade's IP Navigator, Cabletron's Secure Fast Virtual Networking, Cisco's Tag Switching, IBM's Aggregate Route-based IP Switching (ARIS), and Toshiba's Cell Switch Routing, are converging into the IETF MPLS work. In my experience in the working group's mailing list and meetings, there is a sincere interest in establishing an interoperable multivendor standard. Ipsilon's IP switching is the major exception, and Ipsilon is no longer an independent player, having lost its early market share and then being acquired by Nokia.

Technology	Advantages	Disadvantages
L3 switches	Well understood	May not offer functionality of more software intensive routers
Fast IP	High performance Interoperate with existing routed networks Usually support VLANs and some QoS	Vendor dependent Often medium dependent
MPOA	Standard	Requires L3-aware edge devices Potential security holes
MPLS	Emerging standard	Complex

NHRP

Server-based mechanisms rely on NHRP. The edge device uses NHRP to select the path through a Layer 2 switching core. Vendors with products in this area include 3Com, Cisco, Hughes Network Systems, IBM (a licensee of 3Com's FastIP), and Newbridge.

Many of the hybrid mechanisms depend on NHRP. If a given destination address is on the same logically independent subnets (LIS) on the source, there is a basic assumption that the two addresses do not have Layer 2 connectivity. With NBMA media, this assumption is not always true.

The local-versus-remote assumption can be superceded with a route-versus-shortcut decision.

> **Note**
>
> *See the ongoing work of the Internetworking over NBMA working group of the IETF:*
> **www.ietf.org/html.charters/ion-charter.html**

If a given destination address is on a different LIS than the source, a different basic IP assumption is that you need to pass traffic at Layer 2 to the router on your LIS, and that router will use Layer 3 mechanisms to forward packets to their ultimate destinations.

NHRP provides a way to work around the second assumption, and could also help in the first. NHRP will provide the optimal next hop to reach a given destination, which could be:

- A router on the same subnet as the source, if conventional routing to the specific destination remains more appropriate than cut-through

- The transmission system address of the actual destination, if the source and destination share a common transmission system

- A router at an egress point from the source's transmission system, if the destination is not on the same transmission system

NHRP is a client/server protocol that answers the next hop question for originating hosts or ingress routers. It is not a routing protocol, although routing information definitely can be used to populate the NHRP server's database. NHRP is most commonly used with a virtual circuit transmission system, especially ATM, in which multiple LISs map onto a common medium. In an LIS model, the underlying virtual circuits are capable of establishing a shortcut path between logical addresses in different circuits.

The basic cases of NHRP deal with host-to-host and host-to-ingress-router scenarios. Router-to-router (R2R) NHRP is a much more complex topic, beyond the scope of this chapter. The complexity of R2R NHRP comes from a need to avoid loop formation between routers, which is unlikely in the basic scenarios.

Requesting NHRP is initiated in an application-dependent manner by an end host or ingress router. One reason for an application to request a possible cut-through includes application requirements for a QoS that is more likely to be provided successfully by the Layer 2 transmission system. Alternatively, if the application knows it will participate in high-volume traffic exchange that could be made more efficiently with a direct Layer 2 connection, it may request cut-through.

A given host need not make NHRP requests for all its communications. For example, a NHRP-host's DNS client would not make an NHRP request for a simple query, but might make an NHRP request for a DNS zone transfer and would be likely to do so for an FTP session.

To examine the scalability of NHRP, you need to consider the problem in several parts: client, LIS, and domain. At the client level, whether on an end host of a router, there usually are practical limitations to the number of VCs that a given interface can handle.

Scalability in an LIS can be limited by the capabilities of the NHS. Multiple NHSs can share load, using the Server Cache Synchronization Protocol (SCSP) [RFC 2334]. Using multiple NHSs linked with SCSP also eliminates a single point of failure. Cisco deployed its proprietary Simple Server Redundancy Protocol (SSRP) before the SCSP specification was available. SSRP has functionality very similar to that of SCSP.

If the NHRP servers are populated with information from a routing protocol, the scalability of the routing protocol is a limit to the scalability of the NHRP domain. Static routing among NHRP routers can help deployability if some routers do not support NHRP, but there is the fundamental issue of the scalability of static routing for large networks.

If a router receives an NHRP request, but does not support NHRP, the router will silently discard the request. For NHRP to be widely deployable within a routing domain, most routers must support NHRP.

MPOA

Because delay and cost are associated with creating a virtual circuit, and real device interfaces can only handle finite numbers of virtual circuits, the decision to route or to switch over a Layer 2 virtual circuit transmission system is not always easy.

It is most desirable to cut through with a virtual circuit either because you know that a large amount of traffic will move between the source and destination, or because you need controlled QoS to the destination and the Layer 2 service can provide such a QoS. Both these conditions are more likely to be known to the end host than to an ingress relay, unless the host signals to the ingress device using RSVP, or the ingress device is capable of differentiating traffic.

LANE is the ATM Forum's alternative to VLANs. Where VLANs are by definition limited in range, LANE and MPOA potentially are of WAN range because their trunking is over ATM facilities. In practice, their range may be limited by speed of light considerations, but their range is definitely longer than a single campus. One of my clients, a regional telecommunications carrier, runs a single LANE environment mapped onto its inter-office ATM backbone, and operates a single LAN over distances of hundreds of kilometers.

MPOA is a major cut-through extension of LANEv2. MPOA decides whether a cut-through is appropriate based on its traffic monitoring, and then requests a cut-through next-hop address from an NHRP server.

MPOA can be considered a second-generation LANE architecture rather than just an extended set of protocols. In addition to cut-through (the mixture of Layer 2 and Layer 3 routing), MPOA supports QoS.

LANEv2/MPOA supports the IEEE 802.1p classes of service, mapping the service requirements to VCs.

Multiprotocol Label Switching: The Edge Component

MPLS is a complex yet powerful architecture for integrating Layer 2 and Layer 3 forwarding. Its basic model is to determine **path**s using Layer 3 routing or manual traffic engineering, and then associating labels with streams of data. Labels are short, fixed-length fields that can be looked at efficiently and quickly in forwarding engines. These forwarding engines can reside in "routers" or in "switches," and MPLS can operate over a wide range of Layer 2 technologies.

This architecture has significant capabilities for supporting traffic engineering, quality of service, explicit routes, and other advanced requirements. See "MPLS Requirements" in Chapter 14.

MPLS does not directly support virtual networks, and is not a simple alternative to VLANs, VPNs, LANE, and MPOA. Any of these virtual networking technologies can be mapped onto MPLS. In many cases, MPLS will be the provider technology that underlies a user VPN.

MPLS has edge and core nodes. The core nodes are called label switching routers (LSR). An edge node is a relaying device that either connects an MPLS domain to a node that is not MPLS-aware, or to a different MPLS domain. Edge nodes insert the label into packets entering the MPLS domain.

MPLS is of the form of "route first and then switch" paradigm. The route-first part defines the path, and involves distribution of path information and information about how to mark packets to be sent to certain paths. An active label is of link-local significance. It maps to streams of data in FECs.

Figure 13.12 is commonly used to illustrate topologies possible with MPLS. It is sometimes called the "fish" diagram—you can see the reference, if you squint hard and imagine, by looking at the two ISP routers as the tail of the fish.

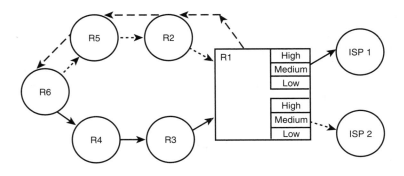

Legend

- - - - - - -▶ Path indicated by interior routing
◀ - - - - Flow of FED information
─────▶ Optimal end-to-end path

FIGURE 13.12 *MPLS can enforce special routing paths that ordinary interior routing does not understand.*

The purpose of the fish diagram is to show that MPLS gives R1 the capability to tell other routers how they should send to it, based on its unique knowledge of utilization and policies for sending to the ISP routers. In this figure, we can also assume that R1 is aware of bandwidth and utilization inside the enterprise, and constructs a path that will give the desired quality of service. Ordinary interior routing, which is only aware of bandwidth, not congestion, cannot define such a path. Although routing methods in development do advertise utilization information, an alternative would be for routers to report link utilization only to R1, which would have special path and FEC software.

Note

Labels may be stacked to form MPLS tunnels. For example, traffic might enter a network with an MPLS label associated with an external BGP connection. The enterprise, however, pushes its own MPLS label on top of the external label, and strips the internal label only when the traffic leaves the enterprise on a different eBGP router. Only one label is actively used in forwarding at any given time.

Streams may be associated with simple Layer 3 destination routes, with route aggregates, with Layer 4 flows, or with flow aggregates. Information about FEC, and the labels to be mapped to FECs, is distributed to Layer 2 or Layer 3 forwarding devices using a label distribution protocol or a function piggybacked onto a routing protocol.

In the specific MPLS context, a FEC is the set of Layer 3 packets that can safely be mapped to the same label. FECs are global to the routing domain, whereas the labels to which are mapped are link-local, much as an ATM VPI/VCI is local to each ATM circuit, and remapped at each switch. There may be reasons, however, for the traffic of a single FEC to be mapped to more than one label. See "Merging" in Chapter 14.

ARP Variants

A variation on the ARP mechanism forces end hosts to ARP whenever sending any packet. They ARP not to the traditional default gateway, but to their own address. Host configuration changes, therefore, are necessary. If the hosts obtain addresses and other parameters from DHCP, and you have the capability to manipulate DHCP's response so that the host address also becomes the default gateway address, manual changes will be minimized.

In such schemes, used on Cabletron and DEC hybrid relays, the switch intercepts the ARP request. These techniques assume a microsegmented environment, so the switch can handle the ARP broadcast before it propagates beyond a single port.

The ingress switch hears all ARP requests, and returns:

- A host MAC address if the destination is on the same subnet

- The MAC address of an ingress router if the destination is on a different subnet and no cut-through is defined,

- A host MAC address if the destination is on another subnet but a cut-through is in place

This model assumes a flattened network; there needs to be considerable intelligence to avoid excessive broadcasts. SAPs, for example, should go only to server ports. The switch knows that it should not propagate ARP requests to other subnets. Cabletron uses an OSPF-like protocol called VLAN Link State Protocol (VLSP) to distribute Layer 3 information to switches.

Looking Ahead

Chapter 14 shows the complement to the edge mechanisms described in this chapter. It deals with the high-performance routing and switching techniques optimized for efficient transfer of traffic categorized at the edge.

New Methods in the Enterprise Core

"Any sufficiently advanced technology is indistinguishable from magic."
—Arthur C. Clarke

"Any sufficiently advanced magic is indistinguishable from technology."
—Seen on a button worn by a contemporary occult practitioner

"Any sufficiently advanced technology is indistinguishable from a rigged demo."
—Muttered at a large networking trade show

This book started with the question, "What is the problem you are trying to solve?" The initial focus of that question was aimed at the application requirements that justify the network. In this chapter, we conclude by looking at requirements inside the network, so that we can solve problems encountered only as networks grow and present new issues. Some of these issues include:

- Effective use of high-capacity resources

- QoS

- Multicasting

- Scalability

- Routing implications of network address translation (NAT), proxies, and other functions that violate the IP end-to-end significance assumption

- Security of routing systems

- Flow- and application-based routing

- Policy- and constraint-based routing

QoS, CoS, ToS…Do I Know Them When I See Them?

Discussions at the 1998 IAB routing workshop concluded that several related terms are commonly used in imprecise ways. They attempted to clarify the definitions.

Type of Service (ToS) makes decisions based on bits in the Type of Service field of the IP header.

Class of service (CoS) is based on service contracts. These contracts may be enabled by mechanisms including prioritization and queuing, and the use of load-shared or inverse-multiplexed paths.

Quality of service (QoS) is a more formal process of managing performance constraints, and includes routing the resource request, finding a path that meets the constraints, and routing traffic over that path.

The workshop concluded, however, that there is no clear distinction between ToS and QoS, other than generally stating ToS is "relative," whereas QoS is "absolute." The current concept of differentiated services was considered ToS++.

They also discussed a concept more general than either CoS or QoS: "constraint-based routing a concept more general than either CoS or QoS: "constraint-based routing." Constraint-based routing deals with both traffic engineering and routing policies, based on the characteristics of specific data streams.

Chapter 13 deals with edge technologies that prepare traffic for transmission over a high-performance core. Do understand that core technologies, of the performance of the new methods discussed here, are largely intended for service providers and large enterprises. If you have a data network with several sites and everyday traffic among them, you may not need any of these methods. Chapter 6 was written with the small network in mind. The techniques discussed in Part IV serve the majority of enterprises very well.

Yet, you should understand what your service provider is doing with your bits, and you should be prepared if you work for a large enterprise that grows to need some of these techniques.

Foundations of Emerging Core Technologies

To understand the technologies that are emerging for core routing and switching applications, you need to understand a number of concepts that may seem new. In many cases, these concepts are formalizations of concepts you have used for some time.

Constraint-Based Routing

Traditional route lookup follows this model:

Does a path exist to the destination?

If there is more than one path, are they of equal cost?

If so, load-balance

Otherwise, use the cheapest path

Else use the default route

In other words, if you can find a path, use it. Constraint-based routing, however, introduces additional considerations as to whether you can use a route that you discover.

The bypass VPN in Chapter 7 has one requirement for constraint-based routing. Consider what happens if there is a failure in the topology (see Figure 14.1).

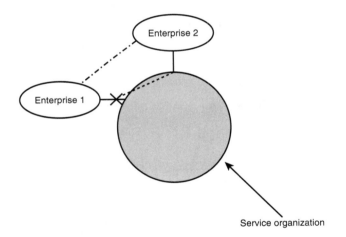

Service organization

Legend

——————— Connectivity to service organization

·—·—·—·— Dedicated or other links with service level agreement, operated by bilateral agreements between enterprises

- - - - - - - - - Tunnels or on-demand facilities operated by service organization

FIGURE 14.1 *Without constraints, a failure in Enterprise 1 causes its traffic to try to flow through its direct competitor.*

Route filtering can prevent a router from being aware of certain routes due to an administrative policy. See "Summarization and Pseudo-Summarization in RIP and IGRP" in Chapter 12 for examples of using route filtering for solving performance problems. Route filtering certainly could be used if there were an administrative policy that a certain source could not send to a certain destination.

Formally, constraints can be specified as a sequence of ordered pairs. The resource class defines a relationship between the class and the trunk; the affinity is a binary variable that states whether to include or exclude the traffic. The affinity also can have a "don't care" value.

Constraints can be an input to dynamic routing processes, especially core routing processes that make decisions using marking done at the edge. There are two basic strategies:

- Opt-out or dense mode, where it is the exceptional class that should be excluded. Before the path determination process, remove (that is, prune) all resources that do belong to the class.

- Opt-in or sparse mode, where it is the exceptional class that should be included. Before the path determination process, remove (that is, prune) all resources that do not belong to the class.

Traffic engineering classes are a major emerging application for constraint-based routing.

Trunks

Trunks are not only one of the defining characteristics of elephants, but also a key concept in network scalability. A trunk is an aggregate of forwarding equivalence classes (FEC). In current thinking, a trunk is an aggregate of unidirectional data that is different than the path over which it travels. This is a revision of the definitions introduced with multiplexing in Chapter 9.

A trunk has an ingress and egress point into the transmission system, a forwarding equivalence class that maps onto it, and a set of attributes. Some of these attributes are interrelated. Usage parameter control in ATM, for example, covers traffic and policing attributes.

Attributes include

- Traffic parameter attributes. These are familiar parameters such as average rate, peak rate, token bucket size, and so on.

- Generic Path selection and maintenance attributes. These are rules for initial path selection and maintenance. Paths can be created manually or automatically. Basic automatic path selection uses a dynamic routing protocol, but more advanced selection involves considering constraints such as congestion avoidance.

- Priority attribute. When the network status changes and it is necessary to reroute trunks, in which order will they be selected for new paths?

- Preemption attribute. Closely related to priority, this attribute defines whether this trunk preempts another trunk if resources are not available for both. Preemption can be associated with high priorities of differentiated service.

  There are four potential preemptor modes, some of which are mutually exclusive. A trunk may be *preemptor enabled*, or authorized to preempt lower-priority trunks, or it can be a *non-preemptor*. A trunk may be *preemptible* or *non-preemptible*. An interesting aspect of preemption comes from emerging work where the "traditional" optical layer protection in optical networks, such as the SONET protection switching discussed in Chapter 2, evolves to protection schemes on very-high-speed routers [St. Arnaud, 1998].

- Resilience attribute. In the event of a failure, should the trunk be rerouted? Even if this is a critical trunk, formal rerouting may not be needed if, for example, the trunk runs over an inverse multiplexed multilink medium.

  Basic resilience says the trunk should be rerouted in the event of a failure. More advanced resilience can specify how and where the trunk is rerouted. The advanced concept isn't that strange; it can be as simple as the quasi-static routing discussed in Chapter 11.

- Policing attribute. What should be done if the workload presented by a trunk exceeds the service contract of the trunk? Actions include rate limiting, buffering, dropping, tagging, or choosing to take no action.

- Adaptivity attribute. Is the path subject to re-adaptation? In other words, can it be rerouted when conditions change, or is it "nailed" or "pinned" to a specific path? The tradeoff in adaptivity is that reacting too fast threatens stability, but reacting too late leads to suboptimal resource use.

  Re-optimization is similar to, but different than, resilience. The capability to re-optimize implies resilience, but the reverse is not necessarily true.

Administratively specified explicit paths are created either by operator interaction or a non–real-time path computation process that automatically configures paths. Paths may be *completely specified* if all intermediate points in the path are specified, or *partially specified* if only some of the intermediate points are defined and a dynamic routing protocol is expected to complete the path.

Because manually specified paths can contain errors, and paths computed in non–real-time batch software may not know the most recent network topology, loop detection needs to be considered. Never underestimate the power of human error.

Ideally, it should be possible to indicate whether an explicit path is *mandatory* or *non-mandatory*. Mandatory paths must be used for the particular requirement. If the resources for the specified path are not available, the path must not be set up, and the traffic should not go to a default route. Mandatory paths are implicitly "pinned" and cannot be changed without being deleted and re-created.

A challenge in creating explicit paths is finding a way to load share across multiple paths. Traffic engineering ideally should have some way to specify how to distribute traffic of the same class over multiple links. Simple schemes such as round-robin and per-destination load balancing tend to be undesirable because they do not consider nonadjacent congestion, and may cause unbalanced load sharing or out-of-sequence delivery.

In MPLS, a trunk is distinct from a label-switched path. A trunk can go through one or more label-switched paths (LSPs). Another way of looking at this concept is to think of a trunk as a routable object, that is, routed over paths. As a routable object, a trunk can be moved onto different paths as operational requirements dictate.

Usable trunks have practical requirements. Because they form a key part of capacity, decent accounting and performance information is necessary.

Although trunks are defined as unidirectional, it is often desirable to couple a trunk in each direction, forming a *bidirectional traffic trunk* (BTT). One trunk is the *forward trunk* to a destination, whereas the *backward trunk* carries traffic back to the source from that destination.

Think of asymmetrical routing and the challenges it creates in troubleshooting. BTTs may be either topologically symmetric, in that both trunks go through the same physical path but in different directions, or topologically asymmetric, where the two directions go over different physical paths but are still created and destroyed as a single unit.

Data and Control Models for Bindings

In the emerging edge and core techniques, there are a variety of requirements to bind edge or end-to-end information with local identifiers, including

- Host addresses to multicast groups

- Multicast groups to trees

- MPLS labels to forwarding equivalence classes

When recognition of a particular data pattern causes bindings to be established or destroyed, the binding is *data-driven*. When control messages cause bindings to be established or destroyed, the binding is *control-driven*.

Both strategies have advantages and disadvantages. Data-driven binding is triggered by real requirements. It does not introduce a new protocol, although there must be a means, frequently manual, of establishing the triggering criteria.

Data-driven approaches have interesting timing issues. Do you wait to see several packets before creating the binding, wanting to make sure that a pattern rather than a single event exists? Or do you trigger on the first recognizable packet? Like most architecture questions, the answer is "it depends."

Dial-on-demand routing, for example, has a mandatory need to trigger on the first packet. Cut-through schemes such as MPOA are optional, and cutting through incurs overhead, so MPOA waits to trigger a binding to a cut-through path after it sees what it considers a significant volume of traffic.

In some platforms, binding is done in a slower management path, whereas forwarding is done in a hardware-assisted high-speed path. As a consequence, data-driven binding may lag behind data transmission.

There is also the question of when to tear down a binding. As described in Chapter 6 of *Designing Addressing Architectures for Routing and Switching* [Berkowitz, 1998a], the issue of bindings from NAT outside port numbers is a complex one when UDP is the transport protocol. Where you can explicitly tear down TCP bindings when you see a TCP disconnect, UDP bindings generally depend on an inactivity timer. Values of this timer are often as long as 24 hours, so, for a busy UDP-based server, you may need extra outside addresses simply to make available more ports than the maximum 62 K for each IP address.

Control-driven methods introduce the complexity and overhead of control protocols, but they are much more predictable than data-driven methods. Because the bindings generally are precomputed and defined in control messages, the problem of binding lagging behind data transfer is much more rare than with data-driven methods.

Merging

Merging of traffic flows into aggregates, and possibly deaggregating them, can be a major positive capability for scaling. The notion of merging was introduced with RSVP. A considerable range of merge techniques are used in evolving core techniques, both at Layer 2 and Layer 3.

Some general terminology will help. A *merge point* is a node in which multiple streams and paths are combined into a single stream over a single path. The *aggregate stream* can be denoted with a label. This label could be an MPLS label, an ATM Virtual Path Identifier, a stack of MPLS labels, and so forth.

In an ATM environment, a *VC merge* combines multiple VCs into a single VCs. In a VC merge, the individual VCs lose their identity. Alternatively, multiple VPs may merge into a single VP, subject to the constraint that the individual VCIs in all merged VPs must be unique among the VPs. A VP merge thus can be deaggregated back into individual streams, whereas a VC merge cannot.

Traffic Engineering

Although the leading edge of work on traffic engineering goes on in service providers, it is happening there because they cannot survive without it. As enterprises grow, however, and have critical performance requirements, traffic engineering becomes important there as well.

Traffic engineering has both traffic-oriented and resource-oriented aspects. Traffic-oriented goals focus on QoS aspects: throughput, loss, latency, and so on. Resource-oriented goals focus on efficiently using the resource of the network, preventing congestion on one extreme and underutilization on the other.

Resource models generally focus on bandwidth.

Traffic engineering, to be scalable, considers trunks that carry multiple data streams.

So what is traffic engineering? In practice, it is a systematic approach to overcoming the limitations of existing interior routing protocols. Principal among these limitations is the computation of a best path based on administratively defined interface metrics, but that does not consider load and congestion in a meaningful way. Defined in the context of ISPs but equally relevant to enterprises, "traffic engineering can be viewed as assistance to the routing infrastructure that provides additional information in routing traffic along specific paths, with the end goal of more efficient utilization of networking resources" [RFC 2430]. Further, it is "performed by directing trunks along explicit paths within the ISP's topology."

O'Dell *et al.* define traffic engineering as "concerned with performance optimization of operational networks. Specifically, the goal of Traffic Engineering is to facilitate efficient and reliable network operations, and at the same time optimize the utilization of network resources" [O'Dell, 1998].

One useful abstraction, illustrated in Figure 14.2, is to think of two components in a network: traffic and the resources that carry traffic. There may be separate optimizations for resources and for traffic, and conventional IP routing is inadequate for some of these.

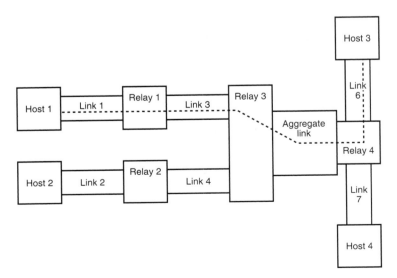

FIGURE 14.2 *The dashed line is a traffic flow that goes through link and relay resources.*

Existing IGPs do not consider traffic. OSPF and IS-IS simply consider routes as the sum of administratively set interface costs. EIGRP, in principle, can consider load, but IGRP and EIGRP can sense load only on directly connected links. The use of load as part of the IGRP/Enhanced IGRP metric leads to oscillation among links and often suboptimal routing past the next hop. By default, load is not considered in the metric, and if you want to use it, you need to understand the implications of doing so. I have never seen it used successfully.

As a result of incomplete information, congestion can occur when the routing system either routes a traffic stream through a medium or router interface that has insufficient available bandwidth, or an excessive number of streams run through the same interface or medium.

Load sharing can help in the first type of congestion, but the second is an inherent limitation of routing that makes local, not global, decisions.

Overlay models are current practice in large provider and enterprise networks. An overlay network (see Figure 14.3) superimposes IP structure on top of an intelligent Layer 2 network that has good performance control capabilities, such as those found in ATM and Frame Relay. From the perspective of the IP routing protocols in the overlay, the underlying performance-controlled virtual circuits are physical circuits. In reality, separate optimizations are possible with the virtual circuits.

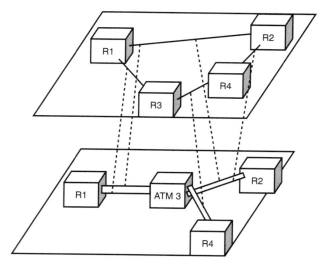

FIGURE 14.3 *Overlay models map from Layer 3 to Layer 2.*

Much of traffic engineering in the overlay model is done at Layer 2, using techniques such as manually configured VC paths, call admission control, traffic shaping and policing, and so on.

Formal definition of trunks is an alternative to overlay models. Trunking is a key concept in the evolution of MPLS, but it conceptually can be applied to any infrastructure. If you are manually optimizing traffic over a small set of high-bandwidth resources (for example, ATM), in an enterprise, the ideas of formal trunking may help you plan.

A graph $G=(R,(P,C))$ of a trunk model consists of a set of routing nodes R and a set of paths P among them, with a sent of constraints C. You may want to think of them hierarchically, in terms of stacked identifiers, an explicit concept in MPLS.

The base network topology can be modeled as a graph $G=(V,E,C)$, in which V is the set of nodes, E is the set of media, and C is a set of constraints for V and E. An object <v,w> is part of the base network topology if v and w are directly connected in G under the restrictions of the constraints.

$H=(U,F,d)$ is the graph of the overlay network, or, in MPLS terms, the *induced graph*, and is a subset of the base network topology G. U is a set of relays that are the endpoint of at least one path.

Whenever resources are not guaranteed for traffic, there is both transient and long-term congestion. Two kinds of long-term congestion exist in a traffic-engineered environment. The first kind is straightforward: inadequate bandwidth to meet the offered load. The second is more complex.

In the second case, the traffic is not optimally mapped onto the available resources. The network could carry the traffic without congestion if the mapping were proper.

Obviously, adding capacity is the most straightforward way to deal with the first kind of congestion. Congestion avoidance and reaction techniques also are relevant, including traffic policing and rate limiting, traffic prioritization and buffering, admission control for connection- and flow-oriented traffic, and so forth.

Traffic engineering techniques are the fundamental method of dealing with the second kind of congestion. Effective load balancing techniques often can deal with these problems, but there may be legal, financial, or other nontechnical policies that must be accommodated by the solution.

OSPF Enhancements

OSPF is the most widely used standard, scalable IGP. Nevertheless, it has limitations, but work continues to enhance it. The alternatives to OSPF for scalable interior routing are IS-IS and EIGRP. IS-IS has been a niche protocol, but active efforts are underway to extend it to make it more of an alternative to OSPF. EIGRP has excellent performance and widespread availability, but has the potential problem of being Cisco proprietary.

The opaque LSA is a fundamental part of many of the new extensions to OSPF, because this LSA offers a means of extending OSPF, now that the limited number of options flags have been exhausted. IS-IS advocates claim their solution is more extensible than OSPF, whereas OSPF partisans point to the greater efficiency possible in OSPF's emphasis on 32-bit-aligned messages that emphasize fixed-length fields.

The Opaque LSA

As both OSPF and general networking have evolved, so have requirements for them. One requirement is distributing "opaque" information to functions that share connectivity through the IP routing mechanism, but are not pure IP routers. They could be routers for workgroup protocols such as Novell or Apple. They could provide network management information such as load on non-local links. They could provide mappings to Layer 2 services.

Because there was an assortment of needs, not all of which were predictable, the OSPF Opaque LSA was created as a general means of extensibility. There are three types of opaque LSA, which differ in the scope of their flooding:

- LSA type 9: link-local. Stays on its local subnet, such as OSPF hellos.

- LSA type 10: area-local. Stays within the area in which it is created, such as a type 2 network LSA.

- LSA type 11: flooded throughout the OSPF routing domain, following the rules established for type 5 external LSAs. LSA-11's are not flooded into stub areas.

Information in opaque LSAs is carried as a set, or a tree, of type-length-value (TLV) triplets.

Traffic Engineering with OSPF

With the availability of the opaque LSA, there is a mechanism for sending information usable in traffic engineering. Equivalent mechanisms have been defined for IS-IS.

Opaque LSAs of area scope are used to carry traffic engineering information of two types: router address and link. These are top-level TLVs, and may contain a substantial number of subordinate TLVs.

The Router Address TLV contains a stable IP address of the router that generates the LSA. Such an address will be available if any of the interfaces of the router are reachable. Think of it as mandatory use of the equivalent of a loopback interface or circuitless interface to generate an OSPF router ID.

Link TLVs describe single links between a local and a remote interface. When the link type is point-to-point, the link ID is the router ID of the neighbor. When the link is multiaccess, the link ID is the address of the designated router (DR) for the link.

A link is further identified by a local interface IP address on the originating router and a remote interface IP address on the neighbor. Links belong to one or more resource classes, also called *colors*.

In the context of traffic engineering, the link metric may differ from the standard OSPF metric. Traffic engineering information about links tells, in the direction from the LSA originator to its neighbor:

- The *maximum bandwidth* value states the true link capacity, or the maximum bandwidth that possibly can be used.

- Maximum reservable bandwidth, which may be greater than the maximum bandwidth if there is a policy of oversubscription.

- Currently *unreserved bandwidth* at each diffserv priority level. At each priority level, the value will be less than or equal to the reservable bandwidth.

OSPFv6

"OSPF version 6" is the name for a new version of OSPF intended to handle IPv6 addresses. I put the term in quotes, because the actual internal protocol version number in the OSPF packets is version 3, to differentiate it from the current version 2. Of course, version 2 has had several versions of its own, as the standards have progressed.

Whatever we number it, OSPFv6 offers some improvements over the widely deployed OSPF. OSPFv2 implementations have had some confusion about secondary addresses, and nodes that can communicate over a common medium but are not in the same subnet. OSPFv6 changes its model from "subnet" to "link," a more general idea.

In general, the design goal of OSPFv6 was to make it much more independent of the network layer addressing in use. Wherever possible, OSPF information is defined in terms of topological relationships among router identifiers, rather than in terms of explicit addresses.

The opaque LSA, now part of OSPFv2, has three flavors of different scope. The idea of scope has been generalized for all LSAs, so that they can be of link-local, area, or AS scope. IPv6 addresses in the global or site-local space must be used as the endpoint of virtual links.

Another extension is the capability to support multiple OSPF routing domains on a single link, as, for example, might be encountered at an interprovider or extranet exchange point. There are also cases where it is convenient to have a link belong to more than one area.

Because OSPFv6 assumes it will run over IPv6, and IPv6 can routinely use the IPsec Authentication Header, authentication functions have been removed from OSPF packets. In addition, the IPv6 checksum covers the entire packet and IPv6 pseudo-header, so an explicit OSPF checksum is no longer needed.

The options field has been extended to 24 bits, and new options have been defined. A new R-bit option allows a router to participate in path determination in the OSPF domain, but not necessarily to forward traffic. There is an assortment of applications for this, such as a router capable of forwarding only IPv4 packets. Another new option bit defines IPv6 capability.

IS-IS' New Trends: ISNT?

IS-IS has been a niche protocol, with a small set of very strong advocates. It does seem to be undergoing a resurgence of interest. Router vendors have, for some time, been implementing IS-IS extensions for things not covered in the original ISO specification. These include header authentication [Li, 1999].

An IS-IS router is either level 1, which has knowledge of destinations in only its own area, or level 2, which has knowledge of other areas. There is no explicit backbone area in OSPF, but the set of level 2 routers forms the backbone.

In the present model of IS-IS, nonzero areas behave much as OSPF stub areas. If there are multiple level 2 routers, the IS-IS equivalent of ABRs, routers inside an area do not have information on inter-area routes that would let them pick the optimal level 2 router to leave the area.

An extension to the model [Przygienda, 1999] allows external information to be selectively injected into non-backbone areas, so L1 routers can make more intelligent selections of the egress router.

People who prefer IS-IS to OSPF point to its much more intelligent backbone restoration model, its extensibility, and the lesser amount of state it keeps on neighbors. OSPF is much more "picky" in establishing neighbor relationships, requiring timers to be identical. IS-IS hello and dead timers are independent, which allows some medium-specific tuning.

By using unicast ACKs, OSPF generates more traffic than IS-IS. OSPF also has more of an LSA refresh overhead than IS-IS LSP refreshes.

Limitations of IS-IS, aside from its more limited availability, included more coarse-grained metrics than OSPF, a limit of 255 pseudonodes in an area, and limited LSP space. The basic protocol does a two-way, not three-way, handshake when establishing adjacencies.

IS-IS was originally specified to run directly over the data link layer. A current implementation technique [Bansal, 1999] enables IS-IS to run on top of IP, which makes it more medium-independent. The original IS-IS relied on Layer 2 checksums for error detection, and this has proven to be an unwise decision. Checksums and authentication mechanisms have been developed.

Not surprisingly, given the ISP interest in IS-IS, traffic engineering [Li, 1999] and optimized multipath [Villamizor, 1999] features have been developed for IS-IS as well as for OSPF.

Foundations of Multicast Routing

A substantial amount of theoretical background underlies multicasting, including a description of the fundamental model [Deering, 1999]. Although the focus here is on IP multicasting, there are certainly Layer 2 multicast technologies on both broadcast-capable LAN media, and simulated on ATM networks [RFC 2022]. Transport protocols such as RTP [RFC 1889] can establish multicasting relationships, and an assortment of application layer protocols do their own multicasting.

An increasing number of applications are evolving for multicasting. They include fault-tolerant computing where a packet is sent to a group of servers, video and audio distribution as in distance learning and on-demand entertainment, stock quotation services, and so forth.

The 1998 IAB workshop on routing [IAB 1998] observed that there are a wide range of multicast applications, which may differ in

- number of sources

- number of receivers

- amount of data

- amount of data in a burst, and length of quiet periods

- number of groups utilized per application or per group of cooperating applications

- amount of time during which the group exists

- topological distance between members of the group

- volatility of membership

Most current multicasting is data-driven, a model which may or may not fit critical or large-scale applications. Multicast models are very much the subject of research. The workshop suggested that current multicast protocols as well as an unpublished model called Express (developed by Holbrook and Cheriton) should be evaluated, as well as the following basic mechanisms:

- Registering with the core or the RP (Rendezvous Point)

- Having the ID of the group include the core, and having joins specify the core

- Having the ID of the group include the core, and having joins and data specify both

- Sending data via unicast to all members

- Sending data via unicast transport to the RP

Multicasting on the scale of the Internet is still a research topic, as is reliable multicasting in which the sender is responsible for delivery.

Several multicast routing protocols are in current use, with new techniques continuing to evolve.

Some general considerations apply to any multicast routing mechanism. With the exception of DVMRP, the multicast protocols rely on an underlying unicast routing protocol. There will thus be different RIBs and corresponding FIBs for the unicast and multicast views of the world.

Multicast Tree Types

Multicast technology is very "green," in that it depends on trees. There are two fundamental kinds of trees in multicasting, *source trees* and *shared trees*, with variants. Source trees have a separate tree for each source in a multicast group. Shared trees use a single tree for all sources.

Not all multicast models solve the same problem. Wall [Wall 80] divided multicast routing into two categories, *minimum delay* and *minimum cost*. A minimum delay model minimizes the metric to the destination, potentially incurring greater overhead and sending multiple copies of the same packet. Minimum cost models optimize the use of bandwidth resources.

For *closed* multicast groups, where all senders and receivers belong to the group, a single tree minimizes cost. Minimizing delay requires several source-routed trees, one per sender.

Open multicast groups are more complex but are closer to most real-world applications, where a server is the sender to multiple receivers, but the server is not itself part of the group because it does not need to receive its own traffic. Open models require per-source trees, losing the advantage of overhead reduced vis-a-vis minimum delay. Shared tree models reduce this overhead but may still demand more overhead—more state—in routers.

In a shared tree environment, in principle, multicast traffic goes over the same tree. There may be some pruning, but fundamentally the routers need to know about all multicast groups. More advanced versions of shared tree algorithms keep a tree for each source.

In source trees, a separate tree is maintained for each multicast group. The routing is more complex to track because a greater number of trees need to be maintained, but source trees also have the potential of reducing traffic and computational load.

Core trees are an advanced tree model with one tree for each multicast group, rather than one tree for the source in each multicast group.

Sparse and Dense Models

Multicast applications tend to have two flavors: applications where most endpoints participate in a multicast group, and applications where participation is the exception rather than the rule. The first case is called the *dense* model (see Figure 14.4), and the latter the *sparse* (see Figure 14.5).

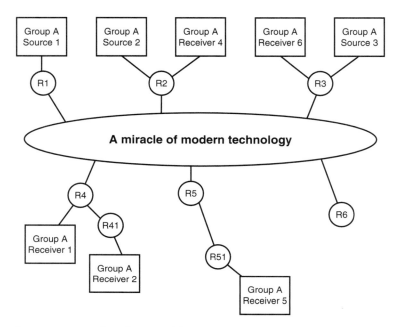

FIGURE 14.4   *In a dense model, most routers and hosts are interested in the multicast traffic. Even though router R5 does not have end hosts interested in Group A, R5 needs to know about the traffic to pass it to R51.*

Dense models are also called *opt-out*. Dave Meyer likens these to radio broadcasts, in contrast to sparse models, which are more like pay-per-view [Meyer, 1998].

Sparse, or *opt-in*, models usually have a *core* or *RP* where endpoint traffic meets to establish the tree. Depending on the multicast protocol, there can be one RP per (source, group) or one per (group). Source tree models generally assume sparseness. An RP reduces traffic, but can also be a single point of failure. You could have a sparse shared tree where all multicast groups use the same RP, or you could have an RP for each group.

Dense mode historically assumed bandwidth was inexpensive, where the newer sparse mode strategies try hard to limit bandwidth use at the cost of additional CPU resources. Dense mode implementations include Distance Vector Multicast Routing Protocol (DVMRP) and Protocol Independent Multicast-Sparse Mode (PIM-SM).

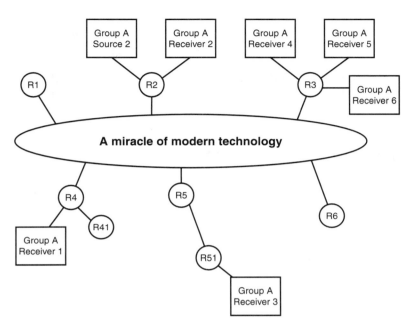

FIGURE 14.5 *In a sparse model, most routers and hosts are not interested in the multi-cast traffic. The cluster of receivers attached to R3 does not detract from the overall topology being sparse.*

Multicast Algorithms

There are several basic ways to implement multicasting. In a flat network, flooding is the natural approach, with the natural limits on scalability. IGMP snooping and CGMP, as discussed in Chapter 13, do help it scale, but more intelligent algorithms allow much more scalability.

Basic Spanning Trees

The next most basic approach is a spanning tree (see Figure 14.6), specifically a *shared tree* used by all routers that do multicasting. In such a tree, there is only one active multicast path between any two routers. The traffic of all multicast groups flows over this path.

When a router in this tree receives a multicast packet, it forwards it out all interfaces in the spanning tree other than the one on which the packet was received. Spanning trees are loop-free and comprehensive, but not ideally scal-able. A single shared tree does not limit traffic. As in a Layer 2 spanning tree, the paths selected can be suboptimal.

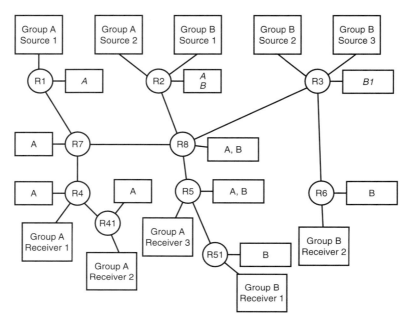

FIGURE 14.6 *In a simple shared tree, all routers must be aware of all groups, even though only edge routers R2 and R5 have both groups connected to them.*

A refinement would keep more than one spanning tree, as shown in Figure 14.7. In this variant, the routers need to maintain state on all routers and hosts in any spanning tree where they have one or more members. Depending on the specific multicast routing protocols, routers that are only connected to sources may or may not need to keep detailed state.

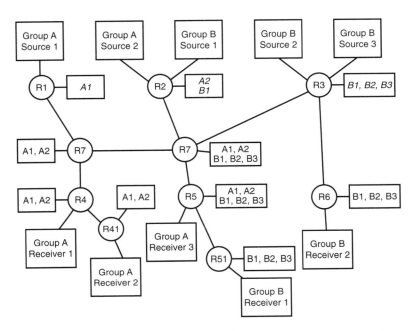

FIGURE 14.7 *Routers need to keep complete state on multicast Group A or multicast Group B if they have any members in the group. Complete state includes knowledge of sources.*

Reverse Path Broadcasting and Truncated Reverse Path Broadcasting

The next refinement is to build a *source tree*, or a separate tree for each multicast (source, group) pair. For Figure 14.7, the trees would have the membership shown in Table 14.1.

TABLE 14.1   SOURCE TREE MEMBERSHIP

Group	Source	Member routers
A	1	R1, R4, R7, R41, R2, R8, R5
	2	R4, R7, R41, R2, R8, R5
B	1	R2, R8, R5, R51, R3, R6
	2	R2, R8, R5, R51, R3, R6
	3	R2, R8, R5, R51, R3, R6

Basic source trees are built with a Reverse Path Broadcasting (RPB) algorithm. This algorithm keeps track of the routing costs to the source of each pair in which it participates. When a RPB router receives a packet on a medium that is the next hop for the lowest-metric path back to the source, the router sends the packets out all its interfaces other than the one on which it received the packet. The interface associated with the lowest-cost path is called the *parent link*, and the interfaces out which the multicast packets are forwarded are *child links.*

A parent router can reduce traffic if it has knowledge of the next-hop child router. If a packet to be forwarded to the child arrives on an interface that the child does not consider lowest-cost, the parent does not forward the packet. The parent knows this information from unicast routing information. When link state routing is used, and the parent has the same topological database as the child (that is, both parent and child are in the same area), the parent can make this determination easily.

If the routing domain runs a distance vector protocol, the parent can learn the child's view by listening to routing updates that either advertise the previous hop, or contain poison reverse information for links other than the lowest cost.

Reverse path broadcasting is one of those things that is reasonable. It is reasonably easy to implement, and imposes a reasonable amount of overhead. It can maintain soft state to know when to stop forwarding, relieving leaf routers of the requirement to send explicit commands to stop receiving data. It finds the shortest path from the source to the destinations. Because it uses separate trees for each source/multicast group pair, the trees tend to distribute over different paths and have better network utilization than a single path.

RPB, however, does not consider multicast group membership when building its distribution trees. As a consequence, it is entirely likely that subnets with no members in a group will still receive traffic from that group, unless supplementary methods such as IGMP snooping or CGMP can block unwanted multicasts at Layer 2.

Truncated Reverse Path Broadcasting (TRPB) improves on RPB by intelligently using IGMP information to prevent traffic for a group from being received on subnets with no members in the group. The term "truncation" means that leaf networks are truncated from the source tree.

TRPB is still limited in its capability to control traffic, because it does not consider group membership when building the branches of the tree, only when sending to leaf networks. This can lead to unneeded traffic on inter-router links.

Reverse Path Multicasting

The next level of improvement on RPB and TRPB, Reverse Path Multicasting (RPM), considers whether branches of the tree that run between routers lead to leaves that have members of a multicast group. RPM builds source-rooted delivery trees that contain only subnets with group members, and routers and inter-router branch links that lead to subnets with group members (see Figure 14.8).

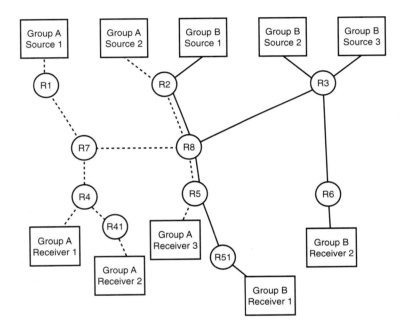

FIGURE 14.8 *RPM builds source-routed trees with minimum replication.*

Each leaf router in the initial tree receives a packet from the source/group flow. If the leaf router does have a connected subnet with a member of the group, which it learned about from an IGMP message sent by that member, the leaf router sends the multicast packet to the group member.

If there is no group member on any of the leaf router's subnets, the leaf router sends a prune back to its previous-hop upstream router. This message tells the upstream message not to forward traffic for this group to the leaf router.

The upstream router, in turn, stores the prune. If the upstream router has no locally attached subnets with group members, and it has received prune messages from all its child routers, it sends a prune message to the next upstream router. Eventually, in this "opt-out" or dense model, the tree prunes back to the minimum tree needed to distribute multicast packets to all group members.

Because membership changes over time, the RPM algorithm uses a soft-state model in which routers periodically delete their prune lists, and allow a new burst of prune messages to flow to the leaves. Based on membership at the time of the new burst, the tree is adjusted.

There are still scaling issues with this approach. The soft state approach means that there will be periodic traffic bursts that may result in no change to the topology. Each router also has to maintain state for each group and each source within each group.

Because routers that do not have child group members still incur the overhead of prune messages for each group, groups that may be sparsely distributed, the RPM technique does not scale.

Core-Based Trees

Core-based trees (CBTs) are an alternative to source-rooted trees. The CBT algorithm builds a single tree shared by all members of a group. The same tree is used for sending and receiving, which might be especially attractive for inherently symmetrical applications such as videoconferencing.

CBT is more scalable than RPM, reducing the amount of state held by routers to the level of groups, rather than (source, group). It also reduces bandwidth by not requiring continuing multicast reports.

Because all traffic concentrates on the core, there may be congestion as traffic approaches and enters the core. Using a shared tree also may lead to some suboptimal routing.

The shared core may consist of one or more routers. As shown in Figure 14.9, traffic is forwarded across a backbone that may include core routers and non-core routers.

As befits a sparse model, each receiver must send an explicit join toward the core. A receiver can send the join to the address of any router in the core. The join is sent as a unicast, and, as it traverses intermediate routers on the way to the core, those routers mark the interface on which they received the packet as part of the tree.

Senders, which may or may not be group members, send unicasts to the core. When these packets reach the core, the core routers multicast the packets onto all outgoing interfaces that are members of the appropriate group delivery tree. These routers do not send the packet back out the incoming interface.

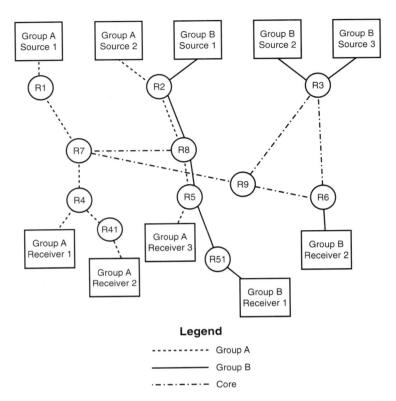

Legend

---------- Group A

——————— Group B

·—·—·—·— Core

FIGURE 14.9 *The backbone is a set of routers, connected with dot-dash lines, that need not be neighbors.*

Multicast Routing Protocols

There is an assortment of mechanisms for multicasting. Flooding alone is really only practical for flat networks of moderate scale. Different routing protocols are scalable to differing extents. Scalability is not a single dimension, because protocols can trade router memory and processing load against bandwidth efficiency.

The major alternatives include:

- Layer 2 schemes

  — MARS

  — IGMP snooping and CGMP

- Layer 3 schemes

  —Interior multicasting

  - Distance-Vector Multicast Routing Protocol

  - CBT

  - Protocol Independent Multicast (PIM)

    —PIM Sparse Mode (PIM-SM)

    —PIM Dense Mode (PIM-DM)

  - Multicast OSPF (MOSPF)

  - Multicast Internet Protocol (MIP)

  - Simple Multicast

  —Inter-Domain Multicasting

  - Border Gateway Multicast Routing Protocol (BGMP)

  - Simple Multicast

  - Multicast Address Set Claim Protocol (MASC)

See Table 14.2, adapted from "Framework for IP Multicast in MPLS" [Sales, 1999], for a comparison of the interior multicast protocols.

TABLE 14.2   SUMMARY OF MULTICAST METHODS

	DVMRP	MOSPF	CBT	PIM-DM	PIM-SM	MIP	SM
Flood & Prune	yes	no	no	yes	no	no	option
Tree Type	source	source	shared	source	both	both	shared
Directionality	N/A	N/A	bi	N/A	uni	both	bi
Loop Free	no	no	no	no	no	yes	no
RPF check	yes	yes	no	yes	yes	no	no
Availability	all major vendors,	public domain	some vendors experimental	a few vendors, experimental	still experimental	many vendors	many vendors

DVMRP

There's a saying that "there's nothing as permanent as a temporary network." DVMRP falls into this category. It was originally developed to deal with the practical need for multicasting IETF meetings. The original specification was RFC 1075, the low number of which shows DVMRP's vintage.

DVMRP originally used a variant of the RPB algorithm, and the RFC specifies this algorithm. Most current implementations, including the reference implementation, use RPM, so they differ substantially from the RFC.

The current DVMRP uses RPF to create on-demand source trees. Routers need to maintain state on each source in each group.

A DVMRP domain consists of physical links between DVMRP routers, and tunnels between multicast "islands" (see Figure 14.10).

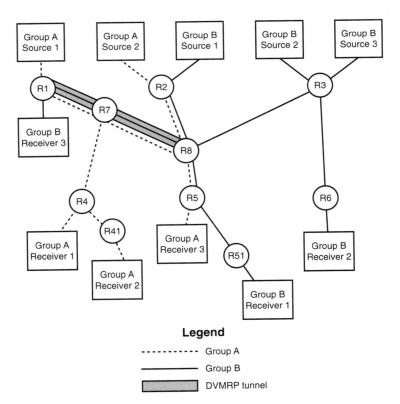

FIGURE 14.10 *A DVMRP tunnel is needed to link the "island" of Group B connected to R1.*

DVMRP limits the scope of flooding using the IP TTL field, as in Table 14.3.

TABLE 14.3   DVMRP TTL VALUES FOR CONTROLLING SCOPE

Initial TTL Value	Scope
0	Host
1	Link-local
32	Site
64	Region
128	Continent
255	Global

As defined by RPM, the first packet belonging to a (source, group) pair is forwarded throughout the network, subject to TTL constraints. Leaf routers send back prune messages if they do not have any members of the multicast group. Prune messages use the poison reverse principle of announcing an infinite cost to the destination address. The prune messages reduce the source tree to a source-specific shortest path tree.

Periodically, the pruned branches grow back; this is a means of arranging connectivity for new devices. There is also an explicit graft mechanism, from previously pruned leaf routers that discover they now have members of a group that they previously pruned. As upstream routers learn the graft information, they cancel prunes they may have sent upstream. The way in which information propagates from the leaves is a good example of how multicast protocols are receiver-driven.

If there are multiple DVMRP routers on a medium, a dominant router will be selected and also have the IGMP querier function.

CBT

The CBT architecture, defined in RFC 2201, creates a single shared tree for each multicast group. This differs from the shared trees of other multicast protocols, which build a source-rooted tree for each sender in a multicast group. CBT proponents suggest it offers better scaling properties than other algorithms.

In CBT, a node or set of nodes is declared the core. The core is a shared tree for all sources and receivers in a group. The core for a given group has a single active core router, but other routers may be defined as backups [RFC 2201].

Each member router explicitly joins the core. If a router on the path already knows about the group and the core, there is a merge, called a graft. When a graft occurs, there is no need to forward the join closer to the core.

By having a single tree per group, rather than a tree for each source and each group, the amount of state that routers need to keep drops from O(S,G) to O(G). Packets may not necessarily traverse the shortest end-to-end path to a destination. In OSPF, when you are in one nonzero area and have a destination in another nonzero area, each nonzero area has two ABRs, and you are summarizing into area 0.0.0.0 from both areas, it is entirely likely, as well, that packets may not traverse the shortest end-to-end path. You are trading off lessened state, more stability, and a more understandable topology against complete route optimization.

PIM

PIM is generally considered the leading available and scalable multicast routing mechanism, although there is always the possibility that one of the methods in a research phase may overtake it. The term "protocol independent" in its name means that it is independent of a specific unicast routing protocol, as opposed to DVMRP and MOSPF.

The requirements for sparse mode drove PIM, with the option of using dense mode when bandwidth is adequate and the member density is appropriate. Dense mode PIM, however, does have advantages over DVMRP.

PIM uses an RP similar to the core in CBT. PIM supports the simultaneous use of shared and source-rooted trees. PIM is complex, and depends on reverse path metrics so that PIM paths are optimal only when links to and from senders are symmetrical.

Consider using one of the forms of PIM when you want independence of the underlying unicast routing protocol, fairly widespread vendor support, and the capability to tune for sparse or dense modes. Do note that even though PIM is independent of unicast routing protocols, it can use OSPF, in contrast to MOSPF, which must use OSPF.

The sparse versus dense distinction is a key part of PIM design thinking. PIM sparse mode architects claim their protocol is much more bandwidth-efficient than DVMRP, which sends multicast packets over links that do not connect to members of the multicast group, and MOSPF, which sends membership information over links that do not include multicast hosts.

PIM advertises a set of core/RP-capable routers. A PIM router can run sparse and dense modes concurrently, using the mode most appropriate for a given group.

PIM-DM

Like DVMRP, PIM-DM is a source tree model that creates source trees on demand. If a source goes inactive, the entire tree is deleted.

Unlike DVMRP, PIM-DM accepts packet duplication so that it can avoid having to build a parent/child database such as that of DVMRP. PIM-DM's model is simply to forward traffic down its tree until it encounters "opt-out" prune messages.

When members on a previously pruned branch become interested in a group, PIM-DM, like DVMRP, sends explicit graft messages to let them join.

PIM-SM

PIM-SM uses an explicit join model, in which receivers send join messages to the RP, and senders register with the RP. Only those receivers interested in a multicast group hear them [Meyer, 1998].

There is only one active RP for each group. In PIMv1, the RP was statically configured, whereas candidate RPs can advertise themselves in PIMv2.

The major difference between PIM-SM and PIM-DM algorithms is that routers must explicitly join distribution trees. Sparse mode multicast routers default to blocking traffic, whereas dense mode routers default to forwarding.

Like CBT, PIM-SM has a concept of a core or RP. When a router creates a group, it selects a primary RP and a list of backup RPs listed in priority order. This list is advertised as a PIM-SM control message, and sparse PIM-SM routers must maintain a state-of-the-RP list. PIM-DM routers are data-driven and do not need to maintain as much state.

If there is more than one PIM router on a multiaccess medium, a PIM-SM designated router (DR) is elected and also becomes the IGMP querier. The DR sends join and prune messages on behalf of all devices on the medium. The DR can decide whether a group is dense or sparse, because different class D addresses have been reserved for SM.

When more than one PIM router is connected to a multiaccess medium, one router becomes PIM-SM DR, and is also the IGMP querier. The PIM-SM DR sends join and prune messages to the RP, and keeps track of the state of the RP.

PIM routers can switch to the shortest path tree for a specific source if they decide that the amount of data from that source exceeds a threshold. Remember, the shortest path tree is actually the shortest only if paths to and from the source are symmetrical.

To switch modes, the receiver DR sends a join toward the sender from which it wants to receive direct transmission. Simultaneously, the DR sends a prune to the active RP to stop sharing the shared tree to the same source.

MOSPF

Multicast extensions to OSPF were introduced in RFC 1984. MOSPF has not been used as widely as DVMRP and PIM, due to scaling issues. When OSPFv6 becomes available, many of the limitations of MOSPF may disappear. MOSPF has its strong partisans for environments where its scaling capabilities are adequate. Perhaps the strongest argument for MOSPF is that it interoperates with non-multicast OSPF routers. Not surprisingly, MOSPF uses OSPF as its underlying unicast routing protocol.

Consider using MOSPF when the implementations in use support it, you have a relatively small multicast requirement in an existing OSPF system, and the means of scoping MOSPF fit your requirements.

Intra-Area MOSPF

Basic MOSPF routing is intra-area. MOSPF routers create a *local group database* that identifies directly attached multicast group members (that is, on directly attached subnets). Multicast group members are identified using IGMP in the conventional way. The IGMP querier function must be on the designated router. Both the DR and backup designated router (BDR) listen to IGMP reports.

This additional requirement for the DR to support the querier function means that the DR and BDR must be MOSPF-capable. You need to set non-MOSPF capable routers on a subnet with an OSPF priority of 0, so that they cannot be elected DR or BDR.

Much as a regular DR floods router and network LSAs, a MOSPF DR also floods group membership LSAs, with area scope.

In an area with MOSPF capability, all routers, whether multicast-capable or not, forward unicast datagrams. Only multicast-capable routers, designated by having the MC bit set in their router LSAs, forward multicast traffic.

You need to consider whether some routers that do not connect to multicast hosts should still be multicast-capable to make the intra-area topology cleaner. If some routers are not multicast-capable, the area might become partitioned with respect to multicasting but not unicasting, as shown in Figure 14.11.

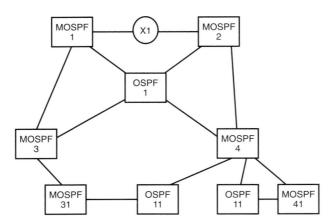

FIGURE 14.11 *Even though every router is at least dual-homed for non-multicast OSPF, a failure at point X1 splits the area into two MOSPF partitions that cannot communicate with one another.*

Alternatively, the area might not be partitioned, but multicast traffic may take a suboptimal path. See Figure 14.12, in which a much better path between Host 1 (multicast source) and Hosts 2 and 3 (multicast receivers) would be taken if router OSPF 2 were multicast-capable.

If the multicast and unicast topologies inside an area become too different as a result of differences in router support of MOSPF, troubleshooting can become complex. Although there is no strict requirement for every router in an area to be multicast-capable, where every router in an area with demand or stub attributes must have the same capabilities, it is often desirable to have all routers either multicast or not.

Troubleshooting can be reasonable with mixed multicast-capable and non-capable multicast routers in the same area, if a reasonably hierarchical design is followed, as shown in Figure 14.13.

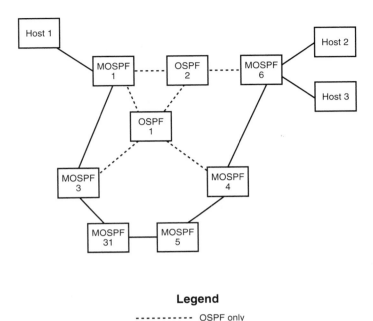

Legend

---------- OSPF only

————— Multicast

FIGURE 14.12 *If OSPF 1 or OSPF 2 were made MOSPF capable, a much better route between Host 1 and Host 2 and 3 would be usable.*

DVMRP uses tunnels but MOSPF does not. Tunnels can control the propagation of multicast information to links that do not need it, but MOSPF will flood information within its scope, such as an area.

In intra-area MOSPF, the Dijkstra algorithm is used much as it is in OSPF, but the Group Membership LSAs are considered when pruning the shortest-path tree for each (source, group) pair. Branches that do not contain multicast group members are pruned.

Inside an area, there is a single multicast tree for each source and each group. MOSPF does not have the OSPF concept of equal-cost multipath.

The MOSPF model is control-driven, building the tree from topology definitions learned through the routing protocol. This is again a difference from DVMRP, where the first packet of a transmission to a group establishes the tree but has to be sent to media that do not have members of the group.

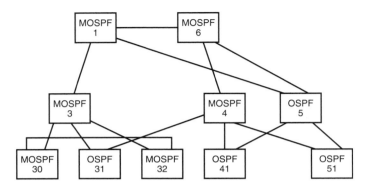

FIGURE 14.13 *This topology has no single point of failure for OSPF or MOSPF.*

Inter-Area Routing with MOSPF

A manually configured subset of the ABRs for an OSPF area, a subset that can include all ABRs, operate as inter-area multicast forwarders (IAMFs). These routers summarize the multicast group information and advertise it into area 0.0.0.0.

In contrast with non-multicast OSPF, the advertising is not symmetrical. Area 0.0.0.0 does not advertise its knowledge of multicasting into the nonzero areas. This means that closest-exit routing applies to all MOSPF communications outside the areas.

Inter-Autonomous System Multicasting with MOSPF

Remember that OSPF standards use an old meaning of *autonomous system*. OSPF's use of the term is more like that of a routing domain, and there could be many OSPF and MOSPF routing domains inside a real AS. MOSPF is not designed for general inter-domain routing in the Internet.

The equivalent of an ASBR is an inter-AS multicast forwarder. MOSPF assumes these routers run a separate interdomain multicast routing protocol.

Dynamic Load Sharing

Advances continue in load sharing, beyond the techniques discussed in the Chapter 13 section "Load Sharing." An idea applicable to OSPF, IS-IS, and MPLS is that of *optimized multipath* [Villamizor, 1999]. It deals with the problem that routers are usually not aware of congestion on non-directly connected links, and may select a next hop based on local information. Selecting a different next hop might encounter more loading on the directly connected medium, but less loading on an end-to-end basis.

OSPF Optimized Multipath (OSPF-OMP) uses the opaque LSA to distribute non-local load information. It has an algorithm that balances adjustment to load against stability.

OSPF-OMP to extend OSPF, IS-IS, and MPLS to provide non-local load information to routers [Villamizor, 1998]. These extensions are quite complex, but it is illustrative to look at the sort of information that would need to be flooded inside an area:

- Link capacity in kilobits. This is comparable to the common default—although not an OSPF requirement—of a bandwidth-based interface cost.

- A measure of link loading in each direction, expressed as a fraction of capacity.

- If available, the fraction of packets dropped in each direction due to buffer overflow.

The point here is that load sharing is not a trivial problem, and has only limited solutions with current technologies.

MPOA

Multiprotocol Over ATM (MPOA) is an ATM-oriented technique that, by default, routes packets between subnets, and does Layer 2 cut-through when the performance benefit of using Layer 2 exceeds the overhead of setting up virtual circuits. MPOA's paradigm is subtly different than either "switch if you can, route if you must," or "route once then switch." It is more "route until you have to switch, then switch."

MPOA builds on LANE and also works with 802.1 VLANs. It seeks to use Layer 2 and Layer 3 information to select an optimal exit from an ATM infrastructure. MPOA and MPLS solve somewhat different, but related problems. Again, which one you select for a given enterprise comes down to the classic "it depends" answer.

MPLS is medium-independent and runs on top of ATM. MPOA is a superset of LANE, and has much more Layer 2 awareness than MPLS. Although it is still a relatively new protocol, there is more field experience with MPOA than with MPLS, and certainly more experience with LANE.

When the edge device is Layer 2- but not Layer 3-aware, LANEv2/MPOA can guarantee service where 802.1p cannot, because 802.1p offers only best-effort. 802.1p advocates counter that it is reasonable to overprovision bandwidth in campus networks, and doing so is much simpler than using ATM.

The term *virtual router* is used extensively in MPOA to describe physical separation of the path determination and packet forwarding functions with the benefits [ATM AF-MPOA-0087]:

1. It allows efficient inter-subnet communication;

2. It increases manageability by decreasing the number of devices that must be configured to perform internetwork layer route calculation;

3. It increases scalability by reducing the number of devices participating in internetwork layer route calculation;

4. It reduces the complexity of edge devices by eliminating the need to perform internetwork layer route calculation.

The MPOA environment contains MPOA clients (MPCs) and MPOA servers (MPSs). These have some similarity to LANE clients and servers. The separation of virtual router functions can mean that an MPC is an edge host or edge switch, whereas an MPS is usually an ATM-interfaced router. Although the MPC does not do path determination, it does, in contrast to LANE and VLAN edge devices, have the intelligence to forward based on Layer 3 information.

The MPS contains the function of distributing Layer 3 information to the MPCs. It contains a full NHRP Next-Hop Server (NHS), and participates in routing protocols. It serves as a NHRP proxy for MPCs.

MPCs forward to LECs until a trigger point for cut-through is reached. When the MPC recognizes that a cut-through is desirable, usually based on traffic volume in a flow, it queries the NHS on how to perform the cut-through.

A default trigger for cut-through is 10 packets per second to a Layer 3 address. Implementations could also trigger based on QoS requirements.

The cut-through is a virtual circuit. Before initiating the cut-through, if the destination is a local MPS, the MPS asks it whether it can accept another VC. Assuming the target client can do so, the MPS sends an MPOA acknowledgement back to the originating MPC. That acknowledgement contains the information necessary to establish the VC.

If the MPS does not have the information to determine a next hop, it queries a higher-level NHRP server to get the information on how to establish the VC.

MANET

In Chapter 13 you saw the mobile IP work, which deals with hosts that move from subnet to subnet. Each subnet has one or more routers, in fixed locations, and tunnels go to these routers as they perform agent functions.

Mobile ad hoc networks (MANETs) go one step further, permitting the routers themselves to be mobile. The routers and hosts are assumed to be connected by wireless links.

The scope of such networks is seen as extending to hundreds of routers. For some time, there have been military tactical requirements for such networks, but there are obvious civilian applications in emergency services, communications in countries without a well-developed fixed telecommunications infrastructure, and so on.

Just because host locations seem to be fixed, do not assume that they will be wired. In Eastern Europe, for example, there are many cases where residential telephone service is cheaper to deliver by not insisting on installing extensive wiring systems in old and distinguished cities such as Budapest, which were not built with wiring in mind. Fixed-topology wireless, with occasional movement of routers, is a perfectly reasonable application.

In large First World cities, wireless high-speed communications may be an extremely fast-to-deploy alternative to entrenching fiber or copper. Many operators prefer this to the depredations of the dreaded backhoe—a T-shirt from one of the NANOG meetings has a backhoe in a crosshairs and the caption, "Let Fiber Live."

Some wireless technologies rely on line-of-sight availability. New construction may block a key line of sight, and the network needs to reconstitute itself to a reachable repeater or router.

PNNI ATM Routing

As the name should suggest, Private Network-to-Network Interface (PNNI) is intended for private, not carrier networks. Carrier ATM networks use SS#7 signaling, but PNNI may be a perfectly appropriate edge extension mechanism. Always remember, however, that your core may be a carrier's edge.

The motivation for PNNI is to scale ATM networks beyond the administrative limits of IISP [Patterson, PNNI]. (IISP, which indeed is very limited, is discussed in Chapter 9.) IISP is little more than a static routing protocol and is labor-intensive. PNNI also extends ATM routing to include QoS capabilities, which in turn can work with IEEE 802.1p LAN QoS mechanisms.

PNNI is quite powerful in creating topologies. At the lowest level, it supports both point-to-point and point-to-multipoint connections, although it does not support broadcast media. It can abstract a "cloud" of PNNI devices into a single logical link, and have a large number of levels of hierarchy.

PNNI's model involves setting up connections using dynamic path discovery, and can route around failed components. PNNI is a link-state protocol; you can think of it as derived from OSPF but with an arbitrary number of levels of hierarchy. Well, with a 13-byte prefix, it's only practical to have 104 levels of hierarchy, hardly a real-world limitation [Jain, 1999].

PNNI understands QoS and can use QoS parameters in setting up links. The capability of PNNI to guarantee bandwidth from end to end is one advantage it has over 802.1p switches, even when those switches use Gigabit Ethernet. PNNI refuses to set up additional calls (that is, Call Admission Control) when the network has no capacity for them, whereas 802.1p accepts the additional load.

ATM switches with PNNI routing capability are called *PNNI nodes*. At the lowest level of the PNNI hierarchy, not surprisingly, these are called *lowest level nodes*. Nodes are grouped into peer groups, which are somewhat analogous to OSPF or IS-IS areas.

In PNNI, a *peer group* is a group of nodes at the same level of hierarchy. This is roughly equivalent to an OSPF area. PNNI *border nodes* correspond to area border routers.

In OSPF, there is the abstraction from a higher layer to a lower. The higher layer conceptually treats a nonzero area as a single unit, which is called a *logical group node* in PNNI. *Child nodes* are any individual node at the lower layer, whereas *parent nodes* are at a level above the current one.

ATM addresses are 20 bytes long, of which the most significant 19 bytes identify unique nodes. Byte 20 is the selector value, used to indicate capabilities of a node. The eighteenth byte identifies the peer group to which a lowest level node belongs, and up to 13 of the most significant bytes can be used to identify higher hierarchical levels in the PNNI topology.

Another way to look at the ATM addresses in PNNI is that they have a variable-length prefix that aggregates peer groups. When a switch contacts another switch over a reserved VC, if the peer groups are equal, the two nodes are in the same peer group and have a *horizontal link*. Horizontal links are analogous to OSPF intra-area networks. Nodes with different peer groups are called border nodes, and are reached with border links.

Inside a group, the nodes exchange hellos over the PNNI routing control channel (RCC) with VPI=0 and VCI=18, and build information on the state and group membership of directly connected nodes, and on the metrics and administrative factors for links. The information is then flooded and synchronized much as are OSPF LSAs. PNNI's announcements, however, are called *PNNI topology state elements* (PTSEs). Neighbors in the same peer group synchronize their databases with information both about their current peer group and more abstract information about remote peer groups.

Each peer group has a peer group leader (PGL), roughly equivalent to an OSPF area border router. Only one PGL can be active at a given time, although a backup PGL can be elected. The idea of having a single PGL is analogous to OSPF's use of a single designated router on links, except that the PGL represents an area-equivalent, not a link-equivalent.

There can be multiple border nodes, but only one PGL is active. The role of the PGL is more to announce the peer group to a higher level group than it is to be the single boundary router.

A PGL is needed only if the PNNI system is actually hierarchical. Early real-world PNNI deployments often use PNNI without its hierarchical structure, and do not have a PGL. Vendor implementations of PNNI may or may not contain the PGL and hierarchical functionality. Nonhierarchical PNNI is still more scalable than IISP, just as RIP is more scalable than static routes in other than a strictly hierarchical topology.

PNNI specifications define two kinds of topology aggregation, which is the systematic hiding of details of the peer group internal structures along a path. Hiding internals increases stability at the potential cost of suboptimal routing. Hiding internals also can provide security if the internal structure of peer groups is sensitive.

PNNI does two kinds of topology aggregation: link and node. Link aggregation treats a set of links between two peer groups as a single link, much like a tunnel. Nodal aggregation treats an entire child peer group as a single node in the parent peer group.

Designated Transit Lists, Call Admission Control, and Crankback

Several mechanisms work together in PNNI to improve call setup. In ordinary routing protocols, it is not necessarily assured that a path can reach a destination. The PNNI assumption is source-route based. The ingress PNNI node decides whether it can create an end-to-end path called the Designated Transit List (DTL), which is a sequence of node or port identifiers that reach from end to end.

When the DTL is being set up in a hierarchical PNNI environment, it may start as a list of peer groups. Each ingress node into a peer group (that is, a border node) selects the path through the peer group. The DTL is not necessarily optimized end to end, but may be an optimal sequence of peer groups with local optimization inside each peer group.

QoS factors could be involved in each switching decision in creating the path, and Call Admission Control (CAC) might either direct a call, redirect a call, or indicate that a DTL cannot be constructed at the moment given current requirements.

The specific decisions in CAC are not part of the PNNI standard. Because different nodes may have different CAC criteria, there is no practical way to predetermine the feasibility of a DTL. It is necessary to try to set it up and see whether CAC makes any part of the DTL infeasible.

As the path is set up, each switching element does or does not accept a connection. This is actual CAC (ACAC). If, during the lifetime of a call, the network or node condition changes, new PTSE is originated.

Generic CAC (GCAC) attempts to predict the real-world CAC decision. GCAC runs on an ingress switch, and predicts based on a generic set of QoS and topology parameters.

The source route, through the use of aggregation, may contain recursive definitions of elements along the path. In other words, each element in a DTL may actually represent a stack of subordinate elements.

When the DTL is being built, a node about to send out a next-hop query stores the setup information, in case the selected next hop cannot service the call and an alternate next hop needs to be tried, using the same setup information.

A node uses its best knowledge of the forward path to select nodes that will not block the call request, but, in the real world, some requests are blocked. In such cases, the *crankback* mechanism comes into play. When a requesting node denies a call request along the path, the information is "cranked back" to the originator of the DTL. Remember that the DTL is recursive. The originator may select an alternate next hop through which it will try to route the call, or it may crank the request back to the node that gave it the DTL request.

Metrics in PNNI

Metrics in PNNI, as one might expect, include the various components of ATM performance, plus an administrative weight. The components are as follows:

- Maximum Cell Transfer Delay (MCTD)

- Maximum Cell Delay Variation (MCDV)

- Maximum Cell Loss Ratio (MCLR)

They also include the attributes of available cell rate and cell rate margin.

PNNI routing also considers attribute flags. The first attribute flag is the *branching flag*, which indicates whether or not point-to-multipoint traffic is supported. The *restricted transit flag* indicates whether or not the link supports transit traffic.

Other attributes to consider might include security and administrative policies.

MPLS

Review the concept of a forwarding equivalence class (FEC). Let's say you have an external router that has one internal network interface, and interfaces to two separate ISPs. This router exchanges full BGP routes with both ISPs, and thus has 57,000 or so routes in its RIB. But, from the perspective of the enterprise, there are only two ways to leave the router. Formally, these are two FECs. The tens of thousands of routes map to one or the other interface.

Another way to look at this is to consider that a packet header contains much more information than is needed for a simple next hop determination. Next hop selection actually involves two functions, the first being analysis of the packet header to determine the FEC to which it belongs, and the next mapping that FEC to the next hop on a path to the destination.

Layer 4 or 7 information can go into defining an FEC. Higher-layer information is more often used to determine a class of service than a different interface, but if you have multiple priorities for leaving an interface, these each belong to a different FEC.

If the FEC is represented with a label, the set of link-local labels along the end-to-end path defines a label-switched path (LSP). LSPs are quasi–virtual-circuits defined by sequences of labels. You can think of labels as an in-band, explicit means of identifying traffic that belongs to an FEC.

Labels can assume specific Layer 2 technologies, or, as discussed later in this section, can be Layer 2 independent. One of the first Layer 3 switching implementations, Ipsilon's IP switching, was ATM dependent.

At the forwarding level, MPLS uses a label FIB (LFIB—called a TFIB in tag switching). The labels in the label forwarding LFIB correspond to FECs. FECs are global to the routing domain, whereas the labels to which they are mapped are link-local, much as an ATM VPI/VCI is local to each ATM circuit, and remapped at each switch.

Ipsilon's Layer 3 switching was ATM dependent because it used ATM VPI/VCI fields to hold the equivalent of a label. In Tag and MPLS, the label is a shim header inserted between the Layer 2 and Layer 3 headers, making MPLS independent of the transmission medium. The actual label is a 20-bit part of a 32-bit shim header. It is possible to stack multiple shim headers between Layer 2 and Layer 3 headers.

Typically, the egress router determines the FECs *after* routing tables are built. It uses a tag or label distribution protocol (TDP/LDP) to send the FEC information back to routers along the path, which map the FECs to link-local tags. Eventually, the information propagates back to an ingress router, which does the initial tagging.

Although the specific term FEC isn't used in LANE and MPOA, the same logic is there. Especially in LANEv2 and MPOA, you reasonably can think of an ATM VC to an FEC, but the FEC is associated with a sequence of VCs among ATM devices.

MPLS Requirements

MPLS must be general and work with a wide range of existing and future routing protocols and data link technologies. At the same time, it must simplify packet forwarding in a useful manner that lowers the cost of forwarding while raising forwarding performance. Luckily, the technologies available make those forwarding goals more plausible than the classical political promise to lower taxes while increasing government services.

A controversial area of MPLS is the extent to which MPLS is required to prevent loops or mitigate loops that are formed due to incorrect information being passed to MPLS. The controversy comes in because modern routing protocols generally create loop-free paths, and there is a concern that having MPLS track time-to-live imposes unneeded overhead.

MPLS must operate in hierarchical environments and support aggregation of data streams defined either by traditional Layer 3 routing (that is, in terms of destinations), and by higher-layer flow information, typically with QoS requirements. It must work with both unicast and multicast traffic, and understand Integrated Services and RSVP.

Another aspect of working effectively in a hierarchy includes the capability to merge streams whenever practical. Multipath, parallel operation is an essential capability.

A fundamental requirement is that MPLS must be able to drop into existing networks without breaking operational tools. If MPLS does break a tool, it must provide hooks for an equivalent capability. Again at a fundamental level, MPLS switches must not impose any additional configuration requirements on non-MPLS switches that interoperate with them. MPLS must be able to coexist with existing Layer 2 mechanisms such as ATM signaling.

Labels

Labels are fast-lookup equivalents of a full packet header, subject to additional constraints. A simple way to think of a label is as shorthand for a stream or an aggregate stream. In simplistic terms of traditional routing, this is an adequate model.

A label corresponds to an FEC, which, in turn, can map to:

- A destination prefix, as in conventional routing.

- An aggregated destination prefix, as in conventional hierarchical routing.

- A source-destination pair—a flow identifier—that can be an IP address pair, or go beyond to consider higher-layer identifiers. Either source or destination can be a wild card.

- An aggregate of source-destination pairs. This is called a *traffic trunk* in some of the MPLS traffic engineering literature [RFC 2430].

  A traffic trunk can be treated as an object that can be routed itself. Doing so allows you to merge streams of traffic onto a common Layer 2 mechanism such as a virtual circuit. The trunk maintains a conceptual identity beyond that of the LSP it traverses.

But the power of MPLS comes from a broader meaning of labels. Because labels and label switching come in as an "overdrive" after conventional routing, think of them more as a means of optimization than as a basic operating mode. In general routing, the forwarding router has no way to know whether it is sending a packet into a blackhole, into congestion, or into a loop. MPLS labels can be part of a larger path, and the MPLS mechanism can check for bad next hops.

If, for example, the MPLS label setup mechanism derived from an IP or ATM routing protocol that is loop-free, then sets of labels derived from them also will be loop-free. If a set of labels derived from a congestion-aware routing system, which set up the initial set to avoid congestion and can re-optimize the path later to avoid transient congestion, the set of labels will be a path that avoids congestion.

These labels can be created dynamically as an "overdrive" to routing protocols, or can map to explicit paths. The explicit paths might be manually configured, or determined by new constraint-based methods that probe for an optimal path, Another option, used today by some providers, is to compute explicit paths with non–real-time software programmed with the topology and constraints.

Packets are assigned to FECs at the ingress router, and the label associated with that FEC *at the ingress router* is prepended to the packet. The label and packet are then sent to an outgoing interface, encapsulated in the appropriate Layer 2 protocol, and forwarded to the next hop.

At subsequent label switched routers, the packet header is no longer examined. Instead, the label is looked up in a label information base (LIB) and a new next hop and label value retrieved. The new label replaces the old, and the packet is forwarded to the interface indicated by the LIB for Layer 2 encapsulation and forwarding to the next LSR. This process of looking up a label, determining the outgoing label and interface, replacing the label, and forwarding, is called *label swapping*.

Labels can be stacked. A labeled packet can contain a last-in-first-out *label stack*. A label switch always makes its decision based on the top label.

Stacked labels are associated with tunnels. If some router, RA, wants a packet to be sent to RB, but RA and RB are not neighbors on the hop-by-hop path, the packet for RB can be encapsulated inside another packet and tunneled to the next hop(s). The delivery header is associated with a new FEC from router R1 to R2 to R3. R3 will deliver the packet to RB.

For example, an enterprise runs a BGP confederation connecting several of its divisions. We are concerned here with the labels involved in running MPLS through this particular division. Assume it is a confederation AS that provides transit to other ASs in the company.

There needs to be iBGP connectivity among the BGP speakers in an AS. The actual connectivity in AS64000, however, goes through three non–BGP-speaking routers, R1 through R3.

A labeled packet arrives from AS64000, associated with an FEC that has router C2 as its destination. Router C1 looks up the label, and finds that it does not have a direct LSP to C2, but does have a tunneled path whose next hop is R1.

Unicast labels can correspond to specific destination routes or to aggregated routes. They can have additional semantics of a specific next hop of a QoS requirement.

Multicast labels bind to the subset of a multicast tree that is the branch of a multicast group that extends from a specific physical interface. In shared trees, this is (*,G), whereas in source trees, it is (source, group). Labels could have additional semantics of policies or QoS requirements.

> **Note**
>
> Labels for explicit routes correspond to tunnels. Remember that tunnels are most commonly used to build virtual private networks, so stacked MPLS is another implementation technique for VPNs [RFC 2547].

Label Distribution Protocol

LDP announces the existence of LSRs, creates peerings between LDP entities in LSRs, and advertises mappings between FECs and labels. LDP also carries advisory and error notifications.

The LDP discovery message is a hello subprotocol function similar to that in OSPF or IS-IS. In contrast to OSPF, where hellos are sent directly over IP, and IS-IS, where the hellos were originally sent over the data link layer, LDP hellos go over UDP. Neighbors are not required to be on the same subnet.

When an LSR recognizes a neighbor and desires to establish peering, it initializes using TCP. UDP is used only for discovery. LDP does not have the reliable delivery mechanisms of OSPF and IS-IS, relying instead on TCP.

The decision to request a label or advertise one is a local choice of the LSR implementation. The basic principle is to do such things when it makes sense to do so: request a label when the LSR needs a label, and advertise a label when it wants a neighbor to use a label to send to the LSR.

LDP messages are variable-length TLV structures. See "LDP Specification" [Thomas, 1999] for the detailed structure; our concern here is with functionality. There will be an FEC for each label-switched path (LSP). An FEC is a set of one or more FEC elements that maps to an LSP; more than one FEC can map to the same LSP. Currently defined FEC elements are:

- IP address prefix

- Host address

Selecting the LSP for an FEC

Just as there is a procedure for making a best match of a packet destination address to a route in a routing table, there are a series of rules by which a packet is mapped to an LSP. The rules are applied until there is a match:

1. There is one and only one LSP with a Host Address FEC element that exactly matches the destination address in the packet.

2. If multiple LSPs with Host Address elements match the destination address, one LSP is selected based on local criteria in the LSR. These are not standardized, but could include any traffic engineering or QoS criterion.

3. If the destination address matches one and only one LSP associated with a packet, that LSP is selected.

4. If there are multiple LSPs that match the destination address, the longest match is taken.

5. If there are more than one LSP matches of the same prefix length, local implementation criteria are used to select an LSP. These criteria might include load balancing.

6. If the LSR knows the packet must go through a specific egress router, and an LSP matches an address of that router, the packet is mapped to the FEC. The method by which the LSR learns about specific egress routers is not part of the LDP specification.

Label Spaces and Identifiers

LDP defines two types of label space, *per-interface* and *per-platform*. Interface-specific labels relate to interface types that use an interface-specific mechanism for labeling, such as an ATM VPI/VCI or a Frame Relay DLCI. This sort of label is applicable when the LDP peers are directly connected at Layer 2, and this linkage is used for traffic going over the interface. Per-platform labels are used for multiple interfaces on the LSR.

The actual LDP identifier is six octets long. The first four octets are an IPv4 address associated with the platform, presumably a stable address such as a loopback or circuitless interface. The low-order two bytes identify a label space, either with zeroes for a platform-wide space or an identifier for each per-interface space. LDP identifiers are written:

```
IP-address, label-space-id
```

as in the following example:

```
171.32.27.28:0, 192.0.3.5:2
```

One LSR might need to advertise more than one label space to another if it is using tunneling.

MPLS Advanced Capabilities

In dynamic QoS routing, there is a constant tradeoff between the overhead of sending current load information and picking the optimal path judged in relation to load. There is even a danger of oscillation if load information is updated too quickly.

To reserve bandwidth, it is impractical for the routing system to maintain information on the best path for all potential bandwidth requirements to all destinations. RSVP-style, on-demand path computation by a first node, which specifies an explicit path, is much more scalable.

So, a scalable trunking mechanism needs to support explicit paths, both administratively specified by operator action, and dynamically created by mechanisms such as RSVP. MPLS is an attractive mechanism for specifying explicit routes. Alternatives could include, in moderately sized networks, non–real-time generation of static routes that are automatically configured into routers.

The capability to do traffic engineering was a substantial motivation for MPLS. Attaching labels to traffic gives a level of control that simply is not possible with traditional routing models that make decisions based on destination address only.

Today, providers often do manual configuration of the Layer 2 PVC mechanism among key aggregation points—"superhubs"—in their networks. They accept this labor-intensive activity, which needs quite skilled labor, because it is the only readily available way to distribute Layer 3-identified traffic over Layer 2 bandwidth resources.

Experience has shown that load balancing that only considers the next hop in Layer 3 can have some benefit locally, but cannot consider optimal load distribution beyond the next hop. OMP is one approach that deals with going beyond the next hop, and indeed has an MPLS variant as well as OSPF and IS-IS.

Bibliographic References

[Abe, 1997] Abe, G. *Residential Broadband*. Indianapolis, IN: Macmillan Technical Publishing, 1997.

[Albitz, 1992] Albitz, P. and C. Liu. *DNS and Bind in a Nutshell*. Sebastopol: O'Reilly & Associates, 1992.

[ANSI, X3.102] American National Standards Institute. "Data Communications Systems and Services: User-Oriented Performance." 1983.

[ANSI, X3.141] American National Standards Institute. "Data Communications Systems and Services: User-Oriented Performance Measurement Methods." 1987.

[ATM AF-LANE-0084-000] ATM Forum. "LAN Emulation over ATM Version—LUNI Specification." 1997.

[ATM AF-MPOA-0087.000] ATM Forum. Multi-Protocol Over ATM Version 1.0.

[ATM UNI 3.1] ATM Forum. *ATM User-Network Interface (UNI) Specification, Version 3.1*. Upper Saddle River, NJ: Prentice-Hall PTR, 1995.

[Ballardie, 1998] Ballardie, Tony, B. Cain, and Z. Zhang. "Core Based Tree (CBT) Multicast Border Router Specification." Work in progress, Internet Engineering Task Force, March 12, 1998. See www.ietf.org/internet-drafts/draft-ietf-idmr-cbt-br-spec-02.txt.

[Bansal, 1999] Bansal, Atul, Antoni Przygienda, and Ajay Patel. "IS-IS over IPv4." Work in progress, Internet Engineering Task Force, January 27, 1999. See www.ietf.org/internet-drafts/draft-ietf-isis-wg-over-ip-00.txt.

[Bay, 1998] Bay Networks (now Nortel Networks). "Configuring IP Multicasting and Multimedia Services, BayRS Version 13.10, Site Manager Software Version 7.10 BCC Version 4.10." Part No. 117355-C Rev 00, 1998. Available at support.baynetworks.com.

[Bellcore] Bellcore publication TR-TSY-000253, SONET Transport Systems. Common Generic Criteria.

[Berkowitz, 1975] Berkowitz, H. "Notes on Network Reliability Design." INTERFACE '75, Miami Beach, FL, 1975.

[Berkowitz, 1998a] Berkowitz, H. *Designing Addressing Architectures for Routing and Switching.* Indianapolis, IN: Macmillan Technical Publishing, 1998.

[Berkowitz, 1998b] Berkowitz, H. "Good ISPs Have No Class." Presentation at North American Network Operators' Group (NANOG). 1998.

[Berkowitz, 1999a] Berkowitz, H. "EIGRP Load Balancing," mail list messages at www.groupstudy.com, January 26, 1999.

[Berkowitz, 1999b] Berkowitz, H. "Requirements Taxonomy for Virtual Private Networks." Work in Progress, Internet Engineering Task Force, 1999. See www.ietf.org/internet-drafts/draft-berkowitz-vpn-tax-00.txt or later versions.

[Bernet, 1998] Bernet, Y., R. Yavatkar, P. Ford, F. Baker, L. Zhang, K. Nichols, and M. Speer. "A Framework for Use of RSVP with Diff-serv Networks." Work in progress, IETF diff-serv Working Group, 1998.

[Blake, 1998] Blake, S., D. Black, M. Carlson, E. Davies, Z. Wang, and W. Weiss. "An Architecture for Differentiated Services." Work in progress, IETF Differentiated Services Working Group, 1998.

[Bloomfield, 1997] Bloomfield R., "Performance Measures for Multimedia Applications." Presentation to June 1997 meeting, North American Network Operators' Group (NANOG). See 132.163.64.201/n3/present/nanog597/index.htm. Similar presentation to IETF Real-Time Flow Measurement Working Group, April 1997. See www.ietf.org/proceedings/97apr/ops/rtfm-2/sld001.htm.

[Cabletron, 1998] Cabletron Systems. "LAN Emulation and Multi-Protocol Over ATM." 1998. See www.cabletron.com/white-papers/atm/lan-emulation.html.

[Cabletron, 1999] Cabletron Systems white paper, "Router Reduction Techniques: An Introduction to High-Capacity Switching Systems." 1999. See www.cabletron.com/white-papers/capacity/.

[Caidin, 1989] Caidin, M. *The God Machine*. Riverdale, NY: Baen, 1989.

[Callon, 1997] Callon, R., George Swallow, N. Feldman, A. Viswanathan, P. Doolan, and A. Fredette. "A Framework for Multiprotocol Label Switching." Work in Progress, IETF Multiprotocol Label Switching Working Group, 1997. See www.ietf.org/internet-drafts/draft-ietf-mpls-framework-02.txt.

[Chapman, 1995] Chapman, B. and E. Zwicky. *Building Internet Firewalls*. Sebastopol, CA: O'Reilly, 1995.

[Cheswick, 1994] Cheswick, W. and S. Bellovin. *Firewalls and Internet Security: Foiling the Wily Hacker*. Reading, MA: Addison-Wesley, 1994.

[Cisco CID] Cisco Systems. Internetwork Design Course.

[Coover, 1997] Coover, E. *ATM Switches*. Boston, MA: Artech House, 1997.

[Davie, 1998] Davie, B., P. Doolan, and Y. Rekhter. *Switching in IP Networks: Ip Switching, Tag Switching, and Related Technologies*. San Francisco, CA: Morgan Kauffman, 1998.

[Deering, 1999] Deering, Steve, B. Cain, and A. Thyagarajan. "Internet Group Management Protocol, Version 3." Work in progress, Internet Engineering Task Force, February 19, 1999. See www.ietf.org/internet-drafts/draft-ietf-idmr-igmp-v3-01.txt.

[Doyle, 1998] Doyle, J. *CCIE Professional Development: Routing TCP/IP, Volume I*. Indianapolis, IN: Cisco Press, 1998.

[Ellison, 1997] R. Ellison, et al. "Survivable Network Systems: An Emerging Discipline." Carnegie Mellon University, Software Engineering Institute Report CMU/SEI-97-TR-013. November 1997 (Revised May 1999).

[Escoffier, 1941] Escoffier, A. *The Escoffier Cook Book; A Guide to the Fine Art of Cookery*. New York, N.Y. Crown Publishers, Inc., 1941..

[Estrin, 1998] Estrin, Deborah, V. Jacobson, D. Farinacci, David Meyer, L. Wei, Steve Deering, and A. Helmy. "Protocol Independent Multicast Version 2 Dense Mode Specification." Work in progress, Internet Engineering Task Force, November 6, 1998. See www.ietf.org/internet-drafts/draft-ietf-pim-v2-dm-01.txt.

[Farinacci, 1993] Farinacci, D. "An Introduction to EIGRP." Cisco Systems, 1993.

[Ferguson, 1998] Ferguson, P. and G. Huston. "What is a VPN?" 1998. See www.employees.org/~ferguson/vpn.pdf.

[Floyd, 1994] Floyd, S. and V. Jacobson. "The Synchronization of Periodic Routing Messages." Preprint of paper to appear in April 1994 IEEE/ACM Transactions on Networking.

[Fox] Gleeson, B. and B. Fox. "Virtual Private Networks Identifier." http://www.ietf.org/internet-drafts/draft-ietf-ion-vpn-id-02.txt.

[FRF.11] Frame Relay Forum. "Implementation Agreement for Voice over Frame Relay." May 1997.

[FRF-SVC] Frame Relay Forum. "GENERAL OVERVIEW Frame Relay SVCs." See www.frforum.com/4000/4019.html.

[GateD Policy] Gated Consortium. "GateD Policy Module." 1996. See www.isi.edu/ra/RSd/gatedInternals/config.html#Gated Policy Module.

[Goldstein, 1992] Goldstein, F. *ISDN in Perspective*. Reading, MA: Addison-Wesley, 1992.

[Hedrick, 1991] Hedrick, C. "An Inroduction to IGRP." Unpublished document available from Cisco Systems, 1991.

[IAB 1998] Perlman, R., S. Hares, S. Deering. "Overview of the 1998 IAB Routing Workshop" http://www.ietf.org/internet-drafts/draft-iab-rtrws-over-01.txt

[IEEE 802.1D] IEEE. "Common Specifications: Part 3: Media Access Control (MAC) bridges, incorporating IEEE 802.1P Traffic Class Expediting and Dynamic Multicast Filtering." Also ISO/IEC Final Draft International Standard 15802-3. 1998.

[IEEE 802.1P] IEEE P802.1D/D15. ISO/IEC Final CD 15802-3 "Local and metro politan area networks—Common specifications—Part 3: Media Access Control (MAC) Bridges: Revision (Incorporating IEEE P802.1p:Traffic Class Expediting and Dynamic Multicast Filtering)."

[IEEE 802.1Q] IEEE Project 802, 802.1Q Working Group. "Draft Standard P802.1Q/D8 IEEE Standards for Local and Metropolitan Area Networks: Virtual Bridged Local Area Networks." 1997.

[Ikle, 1991] Ikle, F. *Every War Must End*. New York, NY: Columbia University Press, 1991.

[ISO 9575] ISO Technical Report 9575. "OSI Routeing Framework." 1989.

[ISO 10000] ISO Technical Report 10000. "Framework and Taxonomy of International Standardized Profiles (Part 1 and Part 2)." 1990.

[ISO 10589] ISO Technical Report 10589. "Intra-Domain Routeing Exchange Protocol for use in Conjunction with the Protocol for Providing the Connectionless-mode Network Service (ISO 8473)." 1990.

[Jain, 1999] Jain, R. "PNNI: Routing in ATM Networks Routing in ATM Networks." Ohio State University, 1999. See www.cis.ohio-state.edu/~jain/.

[Katz, 1999] Katz, D. and M. Yeung. "Traffic Engineering Extensions to OSPF." Work in progress, Internet Engineering Task Force, 1999. See www.ietf.org/ internet-drafts/draft-katz-yeung-ospf-traffic-00.txt.

[Keiser, 1995] Keiser, B. and E. Strange. *Digital Telephony and Network Integration, 2nd Edition*. New York, NY: Chapman & Hall, 1995.

[Kleinrock, 1975] Kleinrock, L. *Queueing Systems, Volume I: Theory*. New York, NY: John Wiley & Sons, 1975.

[Kleinrock, 1976] Kleinrock, L. *Queueing Systems, Volume II: Computer Applications*. New York, NY: John Wiley & Sons, 1976.

[Li, 1998] Li, T. and C. Villamizar. "IS-IS Optimized Multipath (ISIS-OMP)," 1998.

[Li, 1999] Li, Tony. "IS-IS HMAC-MD5 Authentication." Work in progress, Internet Engineering Task Force, January 7, 1999. See www.ietf.org/internet-drafts/draft-ietf-isis-hmac-00.txt.

[Malkiel, 1996] Malkiel, B. *A Random Walk Down Wall Street*. Norton, 1996.

[Meyer, 1998] Meyer, D. (Cisco Systems). "Introduction to IP Multicast." Presentation at NANOG meeting, June 1998. See www.nanog.org/ mtg-9806/ppt/davemeyer/index.htm.

[Morissey, 1999] Morissey, P. "The Cost of Security on Cisco Routers." *Network Computing*, 10(4):122 (February 1999).

[Moy, 1998] Moy, J. *OSPF: Anatomy of an Internet Routing Protocol*. Reading, MA: Addison-Wesley, 1998.

[Northern Telecom, 1998] Northern Telecom. "Passport Networking Introduction." Publication 241-7501-310, 1998.

[O'Dell, 1998] O'Dell, M., J. Agogbua, D. Awduche, and J. McManus. "Requirements for Traffic Engineering Over MPLS." Work in Progress, MPLS Working Group, 1998. See www.ietf.org/internet-drafts/draft-ietf-mpls-traffic-eng-00.txt.

[Parsa, 1997] Parsa, M. and J. Garcia-Luna-Aceves. "A protocol for scaleable loop-free multicast routing." *IEEE JSAC*, vol.15, no.3, (April 1997): 316–331.

[Partridge, 1994] Partridge, C. *Gigabit Networking*. Reading, MA: Addison-Wesley, 1994.

[Patterson, PNNI] Patterson, M. "Private Network to Node Interface—Phase One." See www.cabletron.com/white-papers/pnni-1/.

[Paxson, 1997] Paxson, V. "End-to-End Routing Behavior in the Internet." *IEEE/ACM Transactions on Networking*, 5:601 (October 1997).

[Perlman, 1992] Perlman, R. *Interconnections*. Reading, MA: Addison-Wesley, 1992.

[Perlman, 1998] Perlman, R., C-Y Lee, A. Ballardie, J. Crowcroft, Z. Wang, and T. Maufer. "Simple Multicast." IETF draft, work in progress, Internet Engineering Task Force,November 1998. See www.ietf.org/internet-drafts/draft-perlman-simple-multicast-02.txt.

[Perlman, 1999] Perlman, R., S. Hares, C. Perkins, and S. Deering. "Overview of the 1998 IAB Routing Workshop," 1999. See www.ietf.org/internet-drafts/draft-iab-rtrws-over-01.txt.

[Przygienda, 1998a] Przygienda, Antoni. "Maintaining more than 255 adjacen cies in IS-IS." Work in progress, Internet Engineering Task Force, November 24, 1998. See www.ietf.org/internet-drafts/draft-ietf-isis-wg-255adj-00.txt.

[Przygienda, 1998b] Przygienda, Antoni. "Optional Checksums in ISIS." Work in progress, Internet Engineering Task Force, 1998. See www.ietf.org/internet-drafts/draft-ietf-isis-wg-snp-checksum-00.txt.

[Przygienda, 1999a] Przygienda, Antoni and Patrick Droz. "Proxy PAR." Work in Progress, IETF Internetworking over NBMA (ION) Working Group, February 17, 1999. See www.ietf.org/internet-drafts/draft-ietf-ion-proxypar-arch-01.txt.

[Przygienda, 1999b] Przygienda, Antoni and Ajay Patel. "L1/L2 Optimal IS-IS Routing." Work in progress, Internet Engineering Task Force, February 19, 1999. See www.ietf.org/internet-drafts/draft-ietf-isis-l1l2-00.txt.

[Pusateri, 1999] Pusateri, T. "Distance Vector Multicast Routing Protocol." Work in progress, Internet Engineering Task Force, March 3, 1999. See www.ietf.org/internet-drafts/draft-ietf-idmr-dvmrp-v3-08.txt.

[RFC 1001] NetBIOS Working Group. "Protocol Standard for a NetBIOS Service on a TCP/UDP Transport: Concepts and Methods." 1987.

[RFC 1002] NetBIOS Working Group. "Protocoal Standard for a NetBIOS Service on a TCP/UPD Transport: Detailed Specifications." 1987.

[RFC 1034] Mockapetris, P. "Domain names—concepts and facilities." 1987.

[RFC 1058] Hedrick, C. L. "Routing Information Protocol." 1998.

[RFC 1075] Waitzman, D., C. Partridge, and S.E. Deering. "Distance Vector Multicast Routing Protocol." 1988.

[RFC 1136] Hares, S. and D. Katz. "Administrative Domains and Routing Domains A Model for Routing in the Internet." 1989.

[RFC 1142] Oran, D. "OSI IS-IS Intra-domain Routing Protocol." 1990. IETF version of draft "Intermediate System to Intermediate System Intra-Domain Routeing Exchange Protocol for use in Conjunction with the Protocol for Providing the Connectionless-mode Network Service (ISO 8473)," ISO 10589.

[RFC 1191] Mogul, J. and S. Deering. "Path MTU discovery." 1990.

[RFC 1195] Callon, R. "Use of OSI IS-IS for routing in TCP/IP and dual environments." 1990.

[RFC 1234] Provan, D. "Tunneling IPX Traffic through IP Networks." 1991.

[RFC 1242] Bradner, S. "Benchmarking terminology for network interconnection devices." 1991.

[RFC 1256] Deering, S. "ICMP Router Discovery Messages." 1991.

[RFC 1323] Jacobson, V., R. Braden, and D. Borman. "TCP Extensions for High Performance." 1992.

[RFC 1483] Heinanen, J. "Multiprotocol Encapsulation over ATM Adaptation Layer 5." 1993.

[RFC 1582] Meyer, G. "Extensions to RIP to Support Demand Circuits." 1994.

[RFC 1586] deSouza, O. and M. Rodrigues. "Guidelines for Running OSPF Over Frame Relay Networks." 1994.

[RFC 1639] Baker, F. and R. Bowen. "PPP Bridging Control Protocol." 1994.

[RFC 1702] Hanks, S., T. Li, D. Farinacci, and P. Traina. "Generic Routing Encapsulation over IPv4 Networks." 1994.

[RFC 1722] Malkin, G. "RIP Version 2 Protocol Applicability Statement." 1994.

[RFC 1723] Malkin, G. "RIP Version 2—Carrying Additional Information." 1994.

[RFC 1775] Crocker, D. "To be 'on' the Internet." 1994.

[RFC 1812] Baker, F. "Requirements for IPv4 Routers." 1995.

[RFC 1850] Baker, F. and R. Coltun. "OSPF Version 2 Management Information Base." 1995.

[RFC 1879] Manning, B. "Class A Subnet Experiment Results and Recommendations." 1996.

[RFC 1889] Schulzrinne, H., S. Casner, R. Frederick, and V. Jacobson. "RTP: A Transport Protocol for Real-Time Applications." Audio-Video Transport Working Group, 1996.

[RFC 1930] Hawkinson, J. and T. Bates. "Guidelines for Creation, Selection, and Registration of an Autonomous System (AS)." Internet Engineering Task Force, March 1996.

[RFC 1944] Bradner, S. and J. McQuaid. "Benchmarking Methodology for Network Interconnect Devices." 1996.

[RFC 1944] Bradner, S. and J. McQuaid. "Benchmarking Methodology for Network Interconnect Devices." 1996.

[RFC 1965] Traina, P. "Autonomous System Confederations for BGP." 1996.

[RFC 1966] Bates, T. and R. Chandrasekeran. "BGP Route Reflection: An alternative to full mesh IBGP." 1996.

[RFC 1998] Chen, E. and T. Bates. "An Application of the BGP Community Attribute in Multi-home Routing." 1996.

[RFC 2001] Stevens, W. "TCP Slow Start, Congestion Avoidance, Fast Retransmit, and Fast Recovery Algorithms." 1997.

[RFC 2002] Perkins, C. "IP Mobility Support." 1996.

[RFC 2005] Solomon, J. "Applicability Statement for IP mObility Support." 1996.

[RFC 2018] Mathis, M., J. Mahdavi, S. Floyd, and A. Romanow. "TCP Selective Acknowledgement Options." 1996.

[RFC 2022] Armitage, G. "Support for Multicast over UNI 3.0/3.1 based ATM Networks." 1996.

[RFC 2113] Katz, D. "IP Router Alert Option." 1997.

[RFC 2201] Ballardie, A. "Core Based Trees (CBT) Multicast Routing Architecture." 1997.

[RFC 2205] Braden, R., Ed., L. Zhang, S. Berson, S. Herzog, and S. Jamin. "Resource ReSerVation Protocol (RSVP)-- Version 1 Functional Specification." 1997.

[RFC 2208] Mankin, A., Ed., F. Baker, B. Braden, S. Bradner, M. O'Dell, A. Romanow, A. Weinrib, and L. Zhang. "Resource ReSerVation Protocol (RSVP)—Version 1 Applicability Statement Some Guidelines on Deployment." 1997.

[RFC 2236] Fenner, W. "Internet Group Management Protocol, Version 2." 1997.

[RFC 2280] Alaettinoglu, C., T. Bates, E. Gerich, D. Karrenberg, D. Meyer, M. Terpstra, and C. Villamizar. "Routing Policy Specification Language (RPSL)." 1998.

[RFC 2285] Mandeville, R. "Benchmarking Terminology for LAN Switching Devices." 1998.

[RFC 2328] Moy, J. "OSPF Version 2." 1998. (This is the Full Standard edition of OSPF. Several prior versions were called Version 2.)

[RFC 2332] Luciani, J., D. Katz, D. Piscitello, B. Cole, and N. Doraswamy. "NBMA Next Hop Resolution Protocol (NHRP)." 1998.

[RFC 2333] Cansever, D. "NHRP Protocol Applicability Statement." 1998.

[RFC 2334] Luciani, J., G. Armitage, J. Halpern, and N. Doraswamy. "Server Cache Synchronization Protocol (SCSP)." 1998.

[RFC 2335] Luciani, J. "A Distributed NHRP Service Using SCSP." 1998.

[RFC 2338] Knight, S., D. Weaver, D. Whipple, R. Hinden, D. Mitzel, P. Hunt, P. Higginson, M. Shand, and A. Lindem. "Virtual Router Redundancy Protocol." 1998.

[RFC 2362] Estrin, D., D. Farinacci, A. Helmy, D. Thaler, S. Deering, M. Handley, V. Jacobson, C. Liu, P. Sharma, and L. Wei. "Protocol Independent Multicast-Sparse Mode (PIM-SM): Protocol Specification." 1998.

[RFC 2365] Meyer, D. "Administratively Scoped IP Multicast." 1998.

[RFC 2370] Coltun, R. "The OSPF Opaque LSA Option." 1998.

[RFC 2391] Srisuresh, P and D. Gan. "Load Sharing using IP Network Address Translation (LSNAT)." August 1998.

[RFC 2427] Brown, C. and A. Malis. "Multiprotocol Interconnect over Frame Relay." 1998.

[RFC 2430] Li, T. and Y. Rekhter. "Provider Architecture for Differentiated Services and Traffic Engineering (PASTE)." October 1998.

[RFC 2547] Rosen E. and Y. Rekhter. "BGP/MPLS VPNs." 1999.

[RFC 2578] McCloghrie, K., D. Perkins. J. Schoenwaelder, and T. Braunschweig. "Structure of Management Information Version 2 (SMIv2)." 1999.

[Roberts, 1997] Roberts, Erica. "IP on Speed." *Data Communications*. 1997. See www.data.com/roundups/ip_speed.html.

[Rose, 1988] Rose, M. and T. Rose. *The Simple Book: An Introduction to Networking Management*. Upper-Saddle River, NJ: Prentice-Hall, 1996.

[Rosen, 1999] Rosen, E., A. Viswanathan, and R. Callon. "Multiprotocol Label Switching Architecture." Work in progress, Internet Engineering Task Force, 1999. See www.ietf.org/internet-drafts/draft-ietf-mpls-arch-04.txt.

[Sales, 1999] Sales, B., W. Livens, D. Ooms, and M. Fernanda Ramalho. "Framework for IP Multicast in MPLS. "Work in progress, Internet Engineering Task Force, February 25, 1999. See www.ietf.org/internet-drafts/draft-ooms-mpls-multicast-01.txt.

[Sathaye, 1999] Sathaye, S. "The Ins and Outs of Layer 4+ Switching." Presentation at NANOG meeting, January 1999. Slides at www.nanog.org/mtg-9901/ppt/alteon/index.htm.

[Semeria, 1998] Semeria, C. and T. Maufer. "Introduction to IP Multicast Routing." 3Com white paper, 1998. See www.3com.com/nsc/501303s.html.

[Shimomura, 1996] Shimomura, T. and J. Markoff. *Takedown: The Pursuit and Capture of Kevin Mitnick, America's Most Wanted Computer Outlaw-By the Man Who Did It*. New York, NY: Hyperion, 1996.

[Simpson, 1998] Malis, A. and W. Simpson. "Applicability statement for PPP over SONET/SDH." Work in Progress, IETF PPP Working Group, 1998. See www.ietf.org/internet-drafts/draft-ietf-pppext-pppoversonet-update-04.txt.

[Sklower, 1999] Sklower, K. "A Tree-Based Packet Routing Table for Berkeley UNIX." 1999. See www.unix.digital.com/faqs/publications/base_doc/DOCUMENTATION/HTML/gated_html/radix.html.

[Smith, 1997] Smith, R. *Internet Cryptography*. Reading, MA: Addison-Wesley, 1997.

[Smith, n.d.] Smith, T. "Patricia Trie," n.d. See www.cs.waikato.ac.nz/~tcs/courses/c317/HTML/patricia.html.

[Spohn, 1997] Spohn, D. *Data Network Design, 2nd Edition*. New York, NY: McGraw-Hill, 1997.

[Spurgeon, 1998] Spurgeon, C. "Late Collisions." Posting to comp.dcom.sys.cisco newsgroup, October 15, 1998 21:17:01 GMT.

[Srisuresh, 1998a] Srisuresh, P., K. Evegang, and M. Holdredge. "Traditional IP Network Address Translator (Traditional NAT)." Work in Progress, Network Address Translation Working Group, Internet Engineering Task Force, 1998.

[Srisuresh, 1998b] Srisuresh, P. and M. Holdredge. "IP Network Address Translator (NAT) Terminology and Considerations." Work in Progress, Network Address Translation Working Group, Internet Engineering Task Force, 1998.

[St. Arnaud, 1998] St. Arnaud, B. "The Canadian Optical Network." Presentation at NANOG meeting, Fall 1998.

[Stallings, 1988] Stallings, W. *Data and Computer Communications*, Second Edition. New York, NY: Macmillan, 1998.

[Stevens, 1994] Stevens, W. *TCP/IP Illustrated, Volume 1: The Protocols*. Reading, MA: Addison-Wesley, 1994.

[Stoll, 1990] Stoll, C. *The Cuckoo's Egg*. New York, NY: Pocket Books, 1990.

[Tanner, 1996] Tanner, M. *Practical Queueing Analysis*. London: McGraw-Hill, 1995.

[Thaler, 1998] Thaler, D. "Interoperability Rules for Multicast Routing Protocols." Work in progress, Internet Engineering Task Force, August 3, 1998. See www.ietf.org/internet-drafts/draft-thaler-multicast-interop-03.txt.

[Thomas, 1999] Thomas, B., N. Feldman, P. Doolan, L. Andersson, and A. Fredette. "LDP Specification." Work in progress, Internet Engineering Task Force, 1999. See www.ietf.org/internet-drafts/draft-ietf-mpls-ldp-03.txt.

[Villamizar, 1998] Villamizar, Curtis. "OSPF Optimized Multipath (OSPF-OMP)." Work in Progress, IETF OSPF Working Group, 1998. See www.ietf.org/internet-drafts/draft-ietf-ospf-omp-02.txt.

[Villamizar, 1999] Villamizar, C., "MPLS Optimized Multipath (MPL—OMP)." Work in Progress, 1999. See www.ietf.org/internet-drafts/draft-villamizar-mpls-omp-01.txt.

[Wall, 1980] D. W. Wall. "Mechanisms for Broadcast and Selective Broadcast." PhD thesis, Electrical Engineering Dept., Stanford University, June 1980. Also Tech. Rep. 190, Computer Systems Laboratory, Stanford.

[Wang, 1997] Wang, Z., J. Crowcroft, C. Diot, and A. Ghosh. "Framework for Reliable Multicast Application Design." Hipparch '97, Uppsala, Sweden, 1997. See www.cs.ucl.ac.uk/staff/J.Crowcroft/hipparch/hipparch.html.

Index

I

Q

The *Macmillan Technology Series* is a comprehensive and authoritative set of guides to the most important computing standards of today. Each title in this series is aimed at bringing computing professionals closer to the scientists and engineers behind the technological implementations that will change tomorrow's innovations in computing.

Currently available titles in the *Macmillan Technology Series* include:

Directory Enabled Networking, by John Strassner (ISBN: 1-57870-140-6)

Directory Enabled Networks (DEN) is a rapidly developing industry and standards effort in the Desktop Management Task Force (DMTF). DEN allows network architects and engineers to manage their networks through centralized control and provisioning, which yields significant reductions in the cost of ownership. DEN is also a fundamental technology for policy-based networking, which is receiving a lot of attention in the networking industry. The author, John Strassner, is the creator of the DEN specification, as well as the chair of the DMTF DEN working group. *Directory Enabled Networking* is a critical resource for network architects and engineers to consider how to optimally utilize this technology in their networking environments.

Supporting Service Level Agreements on an IP Network, by Dinesh Verma (ISBN: 1-57870-146-5)

Service level agreements (SLAs), which allow those who provide network services to contract with their customers for different levels of quality of service, are becoming increasingly popular. *Supporting Service Level Agreements on an IP Network* describes methods and techniques that can be used to ensure that the requirements of SLAs are met. This essential guide covers SLA support on traditional best-effort IP networks, as well as support of SLAs using the latest service differentiation techniques under discussion in the IETF and other standards organizations. *Supporting Service Level Agreements on an IP Network* provides information services managers and engineers with critical practical insight into the procedures required to fulfill their service level agreements.

Differentiated Services for the Internet, by Kalevi Kilkki (ISBN: 1-57870-132-5)

One of the few technologies that will enable networks to handle traffic to meet the demands of particular applications, Differentiated Services is currently being standardized by the IETF. This book offers network architects, engineers, and managers of Internet and other packet networks critical insight into this new technology.

Gigabit Ethernet Networking, **by David G. Cunningham, Ph.D., and William G. Lane, Ph.D. (ISBN: 1-57870-062-0)**

Written by key contributors to the Gigabit Ethernet standard, *Gigabit Ethernet Networking* provides network engineers and architects both the necessary context of the technology and the advanced knowledge of its deployment. This book offers critical information to enable readers to make cost-effective decisions about how to design and implement their particular network to meet current traffic loads, and to ensure scalability with future growth.

DSL: Simulation Techniques and Standards Development for Digital Subscriber Line Systems, **by Walter Chen (ISBN: 1-57870-017-5)**

The only book on the market that deals with xDSL technologies at this level, *DSL: Simulation Techniques and Standards Development for Digital Subscriber Line Systems* is ideal for computing professionals who are looking for new high-speed communications technology, who must understand the dynamics of xDSL communications to create compliant applications, or who simply want to better understand this new wave of technology.

ADSL/VDSL Principles, **by Dr. Dennis J. Rauschmayer (ISBN: 1-57870-015-9)**

ADSL/VDSL Principles provides the communications and networking engineer with practical explanations, technical detail, and in-depth insight needed to fully implement ADSL and VDSL. Topics that are essential to the successful implementation of these technologies are covered.

LDAP: Programming Directory-Enabled Applications with Lightweight Directory Access Protocol, **by Tim Howes and Mark Smith (ISBN: 1-57870-000-0)**

This book is the essential resource for programmers, software engineers, and network administrators who need to understand and implement LDAP to keep software applications compliant. If you design or program software for network computing or are interested in directory services, *LDAP* is an essential resource to help you understand the LDAP API; learn how to write LDAP programs; understand how to LDAP-enable an existing application; and learn how to use a set of command-line LDAP tools to search and update directory information.

Upcoming titles in the *Macmillan Technology Series* include:

Virtual Private Networks, **by David Bovee (ISBN: 1-57870-120-1)**

Understanding the Public Key Infrastructure, **by Carlisle Adams and Steve Lloyd (ISBN: 1-57870-166-x)**

SNMP Agents, **by Bob Natale (ISBN: 1-57870-110-4)**

Intrusion Detection, **by Rebecca Gurley Bace (ISBN: 1-57870-185-6)**